To The Ends of the Earth

To the Ends of the Earth

The Great Travel and Trade Routes of Human History

Irene M. Franck
David M. Brownstone

A Hudson Group Book

Facts On File Publications
New York, New York • Oxford, England

To the Ends of the Earth

Library of Congress Cataloging in Publication Data

Franck, Irene M.
    To the ends of the earth.

    "A Hudson Group book."
    Bibliography: p.
    Includes index.
    1. Trade routes—History. I. Brownstone, David M.
II. Title. III. Title: The Great Travel and Trade Routes
of Human History.
HE323.F7 1984   909   82-7430
ISBN 0-87196-647-6

Design: Edward Smith Design, Inc.

Printed in the United States of America

10 9 8 7 6 5 4 3 2 1

Typeset by Burmar Technical Corp., Albertson, N.Y.

Contents

The Ambassador's Road and the Burma Road   1

The Amber Routes   17

The Appian Way and the Egnatian Way   33

The California Mission Trail   49

The Cape Horn Route   63

The Cape of Good Hope Route   77

The Eurasian Steppe Route and the Russian River Routes   95

The Great Desert Route and the Persian Royal Road   111

The Great North Road   129

The Great Trek Route and the Missionary Road   139

The Heraclean Way   147

The Inca Royal Road   159

The Incense Road and the Pilgrimage Road   169

The Indian Grand Road   187

The Mediterranean-Black Sea Routes   207

The Mississippi Route   233

The Mohawk Trail   243

The Nile Route and the Sudan Route   255

The North Atlantic Route   271

The Northeast Passage   283

The Oregon Trail and the California Trail   295

The Orient Route   309

The Panama Route   323

The Sahara Routes   337

The St. Lawrence-Great Lakes Route   353

The Santa Fe Trail and the Chihuahua Trail   363

The Silk Road   377

The Spice Route   401

The Trans-Canada Route   429

The Western Seaways and the Tin Routes   439

The Wilderness Road and Other Trans-Appalachian Routes   453

INDEX 461

List of Maps

The Ambassador's Road and the Burma Road in the Early Middle Ages
The Main Chinese Routes in Early Modern Times
The Amber Routes in Prehistoric Times
The Santiago de Compostela Routes in Medieval Times
The Amber Routes in Late Medieval Times
The Appian Way and the Egnatian Way in Roman Times
The California Mission Trail in Colonial Times
The Cape Horn Route
Cape Horn
The Cape of Good Hope Route and the Modern Spice Route
The Main Eurasian Steppe Route and the Silk Road in Mongol Times
The Russian River Routes in the Late Middle Ages
The Mesopotamian Routes in Old Testament Times
The Persian Royal Road and the Great Desert Route in Early and Medieval Times
The Great North Road
The Great Trek Route and the Missionary Road in the Late 19th Century
The Heraclean Way in Greco-Roman Times
The Inca Royal Road, with Detail of the Central Portion
The Incense Road in Greco-Roman Times
The Pilgrimage Road in Modern Times
The Grand Trunk Road in 19th Century India
The Mediterranean and Black Sea Routes in Greek and Phoenician Times
The Mediterranean and Black Sea Routes in Medieval Times
The Mississippi Route in the 1840's
The Mohawk Trail in the Early 1800's, with Detail of Early Colonial Times
The Nile Route and the Sudan Route in the 19th Century
The North Atlantic Route
The Northeast Passage and the Trans-Siberian Railroad
The Oregon Trail and the California Trail in the Mid-19th Century
The Orient Route in Roman Times

The Orient Express Route in the 1920's

The Panama Route

The Early Panama Crossings

The Modern Panama Crossings

The Sahara Routes in the Late Middle Ages

The St. Lawrence-Great Lakes Route in the Mid-18th Century

The Santa Fe Trail and the Chihuahua Trail in the 1830's with Detail of the
    Chihuahua Trail in Colonial Times

The Silk Road and Other Eurasian Routes in Greco-Roman Times

The Silk Road in Central Asia in the 7th Century

The Spice Route in Greco-Roman Times

The Early Trans-Canada Fur Trade Routes and the Modern Trans-Canada Routes

The Western Seaways and the Tin Routes in Greek and Phoenician Times

The Western Seaways in the 10th and 11th Centuries

The Wilderness Road and Other Main Roads to the West in the Early 19th Century

List of Color Plates

The following is a list of color plates in the order they appear. For more information on the routes depicted, consult the chapters noted in parentheses.

"Nurtured in the frozen fjords of Norway…" (The North Atlantic Route)

"Controlling the portage route across Jutland…" (The Western Seaways and the Tin Routes)

"Travelers on the Great Desert Route…" (The Great Desert Route and the Persian Royal Road)

"After the Battle of Lepanto…" (The Mediterranean-Black Sea Routes)

"East India ships left the Netherlands…" (The Cape of Good Hope Route)

"In recent centuries, travelers have found largely ruins…" (The Appian Way and the Egnatian Way)

"This was one of many maps drawn of Eurasia…" (The Eurasian Steppe Route and the Russian River Routes)

"Day and night the Conestoga wagons thundered…" (The Wilderness Road and Other Trans-Appalachian Routes)

"Pilgrims bound for Mecca set off from Baghdad…" (The Incense Road and the Pilgrimage Road)

"Many Moslem romances featured a pilgrimage…" (The Incense Road and the Pilgrimage Road)

"In 1521 the Ottoman Turks drove the Knights of St. John Hospitallers…" (The Mediterranean-Black Sea Routes)

"An old-style Chinese junk and a modern ship…" (The Spice Route)

"Once steamboats of shallow draft had been developed…" (The Mississippi Route)

"Within decades of Columbus's arrival in the Caribbean…" (The Panama Route)

"Long after Venice's great days as a world power…" (The Mediterranean-Black Sea Routes)

"This rather unflattering portrait of Hsüan-tsang…" (The Silk Road)

"On the great liners, first-class passengers…" (The North Atlantic Route)

"Complete with passengers, slaves, and crew, this 12th century Arab ship…" (The Spice Route)

"The canal from the Mediterranean port of Narbonne…" (The Western Seaways and the Tin Routes."

"The sack of Baghdad by the Mongols…" (The Great Desert Route and the Persian Royal Road)

"The road on the cliff below Cannes..." (The Heraclean Way)

"The Cathedral of St. Etienne at Toulouse..." (The Amber Routes)

"Operating for centuries to keep invaders out..." (The Silk Road)

"Even when the port was frozen..." (The Northeast Passage)

"Modern travelers to Rome have often deserted..." (The Heraclean Way)

"When the Moslems controlled the Spice Route..." (The Spice Route)

"Near the ruins of ancient Carthage..." (The Mediterranean-Black Sea Routes)

"A caravan leaves the bustle of daily life in Ankara..." (The Silk Road)

"From Verona, the old Amber Route..." (The Amber Routes)

"In modern times, Antibes and other Riviera towns..." (The Heraclean Way)

"Supposedly depicting Jacob's journey into Egypt..." (The Orient Route)

"With Marco Polo testing the product..." (The Spice Route)

"This view of Marco Polo in Venice..." (The Mediterranean-Black Sea Routes)

Preface

Much of the romance and adventure of human history flows from the world's great travel and trade routes, and much of the stuff of human history stems from the development of these routes. The Silk Road, the Santa Fe Trail, the Appian Way, the Spice Route, the Wilderness Road, the Amber Routes—these and two-score other highways and seaways have for tens of thousands of years shaped the course of history. These great routes have carried with them the stories of people pushing across continents and seas, of armies sweeping out in conquest and retreating in defeat, of empires built on trade goods later falling as new routes pass them by, of ideas and cultures flowing and merging along the way.

The names of many of these routes are well known to those who are fascinated by travel throughout history. But in modern times some routes have been buried under concrete and asphalt, and others have been bypassed as technology has cut new routes elsewhere. Astonishingly little has been written about many of them; indeed, this is the first and only historical guide to all of the world's main travel and trade routes. In it, we have told the stories of almost 50 routes, tracing the course of each and following its history, sometimes for millennia. Hundreds of first-hand accounts, illustrations, and maps have been included to help bring each route and its history to life, and to illuminate the great events—the migrations, settlements, conquests, wars, trade, and adventures—that shaped it. Routes have been selected from all parts of the world both for their significance in history and for their unique qualities.

We have long thought that the Earth is, in essence, only a single place, and that political boundaries only temporarily fracture the interconnections between all the people and areas of the world. We discovered abundant evidence to support that view in writing this book. Wherever we looked, we found that—long before the dawn of recorded history—people had been marking out the world's great natural highways, the most accessible routes through formidable mountain ranges, across barren deserts, over treacherous waters. Tens of thousands of years ago, when humans were producing the great cave paintings of Western Europe, some of their kin had already traversed the more than 8,000 miles of the Eurasian Steppe Route. European traders on the Santa Fe and Chihuahua trails were following pathways taken by Native Americans thousands of years before, as they coursed down through the Americas. While humans were still working with stone alone, people were routinely traveling across the Sahara Desert. When China sent its first recorded emissaries along the Silk Road, at the beginning of the Christian era in the West, they heard there ancient legends of Chinese travelers from long before. And when the Egyptians were building their great pyramids, shipments of precious cinnamon were reaching them by sea from East Asia.

In doing this book, we had a great deal of indispensable help from others. Most important was the assistance of the Chappaqua Library. Doris Lowenfels, Director, gave us her full support throughout the entire preparation of the book. The reference staff, especially Mary Platt, Linda Goldstein, Karen Baker, and Paula Peyraud, were extremely helpful in helping us track down esoteric and long-out-of-print books from faraway libraries. Marcia Van Fleet and her circulation staff were unfailingly helpful, efficient, and friendly as they handled the seemingly never-ending stream of books being funneled through the library to us. We should also thank all the many people who operate the Interlibrary Loan System in the Northeast; without them we should never have hazarded and should certainly never have completed the work, involving as it did research into all the human world and time.

We also very much appreciate the interest and support of our publishers, Facts On File, Inc., especially Edward Knappman, Kate Kelly, Martin Greenwald, Rachel Rephan Ginsburg, Ann Forstenzer, Joe Reilly, Robin Smith, Fran Fishelberg, and Susan Brooker.

Our thanks also to cartographer Dale Adams, book designer Ed Smith, and cover designer Ed Smith, who have made such fine contributions to the book.

We also appreciate the excellent work of our able and patient typists, Shirley Fenn and Nancy Fishelberg, and Mary Racette, who also helped with the bibliographic and illustration research.

We would also like to acknowledge the permission of several publishers to reprint selections from their works: Excerpts on pp. 194 and 388 are quoted from *The Travels of Fa-Hsien (391–414 A.D.) or Record of the Buddhist Kingdoms*, translated by H. A. Giles and published by Cambridge University Press in 1923. Excerpts on pp. 382-383 are quoted from *Records of the Great Historians of China*, translated from the *Shih Chi* of Ssu-ma Chien by Burton Watson, copyright © 1961, Columbia University Press. Excerpts on pp. 11, 105-107, 263, 344, and 395 are quoted from Ibn Battuta's *Travels, A.D. 1325-1354*, translated by H. A. R. Gibb, published for the Hakluyt Society by Cambridge University Press, 1958-71. The excerpt on p. 17 is quoted from Pliny's *Natural History*, Vol. X, translated by H. Rackham and published by Harvard University Press in the Loeb Classical Library in 1938; excerpts on pp. 115 and 212-213 are from the works of Herodotus, translated by A. D. Godley,

published by Harvard University Press in the Loeb Classical Library in 1920; excerpts on pp. 39-40 are from Horace's *Satires, Epistles and Ars Poetica,* translated by H. Rushton Fairclough, published by Harvard University Press in the Loeb Classical Library in 1926; all are copyright © Harvard University Press. The excerpt on p. 275 is quoted from *The Vinland Sagas; The Norse Discovery of America,* translated by Magnus Magnusson and Hermann Pálsson, published by Penguin in 1965, copyright © Magnus Magnusson and Herman Pálsson, 1965. The excerpt on p. 207 is from Homer's *Odyssey,* translated by E. V. Rieu, published by Penguin in 1946, copyright © the Estate of E. V. Rieu, 1946. The excerpts on pp. 10-12, 104-105, 394-396 and 414-415 are from Marco Polo's *The Travels,* translated by Ronald Latham, published by Penguin in 1958, copyright © Ronald Latham, 1958.

Many other people helped us in our search for just the right book, excerpt, or illustration. They are too numerous to name here, but we would be remiss not to note the special kindness of Willie K. Friar of the Panama Canal Commission.

We would also like to express our very personal thanks to Gene R. Hawes, who has contributed time and thought to every aspect of the book over the years.

A work like this must, of necessity, rely very heavily on other historical works, even when many firsthand accounts are being used. Wherever histories have particularly useful information on a route, we have included them in the specific bibliography at the end of each route, for those interested in digging further into the histories of these pathways.

The development and writing of this book has been a shared experience. Irene Franck first conceived of the work and wrote most of it, in addition to researching the maps and illustrations. David Brownstone edited her work and wrote several of the articles on North America, South Africa, and the North Atlantic, which she then edited. The result is truly a joint work. We hope that others will be as fascinated as we have been with the stories of the great routes of human history.

Irene M. Franck
David M. Brownstone

Chappaqua, New York
Summer 1984

To The Ends of the Earth

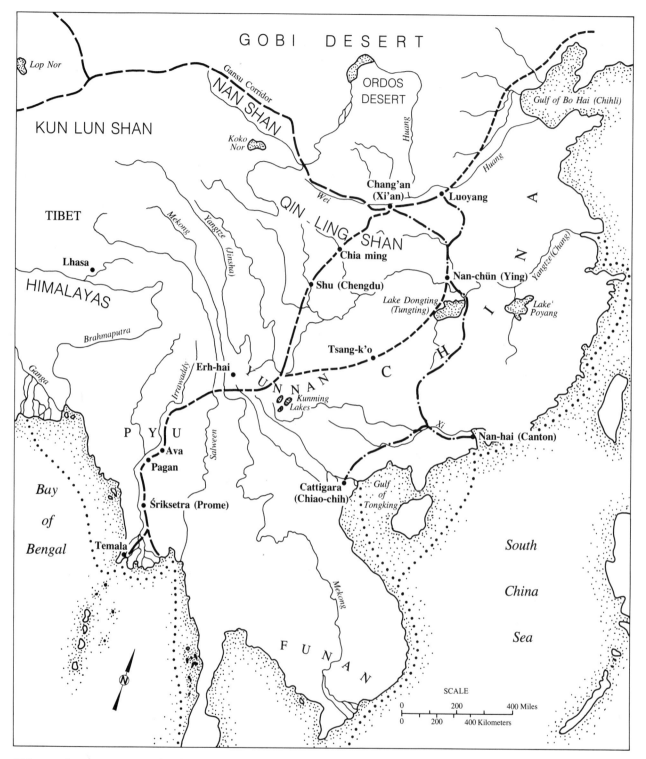

The Ambassador's Road and the Burma Road in the Early Middle Ages

—·—·— Ambassador's Road

— — — Burma Road

— — — Silk Road

- - - - - Main Connecting Routes

· · · · · · · Spice Route

The Ambassador's Road and the Burma Road

In the late 18th century, the British sent an envoy, Lord Macartney, to Peking, requesting that they be allowed to have a permanent representative in the Chinese capital. The Ch'ing emperor's refusal was firm but polite, noting that the British, on their "lonely, remote island" far away could have little knowledge of the "dynastic usage" that made such a proposal unacceptable. He put the situation quite plainly:

> Hitherto, all European nations, including your own country's barbarian merchants, have carried on their trade with Our Celestial Empire at Canton. Such has been the procedure for many years, although Our Celestial Empire possesses all things in prolific abundance and lacks no products within its own borders. There was therefore no need to import the manufactures of outside barbarians in exchange for our own produce. But as the tea, silk, and porcelain which the Celestial Empire produces are absolute necessities to European nations and to yourselves, we have permitted, as a signal of favor, that foreign *hongs* [Chinese business associations] be established at Canton, so that your wants might be supplied and your country thus participate in our beneficence.

Request denied—as it had been at many other times in China's history. Although China has sometimes been open to foreigners, its borders have been closed for long periods of time, and the few travelers permitted to pass through the land were generally kept to one imperial highway; because foreign envoys were limited to this single route, it came to be called the Ambassador's Road.

China is not a naturally united country. Its main centers of culture lie along three horizontal strips, separated by broad swaths of mountains and hills. The oldest and northernmost of these strips is composed of the valleys of the Wei and Huang (Yellow) rivers. There the fertile plains were conducive to farming, even though the Huang has, throughout history, flooded disastrously and sometimes changed the direction and course of its eastern end by hundreds of miles. China's second center lies in the valley of the Yangtze, a powerful river so long it has two names; the eastern half is called the Chang, while the western half—past the great rocky gorges of the center—is called Jinsha (the River of Golden Sand). While China's political center has remained in the north, except when forced southward, the Yangtze has long been her economic heartland. The third of China's cultural strips was the least attractive of all: the humid, malarial southeast coast. For many centuries travelers justly feared the fevers that bred in the swamps of the "jungle forest." A seventh century A.D. T'ang folk-poem noted of the fever-ridden route that led along the coast into Annam (now North Vietnam):

> The customs barrier at Ghost Gate—
> Ten men go out,
> Nine men return.

1

Trestle roads like this one have been built in the Qin Ling Shn (Mountains) for thousand years. (Anonymous photograph)

This region attained its importance primarily because its ports faced the Southern Seas, over which came sailors for thousands of years, plying the Spice Route for China's unique and exotic luxuries.

That these disparate regions became bound together—so that they are, today, indistinguishable to out-

siders as anything other than, simply, "China"—is due in no small measure to the great road system that the Chinese built. Comparable in length and effect to the Roman road system, although begun considerably earlier, the imperial highways eventually brought Chinese language and culture throughout the land, while always maintaining the prestige and primacy of the northern heartland. The two main roads in this welding process were the Ambassador's Road and the Burma Road.

The Ambassador's Road was China's great southern route. From her main early cities—Chang'an (near modern Xi'an) on the Wei River, and Luoyang on the Huang River—routes fed together to form the Ambassador's Road, crossing over the intervening hills that divided the northern wheatlands from the central and southern wet ricelands. Arriving at Nan-chün (Ying) on the Yangtze, the route followed the north bank of the river, crossing it past the head of Lake Dongting (Tung-ting), and then continuing south to the seaport of Nan-hai (Guangzhou, or Kwangchow, better known to Europeans as Canton). A spur of this main route followed the course of Xi (West) River around the Gulf of Tongking to the early port of Chiao Chih (today Hanoi and Haiphong) in Annam (now North Vietnam). It was these two ports—China's openings onto the fabled Spice Route—that determined the line of the Ambassador's Road from the earliest times. Although the route fed through some hills and crossed many watercourses, it was not especially difficult.

The same could not be said for the Burma Road, which headed into the mountain redoubts of southwestern China and then crossed through overland jungles to inaccessible inner Burma. Immediately south of Chang'an, the road had to force its way into the Qin Ling (Ch'in-Ling) Mountains of Shaanxi (Shensi) province, along precipitous passes, some of them close to 6,000 feet high. Through these and other lower, but still formidable mountains, the route worked its way into the main southwestern city of Shu (Chengdu, or Chengtu), heart of Sichuan (Szechuan) province. From there it worked its way across the Yunnan uplands, essentially a tail of the great Himalayas to the west, crossing the headwaters of the Yangtze, Mekong, and Salween rivers in quick succession; on reaching the Irrawaddy in Burma, it followed that river's east bank down to its many and shifting mouths at the Bay of Bengal. At times an overland spur fed from the middle reaches of the Irrawaddy, across through Bengal to the Ganga River in India, there linking with the India Grand Road. The Burma Road may have a modern name and importance, especially in the 20th century, but its history goes back long before Christ, as this route reached out toward the Spice Route trade on the Bay of Bengal.

The early Chinese were a Mongol people who gradually split off from their nomadic kin to the north and west, adopting instead an increasingly agricultural life. (A fortified embankment known as the Great Wall would

For two thousand years, the middle lane on China's imperial highways, as on this Peking bridge, was reserved for imperial traffic. (Museum of the American China Trade, Milton, Mass.)

The Yunnan Hills in the background mark the traditional border between Burma and distant China on the old Burma Road. (Delia and Ferdinand Kuhn)

for centuries mark the line between the two). The loess fields of the Huang River plain provided an attractive homeland and, with the introduction of some technical advances from the West, the Chinese soon developed an enviable civilization. By the middle of the second millennium B.C., as legend begins to give way to history, we find that cowrie shells are used as a medium of exchange by

the Shang civilization; the shells came from south of the Yangtze, and (along with other items) imply a trading chain, in which goods were bartered from tribe to tribe over long distances. By this period also sericulture — the production of the fabulous silk that would draw traders from around the world — was well advanced. (Tradition dates discovery of the silk-production techniques back to

4

the third millennium B.C.)

From their center on the lower curve of the Huang River, the Chinese spread westward on the Wei River, eastward to the Huang's mouth on the Gulf of Bo Hai (Chihli), southeastward to the mouth of the Huai River, and south to the Yangtze River, reaching it first in the area of Lake Dongting. Along tracks that would become the Burma Road and the Ambassador's Road, tribute and trade goods made their way, partly by road, partly by water. From the mountains of Shaanxi and Sichuan came wild animals and precious metals. The Yangtze River basin sent exotic goods like feathers, bamboo, ivory, pearls, cinnabar, and tortoise shells used for divinations, along with the more mundane hides and metals. From here also came silk, which gradually became so widespread that bolts of the fabric became the main medium of exchange; indeed, later, even taxes were payable in silk. The women in each family—including the emperor's—were employed for much of the year in raising the silkworms and preparing the precious threads on which depended so much of their livelihood.

Under the Chou dynasty, which bridged into the first millennium B.C., China expanded into a wide variety of fiefdoms, sharing a common language and culture, and a similar concern with effective transportation. Each ruler had his own series of footpaths and roads throughout his territory, on which traveled messengers bearing word from watchtowers and outposts at strategic points around the province, often conveying messages by means of beacon fires. That these roads were built and maintained with some considerable care is indicated by a poem from the ninth century B.C.:

> The roads of Chou are [smooth] as a whetstone,
> Straight as an arrow;
> Ways where the lords and officials pass,
> Ways where the common people look on.

Roads continued to be a main Chinese concern throughout the Chou dynasty and even in the Warring States period, which lasted from the fifth to third centuries B.C., with military use as important as commercial travel.

In 221 B.C., the state of Ch'in became dominant and unified China for the first time. Huang Ti (the Yellow Emperor) quickly set the pattern of centralized administration that would obtain in China throughout its history. The nobility, his potential rivals, were removed from their local power bases, and the roads that had once served only provincial needs were welded into an imperial system centered on the capital of Chang'an. So concerned was he with effective transportation that he standardized the width of chariot wheels at six feet. Over the centuries China had extended to the northwest and east; but it was barred there, by the sea and by the nomads, especially the Hsiung-nu (Huns). It found expansion easier to the

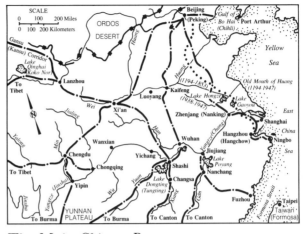

The Main Chinese Routes in Early Modern Times
——·——— Main Highways
············· Grand Canal
—■—■—■— Great Wall

south and southwest. Under the Ch'in dynasty, control spread to the mouth of the Yangtze and part-way down the coast; into Sichuan to past the provincial capital of Shu; and along a corridor straight south from Lake Dongting to Nan-hai (Canton), with its incomparable port on the South China Sea. Huang Ti's work in uniting this large empire was celebrated by a chronicler half a century later:

> He also ordered the building of the post-roads all over the Empire...around the lakes and rivers, and along the coasts of the sea; so that all was made accessible. These highways were fifty paces [probably feet] wide, and a tree was planted every 30 feet along them. The road was made very thick and firm at the edge, and tamped with metal rammers. The planting of the green pine trees was what gave beauty to the roads. Yet all this was done so that [his] successors should not have to take circuitous routes.

It was in this period that the main line of the Ambassador's Road was set from Chang'an south to Lake Dongting and down to the low hills north of Nan-hai. There, faced with five passes, the road at first took the one that fed straightest to Nan-hai; but the westernmost of the passes was soon adopted as the main path. Even though it meant a wide swing in the route, it allowed transport by the Xi (West) River on the final leg of the trip to Nan-hai.

More remarkable, the Ch'in broke a new road to the southwest, to replace the old, deficient paths to Sichuan.

Surveyors were sent into the Qin Ling Shan, whose snowcapped peaks towered over the Wei Valley, to mark out a more direct route. Unlike the tamped earth roads of the plains, this one would have to cross deep river gorges and slide along sheer rock faces. The Ch'in engineers were up to the task that faced them, for they had developed appropriate techniques in the previous centuries. They bridged gorges with wooden trestles, and hung wooden balconies on cliff faces, sometimes built out from narrow ledges and sometimes hung from brackets driven into solid rock. The achievement was considerable, and the Chinese commemorated the feat by naming one leg of the new route "the Linked Cloud Road."

After barely a quarter of a century, the Ch'in dynasty was replaced by the Han, which would last for over four centuries. The Han continued and expanded on the Ch'in work, using corvée and convict labor. The building and maintenance of roads was placed under bureaucratic administration, in what would be the classic Chinese pattern. According to a second century B.C. document, an imperial lieutenant was responsible for studying maps "in order to obtain a perfect knowledge of the mountains, forests, lakes, rivers, and marshes, and to understand the [natural] routes of communication." He was also responsible for "planting trees and hedges along [the roads] for defense," and placing guardposts at all strategic points. In case of danger, he had additional charges:

> If there is alarm in the empire he fortifies the roads and difficult points, halts wanderers, and guards the positions with his men, letting past the barriers only those with the imperial seal.

These roads ranged from simple footpaths to multi-lane highways. Within the capital and a few other main cities, the primary arteries were built to carry nine chariots, or even more, abreast; ring-roads around the cities were seven-width roads; while imperial highways, among them the Ambassador's Road to Nan-hai, were generally five lanes across. The middle lane of the imperial highways were supposed to be reserved for the private use of the emperor, his family, and his immediate deputies; although that custom was most likely honored in the breach on roads some distance from the imperial capital, Chinese annals record at least one execution for the crime of riding in the emperor's lane.

Chinese road-building techniques became a weapon of expansion when the Han had reason to open the unknown territory southwest of Shu. In 128 B.C., the Han envoy Chang Ch'ien crossed Central Asia on China's first known mission to the West; halfway across Asia, at the city of Bactra (now in northern Afghanistan), he was astounded to find for sale bamboo from south China and cloth from Shu. When he asked how they had gotten such articles, he was told: "Our merchants go to buy them in the markets of Shen-tu." This was China's first word of the great land of India—and first inkling of a connection between lands south of the Yangtze and other countries on the Southern Seas; China was, after all, still a rather small nation in the north of the land. Chang Ch'ien immediately saw the advantages of a route from Sichuan to Shen-tu, reasoning (as chronicler Ssuma-Ch'ien recorded):

> Now if the kingdom of Shen-tu is situated several thousand *li* [a *li* = about one-third mile] southeast of Ta-Hsia [Bactra] and obtains goods which are produced in Shu, it seems to me that it must not be very far away from Shu.

Noting that hostile nomads barred the way west through Central Asia, Chang Ch'ien concluded: "It would seem that the most direct route, as well as the safest, would be that out of Shu."

The Han had already made some probes beyond Shu, but had been dissuaded from continuing by the lack of roads and the hostility of the tribes there. The existence of Shen-tu placed a new light on the matter, and the Emperor agreed that Chang Ch'ien should lead a mission to the southwest. There they met various tribes, some of whom, he reported, "have no chiefs and were given to robbery; the Chinese envoys would have been killed or captured." Blocked in their mission, they nevertheless learned of an elephant-riding state called Tien (Yunnan, or Burma), where Shu traders sometimes went with their goods on "unofficial trading missions." Undaunted, the Hans slowly pressed westward into Yunnan, pushing ahead of them a number of peoples who then settled in Burma. Chinese roads went hand-in-hand with their expansion, reaching across the headwaters of the Mekong River. From Shu the road curved southeastward to cross the Yangtze at Pa (near modern Chongqing); it then turned back southwestward past the Kunming Lakes and Erh-hai Lake to a point between the upper Mekong and Salween Rivers. This was, however, no multi-lane highway. Many sections required the trestle-and-balcony construction developed in the Qin Ling Shan, and parts of the route were only a few feet wide, giving the road its name: "The Five Foot Way."

Somewhat later in the dynasty, the Han spread Chinese dominion further south around the coast of Annam, securing a second major port on the South China Sea: Chiao Chih, which the West would know as Cattigara (Hanoi and Haiphong). A main spur of the Ambassador's Road to Nan-hai split off to connect with Cattigara. These were some of the great early days on the Spice Route, which followed the southern coast of Asia from Egypt to China; Indian and Malayan sailors had long plied the waters, bearing goods from both East and West. Some Eastern goods had reached the sea by traveling overland

On either side of the Yangtze River's gorges were rock-cut towpaths for "trackers" who hauled boats upstream against the swift current. (Museum of the American China Trade, Milton, Mass.)

on the Burma Road and down the Irrawaddy River to the Bay of Bengal; some had even crossed the jungles of Burma overland into India. But as the Roman Empire's hunger for exotic goods grew in the West, the Spice Route became increasingly dominant; the ports of Cattigara and, to a lesser extent, Nan-hai became major entrepôts, and the Ambassador's Road quite overshadowed the Burma Road. In addition to being a major artery of internal communication, the Ambassador's Road funneled all manner of trade goods into these two seaports for the Western markets.

The Western trade, while primarily carried on by Indians and Malayans, also brought others from further away to China's shores. In 120 A.D., a group of Syrian jugglers and acrobats arrived in China, apparently via Burma, and were taken north to provide the emperor with his New Year's entertainment. The Chinese chronicle *Hou*

Han Shu reported that they could "conjure, spit fire, bind and release their limbs without assistance, interchange the heads of cows and horses, and dance cleverly with up to a thousand balls." Magicians and conjurors from India, too, found their way along the Ambassador's Road to the imperial court. Chinese annals also record the appearance in 166 A.D. of a mission from "the king of Ta-Ch'in, An-Tun," presumably Emperor Aurelius Antoninus of the Roman Empire. These were probably not official Roman envoys, but free-lancing merchants attempting to open new markets. Arriving in Annam, they offered ivory, rhinoceros horns, and tortoise shells to the Chinese, clearly items they had picked up in various exchanges along the way. The *Hou Han Shu* did, however, note: "From that time dates the [direct] intercourse with that country [the Roman Empire]." And from this period dates the Western knowledge of the great port of Cattigara (Chiao Chih). At least one

Carried by porters rather than riding in a wheeled vehicle, this mandarin is protected from the many bumps and holes in the road. (By Thomas Allom, from G. N. Wright, China in a Series of Views, *1843)*

Syrian trader from the Roman Empire traveled all the way from Cattigara on the Ambassador's Road to Chang'an, to visit the emperor, "who asked him for a report on his native country and its people," before returning home with some dwarfs, an imperial gift. Later, when the Roman Empire declined, such missions ended, although Indian and Malayan traders continued to frequent Cattigara and Nanhai.

But most travelers on the Ambassador's Road and Burma Road were—as they would always be—natives, not foreigners. China itself was still based in the north, and had only modest control over the territories of the south. She had established military-farming colonies in the region, but these were primarily concentrated along the main highways, and large numbers of people in the southern lands had as yet barely heard of "China." On the Ambassador's Road were seen a dizzying variety of two-wheeled chariots, from crude dished-wheel country carts to racing chariots with four horses abreast to fashionable open carriages with an umbrella-like awning to shade their privileged occupants. Two wheels were favored over four because they turned more readily and

were easier to drive over narrow winding roads. Single-wheeled vehicles were even better-suited to these conditions, and seem to have been developed during late Han times. Though some of these were like the wheelbarrows we know in the West, others were large vehicles which could carry several passengers, or a considerable load of goods, sometimes with the aid of draft animals and later even a sail, to take advantage of a favorable wind. The Burma Road was most frequented by traders on foot, using pack animals or human bearers to carry their goods.

As is proper for a civilization whose river valleys are so important, the Chinese also paid close attention to the interconnections between land and river routes. In the later Han period, for example, part of the Linked Cloud Road toward Shu was replaced by a new route called the Northern Trestle Road. Chronicler Ssuma Ch'ien quotes the official report on the matter:

In order to reach Shu [traffic] goes through the Marches of the Old Road where there are many rocky descents and long detours; if we now pierce a road between the Pao and the Yeh [rivers] the gradients will be much less difficult and the distance will be shorter by 400 *li*...[And] we should be able to use them [the rivers] for grain transport by boat.

For navigation, the Yangtze—crossed by both the Ambassador's Road and the Burma Road—was pre-eminent among Chinese rivers, and tracks were gouged out of the rock faces in her famous gorges for haulers to follow, as they pulled transport boats upstream. The Chinese had already built, as an aid to their conquest of the south, the "Magic Canal," which ran from the Yangtze River through Lake Dongting and canalized links with several smaller rivers to Nan-hai itself. But the Han also built an even more ambitious canal, joining the Huang and Yangtze rivers via Lake Hongze on the Huai River between them; this astonishing accomplishment formed the basis for the Grand Canal of later times. On these water routes went most of the bulk traffic, such as grain, which was uneconomical to transport by road.

The Ch'in and Han dynasties were the great period in the history of transportation in China. In the coming centuries, China would fragment and reunify several times, and at times would rebuild or improve upon neglected road and water systems, but the foundation was laid in this early period. Much as in the contemporary Roman Empire, the great road system would have no peer until modern times.

For the Ambassador's Road and the Burma Road, the breakup of China at the end of the Han period in 220 A.D. signaled the beginning of a long decline. Indeed, the roads seem to have been ill cared for even in the later Han, for in the late second century official travelers had increasingly abandoned carriages and taken to riding horses, which were less sensitive to badly maintained roads. Slow, heavy carts, pulled by draft animals rather than swift horses, came to be the most common vehicles on the wide roads; while in narrow, winding sections the rich were more often borne by man-hoisted litters or in single-wheeled vehicles, both of which rattled passengers less than a multi-wheeled carriage on a bumpy road. Aside

from the vehicles, the roads were filled with walkers; some of them were themselves beasts of burden, who carried rich travelers on their shoulders. Under the circumstances, traffic increasingly went by water routes over the coming centuries, and the roads gradually passed from civilian control to the military, who handled any repairs or rebuilding. Some of the southern regions around Nan-hai recognized only the slightest of connections with the imperial center of the north.

Conditions changed only with the reunification of China under the T'ang dynasty in 618. Like the Han centuries before, the T'ang sent military colonists to settle the south, attempting to re-establish Chinese hegemony there. The late arrival of the coastal peoples into the Chinese fold is, in fact, still enshrined in the popular parlance; they call themselves T'ang Jen (Men of T'ang), while their central Chinese neighbors see themselves as Han Jen (Men of Han). It is no coincidence that the absorption of Nan-hai and the rest of the southeast coast in this period occurred when the Moslem world was rising in west Asia, for Arab sailors soon made their presence felt on the Spice Route, arriving in Canton (as Nan-hai was known in the West) in great numbers. In the eighth century, minister Chang Chiu-ling was assigned to repair and partly rebuild the southern portion of the Ambassador's Road. He described the condition of the old road in poetic form:

Formerly, an abandoned road in the east of the pass,
An unswerving course: you clambered aloft
On the Outskirts of several miles of heavy forest,
With flying bridges, clinging to the brink
Halfway up a thousand fathoms of layered cliffs...

Of the reasons for repairing the road, he had no doubt:

The several nations from beyond the sea
Use it daily for commerical intercourse;
Opulence of teeth, hides, feathers, furs;
Profits in fish, salt, clams, cockles.

At Beijing (Peking), China's great waterway, the Grand Canal, met the camel trains from across the Eurasian Steppe. (Museum of the American China Trade, Milton, Mass.)

Not to mention silk, of course. All these things and more brought foreigners to Canton, among them Indians, Malayans, Indochinese, Persians, and Arabs, who formed a cosmopolitan merchant class within the old city.

Relations in the city were not always smooth, however. Foreign merchants operated under considerable restrictions, and also had to contend with much corruption from the many levels of the Chinese bureaucracy. Sometimes the Chinese exactions became so intolerable that Western merchants forsook Canton altogether for Cattigara—or took matters in their own hands. In the mid-eighth century, a group of Arabs and Persians conducted a devastating raid on Canton, looting and burning the always fire-prone city, and making Cattigara the main port for some decades. Canton, still on the wild frontiers of China, was also vulnerable to internal strife, with occasional rebellions of regional eunuch rulers; the worst such event was an anti-foreign attack in the mid-ninth century. Many thousands of foreign merchants—Chinese records say 120,000—were massacred, the great mulberry groves that fed the precious silkworms were destroyed, and Canton was ruined. Cattigara once again took up the slack, but Canton never fully recovered until modern times.

Under the T'ang dynasty, China was relatively open to the world, and many foreigners traveled along her roads, some to stay. They were closely monitored, however, and were most likely to be found on the Ambassador's Road to Chang'an. But, as water routes became increasingly important for internal shipment, many foreigners found themselves joining natives on a more easterly route. This fed from Canton northeast to Lake Poyang on the Yangtze and from there downriver to the canal network that linked the Yangtze and the Huang.

Throughout this period the Burma Road had operated fitfully, always playing second fiddle to the Ambassador's Road. But in 698 A.D. the provincial governor of Sichuan, facing increasing harassment from the Burmese people, noted to the emperor:

> Yunnan was kept open in earlier dynasties because through Yunnan China was connected in the West with Ta-Chin [the Roman Empire] and in the south with Indo-China. Tax receipts in cloth and salt are now declining and precious tribes fail to come. We press our people to garrison the territories of the tribes to no purpose. I therefore suggest that we withdraw from Yaochow [west of Kunming Lakes] and leave the tribes south of the Lu [Yangtze] River as vassal states and prohibit all traffic except by special permission...

So the road was closed, except for unofficial smuggling, for some centuries. The northern part of the route, between Chang'an and Shu, however, continued in heavy use.

With the fall of the T'ang dynasty in the 10th cen-

tury, China underwent enormous upheavals. The successor kingdoms, under increasing pressure from northern nomads, moved their capital south, first to Kaifeng, then to Hangzhou (Hangchow), a well-protected port city on the east coast. During this period the Ambassador's Road lost some of its dominance, as other main roads fed toward the east coast, linking with the new capital. As roads were neglected, canal routes became increasingly important. Along with grain, and other bulk products appropriate for the water routes, came precious salt, plentiful on the east coast, dear in the interior. Ninth century Japanese travelers noted over three dozen salt barges, two or three abreast, being pulled along one feeder canal by just two water buffaloes on the towpath alongside; on the main canals, the salt boats might be three to five abreast stretching for miles. So vital were these routes that storehouses were built along the way so that, if floods or low water hindered shipping, grain and other necessities could be stored temporarily. When the Sung dynasty was forced south, much of China's cultural center moved with it; by the 12th century, the southern territories were finally sinicized, becoming fully part of China proper for the first time.

In 1260, the Mongols established the Yuan dynasty in China, bringing new blood to an old land, and changing the country in some permanent ways, rebuilding, restoring, and expanding. True to their northern origins, they established their new administrative capital at a site they called Khanbaligh (City of the Khan) north of Luoyang; the great metropolis they built there awed even Europeans used to the splendors of Venice and Rome, and it has remained China's capital (except for short periods) until now, under various names, currently Beijing (Peking, or Northern Capital). The main roads of the land, now all linked with the new capital, were quite revived, as Marco Polo related:

> Now you must know the Great Khan has bidden that on the highroads along which his messengers, as well as merchants and other people travel, trees should be planted on both sides, at a distance of two paces from one another. And truly they are so high and big, that they can be seen from afar. The Great Khan has had this done so that people should be able to see the roads and not miss their way, for you will find these trees even along desert roads; and then they are of great comfort to traders and wayfarers... on rocky mountains, where it would be impossible, he has stone cairns and pillars set up to show the way. And he has certain barons to whom he has committed the task of seeing to it that those roads are constantly kept in good condition.

Since Polo arrived in Peking in 1275, only 15 years after the Mongols took China, the large trees are most likely remnants of the road system established long before, refurbished under the Khans.

As was necessary in a vast empire, which stretched from one end of Asia to the other, the Mongols had an elaborate communication system; Marco Polo was not alone in his praise of the post-system in China:

> ...the way the Great Khan's messenger-service works is truly admirable; it is indeed arranged in a most excellent manner...the envoy of the Great Khan who leaves Cambaluc [Beijing] and rides twenty-five miles, reaches at the end of that stage...a horse-post station. There the envoy finds a very large and fine palace, where the Great Khan's envoys lodge, with splendid beds, furnished with rich silk sheets, and with everything else that an important envoy may need. And if a king should go there, he should be splendidly lodged. Here the envoys also find no less than four hundred horses, always kept there by the Great Khan's orders, in readiness for any envoys of his that he may send somewhere.
>
> And even when the envoys have to traverse... mountainous regions, without horses or hostels, the Great Khan has had post-stations built there, with. . . all the other things, such as horses and harness, that the other stations have. Only the distances are larger, for they are placed at thirty-five, and even more than forty miles, from one another. The Great Khan also sends people to live there and till the soil, performing the necessary services for the posts. Thus large villages are formed.

One of the regions in which such post-villages had to be established was Yunnan. The Mongols spread further into the southwest region than the Chinese ever had, reaching all the way to the Irrawaddy River in Burma. Traveling in the region as an adviser to Kublai Khan, Marco Polo found many cities and villages around the Kunming Lakes with traders and craftsmen aplenty; but beyond that was a land of snakes and serpents, quite desolate except for an occasional market town on the old Burma Road:

> ...the way leads steadily downhill for fully two days and a half. The only thing worth noting on this stretch of the road is a great market-place, where all the people of the country come to market on the appointed days...Merchants come here from a great distance to change their silver for the local gold... As for the natives who bring the gold, no one can go to their dwelling places to do them harm; they dwell in such impregnable and inaccessible spots. Indeed no one knows where their homes are, because no one goes there but themselves.

After descending from the Yunnan Plateau, the traveler still had to travel for 15 days "through very inaccessible places and through vast jungles teeming with elephants, unicorns, and other wild beasts" before reaching settled country once more. Only on the Irrawaddy River did travelers come on a city "of great size and splendor"; Polo

called the city Mien, probably referring to the trading town of Taguang on the upper reaches of the river. In this period the overland route from India through Bengal to Burma was operating, for Polo noted:

> The Indians come here and buy the eunuchs...who are very plentiful here because any prisoners that are taken are immediately castrated and afterwards sold as slaves.

Under the Mongols, foreigners were confined to no one route and the security of all travelers was assured with a system described by the great 14th century Moslem traveler Ibn Battuta:

> China is the safest as well as the pleasantest of all the regions on the earth for a traveler. You may travel the whole nine months' journey to which the empire extends without the slightest cause for fear, even if you have treasure in your charge. For at every halting place there is a hostelry superintended by an officer who is posted there with a detachment of horse and foot. Every evening after sunset, or rather at nightfall, this officer visits the inn accompanied by his clerk; he takes down the name of every stranger who is going to pass the night there, seals the list, and then closes the inn door upon them. In the morning he comes again with his clerk, calls everybody by name, and marks them off one by one. He then dispatches along with the travelers a person whose duty it is to escort them to the next station, and to bring back from the officer in charge there a written acknowledgment of the arrival of all...In the inns the traveler finds all needful supplies, especially fowls and geese.

Safe they may have been, but in the long centuries during which roads had been neglected, water travel had come to predominate over land transport; that pattern continued under the Mongols, and even intensified with the building of the Grand Canal.

The northern section of the old canal between the Huang and Yangtze Rivers had been destroyed by the Sung in the effort to stop the Mongol advance in the 12th century. But more to the point, this canal would not have served the new capital: Beijing. Drawing on the great Chinese traditions in engineering, the Mongols had a new canal cut on a more easterly course, as Polo explains:

> The great Khan has made very great channels, both broad and deep, from the one river to the other and from one lake to the other; and makes the water go through the channels so that they seem a great river; and quite large ships go there with...grain loaded from [the Yangtze] up to the city of Cambaluc [Beijing] in Cathay [northern China].

Porcelain for the Western markets was transported overland to the main port of Canton. (Anonymous Chinese artist, late 18th century, British Museum)

This truly Grand Canal—over 1,000 miles long, from Beijing to the former capital of Hangzhou, south of the Yangtze on the east coast—was a vital artery; the Chinese called it "River of Transport." It was even accompanied by a land route, as Polo notes:

...alongside the waterways there runs a causeway.
So that there is a way...by land and water alike.

Polo even avers that "all the high roads and causeways" of southeast China were paved with stone and brick, "so that it is possible to walk dry-shod through the length and breadth of the land." Such an innovation was not without its disadvantages, however:

...since the Great Khan's couriers could not ride post-haste on horseback over paved roads, one strip of road at the side is left unpaved for their benefit.

The Ming dynasty, native Chinese rulers who overthrew the Mongols in 1368, benefited from the Mongol advances, especially the Grand Canal. They also expanded Chinese sea power to reach Africa and Arabia, exacting tribute from ports around the Indian Ocean with a show of maritime might. But after some decades—and a shift of their capital from Nanking, near the mouth of the Yangtze, to Beijing—the Ming dynasty for its own private reasons withdrew from the world. The great eastern ports, which Polo and other world travelers had pronounced some of the largest and most splendid in the world, were closed down, and the Ming confined foreign trade to just the southern port of Canton—and that only grudgingly. A century later, Europeans would be knocking at the door, and the Mings would adopt a full siege mentality, barring entry to their seaports as well as building the modern version of the Great Wall to keep out intruders from the north.

Under the Ming dynasty, the road system carefully restored by the Mongols once again fell into disrepair. The Burma Road was closed, as that region once more became independent; Annam, which had broken free from the Mongols, was partly restored to the Chinese for a time, before the coastal strip and the prime port of Hanoi were lost once again. The line of the old Ambassador's Road, from Canton via Lake Dongting north, continued in use, now extended to Kaifeng and Beijing. But alien ambassadors generally followed the more easterly route, angled toward the coast and the Grand Canal. Foreign envoys would be housed in segregated quarters in Canton, while word of their presence was sent to Peking; if approved, these visitors were summoned north to the imperial court. From Canton the envoys were led on a route through the Mei-ling Pass in the low intervening mountains to Nanchang near Lake Poyang. From there, travelers going overland passed through Luchow and Suchow, then crossed the Grand Canal and the Huang River on the north road to Peking. Travelers preferring the water route would follow the Yangtze to the Grand Canal, where they would embark on a boat for the north, a slow choice, since the canal was always filled with barges. Either way, they traveled only with official permission and escort; no "barbarians" were allowed to travel on their own in China, and Chinese were forbidden to aid such travelers. In early Ming times, many foreign ambassadors were tributebearers, come to pay tangible homage to Chinese seapower. Even later, visitors for whatever purpose were treated as tribute-bearers, and were expected to "kowtow" – to kneel and literally knock their heads against the floor – in the presence of the emperor; many were spared this humiliation, for they met only the imperial eunuchs, who increasingly handled official business.

The first Western Europeans to arrive in China in the modern period were the Portuguese, a party of whom appeared in Canton in 1517. The first contact was illstarred. The Portuguese announced their arrival by firing their ship's guns at the city of Canton; the Portuguese representatives, taken to Peking and later returned to Canton after the emperor's sudden death, were imprisoned and ill-treated, one of them dying in jail. They regained some favor by helping the Chinese put down troublesome coastal pirates, and in turn were allowed to settle on the peninsula of Macao, downriver from Canton, where they established a permanent trading post. The Portuguese were followed by other Europeans, notably the Spanish, the Dutch, and the British, all of whom went through the same induction process, though somewhat more peaceably. Indeed, some European visitors were given special favor, among them some Jesuit priests who arrived in the late 16th and early 17th centuries. They were even allowed to establish a few selected missions; while these were not always welcomed by the general population, who exhibited considerable xenophobia, many in the court were honored as scholars. One Jesuit priest, Matteo Ricci, after losing his mission west of Canton, was brought north to Peking; there he spent nine years, traveling freely through T'ien An Men (the Gate of Heavenly Peace) into the palace grounds. The Jesuits brought to China word of new discoveries that had been made in the West while the Chinese had been behind closed doors – new continents, but also new scientific techniques, along with some startling new inventions, like guns.

Under the Ming dynasty, Chinese roads were more used than repaired. Yet, in comparison with European roads at the time, Western visitors found much to praise, like the French traveler Louis Lecomte at the end of the 17th century:

> One can't imagine what care they [the Chinese] take to make the common Roads convenient for passage. They are fourscore foot broad or very near it; the Soil of them is light, and soon dry when it has left off raining. In some Provinces there are on the right and left hand Causeways for the foot Passengers, which are on both sides supported by long rows of trees, and ofttimes terrassed with a wall of eight or ten foot high on each side, to keep Passengers out of the fields. Nevertheless these Walls have breaks, where Roads cross one the other, and they all terminate at some great Town.

Posthouses and guard stations were, as always, placed along the road at strategic points. And Europeans were still much impressed by the trestle-and-balcony construction still to be seen in some mountainous terrain.

But China was, in truth, entering into an ever deeper decline. Europeans continually chafed at being allowed to trade only at Canton, and then on restricted terms; after three centuries of fruitless embassies to Peking, they succeeded in opening trade with other Chinese ports after a series of Opium Wars in the 1830's and 1840's. Canton lost its primacy, and as foreign – especially British – influence spread, the old Ambassador's Road and its easterly counterpart lost their special purpose. Visitors complained that the roads were so dilapidated that travelers sometimes made a parallel new road in fields alongside, until the forces of nature had once again smoothed the main road's surface, making it fit for travelers.

In the 20th century, the end of the empire brought few changes to the old roads of China. The main northsouth lines of travel remained as they had for centuries. Parts of the Grand Canal, too, remained open, although the northern section was unusable. Even the old trail to Burma still operated, in its own rough way. Writing at the turn of the 20th century, the Chinese expert E. H. Parker noted that:

> ...as many as 5,000 Chinese mules from Yün Nan may be seen any day during the autumn trading season picketed amongst their burdens in the vacant fields around Bhamo [on the upper Irrawaddy].

This route was destined to play a special role in World War II. When the Japanese overran the eastern half of China, the Chinese were forced to remove their capital to the southwest, to Chongqing (Chungking), on the Yangtze. In an effort to supply their comrades, the Allies built the famous Burma Road; from the rail link that branched eastward from the Irrawaddy at Mandalay to Lashio, they carved a road out of the jungle across the Yunnan Plateau to beleaguered Chongqing. The road

13

operated for only a short time, however; air supply soon had to take over, and the Burma Road was let lapse once again, after its brief moment of world fame.

After its revolution in 1949, China once again closed herself off from the outside, but this time more briefly; intrepid travelers today can once again bump along the old trail to Burma, or through the mountains of Sichuan. Those who choose the smoother rail ride may well find themselves following the main line of the old Ambassador's Road, familiar to centuries of travelers, from Can-

ton north to Lake Dongting, detouring eastward to the modern river port of Wuhan—home of the great steamships of the Yangtze—then heading north past Kaifeng to Peking. Though the human beasts of burden—the oppressed underlings of imperial times—no longer ply the roads, modern automobiles are few and far between. Wagons and walkers still dominate the Ambassador's Road and the Burma Road, as they have in centuries past, along with the now-ubiquitous modern bicycle.

Selective Bibliography

Buxton, L. H. Dudley. *China: The Land and the People, A Human Geography* (Oxford: At the Clarendon Press, 1929). A dated but interesting work on the modern period, with numerous illustrations.

Cameron, Nigel. *Barbarians and Mandarins: Thirteen Centuries of Western Travelers in China* (Chicago: University of Chicago Press, 1976; reprint of 1970 edition by John Weatherhill, Inc.). Despite the subtitle, focuses on Mongol, Ming, and modern travelers, with many excerpts, paraphrases, and illustrations.

Journey Into China (Washington, D. C.: The National Geographic Society, 1982). An unusually well-illustrated volume, with a series of articles on themes and regions, along with useful maps.

Lattimore, Owen, and Eleanor Lattimore, eds. *Silks, Spices and Empire: Asia Seen Through the Eyes of Its Discoverers* (New York: Delacorte Press, 1968). Part of the Great Explorers series. Well-annotated excerpts of Western accounts of Asia.

Morse, Hosea Ballou. *The Trade and Administration of China,* Revised Edition (Shanghai, Hongkong, Singapore & Yokohama: Kelly and Walsh, Ltd., 1913). Focuses on the mechanics of trading in the modern period.

Needham, Joseph. *Science and Civilization in China* (Cambridge: At the University Press, 1965-). An invaluable work with extremely useful maps and illustrations; Volume I gives an historical overview of travel, while Volume IV, Part 3, includes detailed sections on roads and canals.

Parker, E. H. *China: Her History, Diplomacy, and Commerce, From the Earliest Times to the Present Day,* Second Edition (London: John Murray, 1917). A detailed early work stressing the modern period.

Polo, Marco. *The Travels.* Translated by Ronald Latham (Harmondsworth, Middlesex: Penguin, 1958). A well-indexed and helpfully annotated edition of the unabridged text.

Purcell, Victor. *The Chinese in Southeast Asia,* Second Edition (London: Oxford University Press, 1965). Reviews Chinese presence and influence from early times in each major area, stressing the modern period.

Reischauer, Edwin O., and John K. Fairbank. *East Asia: The Great Tradition* (Boston: Houghton Mifflin, 1958). Volume I of *A History of East Asian Civilization.* A good, standard history.

Schafer, Edward H. *The Golden Peaches of Samarkand: A Study of T'ang Exotics* (Berkeley and Los Angeles: University of California Press, 1963). An interesting study of the beings and items that traveled through China during the T'ang period.

_____. *The Vermilion Bird: T'ang Images of the South* (Berkeley and Los Angeles: University of California Press, 1967). A diverse work on the people, flora, and fauna of the coastal regions, including Vietnam.

Schurmann, Franz, and Orville Schell, eds. *Imperial China: the Decline of the Last Dynasty and the Origins of Modern China, The 18th and 19th Centuries* (New York: Random House, 1967). Volume I of the China Reader series. Combines excerpts of first-hand accounts with analytical essays.

Tregear, Thomas R. *A Geography of China* (London: University of London Press, 1965). A very useful overview, containing a substantial section on historical geography.

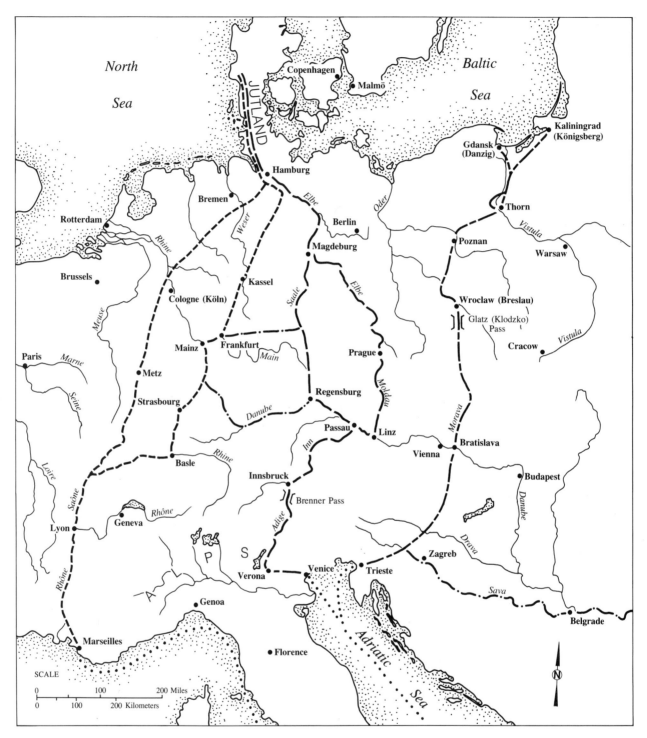

The Amber Routes in Prehistoric Times
(Modern Cities Noted for Reference)

— — — Brenner Pass Route   — · — · — Main Connecting Land Routes

– – – – – Rhône-Saône Route   · · · · · · · Main Connecting Sea Routes

— – — – — Vistula Route

The Amber Routes

*T*he Roman writer Pliny the Elder told of an unusual journey northeastward from Italy to the source of that most prized of ancient gems, amber:

> The distance from Carnuntum [near the junction of modern Austria, Czechoslovakia, and Hungary]...to the coasts of Germany from which amber is brought to us is some 600 miles, a fact which has been confirmed only recently. There is still living a Roman knight who was commissioned to procure amber by a Julianus [who]...was in charge of a display of gladiators by the Emperor Nero. This knight traversed both the trade-route and the coasts, and brought back so plentiful a supply that the nets used for keeping the beasts away from the parapet of the amphitheatre were knotted with pieces of amber. Moreover, the arms, biers and all the equipment used on one day...had amber fittings. The heaviest lump brought by the knight to Rome weighed 13 pounds.

This journey, though apparently not repeated by the Romans in the first century A.D., was less unusual than it might seem, for by then amber had been arriving in southern Europe for 2,000 years.

The several pathways by which amber reached the Italian peninsula—and the Mediterranean on either side of it—were developed by intrepid early peddlers, who laid down the main lines of travel in Europe. For some thousands of years—we know not how long—goods were traded across Europe in the ancient way, from tribe to tribe. Well before 4,000 years ago, specialist craftsmen-traders—experts in preparing stone knives and axes—wandered over the continent, selling their goods to peoples along the way. Rather than carry their full stock with them all the time, they left behind carefully hidden caches of tools—some freshly made, others worn but kept for refurbishing and resale—and other goods. Many traders never lived to return for their goods—an indication of the danger faced by these bold venturers—but their loss is our gain. For it is by uncovering such secret hoards and roadside graves that modern archaeologists have traced the trade routes they laid down across Europe. These are called the Amber Routes because that gem (fossilized resin) is almost indestructible and readily identifiable as to origin, so it is possible to trace the course of the amber—and therefore of the ancient trade routes—from the North and Baltic seas through France, Germany, Switzerland, Austria, and Poland down to the Mediterranean Sea.

Far more than amber was traded on these routes, of course. Some items—like vital salt and always-prized furs—were perishable and have left little trace. Other items indicate the surprising breadth of contact among these early traders. For example, in Central Europe archaeologists have found cowrie shells, native only to the Indian Ocean or the South Pacific, and ivory from Africa or Asia.

The earliest Amber Route across Europe seems to have been the Brenner Pass Route. Starting on the west coast of Jutland, where amber was commonly washed up

Across the great rivers of northern Europe, ferries have operated for thousands of years, like this one on the Vistula. (By Daniel Chodowiecki, 1773, Kupferstichkabinett und Sammlung der Zeichnungen, Berlin)

on the shores of the North Sea, traders made their way with the precious substance to near modern Hamburg, then south along the Elbe River to the region of Magdeburg. There, the east branch of the route continued through Bohemia down the Elbe and then the Moldau rivers past Prague, then crossing to the upper Danube River near Linz. The western branch of this route diverged at Magdeburg down the Saale River, crossing Bavaria to the upper Danube near Regensburg. The two branches then converged near Passau and, leaving the Danube, passed up the Inn River as far as Innsbruck; cutting south through the Alps, the route traversed the 4,500-foot-high Brenner Pass, one of the gentlest of all the Alpine passes. Once in Italy, the route picked up the valley of the Adige River to Verona, with its ready access to both northern Italy and the Adriatic, in later times especially Venice and Rome.

Amber had been reaching Bohemia even in earlier times, but by the early second millennium B.C. it was being carried all the way into northern Italy, especially to the eager markets of Etruria in the northwest. Among the other items traded in return for northern amber seems to have been Bohemian tin, necessary for alloying with copper to make bronze; indeed, some experts feel that it was by the Amber Routes that the techniques of bronze-working traveled to the peoples of Northern Europe. This

trade continued to develop over some centuries, during which time the wandering merchants gradually refined the Brenner Pass route, finding the best fords and passes, and occasionally improving the way slightly with a modest wooden bridge, or with layers of logs called a "corduroy road," to ease the passage through a marsh. During this period, amber from Northern Europe was even reaching as far as Assyria in the Near East. Rarely, if ever, would one trader traverse the whole Brenner Pass Route, however; more likely traders would have a certain "territory," and the valuable goods would be passed from one to another from Jutland on down to Italy. During the later part of the Bronze Age, invaders into Bohemia made the eastern branch of the Brenner Pass Route less safe, but trade continued on the western branch, declining only in the last few centuries before the birth of Christ.

Meanwhile a new Amber Route was being opened to the West, after about 1800 B.C. With the Bronze Age under way, this route is traced not only by amber but by the worksites and caches of traveling bronze workers, ancestors of the more modern tinkers, who would both make new objects and repair old ones, as did stoneworkers before them. Also proceeding from Jutland to Hamburg, this route left the Elbe by one of two branches. The eastern branch cut south to Frankfurt on the Main River, cutting west along the Main to Mainz on the Rhine; there archaeologists have found the remains of many ancient wrecked ferries on what must have been a difficult crossing. Passing southward through the German forests, this east branch reached the upper Rhine at Basel in Switzerland, then cut westward to the Saône River. The western branch of this new Amber Route cut sharply southwest from Hamburg, crossing the lower reaches of the Rhine near modern Cologne (Köln), then passing over the lowlands to meet the eastern branch at the Saône. The route then headed down the Saône and the Rhône to the Mediterranean.

The eastern branch of this Rhône-Saône Route had a special advantage because the Alpine peoples worked the amber into ornaments before it was sent on (clearly the modern Swiss are following a long tradition as consummate craftsmen). Indeed, the Etruscans of northwestern Italy exported their inferior amber north, preferring instead the North Sea amber refined by Alpine artisans. Like the Brenner Pass Route, the Rhône-Saône Route operated—surely with occasional interruptions, but no real breaks—for many centuries. It became increasingly important as Cretan, Phoenician, and Greek traders began stopping to trade at the mouth of the Rhône; it was the Greeks who stayed to found Massalia (Marseilles) just east of the Rhône's swampy delta in about 600 B.C. Although the routes marked by traders'—and probably also robbers'—caches are primarily overland pathways, early traders may well have used the Saône and Rhône on the downstream passage, even though the rivers are fast-flowing and rather variable.

The third and latest of the Amber Routes is the Vistula Route. The coastlands of the eastern Baltic Sea, especially between Gdansk (Danzig) and Kaliningrad (Königsberg), were rich in a high-quality amber; a Greek maritime explorer, Pytheas, noted in the fourth century B.C. that:

...[On the sand flats] amber is washed up by the waves in the spring, scum from the condensation of the sea. The inhabitants use it as fuel instead of wood and sell it to their...neighbors.

Some of this amber had been traded to Central Europe (and Russia as well) even before the second millennium B.C., but that trade was later interrupted. Then at the turn of the first millennium B.C., a new trans-European Amber Route was opened. Following the Vistula River down to Thorn, where the waterway begins its great eastward curve, the route angled southeastward across the Polish plain and the Sudetenland, picking up and following the Morava River down to its junction with the Danube; here, near modern Bratislava (Pressburg), stood Carnuntum, which the Roman knight visited on his way to the amber markets. The Vistula Route then made a long slow curve across the headwaters of the Drava and Sava rivers to reach the northeast corner of the Adriatic Sea near Trieste. From there the amber was picked up by Greek and other traders, who distributed it to Italy and other parts of the eastern Mediterranean.

It was some time before the amber trade was extended the whole length of this trail, but by 700 B.C., trade on the Vistula Route was well underway, while the Brenner Pass Route and the Rhône-Saône Route were beginning a long, slow decline. Suitable to a more highly organized trade, many parts of the Vistula Route were improved; parts were corduroyed (some sections have been preserved in the northern European bogs until modern times), while some parts where bedrock was exposed show grooves cut into the stone, as tracks for carts with a standardized wheel-gauge of about a yard. So great was the volume of traffic on this early route that archaeologists have found some traders' depots holding well over a ton of amber—some rough cut, some partly worked—along with a wide variety of tools employed at these "refineries."

Trade on the Vistula Route, and to a lesser extent on the other Amber Routes, continued for some centuries, at least while the Etruscan market was undisturbed. During this period Greek traders were gradually filtering through southern Europe, exploring the main Alpine passes and becoming actively involved in the amber trade. But for the Greeks themselves, amber fell temporarily out of fashion. When, in the fourth century B.C., the Romans became the new power in Italy and came under the cultural spell of the Greeks, the amber market plummeted. Trade continued on all these routes, of course, but it was not quite as brisk, without the desire for amber as its main motor. By the time amber was once again back in fashion in Rome, the European world had become quite a different place, under Roman rule; and these Romans would transform the Amber Routes—the parts they controlled—into Roman roads.

The Romans paid little attention to the Amber Routes in early times. They were farmers, not traders, and were happy to have others bring goods to them, without questioning the source. Not only that, they were fully occupied with rivals on the Mediterranean. Although the Romans early developed a coastal route—the Heraclean Way—to Spain, they knew so little about the mountains to their north that Hannibal was able to surprise them with an Alpine crossing, aided by Celts who were used to guiding traders in exchange for appropriate tolls and tribute.

It was Julius Caesar who in the first century B.C. moved beyond the coastal district, which was considered almost part of Italy itself, into the hinterland of Gaul, which he pronounced was divided into three parts: Aquitania in the southwest, Lugdunensis in the center, and Belgica in the northern lowlands. He pushed a new road through the Alps, following an earlier traders' path along the 8,000-foot-high Great St. Bernard Pass to the upper Rhône and Lake Geneva. In a series of stunning campaigns 50 years before the birth of Christ, Caesar won all Gaul for Rome, and his route through the Alps was extended to Lugdunum (now Lyon, named for the Celtic god, Lug), at the Rhône-Saône junction. The Alpine connection with Italy made Lugdunum the main city on the Rhône-Saône Route in Roman times. Traders from Massilia—now under Roman control—would thread their way up the Rhodanus (Rhône) River Valley to Lugdunum; as Roman rule extended further north, the road did likewise. From Lugdunum it followed the Arar (Saône) River north, crossing to pick up the valley of the Mosella River, to Augusta Trevororum (Trier, or Trèves), founded in 16 B.C. As the Romans gradually extended their rule into Germania, across the Rhenus (Rhine) River, the route was extended through the Arduenna Silva (Ardennes Wood) to the prime city of Colonia Agrippinensis (Cologne, or Köln) founded in 38 B.C. by order of Caesar Augustus. This rapidly became a flourishing commercial city, northern terminus of the Rhône-Saône Route in Roman times and long the largest city on the Rhine.

As they would everywhere they spread, the Romans built firm roads throughout their territory. These were not always the uniform, straight roads of their popular reputation, but were very much tailored to the terrain. In mountainous or rocky country, Roman engineers were in their element, carving roads out of the sides of hills and building their famous well-drained, solid, stone-paved highways and causeways. But in the lowlands of northern Gaul, they adopted road-building methods that had already been used in the region for over 2,000 years, building log roads across marshy regions, standardizing them to a 10-foot width, and often adding to them a top layer of gravel or sand, for firmer footing. Where the heavy, stone bridges characteristic of the Romans dominated in southern Gaul, in the lowlands wooden bridges were more common; portable pontoon bridges were sometimes covered with earth and gravel when semi-permanently in place. Log roads and bridges were also the tools of invasion, and when the Romans took their armies across the Rhine, log roads were aimed deep into Germania, one apparently following the general line of the old Amber Route up to the Albis (Elbe) River. But after a disastrous defeat across the Rhine, the Romans effectively gave up the attempt to invade Germania, and contented themselves with the Rhine as a frontier, creating a cleared, fortified buffer zone on the far side of the river, extending down the Rhine to Mogontiacum (Mainz) where it turned to follow the Main and later cut across to meet the Danuvius (Danube).

Gaul—and its lifeline, the Rhône-Saône Route—was extremely important to Rome in its early days of empire. Emperor Claudius was born in Lyon, and generals and heirs apparent were sent to the Rhine to make their names. Julius Caesar had used the Rhône-Saône Route as an entrée to Britain; Claudius made it a full-scale invasion route,

in the first century A.D. From Rome the main connecting route to Gaul fed through the Alps via the Great St. Bernard Pass opened by Julius Caesar, which the first century Greco-Roman geographer Strabo noted was "passable for vehicles over most of its length." (An alternate route over the Little St. Bernard was not, being "steep and narrow.") That Lyon was the hub of Gaul was clear to Strabo:

> Lugdunum lies in the center of Celtica, of which it forms in a way the citadel, since it lies at the confluence of the rivers and is conveniently placed for the different parts of the country.

Traders from the north found Lyon a prime marketplace at which they could exchange goods, and then either travel down the Rhône to Arelate (Arles) and Massilia or over the Great St. Bernard through Augusta Taurinorum (Turin) to Italy.

During Roman times, the Brenner Pass Route was sharply truncated. Although an important connecting route—the Via Claudia Augusta, named for its builder Emperor Claudius—ran between Verona in the Po Valley across the Brenner to Augusta Vindelicum (Augsburg), no main connecting route extended across Bavaria north to Jutland, as it had in the days of the early amber trade. The Romans built numerous other roads through the Alps as well, through passes like the Simplon, St. Gotthard, San Bernardino, Splügen, Arlberg, and Grossglockner. These roads—some of them stunningly cut along cliffsides—primarily fulfilled strategic purposes, however; while these passes were often-used in Roman times (and have become well-known in modern times, when technology has reopened them as highways), they were exceedingly difficult routes. As a result, they never supplanted the old Amber Routes as main highways, even at the height of the Roman Empire.

On the main routes, chariots and carriages could easily be used; Claudius even had a special carriage built so he could play dice en route through Gaul. Lesser routes were probably like those the Roman writer Apuleius complains about, which were rough tracks "heavily rutted, now a morass of stagnant water, now covered by a layer of slippery mud." Where possible, travelers would stay at the home of a friend—or the friend of a friend, for letters of introduction were often supplied to traveling acquaintances; those on military campaigns would generally camp with their soldiers at sites along the way. The rest had to make do with inns, which often left much to be desired, both in terms of safety and comfort; it was not unheard of for a traveling stranger to be abducted from an inn and enslaved, and more than one complained about the sleeping accommodations, like Apuleius: "My couch, besides being rather short, had a leg missing and was worm-eaten." Perhaps more than anything, road travel was tedious, and the practice of telling tales to while away the time—which

Beggars, vagrants, and pilgrims were always common on the Amber Routes of Europe. (By Lucas van Leyden, 1520, Kupferstichkabinett und Sammlung der Zeichnungen, Berlin)

would be so characteristic of medieval pilgrimages—was well-established in Roman times.

Travelers were also caught in a peculiar bind; because they feared attack by robbers, they often banded together in large groups—sometimes only to be suspected as robbers themselves. Apuleius explains:

> When the farmers on a country estate near which we were passing saw us in such numbers, they thought we were brigands...They sent after us huge dogs.

Indeed, some of these dogs were "enormous, savage creatures, accustomed to feeding on corpses left in the fields and trained in addition to bite without any distinction all passing wayfarers." These great Roman roads—some over 25 feet wide in Gaul, where land was cheap—were also drovers' roads. Farmers drove their livestock to nearby cities, sometimes for hundreds of miles to Rome itself, to find the best market prices.

During this time, the Vistula Route was also divided between the Romans and the "barbarians." Aquileia had been founded at the head of the Adriatic—"as a fortress against the barbarians who were situated about it," according to Strabo—in 181 B.C.; but as the Romans gradually pushed their frontier eastward, to give better protection against invasion, Aquileia became a prime commercial city as well, terminus of the Vistula Route. Carnuntum became the Romans's furthest outpost on the Vistula Route, acting as both a fort and a trading post, to which Celtic traders brought amber and furs from the north, to exchange for the finely worked items created by Roman craftsmen. As Aquileia had been the base for the conquest of Noricum (Austria), so Carnuntum became a prime forward base for legions guarding or crossing the Danube.

While the Romans brought some order to the lands they controlled, especially in the first century A.D., they came under increasing pressure from across the frontier as the centuries wore on. For some time, the Romans pursued a rather successful policy of bringing into their fold potential invaders, in effect seducing them with the blessings of civilization. But that policy grew less effective as Rome's central hold weakened, and the regional armies vied with one another for power. As the justly feared nomadic Huns pressed westward out of the Eurasian Steppe, they pushed ahead of them other peoples, among them Vandals and Goths; the Romans reluctantly accepted these refugees, and attempted to settle them in Roman territory. But they could not be contained, and gradually spread across western Europe, often giving their tribal names—such as Burgundians, Lombards, and Franks—to the regions where they eventually settled. The Hunnish invaders followed them into Europe in the fifth century; these overextended themselves and were driven out

by the other inhabitants of western Europe, new and old. But the damage was done.

In these times of flux, with large population shifts and no central order, the Amber Routes that had, for a time, become Roman roads, fell into disrepair. The Vistula Route, and with it the port of Aquileia, was particularly hard hit, and would be subjected to successive onslaughts over the centuries, especially from the Avars, the Slavs, and the Magyars. The Brenner Pass Route was likewise disrupted, as wave after wave of invaders poured over it into northern Italy. Only along the Rhône-Saône Route was any semblance of order restored, as the Franks migrated from the lower Rhine into the heart of Gaul, beginning the process by which this country would be transformed into France.

But in all these areas, the roads suffered. Many of the old Roman highways, not simply the more daring Alpine routes, were abandoned to nature, and soon became filled with trees and gaping holes. Although local rulers might repair some sections for regional use—as Charlemagne did in France—no central power had the will or the ability to keep the whole network open, safe, and in good repair. Indeed, good roads were not always an advantage, for they led invaders easily into the heart of the land; this was perhaps clearest on the Brenner Pass Route, which allowed Goth, Huns, Lombards, and others to swarm through the Tyrol into northern Italy, in the days when the Roman road was still in repair. Cities whose existence had depended on the traffic that coursed along the roads in Roman times often declined to small villages; those that remained were generally those on one of the main waterways, like the Rhine or the Rhône, which increasingly replaced roads in handling transport, especially of heavy goods.

The roads that remained were often unsuitable for the swift chariots and fashionable carriages they had seen in Roman times; large, crude farm wagons, their heavy wooden wheels often studded with iron nails, were more common for hauling bulk goods, and even then usually only for short distances. Increasingly, riding or walking became the dominant mode of travel, being less vulnerable to bumps and holes than wheeled vehicles. Except for bulk goods, like wheat, most items in the modest early medieval trade were transported on caravans of pack horses or asses. Men and women rode mounted, when they could afford it, or walked. As in Roman times, travelers often formed groups for protection on the road; and, as Western Europeans adopted the heavy mounted cavalry of the nomadic invaders from the steppes, knights or other armed horsemen were often engaged to accompany travel parties. There was, in any case, not much travel in early medieval times.

The picture really began to change only in the 10th century; then, with the cessation of the great invasions that had beleaguered Europe from all quarters, a relative calm was once again restored. Messengers, merchants, minstrels, healers, traveling artisans (journeymen), and wayfarers were seen in increasing numbers—and were joined by another kind of traveler: the *peregrine* (wanderer), whom we know as the pilgrim. Pilgrims had wandered European roads for centuries, at least since the Emperor Constantine had adopted Christianity and restored Jerusalem in the fourth century A.D.; some of these early pilgrims had even made their way all the way to the Holy Land. But the practice of Christian pilgrimage only became widespread in the 10th century.

Pilgrims themselves were distinguished by their destination, as Dante later described in his *La Vita Nuova*:

> ...there are three separate denominations proper unto those who undertake journeys to the glory of God. They are called Palmers who go beyond the seas eastward [to Jerusalem] whence often they bring palm-branches. And Pilgrims...are they who journey unto the holy House of Galicia [Compostela]; seeing that no other apostle was buried so far from his birth-place as was blessed St. James [Santiago]; and there is a third sort who are called Romers; in that they go...unto Rome.

Palmers generally took the Orient Route from the upper Danube across to Constantinople, and then traveled overland to the Holy Land. In later times, when the Crusaders had established Christian communities in the eastern Mediterranean, many bound for Jerusalem would filter through the Alps on the Brenner Pass Route, embarking for the Near East on a ship from Venice—whose prosperity owed not a little to this traffic. Romers (or Roamers) bound for the tombs of St. Peter and St. Paul in Rome would follow either the Brenner Pass Route from Germany or the Rhône-Saône Route to Lyon, proceeding to Italy either by the Great St. Bernard Pass or by the 6,800-foot-high Mont Cenis Pass opened in Charlemagne's time, in about the eighth century.

The third group of pilgrims opened a new route altogether. Their destination was Compostela in Spain, where medieval Christians believed the body of St. James (St. Iago, or Santiago in Spanish) was buried. Although Santiago de Compostela lay on no main road, it was an attractive destination, especially for pilgrims from France, Britain, and western Germany; indeed, it had parity with Rome in many important respects, such as granting indulgences or fulfilling penances. So medieval pilgrims began to carve out a new network of pathways known collectively as the Santiago de Compostela Routes. From the north, pilgrims headed toward Paris, becoming France's dominant capital on the Seine River, to the shrine of St. Denis, and then headed south through Orléans, Tours, Poitiers, and Bordeaux, crossing the Pyrenees into Spain at St. Jean Pied-de-Port. From central France, the first station of the route to Santiago de Compostela was general-

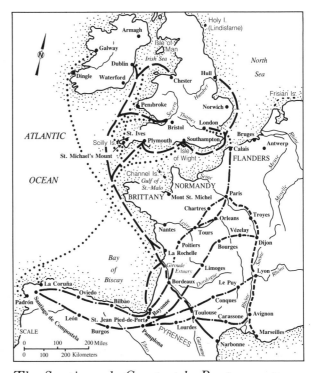

The Santiago de Compostela Routes in Medieval Times

——·——·—— Land Routes to Santiago De Compostela
·············· Sea Routes to Santiago De Compostela
—— —— —— Tin and Wine Routes
–––––––– Main Connecting Route

ly the great cathedral at Vézelay, and then through Bourges and Limoges to join the northern route near the Pyrenees. Pilgrims from further east, from the Rhineland or Switzerland, more often took the Rhône-Saône Route to Lyon, and then cut southwestward through Le Puy, Conques, and Cahors to the Pyrenees, being joined by others who had come by way of Narbonne, Carcassone, and Toulouse or Lourdes. Once in Spain, the pathways generally formed a single main route through Pamplona, Burgos, and León to Compostela; because this city was near the coast, these pilgrims had as their symbol a scallop shell.

Along all of these routes there developed a series of cathedrals and lesser shrines, often built with very wide aisles to accommodate crowds of pilgrims. Hospices, too, were set up by religious orders, to provide shelter and medical care, if necessary, along the way; where these were not available, travelers often had to pay dearly for mean, crowded, vermin-ridden quarters. Because of these hazards, itineraries—the medieval version of travel guides—were widely circulated, noting good places to stay, and detailing special hazards along the way. Aimery Picaud's *Guide du Pelerin*, for example, warned pilgrims on the road to Santiago de Compostela about extortion from riverboatmen who were so greedy they sometimes overloaded their ferries and drowned all passengers. Similarly, toll officials

This 1842 illustration well conveys the amount of pushing, walking, and just plain waiting involved in stagecoach travel. (From Jean Grandeville, Die kleinen Leiden des menschlichen Lebens)

near St. Jean Pied-de-Port, who were supposed to tax only merchants, often extorted fees from pilgrims by force; Picaud's opinion was unequivocal: "...quite frankly they should be sent to the devil." Pilgrims were especially numerous during the periodic Holy Years, the first of which was in 1300; then tens or hundreds of thousands of Christians would make their way to Rome, seeking full pardon for all their sins.

Many pilgrims had purposes other than purely religious ones in mind. Some were required to make pilgrimage as punishment for a crime. Many simply wanted an excuse to travel. Indeed, the pilgrimage was often a far-from-elevating experience. Some churchmen even disapproved of pilgrimage, especially for women, who they thought were in danger of losing their virtue en route. The problem is well-illustrated by Brother Felix Fabri, who made two pilgrimages to Jerusalem in the 15th century:

> ...we all decided that no more games of cards or dice should be played on board of the galley, that no quarrels, swearing or blasphemies should be allowed, and that the clerks and priests should add litanies to their usual daily prayers...for men were gambling morning, noon and night, especially the Bishop of Orléans with his suite...

Because these pilgrims traveled far and wide, they often doubled as merchants and private postmen, delivering messages and packages for officials and friends.

These medieval travelers began to make the roads usable once again. Though far rougher than the old Roman roads, the largely dirt medieval roads did reasonably well for travelers who mostly walked or rode, as long as they were not too fastidious about dust, mud, or manure from horses and cattle. Merchants from the main north Mediterranean ports, enriched by the increase in travel, took their trade goods further and further inland, quite naturally following the main line of the old Amber Routes. From Marseilles, the old Rhône-Saône Route fed north through Lyon and Dijon but then angled slightly westward, through Troyes to Bruges, for this was the main trading route across the English Channel to increasingly important London. The Italian city-states of Genoa and Pisa sent their traders, as of old, across the Great St. Bernard pass to Lyon or to Dijon. But many traders and pilgrims preferred the route to Lyon via the Mont Cenis Pass. From Turin, rather than curving north around Lake Geneva, this route cut more directly westward to Lyon; since it also avoided the difficult passage through the Jura Mountains between France and Switzerland, the Mont Cenis Pass became the most used crossing between Italy and France, though it never fully replaced the Great St. Bernard, which continued to attract much traffic. Other routes, through central Alpine passes like the St.

Gotthard and the Septimer, also became heavily used in this period by traders heading directly for Bavaria. As a result Milan (to the Romans, Mediolanum), at the junction of various routes, joined Turin as a major northern Italian crossroads city.

From the Adriatic, Venice sent her traders along the Po to Verona on the Brenner Pass Route to the old Roman settlement of Augsburg and north through the newer towns of Nuremburg and Leipzig toward the Elbe. From Augsburg, there also ran an alternate route to the northwest, headed toward Frankfurt-on-Main (which was replacing Mainz as the main market city in the region), and then on through Cologne to Bruges. Italian traders on the Rhône-Saône Route or the Brenner Pass Route did not, however, usually reach all the way north to Hamburg and Jutland; this was Hanseatic League territory, where river routes prevailed and trade was strictly controlled. A 13th century regulation from Cologne indicates the problem faced by southern and central European merchants:

> Any merchants attempting to pass through Cologne on their way from Hungary, Bohemia, Poland, Bavaria, Swabia, Saxony, Thuringia and Hesse or from Flanders, Brabant and the other Low Countries...can be taken into custody by any citizen of Cologne who catches him...

The punishment being a large fine, merchants were certainly discouraged from encroaching into Hansa territory.

The rival Hanseatic League did not, however, block full use of the Vistula Route. From Venice itself the route angled eastward toward the now-important city of Budapest on the Danube, then cut northward. It split into two branches—one westward to Breslau (Wroclaw) on the Oder River, the other following the line of the Vistula River through Cracow and Warsaw; these recombined at Thorn and proceeded to Danzig (Gdansk) on the Baltic Sea. Here, too, traders sometimes followed a connecting route westward from Cracow through Breslau and Leipzig to link up at Frankfurt-on-Main

Initially, such trade ran into several obstacles. Every fiefdom and principality would try to charge customs duties on each load of goods that passed across its borders. This was especially true on the Brenner Pass Route, which passed through the many petty states of Germany, cantons of Switzerland, and duchies of Italy. Anglo-Saxons traveling from their homeland in northern Germany to Lombardy, in northern Italy, for example, had to pay duties at 10 customs houses in the Alps alone, "on horses, male and female slaves, woolen, linen, and hemp cloth, tin, and swords," according to court regulations of 11th-century Pavia. This provoked an angry response, as the regulations continue:

> ...the Angles and Saxons...were wont to come with their merchandise and wares. And [formerly], when

25

they saw their trunks and sacks being emptied at the gates, they grew angry and started rows with the employees of the treasury. The [parties] were wont to hurl abusive words and in addition very often inflicted wounds upon one another.

To solve the problem, the two nations made a trade agreement whereby the Angles and Saxons would pay no duties and would be given safe-conduct through Lombardy, in return for a yearly payment of gold and goods. Agreements such as this oiled trade on the Amber Routes in late medieval times. International fairs—some begun centuries earlier as regional fairs—also served the same purpose, allowing merchants to meet together in a safe place with standardized taxing arrangements. The fairs at Lyons (noted for its silk mart), Frankfurt-on-Main, Geneva, and the cities of Champagne in northeast France were among the most important. These great fairs attracted even Syrian and Jewish traders from across the Mediterranean, who came to trade Eastern luxuries like silk and gems for the products of Northern Europe, especially wools and linens from Flanders. International trading cities generally set aside special quarters for foreign merchants, for their safety and the government's ease of surveillance.

Such systems were much damaged in the 14th century, when plague—largely spread inland along the Amber Routes by traders and travelers—and peasant risings undermined the already weakened feudal order. The emergence of Protestantism in the next century had perhaps even more profound effects on the Amber Routes. With the wave of reform came the suppression of monasteries, sometimes even in Catholic countries, leaving wayfarers without

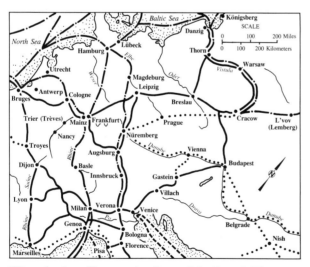

The Amber Routes in Late Medieval Times
——————— Main Italian Trade Routes
——·—·—·— Main Hanseatic Trade Routes
·········· Other Main Land Routes
— — — — — Other Main Sea Routes

hope of hospices for safe shelter on the road. The practice of pilgrimage sharply declined, though the faithful continued to travel to the main shrines, especially to Rome during the Holy Years, which were now being held every 25 years. But perhaps most important, Europe was divided between Protestant and Catholic. Country was ranged against country and party against party, both equally disastrous to peaceful travel. In the 14th century, Italian merchants increasingly took the Western Seaways from the Mediterranean to the English Channel ports to avoid trouble on the land routes to northern France and Flanders. The result was a disruption of travel from which the Amber Routes would not fully recover until modern times.

But while roads and travel conditions were declining, expectations were rising. Medieval travelers had largely been satisfied to walk or ride a horse, but the Europeans of the 16th century increasingly wanted to travel by carriage. The clash of expectation and reality led to a torrent of abuse for European roads in early modern times. Criticism was surely justified. On many routes, the bridle paths were in far better shape than the roads they paralleled. Many routes in northern Europe were ill-maintained corduroyed pathways, with their few wooden bridges not to be trusted; toll ferries and fords were the order of the day. In many parts of Eastern Europe, the main road was simply a slightly cleared beaten path through the forest; some regions of Poland, especially around the middle Vistula, were so ill-connected with the more settled and populous parts of Europe that they even escaped the main plagues that had devastated their Western neighbors. Passengers often carried large planks and loads of twigs, for use in extricating their carriages from mudholes. If they were not helping to haul their vehicles out of the mire, coach passengers were often found overturned into a stream or a snowbank, or standing by the roadside while the coachman or the local smithy attempted to fix a broken wheel or axle. Such travel was excruciatingly slow and accordingly expensive; it was also literally bruising, for the virtually springless carriages were (in the words of the 19th century German writer Adolph von Schaden) unsuited for anyone "who does not possess a breast of iron, innards of copper and a posterior of platinum."

Improvements came very slowly, and then more in travel conditions than in the roads themselves. First came the development of a regular postal system, to suit a Europe that was becoming an interconnected world once again. Throughout medieval times, messenger service had been distinctly ad hoc; kings, prelates, and rich merchants had private couriers, while pilgrims and various itinerant travelers were occasionally pressed into service to convey a message or package. Such methods were slow, unreliable, and often expensive. Among these private courier services, one operated by Venice had, since the early 14th century, employed members of the Taxis (Tassi) family. So, when

In Eastern Europe, travelers were often obliged to sleep in public rooms on pallets of straw. (By Daniel Chodowiecki, 1773, Kupferstichkabinett und Sammlung der Zeichnungen, Berlin)

the Holy Roman Emperor Maximilian I desired to set up a faster, more regular postal service, he quite naturally turned to the Taxis family. It was they who re-established in Europe the kind of postal relay system that had gone out with the Romans. From their base at Innsbruck, on the Brenner Pass Route, the Taxis organization built a set of relay posts connecting the emperor's far-flung territories, from Belgium to Spain. Letters sent in sealed bags were transferred to a fresh horse and rider at each post, with the progress of each pouch recorded in logs along the way. At first, these were supposedly only royal messages, but the Taxis messengers informally began to carry private messages besides. The system quickly became so successful that it spread elsewhere in Europe. Where before a traveler might count himself lucky to make 20 miles a day, barring accidents, the postal relay allowed messages to travel from Brussels to Rome – a distance of about 1,000 miles – in 10–12 days, depending on the weather. While the Taxis post would predominate in Central Europe for over three centuries, other postal systems grew up along side it. Towns along main and less-served minor routes began to set up their own relays, so a mail pouch might be sent from Antwerp to Frankfurt via the Cologne post, and then be picked up by the Augsburg post and conveyed to Venice or Genoa.

Gradually mail coaches began to carry passengers, and the post-chaise system developed, in which passengers would take a series of coaches to cross Europe. These coaches were extremely slow, since the roads were still in abysmal condition and the coach would stop overnight. Even so, Europeans were ready to travel. Such arrangements, which did not require each traveler to own a private coach, brought travelers on the Amber Routes in increasing numbers. No longer was pilgrimage the object; now the aim was to see the world, especially Italy, for, as one chronicler put it, if Europe were a ring, Italy would be its diamond. Travel was still long and arduous; as in medieval times, travelers routinely put their affairs in order and made a will before leaving home. The cost of trips that might take months was considerable and were not undertaken lightly, especially by one of little means. There were not just the coach fare and inn expenses to consider; there were also the onerous tolls at all border crossings along the way. These were levied not only on affluent travelers but also on young journeymen who, having completed their apprenticeship, would travel the land plying their trade for a year or two before settling down to become master artisans. A tanner, Johann Eberhard Dewald, describes the problem that he found even as late as the early 19th century:

These eternal frontiers in Germany are truly invented by the devil. The constant passing of turnpikes and the prying into one's walking records by constables and town guards of all sorts, is a great annoyance...Toll barriers stretch across the country like a spider's web in which the most honest man can be caught.

Travelers were also required to have health certificates showing them free from contagious diseases and sometimes were regardless held in quarantine for the specified 40 days or more, before being allowed to pass on.

But through all the hardships, travel persisted and even expanded. Only belatedly were roads improved to meet the growing demand, which had only worsened their condition. The leader in road improvement was France, where civil engineers in the 18th century began to build roads with graded layers of stones to provide both a firm base and good drainage. In 1720 the French even laid down specifications for main roads, including the Rhône-Saône Route; they were to be 60 feet wide, with six-foot-wide ditches on either side and trees lining the sides at 30-foot intervals. Begun under the monarchy, such work was continued after the French Revolution, supported by funds from the central government, as well as by local taxes. Travel time was cut in half in many places; from Paris to Lyon took five days, whereas in the 17th century it had taken ten.

In Switzerland, northern Italy, Bavaria, and Austria, the main old Amber Routes were also much improved in this period; many travelers from Italy to Frankfurt, Nuremberg, or Vienna praised the "good, hard roads" and the comfortable inns. Further north and east, among the many states of Germany and still-rural Poland, the roads were far less satisfactory. There the road was simply a pair of ruts cut sometimes axle-deep into a broad dirt swath, alternately mire or caked earth. Unless a carriage had a wheel gauge exactly matching the local one, it would be obliged to travel in the field along the side—with all the extra hazards that might entail. Nor were accommodations all that might be expected; instead of a comfortable inn at the end of a day's journey, the unwary traveler might often find simply a stable for his horses, with passengers expected to sleep on a bed of straw on the floor.

But on the Rhône-Saône Route, the French continued pioneering. Napoleon, unsatisfied with the Great St. Bernard Pass crossing into Italy, ordered his civil engineers to open a new route at the Simplon Pass. In work such as the Alps had not seen since Roman times, they hewed a road out of solid rock faces, building astonishing bridges across gorges thousands of feet deep; this work set a standard for the transformation of other Alpine mule tracks into full-fledged carriage roads, even though the Simplon was opened before many modern technological developments had been made.

The Napoleonic Wars that convulsed Europe in the early 19th century severely disrupted travel on the Amber Routes. But when the wars were over in 1815, travelers began to appear in Europe in even greater numbers. Affluent young men resumed their Grand Tours of the Continent, and they were increasingly joined by people from the rising middle classs, who formed the new class of "tourist." With the rise of Romanticism and its new view of Nature, the Alps and the great Northern European rivers, like the Rhine, became objects of pilgrimage in themselves, not just things to be passed on the way to Italy. In this period also, the Europeans instituted the express post, adopted from Britain, in which the coach traveled continuously, with just a change of horses and driver, rather than stopping at specified inns overnight. They continued one tradition, however: As had been true since the institution of the Taxis post, the postilion was required to blow his horn all the way from the city gate to the post-station. Yet though travel had become far more comfortable, cheaper, and faster, it fell short of romantic expectations, as these new travelers also faced the reality of the road. Diplomat Alexander von Villers commented:

> This rushing from place to place, pack, unpack, get tickets, change carriage, inns with impertinent dandified waiters, terrible food, marrow-chilling bills, robbery without sword or pistol, money, money, always money, nothing but money—what must one be like to endure all that? Let nobody talk to me about the joy of that kind of travel. I don't believe in it.

Modern travelers might sympathize. Indeed, it was to meet these kinds of problems that the package tours developed, allowing large numbers of people to travel with fewer arrangements necessary; the 19th century was the heyday of the Cook's Tour.

But no sooner had coach roads reached their height than they were challenged by modern technology in the form of the railroad. Iron rails pushed across the continent, through marshes and mountains, linking Europe as never before, and changing its character forever. Less than a century later, automobiles made their appearance, and in the 20th century great concrete highways have been built alongside the railroad lines, the two binding the continent together.

In all the turmoil of the last two centuries, only the Rhône-Saône Route—of the three Amber Routes—has survived as a major through route. A main line runs from Hamburg on the Elbe across the north German plain to the great industrialized strip along the Rhine, including Cologne and the West German capital of Bonn; from there one branch runs through Trier, Nancy, Dijon, and Lyon to Marseilles, while another branch follows the Rhine to Mainz or Frankfurt-on-Main and on south to Basle, then forking either toward the Rhône or into northern Italy. Further east, the Brenner Pass is still the easiest route through the Alps and is the main route north from Verona, as of old; but the route that once swung north to Jutland is now blocked by the barrier between the two Germanies, and angles instead westward toward Frankfurt. As for the easternmost of the Amber Routes, Trieste has long since replaced Venice as the main port on the Adriatic, but its land connections are primarily to the east, along the Sava and Drava rivers. The Amber Route which once crossed through Austria to northern Poland is fragmented by politics.

In truth, however, the Amber Routes emerged at a time when the highest civilization centered on the Mediterranean; but now, when Northern Europe is dominant, and airplanes threaten to overshadow land routes, the Amber Routes are something of an anachronism. Yet Europeans are proud of their heritage, not just of the classical civilizations, and many an amateur archaeologist in Northern Europe will tell you proudly, "I live on the Amber Route."

Even after the roads had been improved, 19th century travelers often preferred to walk or ride than to hazard stagecoaches on narrow passes like St. Gotthard. (From F. Schoppe and C. W. Gropius, Malerische Ansichten Gegenden . . . auf einer Reise durch Oesterreich . . . und Unteritalien, *1823-25, Germanisches Nationalmuseum, Nuremberg)*

Selective Bibliography

Bautier, Robert-Henri. *The Economic Development of Medieval Europe* (London: Thames and Hudson, 1971). Part of the Library of European Civilization. A well-illustrated useful work.

Braudel, Fernand. *The Wheels of Commerce.* Translated from the French by Siân Reynolds (New York: Harper & Row, 1982). Volume II of *Civilization and Capitalism, 15th–18th Century.* A useful and detailed work.

Chevallier, Raymod. *Roman Roads.* Translated by N. H. Field (Berkeley and Los Angeles: University of California Press, 1976). A useful review of archaeological and literary information on the construction and life of the roads.

Clark, J. G. D. *Prehistoric Europe: The Economic Basis* (London: Methuen, 1974; reprint of 1952 edition). An invaluable work, with many illustrations of archaeological artifacts.

de Navarro, J. M. "Prehistoric Routes Between Northern Europe and Italy Defined by the Amber Trade." *The Geographical Journal,* Vol. LXVI, No. 6, December 1925. A still-useful review of the ancient routes.

East, W. Gordon. *An Historical Geography of Europe,* Third Edition (London: Methuen, 1948). An extremely useful overview.

Heichelheim, Fritz M. *An Ancient Economic History: From the Paleolithic Age to the Migrations of the Germanic, Slavic and Arabic Nations,* 3 vols. Translated by Joyce Stevens (Leyden: A. W. Sijthoff, Vols. 1 & 2 1968, Vol. 3 1970). A comprehensive work with much fascinatng detail.

Hindley, Geoffrey. *A History of Roads* (Secaucus, New Jersey: Citadel Press, 1972). A slim but sound work emphasizing construction.

Kendall, Alan. *Medieval Pilgrims* (New York: Putnam, 1970). Part of the Putnam Documentary History series. An interesting brief review, with selections from many firsthand accounts.

Leighton, Albert C. *Transport and Communication in Early Medieval Europe, A.D. 500–1100* (Newton Abbot: David & Charles, 1972). A useful overview of a neglected subject.

Löschburg, Winfried. *A History of Travel* (London: George Prior Associated Publishers Ltd., Edition Leipzig, 1979). A popular work of much illustration and light text, emphasizing travel in modern Europe.

Merrick, Hugh. *The Great Motor Highways of the Alps* (London: Robert Hale, Ltd., 1958). A description of the main passes, focusing on modern information, but with some historical notes.

Piggott, Stuart. *Ancient Europe: From the Beginnings of Agriculture to Classical Antiquity* (Chicago: Aldine, 1965). A fine standard review.

Pliny the Elder. *Natural History,* 10 vols. Translated by H. Rackham (Cambridge, Massachusetts: Harvard University Press, 1938). Part of the Loeb Classical Library. A fine bilingual translation.

Pounds, Norman J. G. *An Historical Geography of Europe, 450 B.C.-A.D. 1330* (Cambridge: At the University Press, 1973), and *An Historical Geography of Europe, 1500–1840* (Cambridge: At the University Press, 1979). A comprehensive and very useful two-volume set.

Schreiber, Hermann. *The History of Roads: From Amber Route to Motorway.* Translated from the German by Stewart Thomson (London: Barrie and Rockliff, 1961). Contains chapters on the Amber Routes and their medieval and modern incarnations.

Von Hagen, Victor W. *The Roads That Led to Rome* (Cleveland and New York: World, 1967). A well-illustrated, readable work by the director of the Roman Road Expedition.

Zilliacus, Laurin. *Mail for the World: From the Courier to the Universal Postal Union* (New York: John Day, 1953). A popular history.

The Appian Way and Egnatian Way in Roman Times

——·—— Via Appia

········· Main Connecting Land Routes

-------- Via Appia Traiana

————— Appia-Egnatia Sea Connection

——— —— Via Egnatia

The Appian Way and the Egnatian Way

*I*n 52 B.C., a time of great civil strife in Italy, a murder was committed on the Appian Way that shook the unsteady government of Rome itself. Two bitter enemies—Milo and Clodius—each with an entourage of over 200 armed guards, met accidentally on the Via Appia outside Rome. A street battle that apparently began with insults bandied by the bodyguards resulted in Clodius being wounded and then later hacked to death, his corpse left on the Appia. Such "gang wars" were common at this time, but this one caught the attention of the masses. Milo himself was a widely respected senator, while Clodius was a well-known blackguard, who had himself murdered another on the Appian Way in similar circumstances. But no matter that Clodius was a notorious villain; the people of Rome were shocked that he had been butchered on the very road built by and named for his ancestor, Appius Claudius, the highway that formed the spine of the Roman Empire.

Although Clodius had not been tried for the earlier murder, Milo was brought to trial for his offense and was tried by no less a personage than the great Cicero (himself wronged by Clodius). Cicero protested that Appius Claudius had built the Via Appia for the use of the people, not for his descendants to kill and pillage upon, noting:

> When this same Clodius, still on the Appia, killed the worthy Roman Marcus Papirius, this was not a crime to be punished. Yet now the name of that same Appia comes up again amid so many tragic laments. That road which first, the fruit and work of an honest man, was not even named, today makes everyone speak of it because it drank the blood of this brigand and traitor to his country.

Yet the feeling of the people ran so high against the desecration of the Appia by Clodius's death, that Milo was forced into exile.

As this incident suggests, the Appian Way occupied a unique place in the history of Rome. It was the Via Appia that first bound together the disparate peoples of Italy into the core of the Roman Empire. The great highway laid the basis for the entire Roman road system that would bring a higher civilization to most parts of the empire and give large numbers of people both the means and the freedom to travel, as they would be unable to do for over 1,000 years after Rome's passing. When the empire expanded to the East, the Via Appia was joined to the Via Egnatia through a connection across the Adriatic Sea, the two forming the "Great East Road" from Rome to the empire's second capital at Byzantium (later Constantinople, now Istanbul).

The Appian Way began, as would all Roman roads, from the Golden Milestone (*miliarium aureum*) at the Forum in Rome, the point from which all distances in the empire were measured. From the Porta Capena, a gate in the early Roman wall, the Appia coursed through a virtual tunnel, formed by villa walls on either side, for about a mile; it left the great outer wall of the city through

This is a 19th century reconstruction of the Appian Way, running between walls of villas, where Clodius was murdered. (By Canina, German Archeological Institure, Rome)

the Porta Appia (now Porta San Sebastiano) and then headed southeast along the line of the peninsula. Passing the Alban Hills to the east, and spanning the gorge of Aricia (Ariccia), the road pushed straight across the fetid Pontine Marshes, by causeway and parallel canal, reaching the shore of the Tyrrhenian Sea at Tarracina (Terracina). There, faced with a rocky projection toward the sea, the Via Appia in early times moved inland around and over it, but later followed a stunning cliffside cut facing the sea. Heading inland again, the route reached the shore once more at Formiae (Formia) and followed the coast to Sinuessa (Bagni Mondragone). There a coast route continued down to the Bay of Naples, to the ports that would serve virtually harborless Rome for centuries: Cumae (Cuma), Puteoli (Pozzuoli), Neapolis (Naples), Pompeii and Herculaneum (both buried by Vesuvius's eruption in 79 A.D.) and Salernum (Salerno).

But the Via Appia itself cut inland from Sinuessa and headed further east; passing through the major cities of Capua and Beneventum (both of which sent important spurs down to the Bay of Naples), the road climbed onto the rocky Apennine Plateau, reaching the Ionian Sea at the instep of Italy's boot in the city of Tarentum (Taranto).

From there, the road moved across the boot's heel to Brundisium (Brindisi), the main port to the East, and to the bottom of the heel at Hydruntum (Otranto), a secondary port. In the later years of the Roman Empire, another route developed—the Via Appia Traiana—which cut from Beneventum over the Apennine ridge through Canusium (Canosa) and then to the Adriatic at Barium (Bari) and down the coast to Brundisium.

But the Via Appia was only one-half of Rome's Great East Road. True, many Romans set sail from Brundisium for Greece, Asia Minor, the Levant, or Egypt. But Romans were always more comfortable on land than on sea; the sea routes, in any case, were unusable in winter except in extreme emergencies. Also, their eastern capital lay at the meeting place of Europe and Asia, in Byzantium on the Bosporus. So the second half of the route to the East lay on the far side of the Adriatic: the Via Egnatia.

From Italy, travelers were ferried across the 47-mile-wide Strait of Otranto to the port of Dyrrhachium (Durrës, or Durazzo), in Illyria, or sometimes to the more southerly Apollonia (Avlona, later Vlorë), in Epiros. (Both are now in Albania.) On the rugged Balkan Peninsula, the mountains—notably the Dinaric (Albanian) Alps—come right down to the rocky Adriatic coast; the small stretch of coastal plain between Dyrrhachium and Apollonia offers the only natural opening to the east. Even so, the route is difficult. From these two ports the joint road followed a narrow valley into the Candavian Mountains and took a tortuous route down the east slope of the range, passing north of the two large lakes in the region: Lychidos (Ochrid) and Melitonus (Préspa). Near Heraclea (Bitola, also called Monastir), the road was joined by the main north-south route from the middle Danube. It then funneled through the Monastir Gap, a north-south opening in the mountains, emerging onto the coast at Thessalonica, the main Macedonian port on the Aegean Sea. Macedonia's coastal strip is dotted with marshes and lakes—depressions gouged by glaciers and filled with water draining the Balkans—so the road snaked its way eastward between the points of high ground. Following the path trod by Alexander, Darius, and Xerxes long before Roman times, it passed through the historic town of Philippi into Thrace and on to Cypsala (Ipsala) on the Hebros River, largest of the rivers flowing into the Aegean, at the modern border between Greece and Turkey.

At Cypsala the road forked. The main path of the Egnatian Way continued eastward, crossing easily over the midstream island at Cypsala, to meet and follow the north shore of the Propontis (Sea of Marmara)—the waist between the Aegean and Black seas—to the great crossroads city of Byzantium. But one branch from Cypsala followed the Hebros River north to Hadrianapolis (Adrianople, now Edirne); after crossing the Orient Route, which slices into the heart of Europe, it continued northeast along the Black Sea to the Eurasian Steppe. Over the millennia innumerable peoples from Eurasia followed this route into the Balkans—most notably the Greeks themselves, who were among the Indo-European peoples originating north of the Black Sea. The other branch from Cypsala headed east and then south to the Gallipoli Peninsula, which overlooks the Hellespont (Dardanelles), entryway to the Propontis and the Black Sea; in the centuries before the rise of Byzantium, this was the main crossing point between Europe and Asia, with travelers from Gallipoli ferrying across to Troy (Ilium) on the opposite headland. Though it was a difficult road, the Egnatian Way had a special importance for the Romans, for it was a link with their traditional roots in Asia Minor; Troy was the home of the legendary Aeneas, ancestor of Romulus and Remus, traditional founders of Rome itself. While the Appian Way was, as many called her, the Queen of Roads, with no peer at the height of the Roman Empire, the rougher Egnatian Way had a longer and in some ways greater history, especially in its eastern portion.

When the Italian peninsula was still the home of many petty tribes, the Aegean was developing a high civilization. Early traders from Greece and Asia Minor

sailed around the Aegean and Ionian seas (often crossing at the Isthmus of Corinth) and worked their way inland. The Hellespont, with its fast-flowing westward current, was still a major hindrance for sea-craft, so travelers often crossed overland from Troy to Europe via the Gallipoli Peninsula. It was early traders from the Aegean who first opened up the land routes along the Egnatian Way. Some moved from the Hellespont and from the Bosporus overland to Cypsala and west; others, especially from Corinth and Corcyra (Corfu), pushed eastward from Apollonia and Dyrrhachium. They worked their way through the maze of mountains, trying and abandoning one dead end after another, often finding that the longest route was the best, clearing and beating down a person-wide foot trail from either end. Long before the time of the Romans, traders had made this a commercial track, if not a road; Heraclea—roughly midway between Dyrrhachium and Thessalonica—sported wine jars from both the Ionian and Aegean seas.

The route of the Egnatian Way was a battleground for some centuries, as Greeks from the south fought over the territory with Persians from Asia Minor, who repeatedly crossed via the Gallipoli Peninsula and headed across the Thracian coast to Therma (later Thessalonica). Later the Macedonians became dominant over them both, first under Philip II and then under Alexander III, better known as Alexander the Great. It was Alexander who first brought unity to the Egnatian Way, but only briefly. He went off to conquer the world, and the region fell apart again into several states, all threatened by Celts, one of a long series of peoples who would push through the Monastir Gap toward the sea at Thessalonica.

Italy, meanwhile, was still inhabited by a mosaic of tribes, some long-established, others more recent arrivals. These diverse peoples agreed upon little, except that the site of Rome was a superb one. Although marshy in parts, and encouraging malaria (literally, "bad air"), Rome drew people from all directions. Its seven hills were easily defended, the water of the Tiber was sweet, and the river valley fed down to the sea, where salt was to be had. But Rome was simply one small walled city among many in the middle of the first millennium B.C. The track down the coast from Rome to Naples was divided among various peoples, including Etruscans in the north, Italics along the central spine of the peninsula, Illyrians on the east coast, and Greeks in their many colonies (known collectively as Magna Graecia, or Greater Greece) around the sole and heel of Italy's boot. The city that would later become the southern terminus of the Appian Way was then simply a modest Greek settlement called Brentesion (Brindisi). When the Celts invaded from the north in the early fourth century B.C., the peoples in central Italy formed a Latin League for common defense. Rome gradually emerged as the strongest among them and within decades had subdued most tribes in central Italy.

At least one Roman—the famous Appius Claudius—recognized that Rome's future lay to the south and east, in the direction of the great cultures of the east Mediterranean. In 312 B.C. he began building the road that still bears his name. As censor, in charge of public morals and public works, he chose as his route a dirt track leading out of the Porta Capena, the south gate in Rome's defensive wall. The Romans had few models to follow; sea routes had, before then, been predominant in the region and constructed roads were rather an innovation. It was on the Appian Way that they developed the techniques they would apply throughout the empire.

Following the footpath that had been beaten down over the previous centuries, Appius Claudius sent engineers and laborers (many of them convicts) to widen and clear the route, provide drainage ditches and curbing on the side, and build up the center of the road to facilitate run-off. Attempting to keep the road as level as possible, engineers tended to follow the side of a valley (avoiding ill-drained valley floors) where feasible; in crossing a valley, they often avoided sharp grades by carrying the road across on linked stone arches, like the famous viaduct at Aricia, south of Rome near the Alban Hills. Marshes posed a more difficult problem, especially the 20-mile-wide Pontine marshes which had to be crossed before the road reached the sea at Tarracina. In earlier times, ferries had crossed the marshes via canals, and they continued to do so; but the Romans built a causeway across the watery depression, supporting it on piles driven deep into the mud. Bridges were also necessary, but not heavy stone ones, for the Romans in these early years had a superstition against bridges of any material other than wood. The main bridge on this first section of the Appia was across the Volturno River, a few miles before the town of Capua, the territory of the independent Samnite tribes.

Contrary to popular belief, the Roman roads were neither completely uniform nor completely straight. Certainly the Romans tried to avoid sharp curves, especially as their awkward wagons had difficulty turning on a tight radius; for the same reason, they would often cut out sections of rock to ease passage. But, where necessary, they would swing the road around intractable impediments; only where none existed, as in the Pontine marshes, was the road absolutely straight. The width of the road also varied, depending on the terrain and the type of traffic expected on the route; while parts of the Appia were ten to fifteen feet wide, some were only eight feet across. Only later, when traffic became heavier, did the Romans adopt uniform patterns for their roads (though even then distinguishing between carriage roads and bridle paths through mountains).

The same is true for the surface of the road. The first section of the Appia—the 132 miles from Rome to Capua—was originally covered simply with gravel in 298 B.C., while the first mile of the road, from the Porta Capena to the Temple of Mars on the outskirts of Rome, was paved with cut stone. Only in 295 B.C. did Roman engineers begin to use the characteristic heavy-cut blocks of volcanic rock called *silex* as the base of their roads, paving the Appia from the Temple of Mars to Capua. By 280 B.C. they had moved across the plain of Campania to the former Samnite stronghold of Beneventum (passing on the way the site of an earlier rankling defeat at Caudine Forks). Over the next four decades the Appia was gradually extended diagonally across the peninsula through Venusium (Venosa) to Tarentum on the Ionian Sea; here the engineers often dispensed with formal road construction, for the dry bedrock of Apulia sometimes needed little more than to be cleared of undergrowth and loose rocks and provided with drainage ditches. By 244 B.C. the Romans had reached across the heel of the peninsula to the Greek colony they renamed Brundisium, extending soon after that to the more southerly port of Hydruntum (Otranto).

The Romans did not proceed all that way unopposed. At the time they reached Capua, making it the Appia's temporary terminus, Maleventum was still a Samnite city named Maleventum. Advancing into enemy territory, the Romans built a fort at Maleventum to guard their construction corps as they extended the road to Tarentum and Brundisium. While the Appia allowed the Romans to bring in troops—and later colonists—to gain and consolidate their hold on these new territories, roads are non-partisan, serving enemies as well. In 281 B.C., King Pyrrhus of Epiros—coming to the aid of his ally, Tarentum—crossed the Adriatic; through rocky Apulia and up to Maleventum and even Capua, Pyrrhic and southern Italian troops fought Roman soldiers back and fourth along the Appia. Pyrrhus won most battles, yet they drained so much of his strength that he eventually retired to Epiros, leaving us with the still-common phrase "Pyrrhic victory" as a synonym for a too-costly triumph. Indeed, one imaginative sixth century A.D. Greek historian, Procopius, suggested that Maleventum's name was changed at this time. He noted that a fierce *ventus* (wind) blew from across the Adriatic, and that:

> …when this begins to blow, it is impossible to find a man there who continues to travel on the road…Such indeed, is the force of the wind that it seizes a man on horseback together with his horse and carries him through the air to a great distance…And it so happens that Beneventus [being opposite the Adriatic]…and situated on rather high grounds gets some of the disadvantage of the same high wind.

In what was perhaps a flight of fancy, Procopius proposed that the Roman success over Pyrrhus led them to change Maleventum (ill wind) to Beneventum (favorable wind).

Hannibal, too, threatened the Appian Way and Roman hegemony in the third century B.C. Arriving over the Alps and heading south along the Adriatic coast, he tramped across the peninsula to the Campania, severed the Via Appia at Sinuessa, and cut off Rome's food supplies from the south. The Romans tried to box Hannibal in by fortifying the crossing of the Volturno Rver and the narrow mountain passage at Tarracina, but Hannibal broke out of the trap, and the following year returned to cut the road again at Capua. But Hannibal was in unfriendly country, cut off from his own supplies across the Mediterranean; finally he, like Pyrrhus, was forced to retire from Italy in 202 B.C.

With Hannibal and his Carthaginian army gone, the Appian Way began to recover. Rome confirmed its hold on the peoples along the Via Appia, sending colonists out to repopulate the ravaged towns along the way and to establish settlements. Many of these grew up where inns or public houses were established for the needs of official couriers—and of the increasing number of ordinary travelers on the Appia, including traders, beggars, actors, philosophers, teachers, and all manner of quacks and charlatans, who were being drawn to Rome, as they would be for centuries. In the second century B.C. the Romans began building the heavy stone bridges whose arches would remain to remind us of their former greatness long after the empire itself was gone. The old wooden bridges—including the Pons Sublicius across the Tiber, immortalized in the story of Horatio at the bridge defending Rome against the Etruscans—gave way to solid structures, built to carry the heavily loaded wagons that brought food to rapidly growing Rome and to support the carriages for the massive siege equipment developed by the army. No longer did Rome need temporary bridges that could be hauled up, or boat bridges that could be dismantled in case of invasion. The Via Appia was secure. The Romans were properly proud of their achievement; Pliny was typical in his enthusiasm about the causeway across the Pontine:

>...we may say it was a miraculous work in filling up that troublesome marsh as if another Hercules were forcing up the road by great and spacious banks to bear the burden of immense stones of the Appian Way.

With its home base secure, Rome looked across the Adriatic. She already had allies there, notably two main ports she had taken under her protection in 229 B.C.: Apollonîa and Dyrrhachium (which the Greeks had called Epidamnon). Macedonia had allied itself with Hannibal in the Punic Wars, and provided Rome with a motive—if one were necessary—for carrying its empire to the East. From their main base at Apollonia, the Romans in 200 B.C. sent an army—including Hannibal-inspired elephants—along the eastward trail past the Macedonian borders near Lake Lychnidos to Heraclea; there they sharp-

ly defeated Philip V of Macedon, whose army retreated to block the narrowest parts of Monastir Gap. But the Romans hammered their way through the wooden barricades and forced the Macedonians to retire beyond Edessa. Initially satisfied with separating Macedon from her Greek possessions, the Romans later swept across Thrace and into Asia Minor. Firmly implanted on the eastward route, the Romans now absorbed Macedonia. Following the pattern developed on the Via Appia, they began to shape a road out of the rough track they found, carrying both soldiers and colonists into the alien country. This 500-mile route soon became known as the Via Egnatia. The source of the name no one knows; while it may have had some connection with the minor Italian port of Gnathia, north of Bari, it is more likely that one of the main builders was called Egnatia (Ignatius).

The Via Egnatia was, first and foremost, a *via militaris*—a military road. Even after the subjugation of Macedonia, the Romans had to contend with the unbridled mountain peoples along the way; Cicero rightly noted that Macedonia was "adjoined by so many barbarian tribes that its governors have always held that the boundaries extend only as far as swords and javelins can reach." The road allowed the Romans to bring their might to bear on the interior, especially on the region between the Adriatic and the Aegean port of Thessalonica. Like other Roman roads, the Via Egnatia had an arched roadbed, high in the center to promote run-off of water, with curbs and drainage ditches on either side (from which had come the earth for building up the center). The road, generally nine to twelve feet wide, so that wagons could pass, varied from as little as six feet in some mountain defiles to over a dozen yards near some cities. Post-stations were set at appropriate intervals along the way, and mounting stones were provided for riders (the stirrup not yet being in use). Milestones every 1,000 paces gave the distances between cities and advertised the achievements and virtues of the builders, sponsors, and later repairers of the road. The road surface itself was built up in layers, with the base being formed of rough stones joined by cement or clay, its depth varying with the terrain. On top of this came a thin layer of pebbles (sometimes pieces of brick), then a layer of gravel or sand, and finally large cut stones with flat surfaces, sunk into the previous layer to form the actual roadbed. Limestone, common in the Balkans, predominated as the surface stone of the Egnatia, and surviving parts of the road still show the tracks of wheels from thousands of years ago.

The region around the Via Egnatia was divided into Roman provinces. From the coastal ports of Apollonia and Dyrrhachium eastward to past Philippi was the province of Macedonia, with its capital at Thessalonica. East of that was the province of Thracia, with its capital at Perinthus, on the Propontis, and its border just east of that city. Byzantium, which had allied herself with the

Romans against the Macedonians, was given a special status under the emperor, and was considered part of the province of Bithynia in western Asia.

Rome's presence did not mean peace on the Via Egnatia, however. Throughout the second century B.C. and into the first, the Romans continued to fight against mountain peoples; some of these were supported by outside allies, like King Mithridates from the coast of the Black Sea, who urged on the truculent Thracians. Even as late as the middle of the first century B.C., tribes from the north penetrated down to Thessalonica. But these conflicts paled when the Roman Empire itself was riven by civil war.

This was the turbulent period when the infamous Clodius was killed on the Via Appia, and when the struggle for power between Julius Caesar and his son-in-law, Pompey, reached a head. When Pompey emerged as the most significant power in Rome, Caesar chose to defy senatorial orders and crossed the Rubico River into Italy with his army, to challenge Pompey's authority. This action precipitated a series of internal wars that were to rock the Appia and Egnatia for decades.

Shortly after Caesar had crossed into Italy, Pompey retreated down the Via Appia to Brundisium, intending to garner the resources of Macedonia and the East for his army. Caesar, after quickly securing Italy and the western provinces, headed eastward himself, surprising Pompey by making a winter crossing from Brundisium to take the Epiros coast from Apollonia south. Rejecting a negotiation which Caesar's urgent post-messenger bore along the Egnatian Way, Pompey quickly realized that Caesar's objective was Dyrrhachium. The opposing forces converged on that prime port, Caesar being joined by Mark Antony's army, which had also sailed from Brundisium. But the result was a stalemate. Attempting to out-feint each other, the two armies headed eastward, sometimes on the Egnatia, sometimes on bypasses. In the end Caesar defeated Pompey in Thessaly, in 48 B.C. Pompey retreated to Egypt, there to be killed, while Caesar headed eastward to defeat Mithridates's successor near the Bosporus. (This victory gave rise to Caesar's famous statement "Veni, vidi, vici" – "I came, I saw, I conquered.") He returned home to a triumphant reception such as no Roman general had ever seen.

Children of wealthy Roman families had their own chariots, like this one drawn by an ass. (Louvre)

But peace along the Appia and Egnatia was to be short-lived. In less than a decade, Caesar was assassinated, for an army and a fleet, Brutus from Illyria, Cassius from Asia Minor. To head them off, the army of Octavian and Antony crossed from the Appia and onto the Egnatia—which the chronicler Appian called "the only known route of travel from Asia to Europe"—to meet their foes. Brutus and Cassius, having plundered in Asia Minor, crossed the Hellespont and headed westward. The two sides met on the plains of Philippi in 42 B.C., where Brutus and Cassius, initially successful, finally fell to defeat, both committing suicide. A decade later, the winners fell out, with Antony and the Egyptian queen, Cleopatra, making a losing bid for power at the Battle of Actium, off the west coast of Greece. By 27 B.C. Octavian ruled alone, being honored with the title of "Caesar Augustus." It was under his rule that peace finally came to the Appian and Egnatian ways.

In the transition from Republican to Imperial Rome, citizens lost considerable political freedom; they did, however, gain the ability to travel for thousands of miles in all directions from the center of the empire. These were the great days of Roman travel. Travel was heaviest around Rome itself. Few people stayed in Rome by choice during the summer; those who could left the heat and malaria behind for country villas, north or south of the city. Some even commuted 20–25 miles out of the city each day. But Rome was a nexus—the Emperor Constantine would call it the navel—of long-distance travel as well. Teachers, students, philosophers, and soldiers fanned out around the empire, especially on the Appian and Egnatian ways, the main pathway to the high culture of the East. Others were drawn inward to the capital by the hope of fame or fortune; actors, doctors, itinerant craftsmen, country boys seeking riches in the great city, all these and more found their way to Rome. In the daytime, the Appia would be crowded with litters, chariots, and horse-drawn carriages, along with the riders and walkers; at night the carters would take over, bringing heavy loads and produce into the cities, whose streets were so crowded that wheeled vehicles were forbidden within city walls during the day.

Ostentation was the pattern of many travelers—more than one young man spent his patrimony in making a great show on the road, and then had to join the army when he ran out of money. Others went to the opposite extreme, feigning poverty or catastrophe. Seneca, for example, boasted that he traveled as if he had been shipwrecked, sojourning "with very few slaves—one carriage load—and no paraphernalia...The mattress lives upon the ground, and I upon the mattress."

The reasoning behind this approach was sound: Highwaymen, many of them escaped slaves, looked for rich targets at any vulnerable place along the road, like the viaduct at Aricia, the Pontine Marshes, or a defile in any unpopulated area, where travelers might be trapped and shorn of their goods. Some of these highwaymen captured the popular imagination, like Italian Robin Hoods; one and civil war once again raged. Popular feeling forced the killers to leave Rome, although several were given responsible posts in foreign territories, among them Brutus and Cassius. But, disaffected, the two began to raise money brigand named Felix Bulla led a network of some hundreds, with informers alerting him as to the imminent arrival of likely victims, who would be fleeced and sent on their way. The social origins of this land piracy were apparently clear to Bulla; at one point he sent this message to the Roman authorities: "If masters treated their slaves better, there would be no robbers."

These large numbers of disaffected slaves and criminals gave rise at one point to a full-scale rebellion, under a Thracian slave named Spartacus. Forming a band near Mt. Vesuvius, on the Bay of Naples, in the first century B.C., Spartacus was soon joined by tens of thousands of recruits. They marched north on the Appia but—to the great relief of the capital's citizens—bypassed Rome, originally heading for freedom in the Alps; but, most soldiers preferring to pillage in Italy, the army turned south again, hoping to sail to Sicily or Africa. But their sea connections failed; the Roman army, which they had defeated on several earlier occasions, cut them to pieces.

Those rebels who did not die in battle, like Spartacus, or escape to the hills, were nailed to crosses, a standard punishment for robbers and other criminals at the time; for months their crucified corpses lined the Via Appia between Capua and Rome. Other highwaymen, like Felix Bulla, were sentenced to be thrown to the lions in the bloody circuses of the empire. To deal with highwaymen and potential rebellions, the Romans stationed troops to guard strategic spots along the way: on the Appia, notably at Fort Anxur, at Tarracina; on the Egnatia, at Dyrrhachium, Pella, and Philippi. Hazards along the always-rougher Egnatia were greater than on the more refined Appia, but even so, travel on these routes was safer than it would be for many centuries, in some cases until the 20th century.

Travel along the Appia even drew attention from poets; the best-known description, a satire by Horace, gives a vivid picture of life en route to Brundisium. Stopping first at "a modest inn at Aricia," he found Forum Appii "crammed with boatmen and stingy tavern-keepers." "This stretch," he noted, "we lazily cut in two, though smarter travelers make it in a single day: the Appian Way is less tiring, if taken slowly." There is no doubt about that, for carriages in those days had no springs, and the unyielding and somewhat uneven stone surface was surely a trial for any traveler; indeed, litters were popular because the carriers—whether animals or men—tended to absorb most of the shocks and bumps of the road. Modern travelers can still sympathize with Horace's complaints about the villainous water and the delays en route, which caused them—being towed through the canal, rather than taking the causeway—to cross the Pontine Marshes when it was dark:

> Then slaves loudly rail at boatmen, boatmen at slaves: "Bring to here!" "You're packing in hundreds!" "Stay, that's enough!" What with collecting fares and harnessing the mule, a whole hour slips away. Cursed gnats and frogs of the fens drive off sleep, the boatman, soaked in sour wine, singing the while of the girl he left behind, and a passenger taking up the refrain. The passenger at last tires and falls asleep, and the lazy boatman turns his mule out to graze, ties the reins to a stone, and drops a-snoring on his back. Day was now dawning when we find our craft was not under way, until one hot-headed fellow jumps out, and with willow cudgel bangs mule and boatman on back and head.

The long night's travel was capped by arrival at Tarracina, with the travelers "crawling on three miles climb up to Anxur, perched on her far-gleaming rocks."

Like many other Roman travelers, Horace detoured off the main route of the Appia to visit friends. He was traveling with some friends on semi-official business, however, so they sometimes stayed at way-stations provided for government travelers; he noted:

> The little house close to the Campanian bridge put a roof above our heads, and the state-purveyors, as in duty bound, furnished fuel and salt.

At other times, Horace took his chances at inns along the way, like that at Beneventum:

> ...where our bustling host was nearly burned out while turning lean thrushes over the fire. For as Vulcan slipped out through the old kitchen the vagrant flame hastened to lick the roof. Then you might have seen the hungry guests and frightened slaves snatching up the dinner, and all trying to quench the blaze.

At a certain point Horace succumbs to the dazed feeling known to every long-distance traveler, where scenes of familiar countryside are mixed with cloudy memories of green wood fires and dust causing smarting eyes; of waiting for a "faithless girl" at a wayside inn; of being whirled in carriages through half-remembered towns; of a long slog on a muddy road. We can sympathize with Horace when he concludes: "Brundisium is the end of a long story and of a long journey."

For most travelers, however, it was far from the end of the journey. As Rome's territories and interests continued to expand in the East, travelers increasingly took ships from Brundisium (which became the main port, over

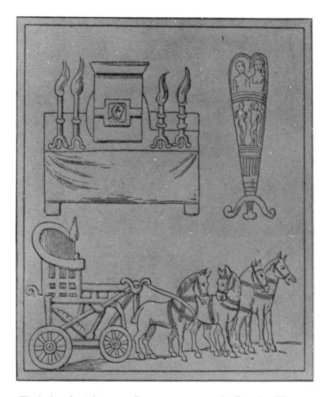

The badge of a 4th century Roman governor on the Egnatian Way quite naturally includes a four-horse chariot. (New York Public Library)

both Hydruntum and Barium) to points around the eastern Mediterranean. Ships were fine for long distances and good weather, but from late autumn through winter the Mediterranean was best left alone. Winds were also unreliable, making the sea route often take longer than the land route. As a result, the Egnatian Way was favored for many purposes as the most reliable all-weather route, where even snow rarely stopped travel in the mountain passes for more than a week at a time. This was the main route for the imperial post that Augustus initiated for the cities to the East. It was also the main route for soldiers.

At the beginning of the Augustan period, the Egnatian Way was still much troubled by incursions of peoples from the Balkans. The Roman army conducted many campaigns to pacify these tribes; they also sent large numbers of veterans to colonize the region. In the end, they used the Egnatian Way as their main line of communication and supply in their campaigns to extend the imperial frontier north to the Danube and beyond, in an effort to gain peace for this vital pathway. A fourth century observer, Ambrosius, noted the special arrangements that were made for armies on the march:

> When a soldier sets out on the Way he does not decide the order of march for himself, nor does he choose the route according to his own will, take pleasant shortcuts or fall behind the standards. He

receives an itinerary from the emperor and keeps to it. He advances in the prescribed order; he marches with his weapons and covers the route by the right road—so that he may find supplies waiting in places where they have been got ready. If he took some other route, he would not get his rations or find the proper billet, for the commander gives orders for these to be prepared for those who follow him...the officer does not consider what will suit himself but what is possible for all. That is why he arranges for halts. The army marches three days, and rests on the fourth. Cities are chosen which lie at three or four days from each other, or even more, if there is plenty of water and supplies are abundant; so the journey is done without fatigue, until they reach a chosen, as it were royal city, in which tired armies find refreshment.

But the Roman roads found themselves being used by quite a different army in the first century A.D. In their eastern territories, there had arisen a new religion—Christianity—which was to use those roads to conquer the Roman Empire without force of arms. The advance guard of this invasion was formed by apostles whose names are known to every reader of the Bible. Acts 16:9–12 tells the beginning of the story for the Egnatian Way:

> And a vision appeared to Paul in the night. There stood a man of Macedonia, and prayed him, saying, Come over into Macedonia, and help us.
> And after he had seen the vision, immediately we endeavored to go into Macedonia, assuredly gathering that the Lord had called us for to preach the gospel unto them.
> Therefore loosing from Troas [the region around Troy in Asia Minor], we came with a straight course to Samothracia, and the next day to Neapolis;
> And from thence to Philippi, which is the chief city of that part of Macedonia, and a colony: and we were in that city abiding certain days.

It was here that Paul and Silas were bound in jail and freed by an earthquake (far from the last to disturb the Egnatia's

Activity at a coastal post-station—with mail coach, two wheeled chariot, mounted horseman, and freighter—are detailed in this 19th century drawing. (By Ludwig Burger)

41

stones), which loosened their bonds. As early Christians, they were persecuted by the Romans. Those who were, like Paul, born Roman citizens were often sent to Rome itself for trial. Aside from the many Christians who were consigned to the bloody circuses of Rome, many others were set to work at the post-stations along the Roman road system; this was especially true along the wild and unsettled portions of the Via Egnatia. Despite oppression, these Christians maintained their common belief and practices, in no small measure because of the Roman roads, which allowed continuous contact between communities separated by thousands of miles. Indeed, some Christians served as voluntary messengers, carrying letters between communities; a number of these messages of support and encouragement have been preserved in the New Testament, such as Paul's epistles written to or from Thessalonica or Corinth.

As traffic on the Appia and Egnatia increased, both were periodically repaired, with milestones set up to applaud the event getting progressively more effusive. In the early second century A.D., the Emperor Trajan decided to promote an old bridle path over the spine of the Apennines into a full-fledged main road. From Beneventum, the new road cut across the ridge and then along it to Canusium, reached the sea at Barium, passed through Gnathia, and arrived at Brundisium. He also carried out a major renovation of the Via Appia, repairing causeways and building bridges to replace ferries. At Tarracina his workmen produced an astonishing cut out of solid rock, so the road could proceed along the side of the hill, rather than crawling over it. The result of these two changes was to save perhaps half a day for travelers bound for Capua or the Bay of Naples; for the total route between Rome and Brundisium, the gain was a full day, requiring all itineraries to be revised. Trajan also overhauled at least the western part of the Egnatian Way.

Gradually the center of gravity of the Roman Empire shifted eastward. Where once emperors were likely to have come from Rome or the western provinces, from the third century on many were drawn from the East—and there they made their headquarters. In the late second century B.C., Diocletian set up his capital at Nicomedia, across from Byzantium in Asia, while his co-emperor resided at Thessalonica after 300 A.D. In the beginning of the fourth century, Constantine went even further than these, establishing a "New Rome" on the site of Byzantium. The city later became known as Constantinople in his honor, and—after he made Christianity the state religion in 333 A.D.—it became co-equal with Rome in both politics and religion. In this period the empire began to split into western and eastern halves. Attention was also focused in the East because the imperial frontier was increasingly being threatened from across the Danube. The Egnatian Way, which had grown rather neglected in times of peace, was once again transformed into a military road.

Some Goths reached Byzantium, Perinthos, and Thessalonica as early as the mid-third century; by a century later, they had taken most of the Balkans, confining the Romans largely to the corridor of the Via Egnatia, and threatening to cut the highway, splitting Rome and Constantinople apart. By the beginning of the fifth century, Goths were marching along the Egnatian Way into Macedonia and Greece; some headed up the Illyrian coast (where the Romans had built a convenient road) around the Adriatic and into Italy, shocking the world by sacking Rome. (The western government had virtually yielded the city to them, retiring to safety in the water-fortified island city of Ravenna, south of Venice on the Adriatic.) While Goths headed westward, Constantinople redoubled its fortifications, building a Long Wall across the peninsula on which it stood and building into its city wall the famous Golden Gate, through which travelers from the Egnatian Way entered. (So popular was this gateway for ceremonial entrances that some sea travelers disembarked at a port somewhere on the Propontis, so they could finish their journey on the Via Egnatia.) One did not enter directly, however, for Constantinople had a double wall for defense, forcing travelers to approach along a road between the two concentric rings before entering the Golden Gate.

The arrival of the Goths in Italy was not a total disaster for the country; they had been much influenced by Roman culture and aspired to be its heirs. Indeed, the Visigoths even carried out some restoration and repair on the Via Appia, which had been neglected in Rome's decline. But in these centuries the Appian and Egnatian ways continued to separate, no longer joining a single united empire. On the Appia, the section between Rome and the Bay of Naples became the most important, with vital supplies being carted in from the southern ports. The Romans attempted to absorb the Goths by making them part of the empire, but as other people moved into Italy, the peninsula became fragmented into a variety of petty states, as did the Appian Way itself.

Under these circumstances, the Egnatian Way retained its importance as Constantinople's lifeline to its few remaining western territories, notably around Ravenna and the boot and heel of Italy. In the mid-sixth century, Justinian even rebuilt the defences along the Via Egnatia. But within decades, a new threat—the Avars—appeared from the Eurasian Steppe; they were a sufficiently formidable opponent for the Byzantines to call for the help of some Slavic peoples, the Serbs and the Croats. With their help, the Byzantines drove the Avars back onto the Hungarian plain, but the Slavs stayed, filtering through the Balkans, along with the Bulgars, who arrived at the same time, and, a little later, the Wallachs (Vlachs), who came to operate as the main carriers on the route. Settling along the Egnatian Way, these peoples for a time cut overland communications between Constantinople and the remnants of the Western Roman Empire, which were reached mainly by sea in the seventh and eighth centuries. With the Bulgar Empire settled astride the Egnatian Way in the ninth and tenth centuries, many cities in the regions received new or modified names. Lychnidos became Ochrid; Heraclea was transformed into Bitola or Monastir (for a well-known Christian monastery there). Further west, Apollonia was mostly abandoned, being replaced by a new settlement called Avlona (later Vlorë) across its small bay; Dyrrhachium was well on its way to becoming Durrës or (to the Italians) Durazzo.

In this period a split began to develop along the Egnatian Way that would have widespread consequences in the world. As Christian culture was adopted by the newer immigrants along the way, those regions to the east of Bulgaria were mostly influenced by Constantinople, and those to the west by Rome. The difference was to a large extent one of language – Rome spoke Latin, while Byzantium (even though it called itself Roman) spoke Greek. But there were cultural questions, too, and the two groups began to differ in many ways over the centuries. Some of these were small – questions of shaving, eating meat, eating unleavened bread, counting days of Lent, kneeling or prostrating – but cumulatively they became increasingly divisive. It is not surprising, then, that the Great Schism between the Eastern and Western churches was sparked by a question of which had authority over the bishopric of Ochrid.

But the Christians were soon forced to fight together, schism or no. While pilgrims had been allowed access to Christian shrines in Moslem territory over the centuries, the Turks – newly arrived in the Near East – wanted no part of the Christians, closed the pilgrimage

In the 17th century, an eruption of Vesuvius disturbed travel on the Naples spur of the Appian Way, as an earlier one had destroyed the city of Pompeii. (From Jean Blaeu, Nouveau Théâtre d'Italie, *1704)*

In the 17th century, as today, travelers on the Appian Way followed the old Roman cut around the hill of Terracina. (Engraving by Braun, Florence; Autostrade S.P.A.)

routes, and seriously threatened Constantinople. Alexius Comnenus, the Byzantine leader, appealed to the Latin pope for aid, and the First Crusade resulted. Not surprisingly, since the Christian states were temporarily united, one of the main routes for the Crusaders from Italy was down the Appian Way, across the Adriatic (where they were joined by others who had journeyed down the Illyrian coast), and along the Egnatian Way to Constantinople. One errant group of Normans, erstwhile Crusaders, chose to ignore the Turks and returned to attack Byzantine territory. A chronicler traveling with the Normans noted that from Dyrrhachium, they "passed into the regions of the Bulgarians, through steep rocks and deserted places." Not completely deserted, however, for they found an "abundance of corn and wine and food for the body." Forewarned of the Normans' invasion, Alexius blocked the main passes on the route, especially those in the Monastir Gap, and after much hard fighting defeated the Normans. The Egnatian Way was, by this time, in sad condition, with parts apparently unusable for wheeled vehicles; after this set of battles, some parts of the Way were closed, never to reopen. In particular, the route over the Candavian Mountains was largely abandoned, being replaced by a variety of lesser paths for local use. The eastern part of the Egnatian Way continued in use, however, with western traffic often arriving by ship at the main ports, especially Thessalonica. In the early 13th century, a Frankish soldier, Geoffrey of Villehardouin, noted that "the land from Salonica to Constantinople was as well pacified and the roads so safe that one could come and go as one pleased — and twelve long days' journey was needed from one city to the other."

The continual battles between Latin and Greek armies weakened the Eastern Roman Empire, however. When the Serbs began a drive along the Egnatian Way, the Byzantines had to call in Turks to help drive them out. Unfortunately for Constantinople, the cure was worse than the illness. From the middle of the 13th century on, Turks in increasing numbers moved out along the Egnatian Way — often driving the local settlers up into the hills, or across the Adriatic into Italy. By the turn of the 16th century, they had driven the Italians out of Durazzo. The fall of shrunken Constantinople in 1453 was, in a sense, an anticlimax, for its greatness had long since gone, as her territories were stripped away one by one. The Egnatian Way received some other migrants in this period, notably Jewish refugees from Spain and Portugal, large numbers of whom settled in Thessalonica, making up perhaps half of the population.

The coming centuries saw mostly decline on the Egnatian Way. The Turks repaired only those sections of the road they found useful. By the 16th century, a Frenchman, Pierre Belon, noted that, in the region between Philippi and Ipsala, the road had been so let go that trees grew in the middle of it; bypaths had developed to the

left and right of such obstacles of neglect, distorting the once-straight Roman road. The western portions of the Way were, of course, in the worst condition. In the early 19th century, the French visitor François Pouqueville called the region near Ochrid "certainly the wildest and least known of any of the Turkish portion of Europe," which he imagined to be much as it was before the Romans came.

In this period, the Via Appia was seeing activity of a different sort. In the long centuries of the Middle Ages, the road had suffered a great decline. Large sections of road had been abandoned to brush and scrub, and the great causeway across the Pontine Marshes had rotted away, forcing the southern route on a long detour inland, before returning to the coast. The jubilee years of 1575, 1600, and 1625 brought many hundreds of thousands of pilgrims to Rome, and many lamented the passing of the old Appia. One young German traveler, Stefan Pighius, noted in 1575 that in "the vast but watery Pontine fields where once passed the superb straight line of the Via Appia...now one sees only the miserable ruins under the water, while on both sides appear mausoleums, tombs, buildings, villas and palaces which once ornamented it." Even these were not to last. In a process that had started in the Middle Ages and sped up with the economic revival of the Renaissance, the Italians raided the Via Appia and its monuments for building materials. Many a church and hospice was built with the stone from a former monument or post-station, or from the flagstones of the Appia itself. Tons of marble lay untouched in the port of Ostia, but blocks from the Appia were ready-dressed and closer to hand.

Some popes attempted to stop the dismantling of the Roman remains. In the 15th century, Pope Pius II told of "going out by the Porta Appia on the road toward Naples" and seeing on the way "many ruined villas and an aqueduct borne on lofty arches but broken in many places." Further on, near the Alban Hills, he found "the Appian Way paved with very hard black stones and on either side the huge bulk of towerlike tombs stripped of their marbles." Although he found the road "in many places more beautiful than at the height of the Roman Empire, since it was shaded on the sides and overhead by leafy filbert trees," he was irate to see the destruction continue. Speaking of himself in the third person, he reported:

> ...here a man was digging out the pavement and destroying the road, breaking up the great rocks into small pieces to build a house near Nemi. The Pope sharply rebuked him, and instructed...the owner...not to allow the public road, which was the Pope's responsibility, to be touched thereafter.

Some popes took this responsibility seriously. In the 17th

and 18th centuries they drained the Pontine Marshes and reopened a road across the reclaimed land. Others felt differently, wanting only to clear the Appia of ruins, while restoring sections of road for modern use.

The section of road between Rome and Naples was still the most important, connecting the capital with its supply port. This became increasingly true in Napoleonic times, when the British were blockading the French at sea; important supplies from southern Italy were carted north on the inland route out of harm's way. But with the passing of Napoleon, the British became a dominant force in the Mediterranean. They were fascinated by things classical, and sent innumerable travelers to Italy—among them many who would begin the archaeological study of the Roman past. The British also increasingly crossed the Mediterranean to Egypt or the Levant, on the way to their eastern territories. Nothing could have been more natural than to revive the overland route to the eastern Mediterranean, and the port of Brindisi once again came alive with travelers headed eastward. This port might well have thought her day was over, for her channel to the sea, blocked centuries before to keep out the Turks, had made her port virtually worthless, until the channel was cleared in the late 18th century. When, in 1869, the Suez Canal opened, Brindisi became a major international port and once again housed the Italian navy.

While the Appian Way was reviving, the Egnatian Way was in its deepest decline. By 1912, Turkey's domains in Europe had—like Rome's in the fourth century A.D.—been trimmed to just the Egnatian corridor. When an assassination in Serbia brought the world powers more directly into the region, the Turks even had to withdraw from much of that territory, leaving the Balkan peoples to fight over the region between Durazzo and the Hebros River—while the Western powers watched and waited. In the end Albania kept the mountainous region at the western end of the Egnatian Way, including the main ports of Durazzo and Vlorë (Avlona); Turkey was cut back to the Hebros River; and Greece was left with the coastal strip between them along the Egnatian Way. At this time the Egnatian Way also underwent a different kind of upheaval, for the enmity and nationalist feelings of both Greece and Turkey prompted a massive population exchange. Many hundreds of thousands of ethnic Greeks, some of them residents in Turkey for long centuries, emigrated to Greek territory, especially to Thrace. Likewise, many Turks left their long-time homes along the

Egnatian Way to live in the new republic of Turkey that emerged after the war.

In the 1930's, Benito Mussolini dreamed of reviving the old Roman Empire. As had so many Romans before him, he headed for Brindisi and Bari, and sent his armies across the Adriatic to Albania; when the war began in earnest, the Germans also entered the lists, striking down the north-south route at always important Thessalonica and passing on into Greece. (Most of Thessalonica's large Jewish population was deported and exterminated at this time.) When the war was over elsewhere, it continued along the Egnatian Way, for Greece became embroiled in a civil war, between Western-supported forces and Communist forces supplied by the now-Communist countries to its north and west. The final battle between the two groups was, fittingly, fought in the Monastir Gap, that central passageway along the Egnatian Way. The Communists were decisively defeated, and the borders along the Egnatian Way settled into their modern position. But in modern times, a traveler would find it almost impossible to travel along the old Egnatian Way from one end to the other. Roads and railroads now exist, where few did a century ago; some follow closely the line of the old Egnatian Way, others deviate where modern technology suggested a different choice. The problem is political. Albania's borders are closed to almost all comers. Greece and, at the far eastern end of the Way, Turkey allow freer travel, but either is capable of closing the road summarily for its own purposes.

The picture along the Via Appia is rosier. True to their heritage, the Romans have in modern times fallen in love with automobiles and built great new highways on which to drive them. While the superhighways run further inland, the old two-lane main road follows the line of the old Via Appia—for if much has changed, that has not. Today, Strada Statale (State Road) 7 still curls around the rockface at Terracina, first cut by Roman laborers many centuries ago, on to Capua, Beneventum, and finally Brindisi. There, though little remains, travelers will find still standing one of the two columns that once marked the end of the Via Appia. At both ends of the route, many maps still mark the road "Via Appia Antica." And if not every Italian knows who Appius Claudius was, his achievement is surely remembered every day; ask for directions south from Rome, and you will be told, "Take the Appia…"

Selective Bibliography

Charlesworth, Martin Percival. *Trade-Routes and Commerce of the Roman Empire* (London: Cambridge University Press, 1924). A classic, packing considerable detail into a small space.

Chevallier, Raymond. *Roman Roads.* Translated from the French by N. H. Field (Berkeley and Los Angeles: University of Calfornia Press, 1976). A detailed work, focusing on literary evidence and existing remains.

Hamblin, Dora Jane, and Mary Jane Grunsfeld. *The Appian Way: A Journey* (New York: Random House, 1974). Explores various aspects of the route, with notes on remains to be seen and some fine black-and-white photographs.

Leighton, Albert C. *Transport and Communication in Early Medieval Europe, A.D. 500–1100* (Newton Abbot: David Charles, 1972). A helpful overview.

O'Sullivan, Firmin. *The Egnatian Way* (Harrisburg, Pa.: Stackpole Books, 1972). Treats the route up to modern times, with special attention to remains to be seen by travelers.

Rose, Albert Chatellier. *"Via Appia* in the Days When All Roads Led to Rome."*Smithsonian Report for 1934,* pp. 347–70. A useful summary, focusing on construction methods for the Appia and other Roman roads.

Rostovtzeff, M. *The Social and Economic History of the Roman Empire,* 2 vols. Second Edition revised by P. M. Fraser (Oxford: At the Clarendon Press, 1957). A full standard work; Volume 2 contains notes and indexes only.

Sitwell, N. H. H. *Roman Roads of Europe* (New York: St. Martin's, 1981). A beautifully illustrated work with many useful detailed regional maps.

Skeel, Caroline A. J. *Travel in the First Century After Christ: With Special Reference to Asia Minor* (Cambridge: At the University Press, 1901). A brief gem, more general than the subtitle indicates.

Von Hagen, Victor Wolfgang. *The Roads That Led to Rome* (Cleveland: World, 1967). A useful well-illustrated general survey of the Roman road system.

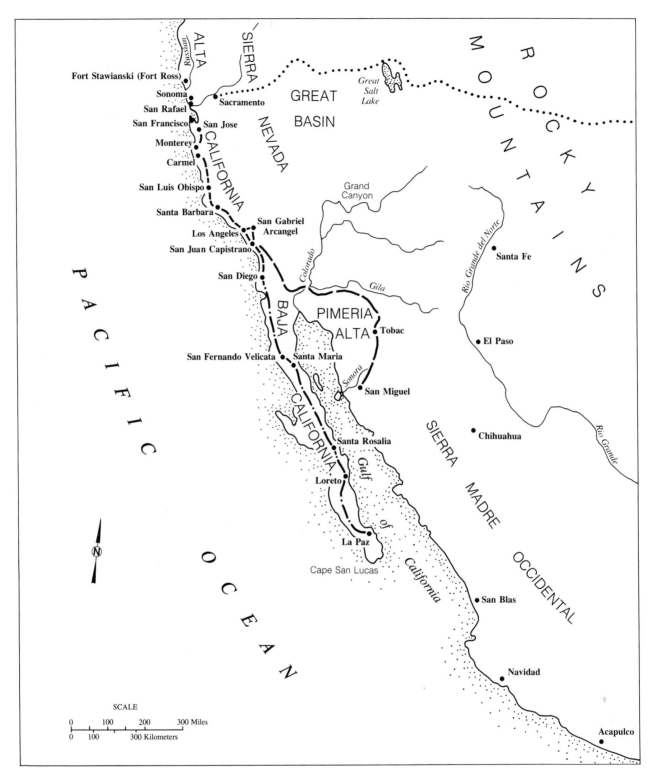

The California Mission Trail in Colonial Times

-------- California Mission Trail (El Camino Real)

———— El Camino Del Diablo (Anza Trail)

—·—·— Baja Mission Trail

········· California Trail

The California Mission Trail

*I*n the year 1775, Captain Pedros Fages, *commandante* at Monterey, reported to his superior, the Viceroy of New Spain, about the difficulty of traveling in California:

In order to travel and transport goods from San Diego to Monterey it is necessary to pass twenty or more Indian towns either directly through them, along their borders, or at least within sight of them at about gunshot distance and there are numerous cliffs, bluffs, and difficult passages where the natives might, to advantage, dispute the way and even prevent travelers from passing. Instances of this are not lacking. For example, in the year '72 they threw stones and darts at me when I was going down to San Diego at a place which we call El Rincon; the Indians took advantage of an opportunity to surprise me and my escort when we were occupied in effecting a difficult passage, and we found ourselves in such straits that it was necessary, assuming the defensive, to punish the boldness of the insolent fellows, killing one or more of them but losing none of our men. Since then they have shown some caution but whenever they see a small number of travelers not well armed the Indians do not hesitate to try their fortune. It is plain to see that there is no means of forfending these injuries than to establish presidios [forts] and missions in suitable places.

The idea of a "mission trail" was hardly new, and California itself had been discovered by Europeans almost two centuries before Fages came to Monterey, but the world paid little attention to California in colonial times.

For over 300 years, California was a state waiting to be born. Isolated from the world in all directions, it was claimed by Spain but never much settled, being regarded only as a buffer against Spain's rivals in the north: the Russians, French, English, and later Americans. Only a fragile network of missions strung out along a coastal trail united the area until, in the 19th and 20th centuries, millions of people poured into the state, lured first by gold and later by land, climate, and commerce. For the last century and a half, California has been for many a promised land, the end of a long journey that started on the other side of the Atlantic or the Pacific, or south of the border. As missionaries were replaced by miners and later movie stars, and as the Spanish and native Americans mixed with northern Europeans and East Asians, California created a unique culture. And the California Mission Trail grew to be one of the most heavily used highways in the world, with one of the world's most populous cities—Los Angeles—spread out from the site of a once-solitary mission.

Unlike most North American routes, the Mission Trail did not follow an already established native American pathway. California's native Americans lived in relatively isolated groups, with no regular long-distance pattern of contact and communication among them. They seem to have filtered across the inland barriers, from the Great Plains, where their ancestors first arrived, and over several millennia to have established themselves in the

Even 150 years after its founding, the Mission of San Carlos Borromeo, near Monterey, was a modest settlement, with post riders arriving on the Mission Trail. (By Capt. W. Smyth, R. N., from California: A History, *by Alexander Forbes, 1839)*

coastal areas. The terrain divided them from each other and protected them from potential conquerors. To the north and east, California is cut off from the rest of the continent by two ranges of mountains—the range the Spanish named the Sierra Nevada and, further east, the Rocky Mountains—with the vast desert called the Great Basin in between. To the south, desert and rugged mountains also act as a barrier. To the west, the ocean was long an effective bar to invaders; the strong coastwise winds made the California shore a dangerous place for sailing ships, as many a Spanish galleon captain was to learn. So the area was before the Spanish came.

It seems appropriate that California, land of dreams and fables, was named for a fiction. Less than 20 years after Christopher Columbus sailed into the Caribbean, a Spanish author, Garcia Ordonez de Montalvo, wrote a romantic novel in which he described "...an island called California, very close to the side of the Terrestrial Paradise; and it was peopled by black women, without any men among them, for they lived in the fashion of Amazons....Their island was the strongest in all the world, with its steep cliffs and rocky shores. Their arms were all of gold, and so was the harness of the wild beasts which they tamed to ride; for in the whole island there was no metal but gold." Though clearly intended as a fiction, the story spurred on various explorers, including Cortés, in their search for riches. Two decades later, when a peninsula was discovered to the west of Mexico, Cortés

officially named it Santa Cruz but—in jest, so the story goes—may have laughingly tagged it "California." In any case, California it was from then on. The fictional name for this unknown land also fed the idea that California was an island, bounded on the north by a passage that would link the Atlantic and Pacific Oceans.

It was the search for this mythical passage (which was called the Strait of Anian, after a reference in Marco Polo's writings) that drew explorers to California. The first of these explorers was Juan Cabrillo, who in 1542-43 sailed up the west coast of North America from Navidad, on the mainland north of Acapulco, to the modern Oregon border, taking shelter on the way at San Diego (which he named San Miguel) and Santa Barbara, but discovering no strait. Three decades later, the British sailor Francis Drake came on the same search, pirating Spanish galleons on the way and putting in at the area still known as Drake's Bay. Leaving a brass plate to mark his country's claim to the land, he named the territory Albion:

> ...and that for two causes: the one in respect of the white banks and cliffs which lie toward the sea; the other that it might have some affinity, even in name also, with our own country, which was sometime so called.

The Spanish soon had some other reasons to explore the land they called California. Drake's exploits brought eager pirates to the west coast, and Spain's galleons between Mexico and the Philippines now had to contend with not only scurvy, crosswinds, illness, and lack of water, but also piracy. Because of these problems, Sebastián Vizcaíno was charged with breaking a land trail along the California coast and establishing a harbor for the Manila galleons. He started in the area called Baja (Lower) California, but failed to make a usable land route—not surprisingly, since it is still extremely rugged country for travel—and chose to search by sea. En route, he named many of the common points along the coast, among them Capes Concepción, Piños, Año Nuevo, and Reyes, as well as the bays of San Diego and Carmel. But he is best known for his discovery—and quite fanciful description—of Monterey Bay, about which he said:

> ...it is all that can be desired as a harbor for ships making the voyage from the Philippines...surrounded by settlements of friendly Indians...with plenty of food and water.

But Spanish policy changed, and California was left to the native Americans for another century. Vizcaíno's only legacy was a better-charted coast, and a fiction regarding Monterey which would cause mischief long after his death years later.

Meanwhile Jesuit missionaries had been moving northwestward from Mexico City, establishing missions in the area called Sonora. In the late 17th century their efforts were strengthened by bequests from the Pious Fund of California, established by wealthy Catholics in Spain who wished to buy salvation. More important, their work was sparked by an extraordinary priest, Eusebio Francisco Kino, a scholar newly arrived from Europe. He established two missionary colonies on Baja California, one at La Paz, which was abandoned after two years, and a more permanent one at Loreto, 200 miles north on the Gulf of California. He then moved into the desolate northwest area of New Spain called the Pimeria Alta, on the border of present-day Arizona and Mexico. With his companion, Father Juan Maria Salvatierra, he explored farther to the northwest, founding missions as he went, across desert country to the Colorado River, a route later called El Camino del Diablo (the Devil's Highway) for the extreme difficulties it presented. Arriving at the upper end of the Gulf of California, Father Kino confirmed his suspicion that California was not an island, although the belief persisted for many decades yet. It was Father Kino who planned the mission trail, which he saw extending from the southern tip of Baja California at Cape San Lucas up to the famous port of Monterey, in Alta (Upper) California, and perhaps even beyond.

With money from the Pious Fund, Kino began to implement his plan. From the base at Loreto, a trail of missions began to stretch north and south on Baja Cali-

fornia, with a permanent mission being founded at La Paz in 1720, and one even farther south on the Cape itself. Through dry, rugged country, abounding in mountain lions, snakes, and insects of all sorts, the dusty trail linked a string of missions that, by 1767, had reached three-quarters of the way up the Baja Peninsula. Then the king of Spain suddenly expelled all Jesuits from New Spain and took their holdings in the name of the crown. At the same time, there came a rumor that the Russians were advancing on California. That rumor was—like many others over the following decades—false, but it temporarily focused Spanish attention on Alta California. While not thought valuable in itself, Alta California was seen as a buffer protecting New Spain's truly valuable land in Mexico, especially the rich silver mines of the north. So the area fell under the control of Jose de Gálvez, Visitador General, sent by the king to put down protests resulting from the expulsion of the Jesuits and to establish defensible ports at San Diego and Monterey. (San Francisco Bay was as yet undiscovered by any Europeans.)

Gálvez outfitted three ships for the purpose, but a six-week voyage from San Blas, on the west coast of New Spain, to Cape San Lucas against heavy coastal winds, convinced him that a land route was necessary. Stocked with livestock and supplies taken from the former Jesuit missions along the Baja mission trail, a party assembled at the northernmost mission on the trail, Santa Maria. The soldiers in the party were commanded by Captain Gaspar de Portolá, while the Franciscan priests, sent from Spain to replace the Jesuits in spreading Christianity among the native Americans, were led by the newly arrived Father Junipero Serra, limping from a spider bite suffered as he walked from Vera Cruz to Mexico City. In the spring of 1769, half of the party headed north toward Alta California, blazing a fresh trail along the coast, with eight soldiers going ahead to clear the way, where necessary, with spades and crowbars. After two months they arrived at San Diego Bay, where they found waiting two of their three ships, which had arrived earlier. Unfortunately, many of the seamen were dead or dying from scurvy or other diseases, while the third ship had been lost at sea. The rear party, including Portolá and Serra, arrived six weeks later and founded a mission and a presidio on the site. While one ship returned south for supplies, and the other lay at San Diego for lack of a crew, half of the land party resumed the northward journey on July 14, 1769.

The party advanced about six miles a day, with camp pitched in early afternoon to allow scouts to explore the next day's route. Sometimes especially rough country, a difficult march, or a stampede might keep the party in camp for several days. The mules used as pack animals (and occasionally food) were skittish, easily stampeded by the teasing of native Americans they met along the way or by earthquakes, the first of which—"it lasted about half as long as an Ave Maria"—the party encountered a week north of San Diego. Naming as they went, the party passed through Santa Ana and Nuestra Señora de Los Angeles de Procuincúla (later shortened to Los Angeles), moving along a natural coast trail to the Santa Barbara Channel, which they recognized from the descriptions of the early explorer, Juan Cabrillo. There a group of native Americans the Spanish called Canaleños, for their skill in boat-building, conveyed by sign language that two months before they had seen a boat with men who looked like the Spaniards; while some thought that meant Russians were in the area, others decided it was one of their two surviving ships, which had originally overshot San Diego on its voyage north. Throughout the trip, relations with the native Americans were non-violent and friendly, as one of the officers wrote:

> The Indians came voluntarily to nearly every place where our men camped that they might present themselves to us and show us honors demonstrating the most complete confidence...Our men made themselves understood by signs and they in like manner indicated to us the road, the watering places and other matters concerning which we required information for our guidance on the march. It was never necessary for us to use our weapons for any purpose save to obtain some game which was generally bears whose flesh had a pleasant flavor.

Clearly, also, the route they were blazing was not a completely new one, but sometimes followed local trails.

The party continued along a relatively easy route until they reached the site where San Luis Obispo would later be founded. This was—and is—a natural dividing line between northern and southern California. At this point, since they were approaching the spot where the fine bay of Monterey was supposed to be located, Portolá's party decided to stay as near the coast as possible, forsaking natural trails. This was easier said than done, for in the area of San Simeon the cliffs of the coastal range, the Sierra de Santa Lucia, drop sheerly down to the sea. After days of struggling through inhospitable terrain, crossing innumerable *arroyos*, they finally turned inland to the valley of a northward-flowing river we know as the Salinas. Following this valley, they reached Monterey Bay—and understandably failed to recognize it, since it bore little resemblance to the grand bay described by Vizcaíno. Father Juan Crespí, a member of the party, put it bluntly:

> At Punta Piños there is no port, nor have we seen in all our journey a country more desolate than this, or people more rude, Sebastián Vizcaíno to the contrary notwithstanding.

In the late 18th century visitors were so rare that they received a full-scale welcome, as did the Comte de La Pérouse in Carmel in 1786. (Museo Naval, Madrid)

52

Carrying passengers and the vital mail, the stagecoach pounds to keep its schedule along the Mission Trail. ("Stage Arriving in California," by Einar Petersen; California Historical Society/Title Insurance and Trust Co., Los Angeles)

Continuing up the coast, Portolá's party found other recognizable points and, from a high point on a hill, saw an "immense arm of the sea or estuary, which extended inland as far as they could see..." But so dispirited was Portolá at his failure to find Monterey, that he never even explored or reported on this discovery of San Francisco Bay (although he did mention finding a new type of tree with red wood, the *palo colorado*). Instead, he returned to San Diego in disgrace, having traversed for the first time what would be known as the California Mission Trail.

The man who would be most responsible for that designation, Father Serra, waited at San Diego, where his party was also in sad condition, having lost many men to illness and having made no converts. Just as Portolá (but not Serra) was about to abandon Alta California, a supply ship arrived. With his orders still standing, Portolá returned overland, arriving at Monterey before Serra's party, whose ship was held up by the difficult coastal winds. There in June 1770 they founded a presidio and a mission, providing a northern base from which to defend California from Russian, English, or French invaders. More important, since the fort would provide little real defense and Portolá left California for good immediately thereafter, from this mission—or more accurately from the mission at Carmel, where Serra moved the following year to separate himself from the army—Father Serra planned

and executed Father Kino's dream of a mission trail. Over the next 14 years, until his death in 1784, Serra personally founded a network of missions, all approximately one day's journey away from each other, so the missions could aid each other and travelers could find a safe shelter on El Camino Real (the Royal Road) anywhere between the Mission at San Diego and the Mission San Carlos Borromeo, at Monterey. The first three missions between these two ends of the trail were San Antonio de Padua, about 70 miles south of Monterey; San Gabriel Arcangel, near modern Los Angeles; and San Luis Obispo de Tolosa.

As Serra and his followers continued to fill out the trail in the next few years with San Juan Capistrano and Santa Clara Mission, they also extended the Mission Trail northward to San Francisco de Asis, named after the founder of the Franciscan Order. This site, on the southern point of the "Golden Gate" formed by the opposing high cliffs at the neck of the great bay, was so prime that the soldiers also built a presidio there to guard it. The bay itself was finally recognized as the magnificent harbor it was; Father Pedro Font's 1776 rave is typical:

The port of San Francisco...is a marvel of nature, and might well be called the harbor of harbors, because of its great capacity and of several small bays which it enfolds in its margin...Indeed, although in my travels I saw very good sites and beautiful country, I saw none which pleased me as much as this.

In later years, Serra's successors crossed the bay and on the northern shore founded Missions San Rafael Arcangel and San Francisco Solano de Sonoma, which remained the northernmost mission on the thousand-mile trail from the southern tip of Baja California.

A trail it certainly was and would be for another century and a half. A trail for pack animals and people on foot, not for wagons; it had no bridges, no graded crossings or causeways, and in the southern part where it ran along the shore, especially near Santa Barbara, it was often submerged at high tide. In this period it was merely tamped down by the feet of priests, their native American converts, and livestock driven back and forth along the trail to bring supplies to new missions from the old.

The missions along the trail were far from self-supporting, however. At first they were supported by ship from La Paz, on the Baja, and San Blas, on the mainland, but that was both difficult and expensive; yet the land route up the Baja Peninsula was no more attractive. A land route was sought by which the young missions might be supplied from the long-established mission in Sonora. It was a soldier, Juan Bautista de Anza, who reopened a route traversed decades before by the Jesuit Father Kino; formerly called El Camino del Diablo, it was now also known as the Anza Trail. The Anza Trail came to be the main supply line for the California missions in their infancy. Over this route Anza brought not only food from the prosperous Sonora missions, but also the first Spanish colonists to California: 240 men, women, and children, who arrived on the California Mission Trail at the Mission San Gabriel Arcangel and moved north to settle in the San Francisco area in early 1776.

While revolutions occurred in Europe and even on the far side of the same continent, California was largely ignored by everyone, including the Spanish government. The priests steadily converted native Americans, who were treated harshly and virtually enslaved, being locked in closed quarters at night; yet the soldiers were worse and the priests offered some protection from military violence and murder. An occasional ship would put into port, but maritime visitors were so rare—sometimes none were seen for years—that visitors were warmly greeted regardless of their nationality, and some were even given a guided tour down part of El Camino Real. A French visitor, Jean François Galaup, Comte de La Pérouse, was given such a treat in September 1786, on the road from Monterey to Carmel:

...we ascended the hills and heard the sound of bells announcing our coming. We were received like lords of a parish visiting their estates for the first time. The president of the mission, clad in cope, his holy-water sprinkler in hand, received us at the door of the church illuminated as on the grandest festivals; and chanted a *te deum* of thanksgiving for the happy issue of our voyage.

The colonists sometimes bartered with their visitors for needed goods (having no mutually acceptable currency), by which process potatoes may have arrived in western North America and longhorn cattle first been sent to Australia. It was from the first American guest that the people of Monterey confirmed rumors—in 1796—of a new nation across the continent called the United States of America.

As the number of visitors increased, Spanish policy changed, and strangers were not allowed inland along El Camino Real and were treated more warily, especially the Russians, who had long been in Alaska (and had even left a legacy of some blond Indians to the north) but who now were edging south. The Russians had a dual purpose: to establish a southern base, which they did at Fort Stawianski just north of the Russian River, and to obtain food supplies, for the trappers had many furs but no produce. The Spanish and Russians established an uneasy trade and, with the uncertainty of alliances in the Napoleonic period, the Spanish took no active steps to dislodge the Russians from Fort Stawianski, which they called El Fuerto de los Russos (the Fort of the Russians), later to become Fort Ross.

From the earliest colonial times, California had been largely ignored by the authorities in New Spain; the settlers and defenders there were largely on their own. But even that token support crumbled and then vanished in the second decade of the 19th century. The American colony of New Spain began agitating for independence and gained it in late 1821. In these turbulent times, pirates replaced friendly visitors, and more than once women and children were sent away from bay areas along the Mission Trail to inland missions for safety. The defending soldiers were generally ineffectual; pirates took whatever was left behind for them, although they did not think it worthwhile to venture inland along the still wild and unsettled Camino Real.

In this same period, the mission trail in Baja California (now under Dominican priests) and the Anza Trail to Sonora fell into disuse. That left California completely on its own, a few ranchos strung out along the Mission Trail on the coast, with the inland area still *terra incognita*. And a thin line it was, indeed, for as late as 1800, there were only 740 Spanish males of all ages in Baja and Alta California combined. The Trail had been widened a bit by use in some places, especially between San Diego and Mission San Luis Rey, and between Mission San Gabriel Arcangel and the developing hamlet of Los Angeles. But conditions were still quite primitive. Father

But for the two bicyclists and the telegraph poles, this road—Cahuenga Pass through Hollywood—in 1899 is much as it was in the early days of the Mission Trail. (Security Pacific National Bank Photography Collection, Los Angeles Public Library)

Pedro Font noted that near Santa Barbara the road ran "along the sea beach almost touching the waves," which he thought would have been more "diverting...if the day had been clear and not so murky from fog." Further on, he continues:

> In places there is no other way except along the beach and in other stretches there is a road which they call "along the heights" which runs on the edge of the sliced off part of the hills with great precipices from which the sea is visible far below.

Vehicles, too, were primitive. Wooden-wheeled *carretas* (ox carts) joined couriers and drovers who walked or rode horses or mules passing information and supplies along the route. As late as 1847, when William Tecumseh Sherman, later a famous Civil War general, arrived at California's capital as a young artillery lieutenant, he was surprised to find that: "Not a single modern wagon or cart was to be had in Monterey, nothing but the old Mexican cart with wooden wheels, drawn by two or three pairs of oxen, yoked by the horns..."

Into this vacuum stepped the Americans. Although that name could apply to settlers anywhere in the American continents, they adopted the label "American" as peculiarly theirs, reflecting both their arrogance and sense of purpose. Venturing into the East Asian sea trade, Boston ships on the Cape Horn route began to stop in California and found there a hungry market cut off from both nations that claimed it. The Californians, for their part, had an enormous surplus of cattle, which gave them valuable hides and tallow greatly valued by the United States. A trade quickly developed, with the arrival of the Boston ships in Monterey being announced by leaflets distributed up and down the Mission Trail. Once cleared at the customs house in Monterey, the ship agents would travel along the trail, trading with missions and ranchos along the coast; even the priests joined in the trade, setting up small stores selling notions. The Mission Trail became a trade route; hides were sent overland to San Diego for curing and loading onto ships, while imported goods were distributed at the missions and ranchos along the trail. The unsophisticated Californianos were easy prey for the Boston traders, who sometimes made a profit of 300% on their goods; once relations with Mexico were re-established and California came under its wing, newly trained priests were sent to handle the trade, acting as unofficial agents and bankers for the Californianos. The riches to be had in the land were becoming obvious, and many of the Boston traders and sailors left their ships in California, converted to Catholicism—"leaving their consciences at Cape Horn"—and married into the now-wealthy Spanish

Where buggies and bicycles once ruled, cars and paved roads began to dominate, as here at Cahuenga Pass in 1928. (Title Insurance and Trust Co., Los Angeles)

families. The riches may also have spurred the downfall of the Franciscan mission; in 1833 half of the Franciscans' holdings were awarded to the state—meaning the politicians—and half supposedly to the "freed" native Americans, although little remained for them in fact when the wheeler-dealers were finished. The missions became parishes, and the Franciscans simple priests.

The change made an enormous difference along the Mission Trail. Before secularization, the relatively few travelers—even strangers—were always sure of a welcome, a good meal, and a clean, safe bed in one of the missions or ranchos along the route. While the mission buildings remained after secularization, they and their grounds were no longer kept up, and the wayfarer was offered flea-ridden beds and poor food at high rates; travelers could not complain, since no alternatives existed. The open Spanish hospitality at the ranchos gave way to a wariness of strangers. The road itself became truly dangerous for the first time since its opening, for it was haunted by disenfranchised and much-abused Native American refugees. These were soon joined by Californian renegades, some of whom became outlaws after an unsuccessful revolt against Mexican authorities, in a battle fought in 1831 at Cahuenga Pass, the main route out of Los Angeles.

The Russians abandoned Fort Ross in 1840, signaling the end of their eastward expansion across Eurasia and into the Americas. The British, on the other hand, exhibited much more than a casual interest in California, especially since they held Mexico in debt for $50 million. But the American westward advance across the continent ultimately proved irresistible.

During the second quarter of the 19th century, Americans continued to trickle into California, some by ship, some by an overland route through the Sierra Nevada opened by Jedediah Smith in 1826, and a few by the southern overland route along the Gila River Valley, joining the old Anza Trail from Sonora. After other former Mexican territory—Texas and New Mexico—fell to the Americans, California seemed next in line. In 1846 some Americans, led by Captain John Frémont, prematurely claimed California for the United States, and various skirmishes were fought on or near the Mission Trail over the next two years. The question was settled in 1848 when the treaty of Guadalupe Hidalgo gave the United States all the territory north of a line 10 miles south of San Diego. After that, Alta California was simply California, becoming a state in 1850. With the discovery of gold in 1848, the flood of Americans began in earnest, following routes by land and sea. At first, many of the towns along the Mission Trail emptied, as everyone raced to the diggings; but some soon realized that they could also become rich selling goods and services to the prospectors. The coastal hamlets became boom towns, with hotels, restaurants, and stores springing up all along the route, in addition to the gambling houses and brothels built to fleece the successful miners. During this boom, more injustices and oppressions were added to the long list already suffered by Californians, for many Mexicans and most native Americans remaining on land granted to them were driven off their property when they were unable to "prove" their ownership to the new American political overlords. Driven into poverty and many into seeking revenge, these people swelled the already large groups of bandits living in the hills along the Mission Trail, preying on travelers, and sparking the formation of vigilante groups in the towns.

The Mission Trail in this period was a sorry sight. In some populated and heavily traveled areas, the route deserved to be called a road; the suburbs of San Francisco, for example, were served by a 40-foot-wide toll road of planks and then hard-packed surface. Elsewhere, some work had been done to ease a river crossing or shore up a bank of the road, but quake damage was seldom repaired. The occasional ferries charged exorbitant prices in boom times—$50 for the Golden Gate crossing—so most travelers simply forded rivers and pushed on through the surf along the shore. Outside of the towns, the route was simply a line of wheel ruts amid fields or sand dunes, with wide drovers' paths on either side where herds were driven along the route. Altogether travel on the Mission Trail in the mid-19th century was both rough and dangerous, a fact that changed little with the coming of regular stagecoach service in 1858. While mail had previously been sent from the eastern United States across the Isthmus of Panama and from the Southwest and Mexico by mule service, the new stage line followed the so-called Ox-Bow Route from St. Louis along the southern border of The United States to San Diego and then up the Mission Trail. The traffic and the new business it brought were sufficiently attractive for some towns in southern California, Los Angeles and Santa Barbara particularly, to pass bond issues to pay for filling in and grading sections of the road. But that took some persuasion for, as late as 1855, the local Santa Barbara newspaper was urging that the local population "tear themselves away from the blandishments of keno, billiards and cards long enough to examine the route for a post road" and especially to clear the Gaviota Pass, northwest of the town, of boulders. At best, modest bridges were built in some areas and boggy portions filled in, and relay stations were set up for exchange of horse teams.

With stagecoaches, the age of advertising arrived in California. California was the far edge of the romantic West, and made the most of it. Writers, both professional and amateur, wrote back East of the daring, wide-open, new culture that was now part of the United States of America. And company advertisements paid little heed to reality, as indicated by this stage company description of the ride along the Mission Trail:

There is no more charming drive in California than that from San Francisco to San Jose and as one is whirled rapidly through the oak openings and across the level plains. . .he finds that pleasure is united with business and wonders why he has never made the trip before.

The only truth in the description was by default—no other ride in California could match it, for there were hardly any other roads, only a few feeder routes into the main Mission Trail. More to the point were the comments of Frank Marryat, a British traveler who rode the route in 1855: "...no one knows what a wagon will undergo until he has mastered California trails and gulches." In this period Sacramento, instead of San Francisco, was the focus of many stage lines, being closer to the gold fields and having easy access to the northern overland route from the East and to Oregon and Washington. The stage lines brought to California "proper" coaches, generally the Concord type, in which the coach was slung on two leather straps—"an imposing cradle on wheels," Mark Twain called it—whose swaying was supposed to absorb the shocks of the road, but which made many people seasick. But the stagecoaching days lasted for only about 15 years until the Butterfield Overland Mail and Wells Fargo were eclipsed by the railroad.

Rumors of the railroad sparked another enormous land boom on the Mission Trail, which swiftly collapsed when the Southern Pacific Railroad chose to lay its route not along the coast but, from Los Angeles, across the Mojave Desert and up the San Joaquin Valley. Coastal California was what the Southern Pacific had to sell, however, and sell it the company did. Having laid a track to the west at enormous expense, the railroad at first did not have enough trade and traffic to pay for the line, so a full staff of writers, lecturers, and publicists were employed to portray California as a paradise—and they succeeded. Tens of thousands of people flocked to California to take up farming; cities exploded off paper into reality, with some like Los Angeles and San Diego growing at the rate of 1,000 or 2,000 people a month; and the rich, the famous, and the affluent invalid were convinced that California was the place for a cure. Along the coast, great resort hotels were built as destinations for the rich; hotels like the Del Coronado in San Diego, the Arlington at Santa Barbara, the Palace in San Francisco, and the Del Monte in Monterey, attracted princes and presidents where, a few years before, only raw frontier had existed. In all, approximately one million people were attracted to California by the railroad blitz, and most of those who stayed settled near the old Mission Trail.

After stagecoaches were reduced to short hauls, ferrying tourists from their hotel to local sightseeing spots, the roads were little improved. But soon there were new kinds of vehicles, their owners clamoring for better roads.

First among these were the bicyclists, who came on strong in the 1880's, forming an organization for better highways and producing what was probably the first road map of the Mission Trail, El Camino Real, in their magazine, *The American Bicycler*. By the turn of the century, they were joined by automobilers, who formed their own clubs to combat public antagonism to cars and to build public sentiment for highway improvement. Gasoline began to be offered along the Mission Trail, at first by general stores or livery stables, and speed records were set, with drivers making the trip from Los Angeles to Santa Barbara in 13 hours. But in 1906 the same earthquake that made San Francisco a shambles contorted the northern portion of the Mission Trail, splitting open the highway by as much as 20 feet and closing the road in many places with rock and mud slides.

Many refugees from the area fled to Los Angeles, some of them permanently; their experience of the terrible condition of the Mission Trail, even in its undamaged portions, made the state's population more sympathetic to highway improvement. Citizens in communities along the route contributed their labor on designated days to rebuild the road, fill in holes and ruts, and mark especially troublesome areas. It was still only a dirt road, however, and during winter rains was so muddy that local residents made a handsome side income towing cars out of mudholes. (Human nature being what it is, some also took to creating road hazards for drivers who were, after all, still primarily rich people at this time.) In this same period, Californians began to discover—and to create—their own history; the Mission Bell Association set up mileposts, each with a bell hung from a staff imitating those of the Franciscan friars, all along the 450-mile route. Jitney services were established, often using second-hand automobiles, and these quickly replaced the remaining stagecoaches. By World War I, more horses were to be found on the lots of southern California's developing movie industry than on El Camino Real. Livery stables were gradually replaced by stations that sold gasoline and fixed automobiles; and in place of the long-gone stage bandits, car thieves began to create a brisk trade across the border with cohorts in Mexico. At Rincon Point, near Santa Barbara, a wooden viaduct was built so automobiles would not have to splash through the surf, as stagecoaches had always done.

Not until the early 1920's did the Mission Trail as a whole begin to be paved, and then it was sparked by money from the federal government and surplus equipment left over from World War I, the Californian contribution coming from a tax on gasoline. Over the decades, the Mission Trail had begun to change from a zigzag path connecting missions, as it was in Father Serra's time, to a straighter road connecting the towns and cities that had grown up along its route. Now, for the first time, engineers and surveyors gave the Mission Trail a modern aspect, widening the road, especially the passes, easing difficult grades, cutting into rock along sections of sheer cliff, and building concrete road bridges. Work was hindered by a large earthquake in Santa Barbara in 1925, and a burst dam in Santa Clara Valley in 1928.

As new settlers continued to swell California's population, alternate routes were developed through major cities. In Los Angeles, the long-used Gaviota Pass was supplemented by another old route, through the San Marcos Pass, as well as other new routes. Out of San Francisco, at least three routes traveled southward, including a tourist road that led to Monterey and then down along the cliff-lined coast of Sierra de Santa Lucia to San Simeon (a road that was also—many charged—a private luxury for the rich families, like the Hearsts, who had mansions along the route). Further south, the route's aspect was also being changed by the arrival of oil derricks. In the mid-1920's, the now-modernized route of the Mission Trail was given a number under the new federal designation system; the section of the Mission Trail from San Diego to Los Angeles and then north through the San Joaquin Valley—the route previously chosen by the railroad—was labeled Route 5. El Camino Real from Los Angeles north became U.S. Route 101.

California continued to grow and the new free road maps used by tourists and immigrants required frequent updating to show new towns, mixing more English names among the old Spanish ones. By 1925, the first motel in California, perhaps in the world, catering to overnight travelers was established on Route 101 at San Luis Obispo. Motor buses came into use along the route and began to eclipse the Southern Pacific Railroad. Heavy trucks started to operate on Route 101, hauling produce from fertile California farms, as well as bootleg liquor from across the Mexican border. During the Depression years, Route 101 was crowded with refugees from the rest of the United States, especially the Great Plains; drawn by the widespread image of California as paradise, many abandoned their cars by the side of the road when they ran out of money to fuel or repair them. Hitchhikers and hobos wandered along Route 101, some being stranded there after driving new cars on contract to California, with a false promise of return fare. Federally funded transient camps were set up along Route 101, as elsewhere in California, and many of the unemployed were put to work in New Deal projects repairing the road, which required heavy maintenance because of its now-heavy load of traffic. In 1937, the Golden Gate Bridge was completed, replacing the ferries that had formerly connected the old Mission Trail with the continuation of Route 101 northward to San Rafael and Sonoma and out along the coast into Oregon and Washington.

World War II brought even greater changes to the old Mission Trail. California became the focus of the Pacific war effort, with major naval bases at San Diego, Los Angeles, and San Francisco, and with training centers and defense plants clustered north and south. The influx of millions of people—to work in the plants, to serve in the armed forces, and to visit those headed for battle—made congestion in both northern and southern California extreme. Plans were made to redo Route 101, but such plans had to wait. During the war, 101 served as a major transportation route, with blackouts and dimouts along its length and beaches closed and strung with barbed wire against the possibility of enemy attack. The Mission Trail also saw the forced evacuation of people of Japanese descent to temporary centers in Salinas and nearby, before internment inland; many lost their homes and land, much of it along Route 101. Some old hotels along the route, such as the Del Monte Hotel, were also taken over for military housing. By the end of the war California's population had grown to almost nine million people. While the administrative center had always been in northern California, from the time Serra settled in Monterey, and the state capital had from 1854 been in Sacramento, the concentration of population—and the attraction of the movie industry—made southern California increasingly dominant in postwar times.

In 1945, the California Mission Trail was well on its way to developing into a "road city," especially at its northern and southern ends. But the road itself was still little more than a city street, with cross streets, traffic lights, left and right turns, and occasional toll stations. The highway engineers who examined the sad state of Route 101, badly battered from years of heavy defense transport and steady traffic with little maintenance and repair, came up with a new concept that would be the prototype for the modern highway. They visualized a multiple-lane turnpike with no stops, turns, or crossings all the way from San Diego to San Francisco, with access limited to ramps feeding vehicles on and off the road at interchange points, and with shrubbery in a median strip between the three north and the three south lanes, to minimize accidents and cut down on glare from oncoming headlights. Approval of the proposed freeway set off another land boom along Route 101, with people buying up land along the expected route, anticipating a big profit. Some of these speculators were disappointed when the route was straightened to bypass certain towns along the old route, and many small business owners who had made their living from motorists on Route 101 went out of business as the new freeway went in. The immense project took 15 years, not being fully completed all along the route until 1960. So high was the cost that the freeways were sometimes called "gold-plated highways," but early criticism of the project soon gave way to complaints that the road should have been built even wider, not surprising considering that the Hollywood Freeway was used by 168,000 vehicles daily in 1954, and was at the time probably the most heavily used road in the world.

Whatever the undesirable aspects of the freeway system, it became a necessity by the mid-20th century for those millions of mobile people who concentrated along the route of the old Mission Trail. Gone are the mountain lions who used to leap from nearby *arroyo* banks to attack travelers on the route of Father Serra. Gone, too, are the deer and bears that, in the early years of the freeway, used to congregate along the fences of Route 101. In their place are millions of people in a largely concrete landscape. But the massive highway did not create *all* of the modern problems along its route; the famous Los Angeles smog far predated the automobile and was noted by many visitors, the earliest being the Spanish explorer Sebastian Vizcaíno, who named the coastal area Bahia de los Humos (Bay of Smoke). Nor will nature allow Californians to forget her. Earthquakes, land slips, mud slides, and brush fires continue all along the modern Route 101. And at Rincon Point near Santa Barbara, motorists can still be splashed by occasional heavy waves crashing against the built-out highway, where travelers on the earlier Mission Trail would get wet sloshing through the surf at high tide.

Selective Bibliography

Bolton, Herbert E. *The Spanish Borderlands: A Chronicle of Old Florida and the Southwest.* (New Haven: Yale University Press, 1921). Volume 23 in the Chronicles of America series. Contains well-written accounts of exploration and colonization.

Corle, Edwin. *The Royal Highway (El Camino Real).* (Indianapolis: Bobbs-Merrill, 1949). A popular account up to the early 20th century.

Lummis, Charles F. *The Spanish Pioneers and the California Missions.* (Chicago: A. C. McClurg & Co., 1931). A highly pro-Spanish account.

Riesenberg, Felix, Jr. *The Golden Road: The Story of California's Spanish Mission Trail.* (New York: McGraw-Hill, 1962). Part of the American Trails Series. A popular account up through the 1950's.

Winther, Oscar Osburn. *Express and Stagecoach Days in California: From the Gold Rush to the Civil War.* (Stanford University, California: Stanford University Press, 1936). A detailed account of the limited stagecoach period.

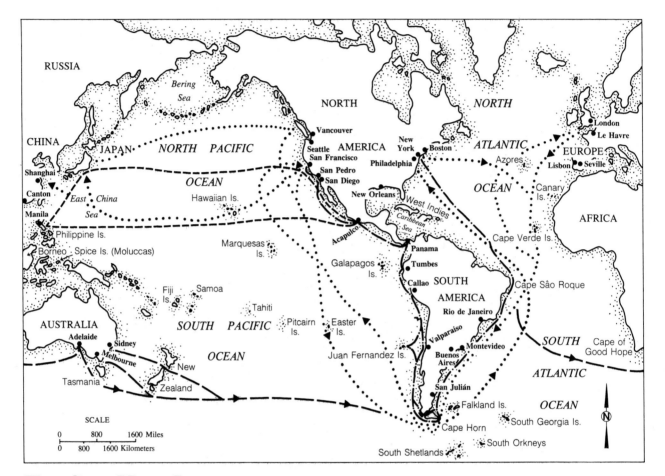

The Cape Horn Route

— · — · — Early Sailing Routes

· · · · · · · · · Late 19th Century Sailing Routes

- - - - - - - Manila Galleon Route

— — — Round-the-World Route

The Cape Horn Route

For five weeks I was beating and banging off that horrid place. It seems as though all the furies of the infernal region were let loose. Tremendous gales, snow and hail continually, nights eighteen hours; sun nine degrees high and sometimes not see him for a week. A small vessel, all hands wet continually, and no chance to dry their clothes. Any person thinking there is pleasure in going to sea, I would advise them to double Cape Horn.

Yankee Captain Francis A. Thompson's description of the passage around Cape Horn, the southernmost tip of South America, would be instantly recognizable to any of his fellow sailors over the centuries. With its icy waters, turbulent winds, and treacherous currents, the Cape Horn Route has always been perilous—so much so that many chose to go to the East by the Cape of Good Hope route around Africa or across the Isthmus of Panama, even before the building of the Panama Canal. Even so, the route around Cape Horn played a major role in world history, at least for one brief period, as Yankee ships swung down the east coast of the Americas and up the west, gathering goods—everything from ginseng and fur pelts to ice and birds' nests—to be sold in East Asia, and in the process laying the basis for annexation of California and Oregon and for domination of the Pacific.

The voyages that led to the discovery of the Americas had their origins in the desire for a sea route westward from Europe to Asia. Although continental land masses were found barring the way, explorers in the decades following Columbus's discovery continued to search for a passage through the Americas to Asia, which Europeans of the time were sure lay only a little way beyond. While northern European explorers searched for such a passage along the North American coast, southern Europeans explored from the the Caribbean southward. In 1513, Balboa crossed the Panama Isthmus and saw the South Sea (El Mar del Sur, later named the Pacific Ocean), confirming the view that there, at least, the land was narrow enough that a strait through it *ought* to exist. In 1516 a Spanish expedition under an explorer named Juan Diaz de Solis thought it had found the desired strait when it sailed into a great river far down the South American coast. De Solis named it El Mar Dulce (the Freshwater Sea), later renamed Rio de la Plata. He himself was killed by native Americans on the river bank, and his crew returned to Spain without exploring further.

The first European mariner to find a route through the Americas was Ferdinand Magellan, a Portuguese sailor leading a Spanish-sponsored expedition. On September 20, 1519, Magellan and five old, much-repaired ships set off with an international (though mostly Spanish) crew from the Guadalquivir River, home of the Spanish Indies fleet, and headed for the South Atlantic. Previous explorers had determined that no strait existed north of the great eastward bulge of South America; below that Magellan and his crew explored every likely inlet, including the bay of Rio de Janeiro and the Rio de la Plata, charting and naming the site of Montevideo near the mouth of that river. In late March of 1520, as the southern winter approached, Magellan set up winter quarters in the Bay of Port St. Julian off southern Patagonia. Magellan's decision was a poor one. The fleet was continually subjected to the strong eastward winds of the "Roaring Forties," the latitudes where winds blow steadily, often at gale force, around the world. Jealousy and fear, which had been fermenting ever since the departure from Spain, grew stronger over the idle winter months. As a result, by the time the fleet left its winter quarters in August, Magellan had roughly put down a mutiny among his crew, including some of his senior officers.

Exploring steadily southward, on October 21, 1520, the fleet approached a high promontory overlooking a strait which they "denominated the strait of the Eleven Thousand Virgins, in honor of the day" (the day being St. Ursula's and the point now being called Cape Virgenes). The crew, too often disappointed, were "firmly persuaded that this strait had no western outlet," but Magellan insisted on the exploration, which they did over the next 38 days. The way was not easy, as Antonio Pigafetta, who sailed on and chronicled Magellan's voyage, described:

> This strait is enclosed between lofty mountains covered with snow, and it is likewise very deep, so that we were unable to anchor except quite close to shore, where was from 25 to 30 fathoms of water....
>
> At night came on a terrible hurricane, which lasted six and thirty hours, and forced us to quit our anchors and leave our vessels to the mercy of the winds and waves in the gulf.
>
> The two other vessels, equally buffeted, were unable to double a cape in order to rejoin us, so that by abandoning themselves to the gale, which drove them constantly toward what they conceived to be the bottom of a bay, they were apprehensive momentarily of being driven onshore. But at the instant they gave themselves up for lost, they saw a small opening, which they took for an inlet of the bay. Into this they entered, and perceiving that this channel was not closed, they threaded it, and found themselves in another, through which they pursued their course to another strait leading into a third bay still larger than the preceding.

At this point they decided to return and report to Magellan, who had almost given them up for lost. The ships joined forces and continued the exploration (one ship choosing this moment to desert back to Spain, under cover of night, with much of the expedition's supplies). After several more days:

> ...the sailors sent on this expedition returned, and announced their having seen the cape where the strait ended, and with it a great sea—that is to say, the ocean. We wept for joy. This cape was denominated Il Cape Deseado (The Desired Cape, or The Cape of Good Hope) for in truth we had long wished to see it.

Once back in Europe writing his report, *Voyage Around the World*, Pigafetta was carried away by his enthusiasm for their discovery of the "Strait of the Patagonians";

> ...At every half-league it contains a safe port, with excellent water, cedarwood, sardines, and a great abundance of shellfish. There were here also some vegetables...In short, I do not think the world contains a better strait than this...

Pigafetta may, perhaps, be forgiven for painting such an overly rosy picture, but later voyagers attempting the passage of the 320-mile Strait of Magellan between the Atlantic and the Pacific would hardly agree with his portrait.

For Magellan's expedition, however, the worst was yet to come. Thinking Asia much nearer than it was, they embarked across the wide, uncharted ocean with much courage but far too few provisions. As Pigafetta tells it:

> ...we sailed the space of three months and twenty days, without tasting any fresh provisions. The biscuit we were eating no longer deserved the name of bread; it was nothing but dust, and worms which had consumed the substance; and what is more, it smelled intolerably, being impregnated with the urine of mice. The water we were obliged to drink was equally putrid and offensive.
>
> We were even so far reduced, that we might not die of hunger, to eat pieces of the leather with which the mainyard was covered...constantly exposed to the water, sun, and wind, [these pieces] were so hard that they required being soaked four or five days in the sea in order to render them supple; after this we broiled them to eat. Frequently indeed we were obliged to subsist on sawdust, and even mice, a food so disgusting, were sought after with such avidity that they sold for half a ducat apiece.

Others who would cross the Pacific after him would be forewarned by Magellan's experience, but for two and a half centuries they would share with him the dreadful scurvy,

> ...in which the gums swelled so as to hide the teeth...whence those affected were thus incapable of chewing their food...Besides those [nineteen] who died, we had from twenty-five to thirty sailors ill, who suffered dreadful pains in their arms, legs, and other parts of the body...

64

Cape Horn sailors found Tierra del Fuego (Land of Fire) a peculiar name for this land of ice and desolation. (National Maritime Museum)

But for all that, the majority of the sailors survived to make the first known crossing of the Pacific, making landfall on some desert islands and eventually arriving at the island group later known as the Philippines, where Magellan himself was killed by natives. The survivors, having linked up from the east with the "known world," straggled in a homeward direction. Of the five ships in the original fleet, only one actually completed the voyage around the world back to the Rio Guadalquivir, but just that one ship's load of spices more than paid for the great cost of outfitting Magellan's expedition. More importantly, the voyage had opened a new sea route by which Europeans could reach the fabled Asian markets.

Attempting to make this a viable commercial route, Spain sent other expeditions through the Strait of Magellan. In 1525 a fleet of seven ships was sent from Spain. They encountered much rougher weather than Magellan had, including a violent storm off the Rio de la Plata and eastward winds so strong that they foiled the fleet's first attempt to enter the Strait of Magellan and forced considerable repairs before the second and successful attempt. With deaths (including those of four successive commanders) and desertions, only three ships passed through the strait, of which only one reached the Philippines. (One went to the west coast of Mexico, where it later was used to explore routes across the Pacific.) In the 1530's another expedition was sent, but that fleet never succeeded in negotiating the Strait of Magellan

and returned to Spain. A little later, another fleet was sent to set up commercial shipping between Spain and its new colonies of Peru and Chile, but only one ship completed the passage to Callao, the port of Lima, Peru's capital. Because the route was so difficult, it saw little traffic later in the 16th century. The Spanish found it easier to break apart ships in the Caribbean, transport them overland at the Isthmus of Panama or in Mexico, and reassemble ships on the west coast, rather than bringing ships around South America on a regular basis. Using such reconstructed ships and other ships built for the purpose, Spanish sailors in the 1560's opened a commercial trans-Pacific route between Acapulco in Mexico and Manila in the Philippines, and a coastal route between Acapulco, Panama, and Callao. Magellan's route was allowed to languish.

During this period, European sailors thought that the land composing the southern side of the Strait of Magellan (named Tierra del Fuego, or Land of Fire, by Magellan for the many fires he saw in the hills) was part of a massive southern continent. That view was not challenged until Francis Drake, carrying the English flag in the search for routes through the Americas, passed through the Strait of Magellan, and then was driven southward through open waters by the Pacific winds. Thereafter, many European maps were modified to show open waters in that region. Drake's voyage had other results as well. Working his way gradually back to the west coast of South America, Drake attacked and plundered colonial ships and settlements on his way north, gaining both booty and valuable maps of the trans-Pacific routes. Passing beyond Spanish territory, he landed north of modern San Francisco, laying claim to the region he called Nova Albion (New England) in the name of Queen Elizabeth, before following the Spanish routes across the Pacific. A second English pirating expedition, under Thomas Cavendish, was a striking success. As Cavendish described it:

> I navigated along the coast of Chili [sic], Peru and Nueva Espanna [sic] [Mexico], where I made great spoiles; I burnt and sunk nine sailes of ships small and great. All the villages and townes that ever I landed at, I burnt and spoiled...

Later pirating voyages, however, were failures, with great losses in men and ships but little compensation in loot, although one of them did discover the Falkland Islands. Faced with attacks on their monopoly, the Spanish attempted to fortify the Atlantic entrance to the Magellan Strait, but most of the would-be colonists perished in the severe climate of the region or were killed in attacks by the native Patagonians, while the survivors were captured by the English.

The Dutch, too, sent expeditions through the Strait of Magellan, attempting to enrich themselves with gold and silver from Peru, Mexico, and Bolivia. It was two Dutchmen who first discovered an alternative to the Strait of Magellan. Knowing that the experience of Drake and others made questionable the existence of a southern continent, Jacob Le Maire and William Schouten in 1615 led an expedition down the east coast of South America past the Strait of Magellan and around the southern tip of the continent, which they named Hoorn (later Horn), after Schouten's home town in Holland. They were the first European explorers to enter the maelstrom off Cape Horn, caused by the mixing of waters from three oceans—the Atlantic, the Pacific, and the Antarctic (as yet unknown and unnamed). Some Dutch traders attempted to exploit the Cape Horn Route, as did the Spanish when they heard about it, but neither was successful, for the weather in the area still took a heavy toll. By the mid-17th century, Dutch traffic had adopted the Cape of Good Hope Route around Africa, and the Spanish were content to avoid the Cape Horn Route, whose very severity provided protection for its west coast colonies. Indeed, Spain codified that decision, prohibiting direct trade between west coast ports and Spain, and decreeing that all traffic should go overland across the Isthmus of Panama or Mexico to authorized east coast ports. Although some piracy continued on the west coast, most Europeans contented themselves with illicit trading at Spanish ports in the Caribbean and the South Atlantic. The great port of Buenos Aires was primarily developed by Europeans conducting illicit trade with Spanish

Like this sealing crew in the Falklands, Cape Horn traders gathered goods wherever they could. (Authors' archives)

colonials, and the Rio de la Plata (River of Silver) was so named for the quantity of the precious metal brought illegally out of the rich mines in what is now Bolivia. Wars in the 17th century also kept the major commercial powers busy back in Europe, with little attention to spare for the Cape Horn Route.

Only in the second half of the 17th century, when relative peace returned, did expeditions reappear in the region, now with scientific as well as commercial and political purposes. Some of these explored Tierra del Fuego, the triangular archipelago between the Strait of Magellan and Cape Horn. Others charted previously undiscovered islands, such as the South Georgia Islands, and filled in details on many smaller islands that had been located in the previous century. Perhaps the most important explorations for the Cape Horn Route were Captain Cook's three round-the-world voyages in the late 18th century. Cook's discoveries in the Pacific caught the imagination of the world, especially after accounts of them were published in 1784. On the last of his three Pacific voyages, Cook had taken some sea otter pelts from the northwest coast of North America to be traded in Asia; what Cook had obtained from the native Americans for a few trinkets Cook's crew (after his death) sold in China for an enormous profit. Learning of this, English merchants quickly moved to develop the Cape Horn Route. They were soon joined by New England merchants, who had only recently won their political independence from Britain and now needed to establish economic independence as well.

The coming century would see the Americans and the British systematically stripping the islands and coasts of the Atlantic and Pacific of any products that might possibly interest China, for that sophisticated country wanted little from the outside world, while its products were prized by the most advanced European nations. At first the Chinese wanted only sea otter fur and ginseng, a highly prized root that grew only in Manchuria and parts of the Americas. In return the Chinese sent tea, medicines, silk, and porcelain—so fine that all high-quality porcelain came to be known as "china." The first shipload of ginseng was shipped in 1783 from Boston to Canton, China's single open port, even before Cook's journals were published. This first Boston ship took the Cape of Good Hope Route around Africa, but instead of sailing on to China, it sold its ginseng to a British merchant ship off Africa and returned with a tidy profit. In the early years of the China trade most European ships, and many American ships leaving North America in the spring, took the Cape of Good Hope Route, for the winds were favorable and ships did not have to hazard a winter passage around the Horn. American ships leaving late in the year generally took the Cape Horn Route, which afforded a summer passage and a more favorable approach to China from the Pacific. Over the decades, however, most American ships chose the Cape Horn Route, for they picked up much of their load of trade goods, often in the form of fur pelts, on the way.

Europeans, especially the British, initially had the advantage in the China trade, having more to sell than the Americans, but the French Revolution and the Napoleonic Wars disrupted commerce, leaving the way open for Yankee traders. For a few decades sea otter pelts from the Oregon coast and Pacific Ocean islands were the prime trade goods for China, at one point amounting to $500,000 annually; later, when they became more scarce—and when the Northwest Coast tribes wanted more than valueless trinkets for their pelts—Yankee traders searched elsewhere for other pelts, notably seal pelts, which were plentiful in many parts of the South Atlantic, including the Falkland Islands and Tierra del Fuego, and of the Pacific. (It was a sealing ship that in 1820 first discovered Antarctica, the southern continent, long thought to be mythical.) The Pacific also yielded other products for the China trade, among them fragrant sandalwood; birds' nests used in Chinese soups; bêche-de-mer, foot-long edible sea slugs; coral moss, also used as food; and mother-of-pearl. These products were obtained from the many islands of the South Pacific, especially Hawaii, Fiji, and the Marquesas; while Yankee traders were on purely private commercial ventures, they inevitably brought these South Sea islands into the American sphere of influence.

In the same way, Yankee traders opened up California. Although foreign trade was forbidden by Spanish colonial policy, California was geographically cut off from direct contact with Spain and was largely ignored by authorities in New Spain (later Mexico), especially between 1810 and 1821, when that colony was winning its independence. New England goods found a hungry market, for the Californians had a great surplus of cattle and nothing to buy with it. Yankee traders solved the problem by taking cattle hides and tallow in exchange for all manner of trade goods. The exchange suited perfectly, for the developing industries of the East Coast had products to sell, while they needed the tallow and hides (called "California banknotes") of the West Coast. For the first time, a North American trade was developing that did not depend on any Old World nations. (Of course, standards were low; the hides valued by the Americans were—after months in the soggy hold of a ship passing around the Horn—often of a quality unacceptable to more demanding European markets.)

Yankees also found other sources of wealth in the Pacific: whales. New England whalers, many of them sailing out of Nantucket, had long been operating in the North Atlantic. During the 18th century, they had moved across the ocean as far as the Cape Verde Islands off Africa and into the South Atlantic. During the years of the American Revolution, whaling was halted, for the

Sailors found Hawaii a prime spot for making repairs and reprovisioning—and a source of delicacies favored by the Chinese. (Peabody Museum of Salem)

ships were requisitioned for war use; losses were so great that only a few ships remained in American ports after the Revolution, forcing many Yankee whalers to sail on British ships out of Canada or on French ships out of Dunkirk. It was a British ship, manned by expatriate New England whalemen, that rounded Cape Horn in search of Pacific whales in 1787. That was the first of many whalers, British and American, to cruise the Pacific, at first concentrating on the coastal waters off Chile, but later spreading across the whole expanse of the ocean. At the turn of the 19th century, the Galapagos Islands (about 600 miles west of Ecuador) were at the center of a whaling industry comprising hundreds of ships; one of the islands—the small, uninhabited Santa María—even acted as an unofficial post office, a mail drop where sailors on two-to-four-year voyages left letters to be picked up by homebound vessels, or picked up letters dropped by ships fresh from ports like Nantucket or New Bedford. By the mid-19th century, New England whalers were operating off Japan and even beyond the North Pacific in the Bering Sea. (In the 1870's some whaling ships stayed in Arctic waters so late in the season that they were trapped in ice and crushed.) Yankee traders and whalers working in the northern Pacific often

met their Russian counterparts, who were moving from the opposite direction in search of furs, which took them down the North American coast to just north of San Francisco. The whaling life was difficult—as recounted in Herman Melville's *Moby Dick*—but the risks were worth taking, for whale oil was prized for lighting throughout the world, as were whalebones for use in the clothing of the day.

Yankee trading activity required a good deal of support. Ships leaving the North Atlantic needed stops on the way for securing provisions (including precious water) and making repairs; common choices were Rio de Janeiro, the Cape Verde Islands, or the Falkland Islands, which were particularly favored because they were closest to Cape Horn. While some found them barren and uninviting, others found them strikingly beautiful, such as Yankee sealer Nathaniel Appleton, who said the Falklands had:

some of the grandest seans [scenes] that can be conceived of, precipices 200 feet high, exactly perpendicular, looks more like work of art than of Nature, below you see the sea breaking & dashing against the bottom.

Then it was time to face the Horn's directly contrary eastward winds (which led to the nickname "Old Cape Stiff"), and the storms and whirling currents cooked up by the meeting of three oceans. Richard Henry Dana, Jr., in his *Two Years Before the Mast*, described the change from a fine sunny day on the South Atlantic:

> ...hurrying upon deck, we found a large black cloud rolling on toward us from the south-west, and blackening the whole heavens. "Here comes Cape Horn!" said the chief mate; and we had hardly time to haul down and clew up, before it was upon us. In a few moments, a heavier sea was raised than I had ever seen before and...the little brig, which was no better than a bathing machine, plunged into it, and all the forward part of her was under water; the sea pouring in through the bowports and hawse-hole and over the knightheads, threatening to wash everything overboard. In the lee scuppers it was up to a man's waist. We sprang aloft and double reefed the topsails, and furled all the other sails, and made all snug. But this would not do; the brig was laboring and straining against the head sea, and the gale was growing worse and worse. At the same time sleet and hail were driving with all fury against us.

Nor was this all the Cape had to offer, for massive icebergs also haunted the Antarctic waters, sometimes rising out of the water like ghost ships; more than one crew had, in Dana's words, left their "ship's old bones adrift in the Southern ocean" after colliding with a floating ice island.

Those who survived all these hazards—and many did not—were sorely in need of another stop for rest and repairs. Preferred "watering spots" were Juan Fernandez Island, which, Dana said, rises "like a deep blue cloud out of the sea" off the coast of Chile, and on the mainland, Valparaiso; other stops farther north might be made at Callao, Payta, or Tumbes (the port where Francisco Pizarro had first landed in Peru centuries before). Farther out in the ocean, Honolulu became the prime port for resting, reprovisioning, and refitting. San Francisco, San Diego, and San Pedro (port of Los Angeles) were main stops for the hide-and-tallow traders, but were not much favored by other ships, for even before gold was found, California's fabled riches were a magnet for sailors, many of whom deserted, converted to Catholicism, and married into wealthy Spanish-American families, a process called "leaving their consciences at Cape Horn." In the 19th century the Pacific Ocean, for two centuries nicknamed the "Spanish Sea," went very far toward becoming an American Sea, especially after Spain's Manila galleons stopped plying the Pacific in 1815.

The way was not without obstacles, however. British whalers operated in the Pacific, and during the various wars of the early 19th century, American ships were fair game for British and sometimes French privateers. The then-small U. S. Navy was called out to protect American interests. During the war of 1812, a frigate was sent to

After the discovery of gold in California, a forest of ships crowded San Francisco's harbor. (Lithograph by W. Roosen after a drawing by Capt. Collinson, National Maritime Museum)

the Pacific to prevent the seizure of American whalers by clearing British whalers from the Pacific; it succeeded, virtually ending British whaling in the region. Later the U. S. Navy established regional headquarters at Valparaiso, from which its ships patrolled the Pacific. Not incidentally, American sailors—whether navy or civilian—brought with them ideas of independence, congenial to colonies seeking freedom from Europe, which was now embroiled in internal conflicts. New Englanders—and Europeans, too—introduced other ideas as well, as missionaries from the Atlantic followed traders to the Pacific, bringing islands like Hawaii further under Western influence.

As the Spanish-American colonies asserted their independence in the 19th century, Americans were sometimes caught between colonial and imperial interests, but they were usually able to protect their own. When the Mexican War broke out in 1846, the U. S. Navy was in a position to assert its government's claim to California, taking both Lower (Baja) and Upper California, although the treaty between Mexico and the United States later left Baja with Mexico. (The U. S. Navy had, in fact, seized Monterey temporarily four years earlier, thinking that Britain was about to do so first.) In the same period, the United States and Britain resolved their boundary dispute over the Oregon territory claimed by both of them. The West Coast, which had been opened to outside commerce by Yankee traders working the Cape Horn Route, gradually became part of the United States.

No sooner had that happened than an event occurred which would transform the entire route and the areas it served; gold was discovered in California in January 1848. When the discovery was announced in the U. S. Congress in December of that year, a flood of people set out for California by any way available. In the first year the rush favored the Cape Horn Route. Since it was winter when the discovery was announced, the overland route was closed until the warm weather. Some people headed for the Panama Isthmus, but regular West Coast passenger service did not yet exist. In fact, when the news was announced, one of the new breed of vessels—a steamship—was on its way around Cape Horn to begin shuttling between San Francisco and Panama City, and only heard of the gold discovery when it put in for water at Callao. When it arrived in Panama City, it found passengers eagerly awaiting the run to gold country. By the end of 1849, over 300 ships of all sizes and descriptions were anchored at San Francisco harbor. For most of these ships and the ones that followed, this was a one-way trip. Once in California some of the ships were put to use on the coastal rivers. Many others were converted into floating homes, stores, or prisons; broken up for construction on land; left to rot and sink in the harbor; or burned in the great harbor fire of 1851. Some had been so unseaworthy at the start that they had been forced to

stop at Charleston, South Carolina for repairs before proceeding south. Regular trading or whaling ships putting into port at San Francisco often found that virtually their whole crews deserted; many ships avoided California harbors altogether, heading for Honolulu or Valparaiso instead—or else they imprisoned their crews while in gold-country ports. European ships drawn around Cape Horn by gold fever adopted similar measures.

The exodus of ships—good and bad—caused a crisis on the East Coast. Ships were unavailable for regular shipping, nor were there crews to sail them. New ships had to be built, with speed and efficiency uppermost in mind. The result was the famous clipper ship, the sleek, graceful, high-masted sailing ship so thoroughly identified with the Cape Horn Route. Developed in Baltimore, Maryland in the 1830's, the improved clippers of the 1850's were the fastest ships of their day. And their reputation was enhanced considerably by improvement in sailing techniques, based upon better knowledge of the sea.

Before the 1850's, ships heading for Cape Horn would generally trace an arc across the Atlantic toward the easternmost tip of Brazil, often negotiating Cape São Roque with great difficulty; then they would follow the coast to just north of the Falkland Islands. From there routes varied, with some going east of the Falklands and some west; with some passing through the Strait of Le Maire, between Staten Island and Tierra del Fuego, and others swinging wide of both of them before rounding the Horn. (An occasional steamship hazarded the Strait of Magellan, but rarely a sailing ship. And the Beagle Channel, another route through the southern islands, named after the ship in which Charles Darwin carried out his famous scientific investigations, was never a major shipping route.) Those who failed to claw their way around the Horn against contrary winds retired to the Falklands or Rio de Janeiro for repairs before trying again—or sometimes gave up and let the winds blow them eastward around the "bottom of the world" into the South Pacific. The passage up the West Coast was less difficult but very slow, for the winds were offshore much of the way, blowing some ships out almost as far as Hawaii. The trip between Boston and San Francisco generally took six to seven months, a good voyage being under 200 days. Some of the gold-rush voyages, in old, slow packets, were considerably slower than that.

In 1855, U. S. Navy Lt. Matthew Fontaine Maury published a book of wind charts and sailing directions, based on analysis of logs from many ships over the years. Maury recommended that ships take a more southerly route in the Atlantic, approaching the Brazilian bulge from the east for an easier rounding of Cape São Roque, and that they then stay east, away from the shore, both to avoid coastal storms and to be in a better position to take the Strait of Le Maire route around Cape Horn. Once past the Horn, Maury recommended that sailors move south—much as Francis Drake had done involuntarily centuries before—to search for a favorable wind among the variable winds of the region, and that as they moved up the west coast of the Americas, they stay farther out into the Pacific where they could take advantage of the southeast winds rather than fight offshore winds. (Ships on the return voyage could continue to follow the old route, for the winds generally ran with them, not against them.) Maury's recommendations were quickly adopted, and the east-west travel time of the swift clipper ships on the Cape Horn Route dropped to about 90 days.

With fine new ships and improved sailing techniques, Yankee traders were well positioned to take advantage of new markets in the Pacific. Many West Coast cities were extremely short of staples (most workers having decamped for the gold fields) and desirous of luxuries their new riches would buy. Most goods brought around the Horn were sold before they were ever unloaded, for people would row out to trading ships at anchor off the California coast, paying enormous prices for whatever was aboard. While many prospectors died in poverty, trading fortunes were made on the Cape Horn Route during the gold rush. In all their ingenuity, traders made profits out of some unlikely material. Some brought ice packed in sawdust from New England around Cape Horn to sweltering Panama City and other Pacific ports. A German immigrant named Levi Strauss, who had sold most of his stock in San Francisco harbor, created work pants out of his remaining stock of canvas "de Nîmes" (from the French town of Nîmes)—and left the legacy of Levi's denims. Nor was the West Coast the only place where trading fortunes could be made. In the mid-19th century, China and Japan yielded to heavy pressure from Europeans and Americans and reopened their ports to foreign trade, enhancing the importance of the Cape Horn Route.

But even in these years of success, the heyday of the Cape Horn Route was passing. In 1855, the Panama Railroad spanned the narrow Central American Isthmus, taking prime freight business from the Cape Horn Route; in only a few years that route was itself to be eclipsed when the transcontinental railroad reached San Francisco in 1869. During the Civil War in the 1860's, America's shipping was completely disrupted. Most ships in the Pacific were requisitioned for war use and were brought back around the Horn, some to blockade the Confederacy. Confederate cruisers captured several trading ships en route around the Horn to the East Coast, and another cruiser—the *Shenandoah*—cleared the Pacific of most remaining whaling ships. Although whaling resumed after the war, the industry never really recovered, especially after oil wells in the United States began producing in 1859.

Nor did the Pacific trade ever recover its former importance after the Civil War, for it had to compete with the lure of the American West. The riches of China and the Pacific began to pale in comparison to the gold of California and the free, open land of the West, there for the taking. Those who in earlier years might have routinely gone to sea now more often went West to seek their fortunes. Ships on the Cape Horn Route, even the top-of-the-line clippers, had difficulty finding and retaining experienced crews, relying increasingly on untrained immigrants from Europe or Pacific islanders. Written accounts of the Cape Horn voyage certainly served to dissuade recruits, among them Dana's *Two Years Before The Mast*:

> We had now got hardened to the Cape weather ...Our clothes were all wet through, and the only change was from wet to more wet. It was in vain to think of reading or working below, for we were too tired, the hatchways were closed down, and everything was wet and uncomfortable, black and dirty, heaving and pitching. We had only to come below when the watch was out, wring out our wet clothes, hang them up, and turn in and sleep as soundly as we could until the watch was called again.

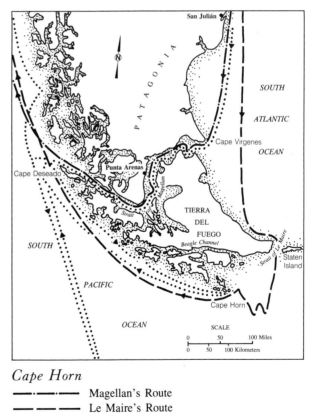

Cape Horn

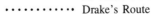

—·—·—·—   Magellan's Route
— — — —   Le Maire's Route
·············   Drake's Route

Before the discovery of gold, San Francisco was a very modest village indeed. (California Historical Society)

But even if some could find romance in dealing with such conditions, there was nothing of the sort to be found in the sailor's position on board, as Dana made clear:

> The captain stood on the...deck, a few feet from [the man in irons], and a little raised, so as to have a good swing at him...A man—a human being, made in God's likeness—fastened up and flogged like a beast!...The first and almost uncontrollable impulse was resistance. But...what is there for sailors to do? If they resist, it is mutiny; and if they succeed, and take the vessel, it is piracy.

Perhaps even worse was the captain's taunting the sailors with his absolute power:

> You see your condition! You see where I've got you all...I'll make you toe the mark, every soul of you, or I'll flog you...You've got a driver over you! Yes, a *slave-driver, a negro-driver*!

Reports by Dana and others documenting the harsh treatment of sailors brought about changes eventually, but not before most Yankee boys had turned their attention in other directions, where they need not trade freedom for adventure.

As the Cape Horn Route passed into decline, so did the clipper ships. With the most lucrative freight being sent by rail, the clippers were left with bulky goods: guano (bird droppings used for manure), nitrates and copper from Chile, and grain from California, the latter being the mainstay on the Cape Horn Route from the 1860's on. Ships traveling westbound from Europe on the Cape Horn Route often took coal to the developing West Coast. But clippers were designed for speed, not bulk, and they were soon replaced by roomier ships better designed for the purposes at hand. In this period, vessels on the Cape Horn Route also included round-the-world ships from European ports which had gone around Africa to Australia and returned with the favorable eastward winds via

Cape Horn, loaded with Australian and New Zealand produce, especially grain.

As steamships gradually replaced sailing ships, the route changed slightly; steamers generally preferred the Strait of Magellan (being not so much at the mercy of treacherous winds and currents as sailing ships were) to the rigors of Cape Horn. By the time steamers were bringing California wine and Hawaiian sugar to the East, the New York to San Francisco trip was down to 60 days. Even that speed was not enough to save the Route for heavy commercial use, although it did play a role in the United States' turn-of-the-century acquisition of a chain of Pacific territories, including Hawaii and the Philippines (the latter taken in the Spanish-American War). In 1908, with the Panama Canal under construction, the Route was taken by one last great fleet: President Theodore Roosevelt sent virtually the entire U. S. Navy on a round-the-world public relations trip, passing through the Strait of Magellan. But in 1914, with the opening of the Panama Canal, the Cape Horn Route was all but dead. Ships trading with coastal ports in Chile and Argentina might still continue to round the Horn, as would ships whose cargo was not valuable enough to warrant payment of the canal toll, but most other traffic went by way of the Panama Canal.

The Cape Horn Route still has a role to play, however. Although the Panama Canal's locks have been successively widened, iron and later steel ships have become increasingly larger during the 20th century and have tended to outgrow the locks. Ships too large for the canal—such as today's largest aircraft carriers, cargo ships, and supertankers—must find alternate routes, among them the Cape of Good Hope Route and the Cape Horn Route. The Cape Horn Route has also served special purposes in wartime, when other routes were unavailable. British and German ships contested it in both World Wars, with German ships haunting the South Atlantic hoping to cut off food supplies to the Allies, not only from South America, but also from Australia and New Zealand around the Horn. The Route also provided "back door" communication lanes between Germany and Japan in World War II.

The Cape Horn Route is unlikely ever again to match its greatness in the period when it laid the basis for America's expansion across the continent to the Pacific, but as the end drew near for the sailing days on the old Cape Horn Route, paeans and poems were sent forth by those who saw themselves as the last of a dying breed; one of them, a sailor named Harry Kemp, in the 1940's wrote in *Cassell's Magazine*:

> I am eighty years old and somewhat
> But I give to God the praise
> That they made a sailor of me
> In the good old Clipper days.
> Then men loved ships like women
> And going to sea was more
> Than signing on as a deckhand
> And scrubbing a cabin floor,
> Or chipping rust from iron
> And painting, and chipping again—
> In the days of clipper sailing
> The sea was the place of men.
> You could spy our great ships running
> White-clouded, tier on tier,
> You could hear their tramping thunder
> As they leaned-to racing near;
> And it was "Heigh-ho and ho, my lad,"
> When we were outward bound,
> And we sang full many a chanty
> As we walked the capstan round.
> Aye, we sang full many a chanty
> As we drove through wind and wet,
> To the music of five oceans
> That rings in memory yet.
> Go, drive your dirty freighters
> That fill the sky with reek—
> But we—we took in skysails
> High as a mountain peak...

Selective Bibliography

Dodge, Ernest S. *New England and the South Seas.* (Cambridge, Mass.: Harvard University Press, 1965). Focuses on their mutual influences.

Greenbie, Sydney, and Marjorie Greenbie. *Gold of Ophir; or The Lure That Made America.* (Garden City, New York: Doubleday, Page, 1925). On the idea of the East as an impetus for opening both sea and land routes.

Hough, Richard. *The Blind Horn's Hate.* (New York: Norton, 1971). A sea lover's history of the southern tip of South America.

McCutchan, Philip. *Tall Ships: The Golden Age of Sail* (New York: Crown, 1976). A celebration of 19th and early 20th century sailing days.

Morison, Samuel Eliot. *The European Discovery of America: The Southern Voyages A. D. 1492-1616.* (New York: Oxford University Press, 1974). A closely detailed account of the earliest explorations.

Penrose, Boies. *Travel and Discovery in the Renaissance, 1420-1620.* (New York: Atheneum, 1965; reprint of 1952 Harvard University Press edition). Excellent; two chapters focus on discoveries along the Cape Horn Route.

Rydell, Raymond A. *Cape Horn to the Pacific: The Rise and Decline of an Ocean Highway.* (Berkeley and Los Angeles: University of California Press, 1952). A prime work on the Cape Horn Route.

Tamarin, Alfred, and Shirley Glubok. *Voyaging to Cathay: Americans in the China Trade.* (New York: Viking, 1976). A well-illustrated book on Yankees in the China trade.

Villiers, Alan. *The War With Cape Horn.* (New York: Scribner's, 1971). A personal, evocative account of the great days of sailing ships on Cape Horn.

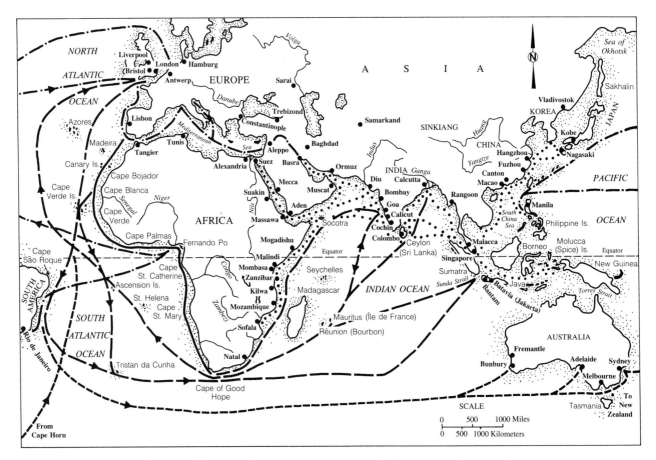

The Cape of Good Hope Route and the Modern Spice Route

————— Early Cape of Good Hope Route

– – – – – Main Cape of Good Hope Route

------- Australia Route

• • • • • • Spice Route

—·—·— Main Connecting Routes

The Cape of Good Hope Route

On June 22, 1596, four Dutch ships arrived in the town of Bantam on the island of Java. These first representatives of the Dutch "Company for Distant Lands" had hazarded a difficult 15-month voyage around the Cape of Good Hope at the tip of Africa, with no certainty of their reception. In fact, the initial response could not have been warmer, with local nobles and notables crowding on board to exchange ceremonial greetings, joined by merchants of all nationalities:

> There came such a multitude of Javanese and other nations as Turks, Chinese, Bengali, Arabs, Persians, Gujarati, and others that one could hardly move.... they...came so abundantly that each nation took a spot on the ships where they displayed their goods, the same as if it were on a market. Of which the Chinese brought...all sorts of silk woven and unwoven, twined and untwined, with beautiful earthenware, with other strange things more. The Javanese brought chickens, eggs, ducks, and many kinds of fruits. Arabs, Moors, Turks, and other nations of people each brought of everything one might imagine.

These Dutchmen may have been newcomers, but some of the others had been trading on the Indian Ocean for well over 1,500 years along the old Spice Route. It was tales of this fabled trade that had drawn western Europeans to find their own sea route to Asian waters, a route that shattered medieval ideas about the geography of the Earth and opened the way for the great Age of Discovery. This was the Cape of Good Hope Route.

From Western Europe, the route ran from the islands off West Africa, notably the Canaries and the Cape Verde Islands, southwest across the mid-Atlantic almost to the great bulge of South America, then southeast back across the South Atlantic with the west winds to the Cape of Good Hope, at the tip of southern Africa. This wide swing out into the ocean allowed sailing ships to make the best use of existing winds and currents; on the return trip, ships followed the coast, for the currents swept them easily back around Africa to Europe. On the outward voyage, traffic diverged at the Cape of Good Hope. One main line followed the east coast of Africa, passing through the Mozambique Channel, west of the island of Madagascar, up to the horn of Africa and across the Arabian Sea to India; to avoid the strong south current of the Mozambique Channel, many northbound ships passed on the eastern side of Madagascar, stopping at islands like Mauritius or Réunion, on their way to India and the international spice markets. The other main route from the Cape of Good Hope cut across the open expanse of the Indian Ocean, with some ships curving north to the Bay of Bengal, while others continued straight for Indonesia, especially for the Sunda Strait between the islands of Java and Sumatra, the gateway to the legendary Spice Islands (the Moluccas). Ships heading for the Sunda Strait were often blown off-course by the powerful west winds, the result being the

Birds and fish sometimes guided early sailors on their way across uncharted oceans. (From de Bry, Petits Voyages, *1601)*

discovery of Australia, which eventually became a third main destination for ships on the old Cape of Good Hope Route

Renaissance Europeans may not have been the first to sail on the route around Africa. Tradition has granted that honor to the Phoenicians, master mariners who sailed the Mediterranean and traded along the coasts of Atlantic Europe and northern Africa. Skilled Phoenician sailors were brought to the Red Sea and Persian Gulf by local rulers, who had neither the wood for their own ships nor the men to build and sail them. From there, Phoenicians

may have sailed around Africa to Europe. The Greek historian Herodotus, writing in the early fifth century B.C. of events that supposedly took place 150 years earlier, relates the story:

Africa proves to be completely surrounded by water except for as much of it as borders on Asia. Of all men of whom we have any knowledge, the Egyptian king Neccho was the first to establish this fact....he dispatched some Phoenicians in ships with orders to sail back into our northern sea by passing

78

through the Pillars of Heracles [Strait of Gibraltar] and so to return to Egypt.

Accordingly these Phoenicians set out and from the Red Sea sailed into the southern ocean. Whenever autumn came, they went ashore wherever in Africa they chanced to be on their voyage, to sow grain in the earth and await the harvest. On reaping the new grain they put again to sea. In this wise, after two years had elapsed, they rounded the Pillars of Heracles and in the third year reached Egypt.

Scholars are sharply divided on whether or not the Phoenicians ever did make such a 10,000-mile trip. Those in favor point to the extraordinary skill of the Phoenician sailors—and to the very strong southward current in the Mozambique Channel, which might have prevented an exploratory ship from returning northward. Detractors stress that Herodotus is an extremely uneven witness; even where archaeological evidence may confirm part of a story, his interpretation is often wildly unbelievable. As for the Phoenicians's trip, Herodotus himself questioned at least part of it, concluding his story by saying: "They said what to me is unbelievable, though some may believe it; that as they sailed around Libya they had the sun on their right hand." Indeed, that is what we should expect for people sailing westward in the Southern Hemisphere. The bulwark of the anti-Phoenician case is that no confirming records exist. The same argument applies to reports that a Greek geographer named Eudoxus sailed around Africa from the Red Sea to Gades (Cadiz) in the second century B.C. Of course, like most early traders, these Greeks and Phoenicians traditionally regarded their routes as state secrets, so we would expect little of such information to have been written down. In any case, if such voyages occurred, knowledge of them was lost to future generations.

The Phoenicians—or Carthaginians, as their colonists in the western Mediterranean were called—do seem to have been the first sailors to trade down the coast of West Africa, conducting silent barter with the native coastal peoples. Such trade may have continued after Carthage fell, for the Romans apparently had some trade with the off-shore islands. The Canary Islands are so-called after the large dogs (canes) found there in Roman times; the Romans themselves knew that archipelago as "the Fortunate Isles," and called Madeira "the Purple Island." With the decline of the classical world, however, such contact ended.

After the great days of the Phoenicians, Greeks, and Romans, the Europeans became a backward people. Great civilizations flourished in the East which were hardly known to the medieval Europeans—except by their exotic goods. These goods—silks, fine Indian cotton, delicately wrought gold and silver, and most of all spices—filtered across the great distances to Europe, however, even in the worst of times; when the western continent began to revive, this trade expanded, making the fortunes of the great Italian maritime states, notably Genoa and Venice, carriers on the Mediterranean. But eventually Islam won the battle with Christianity for the allegiance of Central Asia, and the once-liberal Moslem countries became intolerant of non-Moslems in their midst. Controlling the main sea and land routes to Asia, the Moslems tightened controls on all goods from the East, charging exorbitant duties on them. In the late 13th century, Genoa sent some ships down the coast of Africa to explore a sea route around the Moslems, but the ships were heard of no more. Forced into commercial decline, Genoa and Venice had experienced sailors to spare—and Western Europe had a stake in finding independent routes to those Eastern goods.

The result was the emigration of many skilled Italian mariners to the coastal ports of Western Europe, especially to the Iberian Peninsula, which Christian Europeans were in the process of reclaiming from the Moslems. Spain and Portugal were ready to seek their own place in the sun, and by the early part of the 14th century, they had, with the aid of Italian sailors, moved beyond the Strait of Gibraltar to rediscover the Canary Islands, about 60 miles off the northwest corner of Africa, and the Azores, about 800 miles west of Portugal out in the uncharted Atlantic.

The stage was set for the arrival of a crucial figure in the Age of Discovery and in the history of the Cape of Good Hope Route: Prince Henry of Portugal. Often nicknamed "the Navigator," Henry apparently never sailed beyond sight of land, his major expeditions being across the Strait of Gibraltar to raid the Moorish towns of Ceuta and Tangier. His main contributions were vision and organization. Setting up a base near the town of Sagres, inland from Cape St. Vincent, Prince Henry brought together the best talents of the age, experienced ship pilots, cartographers, astronomers, and mathematicians—for the problems of determining location and direction were paramount in uncharted waters. These experts—many of them Italians experienced in the Mediterranean trade or Jews trained in the fine Islamic centers of learning—were welcomed by tiny Portugal, whose own population numbered less than two million people. In addition to people, Henry collected the pilots' logs and chartbooks and collated information from them, so that future navigators might know which anchorages were safe and which hazardous; could identify landmarks for getting their bearings; and could put in at places where food, water, and wood were readily to be found. Such a systematic collection of data was an innovation, but was intended to benefit only the national interests; dissemination to others was strictly forbidden. (This would be true for centuries. Even in the 16th century, a Spaniard named Angelo Trevisan wrote about Cabral's voyage to India: "...it is impossible to obtain a map of this voyage, for the king has decreed the penalty of death for anyone who sends it out of the country.")

Henry's eclectic approach also led to the develop-

Skilled Benin bronzeworkers made this striking representation of a Portuguese slave hunter in around 1600. (British Museum)

a turning point for the 21-year-old Prince Henry. From Moorish prisoners he learned about the rich trade routes across the Sahara to Timbuktu; to his more general desire to find an alternate route to India was added a desire to outflank the Arabs and reach African gold sources directly. Henry immediately set out to colonize the off-shore islands, using them as staging areas for an exploration of the African coast. His first coastal expedition in 1415 reached as far as Cape Bojador (the Bulging Cape), where the coast juts out into the Atlantic. Although insignificant to modern eyes, this sandy barrier presented hazardous reefs, treacherous currents, and contrary winds to sailors from the north, especially from the almost tideless Mediterranean. Many feared the winds were so strong they could not return once they had rounded the cape. To this were added superstitions about the mythical "Sea of Darkness" that lay beyond the cape, and the zone further beyond, where white men were thought to turn black. The result of these terrors was that for 12 years Henry's exploratory expeditions turned back at Cape Bojador, focusing instead on raiding Moorish coastal settlements. Not until 1433 did the Portuguese break that fearful barrier and double (sail around) the cape. Three years later they had reached a spot 400 miles down the coast, well past Arab control; but internal politics engaged Henry's attention for the next few years, and no more was done for a time.

Then in 1441 a momentous expedition was launched. At Henry's behest, a fleet was sent to these southern lands and returned with 10 black Africans, male and female. The prospect of slave labor proved irresistible to the Portuguese, and licenses were granted for the coastal slave trade. Gomes Eannes de Azurara describes the scene of the early raids for slaves:

> The Moors [Africans] having evidently had unfortunate experience with former white visitors, with their women and children were already coming as quickly as they could out of their houses, because they had caught sight of their enemies. But they, crying "St. James," "St. George," and "Portugal," attacked them at once, killing and taking all they could.

On the return of Azurara's expedition with 235 slaves, Prince Henry himself greeted them. It appears that these were far from a homogeneous group of black peoples, for Azurara noted:

> And these, all placed together in that field were a marvelous sight for amongst them were some white enough, fair to look upon, and well proportioned; others were less white, like mulattoes; others, again, were black as Ethiopians.

ment of new lines of ships, combining technical ideas from both the Mediterranean and Atlantic traditions. Most notable of these was the *caravel*, the prime vessel used by explorers in the great Age of Discovery. These craft were quite small—generally under 70 tons and roughly the same number of feet long—but very reliable and maneuverable. Using varying combinations of the square sail and the triangular lateen sail, the *caravel* was equally suitable for coastal exploration and open-sea voyaging. Such ships had little space for comforts; the officers, vital records, and stores might be housed in a raised "castle" at one end of the ship, but the crew had to sleep on deck. The lack of space caused difficulties on long voyages, but even when these early fleets included larger (though more unwieldy) storage craft, expedition leaders often preferred to stay aboard the smaller *caravels*.

The Portuguese capture of Ceuta, a fortified promontory on the Moroccan coast, in 1415, seems to have been

With little shelter or water available in the South Atlantic, the Portuguese fleet would find even barren St. Helena a welcome sight. (From Jan Huyghen van Linschoten, Itinerario, *1589, British Museum)*

But to the Portuguese, in a time of religious hysteria over heresy, these heathens were, as writer João De Barros put it, "outside the law of Christ, and at the disposition, so far as their bodies were concerned, of any Christian nation." Justified in this way, the slave trade flourished from this small beginning, eventually spreading throughout the whole region. On the African coast itself, Arabs would enter the slave trade, and black Africans themselves would sometimes capture their enemies and sell them to the Europeans. In Portugal itself, slaves intermarried with the small native population, with government encouragement, and generally merged into the Portuguese people. But this trade set the pattern of action for Africa for centuries.

For a few years, attention was focused primarily on the slave trade, centered on Arguim Island, off the arid Mauritanian coast. But Henry's vision held. Two Genoese sailors under his sponsorship in 1455 reached the Gambia and Senegal rivers, giving the Portuguese an entrée into the trade of the Sudan (as the whole region south of the Sahara was then known). The following year these Genoese explorers discovered some islands about 300 miles off the westernmost point of Africa, Cape Verde (the Green Cape). Even so, these explorations had gone down the coast of West Africa only as far as Sierra Leone (so named for the thunderstorms that always growled in the mountains) when Henry died in 1460.

King Alfonso V, who continued Henry's policy, attempted to remedy this situation by contracting with the Lisbon trader Fernão Gomes to explore at least 500 leagues beyond the known coast in return for a five-year monopoly on trade in the region known as Guinea. The idea worked. During that time Gomes rounded the bulge of West Africa and followed the coast due east as far as Benin. In the process he opened up to the Portuguese some of the most lucrative trading regions on the west coast. The region now known as Liberia was found to produce a low-quality pepper, giving the region the temporary name of "the Grain Coast." Beyond that was the Ivory Coast and then the Gold Coast (now Ghana), which the Portuguese called Mina de Ouro, where much gold was traded and Gomes's expedition found alluvial gold in the streams. Past the swampy mouth of the Niger River lay the Benin River, where a high-quality pepper was grown—and where the local kingdom would provide many slaves, captives of wars with its neighbors. The Gomes expedition also discovered the lush island of Fernando Po

81

near the inner curve of the West African coast. But, dishearteningly, they found that the coast there turned southward, ending hopes of an easy route to the East. Before his contract expired, Gomes had explored 2,000 miles of coast, down to Cape St. Catherine, 2° below the Equator.

Despite attempts at secrecy, Portuguese success in the area was sufficiently well known to attract others. In the 1470's Spanish, Flemish, and English ships all raided Portuguese settlements at Arguim and along the coast, especially São Jorge de Mina (Elmina) at Cape Three Points on the Gold Coast and Gato in Benin. Both of these were factory-forts, well-protected entrepôts for collecting and holding trade goods for the 12-15 annual trading ships; and both were supplied with food from the fertile Portuguese-held island of São Thomé, just at the Equator in the Gulf of Guinea. Santiago, in the Cape Verde Islands, played the same role for the Portuguese trading posts facing the mid-Atlantic. Portugal fought well and effectively to protect its African monopoly; at the end of the Portugal-Castile Wars in 1479, Spain retained control of some inner Canary Islands, which it had settled, but Portugal kept the other islands and all fishing, trading, and navigation rights to West Africa.

With the accession of John II to the Portuguese throne in 1481, the Portuguese renewed their efforts to find a sea route to India. John provided his explorers with padrões, stone columns topped by a cube and a cross, which they were to set on prominent points along the way,

staking the Portuguese and Christian claim to the new lands discovered. Movement down the west coast of Africa below the Equator was extremely slow, however, for the prevailing winds and currents all ran to the north. Diogo Cao set up padrões for 1,500 miles beyond Cape St. Catherine, including one at a great river now known as the Zaire (Congo). He and others sometimes traveled up some of the rivers, looking for the great inland kingdoms they had heard of, especially for the mythical but widely believed-in Christian kingdom of Prester John. The Portuguese interest in Prester John was not purely religious. As each successive expedition reached further from home, with the coast still running south, the Portuguese badly needed the hope of some friendly kingdom at the end of their voyage, to provide them with food and a secure place to refit their ships.

It was because of this need that the expedition of Bartholomeu Dias in 1487 included a separate store ship to carry supplies. They also carried from Lisbon six recently captured black Africans—two men and four women—to be left at various spots on the coast of southwest Africa, who were to tell of Portugal's might and wish to trade, and perhaps to alert Prester John of their impending arrival; of these "agents," nothing was heard again. As they traveled further south, Dias's party ran into extremely bad weather. For almost two weeks they ran before a gale, with waves so high, one reporter noted, that "...as the ships were tiny, and the seas colder and not such as they were in the land of Guinea...they gave themselves

The Portuguese fort of São Jorge da Mina later became, in Dutch hands, the stronghold of Elmina. (From G. Greenhill, Collection of views of West African forts, *1682, British Museum)*

"A View of the Cape of Good Hope, with a Dutch Squadron at Anchor and an English Squadron coming to Anchor in the Bay." (By J. T. Serres, 1804, Africana Museum, Johannesburg)

up for dead." As the storm passed, Dias set an easterly course to find the coast once again; but when several days brought no sight of land, he headed north, and arrived in what is now Mossel Bay—he had passed the southern tip of Africa without knowing it.

Once they had taken on fresh water, Dias's ships proceeded up the east coast, struggling against the south-flowing current. They reached as far as a large river they called the Rio de Infante (probably the Great Fish River in South Africa), but Dias could persuade his fellow sailors to go no further. It was on their return that the Portuguese explorers had their first sight of the southernmost point of Africa, the Cape Agulhas and its slightly more northerly, but far more famous companion, the Cape of Good Hope. Apparently named Cabo Tormentoso (Cape Stormy) by Dias, the name Cabo de Boa Esperança (Cape of Good Hope) was reportedly bestowed by King John, for its promise of a sea route to India. Certainly the Cape of Good Hope, with the striking Table Mountain behind it, was always a welcome sight to mariners. As the English sailor Francis Drake put it a century later: "This cape is a most stately thing, and the fairest Cape we sawe in the whole circumference of the earth."

Although Dias returned to Lisbon in 1488, the next attempt to further the Cape of Good Hope Route was not made until 1498. The delay, partly caused by the change-over to a new monarch, was put to good use; with knowledge garnered from Columbus's Atlantic crossings in the interim and from their own developing experience of the Atlantic winds, Portuguese sailors developed a better approach to reaching the Cape of Good Hope. As a result, Vasco da Gama's route to India in 1498 took a very different tack than had Dias's. With a well-armed and amply stocked fleet of square-rigged *naos* (unlike earlier explorers' smaller *caravels*), da Gama set what would become the standard route for the South Atlantic run toward the Cape. From Lisbon he passed through the Canaries and on to the Cape Verde Islands, watering at Santiago; from there he worked his way southeast until he encountered the trade winds that would blow him southwest across the ocean toward Brazil. There he found the winds that would convey him back across to the Cape of Good Hope. Brazil itself was as yet unknown, being discovered only in 1500 by the leader of the second Indian expedition, Pedro Cabral. For later sailors following this route, the aim was to reach Brazil south of its easternmost point, Cape São Roque, or risk a difficult passage around that bulge. From there, the winds in some seasons allowed ships to sail more directly south until they picked up the winds of the "Roaring Forties," which blow from west to east around the world. Da Gama himself did not venture so far west, but turned east above the latitude of Cape São Roque and made landfall at one of the rare South Atlantic Islands, St. Helena—having been out of sight of land for 13 weeks, longer than any other known European, including Columbus.

Da Gama rounded the Cape of Good Hope with some difficulty, even in fairly good weather, and passed beyond known territory, fighting against the south-flowing current all the way. An anonymous member of the expedition described the problem they met off Natal (so-called because it was the Nativity season). On December 14th, 1497, they passed by Ilheo da Cruz (Cross Island) on their way up the coast; then on December 20th:

> In the morning we made straight for the land, and at ten o'clock found ourselves once more at the Ilheo da Cruz; that is 60 leagues abaft [behind] our dead reckoning! This was due to the currents, which are very strong here.
> That very day we again went forward by the route we had already attempted, and being favored during three or four days by a strong stern wind, we were able to overcome the currents, which we had feared might frustrate our plans. Henceforth it pleased God in His mercy to allow us to make headway! We were not again driven back. May it please Him that it be thus alway!

Along the southeast African coast, da Gama's party had occasional contacts with black African tribes. Then on March 2nd, they came upon a very different culture, on a secluded bay known as Mozambique, as the anonymous sailor continued:

> The people of this country are of a ruddy complexion and well made. They are Mohammedans, and their language is the same as that of the Moors [Arabic]. Their dresses are of fine linen or cotton stuffs, with variously colored stripes, and of rich and elaborate workmanship. They all wear *toucas* [robes?] with borders of silk embroidered in gold. They are merchants, and have transactions with white Moors, four of whose vessels were at the time in port, laden with gold, silver, cloves, pepper, ginger, and silver rings, as also with quantities of pearls, jewels, and rubies, all of which articles are used by the people of this country.

Da Gama had reached the southernmost port along the old Spice Route, where Arabs had been trading and intermarrying with the local population for well over 1,000 years. Even in those days of geographical ignorance, the Portuguese were not totally surprised to find the Arabs there, however; in the previous decade, the Portuguese had sent a spy to reconnoiter in the western Indian Ocean, so they would know where to head.

Not surprisingly, the Moslems did not take kindly to the Portuguese intruders. In their first contacts in Mozambique and Mombasa, the Portuguese and the Moslems at first followed the form of the time: The visiting commander sent ashore gifts for the local ruler, who reciprocated. The Portuguese gifts were cheap goods—strips of cloth, scarlet hoods, coral necklaces—quite unsuitable for these East African rulers, who draped themselves in silk, velvet, and gold. More to the point, the Arabs realized that the Portuguese were potential competitors in both trade and religion. Through hostages and Arabic-speaking convict interpreters he carried (as was the practice of the time), da Gama learned of a plot to capture his ships at Mombasa and barely got away. Still desperately in need of a welcoming port, for his crew was suffering badly from scurvy through lack of fresh fruit and vegetables, da Gama came to Malindi, where the ruler's rivalry with Mombasa provided da Gama with the safe harbor he needed. Equally important, the local ruler sent him a pilot, Ahmed ibn Majid, one of the foremost navigators in the Indian Ocean and author of some standard nautical texts. It was he who guided da Gama's expedition up the coast of East Africa, across the Arabian Sea—incidentally showing the crew how to troll for fresh fish on the way—through the great island spray of the Laccadives, to the southwest Indian port of Calicut.

With proper intelligence from their spies and advisers, the Portuguese chose their destination well. A Moslem merchant from somewhat earlier in the century described Calicut as "one of the greatest shipping centers of the world in this period," noting that the people of Calicut are "adventurous sailors, and pirates do not dare to attack" their ships. It was not simply that in Calicut "one may find everything that can be desired"; more important was the safety of this port, as Abd-er-Razzak continues:

> Security and justice are so firmly established in this city that the most wealthy merchants bring thither from maritime countries cargoes, which they unload, and unhesitatingly send into the markets and the bazaars, without thinking in the meantime of any necessity of checking the account or of keeping watch over the goods. The officers of the custom-house take upon themselves the charge of looking after the merchandise, over which they keep watch day and night. When a sale is effected they levy a duty on the goods of one-fortieth part; if they are not sold they make no charge on them whatsoever. In other parts a strange practice is adopted. When a vessel sets sail for a certain port, and suddenly is driven by a decree of Divine Providence into another roadstead, the inhabitants, under the pretext that the wind had driven it there, plunder the ship. But at Calicut, every ship, whatever place it may come from, or wherever it may be bound, when it puts into this port is treated like other vessels, and has no trouble of any kind to put up with.

Arriving in Calicut on May 20, 1498, da Gama found that news had (as at Malindi) preceded him, for the sewn Arab ships called *dhows* were considerably faster than the heavy Portuguese ships. While the crew played drums

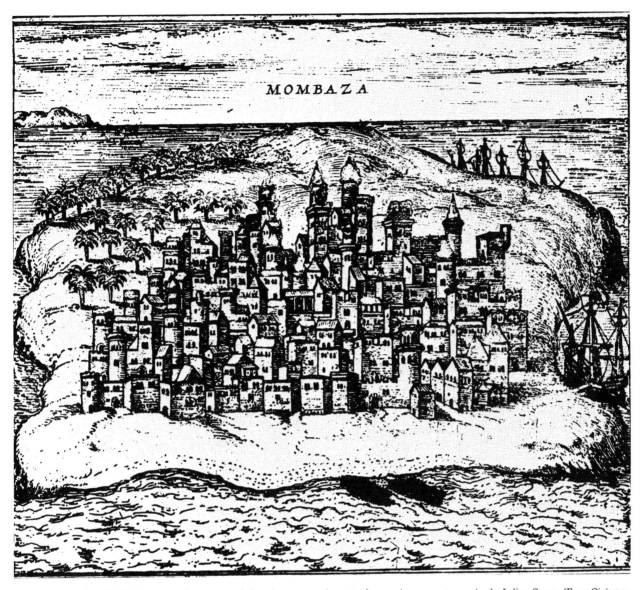

MOMBAZA

Mombasa, where de Gama's party was almost captured, later became a major port of contention among powers in the Indian Ocean. (From Civitates Orbis Terrarum, *1576)*

and trumpets and flew banners, and the chaplains celebrated the completion of this historic journey, the local rulers replied to da Gama's greetings with a local pilot to show the ships to a safe anchorage—for they had arrived on the Malabar (southwest Indian) coast only a few days before the monsoons. Once safely anchored, da Gama led a procession including Portuguese bagpipes through the streets of Calicut to meet the king; his reception, though not hostile, was hardly warm. The king found the Portuguese ceremonial gifts laughable, and the trade goods offered—mostly cloth and hardware—were far inferior to those routinely traded in the region. Religion was not a particular problem; indeed, for a time, the Portuguese took the local inhabitants to be Christians and worshipped in the Hindu temples. Most shipping for this Hindu kingdom was, in any case, carried on by Moslem merchants.

Eventually the Hindu ruler entered into a grudging trade agreement with the Portuguese—perhaps in recognition of their superior arms and the likelihood that they would be followed by others—giving da Gama a modest amount of pepper and cinnamon and a letter to take to his king, noting:

> Vasco da Gama, a nobleman of your household, has visited my kingdom and has given me great pleasure. In my kingdom there is abundance of cinnamon, cloves, ginger, pepper, and precious stones. What I seek from thy country is gold, silver, coral, and scarlet.

The local Moslem traders and sailors were, however, openly hostile, and da Gama was sufficiently wary of his welcome that he would not put his ships ashore and take them apart for the badly needed refitting. The ruler attempted to hold the unsold Portuguese goods as ransom against heavy port duties but when da Gama took some hostages in response, they called it a stalemate, and da Gama left Calicut.

Leaving over a month before the monsoons ended, da Gama had extreme difficulty attempting to cross the Indian Ocean, putting in instead at one of the many islands to refit his ships for the return voyage. Once the winds changed to blow from the northeast in late September, however, he reached the East African coast without difficulty, putting in once more at friendly Malindi. There his crew—over one-third of whom had died, mostly of scurvy—were revived by fresh fruit and vegetables and made fit for the voyage back around the Cape of Good Hope. As it would be for most subsequent voyages, da Gama's return trip was an easy one. Once picked up by the Mozambique Current, the ships were easily carried by a series of inshore currents around the coast—no need to swing out into the Atlantic—back to Portugal, 22 months after they had left.

The Portuguese quickly made use of da Gama's intelligence to mount another expedition. Within six months Pedro Cabral led a trading fleet on the same route; although heavy storms sank several ships, including one commanded by Bartolemeu Diaz, the rest of the voyage went smoothly. Swinging way south of the Cape of Good Hope, to avoid the contrary current, he made the voyage to Malindi in only six months, which would be the standard time for some centuries. With Calicut not disposed to trade, Cabral went further south on the coast to another major port, Cochin, where he obtained permission to build a factory for trade goods. The Portuguese concluded, however, that they could not compete with the Arabs, but must defeat them if they were to profit from this 16,000-mile route they had opened.

Vasco da Gama, returning to India in 1502, opened the campaign by exacting tribute from the rich East African trading city of Kilwa, bombarding Calicut, and defeating with superior gunpower a fleet of Arabs from Malabar. He was followed by Francisco de Almeida, who laid firmer groundwork for Portuguese hegemony by capturing the major East African ports of Sofala, Kilwa, Mombasa, and later Mozambique, as well as the islands of Socotra, off the horn of Africa, and Ormuz, at the mouth of the Persian Gulf. Then in early 1508, off Diu in the Gujarat (northwest India), Almeida's fleet decisively defeated an international Moslem navy. While Almeida established the Portuguese presence on the western end of the old Spice Route, it was Afonso d'Albuquerque who orchestrated their takeover of the route itself. A brilliant strategist, he first captured the major shipbuilding island of Goa off the Malabar coast. Although it strained limited resources in the Indian Ocean, Portuguese ships in 1511 crossed the Bay of Bengal to take the port of Malacca, on the island of Sumatra, commanding the strait through which the Spice Route passed. Aided by a captured Javanese map, the Portuguese by 1513 had reached Canton in China and the fabled Spice Islands—the eastern ends of the Spice Route. Controlling the key points along that route, the Portuguese preyed upon all ships not under their paid protection, largely driving the Arabs out of the trade and establishing the Cape of Good Hope Route as the main route for the desired spices of the East.

In less than two decades, the Portuguese had become the dominant force in the Indian Ocean. They were not the only Europeans in the East, however. A

Traders from this 16th century Portuguese ship have set up an impromptu market on the Japanese shore. (Museu de Arte Antiga, Lisbon)

Spanish expedition from around Cape Horn and across the Pacific arrived in the eastern islands they named the Philippines in 1521, setting the basis for what would become the Manila-Acapulco galleon run. In those days when the shape of the world was unknown, a man named Peter Martyr undertook to explain these new routes to his pope:

> Your Holiness should start at the Columns of Hercules, and proceed to the Islands of Cape Verde...and then follow the route of the Portuguese eastward on to the Golden Chersonesus called by them "Malacca." You are thus half-way round the world; and of the 24 hours, which, according to cosmographers, the sun takes to make his rounds, twelve have gone. In order to embrace the second half start again at the Islands of Cape Verde, but this time with your back turned on the Portuguese ships. The Spanish fleet has followed the setting sun; while the Portuguese ships went ever to the rising, and both have reached the Moluccas.

Despite the Spanish voyage, no other Europeans seriously challenged the Portuguese in the Indian Ocean for decades.

While focusing on the Spice Route ports, especially Goa and the trading colony of Macao established downriver from Canton in 1557, the Portuguese continued to develop their African interests. In addition to West Africa, they focused their attention on three other areas: the Congo and Angola, Mozambique (Portuguese East Africa), and Abyssinia. The Congo and Angola yielded little direct profit, except through slaves in a triangular trade with Brazil and Portugal. In Mozambique, attempts were made to push inland along the Zambezi River, a region they associated with tales of King Solomon and his luxurious trade with the unidentified city of Ophir. Native black Africans, however, strongly resisted and indeed pushed the Portuguese out of some ports, including Kilwa; only with the continued help of the Moslem rulers in Malindi did the Portuguese retain their hold in the area. Abyssinia was associated with yet another myth, that of the Christian kingdom of Prester John. The Portuguese were interested not only in religion but also in the Abyssinian port of Massawa near the mouth of the Red Sea; they had failed to take Aden in southwest Arabia, and still hoped to control the Red Sea—and maybe even build a canal through the Nile to the Mediterranean. In any case, they had not the resources to do so, and Portuguese Jesuits, with their inquisitional stance toward heresy, soured Abyssinia on a closer connection. Because of occasional shipwrecks along the shore, the Portuguese in this period carefully surveyed the known parts of the coast. Oddly, they ignored the prime site of Table Bay at the Cape of Good Hope, possibly because Francisco de Almeida had been killed there by natives on his return home.

Portugal held its monopoly of the spice trade into the 1550's, but then began to lose its hold. The country, small to start with, had been decimated by plague and had lost—to death or overseas settlement—nine out of ten sailors who went abroad. In addition, Portuguese colonies abroad had to continually fight off the native population and Moslem rivals, and at home Portugal was absorbed by Spain in 1578. Meanwhile other countries were entering the competition. English and French sailors had moved into modest trade in West Africa as far as Benin from the 1530's on, often in a triangular trade with Brazil or the West Indies and their homeland, providing the countries with open-ocean experience. In the 1560's the English and the Dutch had also been exploring passages to the northeast and northwest, to little avail. Then in the late 1580's England defeated the Spanish Armada and the Dutch overthrew Spanish rule, and—thus emboldened—were ready to try the Cape of Good Hope Route.

Madagascar and other nearby islands were favored watering spots and pirates' haunts, so fortified villages grew along the coastline. (By Van Linschoten, 1609, Bibliothèque Nationale)

Apart from the challenge of sailing unknown seas, these newcomers faced the very serious problem of scurvy, a debilitating and killing disease only later understood to be caused by lack of vitamin C. Jean Mocquet, who sailed on the Cape of Good Hope Route in this period, describes some of his scurvy symptoms:

> It rotted all my gums, which gave out a black and putrid blood. My knee joints were so swollen that I could not extend my muscles. My thighs and lower legs were black and gangrenous, and I was forced to use my knife each day to cut into the flesh in order to release this black and foul blood...And the unfortunate thing was that I could not eat...because of my great suffering...Many of our people died of

it every day, and we saw bodies being thrown into the sea constantly, three or four at a time...On every side were heard only the cries of those assailed by thirst, hunger, and pain, cursing the hour when they had come aboard.

So severe were the effects of this malady that in these years ships were occasionally found drifting in the open sea with most of their crew dead and the few survivors too weak to run the ship; often ships had to be sent back home with skeleton crews, or even broken up or burned abroad, for there were too few sailors to man them. For Northern Europeans, who had 1,500 miles further to go than the Portuguese on the Cape of Good Hope Route, the problems were magnified.

Their early attempts were disastrous. Even after a fast three-month trip to the Cape of Good Hope, the first three English ships were laid up for a month at Table Bay recovering from the effects of scurvy, and one ship had to be sent back to England for lack of a full crew. The flagship was lost in Mozambique Channel. The remaining ship reached Malaya, plundering all who came near her, but on the return trip storms, mutinies, more storms, and the ever-present scurvy left 13 survivors—and they were carried home in a French ship. These English ships had not been double-sheathed for tropical waters, nor did they have ready ports for provisioning. The same problems plagued the second English voyage—the first to touch mainland India—from which only one sailor survived, on the island of Mauritius in the Indian Ocean.

The Dutch fared a little better—partly because they were better prepared. A Dutch sailor who had sailed on a Portuguese ship to the East Indies had written navigational guides to the route in 1595 and 1596 (much to the dismay of the Portuguese, who had hoped to keep the route secret). The Dutch had long been associated with the East Indian trade, providing both the capital for Portugal's expeditions and the main market—Antwerp—for the distribution of its cargo, neither of which Portugal could have managed on her own.

Putting in at the Cape of Good Hope and at Antongil Bay on the island of Madagascar to recuperate from scurvy, the first Dutch fleet reached Bantam, on Java, in 1596 without losing a ship. Their welcome—warm at first—soon cooled, and some Dutchmen were imprisoned; but they survived to make a trade treaty and load a profitable cargo for home. Although three of the four ships returned safely, two-thirds of the crew had died, mostly from scurvy. Given this mortality rate, the Dutch tried the other southern sea route, the Cape Horn Route, but found that even worse. Other Dutch ships, among them some with English pilots, hazarded the Cape of Good Hope Route, establishing a factory at Bantam in 1599. Finding that the Portuguese were too weak to keep them out, the Dutch concentrated on the eastern end of the Spice Route, especially in the Molucca Islands and Java,

founding the Dutch East India Company in 1602.

Encouraged by John Davis, an English pilot on the 1599 Dutch voyage, the British formed their own East India Company in 1600. Their first voyage around the Cape in 1601 was especially notable because the sailors on one ship, provided with lemon juice en route, remained quite healthy, while the others suffered the full effects of scurvy. Knowledge from this discovery was not widely applied, however, and Table Bay and Antongil Bay remained traditional rest stops for scurvy-plagued ships. It would be another two centuries before British ships were required to provide citrus juices to their sailors, who thereby earned the name of "limeys."

Like the Dutch, the British headed for the Spice Islands, and indeed joined with the Dutch to capture a Portuguese ship in the Strait of Malacca in 1602. The Portuguese held on for a time, maintaining Malacca in spite of a four-year siege by the Dutch ending in 1606 and sharply defeating a Dutch fleet off Macao in 1622. But the balance was shifting. In 1612 the British defeated a larger Portuguese fleet off Surat and in 1622 took Ormuz. In the following two decades, the Portuguese gave up all but a handful of their Spice Route colonies, including Goa and Macao, to other Europeans.

Portuguese possessions on the west coast of Africa came under similar attack. In the 1630's the Dutch took all of the main forts on the Guinea Coast, including the rich fort of São Jorge da Mina, leaving Portugal with only the inferior ports near Bissau. The Dutch also took Angola, but were later rousted, the Portuguese retaining the coast from São Thomé Island down to the Cape of Good Hope, with its active slave trade with Brazil. The Cape itself had continued to be a watering and rest stop for European ships, with no one country laying special claim to the region. Then in 1648 a ship was shipwrecked on the Cape—not an uncommon occurrence, for "Cape Tormentoso" had been an accurate name; while awaiting rescue the crew planted some seeds and harvested a fine crop. As a result, the Dutch in 1652 settled a colony at the Cape, specifically to provide fresh fruits and vegetables for its sailors on the long-distance runs, laying the basis for the present country of South Africa—and, through enslavement and routing of the black African population, for many of its ills.

While the British and Portuguese continued to follow the traditional sailing route up the coast of East Africa to India, using the seasonal monsoon winds of the Indian Ocean—and also avoiding pirates and privateers on islands east of Madagascar—the Dutch developed a new route. Beginning in 1611, Dutch ships rounding the Cape of Good Hope let the strong west winds of the Roaring Forties blow them straight east, and they then arced up across the Indian Ocean to the Sunda Strait, between the islands of Java and Sumatra. Regarding the islands as their territory, and believing that a southern continent—*terra*

Landing in the Bay of Tolaga, New Zealand, October 23-9, 1769. (By James Cook, after Parkinson, British Museum)

australis — existed, as mentioned by Marco Polo, Dutch explorers reconnoitered in the southern seas. One of those, in 1606, is believed to have been the first to sight the continent of Australia, but thought it to be a part of New Guinea. A Spanish vessel bound for the Philippines in the same year was the first to discover Torres Strait, which separates New Guinea from Australia; but Spanish ships generally plied the Pacific, rather than the Cape of Good Hope Route, so their discovery had no practical results. Various Dutch ships, the first in 1616, arrived on the western coast of Australia, which they named New Holland, after being blown off course on the arcing route up to Sunda Strait. Finally, in 1642, Alfred Tasman confirmed that the land was an island by sailing around it (before going on to discover Tasmania and New Zealand); but he did not attempt to explore the coast, for others had written damning accounts of Western Australia. Captain Jan Carsstensz's 1623 account is typical:

It is very dry and barren, for during all the time we have searched and examined this part of the coast to our best ability, we have not seen one fruit-bearing tree, nor anything that man could make use of. There are no mountains or even hills, so that it may be safely concluded that the land contains no metals, nor yields any precious woods, such as sandalwood,

aloes, or columba. In our judgment this is the most arid and barren region that could be found anywhere on earth. The inhabitants, too, are the most wretched and poorest creatures that I have ever seen in my age or time. As there are no large trees anywhere on this coast, they have no boats or canoes, whether large or small.

Small wonder that New Holland was ignored for so long. In these decades, the Dutch established a virtual monopoly on trade with the East Indies. In response, the British decided to concentrate on the Indian mainland, gradually taking over ports along both coasts formerly held by other Europeans.

The Dutch had considerable advantages in this period. Having improved on what they learned from the Portuguese, their new route cut one year off a fleet's turn-around time (since it did not require waiting for the monsoons to clear); they also had more maneuverable boats than other Europeans in the Indian Ocean. More than that, they organized themselves efficiently. They ran all their activities from a single headquarters at Jakarta on the island of Java; the colony, originally established in the old Chinese quarter of the city on a river bank by grant of the local ruler, came to overshadow all other settlements in the region under its Dutch name of Batavia. Reserving their large boats for the long-distance runs between Europe and the East Indies, and allowing them time to refit properly for the turnaround, the Dutch built smaller ships of almost indestructible teak for local use. These worked among the many ports on the Spice Route—what many historians called "country trading"—making the many small trades that were involved in building up a cargo sufficient to fill the holds of large commercial ships. By contrast, the English, as well as the French and Danes, who had also joined in on the Cape of Good Hope Route, had to use their European ships to cruise the Spice Route making trades; often they could not find a market for the full cargo they were carrying, but would have to distribute it piecemeal, not having the central distribution facilities enjoyed by the Dutch.

But while the Dutch had some clear advantages, they were far from dominating the Cape of Good Hope Route. Indeed, while some historians call the period from the mid-17th to the mid-18th centuries the "Interregnum," others call it flatly the "Age of Pirates." It was indeed, a free-for-all period, with no one country ruling the seas, as Portugal had done for the century before. While the various contenders—Portuguese, Arabs, Dutch, British, French, Danes, and the many locally ruled peoples of Southeast Asia—combined and recombined in a kaleidoscopic set of alliances and enmities, often reflecting battles far away in Europe and the North Atlantic, unparalleled assemblages of pirates established themselves throughout the Indian Ocean. Many of these were successors to the previous generations of pirates along the old Spice Route, but some established themselves in new territory. The most dangerous of these along the Cape of Good Hope Route centered on the island of Madagascar, with others based on the Comoro Islands and the Mascarene Islands, notably the Île de France (Mauritius).

The problem was serious enough even in the early 17th century for merchant-rivals—the English and Dutch—to run cooperative convoys in the Indian Ocean. It became even graver in the late 17th century, when pirates forced out of the Caribbean to Sierra Leone chose the more promising location of Madagascar. These freebooters, an international group, though predominantly of English origin, even established a republic on Madagascar, which they named Libertalia. Americans from New York, Boston, and Philadelphia—the first to appear on the Cape of Good Hope Route—supplied the Madagascar community from around 1700. Among these pirates was the famous Captain Kidd, whose alleged buried treasure derived partly from a haul he made in the Indian Ocean. A chief factor (merchant's agent) on the Malabar Coast described him:

This captain is very severe to his people by reason of his commission...procuring him awe and respect from his men, and to this is added his own strength,

being a very lusty man often calling for his pistols and threatening any that durst speak to the contrary of what he desireth, to knock out their brains...They are a very distracted company, continually quarreling and fighting among themselves...We were informed that...in Madagascar is settled great abundance of these villainous people with their families, yearly supplied from New York with liquors, provisions and other goods.

Only gradually did the European trading companies manage to subdue the pirates, partly by more heavily arming their ships, and partly by attracting (and sometimes forcing) pirates to join "legitimate" settlements in the region, such as the French settlements in the Mascarenes and on the island of Bourbon (Réunion).

By the mid-18th century, Britain and France were the two main contenders on the Cape of Good Hope Route. The Dutch, having lost their colonies in North America, were much weakened, especially since their home ports in the Netherlands were limited to relatively small ships, not the more capacious East Indiamen England had been developing. In addition, the Dutch policy of impoverishing and enslaving local populations to maintain an artificial monopoly proved a long-term drain on the colonies. While in the early years the Dutch government had encouraged its traders to bring out their wives and families, in later years they reversed their policy and intermarriage with the natives was the norm. Only at Cape Town did the Dutch establish and maintain a permanent independent colony. Meanwhile, the English and French were on the rise. In West Africa, they ousted the Portuguese and Spanish and took over the slave trade; Portuguese forts were given new life, as São Jorge da Mina became the infamous British slaving fort of Elmina on the Gold Coast. Further east, the British were especially strong in India, where their main port was Surat, a city so rich that some of the streets were paved with porcelain; its southeastern trading center was at Bantam. The French, failing to settle Madagascar, had a base on the island of Bourbon (Réunion) and some ports on the Indian coast, notably that of Pondichéry (Poduca). The French were not nearly so well ensconced as the British, however. The India trade, expanding rapidly as Britain took over more and more of the country itself, became increasingly profitable in the late 18th century, while both the Dutch and French East India companies were going effectively bankrupt, and many of Portugal's trading ships were rotting in their harbors. During its Revolution, France lost more ground; although it regained momentum under Napoleon, with assistance from its Dutch ally, Britain was too strong for them both.

By 1815, Britain had driven its rivals from India and Ceylon; had established itself in Malaya; had taken the Cape of Good Hope (for the second time, having returned it to the Dutch by treaty the first time); had taken some key Indian Ocean islands, notably Mauritius (no longer called Île de France); and had gained a new continent—Australia. So began a new period of colonial development along the Cape of Good Hope Route. The great explorer, Captain James Cook, had in 1768-70 explored the coast of neglected Australia, before going on to his Pacific voyages. What he saw in southeast Australia, which he called New South Wales, presented a very different picture of the land. At a point he named Cape Howe, he found:

> ...the country...had a very agreeable and promising aspect, diversified with hills, ridges, plains, and valleys, with some few small lawns; but for the most part the whole was covered with wood.

They had difficulty finding fresh water, and in landing "by reason of the great surf which beat everywhere upon the shore." Later, however, they found a "tolerably well sheltered" bay with freshwater streams running down into sandy coves; they named it Botany Bay, for "the great quantity of plants...found in this place."

Such a description reopened the question of colonization. After the Revolutionary War in America, there was some talk of sending Loyalists to settle Australia; but nothing came of that, most moving instead to Canada. In the event, the only colonists sent to Australia in the early years were convicts, and the soldiers to guard them. The first of these arrived in Botany Bay in 1788 and settled five miles north at the superior harbor of Port Jackson, now known as Sydney. Australia continued to receive infusions of convict exiles for decades, in New South Wales until 1840 and in Western Australia until 1868. Even so, by the mid-19th century the European population of Australia numbered only about 5,000 people, the land and the convict society not being particularly alluring to skilled Britishers. The situation was similar on the Cape of Good Hope. While the land there was bountiful, the Cape Col-

In the great days of the tea runs, these clippers are racing from China to London. (By Edwin Weeden, from The Illustrated London News, *September 9, 1866)*

ony was peopled mostly by Dutch-speaking Boer farmers, a society whose prospect likewise did not attract the British.

What changed all that was gold and diamonds. In 1851, gold was discovered in New South Wales, and people from all over the world came pouring in to seek their fortunes. The discovery of diamonds in 1871 and gold in 1886 had the same effect on the Cape Colony. From being way stations on the way to the fabulous East, these two colonies became destinations in their own right. The Cape of Good Hope Route changed to meet the need. In the days of Botany Bay, ships from Europe continued to make the wide triangular tack across the Atlantic, often stopping at Rio de Janeiro or Pernambuco (Recife) in Brazil, to take on water and do a little trading, before swinging across to Australia. Ships bound for the Far East often stopped at the island of St. Helena (site of Napoleon's exile in 1815), before swinging around the Cape and up through the Indian Ocean, generally taking the Mozambique Channel to avoid French and other pirates east of Madagascar. But the discovery of gold made speed important and spurred the development of faster and more manageable ships, while analysis of the Atlantic experience allowed navigators to make better use of the trade winds. As a result, ships were able to take a more direct route down the Atlantic; soon clippers were setting records of an astonishing 65 days from England to Australia.

Speed was more important in the Far East, too. As Europe entered the industrial era, the long round trip time—frequently up to two years—for trade goods and messages became unacceptable. With the decline of the Ottoman Empire, Europeans increasingly looked to routes through the Middle East, employing overland routes across the Isthmus of Suez in Egypt or along the Great Desert Route from Mesopotamia to Aleppo on the Mediterranean. Fleets of country traders—increasingly the new steamships, instead of sailing ships—plied the Indian Ocean and the Mediterranean, between these overland crossings, sharply reducing traffic on the Cape of Good Hope Route. The southwest part of the Indian Ocean around Madagascar became a backwater, rarely frequented by sailing ships or steamships, except for new ships being sent around the Cape from England for use along the Spice Route. Even that traffic largely stopped after the opening of the Suez Canal in 1869. The Cape of Good Hope Route became largely aimed at the Cape Colony, Australia, and other islands of the South Pacific. Among the few ships that still swung around the Cape of Good Hope to China were American ships that were unable to round Cape Horn because of unfavorable winds, and chose instead to go eastward.

Faster they may have been, but passengers had no easy time in this period. When the main passengers were convicts, the unfortunate exiles were jammed together in prison ships; early immigrants on the route found conditions little better. These travelers were also responsible for preparing their own food; but bad weather and illness often interfered, leading to malnutrition and starvation. But the lure of gold overcame these conditions. (Once in Australia, crews often deserted their ships to join the rush—forcing more than one British ship to comb local jails for homeward crews, with officers remaining armed and alert the whole voyage.) But in the 1850's, new ships—many operating out of Liverpool, not London—began to be built to accommodate passengers more comfortably, providing different classes of cabins or berths; though far from the luxury liners of the 20th century, these ships sharply decreased the mortality rate on the Australia run, which had often been as high as 50 or 100 deaths per voyage.

The gold fever once past, the population of Australia soon began sending heavy cargoes back home to England, most importantly wool, but later also much meat and still later vegetables; New Zealand, too, populated by new colonists, joined in the trade. Clippers on the Australia run would follow the usual Atlantic route down to Adelaide, Melbourne, and Sydney, and then on to New Zealand. Then, rather than force their way back against the Roaring Forties, they would run with the winds around Cape Horn, at the tip of South America, and back up through the Atlantic. Even after the days of the gold rush, however, ships often had difficulty finding crews for the homeward passage, for Cape Horn was a notoriously nasty part of this round-the-world route.

By the 1870's, iron ships—built at the great British shipyards of Clyde, Mersey, and Aberdeen—began to replace timber sailing ships. Once navigators had found a way to properly shield the ship's compass, so it would not be affected by magnetism, iron ships were found useful, for they could carry more and with less fire risk, even though they were slower. Soon they were themselves replaced by steel ships, also mostly British built. Steamships were tried on the route in the mid-19th century, but the distances were so great, and so many coaling stations had to be provided, that they were unfeasible on the Cape of Good Hope Route. But the opening of the Suez Canal in 1869 tipped the balance against sailing ships, for steamships did not require the costly towing through the canal, nor did they have such difficulties with the Red Sea winds. Steamship liners took over the passenger trade by the 1880's, and much of the cargo trade as well from Australia and New Zealand. Only the bulk cargo trade, like grain and coal, continued for a time in sailing ships on the round-the-world route, after 1914 generally passing through the Panama Canal, instead of rounding the Horn.

But if the Suez and Panama canals changed the character of the Cape of Good Hope Route, it has retained its importance in modern times. Sailing ships have long since passed away, and airplanes have cornered the passenger traffic, but modern vessels still haul heavy cargo from the ports of Africa, Australia, and New Zealand. The Cape of Good Hope Route has also proved its importance in time of war, when the northern seas—and the Suez Canal itself—were too dangerous. Indeed, in the late 20th century, the closing of the Suez Canal for some years forced traffic to take the old route around the Cape of Good Hope. And even with the canal reopened, many of today's supertankers, too large for the Suez passage, have made the Cape of Good Hope Route the lifeline for the precious supply of oil that fuels modern Western economies.

Selective Bibliography

Hart, Henry Hersch. *Sea Road to the Indies: An Account of the Voyages and Exploits of the Portuguese Navigators* (New York: Macmillan, 1950). Detailed account through Vasco da Gama.

Howe, Sonia E. *In Quest of Spices* (London: Herbert Jenkins Ltd., 1939). Focuses on early European activities on the route.

McCutchan, Philip. *Tall Ships: The Golden Age of Sail* (New York: Crown, 1976). Focuses on English and American ships and sailors.

Parry, J. W. *The Age of Reconnaissance: Discovery, Exploration and Settlement 1450 to 1650* (New York: Praeger, 1969).

———. *Trade and Dominion: The European Overseas Empires in the Eighteenth Century* (New York: Praeger, 1971). Both useful accounts; part of the History of Civilization series.

Penrose, Boies. *Travel and Discovery in the Renaissance: 1420–1620* (New York: Atheneum, 1975; reprint of 1952 Harvard University Press edition). Excellent on early exploration.

Tavernier, Bruno. *Great Maritime Routes: An Illustrated History* (London: MacDonald, 1972). Treats the route in various periods, dominated by different countries.

Van Leur, Jacob C. *Indonesian Trade and Society: Essays in Asian Social and Economic History* (The Hague: W. van Hoeve Ltd., 1955). Volume One of Selected Studies on Indonesia. A compilation of evidence and interpretations, in English.

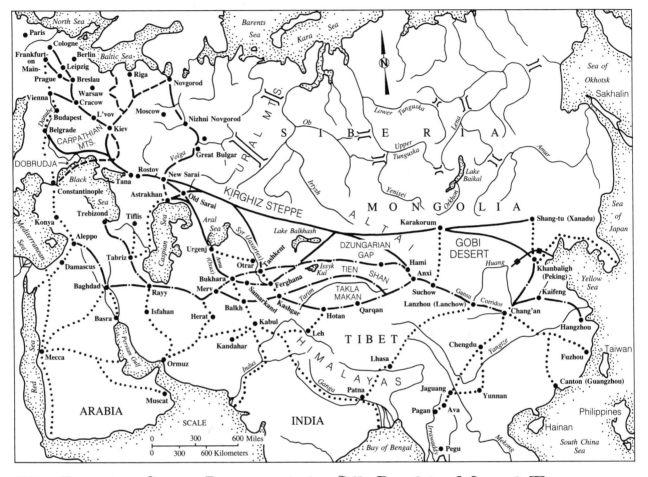

The Eurasian Steppe Route and the Silk Road in Mongol Times

——————— Main Eurasian Steppe Routes   — — — Saracen Route

—·—·—·— Silk Road   ⊐⊏ Main Trans-Siberian Portages

············· Main Connecting Routes   ■—■—■ Great Wall

--------- Varangian Route

The Eurasian Steppe Route and the Russian River Routes

In the early decades of the 14th century, a Florentine named Francesco di Balduccio Pegolotti wrote a book called *The Practice of Commerce,* giving advice to Italian merchants who were considering traveling across Eurasia to trade with Cathay (northern China). Speaking of the journey from the Sea of Azov, atop the Black Sea, eastward to the head of the Caspian Sea, he noted:

> First, from Tana to Astrakhan it is twenty-five days by ox wagon, and from ten to twelve days by horse wagon. Along the road you meet many Mongolians, that is, armed men.
>
> And from Astrakhan to Sarai it is one day by water on a river, and from Sarai to Saraichuk it is eight days by water on a river. And you can travel [both] by land and by water, but people travel by water to spend less [on transportation] of wares.
>
> And from Saraichuk to Urjench it is twenty days by camel wagon...

What is astonishing about this record is that—barely half a century after the Polos had opened the European trade routes to the East—it is all so routine, almost boringly matter-of-fact. Even the reference to armed men, which might have injected a hint of danger, indicates only that these Mongolians were providing safe passage for the traders—although for a hefty fee.

Pegolotti gives a striking account of that unique time in history—a single century only—when the great steppe route across Eurasia was open to all, with security guaranteed by the Mongol overlords who controlled the land mass from the Ukraine east to the Pacific. European traders by the hundreds and thousands pushed eastward to trade with China, a land that a generation before had been known to them only by distant hearsay.

The route followed by these traders, over thousands of miles of steppeland, was far from a new route, however. One of the most natural routes in the world, the Eurasian Steppe Route has been a major human pathway for tens of thousands of years. Human beings walked, and later rode, the 8,000 to 9,000 miles from one end of the Eurasian land mass to the other virtually without impediment. Indo-Europeans, like the Scythians—as well as some of the great scourges of Europe, the Huns and the Mongols— came sweeping out of the plains to bedevil the more settled peoples east and west of them, often because they themselves were being pushed by other, stronger peoples on the route.

And that has always been the Eurasian Steppe Route's great disadvantage: because it was wide open, it was almost always in contention. As a result, it has, through most of its history, been a migration and invasion route more than a travel and trade route. Only in those few times—such as under the Mongols from the mid-13th to the mid-14th centuries—when the route has been peaceful or largely in the hands of one power, has it lived up to its potential as a world-class route. More often it played second fiddle to its more famous kin: the Silk Road.

*The Russian River Routes
in the Late Middle Ages*

———————— Main Varangian Route

——·—·—— Main Saracen Route

· · · · · · · · · Other Connecting Routes

⏝ Main Portages

The heart of the Eurasian Steppe Route is the fertile steppeland that lies between the Russian swamps around the Dnieper and Volga rivers and the great southern seas of Asia, the Black, Caspian, and Aral, and stretches from the Ukraine eastward, south of the Urals, to the vast Kirghiz Steppe of southern Siberia, gradually becoming more arid. This lush land—magnet for countless invaders—has been the fulcrum of the Eurasian Steppe Route from the earliest times.

East of this heartland, the Eurasian Steppe Route—faced with a series of mountains to the east that surround Lake Baikal—dipped southeastward through the Dzungarian Gap, a wide pathway between the Altai Mountains and the more southerly Tien Shan (Celestial Mountains). Crossing the semi-arid prairies and rock-strewn deserts of the Mongolian Plateau, the route traveled past the Mongolian capital of Karakorum and skirted the Gobi Desert to China's modern northern capital of Beijing, either directly or by way of the fabled city of Shang-tu (Xanadu) just to the north. These cities were modern developments, however; the great nomads of the steppes had no settlements but traveled with their tent cities on wagons across the level plain. For much of history, the main centers of

settled civilization lay to the south, and spurs of the Eurasian Steppe Route branched off to join the great trade route called the Silk Road. From the Caspian Sea, passing on either side of the Aral Sea, travelers could pick up the northerly route of the Silk Road along the Tien Shan—perhaps more to the point, nomadic brigands could prey on merchants there. From the region of Karakorum, a spur ran south to meet the Silk Road at the Jade Gate of the Great Wall and the Gansu (Kansu) Corridor, traditional western entryway to China.

At the western end of the Eurasian Steppe Route a similar situation prevailed. Central Europe is somewhat protected by the boomerang-shaped Carpathian Mountains, so the Eurasian Steppe Route fed into Europe on either side of them. From the Black Sea, one branch ran northwest through the crossroads city of Lemberg (L'vov) into Poland and across the northern European plain, either through Cracow and then down to Vienna or straight into Germany via Frankfurt. The other way around the Carpathians into Europe ran southwest from the Black Sea along the coastal plain called the Dobrudja; from there it picked up the Orient Route along the Danube River, which strikes like a spear into the heart of Europe. Attack through the Dobrudja and Danube was most common in early times, especially when civilization centered around the Mediterranean to the south. But in medieval times, northern Europeans opened up the Russian River Routes from the Baltic Sea to the Black Sea via the Dnieper and to the Caspian Sea via the Volga. These routes, with the rise of Russia and northern Europe, became the main modern pathway for war and migration—as witness the activities of Napoleon and Hitler in the past two centuries.

The great fairway of the Eurasian Steppe Route—which early nomads called "The Earth Girdle"—is one of the oldest routes in human history. The unparalleled historian of the steppes, René Grousset, put it quite bluntly: "The first known Eurasian route is that of the northern Steppes." Early humans are known to have lived at the far eastern end of the Eurasian Steppe Route, near Beijing, 400,000 years ago. The people who produced the famous cave paintings of Western Europe tens of thousands of years ago shared aspects of their culture with peoples far to the east, in southern Siberia and northern China. This transmission of culture continued over the millennia; as new ideas and techniques—such as ways of working stone or designing pottery—were developed, they percolated along the route, carried by the bands of hunters who wandered the open steppes. When the peoples of the Near East began to adopt a more settled life, their ideas and practices, too, filtered through to their steppeland neighbors. So the peoples of the Eurasian route learned to domesticate animals—cattle, sheep, horses, and, in dryer areas, goats and camels—gradually adopting the nomadic life of the herder and making seasonal migrations en masse as temperature and availability of water dictated. From the Near Eastern civilizations came other innovations, notably wheeled vehicles in the mid-third millennium B.C. The early clumsy four-wheeled vehicles, drawn by oxen, asses, or small early horses, were of more use to farmers than to nomads; but the two-wheeled vehicle, in which the draft animal bore part of the weight, was much more maneuverable. Wheeled vehicles quickly spread across the Eurasian Steppe, reaching China in short order.

But the Eurasian nomads did not simply transmit the ideas of others; they made contributions of their own. As the wheel was changing the face of Eurasia, these pastoralists were experimenting with riding animals, notably the horse. At first, these slight creatures were better suited as table fare than as mounts; but over the centuries judicious breeding produced more powerful strains that would transform life on the steppes.

We know little directly about the steppe peoples in these millennia, for they left no great cities for archaeologists to plumb. What we know comes from fragments found in ancient burial mounds and garbage heaps and from the surviving records of the more settled civilizations around them; the very names of these nomads are generally those given by others. We do know that, for all the intermixing of peoples along the Eurasian Steppe Route over the millennia, several groups distinguished themselves by language and culture. Prime among these were the Indo-Europeans, ancestors of the culture that would come to dominate most of Europe and western Asia. From their homeland north and west of the Black Sea, the Indo-Europeans had by the mid-third millennium expanded westward on either side of the Carpathians into central Europe, eastward on the steppe past the Caspian and Aral seas, and southward to the valleys of the Oxus

(Amu) and Jaxartes (Syr) rivers. To the north, in the forests of Siberia, the Tungusic peoples pursued their hunting-and-gathering lifestyle. The eastern steppes and borderlands were populated by various groups; among these were the ancestors of Mongols—relatively short, dark-haired people with deep-set eyes and unbearded yellow-brown skin—and the predecessors of the Turks—taller, lighter-skinned, and more hirsute than their neighbors.

But it was in the west that the main early action came on the Eurasian Steppe Route. As the third millennium shaded into the second, the Indo-Europeans began to irrupt in all directions, themselves gradually fragmenting into a variety of distinct peoples. The Iranians made a wide arc around the Aral Sea southwest to the Iranian Plateau. (Some of their kin went further south into India.) In the west, the Hittites swung down the Dobrudja west of the Black Sea to the Aegean and Asia Minor; they were soon followed by several waves of Greeks. Western Europe fell before the Celts, who pushed to the Atlantic and eventually across to Britain. The Indo-Europeans who remained north of the Black Sea came to be known as the Cimmerians, while the Slavs and the Balts occupied more northerly parts of Europe. What allowed this astonishing series of conquests was the Indo-Europeans' skill at managing horses and two-wheeled chariots, plus their development of a compound bow that could—unlike an ordinary bow and arrow—be shot easily and with power from a fast-moving vehicle. The combination was, at the time, unbeatable, and these warrior-nomads swept all before them. Coming into contact with bronze-working in the Near East, they soon spread these techniques eastward as they coursed across Central Asia as well.

Chariot warfare, adopted in self-defense by China in the East, continued to dominate in the coming cen-

On the plains north of the Black Sea, this landowner leaves his comfortable tent home on the left to help defend his lands against the Scythian nomads. (Now-destroyed mural from Panticapaeum, later Kertch, from Rostovtzeff, The Social and Economic History of the Roman Empire)

turies, as Eurasia began to move from the Bronze Age to the Iron Age. Indeed, the wheel became an inextricable part of nomadic life. Seasonal migrations were marked by long strings of carts, on which were loaded all of the clan's worldly possessions. The typical nomadic home was itself placed on a cart, sometimes with wheels 20 feet apart; in a land where trees were rare and life revolved around herds, the mobile tent homes called *yurts* were ingeniously made of wicker frames covered with hides or felt (a fabric of matted animal hair).

Meanwhile, the nomads of the steppes were continuing to develop their skills in riding horses and, although neither the saddle nor the stirrup had been developed at this time, they gradually adopted a change of clothing suited to the life of a rider: Robes and sandals were exchanged for trousers and boots. These nomads developed even more effective archery skills suited to this novel form of locomotion. By the eighth century B.C. the mounted archer had become a force on the Eurasian Steppe. While cattle, sheep, and goats would continue to provide the necessities of life, and camels, oxen, and asses would haul heavy goods in slow caravans, the horse came to dominate the life of the steppe nomads. Each nomad had not just one horse but as large a herd as he could manage; on campaigns each warrior would take a dozen or more mounts, so fresh horses would always be available. Their great speed, their techniques of wheeling and attacking sharply, their ability to surprise and surround an enemy, all made the cavalry the dominant new form of warfare; in the face of this, the war chariot become consigned to ceremonial use, at least on the steppe, and the cavalry of these nomads would become the terror of Eurasia.

The Indo-Europeans were far from alone on the Eurasian Steppe, however. In the East, the main nomadic power of the time were a group the Chinese called the Hsiung-nu, better known to later Europeans as the Huns. An ethnically mixed people, probably more Turkic than Mongol, they pressed hard on the Chinese; early versions of the Great Wall, some of them dating back to the middle of the first millennium B.C., were built in partly successful attempts to keep these nomads at bay. The Indo-European peoples of the steppe had no such protection, and some were pushed westward as the Hsiung-nu expanded, in what would be the classic pattern along the steppe throughout history. Like a line of croquet balls responding to a mallet's blow on one end, or like a row of dominoes falling, peoples all along the steppe have always felt reverberations when any one of their number burst out of its accustomed orbit. In this case the Hsiung-nu pushed before them an Indo-European group the Chinese knew as the Yüeh-chih; these people—known to the West as Scythians—came to rest in the heartland north of the Black Sea, displacing the Cimmerians, who were forced into Europe.

In their new homeland, between the Don River and the Carpathian Mountains, the Scythians came into contact with the high culture of Greece, which was expanding into the Black Sea region. The Scythians remained true to their nomadic origins, however, and roamed the steppe in small groups; like other nomads, their main allegiance was to their family, clan, or tribe, with large confederacies forming only on occasion. During periods of temporary stasis on the steppe, however, some of these groups made up a trading chain that stretched across the Eurasian Steppe. The fifth century Greek historian Herodotus described successive links in such a chain between the Scythians and a people he called the Hyperboreans "who reach to the sea"; though the name means "beyond the north wind," many people feel that the Hyperboreans—known to Herodotus only by hearsay—were the Chinese. The Scythians themselves traveled a long distance to trade with "a people at the foot of lofty mountains," believed to be the gold-rich Altai, as Herodotus described:

> As far as these bald people [presumably a Mongol folk] the country and the nations that inhabit it are well known, for there are Scythians who journey to them, and it is not difficult to obtain information from these or from Greeks of the mart on the Borysthenes [Dnieper] and other Pontic [Black Sea] marts. The Scythians who make the journey do business through seven interpreters in seven languages.

The historian G. F. Hudson has reconstructed the line of the route on the basis of information from Herodotus and other Greek and Chinese chroniclers. Starting from the town of Tanais near the mouth of the Tanais (Don) River at the head of the Sea of Azov atop the Black Sea, traders traveled along a treeless steppe to the great bend of the Rha (Volga) River near modern Stalingrad. On the far side of the river the land became lightly timbered toward the central Russian uplands; as Hudson sees it, the route arced gently northward, so traders could barter for furs with the forest dwellers of the Urals and Siberia while avoiding the more arid southern part of the steppe. He posits a major trading camp in the Dzungarian Gap, south of the Altai Mountains near the upper reaches of the Irtysh River. According to Herodotus, the region traveled by the Scythians was at first "level and deep-soiled," but later more stony and rugged.

Of the route beyond the Altai we know even less. One intrepid Greek traveler named Aristeas apparently traveled to the Altai with the Scythians and then went further east with some other nomads; but his memoirs had been lost by the fifth century B.C., and Herodotus was dealing very much with second-hand information and tall tales. Even he is clear about that, noting that the land further east is "unknown, except for such stories as these peoples tell of it," among them tales of one-eyed men and

Scythian burial mounds, some over 50 feet high, stand out sharply against the level Eurasian Steppe north of the Black Sea. (19th century engraving)

gold-guarding griffins. There was apparently no direct contact between the eastern and western ends of the Eurasian Steppe Route in this period, but trade from either end surely reached the middle. Both from the West and the East came items like fine metalwork and beautiful cloth that could only be produced by settled civilizations, while the higher cultures were satisfied with gold, furs, and (in the case of the Chinese) temporary peace in exchange. This trade along the Eurasian Steppe Route continued for some centuries, but by the fourth and third centuries B.C. the peoples of the steppe were in upheaval again. The Scythian state itself was submerged in the process, coming under attack by its nomadic kin from both East and West. The tenuous trading chain was broken, and—although small-time barter would always continue on the steppe—would not be revived for over 1,000 years.

Throughout the following centuries, the various steppe peoples would push each other back and forth across the land mass, every now and then irrupting into the lands of more settled peoples. They were under little danger of attack themselves. King Darius of Persia, in the sixth century B.C., had circled round the Black Sea via the Dobrudja to go against the Scythians; but the Persian infantry, unbeatable on its own ground, was lost against the Scythian retreat-and-burn tactics. Unable to force the

Scythians into a pitched battle, the Persians had to retreat; the lesson was not lost on others, and the error was rarely repeated—until modern times. When the Roman Empire rose in the West, they adopted the same tactics the Chinese had in the East: they erected a frontier, the *limes,* separating the mobile hordes to the east of the Rhine-Danube axis from the increasingly settled lands of Western Europe. But these defensive positions were of little use to West or East when the great nomad masses of Eurasia began to move once again.

Trouble began in the first century in the East. The Hsiung-nu, many of whom had become rather sinicized along peaceful borders, came under two kinds of pressure. A severe drought caused the loss of much accustomed grazing land, forcing many nomadic groups to seek other, better pastures. In addition, a Mongol group called the Sien-pi began to move out of Manchuria into the former Hsiung-nu territory in Mongolia. The result was like a slow tidal wave sweeping across Eurasia. One group of Hsiung-nu crashed through the Great Wall in the second century A.D., destroying the great northern cities and ending China's unity for some centuries. The rest were continually pressed westward through the Dzungarian Gap onto the Russian Steppe by the Sien-pi, who eventually gave their name—via numerous linguistic transformations—to the region of Siberia. On their forced migration westward, the Hsiung-nu absorbed and mixed with the various peoples it found on its way, in the process becoming the Huns who would strike terror in Europe. The heartland was under pressure from both directions, in fact; the Sarmatians who now held the former Scythian territory were pressed by both the Huns and the Goths of Europe. The Sarmatians were for a time able to hold their own, having the advantage of heavier horses, which allowed them to develop armored cavalry, an innovation in mounted warfare. While some Goths stayed in the heartland (later some even joined with the Huns), others pressed across the Roman frontier as refugees. At first they were ill-received; but later the Romans were glad of their help in defending Europe against a fiercer enemy. In the fourth century the Huns themselves arrived in the heartland, while the Sarmatians retreated ahead of them into the Hungarian plain.

Though the Huns were not very numerous, the Europeans might be forgiven for seeing them as "hordes," for they traveled with their great herds of horses—a dozen or more for each warrior—and numerous cattle for food as well. No farmers, they had to continually keep on the move to new grazing lands; indeed, the Huns' forced evacuation so disrupted the ordinary seasonal migration patterns that many of them had to resort to a more primitive hunting-and-gathering lifestyle to survive. In this period, looking for fresh pastures, some Huns even forced their way through the Caucasus Mountains that largely bar the way south between the Black and Caspian seas. St. Jerome wrote of them:

> They filled the whole earth with slaughter and panic as they flitted hither and thither on their swift horses. They were at hand everywhere before they were expected. By their speed they outstripped rumor, and they took pity neither upon religion nor rank nor age nor wailing childhood.

Still being pushed westward, the Goths arrived in Gaul and Spain, being largely diverted from Italy itself. The Roman Empire itself had long been in decline, and its unity was increasingly a sham, as armies elected their own leaders and asserted their independence. At the same time, the disorganized bands of Huns were being welded into a cohesive force by a series of strong leaders, notably Attila. With more direction and unity of purpose, the Huns in the fifth century broke through the Roman frontier at Belgrade and on into the Balkans. Worse, they struck in the north, crossing the Rhine and flooding Gaul.

But there the Huns faced a stalemate. The great two-pronged push across Europe had sapped much of the Huns' strength; meanwhile the defenders had had time to develop their own cavalry, using Sarmatian-style heavy, armored mounts. In the end, the Huns were allowed to retreat. They did considerable damage, still, in northern

Italy, but with the death of Attila in 453, the Hun confederacy collapsed. Most of the once-fearsome hordes filtered back across the Carpathians into the heartland, settling primarily around the lower Don and Volga. The Goths remained in western Europe, while the Slavs emerged to take control of Eastern Europe.

With Hunnish power spent, a new people arose on the Eurasian Steppe to fill the vacuum in the sixth century. These were the Turks (to the Chinese, Tu-Chüeh), a people of greatly mixed ethnic background who were united primarily by their language and by their extraordinary skill at metalworking. From their homeland east of the Altai Mountains on the Orkhon River south of Lake Baikal, one group spread westward to occupy the lands between the Altai and the Aral Sea south of Lake Balkhash. Luckily for both Europe and China, the Turks were more concerned with internecine battles than with expansion in the early centuries of their dominance. But, though something of a calm settled over the eastern part of the Eurasian Steppe Route, it did not become the major trading route that its geography has always made possible. An ambassador from the Byzantine Empire visited the western Turks in the sixth century, hoping to open up a new route to China, for Byzantium chafed at Persia's control of the Silk road to the south. This envoy, Zemarchus, was impressed by the khan's head camp on the Jaxartes River, as a later chronicler describes:

> They found him [the khan] in his tent, seated on a golden chair with two wheels, which could be drawn by a horse when required...The tent was furnished with silken hangings in various colors cleverly wrought.

In addition, Zemarchus found "a great array of waggons in which there was a vast quantity of silver plates and dishes, besides many figures of animals in silver, in no way inferior to our own." In the end, however, no new transcontinental route was established.

In the West, some offshoots of the Huns continued to bedevil Europe. The Bulgars continued to harass the Byzantine Empire from their base on the lower Volga and Don Rivers. Another Hunnish group called the Avars, driven out of Mongolia by the Turks, came westward also. Adopting a dangerous policy, the Byzantines employed the Avars to help break up the Bulgars. Some of the Bulgars were driven across the Danube into the Balkans; others migrated northward to the great bend of the Volga River, where they established the trading center of Great Bulgar. The Avars, once started, were not easily stopped, however. Like Attila, they broke the Danube line at Belgrade and swarmed into the Hungarian plain, pushing Germanic peoples ahead of them. The Avars continued to bedevil Europe for two centuries, but eventually were driven back across the Carpathians by the Franks in the

The steppe nomads' large felt tents, called yurts, were actually mobile homes pulled by teams of oxen. (From H. Yule and H. Cordier, The Book of Ser Marco Polo, *1903)*

late eighth century. Their main contribution was to bring westward the innovation of the stirrup, which, with the saddle developed somewhat earlier, completed the basic equipment of the cavalry.

Other more stabilizing influences were also at work in the West. In a pocket between the Black and Caspian seas, somewhat protected from the waves of steppe invaders, there had developed the kingdom of the Khazars. Another mixed, mostly Turkic people, the Khazars in the seventh century exchanged a largely nomadic life for a more sedentary trading existence, funneling goods from the steppe westward across the Black Sea to the Byzantine Empire, their main trading partner. To their capital of Itil, at the mouth of the Volga River on the Caspian Sea, came traders from all directions: Christians (largely Greeks) and Jews from the West; Slavs and Volga Bulgars from the North; and Moslems, who filtered across the Caucasus Mountains for trade after some initial military engagements. The Khazars themselves eventually adopted Judaism, and word of this independent Jewish state gave heart to dispersed Jews around the Mediterranean for centuries. Except for the region controlled by the Volga Bulgars, areas to the north of the Khazar base were expected to pay tribute; early chronicles tell how "the Khazars came upon them as they lived in the hills and forests, and demanded tribute from them," generally a

white squirrel skin from each hearth." The Khazars were strong enough to act as something of a bulwark against the marauding nomads of the eastern steppe.

In the lee of the Khazars there also developed settled communities along the great rivers to the north. After the expulsion of the Huns in the fourth century, the Slavs had begun to expand in all directions: across the Vistula River into Poland, south across the Danube into the Balkans, and most of all north. Here the great rivers of Russia offered untouched prime pathways across Europe; not only are the rivers easily navigable, with low gradients and few difficult rapids, but they approach each other closely in headwaters and bends, so portages are relatively easy. The East Slavs spread north from the prime site of Kiev on the middle Dnieper up to Smolensk and on across the headwaters of the Volga to Novgorod and Lake Ladoga, just east of the Gulf of Finland. From there they exacted tribute from the Baltic peoples on the coast and the Finns to the east, trading down to the Black Sea on the Bug and Dniester rivers, west of the Dnieper. The lower Dnieper lay in the hands of the Alans and Magyars, nomads under Khazar control.

The river routes, once opened, attracted attention from others. As part of the great Scandinavian expansion of the ninth and tenth centuries, Swedish Vikings called Varangians moved in. Entering primarily at the head of the Gulf of Finland, they coursed down the two major routes to the south. From Lake Ladoga, the main route headed straight south through Novgorod on the much smaller Lake Ilmen, picking up the Dnieper at Smolensk and then feeding on down the river through Kiev to the Black Sea at the city of Olbia. From here these waterborne raiders threatened Constantinople and swung round through the Black Sea to harass Tana (formerly Tanais) at the mouth of the Don on the Sea of Azov. This route was called the Varangian Route; but the people themselves were known to the Byzantines as the Rus, and their land eventually came to be known as Russia.

The other main route of the Scandinavian raiders arced from Lake Ladoga southeast to the River Volga and then down to the Caspian Sea. But the Bulgars, who still held the great curve on the Volga, and the Khazars at its mouth, were the main traders on this route. Because the Volga Bulgars were Moslems and this route led, via the Caspian, to the Islamic land of Persia, it was called the Saracen Route, that being the European term for Moslems. The early 10th century Moslem writer Ibn Rusta noted that the Volga Bulgars flourished as intermediaries on the Saracen Route:

> ...the Khazars trade with them and buy and sell to them and also the Russes come to them with their merchandise, and all of them on the two sides of the river have different kinds of merchandise, such as sable and ermine and grey squirrel.

In addition to furs, the Rus brought human beings to sell, mostly Slavs—so many of them that their name came to refer to the status they occupied: slave. Moslem writers were quite clear on this, too, noting of the Rus:

> They make raids on the Slavs, coming to them in boats, seizing their people and carrying them off to Khozeran [Khazaria] and to the Bulgars to be sold.

The Rus initially concentrated on the more westerly Varangian Route. Once they settled down to trading, they established commercial relations with the Byzantines—though they sometimes resorted to force to get better terms. Each spring, as soon as the ice melted on the rivers, the Rus would head south in their dugouts, assembling from the various tributaries at the stronghold of Kiev, high on the west bank of the Dnieper. Though the route was rather easy all the way south, it was not without its hazards. Chief among them were the 40-mile-long Dnieper Rapids, on the easternmost curve of the river, fraught with obstructions. The 10th century Byzantine compilation *De Administrando Imperio* noted that at the first of these rocky stretches, the river narrows to the width of a playing field, and:

> ...in the middle there are high and dangerous rocks which stick out like islands. The water rushes up and over them, plunging down the other side with a great and terrifying roar. The Russes do not therefore dare to pass through them; they put in at the bank, landing some of the men, and leaving the goods in the boats; they try out the way with their bare feet lest they strike a rock. While some at the prow and others in the middle do this, those in the stern propel with poles, and so, with the greatest care they get past this first obstruction, keeping in close to the river bank.

Passing other obstructions, many of the men and their human cargo of slaves walked along the bank, while some dragged the boats or even carried them on their shoulders. After a sacrifice to their gods in thanks for a safe passage, the boats had another four days to the Black Sea; there they transformed their boats by adding masts, sails, and rudders, and sailed around the coast of the Black Sea to Constantinople. They apparently abandoned their boats at Constantinople, returning home by unknown routes with their fittings—oars, oarlocks, and the like—to be attached to newly dug boats the following spring for the next trip south.

The Dnieper Rapids exposed the Rus to other dangers as well; since the river sliced through the Eurasian Steppe, Rus traders were often vulnerable to attack from unruly nomads. *De Administrando Imperio* described the problem:

> The Russes cannot come to this Imperial City of the Romans [Constantinople], whether for war or trade, unless they are at peace with the Pechenegs [Patzinaks]. For when the Russes come to the obstructions in the river with their boats, and cannot pass unless they take their boats out of the water and carry them on their shoulders, men of the Pecheneg race attack them, and easily rout them and slay them, since they cannot do two things at once.

Varangian traders on the Russian River Routes hauled or carried their boats on overland portages. (Det Kongelige Bibliotek, Copenhagen)

Since the Pechenegs were vassals to the Khazars, trading rivals of the Rus, the hazard was real. At times, the Rus were forced to adopt a longer route with portages to avoid being exposed on the rapids; in the early 10th century, they sometimes angled over to the Don River and down to the Sea of Azov, where some Russians had established a small state. Despite the problems, however, the Vararŋian Route was in the ninth and tenth centuries a major trade route—indeed the main trade route across Europe, being far preferable to the exceedingly difficult overland routes of Western Europe and the stormy Western Seaways from the Baltic to the Mediterranean.

In attempting to expand their trade on the Saracen Route, however, the Rus made a fatal error. In the late 10th century, they conquered the Volga Bulgars and, with the aid of Byzantium, attacked the Khazars, sacking their capital, Itil. In the process they removed the very state that had been protecting their growth. The nomads of the eastern steppes moved quickly. Pressure had already been building; the Magyars had in the previous century been pushed by the Pechenegs into the Hungarian plain, where they would stay. Now the Pechenegs came in full force against both the Rus and the Byzantines. In 968 they laid siege to Kiev itself and four years later killed the Grand Prince Svyatoslav, architect of the Russian expansion; in a nomadic custom that went back at least to the time of Herodotus, Russian chronicles record that "the nomads took his head and made a cup out of his skull, overlaying it with gold, and they drank from it." The Byzantine Empire held on, and indeed brought the chastened Kievan state into the Christian fold. The 11th century brought worse, for Kiev was sacked and her people enslaved by the nomadic raiders. The Varangian and Saracen Routes began to lose their dominance in these troubled times, as Western Europe began to revive its own commercial routes.

The Pechenegs were but the first of the Turks to move westward; over the centuries many other Turkic peoples would push around the Black Sea, filtering into the Balkans. Even so, the main Turkish advance was to the southwest through Persia into the Near East. In the East, a group of Turks called the Uighurs had been brought in to prop up the weak native administration of China; becoming quite sinicized, these acted as a buffer between China proper and the rest of the Turkish peoples. But the Turks who remained in Central Asia were soon to be subjugated by a different people: the Mongols.

Originating in Manchuria, these descendants of the ancient Sien-pi pushed south and west to the land that now bears their name. One Mongol group called the Khitans had, in the 10th century, moved into north China, shifting China's capital northeast for the first time to the region of modern Beijing (Peking). Their name, transformed from Khitan to Khitae to Cathay, even came to apply to all northern China for centuries. But it was not until the 13th century that the Mongols really hit their

Early Varangian (Russian) traders had to force the Byzantine Empire to open trade with them. (New York Public Library)

stride. From a rather bedraggled and dispersed group of nomads (sometimes called Tatars, from the Chinese *ta-ta*, or nomads, mispelled by Europeans as Tartars), they were welded into a confederacy the like of which had never been seen on the Eurasian Steppe. The prime orchestrator of this feat was a Mongol prince named Temujin (Iron); with the first successes of his federation, he adopted the name Genghis (World-Encompassing). In the early decades of the 13th century, Genghis Khan was pressing at both ends of the Eurasian Steppe Route, at north China and at the Russians on the Dnieper. By 1260, he and his successors had made an empire that stretched from the Black Sea to the Pacific and south to Persia, China, and Burma. This was by far the largest empire the world had even seen, and it was unique not only in its size but also in its administration.

Like other Eurasian nomads, the Mongols had a taste for the finer things produced by the settled civilizations around them; such tastes were generally satisfied at some of the main trading centers on the northern branch of the Silk Road, especially at cities like Samarkand, Bukhara, and Khiva, around the Oxus and Jaxartes rivers in Central Asia. Nomads also valued the skills of these city-dwellers and often enticed or enslaved people to serve them on the move as scribes, metalworkers, and the like. The Mongols carried this tendency to extraordinary lengths. From their raids on Western Europe, which terrorized the populace and drove them north and west into mountains and marshes for safety, they brought back innumerable slaves, many of them skilled artisans. Some of these unfortunates, captured in Hungary, Germany, or Russia, ended their days practicing their trades—be they goldsmiths, scribes, or tent-makers—in far-off Karakorum, headquarters of the Mongols, or after 1264 in their Chinese capitals of Khanbaligh (the Khan's City, now Beijing) or Shang-tu (Xanadu), the fabled Mongol summer residence. These captives were probably the first Europeans to have crossed Eurasia to China since the days of the Scythians. When the Europeans began sending embassies to the Mongols—partly aimed at diverting their attacks from Europe to the Islamic world—these exiles,

103

many of them Christians, were their main informants about the world of the East.

The first of these European embassies left for the East in 1245, in the wake of early Mongol invasions of Hungary and Poland. The Franciscan monk John de Plano Carpini journeyed through Cracow and Kiev to the Mongol camp on the Dnieper. (This region operated as a border, or *ukraina*, from which came the name Ukraine). From there he was forwarded across the lower Volga to the Great Khan's main camp at Karakorum, south of Lake Baikal. Arriving just in time for the investiture of a new Great Khan, he was astonished at the magnificence displayed by these people who lived in mobile tent-homes: sables, ermines, finely worked silk brocades, gold, and gems decorated not only themselves but also their horses and their tents. In 1252, a second envoy, William de Rubruck (Rubruquis) from Flanders, traveled via Constantinople and the Crimean peninsula to the Great Khan; although shorn of his books and robes, he returned back to Europe with word that the Mongols would concentrate their attentions on the Moslems before turning their full force against Europe once again. In truth, once the Mongols moved their headquarters even further east to Khanbaligh, Europe became more distant and less attractive.

Perhaps more to the point, the Mongols recognized that taxing was more profitable than wholesale despoliation, which destroyed hope of further gain. As a result they looked with great favor on the opening of a trade route across the Eurasian Steppe. Nor was European interest long in coming. In 1260—the traditional beginning date for the Pax Mongolica or Pax Tatarica, that great century of peaceful travel in Eurasia—two Venetian merchants,

Nicolo and Maffeo Polo, set out into Mongol territory. Since the Italian city-states now largely controlled shipping on the Black Sea, they naturally began the land portion of their journey at the Crimean Peninsula and proceeded to the Volga; there, because of a border war, they circled south to Bukhara, where they settled and traded for three years, until the new Khan, Kublai, sent word for them to head east. At Khanbaligh, Kublai Khan quizzed them about Europe and sent them home with a request for 100 missionary-scholars to teach the court about Christianity and to argue their religion's merits with other exponents. In the end, the pope sent only two, who turned back, possibly reasoning that they would be used primarily for secular administration, as was the Mongol pattern.

But merchants were hardier and had more incentive. A few years later the Polos returned to the East, accompanied by Nicolo's son, Marco; perhaps to avoid trouble on the steppe, they traveled primarily via the old Silk Road, angling north to Khanbaligh only at the end of their journey. The pope's doubts about Kublai Khan's intentions were perhaps warranted, for all three Polos were inducted into the Khan's service and remained in his employ for 17 years before returning to their homeland. It was Marco's record of these experiences that stunned rough Europeans with its descriptions of surprising grandeur. His description of Khanbaligh, where the Khan lived for only three months a year—December, January, and February—is typical:

All around the city there is a first row of walls, square in shape, each side being eight miles long. All along the wall there is a deep ditch, and in the

Like many other invading nomads, the Magyars headed for the Hungarian plain with all their goods and herds. (Library of Congress)

middle of each side a gate through which pass all the people who come to this city. Then there is a space of a mile, where the troops live. Then you come to another square wall, twenty-four miles long...

In the middle of these circuits of walls rises the Great Khan's palace, which is the...largest that was ever seen...

The inside walls of the halls and rooms are all covered with gold and silver, and on them are painted beautiful pictures of ladies and knights and dragons and beasts and birds and diverse other things. The ceiling is also made in such a way that one sees nothing else on it, but pictures and gold. The great hall is so vast and large that quite six thousand men could banquet there. There are so many rooms as to surpass all belief...The roof is varnished in vermilion, green, blue, yellow, and all other colors; and so well and cunningly is this done, that it glitters like crystal, and can be seen shining from a great way off all round.

A far cry from both the nomadic tents, no matter how accoutred, and the rather more crude European dwellings of the time.

Europeans were, at first, unbelieving, but merchants voted with their feet. In the first half of the 14th century the Eurasian Steppe Route became the great trade route its terrain had always destined it to be. By the 1430's or 1440's, the Florentine writer Pegolotti was writing his essay, *The Practice of Commerce,* for merchants interested in joining the trade. As in former Scythian times, the main route started from Tana on the Don River, with merchants arriving there by land, river, and sea routes from Europe. This was wagon country—indeed, William de Rubruck provided a vivid picture of the nomads' use of wagons in the 13th century. While the male warriors—and many women and children as well—lived on horses, women and children drove the great wagons:

One woman will drive twenty or thirty carts, for the country is flat. They tie together the carts, which are drawn by oxen or camels, one after the other, and the woman will sit on the front one driving the oxen while all the others follow in step. If they happen to come on a bad bit of track they loose them and lead them across it one by one. They go at a very slow pace, as a sheep or an ox might walk.

The Europeans followed suit. From Tana merchants headed toward Sarai, on the Volga end of the portage from the Don, and proceeded by water or wagon to Astrakhan, near former Itil, at the mouth of the Volga on the Caspian.

From there, messengers and envoys would head straight across the steppe, passing from camp to camp to the Mongols' eastern headquarters. This was certainly the route taken by the Khan's couriers, who were so important in the communications system that held the vast Mongol Empire together. But for merchants the central

Mongol archers mounted on their powerful shaggy ponies were Eurasia's consummate cavalry. (Victoria and Albert Museum)

section of the Eurasian Steppe Route was less attractive than the great markets on the northern arc of the Silk Road. As a result, many of them turned south, even though it involved the hardship of crossing deserts like the Kizil Kum, between the Oxus and Jaxartes. Switching to camel wagons for travel through dry country, many headed for Urgenj, near the mouth of the Oxus River, where—Pegolotti vowed—there "is a good market for wares." The Moslem traveler Ibn Battuta, who took this route from Sarai, describes the travel style which had evolved for the desert crossing:

From this place [Sarai] we went on for thirty days by forced marches, halting only for two hours each day, one in the forenoon and the other at sunset. The length of the halt was just as long as the time needed to cook and sup...Everybody eats and sleeps in his wagon while it is actually on the move, and I had in my waggon three slavegirls. It is the custom of travelers in this wilderness to use the utmost speed, because of the scarcity of herbage. Of the camels that cross it the majority perish and the remainder are of no use except a year later after they are fattened up. The water in this desert is at certain known waterpoints, separated by two or three days' march...

Others might choose to swing around the east side of the Aral Sea to the market of Otrar on the Jaxartes River; there they were joined by merchants journeying from Urgenj. Those who then swung north to rejoin the Eurasian Steppe Route would generally continue by wagon. But those who followed the northern arc of the Silk Road, through Almalik and Beshbalik, would change to pack asses for the three-to-four-month trip to Anxi, west gate of the Great Wall, where they switched to pack horses on their way into China. The ultimate destination of all was Khanbaligh (Beijing).

Under Mongol rule, these routes were relatively safe and well-organized—but not completely so, of course. Peoples along the way were supposed to provide safe conduct for merchants, at a payment of so much per pack-load, under the terms of the Khan's rule; in practice, armed nomads often extorted payments from merchant-travelers along the way. Any merchants who died along the road forfeited all their property to the "lord of the country," unless someone else in the party said he was the dead man's brother, "and in this manner the property would be rescued." In addition, Pegolotti warned of danger to strangers at the death of a lord:

> ...in that interval [before the installation of another] sometimes a disorder occurs against the Franks and other foreigners—they call "Franks" all Christians of countries from the Byzantine Empire westwards—and the road is not safe until the new lord is sent for who is to reign after the one who died.

Despite the hazards, the Eurasian Steppe Route was a true international highway between 1260 and 1368.

During this period, the Russians were reluctant vassals of the Mongols. Under pressure of Mongol raids, the Rus—now culturally absorbed by the Slavs and speaking the Slavonic language—had retreated northward into the forests and marshes, where the nomads could not readily follow them. But with the farmlands to the south in nomad hands, they had to find new forms of sustenance; while some reverted to a hunting-fishing-and-trapping lifestyle, others chose to clear forested land in the north, creating new farmland and, in effect, extending the steppe. While Kiev failed to recover its former dominance, being so exposed to the steppe, Novgorod was almost impregnable, being a stockaded island in the middle of a marsh; here was the Russian trading center, on the Varangian Route that still connected the Baltic and Black seas.

Blocked in the south by the Mongols—and on the Volga by the revived Bulgars—the Russians began their long expansion eastward, especially along the Oka and upper Volga rivers. By 1147 they had founded the small settlement of Moscow on a tributary of the Oka River and Nizhni (Lower) Novgorod at the junction of the Oka and Volga. They were still not proof against the Mongols, however. In 1237, the Mongols made a startling midwinter attack on Bulgar; Novgorod itself was saved only by the approaching spring thaw. Russia was, at the time, a congeries of petty principalities and dukedoms, and with the Bulgars out of the running, Nizhni Novgorod assumed temporary dominance on the Volga. Moscow's star was rising, however, and by 1367, she had exchanged the old wooden stockade—symbol of the medieval Russian city—

for the great stone walls of the Kremlin (Citadel). Even Novgorod looked to Moscow, on which she depended for food and safe passage south. With the rise of Moscow, the Volga River became the prime river route to the south, replacing the long-dominant Dnieper; the Volga not only fed into the Caspian Sea but also, via a short portage to the Don River, into the Black Sea as well.

During these centuries, the states of Russia were all still under Mongol authority, however; in the late 13th and 14th centuries, Russian princes—even the great hero Alexander Nevsky—had to make periodic trips eastward to pay obeisance and tribute to the Mongol rulers. Those who failed to do so found their lands devastated and their people enslaved. The southern states suffered especially. On his trip to the East in 1246, Brother Carpini noted of Kiev:

> ...we found an innumerable multitude of dead men's skulls and bones lying upon the earth. For it was a very large and populous city, but it was now in a manner brought to nothing: for there do scarce remain two hundred houses, the inhabitants whereof are kept in extreme bondage.

Travel and trade in Siberia was so crude in this period that the great Moslem traveler Ibn Battuta, who wandered from West Africa to China, went no further north than Great Bulgar, noting:

In the 13th century, the Mongols swept in from the Eurasian Steppe and virtually destroyed Kiev. (New York Public Library)

One travels in these areas only in small carts which are drawn by strong dogs...Only rich merchants, each of whom takes a hundred vehicles with him, are wont to travel in these wastes. The carts are also laden with food, drink and firewood...In exchange for their own goods they are offered skins of sables, white squirrels and ermine...Those who travel to these places do not know whether they are demons or men to whom they sell their goods and with whom they trade; for they never see them face to face.

What Ibn Battuta refers to is the ancient practice of silent barter, known throughout the world, in which peoples who had no common language or long-established contact carried on trade by adjusting their piles of goods until the exchange was mutually acceptable to both.

But by the late 13th century, the great days of the Mongols were passing, as the confederation broke apart. Russia was gradually made free to expand at her own will, but this was the end of the international caravans on the Eurasian Steppe Route. Although trade would continue, it was generally in trading chains among the nomads themselves. Europeans no longer found transcontinental travel safe, if only because the Mongols—after toying with all the major and some minor religions—had finally adopted Islam, with some considerable zeal. At the end of the 14th century Sarai and Astrakhan were destroyed by Tamerlane (Timur the Lame), another in the long series of nomadic invaders. But goods continued to make their way by various routes to the Caspian and Black seas, where the Italian traders came for them. In the 15th century, caravans of as many as 800 camels were still reported in Samarkand, headed for the western seaports. But the cap-

ture of Constantinople by the Turks in 1453 largely broke off that avenue of trade and travel, and within a century the Europeans had begun to turn their attention to their own sea routes—free from the necessity to pass through Moslem territory.

But if the Eurasian Steppe Route was no longer a major international trade artery, a new route was in the process of developing in the East. Over the centuries, the Russians had gradually filtered across the low Urals into the forests of Siberia, seeking furs. They developed a tortuous series of portages that allowed them to proceed mostly by water along the vast network of rivers that laced Siberia, reaching past Lake Baikal all the way to the Pacific Ocean by the end of the 17th century.

The Chinese, meanwhile, had thrown off Mongol rule, replacing it with the native Ming dynasty. Although the Ming had little taste for foreigners, they were not totally averse to profitable trade, as long as others took most of the risks. Under the succeeding Manchus, originally a northern people, China herself expanded, by the end of the 18th century controlling the whole eastern half of the Eurasian Steppe.

Between these two giants—Russia and China—who bitterly contested the region around the Amur River, a new trade route developed. The Russians had acquired a taste for Chinese tea—considerably fresher brought overland than shipped around all of Asia, Africa, and Europe; the Chinese, for their part, were eager for furs. The result was that Russian and Chinese traders met at the border market of Kiachta on a river south of Lake Baikal, north of the old Mongol capital of Karakorum. Chinese caravans, leaving Beijing, headed northwest across the Gobi Desert toward Kiachta, or more precisely toward

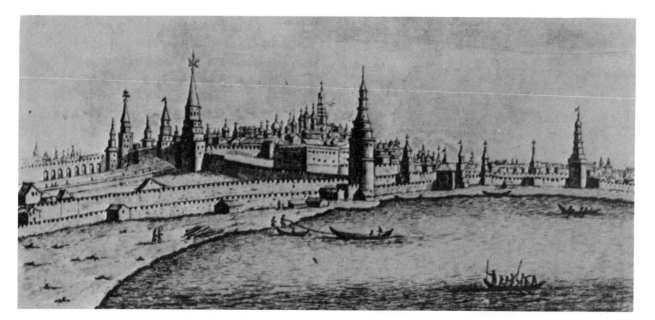

Once a small wooden stockade, Moscow came to be dominated by the great stone fortress called the Kremlin. (From Cornelius de Bruin, Travels into Muscovy, Persia..., *1737)*

their encampment on the Chinese side of the border. At Kiachta they met traders who had crossed the continent from the West. These had not taken the Eurasian Steppe Route, however; allowed to languish after the fragmentation of the Mongol Empire, the heartland was for a long time in the control of Cossacks, "free warriors" who moved into the void and raided in all directions. The Russians preferred a trans-Siberian pathway through the Urals; and not only Russians, but by the early 19th century other northern Europeans were headed eastward on this route to trade with the Chinese.

The English traveler E. D. Clarke followed one such route in 1800, from Germany to Kiev and then northeastward across the Volga into Siberia:

The carriers...go every three years to Tobolsky in Siberia which is a rendezvous for all caravans bound to Kiatka [Kiachta], on the frontiers of China. From Tobolsky they form one immense caravan to Kiatka. From Siberia they bring furs; from Kiatka, Chinese merchandise of all sorts, as tea, raw and manufactured silk, porcelain and precious stones.

Clarke noted that the Chinese brought to the Kiachta products from the Russian settlement of Petropavlovsk (St. Peter and St. Paul) on Kamchatka Peninsula, continuing:

Thus laden, many...[traders] set out for Francfort, and bring back muslin, cambric, silks, the porcelain of Saxony, and the manufactures of England.

On the Russo–Chinese border, traders met to exchange tea for furs and other specialty goods. (By Thomas Witlam Atkinson, from Travels in the Regions of the Upper and Lower Amoor..., *1860)*

Alongside this luxury trade there existed also a rougher trade, largely carried on by Ukrainians, who "with their four-wheeled carriages drawn by oxen" carried vital bulk goods such as salt or corn "in caravans of twenty or forty waggons or even more."

The trans-Siberian route was transformed into a new kind of all-weather route with the coming of the railroad in the early 1900's. And none too soon for those who wished to flee the turbulence of the Russian Revolution and later World War II. Many such refugees made their way across Siberia, crossing from Moscow either through Gorki (formerly Nizhni Novgorod) or Chelyabinsk to Omsk on the Irtysh River and then eastward to Irkutsk at the southern tip of Lake Baikal. From there the main route arced north around the Amur River and down to Russia's Pacific port of Vladivostok. A spur ran straight eastward through Manchuria to Vladivostok, when Russo-Chinese relations allowed, and many refugees settled in Harbin. Another spur in later times fed down through the Mongolian capital of Ulan Bator (southeast of old Karakorum) to Beijing itself. Technology also transformed the Russian River Routes, as a network of canals was formed to replace the old portages and to link the major cities of European Russia with each other and the seas that encircle them.

In modern times, the Eurasian Steppe Route bears no resemblance to an international highway, despite all its natural advantages. The Russians and Chinese are squared off against each other in mid-route, at the Dzungarian Gap and Kiachta. Though some modest local trading is carried on across that border, the Trans-Siberian Railroad now bears most travelers and trade goods across the great expanse of Eurasia, while airplanes bear almost all of the rest. Motor vehicles have never played a major role along the route.

The heartland has never ceased to attract, however. Throughout most of history, invasions were from the East along the Eurasian Steppe Route, but Russia's opening of the rich resources of Siberia and the route to China attracted envious intruders from the West—in the early 19th century, Napoleon; in the 20th century, Hitler. Both of these came out of northern Europe to strike at the new heart of Russia: Moscow. Neither of them, however, was geared to deal with the great distances that were meat and drink to the nomads of the steppe. Even with all the suffering that resulted from these attacks, they reached only a fraction of the distance covered by the Mongols. Western Europeans might, however, be forgiven for feeling that patterns have not changed totally, considering that the Russians swept westward at the end of World War II and continue to occupy Eastern Europe—traditionally vulnerable to invasion from the steppe.

Selective Bibliography

Adams, Arthur E., Ian M. Matley, and William O. McCagg. *An Atlas of Russian and East European History* (New York: Praeger, 1966). A useful work with generalized maps supplemented by textual commentary.

Grousset, René. *The Empire of the Steppes: A History of Central Asia.* Translated from the French by Naomi Walford (New Brunswick, New Jersey: Rutgers University Press, 1970). A comprehensive political history, focusing on the Mongol period.

Hudson, G. F. *Europe and China: A Survey of Their Relations from the Earliest Times to 1800* (Boston: Beacon Press, 1961; reprint of the 1931 edition). An extremely useful review of the main land and sea connections through history.

Lattimore, Owen and Eleanor Lattimore. *Silks, Spices and Empire: Asia Seen Through the Eyes of Its Discoverers* (New York: Delacorte, 1968). Part of The Great Explorers series. A well-annotated collection of excerpts of classical and modern firsthand accounts.

Legg, Stuart. *The Heartland* (New York: Farrar, Straus & Giroux, 1970). A well-written chronicle of Central Asia from the Indo-Europeans to the Mongols.

Mitchell, Mairin. *Maritime History of Russia, 848–1948* (London: Sidgwick and Jackson, Ltd., 1949). A fascinating work, which includes an excellent treatment of the Russian River Routes.

Parker, W. H. *An Historical Geography of Russia* (Chicago: Aldine, 1968). An extremely useful book, with many interesting quotations from firsthand accounts.

Severin, Timothy. *The Oriental Adventure: Explorers of the East* (Boston: Little, Brown, 1976). Tells the stories of many European adventurers and missionaries in Asia in modern times.

Spuler, Bertold. *History of the Mongols: Based on Eastern and Western Accounts of the Thirteenth and Fourteenth Centuries.* Translated from the German by Helga and Stuart Drummond (Berkeley: University of California Press, 1972). A fascinating compilation.

Teggart, Frederick J. *Rome and China: A Study of Correlations in Historical Events* (Berkeley: University of California Press, 1939). A masterly summary of related events on the Eurasian Steppe in the first centuries B.C. and A.D.

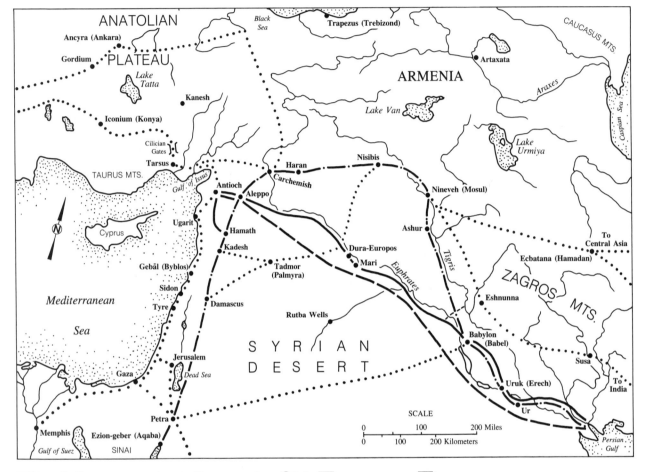

The Mesopotamian Routes in Old Testament Times

——————— Great Desert Route (Early)   • • • • • • • Main Connecting Routes

— — — Great Desert Route (Medieval)   - - - - - Median Wall

— • — • — Fertile Crescent Route

The Great Desert Route and the Persian Royal Road

Neither snow nor rain nor heat nor gloom of night Stays these couriers from the swift completion of their appointed rounds.

This description, borrowed by the United States Post Office in modern times, was actually applied to Persian postal couriers by the Greek historian Herodotus five centuries before Christ. On their Royal Road, the Persians developed the first organized long-distance communications system, laying the basis for the great networks that would bind together western Asia under its many and widely varied rulers, including the Greeks, the Romans, the Moslem Arabs, and the Turks. Its influence spread even wider than that, for the Persian post influenced the development of the great Roman road system in the West and the Indian Grand Road in the East.

In Persian times, as before and since, two main routes cut across western Asia: the Persian Royal Road and the Great Desert Route. The Persian Royal Road headed eastward across the Anatolian Plateau, from Sardes (once capital of the fabulously rich King Croesus) through Gordium (at one time home of the legendary King Midas) to Ancyra (Ankara); it then cut south to cross the upper Euphrates and later the Tigris, passing along the foothills of the Zagros Mountains to the Persian capital of Susa — and on into the hills to the summer palace at Persepolis. Well-supplied with water from the Anatolian and Iranian plateaus, this was throughout history a much-used route.

In the west, it connected with Europe through Greece, through the Danube Valley, and via the Black Sea coast. In the east, it linked with the overland route to India along the Persian Gulf and with the great Silk Road which reached across the continent to China. The route of the Persian Royal Road was, however, often exposed to brigands and immigrants from the hills, so a much-better-protected shortcut was often favored: the Great Desert Route.

Running further west, the Great Desert Route followed the inner curve of the Fertile Crescent formed by the Mesopotamian rivers and the coastal plain. Running along the edge of the Syrian Desert, the route connected southern Mesopotamia with the crossroads city of Aleppo and nearby Syrian ports on the Mediterranean. This was, for thousands of years, the main overland link between the Spice Route of the eastern seas and the Mediterranean.

The desert was not the vast expanse of sand dunes that name usually suggests; the 18th century traveler Bartholomew Plaisted noted:

...this desert has generally been represented as a level sandy plain; whereas in reality the greatest part is a hard sandy gravel like some of our heaths in England. In some places it is full of large loose stones, and in others full of small hills, which are more barren than the valleys or plains.

Horse-drawn war chariots, like this 7th century B.C. Assyrian one, were for a time unbeatable in Mesopotamia. (Louvre)

Nor was there, in this region, generally a lack of water, but more often the water was roiled, brackish, or full of algae. Plaisted noted:

> Even the very best is soon rendered unfit for present drinking; for when you come to a pool, everyone is for taking care of his own camels, and therefore as many of these plunge in at [a] time, that the water soon becomes muddy and unfit for use. I have been forced to take up with it, and have drank it as thick as Turks do their coffee, who always shake the pot before they pour it out...

Travelers on the Great Desert Route were sometimes exposed to predators from out of the Syrian Desert, but were often able to assure a relatively safe passage across the sparsely settled arid steppe by paying off the local chieftains. While most travelers were headed for the Mediterranean, some continued on around the Gulf of Issus to Tarsus (home of St. Paul); from there the route fed through the narrow Cilician Gates, in early times wide enough only for four men abreast, and either headed north

to modern Istanbul or joined the Persian Royal Road and headed west to the Anatolian coast. Mesopotamia—a name literally meaning "in the middle of rivers"—formed the main axis for both the Persian Royal Road and the Great Desert Route. But neither followed a fixed course. Except for those very few places where passes, like the Cilician Gates, or river crossings determined the main route, the route shifted according to changes in politics and climate.

Even the Mesopotamian rivers followed no clear course in the lowlands, changing their beds after serious floods or silting up. The Tigris and Euphrates formed a joint mouth—the Shatt el-Arab—at the Persian Gulf only in the 19th century. For many centuries before that, at least after a great flood in 629 A.D., the Tigris followed a more easterly course, and the Euphrates lay further west, flowing into "the Great Swamp" before entering the sea past Basra. The course of the rivers in ancient times is unclear.

The rivers were certainly better suited for local transport than for long-distance travel. For six months after the winter rains, both were often in flood, with the

Euphrates's whirlpools and the Tigris's wide loops making travel downstream dangerous and upstream almost impossible. (Floods were, indeed, so frequent that "The Deluge" was a frequent theme in Mesopotamian mythology; after the flood described in the Old Testament, Noah was said to have landed his boat on Mt. Ararat, in the Armenian hills near Lake Van.) The rest of the year, travel downstream was slow, as the rafts floated on inflated goatskins that moved at the speed of the sluggish current, and was difficult due to shoals and sandbars. Travel upstream was even slower, as "trackers" towed small vessels against the current, only occasionally helped by a little wind in a sail. Even more serious, travelers, especially merchants, often were preyed upon by the freebooting inhabitants of the river banks.

As a result, travelers throughout history generally preferred the main land routes: the Great Desert Route and the Persian Royal Road. Other routes were possible, cutting straight across the desert, but they were opened and maintained only with considerable effort, rarely having enough water to accommodate trains of hundreds or thousands of men and animals; in general, the cross-desert routes were used only by single fast-moving travelers, such as royal couriers.

Travel along the Great Desert Route and the Persian Royal Road began many thousands of years before recorded history, when feet were the main means of land transport and sledges the only vehicles. Trade along these two routes probably originated in the seasonal migrations of the early nomads and their herds, especially sheep and goats; packing items of interest, these migrants would barter goods from one region to another. Small, light-weight items of considerable value were preferred, like gems or gold. But bulkier goods were hauled, too, for Mesopotamia—so fertile for agriculture—was woefully short of some vital materials, especially wood, copper, and tin.

By the third millennium B.C., the wheel had been invented, and trade had advanced so far that many of the written materials found in the Sumerian city of Ur, on the lower Euphrates, were commercial records of transactions carried on under agreed-upon and standardized rules of conduct. By this time, wood was being imported to Sumer from India, the Zagros Mountains, and Lebanon, along the Great Desert Route and the Persian Royal Road. Copper was brought from Anatolia, the Zagros, and elsewhere; tin—so vital to the Bronze Age—was supplied from unknown sources, possibly from Syria and Armenia. Silver and gold, too, came from the north; and semi-precious stones like lapis lazuli and carnelian came in from the Iranian Plateau, over a route that would later become the famous Silk Road. In these very early times, the main beast of burden was the donkey (domesticated ass), with goods either loaded in a backpack or carried in a cart. (Domesticated camels made their appearance in the region only

later.) Travelers walked beside their animals, riding also being a practice of later vintage.

There was enough travel and trade in these early millennia for many large cities to have foreign quarters, where alien traders kept to themselves, following their own ways. That was the case with the family of one Terah, a Chaldaean who lived in Ur with his family, including his son Abraham. We know about this particular family because they were called to make a special journey in the early second millennium B.C. "Now the Lord had said unto Abraham, Get thee out of thy country, and from thy kindred, and from thy father's house, unto a land that I will show thee...and they went forth to go into the land of Canaan" (Genesis 12:1, 5). Following that call, Abraham, Terah, and their families moved through the heart of Mesopotamia. Although Abraham's northward route is uncertain, he probably passed through the then-capital Babylon, home of the fabled Tower of Babel, on the east bank of the Euphrates; through Ashur on the Tigris, where tradition has it he was strongly offended by the sexually oriented polytheistic religion; and through the provisioning city of Nineveh (now Mosul) on the upper Tigris. The Bible does indicate that Abraham's caravan arced generally westward through arid upper Mesopotamia to the still-existing city of Haran, where they wintered; there Terah died. After the new-year rains had passed, they headed south, probably crossing the upper Euphrates at the ancient ford of Carchemish (near modern Jerablus) and stopping at Aleppo. The southward route is uncertain, possibly running inland like the modern route, but perhaps following the more hospitable Bekaa Valley along its north-south axis before angling eastward again to the ancient city of Damascus. Then, after crossing the River Jordan, "Abraham passed through the land unto the place of Sichem (Schechem) unto the plain of Moreh" (Genesis 12: 6), and was in the land of Canaan. From this journey, dedicated to the primacy of just one God, Yahweh, sprang three of the world's great religions: Judaism, Christianity, and Islam. Sadly, with enmity among the three groups, Abraham's journey would be almost impossible 4,000 years later. In the early 2nd millennium B.C., however, such a journey was almost routine, and had been for at least a thousand years.

The Great Desert Route and the Persian Royal Road were also important migration routes. From the earliest times, waves of people pushed along these natural courses, seeking better pastures, searching for new lands to conquer, or simply being pushed aside by other, stronger peoples. The Sumerians themselves were immigrants, calling themselves "blackheads," in contrast to the native population. In the time of Abraham, Mesopotamia was inhabited mostly by Semitic peoples; in the hills and plateaus surrounding the Fertile Crescent dwelt Caucasians, who had originated from the Caucasus Mountains between the Black and Caspian seas. But several centuries

The Cilician Gates, only wide enough for four soldiers abreast in Alexander's time, still constricted traffic in the 20th century. (By Frances Jenkins Olcott, from The Bridge of Caravans, *W. A. Wilde, 1940)*

before Abraham, a different people began to press toward the region: Indo-Europeans from the Eurasian Steppe north of the seas. One group, the Hittites, crossed onto the Anatolian Plateau and swept down the Mesopotamian routes, sacking the main cities, even Babylon, before withdrawing to northern Syria and the Armenian hills. The other group, the Iranians, swung down from east of the Caspian Sea onto the Iranian plateau.

But travel was changing along the Mesopotamian routes. By 1300 B.C., humans began riding animals, not just using them to bear loads and to pull carts or chariots. At first, Mesopotamian travelers rode donkeys and horses, but by the 10th century B.C. they began to ride one-humped Arabian camels, which had been domesticated on the coast of the Persian Gulf. This camel (more than its two-humped Bactrian cousin) had prodigious stamina in the desert, and gradually became the dominant beast of burden in Mesopotamia, especially on the Great Desert Route. Donkeys, asses, and horses were still preferred on the Persian Royal Road, which was relatively cold and rocky. Wealthy and powerful people—and couriers on missions requiring speed—were privileged to ride camels and horses; most travelers, traders, and soldiers, however, continued to walk, using their "mounts" as pack animals.

Despite Indo-European inroads, Mesopotamia was still dominated by Semitic peoples; under Assyrian rule, they even expanded against both the Hittites and the Iranians. In the Anatolian mountains these conquerors often had to create their own routes, widening a person-wide track into a passage fit for an army. That was certainly the experience of the Assyrian King Sargon II in the eighth century B.C., as he pressed into the Armenian hills:

I set out on the difficult road to Mussassir—I crossed the upper Zeb; between the high mountains, the great heights, the inaccessible mountain peaks which defy description, between them there is no path for the foot-soldiers. Mighty waterfalls rush down and the noise of their fall is like thunder...[The mountains] strike terror into those who penetrate them, where no ruler has yet set foot and whose paths no Prince who lived before me has even seen. I felled the great tree trunks and had their tall tips cut through with the bronze axes; I improved the narrow pass, through which the foot-soldiers had to force their way, and enabled the army to move on. I caused my war chariots to be hauled up with ropes and I took up my position on horseback at the head of my army, and my warriors moved forward slowly and in single file with their horses...

Next to Mt. Everest, the Armenian highlands might look like relative molehills to the modern eye; but to Assyrians living at or near sea level, the 5,000–6,000 foot heights might well have seemed enormous, even granting Sargon's personal puffery.

Then, in around the seventh century B.C., the balance in the region began to change. The Iranians had resolved themselves into two main groups, the Medes and the Persians. The Medes, initially the stronger of the two, began to press their way across Asia Minor; the Assyrians even built a wall between the Euphrates and the Tigris to keep them out. The Medes stretched too far, however, and could not fully control other eager immigrants—Cimmerians and Scythians, with their archers on horse-back—arriving from across the Caucasus. As a result, the Persians gained the upper hand. After establishing a stronghold along the Persian Gulf, they gradually took over the lands that the Medes so tenuously held. Under Cyrus the Great, in the mid-sixth century B.C., the Persians developed the largest empire the world had yet known, extending from Central Asia through Mesopotamia, Egypt, and Anatolia into Greece, where their success earned them enmity but immortality in the classical records. Cyrus's successor, Darius, became famous in his own right, not simply as a ruler but as the creator of the Persian Royal Road.

Clearly recognizing that his vast empire required good communications if it was to survive, Darius laid out his famous post road, which allowed him to send messages from the Persian capital of Susa to the western terminus of Sardes in nine days, ten to the seaports of Smyrna or Ephesus. Even their Greek enemies were admiring; the historian Herodotus, writing in the fifth century B.C., effusively tells how this first-known "Pony Express" worked:

Now there is nothing mortal that accomplishes a course more swiftly than do these messengers, by the Persians' skilful contrivance. It is said that as many days as there are in the whole journey, so many are the men and horses that stand along the road, each horse and man at the interval of a day's journey; and these are stayed neither by snow nor rain nor heat nor darkness from accomplishing their appointed course with all speed. The first rider delivers his charge to the second, the second to the third, and thence it passes on from hand to hand, even as in the Greek torch-bearers' race in honour of Hephaestus.

So famous was this service, that its name—angareion—was a well-known word for "speed" even in the Middle Ages. Caravans, of course, took much longer to cover the route.

Although it incorporated some sections of earlier roads, the Persian Royal Road was unique in being a road built deliberately for long-distance purposes; like modern expressways, Darius's road often bypassed major cities, so that travelers were not deterred by city traffic—nor were the cities made vulnerable by a great, well-appointed road leading enemies up to their gates. Instead, accommodations—and protection—were provided along the road for travelers, as Herodotus notes:

Now the truth about this road is as follows. All along it are royal post-stations and very good inns, and it goes all the way through country that is inhabited and safe...This country is crossed by four navigable rivers, which you must pass over by ferry-boat...There are a hundred and eleven stages in all, and as many inns, on the way from Sardes to Susa...

The actual route of the Persian Royal Road is uncertain, but modern scholars believe that, in the time of Darius, it swung from Sardes on a wide arc over the Anatolian plateau, crossing the Halys River east of Ancyra (Ankara); then at Sivas it headed south to the Euphrates, cut east to the Tigris and south again to Nisibis, then across the Tigris, south to Arbela and Susa, and finally to the summer capital of Persepolis. From there a connecting route on the east side of the Zagros Mountains headed back northwest to Ecbatana (Hamadan) on the Silk Road. Later, however, the route changed. By the time of Herodotus, the most-used route across Anatolia cut through the Taurus Mountains down to the coastal plain near Tarsus, either through the Cilician Gates or by another nearby pass. Travelers then followed the outer curve of the Fertile Crescent across to the far side of the Tigris and down to southern Mesopotamia. Ferries and boat bridges—generally impermanent, given the rivers' tendencies toward flooding—were established at river crossing points where fording was impractical. For travelers on foot or by a slow caravan pace, Herodotus calculated (confirming estimates he had heard) that the trip would take about 90 days. Nor were the stations spaced at even distances; instead they were established with walkers in mind, further apart in easy country, and closer together—sometimes only 12 miles apart—where a day's journey through mountain passes, some of them hewn out of rock, would be difficult.

The Persian Royal Road was, first and foremost, a government road; soldiers and government servants made up a large part of its traffic. It did not eclipse the Great Desert Route, however. Indeed, Persian control of the Persian Gulf brought more trade from the East by land and sea, so the camel caravans on the Great Desert Route flourished. This period saw the rise of the great caravan cities of Syria, especially Aleppo, Hama, Homs, and Damascus, which were on the receiving end of the Incense Road from Arabia as well as of the routes from Mesopotamia. Phoenicians and Greeks added to the activity in the region by building up trade within the Mediterranean basin.

While various Cyruses and Dariuses were amassing fortunes in the richly appointed palaces of Persia, Greeks were planning to return to the Anatolian coast and to Syria. In the spring of 334 B.C., a 22-year-old Macedonian prince named Alexander left home to seek fame and fortune in the East. After winning his first battle over the Persians and regaining several Greek cities along the west coast of Anatolia, he crisscrossed along the Persian Royal Road from Sardes to Gordium. There, unable to untie the "Gordian Knot," he cut it, to signify that he would "rule all Asia." After wintering at Gordium, Alexander went to meet his enemy—King Darius and his Persian army— in the spring, winding down from the high Anatolian plateau south toward the coast. His choice of route was

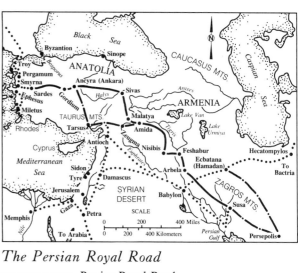

The Persian Royal Road

———————— Persian Royal Road
—·——·——·— Other Main Persian Routes
·········· Main Connecting Land Routes

standard, but dangerous, for it fed through the Cilician Gates; Xenophon had stressed that this defile was "impassible if obstructed by the enemy," who were wont to throw boulders down the cliffs at intruders. But apparently Alexander was fortunate and Darius ill-served, for a night attack easily breached the Persian defenses and Alexander's army emerged on the malarial plains of Tarsus.

The two armies finally met on the Mediterranean plain near where the Gulf of Issus pokes its finger into Asia Minor; the Greeks scattered the Persians into the hinterland, causing Darius to flee on horseback. The next two years Alexander spent in taking cities along the Mediterranean coast in Palestine and Egypt, founding there the most famous of many cities named after him, before turning his attention once again toward inland Asia.

In the spring of 331 B.C., Alexander marched north from Damascus along the Fertile Crescent and then east, crossing the wide upper Euphrates on a specially built pontoon bridge. Then, it being midsummer, he swung wide of the Syrian Desert, following the rim of the Anatolian Plateau on the line of the Persian Royal Road. At the upper Tigris the infantry crossed by wading between rows of cavalry, set to blunt the force of the fast-flowing current. Greeks and Persians met once again on the wide plain of Gaugamela, west of the Royal Road city of Arbela. Once again, Darius with all his numbers could not compete with Alexander's strategy and was forced to flee for his life into the Iranian hills.

With the Persian army routed, Alexander's passage for a time took on the character of a royal progress; through the fertile plains and rich cities of Mesopotamia, he took surrender after surrender, removing Persian overlords and installing his own instead. Not least among these cities was Babylon, where Alexander restored temples ruined by the Persians and directed that Greek plants be included in the famous Hanging Gardens. From Babylon, he proceeded toward the Persian capital of Susa, where surrender was also the order of the day. But there the easy conquests ended. In an astonishing winter campaign, Alexander then forced his way into the Zagros Mountains to the great Persian summer palace at Persepolis. Through these three-and-a-half years of campaigning, the Greeks had often been stunned by Persian magnificence, but never more so than at Persepolis, whose art and craftsmanship drew on the best from the Mesopotamian, Indian, and Greek worlds. It was not to last, however. A conscious decision to destroy a fortress that might support a Persian revival—or a wild impulse brought on by drunken excess—led Alexander to burn the extraordinary palace, destroying it forever. From there Alexander moved on toward Bactria and India, building an even larger empire than the Persian one, and returning to the region only to die, in 323 B.C. With him ended the Persian Royal Road as a distinct highway. Though climate and politics might, at some periods, cause travelers to prefer the northeasterly arc around Mesopotamia, the Great Desert Route—the shortcut between the Persian Gulf and the Mediterranean—now dominated the history of Mesopotamia.

Under the Greeks, trade and travel flourished even more than before, with goods from Syria passing along the Mesopotamian routes and beyond, even into India and Central Asia, possibly as far as China. To deal with the increasing traffic from the Spice Route, various cities in lower Mesopotamia developed as seaports, especially Charax on the Euphrates. Overland traders from India and Central Asia generally made their terminus Seleucia, which replaced Babylon as the main city on the west side of the Tigris; from there, goods were carried on to Syria. The Great Desert Route was the most direct path between these Persian Gulf seaports and the Syrian entrepôts, but rivalry among Alexander's successors sometimes made it unsafe. As a result, many travelers preferred the more northerly course of the Persian Royal Road, crossing the Tigris at Nineveh and the Euphrates at various points, notably Zeugma.

Drawing on the learning of the East—Mesopotamia, Egypt, India—the great Hellenic civilization flowered on the shores of Anatolia, but in Mesopotamia other powers emerged in the centuries after Alexander. The Parthians, an eastern Iranian people, overran both Persia and lower Mesopotamia, monopolizing the routes to the East and forbidding access to all foreigners. Meanwhile the Roman Empire expanded from the Mediterranean coast, taking most of Anatolia, upper Mesopotamia, and a wide swath from northern Syria down to Arabia and Egypt. With Parthia and Rome sparring for advantage, the Great Desert Route and the Persian Royal Road suffered; when the two powers finally reached an accommodation, just before the first century A.D., it was one that effectively cut out both routes, for they funneled traffic across the Syrian Desert through the oasis of Palmyra.

Occasional caravans had taken the cross-desert route since Biblical times, when the oasis was known as Tadmor, but the route was only made suitable for large-scale travel by the Roman builders. With their customary industry, they sank wells and established forts all along the way, guaranteeing Palmyra's safety, neutrality, and—though she was nominally within the Roman frontier—semi-autonomy. The Roman writer Pliny was quite clear about the importance of Palmyra:

> Palmyra is a city famous for its situation, for the richness of its soil and for its agreeable springs; its fields are surrounded on every side by a vast circuit of sand, and it is as it were isolated by Nature from the world, having a destiny of its own between the two mighty empires of Rome and Parthia, and at the first moment of a quarrel between them always attracting the attention of both sides.

These were the great early days of the Silk Road, when Rome and China traded across the vast Asian continent, with India completing the triangle. Trade goods from the East generally arrived first at Ctesiphon (opposite Seleucid on the Tigris) and crossed the Euphrates at the Parthian fortress city of Dura-Europos. Caravans then headed across the arid steppe called the Palmyrena, the northern Syrian Desert, to Palmyra itself. There hundreds of columns lined the road to the great city, many of them still standing today. Historian Michael Rostovtzeff avers:

> The caravan road which traversed Tadmor became in Palmyra one of the grandest avenues to be found in any town in Roman Syria. Hundreds of columns lined it, tetrapylons subdivided it, avenues intersected it, and balconies opened out upon it. Land lying close to the springs at which the caravans halted was wrested from the desert, built over with fine houses, and transformed into the busy centre round which the commercial and the political life of the town was developed...

In that center were the caravanserais, all-purpose quarters for traveling merchants, and a temple, probably old by Roman times, dedicated to the gods of the caravaners: Arsu and Azizu. At Palmyra, Roman caravans—often run by Syrian, Jewish, or Armenian merchants—divided, with some going southwest to Damascus and the Phoenician ports, but with most going northwest to Antioch, which became the main entrepôt for goods headed to Rome itself. This caravan trade made Palmyrenes both wealthy and powerful; many became respected Roman citizens. Some caravan leaders were so highly regarded that statues were erected in their honor, like that for Soados

Ruined Roman columns open to the sky are all that remain of Palmyra, once the crossroads of the Syrian Desert. (Iraq Petroleum Company)

Boliadou, who as caravan leader "in many and important circumstances" had "aided with princely generosity merchants, caravans, and...his fellow citizens." Palmyrene traders spread as far as Egypt, the Danube, and Rome, where they had a temple to their own special gods. Palmyra's dominance lasted into the third century A.D., when its queen, Zenobia, unwisely tried to break completely free of a weakening Rome; for this presumption, Rome not only defeated but destroyed the great caravan empire.

While the main route crossed through Palmyra, the other Mesopotamian routes were in decline. But the main routes in western Anatolia flourished under the Romans. From the upper Euphrates, between Dura-Europos and Zeugma, the Strata Diocletiana ran north, roughly along the Roman frontier, across the Anatolian Plateau to Trapezus (later Trebizond, now Trabzon) on the Black Sea. The other main route through Anatolia arced from the increasingly important city of Antioch around the Gulf of Issus to Tarsus, then threaded through the Cilician Gates, and forked. One branch—so important in Persian and Greek times—headed west to the valley of the Meander River, to the old ports of Smyrna, Ephesus, and Pergamum. The other headed north through Ancyra and across the narrow strait called the Bosporus (Ox Ford), which divides Europe from Asia. Under the Romans, these routes saw a continuous stream of traders and soldiers whose travels knit together the Roman Empire. These Anatolian routes also carried some of the earliest and most important Christian missionaries, among them St. Paul, born in Tarsus. While on his way to Damascus to arrest some Christians, as a Roman official, Paul was himself converted to Christianity; traveling throughout the region, to Antioch, to Damascus, to Jerusalem, and on the main commercial roads to Iconium (Konya), to Ephesus (where he wrote his famous epistles), and Troas (the region around once-great Troy), Paul carried Christianity, helping to lay the basis for the later Roman conversion.

No Roman embraced Christianity more fervently than the Emperor Constantine, for under him it became the state religion. He also changed the orientation of the region, in 330 A.D., by establishing his Eastern capital at Constantinople (formerly Byzantium) on the north side of the Bosporus. As the Western Roman Empire declined, the main roads that had once headed west toward Greece on the axis of the old Persian Royal Road were eclipsed—never to regain dominance—by the road heading north from Tarsus through Iconium (Konya) to Constantinople. Whatever fate befell its Western counterpart, the Byzantine Empire was still large and active. The Sassanid Empire, which replaced the Parthians in Iran and lower Mesopotamia, likewise realized the value of mutual trade. These two powers occasionally warred with one another, notably in the early seventh century, when the Sassanids even threatened Antioch and Constantinople itself; but trade and travel along the Mesopotamian routes was only temporarily unsettled.

Even the irruption of Islam in the seventh century disturbed traffic in the region for only a brief period. By the late eighth century, the Moslems had established their own capital—Baghdad—at the ancient waist of Mesopotamia. Before another century was out, they had spread north to Tarsus and around to the foothills of the Taurus Mountains, the Armenian highlands, and the Caucasus Mountains. With all of Syria and Mesopotamia under Moslem control, the Saracens—as the Europeans came to call them—built a flourishing commercial empire.

It was in this period, especially between the eighth and eleventh centuries, that the Moslem caravans on the Mesopotamian routes began to assume the form they would have until modern times. Merchants and other travelers would join together in caravans under an elected leader called a *bashi*, almost always an Arab sheik, a person of considerable importance in the community. He would oversee the two-to-three month preparations required by a large caravan; these included paying tribute (with all members of the caravan contributing) to the tribes along the proposed route to secure a safe journey. He would employ the services of a special guide, called a *daleel*, and couriers, who were called *basheers* when they bore good news and *nadeers* when the news was bad. Caravans also included a religious leader, called a *muezzin*; a *kahweji*, who made and distributed the coffee to all; and the *bayrakdar*, who carried the caravan's standard at the head of the line of march. Few Christians found their way onto the Mesopotamian routes in these early Moslem times, but Jewish traders—some from distant parts of Europe—would often join Moslem caravans, bribing the *bashi* to camp on the Sabbath, or hiring a special escort to guard them as they rode ahead before, or caught up

with the caravan after, their day of rest. For centuries, they preferred to take the longer Persian Royal Road route to avoid such lone travel in the desert. For other travelers, however, the Great Desert Route became the favored route, a true thoroughfare between the Mediterranean Sea and the Persian Gulf, as Moslem influence grew in both bodies of water.

The general course followed by the caravan was determined by the vital oases on the Great Desert Route, but the precise path varied, as described by the 18th century traveler William Beawes:

> I asked our conductor today by what means they directed their course; who told [me] there are beaten paths throughout the journey (which I afterwards found) wherein the guides constantly keep, and thereby [however] the caravan extraviales [wanders] on one side or other, they are sufficient to keep them in due course. But these paths are sometimes by gales of wind covered with sand, and then the caravan is obliged to halt, and the guides spread themselves, as far as not losing sight of the body will permit, to discover a tract [track]; or, not succeeding therein, wait till night and proceed by the stars. And one evening desiring them to shew me those they particularly observed, there was scarce an Arab but manifested such a knowledge of the heavens as I little expected, and that which they said was their chief director between Bassora and Aleppo, they pointed to, calling Judda [in Arabic, El Jady] and is the north star.
>
> We observed no order in our march, but spread over the waste in different figures; which being so large, the caravan affords a diverting prospect, especially the objects being so various, and to us strange. And one reason for their spreading I suppose may be on account of the camels, who feed as they travel, having absolutely no other provision than they meet with in the way, which hitherto has been only a small sort of farzbush, and that in no great plenty...

The Moslems also continued the postal traditions set by the Persians and carried on by the Greeks, the Romans, and the Byzantines. The Roman *veredus*, which referred first to the post animal and later to the courier and finally the postal system itself, was transformed into the Moslem *berid*. In the eighth century, the Moslems set up their *berid* along the Persian Royal Road route from Baghdad, arcing through Mosul and Rakka to Aleppo. By the ninth century the *berid* had joined with a like system based in Damascus to form a unified postal service which operated with such efficiency through the 11th century that the *Sahib el-Berid*, the chief of the postal system, became—in effect—overseer of all provincial officials under the caliph's control.

Communications along the Great Desert Route were so important that the Moslems even established a pigeon post between the two ends, the Euphrates port of Basra and the Mediterranean port of Iskanderun (known to the West as Alexandretta), which served Aleppo and Antioch. Pigeon towers were established approximately every 50 miles along the route, so that, with pigeon relays, a message might reach from one end to the other in a few days, rather than the tens of days a caravan might take. This pigeon post operated for 1,000 years, until the mid-18th century, when it was closed down for unknown reasons (rumor has it because a pigeon died or was killed and a message fell into the wrong hands). Basra and Iskanderun carrier pigeons were famous throughout the Western world, and merchant caravans on the Great Desert Route often carried homing pigeons with them, releasing them en route to Aleppo or Basra, to indicate their location and warn others of any trouble on the road.

In the early 11th century, travel in the region was disrupted as Seljuk Turks pressed from Iran into Mesopotamia. The Byzantine army only with difficulty held them at the Taurus Mountains, and many Armenians emigrated southwest from their homeland around the Araxes River and Lake Van—only to find themselves surrounded as the Seljuk Turks swept on to take all of Anatolia, save the coastal strip opposite Constantinople.

The weakening of the Byzantine Empire, bastion of Christianity in western Asia, and the capture of Jerusalem by the Turks in 1076 brought European Christians into the Near East in force. Christians who had come overland through Constantinople as pilgrims found that the Turks now barred their access to Christian shrines. In the late 11th century armies of Crusaders came overland, dedicated to wresting the Christian holy places from the Seljuk infidels. In previous centuries, the Byzantine Empire had kept up the roads in Anatolia for their own postal system and trading caravans; but 20 years of battle with the Seljuks had left their highways in a shambles. Steven Runciman, chronicler of the Crusades, describes the conditions the Crusaders found as they crossed from Constantinople toward Antioch:

It was now early October, and the autumn rains had begun. The road over the Anti-Taurus was in appalling disrepair; and for miles there was only a muddy path leading up steep inclines and skirting precipices. Horse after horse slipped and fell over the edge; whole lines of baggage animals, roped together, dragged each other down into the abyss. No one dared to ride. The knights, struggling on foot under their heavy accoutrements, eagerly tried to sell their arms to more lightly equipped men, or threw them away in disrepair. The mountains seemed accursed...

The Crusaders and the Byzantine army regained parts of Anatolia and established various Christian states along the Mediterranean, one centered on Antioch. Jewish merchants soon found themselves acting as middlemen on the Great Desert Route, transferring Eastern goods from Moslems to the Christian Italians—Venetians, Genoans, and Pisans—who increasingly handled trade on the Mediterranean.

But the fragmented Near East soon found itself facing a powerful united force: the Mongols. These Central Asian invaders shocked the Moslem world by sacking the great city of Baghdad in 1258. After that, the center of Moslem power shifted to Cairo, while the Mongols expanded their hold on the Eurasian continent from Mesopotamia across to China. These were centuries of terrible turmoil on the Great Desert Route and the Persian Royal Road, with travel and trade near their lowest point since it had first begun.

But the years that followed were quite a different matter. The Mongols, once in power, established peace and free travel in their domain. Moslem traders once again crossed on the Mesopotamian routes to Basra and the Spice Route to the East, while others continued overland toward China. This was, indeed, a unique time in human history, for only under the Mongols—from the mid-13th to the mid-14th centuries—were individuals able to travel all across Central Asia on the great Silk Road. In this period, the Great Desert Route and the Persian Royal Road became, to some extent, extensions of that fabled route. In western Asia one branch of the Silk Road headed to the Mediterranean via the revived city of Baghdad, while the other more heavily used branch headed northwest through the Armenian hills to the city of Trebizond on the Black Sea or to Constantinople.

But when the Mongols lost control of Asia in the late 14th century, the Great Desert Route once again became the preferred highway, being better protected from the turbulence of the warring powers to the east. Venetians, Pisans, Catalans from Barcelona, and Genoans established warehouses called factories in the main Syrian cities, including Aleppo, Damascus, and the seaports of Beirut and Tripoli.

In the 15th century came the last of the great Central Asian invaders: the Ottoman Turks. Moving swiftly across Anatolia, they captured Constantinople—the only remaining stronghold of the once-powerful Byzantine Empire—in 1453, and then spread southward along the Mediterranean coast. While the Ottomans were busy building the empire that would, by 1600, reach to Belgrade, Odessa, Basra, Mecca, Cairo, and Algiers, trade with Europe withered. The effect was earth-shaking: Europeans, cut off from ready access to Eastern goods, decided to seek new routes to the East. In the process they discovered the Americas, and the Portuguese sailed around Africa to the Indian Ocean. For a time in the 16th century, transcontinental trade on the Great Desert Route was practically nonexistent. But tiny Portugal could not alone handle all the Eastern trade, and Moslems soon resumed sea trade to Basra.

During the Mongol period, traders from Central Asia would often pick up the route of the old Persian Royal Road, passing through Armenian towns like this one to the Black Sea. (From Livre des Merveilles, *1375, MS. Fr. 2810, f. 7, Bibliothèque Nationale)*

As trade revived, European Christians began to join Moslems and Jews on the Great Desert Route. Their numbers were few, at first, and they were generally not traders but couriers sent on the lone and dangerous journey across the Syrian Desert. Among the Europeans, the Portuguese initiated this overland courier service for important communications with the home country, because the turnaround time on the Cape of Good Hope Route around Africa could be as long as 24 months.

The Ottoman Turks developed their own courier service to replace the older *berid*. Their multilevel system used local couriers to serve provincial needs and imperial services to provide communications between their capital, Constantinople, and the major cities — and to handle most of the commercial business of the empire. In addition, the Turks had a special corps of dispatch-bearers, called *tatars* (misspelled *tartars* by Europeans); these carried important government communications, edicts, and bullion. These *tatars* were given strict deadlines and were expected to press on with all due speed, picking up fresh horses at relay stations: reports of European observers indicate that *tatars* often covered the 1,400–1,500 mile distance between Baghdad and Constantinople in 12–13 days. *Tatars* could also, by special permit, be used to carry urgent private messages, when they were not otherwise engaged on government business. The Ottomans continued or revived the pigeon post as well, breeding special homing pigeons specifically for government use; some 19th century Europeans even noted that the pigeon post,

before it was discontinued, was more popular than the courier services in Mesopotamia.

In the early 1600's, Europeans began to build new empires in the East. Most used the Cape of Good Hope Route, establishing sea-supported colonies. But others established themselves on the east Mediterranean coast, at the head of the overland routes from the East. The British, for example, set up the Levant Company in 1605, with consuls appointed to represent member merchants in many Near Eastern cities, among them Aleppo, Tripoli, Smyrna, and Constantinople. With their interests in India continually growing, the British also established their own overland courier system. While the Portuguese and Venetians had favored the easterly Baghdad-to-Aleppo route, the British followed the Great Desert Route between Basra and Aleppo; in the early 17th century, mail packets were sent via this route in duplicate, for surety. European traders and travelers in this period also began crossing on the Great Desert Route from Aleppo to Basra each year, in April and September, with the large merchant *kafilas* — an Arabic word for "companies of people and camels."

Unfortunately, the Ottoman Turks exacted so much official tribute and bribes that the European merchants found trade unprofitable, even as compared with the long and expensive sea voyage that was the main alternative for Eastern goods. Worse than that, the overland routes were unsafe; desert Arabs, resenting Turkish domination, periodically irrupted from out of the Syrian Desert, while the Turks were also troubled by occasional rebellions of *pashas* in major cities, such as Aleppo, Baghdad, and Basra. The overland routes became so dangerous that for almost a century—between 1663 and 1745—no Europeans are known to have taken them; one group of Europeans did venture into the Syrian Desert and were stunned to discover, in the midst of the wasteland, the ruins of the once-great city of Palmyra.

By the 1740's, turbulence in the region had died down and Europeans once again ventured to use the Great Desert Route as a shortcut to the East. These were mostly British and French travelers, whose empires had grown considerably in the previous century. Like the Portuguese before them, the English and French sent special couriers along the Great Desert Route when circumstances demanded it. But many individuals—merchants and adventurers—also made the overland crossing, generally following the Great Desert Route between Aleppo and Basra, where they took ships for Persia and India. Merchants sometimes took a more easterly route, from Aleppo to Mosul and down the Tigris to Baghdad and Basra, partly following the axis of the old Persian Royal Road; but that had its disadvantages for travelers desiring speed and wishing to save money. William Beawes, traveling on the Great Desert Route in 1745, described the problems presented by the alternate route:

This is the common route of merchants and travellers, but has these inconveniences. Firstly, the journey to Mosul is often tedious, the Caravan loitering at places on the road, either to procure the vent of merchandize, and fresh freight, or to avoid the Gordeens [Kurds] who frequently plunder or oblige them to the expence of a guard where the passes are dangerous. Secondly, the water carriages from Mosul to Bagdat being only supported by skins swelled by the induction of air, they sometimes burst and several accidents have happened.

On this route, also, travelers faced "the impertinence of Turkish officers," and tolls and duties levied by each city on the way.

Another alternative was to take a four-day journey overland from Aleppo to the Euphrates, and take a boat downstream to Basra; Beawes was informed that the water passage would take about 20 days and "would be the pleasantest and most commodious of any" except for one problem:

...both merchants and travelers are deterred from steering this course, being liable everywhere to impositions and in some places to being plundered, tho' I've known Armenians that had gone that way, without any such grievous impediments, and who gave me a different character of these people...

As a result, in this period, most travelers still preferred the Great Desert Route. It was not totally secure, of course. Caravans had to pay tolls to the various sheiks en route; even so, they often met with wild bands of brigands, hiring extra guards for protection. Strangers also sometimes faced extortion from the *bashi* himself, once underway.

The caravans themselves were often very large, sometimes having as many as 2,000 camels, like the one Beawes joined:

Our caravan is reckoned large, consisting of two thousand odd hundred camels, of which about four hundred are loaded with merchandize, and near as many more with passengers and baggage, the rest mounted by the Arabs themselves or empty for want of freight, the returns from Aleppo being considerable compared to what is carried from Bassora [Basra]; and what likewise renders the caravan numerous, independent of merchants, are the armed Arabs in case of necessity. The Shauks [Sheiks] and their attendants and many poor Arabs join the caravans from Bassora with one, two or three camels, either loaded with things of small import to barter at Aleppo, or in hopes the greater cameleers may favour them with some freight back again. We have several horses and mules in the caravan which are carried for sale, being cheap in Aleppo and afford a good profit at Bassora; but they arrive there such skeletons that many months are necessary to [recover] them, especially those that have performed the journey mounted...

Travelers on the Great Desert Route had to make considerable preparations, renting camels and, if desired, litters in which to ride; hiring servants to care for the camels and prepare the food; and paying for camels to carry water in skins, which were refilled, when possible, at oases en route. The main food stores carried were rice, bread, coffee, and ghee (boiled butter); Europeans sometimes carried alcoholic drinks, but Moslems generally did not, it being forbidden by their religion. Beyond that, herds would find forage along the route, and humans would hunt fresh game, especially gazelles, hares, and birds; caravan animals that weakened or died were also immediately slaughtered and eaten, including camels and donkeys. Other animals were found along the way as well, including wolves, foxes, tigers, and lions (even as late as the mid-19th century). Travelers carried tents for themselves and their servants; Europeans also often carried cots, which Beawes said "we made to stand a more than ordinary distance from the ground, as a security from the snakes and scorpions that are common it seems in the desert." The tents were best pitched "somewhat apart from and to windward of the rest of the caravans, as else at the time of cooking you are molested with smoke and also with dust from the camels continually rambling about you."

Many travelers on the Great Desert Route stopped at Meshed Ali, or Najaf, tomb of the founder of the Moslem Shi'a sect. (From Carruthers, The Desert Route to India)

Dust on the road was also a problem, as another European traveler, Bartholomew Plaisted, described in 1750:

> ...the north-west wind...blows directly in your face, and is as violent as if it came from a glass furnace, and penetrates into your very lungs...The Arabs turn a part of their turbant before their mouth and nostrils, by which they find a small alleviation. It likewise greatly affects the eyes; which perhaps might be remedied by green glass, worn like spectacles, and tied behind the head to keep them fast...

The pattern of the day varied with the size of the caravan and the decisions of the all-powerful *bashi*. For Beawes's caravan, the day shaped up this way:

> The order for diet in the caravan is coffee in the morning before mounting; then when they stop about noon for an hour coffee again and what else any has ready drest; in the evening it is pleasant for anyone to observe soon after encamping there appears almost as many fires as men and all hands set to preparing...what...their stores may afford...

The day would often last for 12 or 13 hours, starting around dawn and being extended if an oasis was found to have insufficient water for the thousands of men and animals. Camels were generally unloaded at the midday break, though Beawes noted, "I think to little purpose, for in half an hour we were again under way." On occasion the schedule was determined by different considerations, as Beawes found:

> Today being the Jews Sabbath, they prevailed on the Caravan Bashi with (30) thirty dollars not to proceed, which seems a trifling sum to detain so large a company; but he commands and it may be supposed that nobody bid against him.

The *bashi* made all major decisions concerning the conduct of the caravan. Beawes noted:

> This conductor in chief is always a man of extraordinary note amongst the Desert Arabs in general...and his business is to protect the caravan from being molested by any tribe we may meet in our way, for which he receives (a certain sum) per load. But altho' this man is principally necessary for the security of the caravan, he is not absolutely sufficient, for we have also several others of different tribes, who likewise receive a gratuity for their protection, and this expense amounts to the merchants in the whole, from Aleppo to Bassora, to about (14) fourteen dollars each load...

123

Approaching Antioch from Aleppo, the Great Desert Route passed through protective coastal mountains. (From Carruthers, The Desert Route to India)

What Beawes here speaks of is the *rafeek* system. When the *bashi* made appropriate payments to the ruling sheik of a locality en route, the sheik sent along with the caravan a member of the tribe, called a *rafeek,* who was—in effect—a human passport. Riding at the front of the caravan and carrying his tribal banner, he was a personalized warning to all that the caravan should not be interfered with by any who respected the sheik. With the elaborate interconnections and alliances formed by the Arabian tribes for the purposes of co-existence, this *rafeek* system worked rather well in settled times, lessening the need for hundreds of expensive armed guards. But in turbulent times, especially when tribes from Arabia intruded into the Syrian Desert, the system broke down, and the caravan's safety had to be guaranteed by armed escort, sometimes drawn from the local territory it was passing through. These soldiers would, Bartholomew Plaisted noted, "keep about the middle with a small flag" if no danger seemed imminent, "but if there is any alarms they divide themselves, part on one side and part on the other. When the caravan comes near a hill, or any suspicious place, they send out scouts to reconnoitre the road, and see whether any men lie in ambush ahead."

While the land around Aleppo was hilly and uneven, a caravan en route to Basra soon found itself on "a plain unbounded almost every way by anything but the horizon." Nor was much relief offered by the upper Euphrates, although Beawes thought the river there nearly as broad as the Thames at London: "we expected to have been regaled with verdure and those pleasant scenes that generally such copious rivers produce; but here the bounty of nature finds no returns...for since our leaving Aleppo we have not had such a wretched prospect." Further along, part of the caravan turned east toward Baghdad, generally crossing the Euphrates at Anna, while the rest continued for Basra. Melons, dates, and fresh meats were occasionally to be had from villages along the route; travelers sometimes spent the night in the charity-supported caravanserais or profit-making khans in the villages, but were not always more comfortable than out on the desert. In fact, though Beawes found the heat of the day fatiguing, when camping at night under the stars, he found "the night so cool that a quilt double was scarce sufficient to keep me warm"; by contrast, he complained of the heat when he spent the night in a town. Further to the southeast, the shrubs became more varied and plentiful, and the country somewhat more interesting. When water was plentiful, caravans (especially small ones, which needed less) often cut straight across the desert; others stayed nearer the inner curve of the Fertile Crescent, to be sure of refreshment, avoiding both the cities and hazard from the tribes that frequented the Syrian Desert. Even so, Arabs straggling in from the desert sometimes caused the alarm to be raised in the night; and the appearance of nomadic Arabs would occasion "our caravan to travel close and with...arms in readiness, being...necessary, tho' the others were professedly friends." The last part of the journey, Beawes—like many others—found "the worst part of all the journey." From Meshed Ali, tomb of Mohammed's nephew and a sacred Shi'a site, to Basra:

> ...the country [was] exceeding bare and sandy; the weather hotter and water tho' frequent very brackish, and foul in most places, which often disorder our bowels and occasion severe sickness of the stomach...

For large merchant *kafilas* the whole trip between Aleppo and Basra—750–800 miles—took anywhere from 30 to 70 days, depending on conditions on the road and the precise route taken; the northeasterly route through Mosul averaged 55–60 days, while the shorter desert route from Baghdad to Aleppo generally took 25–35 days.

What travelers found in Basra depended largely on the time of the year, for—as in centuries past—the city came fully alive only in those months when the monsoons brought Spice Route ships up the Persian Gulf. Large merchant caravans to and from Basra would be timed accordingly. But such arrangements were always very general and fluid, as Bartholomew Plaisted found when he arrived from the East in 1750:

> On the 20th of April I landed at Busserah, and was informed that there was a caravan ready to set out in fifteen or twenty days, which I was advised by everyone to wait for; but in this they were deceived, and consequently I was so too...Here I was obliged to abide fifty-three days...

Certainly that delay did not encourage Plaisted to take a rosy view of the city, for he continues:

> ...I had a sufficient opportunity to make some remarks upon the place, if there had been anything worth observation; for though this city is large it has the meanest aspect and is the worst built of any I ever saw. The houses are generally two stories high, flat on the top, and constructed with bricks burnt in the sun, but in such a clumsy manner that the Governor's own house was no better than a dog-hole. There is not the least appearance of architecture in any part of the town except in the mosques, and they lean in such a manner that they seem ready to tumble down...

Traveling in the opposite direction from Basra, those who had little time or money to spare always preferred the Great Desert Route. But large caravans heading for Aleppo left only twice a year, waiting until the expected store of goods and people had arrived with the trade winds. Smaller caravans might cross at any time of the year, except that the summer would bring a hot wind, full of fine desert dust, which could suffocate the unwary. Occasional caravans left for Aleppo consisting solely of unloaded camels for sale; these moved much faster than the loaded caravans and took with them only travelers willing to travel light, often with only what they could carry in their saddlebags. The camel traders, returning to Basra with ready cash, generally traveled with the large merchant caravans for safety. Lone travelers, including specially deputed couriers, also made the desert crossing, but only when necessary; more than one such venturer arrived in a Mesopotamian city wearing only a newspaper, everything—including the shirt off his back—having been stolen. In the off months, merchants wishing the security of a large caravan would generally head from Basra for Baghdad, from which caravans left for Aleppo more frequently. If none were in the offing, travelers could follow the Tigris northwest to Mosul.

Either way, all roads led to Aleppo. The city itself, better known to the Arabs as Haleb, was "built on eight small hills or eminences, on the highest of which the castle is erected." Bartholomew Plaisted continued: "It is incompassed by an old wall not a little decayed, and a broad ditch, now in most places turned into gardens. It is about three miles and a half in circumference, but with the suburbs eight." From Aleppo's fertile plain, travelers descended to Antioch, which Plaisted found "not above a sixth part so large as it formerly was, which appeared from the ruins of the old walls, which run up a steep hill, and when they have reached the top, advance along, descending down again on the other side. But there are now few traces of its former grandeur."

From Antioch, travelers threaded through the Beilan Pass, summer retreat of officials from the sultry coast. There Plaisted found the people in all the villages "extremely civil and obliging, particularly to Europeans"; this was not surprising, for European Christians had long been established there. From Beilan and its surrounding chain of coastal mountains, the road descended finally to the main seaport of Alexandretta (Iskanderun) for goods and people headed to Europe. The city being a "sickly place," however, most travelers preferred to wait for their ships in Antioch or Beilan, or even Aleppo, being informed of marine arrivals by pigeon post, which operated into the 19th century. *Tatars* might also be employed, for they still operated from the Turkish capital at Constantinople, following routes through the major cities, where their business was conducted and where post-stations were provided. Indeed, to supplement their fast-riding dromedary post, which took a shortcut over the Syrian Desert, the British continued to send duplicate packets of important papers by *tatar* along the Baghdad-Aleppo route.

As British interests developed in Egypt, however, the overland route at Suez gradually eclipsed the Great Desert Route. The two competed through the mid-19th century, but regular steamship connections were established at Suez, making it the favored choice. Then, with the opening of the Suez Canal in 1869, the question was irrevocably decided against the Great Desert Route. The *tatars* continued to operate on the route, known to the Arabs as Darb es-Sa'i (Road of the Courier), until the Turks lost control of the region in World War I, but its days as a great international passageway were over.

European technology, which had favored Suez, also for a time revived the northeasterly route, with the dream of a Berlin-to-Baghdad Railway. In the 1830's, the British had for a time been interested in a railroad from the revived port of Smyrna, partly along the line of the old Persian Royal Road, but the success of Suez squashed that. The Germans, entering the imperial lists, then broached the idea of a railroad from Berlin to Constantinople and over the Anatolian Plateau to Baghdad. In 1889, the Anatolian Railway was begun, heading through Ancyra and Konya and then, after disputes over the routes had been resolved, on to Aleppo by 1908; meanwhile a southern section was built from Baghdad to north of Mosul. Work continued during World War I, with Germany aiding her ally, Turkey, but the end of the war also saw the end of the Ottoman Empire. Although the railway connections were later completed, the route served only local purposes, never fulfilling its promise as a long-distance track, for the Near East fractured into a cluster of warring, fiercely nationalistic states.

What spelled doom for the railway also spelled doom for the long-distance roads. Roads that had seen the passage of countless international travelers, from long before the time of Abraham, came to have closed borders. But the old ways were passing in any case. A new technological marvel—the automobile—was about to transform the life of the region. Automotive transport had been used on the Great Desert Route during World War I; after the war, British and later American experts led the search for oil to fuel the greedy monsters. Their success and the rapidly increasing world reliance on oil-fueled machinery transformed the region. The rich in the region soon traded in camels for cars. And, as the 20th century advanced, the very wealthy abandoned the road altogether for the air; airplanes at least had the advantage of bypassing the patrolled borders—sometimes armed frontiers—that have continued to hinder international crossings. For the rest, the great international road system fell into disrepair, used for local purposes by ramshackle vehicles and by the still-present camels in the desert and donkeys in the mountains. To follow Abraham's or Alexander's path today would require a particularly hardy, persistent, and intrepid traveler, visas being very difficult to arrange over the various borders, including Iran, Iraq, Syria, and Turkey. But even within one of these countries, travel is not for the weak of heart; Evelyn Lyle describes a bus trip in the mid-1960's on what had been an old main route heading south, down from the 5,000-foot high Anatolian Plateau:

> The road worsened as we climbed into valleys filled with giant boulders often higher than the bus itself. Once or twice the bus squeezed through between rocks towering above it, with merely a fraction of an inch to spare; it was easy to believe that this was the original caravan road of the past few thousand years.

Unfortunately, most interior portions of Anatolia and Mesopotamia are no longer geared for catering to long-distance travelers. The traveler may find little food and water beyond that provided by impromptu tent restaurants set up along the way, and must often be prepared to sleep in or near the bus or truck for, unlike in centuries past, no caravanserais or khans await the traveler at the end of each day's journey.

Selective Bibliography

Carruthers, Douglas, ed. *The Desert Route to India: Being the Journals of Four Travellers by the Great Desert Caravan Between Aleppo and Basra, 1745–1751* (London: Hakluyt Society, 1929). Series II, Vol. LXIII. Classic travel accounts.

Grant, Christina Phelps. *The Syrian Desert: Caravans, Travel and Exploration* (New York: Macmillan, 1938). An extremely useful survey from earliest to modern times.

Hitti, Philip K. *The Near East in History: A 5000 Year Story* (Princeton, New Jersey: D. Van Nostrand, 1961). A general view of the region.

Hoskins, Halford Lancaster. *British Routes to India* (New York: Octagon Books, 1966; reprint of 1928 edition). Contains several sections on the Great Desert Route.

Lyle, Evelyn. *The Search for the Royal Road* (London: Vision, 1966). A popular account of a modern journey along the Persian Royal Road.

Rostovtzeff, M. *Caravan Cities* (Oxford: Clarendon, 1932). Includes an historical survey of the caravan trade, and accounts of visits to ruined cities.

Stark, Freya. *Alexander's Path: From Caria to Cilicia* (New York: Harcourt, Brace: 1958). Memoirs of modern travels in Anatolia.

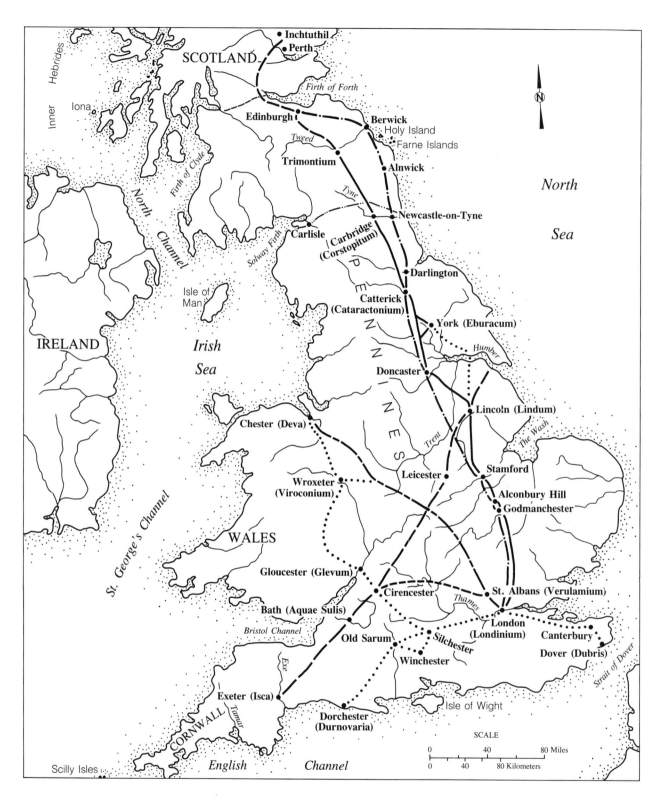

The Great North Road

——————— Main Roman North Road (Ermine Street)	– – – – – Roman Akeman Street
– – – – – Route Uncertain	— – — – Fosse Way
—·—·— Modern Great North Road	·········· Main Connecting Roads
– – – – – Roman Watling Street	—··—··— Hadrian's Wall
	——————— Antonine Wall

The Great North Road

The wind was a torrent of darkness among
    the gusty trees,
The moon was a ghostly galleon tossed upon
    cloudy seas,
The road was a ribbon of moonlight over the
    purple moor,
And the highwayman came riding—
    Riding—   riding—
The highwayman came riding, up to the old
    inn-door.

The highwayman is gone now; indeed, he had been gone for more than half a century when Alfred Noyes recreated him in 1906. By then, the great stagecoach post roads of England, Scotland, Wales, and Cornwall had long since been overtaken by the railroad, and the motorways they would become had already begun to develop. But the memory remains still, as does the aura of romance that has always surrounded the great days of coaching in England. The inn is likely to still be there, for there are many in Great Britain who continue to agree with Samuel Johnson that:

...there is nothing which has yet been contrived by man, by which so much happiness is produced as by a good inn or tavern.

And the roads remain, the coaching roads of Britain, so many of them Roman roads almost 2,000 years ago. The greatest of them all is the road known in Roman times as Ermine Street, then the Old North Road, and since coaching days as the Great North Road. From the great crossroads city of London, this highway pushes northward across the sodden clays of the Midlands and up along the eastern side of the island, past Lincoln, past York and the moors of Yorkshire, across the Humber, the Tyne, and the Tweed to Edinburgh, twining itself into the fabric of the country it has bound together for two millennia.

In the summer of 55 B.C., Julius Caesar and two Roman legions landed at Dover. It was more a reconnaissance in force than an invasion. After successfully warring with the Britons, the Romans retired back across the English Channel to Gaul. Caesar returned the next year with five legions, again to fight and win but not to stay. The Roman conquest of Britain was to come almost a century later.

In the summer of 43 A.D., the Emperor Claudius carried through the planned Roman invasion of Britain, by this time able to draw his resources from a well-established Roman empire that had, by then, been in possession of much of Western Europe for a hundred years. He brought in three legions from the Rhine, one from the Danube, added cavalry and auxiliaries, and held camels and elephants in reserve at his headquarters at Lyon. Landing at several Channel coast points, the Romans drove to and united at Canterbury; then, following a well-established trackway, they moved inland. After defeating the Britons on the Medway, east of London, they took the prime settlement they called Londinium, astride

Aerial photographs still show the old line of Roman Ermine Street, running straight across the field, while the more modern Great North Road curves in from the right near Stamford. (British Air Ministry)

the Thames River. Following pathways that had been laid down by the Celts (themselves invaders from the mainland some centuries before) and their predecessors and carving new routes when necessary, the Romans quickly began building the network of military centers and roads that would enable them to take and hold all of what is now England for three and a half centuries.

During the next three decades, they expanded to control all of southeastern England. Two main roads crisscrossed this region. Watling Street ran northwest from London, eventually crossing all the way to Chester (Deva), on the Irish Sea; Fosse Way, with a protective line of forts, angled from Exeter (Isca), in Cornwall, northeast of Lincoln (Lindum) and on to the Humber estuary. Fosse Way, like all major Roman roads, was elevated, with ditches to carry off water, and itself therefore functioned to some extent as a long fortified wall, shielding the conquered portions of Britain from attack. In the same period, the Romans also built the southern portion of Ermine Street from London to their garrison town of Lincoln. It was along Ermine Street that they moved north, starting in 71 A.D.; no longer following the beaten path, they cut a new road, making Ermine Street their main military highway as they completed their British conquests.

The Great North Road the Romans built crossed the Thames and went through Bishopsgate and Tottenham to Braughing. Here the 20-foot-wide main road traversed

Alconbury Hill and went on to Godmanchester, where it became a four-foot-high, 42-foot-wide elevated road through Stamford and on to Lincoln. To Stamford, it generally paralleled today's A-1 highway. At Lincoln, the road went on the Humber estuary, which was crossed by ferry, and then on to York (Eburacum). Later, the road was shifted further inland, going through Doncaster to York, again generally paralleling today's A-1.

In 80 A.D., the Romans under Agricola pushed the road even further north, inland through Catterick (Cataractonium) and Carbridge (Corstopitum), crossing the Tyne and reaching as far north as the Tweed. Smaller Roman roads went even further north, beyond Edinburgh and the Firth of Forth, to the outpost of Inchtuthil.

It was from here that Agricola went north in 83 A.D. to meet the main Caledonian army in the Highlands on the field of Mons Graupius. The Roman invaders won, but the battlefield speech Tacitus attributes to Calgacus, the Caledonian leader, foreshadowed the centuries of northern resistance that would follow. Of the free people of the north facing Roman tyranny, Calgacus said:

> We, the choicest flowers of Britain...kept even our eyes free from the defilement of tyranny. We, the last men on earth, the last of the free, have been shielded until today by the very remoteness and the seclusion for which we are famed...But today the boundary of Britain is exposed; beyond us lies no nation, nothing but waves and rocks and the Romans...

Of the "peace" that Rome imposed on its conquered peoples, he said bluntly: "They create a desolation, and call it peace."

Throughout Roman times, Ermine Street—the Great North Road—was to be primarily a military road, and especially so in its northern portions. War chariots were more common than carts on the rough dangerous moorlands. Not surprisingly, Rome did not hold the north country for very long. In 142 A.D., the Romans built the 37-mile-long Antonine Wall, from the Firth of Forth to the Clyde, their road only effectively running that far. Later in the same century, they were obliged to pull back to Hadrian's 71-mile-long wall across Britain from Newcastle-upon-Tyne to Carlisle, built 20 years earlier. This would, for centuries, be the northern border of Roman Britain—and the end of their Great North Road.

By the late fourth century A.D., Roman power was waning. Starting in 367 A.D., Pictish raiders came over Hadrian's Wall and in that period began to come by sea as well. After the first decade of the fifth century, no more troops and supplies came from Rome, and Roman rule began to disintegrate, a process essentially completed by the end of the century. This began the period of the Saxon immigrations and the breaking up of what had been Roman Britain into many small states. Maintenance and long-distance use of the Roman road system was at an end, and Britain would not have as good a system of roads for over a thousand years.

The Anglo-Saxon England that evolved from the sixth century through the eighth century had little use for the Great North Road and the other Roman roads. Nor did the Danes who followed. From the end of Roman rule to the Norman Conquest in 1066, no single power really held and administered England, and no one seriously tried to knit England together, as the Romans had done with their roads and military bases. A late ninth century map shows the Great North Road passing through Wessex, East Anglia, Danish Mercia, York, Northumberland, and Scotland, all themselves cut up into smaller, often nearly independent principalities.

With the Conquest, the outlines of what would become modern England began to emerge, and with it new reason for the development of the high road north to Scotland. As the country gradually became unified, trade began to flow more freely, and in the 11th and 12th centuries, the great English fairs developed at Stourbridge, St. Ives, Winchester, and scores of other market towns throughout the country. For eight centuries, British

drovers took their livestock to market at such fairs and later into the cities as well, traveling along a web of "green roads" to the market towns.

Pilgrims also swelled the traffic on the road. Throughout the medieval period, the institution of the religious pilgrimage grew. After the mass Saxon conversions to Christianity of the seventh and eighth centuries, pilgrimages to Christian shrines at home and abroad became increasingly common. Historian J. J. Jusserand tells us that by late medieval times, the roads were thronged with religious travelers:

Pilgrimages were incessant; they were made to fulfil a vow as in cases of illness or of great peril, or in expiation of sins. Confessors frequently gave the going on a pilgrimage as penance, and sometimes ordered that the traveler should go barefoot or in his shirt. "Commune penaunce," says Chaucer's parson in his great sermon, speaking of atonement which must be public, "commune" because the sin has been public too, "is that prestes enjoynen men comunly in certeyn caas, as for to goon, peradventure, naked in pilgrimage or barfot," that is to say, naked in their shirts...

Heavily loaded freight wagons, like this one in 19th century Northamptonshire, carved up the dirt roads in the years before the turnpike system. (After G. S. Shepherd, 1836, authors' archives)

131

Another motive for pilgrimages, and, more than any other, characteristic of the times, was to annoy the king...

Apart from pilgrimages [abroad]...English people usually went to Durham to visit the tomb of the holy Confessor Cuthbert...to the shrine of King Edward the Confessor in Westminster; to St. Albans, St. Edmund's Bury, St. David's...to Chichester, to worship the body of St. Richard the Bishop; to Glastonbury, with its holy thorn-tree, and its church founded by St. Joseph of Arimathea; to Waltham...Lincoln, York, Peterborough, Hayles with its Holy Blood, Winchester, Holywell, Beverly with its St. John...but none could stand comparison with Walsingham and Canterbury.

From London to Lincoln to York, the Great North Road was dotted with shrines and was also a main highway for those going further, to Canterbury, Rome, Jerusalem, or Santiago de Compostela.

There were many other kinds of tradespeople and travelers abroad as well, some of whom made their livings on and from the roads, among them innkeepers, herbalists, charlatans or quacks, minstrels, jugglers, tumblers, messengers, merchants, peddlers, outlaws, wandering workmen, peasants out of bond, itinerant preachers, and friars. Jusserand describes the traditional herbalist:

The most popular of all the wanderers were naturally the most cheerful, or those held to be the most beneficent. These latter were the folks with a universal panacea, very numerous in the Middle Ages; they went about the world selling health...

The traditional outlaw was quite another matter. England's medieval brigands and cutthroats were scarcely the figures so often enshrined in English and American folk myth. Noyes' *Highwayman* is a romantic hero; the real English highwayman was always a nuisance and in some periods a scourge, from medieval times until the early 19th century. As early as 1252 Henry III directed the sheriff to help prevent ambushes along the Great North Road by clearing underbrush.

In medieval times, the main British roads were wide roads, composed of several parallel tracks in the soft sod created by drovers taking their cattle to market and sometimes quite long distances to major fairs. In this, they were much like the 19th century Santa Fe and Oregon Trails across the Great Plains of North America. But they were unsafe; there were many hollows and patches of trees and brush providing excellent cover for outlaws victimizing travelers between the market towns. In 1285, Edward I's Statute of Winchester ordered clearance of the ground

Snow and mud alike posed hazards to coaches; here the precious mail is being sent on ahead by a mounted courier, while help is being summoned. (After James Pollard, 1825, authors' archives)

THE GREAT NORTH ROAD

for 200 feet on each side of the road so that there remained, as Jusserand writes:

> ...neither coppice nor brushwood, nor hollow nor ditch which serve as shelter for malefactors...Only large trees such as oaks might be left. The owner of the soil had to do the work; if he neglected it, he would be responsible for robberies and murders, and have to pay a fine to the king. If the road went through a park, the same obligation lay on the lord, unless he consented to close it by a wall or a hedge so thick, or by a ditch so wide and deep, that robbers could not cross them...The king sets the example and orders such clearings to be made at once on the lands belonging to the crown.

Drovers from Scotland, Northumberland, and Yorkshire especially valued the Great North Road's wide green verges as drovers' paths. (In later years, when the roads became hard surfaced, cattle inevitably cut their hoofs on gravel—and cattle farriers along the Great North Road developed a considerable trade in cattle-shoeing.)

Until Tudor times, most long-distance travel on the Great North Road and other such main roads was on horseback, with baggage and trading goods carried by pack-mule trains. There were carts—there had been carts and war chariots even before Roman times—but these were much more often found in use on those parts of the roads traversing hard ground than those traversing Defoe's "clayey dirty" Midlands or the boggy section of the Great North Road just north of London, which one traveler described as having "swallowed up at least 20,000 cartloads" of fill.

By Elizabethan times, carriages and heavier transport wagons had begun to travel the Great North Road, putting a much heavier burden than before on road maintenance. Not the least of the new burdens was Elizabeth's entourage itself. She was a great traveler, moving throughout her kingdom in an open carriage, accompanied by hundreds of nobles, functionaries, and servants, and by many hundreds of baggage cars and wagons drawn by thousands of horses.

In the early 17th century, heavy four-wheeled wagons drawn by as many as 10 horses began to appear so frequently that harassed local justices imposed a five-horse limit on wagons in 1618, and an increasingly strict weight limit on loads in 1622 and therafter. Yet, even though the roads would not see substantial improvement until turnpike maintenance began to really take hold in the 18th century, road use—especially on the Great North Road—continued to increase from Elizabethan times on. In the 1640's, long-distance stagecoach runs began on the Great North Road, and with them the development of what would become the roadside inns of coaching days.

The inns of the Great North Road were especially notable, for this London-Edinburgh road was traveled by the English and Scottish nobility for centuries. Margaret

Tudor stayed at the Crown at Tuxford on July 12, 1503, on her way north to Edinburgh to marry James IV of Scotland. Richard III signed Buckingham's death warrant at the Angel in Grantham on October 19, 1485. Charles I stayed at the George at Stamford on August 23, 1645. As W. Outram Tristam puts it:

> All were here we may be well assured, at such noted halting-places on the main artery of travel between two countries—all and of every rank, in a motley assemblage of confused travel—kings, queens, statesmen, highwaymen (the North Road around Stamford was celebrated for these gentry), generals, poets, wits, fine ladies, conspirators, and coachmen. All were in such houses as this George at Stamford at one time or another in the centuries, and ate and drank, and robbed, or were robbed, and died, and made merry...

The Great North Road that developed from medieval times on in many sections paralleled the old Roman Ermine Street, as it generally parallels today's A-1. It ran out of London north through Barnet, Stevenage, and St. Neots to Stamford. But rather than following the old line of Ermine Street northeast to Lincoln, it ran more directly north through Newark to Doncaster and Tadcaster. From there, it continued north to Catterick, bypassing York. Out of Catterick, it again diverged from the main Roman route, going north through Darlington, Durham, Newcastle-upon-Tyne, Alnwick, and Holy Island to Berwick, and from there to Edinburgh.

As Britain emerged into the modern period, the Great North Road became the main route between two kingdoms, and then—after the union of England and Scotland—the much-traveled main highway between London and Edinburgh, by far the best-known high road in the British Isles.

It continued to be the main north-south military road until the end of armed Scottish resistance to English domination. In fact, the last great Scottish rising, in 1745, contributed to improvement of the Great North Road, as the bad condition of the northernmost section of the road made English troop movements difficult. After the rising had been crushed, considerable rebuilding and improved maintenance were undertaken in the north.

The Great North Road was also the main post road north, running officially from the General Post Office in London to the General Post Office in Edinburgh. And it was the royal road north and south, the greatest road of coaching days, and the road of the famous highwaymen, Dick Turpin and his kin. Even so, as it entered its great coaching days, the Great North Road was in terrible condition, so terrible that it became a favorite source of lament for 17th and 18th century travelers. Daniel Defoe described the problem as one of soil:

> The soil of all the midland part of England even from sea to sea, is of a deep stiff clay, or marly kind,

and it carries a breadth of near 50 miles at least, in some places much more; nor is it possible to go from London to any part of Britain, north, without crossing this clayey dirty part...

Yet the distances were short, for geographically Britain is a small place; here was no Eurasia or North America to cross. At the turn of the 17th century, no part of England was more than a fortnight's ride from London. And in 1603 Sir Robert Carey was able to ride the 382 miles from London to Edinburgh on the Great North Road in three days, spending 60 hours in the saddle, carrying the news of Elizabeth's death to King James, in Scotland.

The solution to the road problem lay in the development of a system of turnpikes, of which the Great North Road was the first, under an Act of Parliament in 1663. It was a much-maligned and heartily disliked system of turnpikes; throughout England, in the 18th century, toll-

After each stop, the stagecoach would set off again with a great bustle; here the postilion brandishes his horn in a farewell wave. (By Herbert Railton and Hugh Thomson, from W. Outram Tristram, Coaching Days and Coaching Ways, *1888)*

road travelers broke down tollgates, sometimes burning them as well, and abused tollgate keepers. Britons complained about the turnpike system for two centuries, even as it slowly but surely turned the terrible roads of medieval times into the excellent and happily used roads of the great days of coaching.

Travel on the Great North Road grew prodigiously after 1784, when the mail began to be carried by coach rather than by messengers. So did the number and size of the inns that served travelers, for by the late 18th century every aspect of trade and travel had increased enormously. Now scores of mail coaches left London every day, each carrying the mail, four to six passengers inside, and a driver and armed guard on top. The Great North Road was in good condition, and the volume of travel itself began to discourage highwaymen, as did more diligent law enforcement.

These were the very short-lived great days of coaching, so celebrated by Dickens and his contemporaries, so romantically remembered by many who came after. Traveling the high roads of Britain became a national pastime. Here is Charles Dickens, dwelling upon the pleasures of coaching in *Pickwick Papers,* just before the end of the coaching era:

They have rumbled through the streets, and jolted over the stones, and at length reach the wide and open country. The wheels skim over the hard and frosty ground; and the horses, bursting into a canter at a smart crack of the whip, step along the road as if the load behind them — coach, passengers, codfish and oyster-barrels, and all—were but a feather at their heels. They have descended a gentle slope, and enter upon a level, as compact and dry as a solid block of marble, two miles long. Another crack of the whip, and on they speed at a smart gallop, the horses tossing their heads and rattling the harness, as if in exhilaration at the rapidity of the motion; while the coachman, holding whip and reins in one hand, takes off his hat with the other, and resting it on his knees, pulls out his handkerchief, and wipes his forehead, partly because he has a habit of doing it, and partly because it's as well to show the passengers how cool he is, and what an easy thing it is to drive four-in-hand when you have had as much practice as he has. Having done this very leisurely (otherwise the effect would be materially impaired), he replaces his handkerchief, pulls on his hat, adjusts his gloves, squares his elbows, cracks the whip again, and on they speed, more merrily than before...

And now the bugle plays a lively air as the coach rattles through the ill-paved streets of a country town; and the coachman, undoing the buckle which keeps his ribands together, prepares to throw them off the moment he stops.

He throws down the reins and gets down himself, and the other outside passengers drop down also; except those who have no great confidence in their ability to get up again; and they remain where they are, and stamp their feet against the coach to warm them—looking, with longing eyes and red noses, at the bright fire in the inn bar, and the sprigs of holly with red berries which ornament the window...

...[Then] the coachman shouts an admonitory "Now then, gen'l'm'n," the guard re-echoes it; the old gentleman inside thinks it a very extraordinary thing that people *will* get down when they know there isn't time for it; shawls are pulled up, coat collars are readjusted, the pavement ceases, the houses disappear; and they are once again dashing along the open road, with the fresh air flowing in their faces, and gladdening their very hearts within them.

The road continued to improve, with new road builders applying both orthodox and unorthodox methods to good effect. Of the orthodox road builders, Thomas Telford was most notable; he built roads with a firm foundation of large rocks, covered that foundation with a six-inch layer of broken rocks, and laid gravel atop that, taking care to allow enough surface curvature to carry off water into excellent drainage channels. John McAdam quite effectively built roads which did not depend upon a firm foundation, but instead relied on a relatively thin surface composed of coarse aggregates, usually broken rocks, bound together by stone chips and dust. In this, McAdam applied an existing European experimental process on a wide scale to British roads.

But coaching days, and with them the days of the Great North Road, ended when the railroads came. In 1838—the year after Dickens wrote his paean to coaching in *Pickwick Papers*—the mails began to go by rail rather than road; by 1850, over 6,000 miles of track were open in Britain. A decade after the opening of the main railway lines, most turnpike trusts were bankrupt, and the stagecoaches had all but disappeared, to be recalled only by pictures and by timetables carefully framed and put up on old inn walls.

Today's multilane highway, the A-1, generally follows the route of the Great North Road of coaching days, except that it seldom passes directly through town and city centers, following the modern tendency to create bypass roads for the sake of speed and convenience. Much of the Great North Road can still be seen, though, as well as its inns and the main old structures of the places it passed through. A bit of the old Roman road can also be seen in some places, though not nearly as well as the remnants of Hadrian's Wall. Both the Great North Road and Ermine Street are considered parts of Britain's heritage, and a substantial effort has been made by the nation and by many individuals to preserve them.

Unhappiness over the toll system led to complaints and fights for many years; here a stagecoach awaits the outcome of a fight before passing through the gate. (By Herbert Railton and Hugh Thomson, from W. Outram Tristram, Coaching Days and Coaching Ways, *1888)*

Selective Bibliography

Addison, William. *The Old Roads of England* (London: Batsford, 1980). An excellent, detailed, and anecdotal survey of the development of British roads from prehistory to the end of coaching days in the 1840's.

Cottrell, Leonard. *A Guide to Roman Britain* (Wilkes-Barre: Dimension, 1966). Detailed popular description of Roman remnants in modern Britain with useful discussion of their backgrounds, within the context of a traveler's guide.

Harper, Charles G. *The Great North Road: The Old Mail Road to Scotland, Vol. I: London to York; Vol. II: York to Edinburgh* (London: Chapman & Hall, 1901). A popular anecdotal work with many illustrations and odd details.

Hindley, Geoffrey. *A History of Roads* (Secaucus, New Jersey: Citadel, 1972). A sound, basic, brief survey of the history and construction of roads, with a good section on Britain.

Jusserand, J. J. *English Wayfaring Life in the Middle Ages* (New York: Putnam's, 1889). Classic description of the life of the British roads in late medieval times.

Morley, Frank. *The Great North Road* (New York: Macmillan, 1961). A rambling, interesting, anecdotal, sometimes relevant work on the Great North Road and rather loosely associated matters.

Sitwell, N. H. H. *Roman Roads of Europe* (New York: St. Martin's, 1981). A substantial, illustrated work on all major Roman roads, including those in Britain.

Trevelyan, G. M. *English Social History* (London: Longman, 1942). A standard and classic work on British social history from Chaucer's time to the end of the 19th century.

Tristram, W. Outram. *Coaching Days and Coaching Ways* (London: Macmillan, 1888). A romantic, anecdotal work, glorifying the great days of coaching and full of interesting detail.

Von Hagen, Victor W. *The Roads That Led to Rome* (Cleveland: World, 1967). A good, detailed treatment of all major Roman roads; includes a useful section on Britain.

Walbank, F. Alan, ed. *The English Scene* (New York: Scribner's, 1946). An excellent book of quotations on many aspects of British life, from 1700 through the 1920's.

Wood, Anthony. *Nineteenth Century Britain* (London: Longman, 1960). Contains a brief, sound discussion of the early development of the British railway system within a much larger work on British development.

137

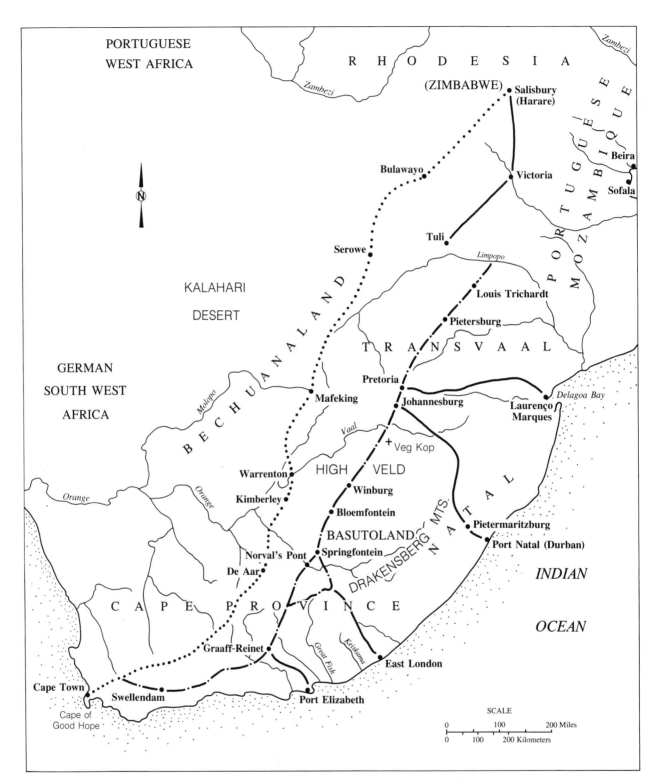

The Great Trek Route and the Missionary Road in the Late 19th Century

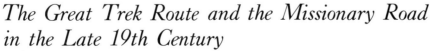

—··—··— Great Trek Route   ——— Main Connecting Routes

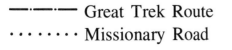

········· Missionary Road

The Great Trek Route and the Missionary Road

On October 19, 1836, in the Transvaal, the plains beyond the Vaal River in southern Africa, Dutch migrants called Boers for the first time met in battle a large force of African soldiers, the Matabele Zulus. The numbers of the two sides in this Battle of Vegkop were vastly different. The Boer party was a wagon train of only about 100 wagons, while the Zulus fielded thousands of infantrymen. Even attacking in phalanx (a Zulu innovation in Africa), however, the African force was no match for the Dutch. They were unable to penetrate the Dutch *laager,* a circle of wagons joined together, with the openings plugged by thorn bushes and a smaller group of wagons inside sheltering noncombatants and horses. Fighting with spears and short swords, which were useless except in hand-to-hand combat, the Zulus suffered massive casualties from the Boer guns; eventually they withdrew, taking with them the Boer livestock. For their part, the Boers were left stranded, unable to travel without their oxen, until relief parties joined them and covered their retreat.

It was not by coincidence that these two groups faced each other. For centuries, the Bantu peoples had been pressing southward from the rain forests of central Africa down the great Rift Valley of eastern Africa and into the southern regions, controlling territory as far as the Great Fish River. The most powerful of the Bantu in the 19th century were the Zulus, occupying the plains between the Drakensberg Mountains and the southeast coast of Africa. (This region was known as Natal, because

the first Portuguese visitors in the late 15th century had arrived on Christmas Day.) The most effective South African fighting force, the Zulus were expanding rapidly in this period, moving both north and south on the coastal plain, as well as west through the Drakensbergs onto the inland plateau called the High Veld, often pushing other, weaker peoples before them. The Dutch had, by this time, been in South Africa for almost two centuries. Though their main settlements were concentrated in the southwest, around Capetown in the Cape Colony, these Boers were pressing east and north from there, driven by land-hunger and disaffection with British rule. From the collision course of these two peoples emerged the Great Trek Route and the more westerly Missionary Road, the two main routes in modern South Africa.

From Capetown these two routes headed eastward on an inland course. Part-way across the tip of the continent, the route later known as the Great Trek Route arced gently northeast on the inland side of the Drakensberg Mountains, across the Orange River to the region of modern Johannesburg and Pretoria, and north across the Transvaal to the Limpopo River, the border between modern South Africa and Zimbabwe (formerly Rhodesia). The Missionary Road, also called the Old Transport Road, ran more up the center of South Africa on an arid course that skirted the Kalahari Desert to the west. From Capetown, the Missionary Road arced northeast somewhat sooner than the Great Trek Route, passing through De Aar, Kimberley (with its famous diamond mines), Mafeking, and Bulawayo, extending all the way north to Harare (formerly Salisbury) in Zimbabwe.

Human beings and their immediate antecedents had been traveling in these regions—from southern Africa up the great Rift Valley into Kenya—for over a million years; it is along this axis that traces of our earliest ancestors have been found. But the Great Trek Route and the Missionary Road are modern routes, developing only after European settlements in the region—and late at that, becoming main trails only in the mid-19th century with the Boer migration northeastward out of the Cape Colony, which set the basis for much of what would follow in modern South Africa.

Europeans had been living at the Cape of Good Hope for almost two centuries before the Great Trek. British and Dutch ships rounding the Cape of Good Hope had put in at Table Bay for water and food since early in the 17th century, and the first permanent European settlement was established at Capetown by the Dutch in 1652. By 1658, the Dutch were bringing in West African slaves; a little later, they began to import convict laborers from the East Indies.

Late in the 17th century, the colony had begun to expand to the south and east in the direction of Natal, with settlers in outlying areas paying five pounds a year for the use of 3,000 *morgen,* or 6,000 acres of land. These settlers were cattle and sheep raisers, farming only a few acres of land for food and moving with their herds during the year; they came to be known as *Trekboers,* literally migrant farmers.

All during the 18th century, the Trekboers continued to expand inland south of the Orange River and to the east along the coast, taking the lightly defended land of the Bushmen and Hottentots. Late in the century, in 1779, they encountered the southernmost of the Bantu peoples, the Xosa, and fought the first in a series of eight engagements known as the Kaffir Wars.

Throughout this period, the Cape Colony was held by the Dutch East India Company; then, in 1795, outlying settlers in Swellendam along the southern coast and Graaf-Reinet to the east set up independent Boertrekker republics. But in the same year, as part of the world struggle between European powers, British forces seized the entire Cape region, including the new republics. The British held the Cape until 1802, then returned it briefly to the Dutch, before taking it back permanently in 1806. The Cape Colony, by then, had 27,000 Europeans, mostly Dutch, 30,000 slaves, and 17,000 surviving Hottentots.

With the British came change, for soon Britain was deeply affected by the anti-slavery and other humanitarian movements; she also had historically attempted to make and to keep treaties with indigenous peoples. From 1810 on, British missionaries began to mount a campaign against Boer mistreatment of African free people and slaves. Writing later in the 19th century, James Bryce describes the role and impact of the missionaries:

In the early 19th century, British governors and settlers, like these in 1820, began to change the character of the Cape Colony. (By Graham Winch after Thomas Baines, from John Noble, Official Handbook of the Cape of Good Hope, *1886)*

The missionaries, and especially those of the London Missionary Society, played...a prominent role in politics...Within and on the borders of the Cape Colony they were, for the first sixty years of the present century, the leading champions of the natives, and as they enjoyed the support of an active body of opinion in England and Scotland, they had much influence in Parliament and with the Colonial Office. Outside the Colony they were often the principal advisors of the native chiefs...Since, in advocating the cause of the natives, they had often to complain of the behavior of the whites, and since, whenever a chief came into collision with the emigrants or with colonial frontiersmen, they became the channel by which the chief stated his case to the British government, they incurred the bitter hostility of the Boers...

In 1828, Hottentots and other "free colored" people were granted equal private civil rights with "whites"; in 1834, slavery was abolished. Many slaveholders were able to continue to hold slaves, calling them "apprentices" and "servants," but it had become clear that, in the British Cape Colony, slavery would soon be abolished in reality.

Equally important for the future of the Great Trek Route was the outcome of the Fifth Kaffir War, in 1834. In that year, the Cape Colony defeated the Xosa along the Great Fish River, and forced them to withdraw, opening up another large area along the coast for Boertrekker expansion. But this time, the British Colonial Office, blaming the Boers for provoking the war by their illtreatment of the Xosa, forced the Cape government to give back the Xosa land, restoring the status quo on the Great Fish River, and making it clear that Boer territorial expansion, like Boer slavery, would soon be a thing of the past.

Other events contributed to the rise of tension between British and Boer in South Africa, as well. English was adopted as the official Cape Colony language, and local Boer council authority was sharply limited. Given the developing pattern of British rule in the Cape Colony and the profound differences between the British and the Boers on such basic matters as slavery and expansion, it was for the Boers clearly a time for revolution, capitulation, or exodus. Revolution was impractical in the face of British power. Capitulation, theoretically unthinkable, was the path chosen by most of the Dutch. Exodus was the course chosen by a few. It was they who made up the body of the Boer Trek and opened up the Great Trek Route. Actually, only about 20 percent of the Dutch population—most of them frontier Boers—emigrated from the Cape Colony during the Boer Trek, though many more went north in later decades.

Their manifesto was grand. Boer leader Piet Retief published a statement in 1837 that caught the imagination of many Boers, greatly spurred migration, and served to a considerable extent as a declaration of Boer independence from the British. He said in part:

The story of the Boers and the Zulus is full of negotiations, broken treaties, and sporadic wars. (Illustrated London News, *December 6, 1902*)

As we desire to stand high in the estimation of our brethren, be it known...that we are resolved, wherever we go, that we will uphold the just principle of liberty; but whilst we will take care that no one shall be in a state of slavery, it is our determination to maintain such regulations as may suppress crime and preserve proper relations between master and servant...We will not molest any people, nor deprive them of the smallest property; but, if attacked, we shall consider ourselves fully justified in defending our persons and effects to the utmost of our ability...We propose...to make known to the native tribes our intentions, and our desire to live in peace and friendly intercourse with them. We quit this colony under the full assurance that the English Government has nothing more to require of us, and will allow us to govern ourselves without interference in future.

Of such manifestos are myths made. In reality, the causes of the Boer inland migrations were a compound of three things: a drive for more and more grazing land that had by then been proceeding uninterruptedly for well over a century; a hard-held determination to continue to hold slaves, whatever they were called, in defiance of the emancipation of all slaves within the British Empire in 1834; and a shared set of frontier attitudes, which resisted any encroachment upon individual prerogatives.

The Boer Trek—or Great Trek, as it is called by

many South Africans—was, in reality, a migration of modest size, over mostly easy-to-traverse terrain, accompanied by a war of conquest, in which the guns and horses of the Boers prevailed over the spears, swords, and clubs carried by the massed, numerically superior infantry of the African nations they defeated.

Between 1836 and 1838, 10,000–14,000 Dutch frontier farmers, acting as individuals but along generally agreed-upon lines, crossed the Orange River north out of the Cape Colony, accompanied by some thousands of African "servants" and "apprentices," most of whom were, in fact, slaves. Proceeding north in separate groups, they traveled west of the 10,000-foot-high peaks of the Drakensberg Range onto the High Veld. The main body of the emigrants crossed the northern Drakensbergs into Natal, while a smaller body stayed on the west side of the mountains and pushed north across the Vaal River into the Transvaal. In both places they came into conflict with the rising Bantu power: the Zulus.

Between 1818 and 1828, under the leadership of Shaka, the Zulus had built a military force that no other southern African force could withstand. The Zulu army Shaka created was a large disciplined mass of infantry fighting in regiments, which attacked in phalanxes, used spears at shorter ranges than before, and introduced short-bladed swords called *assegais* for hand-to-hand fighting. No such instrument of conquest had existed before in southern and central Africa; with it, the Zulus under Shaka had embarked upon a career of ruthless conquest.

More than ruthless, really, for Shaka was an habitual mass murderer, as cruel and destructive as the Europeans in the Caribbean of the 16th century and the Nazis in

the Europe of the 20th century. Shaka was irrational, as well, falling out with several of his chief lieutenants in the short 10 years of his rule and forcing them to flee with their peoples in a series of major Bantu conquests and migrations that were to change the ethnic and political face of south and central Africa. Shaka's years of rule were the years of the *Mfecane*—The Crushing.

One of the Shaka's fleeing lieutenants was Mzilikazi, who fled across the Drakensbergs to the High Veld in 1817 with his people, the Matabele Zulus. Settling on the plateau, he forced the previous African inhabitants, the Sotho, westward into the Kalahari Desert; welcomed Christian missionaries; made a non-aggression pact with the British in Cape Town; and built a Zulu army on Shaka's principles that could field 20,000 infantrymen.

A European missionary, Edouard Casalis, traversing the High Veld during this period, described the empty, blasted country left by the Matabele:

> Arriving here, what struck us most was the solitary and desolate aspect of the country.
> We looked in vain for villages…Everywhere we saw human bones whitening in the sun and rain, and more than once we had to turn our wagon off its course to avoid passing over such remains…

The main body of the Zulu nation remained in Natal and on the fertile coastal plains just to the north. Shaka's rule ended with his assassination by his half-brothers, one of whom—Dingane—took over as ruler. Under Dingane, the Zulus continued their military expansion, focusing their attention on African rivals, like the Xosa to their south. They had not yet come into conflict with the Europeans, who had established a small coastal town at Port Natal (now Durban). The stage was set for a classic confrontation as the Boer Trek began.

Two small Boer parties—the van Rensburg and Trigardt parties—preceded the main Trek, going north all the way into the Transvaal in 1835. These parties consisted of only a few large covered Trekker wagons, each drawn by six to twelve oxen. Like all such trains that were to follow, they traveled no more than five or six miles a day, the pace most comfortable for their sheep, and generally rested on Sundays. They and later trekkers encountered few other people south of the Vaal River, for the country they traversed was the High Veld that had been substantially depopulated by Mzilikazi's Matebele Zulus, for whom this was essentially a border region. Only a few small tribes remained; one group, the Basutos, retired to mountain fortresses, later mastering European guns and horses and founding independent Basutoland (now Lesotho).

Once in the Transvaal, the two Trekboer parties separated. The van Rensburg party went on north and east and were never heard from again. The Trigardt party settled north of the Vaal, in Matabele country. They lived

Trekboers headed for Natal had to traverse passes like this one as they crossed the Drakensberg Mountains. (By Col. C.C. Mitchell, Africana Museum, Johannesburg)

there for a year without being attacked but found the isolation too hard to bear, so they traveled across the northernmost Drakensbergs to the Portuguese settlement at Delagoa Bay, on the Indian Ocean at the mouth of the Limpopo River. The trip was desperately difficult. They had to find and cut their own trail through the mountains, often dismantling the wagons and carrying the pieces through narrow passes, reassembling them on the far side. Worse than that, this was fever and tse-tse fly country. Their animals died on route to the coast and so did most of the Trigardt party, only a few surviving to be eventually shipped back to Natal by the Portuguese. That is why the Limpopo was always to be the outermost limit of Boer migration.

In 1836, the main body of the Trekboers left the Cape Colony and began to open up the Great Trek Route. Most emigrants reached the Orange River crossings on their own, in single wagons or in small groups, following no one course. They bivouacked on the north side of the Orange, usually at the Norval's Pont crossing, and then proceeded north in small, but now mutually dependent groups of wagons, to what became the migration's main staging area, on the Blesberg. The wagon-rutted path from Norval's Pont to the Blesberg, known as the Trekker's Road, was then extended north to the vicinity of Winburg, where the main body of the Trekkers encamped late in 1837. There, they eventually formed an embryo government, headed by Piet Retief, and debated whether to go east across the Drakensbergs into fertile, better-watered Natal or north into the dryer Transvaal.

Two large early parties—the Potgeiter and Cilliers parties—did not wait for the main body; joining at the Orange, they moved north, 100 wagons strong, not stopping at the Blesberg, nor at the Vet, but moving on across the Vaal. Inevitably, they met the Matabele, who viewed them as invaders. This was the first main engagement between Zulus and Boers, the Battle of Vegkop, on October 19, 1836. After these parties retreated to the Blesberg, the emigrants disagreed and split. A minority continued north, across the Vaal, had several indecisive engagements with Msilikazi's Matabele during 1837, and eventually defeated the Matabele, thereby taking the entire Transvaal for the Boers. The Matabele themselves then trekked north—fleeing from the Boers, as they had fled Shaka's army two decades earlier—ultimately settling in what later became southern Rhodesia.

The majority of the Boers decided to proceed across the Drakensbergs into Natal. Piet Retief and 15 men went ahead of the main body, leaving instructions that wagons were not to cross over the mountains into Natal until Retief had completed negotiations with Dingane and his Zulu nation. Retief and his party went on to Port Natal, where they found English guides who would take them to Dingane's capital.

Unfortunately, the main body of the Trekkers disregarded Retief's instructions, and 1,000 Trekker wagons came over the passes in his absence, scattering over a wide area in the upland valleys on the east slope of the Drakensbergs. Retief compounded the problem by sending a message to Dingane that was more ultimatum than greeting, in which he called Dingane's attention to the Boers' recent triumph over the Matabele in the Transvaal. Then he took about a hundred men and went to meet Dingane, in spite of many clear warnings as to Dingane's real intentions—which were, by then, to destroy the Boer invaders. War may have been inevitable, in any case; the size of the Boer invasion may have made it inescapable. But the foolishness of the Boer leadership and the anarchic disposition of their wagons invited disaster.

Disaster came. After two days of negotiations, Dingane signed a deed granting the Boers a substantial part of Natal. He then invited the Boer negotiating party into the center of his camp. They came unarmed, to drink a final toast to the new treaty. At the conclusion of the toast, Dingane rose, and shouted "Kill the wizards!" At his cry, thousands of Zulu infantrymen, who had been hidden in the huts surrounding the central *kraal*, seized the unarmed Boers and killed them, one by one, also killing their African servants at the main gate. The only survivor was one young English interpreter, who escaped. Dingane then sent three regiments to attack the widely dispersed Boer wagons on the slopes of the Drakensbergs, taking them completely by surprise. The Boers suffered several hundred dead, many more wounded, and the loss of most of their livestock. Had the Zulus pressed the surprise attack with more regiments, they might, indeed, have destroyed the main body of the Boer emigration and quite changed the course of South African history. As it was, the main Boer force, although seriously damaged, lived to fight and win another day.

The Zulu-Boer war continued sporadically during 1838 without major battles, although the Zulus won minor engagements with the Boers in March and August and defeated an English force out of Port Natal that spring. But by the end of the year, the inevitable had occurred. A Boer force of about 500 men defeated the main Zulu force at the Blood River in northern Natal. The Boers had a few casualties and no dead; the Zulus had approximately 3,000 dead and many other casualties. The Zulu infantry had attacked a strong Boer *laager* again and again, but had come nowhere near breaking the Boer square; their remaining troops eventually broke and fled from the Boer cavalry when it sortied out of the *laager*.

Meanwhile, a small British force had landed at Port Natal. The British commandant managed to negotiate a peace settlement between the Zulus and the Boers, now led by Andries Pretorious, in which the Zulus gave up half of Natal and made heavy reparations to the Boers. The British force then removed themselves, sailing away on Christmas Eve, 1839. Aided by a division within the Zulus, the Boers reopened hostilities, appropriating tens of thousands of head of Zulu cattle and taking 1,000 Zulu children home with them as "apprentices." The Boers then declared the existence of the Natal Republic and asked for British recognition.

All of this was unpalatable to London, which was not eager to give a potentially hostile Boer power access to the Indian Ocean. Many in Britain—including Lord John Russell, the British Secretary of State—were also outraged by the Boers' harsh treatment of the Bantu. Russell ordered Sir George Napier, the British commandant at Capetown, to reoccupy Natal, promising reinforcements as necessary. In May 1842 a small British force of 250 men marched into Port Natal.

And now the Boers themselves faced the inevitable; they could not withstand a British force capable of being reinforced by sea, having no sea force of their own. Pretorius's Boer troops laid siege to the British at Port Natal for almost two months, until relief arrived in the form of a 50-gun frigate, the *Southampton,* and five companies of troops detoured from their voyage around the Cape to Afghanistan. Three weeks later, and with no further fighting, the Boers surrendered.

That was effectively the end of the Natal Republic and of the Boer Trek. A year more of contention was to follow in Natal, but in the end British troops were able to hold the province without any further major fighting. The remnants of the Zulu nation came over to the British, and some of the formerly defiant Boers decided that they were able to live under British rule. Many drifted away, back over the Drakensberg passes, to join other Boers who had taken the High Veld and the Transvaal from the Matabele. There the Boers built the Orange Free State on the High Veld and the South African Republic in the Transvaal. Both were recognized by the British in 1854—and both were taken by the British at century's end in the Boer War.

Aside from the 150 miles or so of the well-defined Trekker's Road from the Orange River to Winburg, no single road can properly be identified as the Boer Trek road north. Beyond Winburg, the Boers spread out, taking the land and enslaving the local people, some of whom had been their allies against their former oppressors, the Matabele.

David Livingstone, later to become the best-known of Africa's European missionary-explorers, was working in Bechuanaland near the border of Transvaal in the 1840's. He describes how the warm reception first accorded the Boers as deliverers from the tyranny of the Matabele changed in the northern Transvaal:

> They [the Boers] came with the prestige of white men and deliverers; but the Bechuanas soon found, as they expressed it, "that Moselekatse [Msilikazi, leader of the Matabele] was cruel to his enemies, and kind to those he conquered; but that the Boers destroyed their enemies, and made slaves of their friends..."

> I have myself been an eyewitness of Boers coming to a village, and, according to their usual custom, demanding twenty or thirty women to weed their gardens, and have seen these women proceed to the scene of unrequited toil, carrying their own food on their heads, their children on their backs, and instruments of labor on their shoulders...

Livingstone also had more personal experience of the Boer expansion and its effects. In 1852, a Boer force attacked the Bechuanas with whom Livingstone had been working as a missionary:

> The Boers, four hundred in number, were sent by the late Mr. Pretorius to attack the Bakwains in 1852...they assaulted the Bakwains, and, besides killing a considerable number of adults, carried off two hundred of our school children into slavery. The natives under Sechele defended themselves till the approach of night enabled them to flee to the mountains, and having in that defense killed a number of the enemy, the very first ever slain in this country by Bechuanas, I received the credit of having taught the tribe to kill Boers!

> My house, which had stood perfectly secure for years under the protection of the natives, was plundered in revenge...The books of a good library—my solace in our solitude—were not taken away, but handfuls of the leaves were torn out and scattered over the place. My stock of medicines was smashed; and all our furniture and clothing carried off and sold at public auction to pay the expenses of the foray.

After the Boer conquest of the High Veld and the Transvaal, British missionaries were effectively expelled from Boer territory, and many—like Livingstone and his father-in-law Robert Moffat—went further north into the interior of Africa, thereby establishing a major British path from the Cape into central Africa.

Running on a corridor between the Boer republics and the Kalahari Desert, this Missionary Road pushed north beyond the Limpopo and through eastern Botswana (Bechuanaland) to what is now Zimbabwe. There, the British missionaries once again met Msilikazi and the Matabele Zulus, who had fled north across the Limpopo, crushing, terrorizing, and conquering the peoples of the Zimbabwe plateau. Robert Moffat developed an extraordinary personal relationship with Msilikaze, however, which enabled the British missionaries to work with the Matabele and with the conquered peoples as well.

British traders and commercial adventurers also went north on the Missionary Road, which some of them called the Old Transport Road. Later in the century, this was the path taken by Cecil Rhodes and his associates, on their way to establish British settlement and rule over the country that became Rhodesia.

It was along these two paths—the Great Trek Route and the Missionary Road—that the modern country of

In 1888, Johannesburg was still a small settlement on the northern part of the Great Trek Route. (Africana Museum, Johannesburg)

South Africa developed, united by the British after the Boer War at the turn of the 20th century but increasingly under the influence of the descendants of the Trekboers.

Today, a major South African highway and a generally parallel railroad run north from the Orange River crossings to Johannesburg and Pretoria, the capital of the South African state. A little to the east of Johannesburg is Krugersdorn, named for the first president of the 19th century South African Republic, Paul Kruger, who was a boy of 10 when he and his family trekked north with the Cilliers party in 1837. The road and railroad continue north to the South African border at the Limpopo, passing near the border through the town of Louis Trichardt, named for the leader of the ill-fated Trichardt (Trigardt) party of 1835.

The Boer pathway across the Drakensbergs from the High Veld to Natal is no longer heavily used. Now the main road from Durban (once Port Natal) runs north of the Drakensbergs to Johannesburg, there joining the roads running north to the border. On the way, it passes through the town of Pietermaritzburg, named after another Boer Trek leader, and the capital of the short-lived Natal Republic.

Another much longer modern road and railroad run north into the interior of southern Africa, all the way from Capetown to Harare (once Salisbury), capital of Zimbabwe (once Rhodesia). Road and railroad generally follow the path of the old 19th century Missionary Road. The modern path goes north through Kimberley and forks at Warrenton; a short eastern section cuts eastward to Johannesburg, while its much longer original main route continues north through Mafeking, across the Limpopo, and through eastern Botswana to Zimbabwe.

Given current national and racial tensions in southern Africa, the Missionary Road from Capetown north to Zimbabwe is relatively little used, while the Great Trek Route north is a major modern internal South African pathway. South Africa has for the last quarter of a century been essentially a Boer state, and a Trekboer state at that. The ideas and practices of the people of the Boer Trek continue to tear South African society apart; in that sense, the Great Trek has not yet ended.

Selective Bibliography

Bryce, James. *Impressions of South Africa* (New York: Century, 1897). A well-done 19th century history of South Africa, with an excellent treatment of the Boer Trek.

Davidson, Basil. *The African Past* (Boston: Little, Brown, 1964). An excellent collection of source materials, some of which relate to South Africa and the Boer Trek.

Galbraith, John S. *Reluctant Empire* (Berkeley: University of California, 1963). A substantial, very detailed study focusing on British colonial policy in South Africa during the period of the Boer Trek and until 1854.

July, Robert W. *A History of the African People* (New York: Scribner's, 1974). A sound, detailed, scholarly, general history of Africa and its people.

Morris, Donald R. *The Washing of the Spears* (New York: Simon and Schuster, 1965). A substantial history of the rise and fall of the Zulu nation in the 19th century, told from a European point of view, and focusing on the Zulu-Boer-British wars of the period.

Oliver, R., and J. D. Fage. *A Short History of Africa* (Middlesex: Penguin, 1968). A concise, useful African history, with South African material presented in a wider African context.

Walker, Eric A. *The Great Trek* (London: A. & C. Black, 1960). A standard, very detailed work on the Boer Trek, but quite notable for its pro-Boer leanings.

Wilson, Monica, and Leonard Thompson. *The Oxford History of South Africa*, 2 vols. (New York: Oxford, 1969). A full-scale scholarly history of South Africa, from prehistory through the modern period.

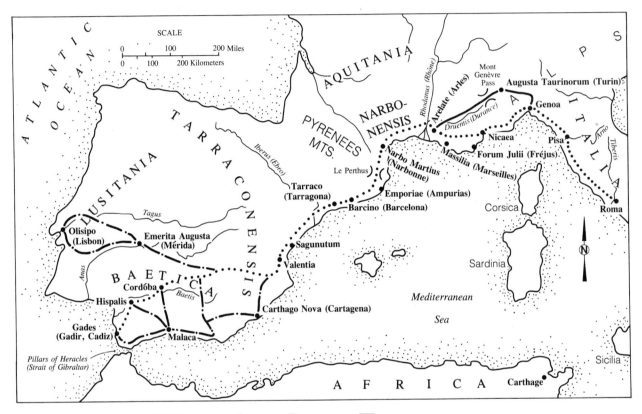

The Heraclean Way in Greco-Roman Times

· · · · · · · · The Heraclean Way   —————— Alternate Routes in Gallia

—·—·—·— Alternate Routes in Hispania

The Heraclean Way

Heracles or (to give him his Roman name) Hercules is one of the great Western heroes, famed for his strength and skill. Linked with many early Greek explorations around the Mediterranean world, he sailed with Jason and his Argonauts, and almost every major Alpine pass carries its legend of Heracles's passing. The first century B.C. Greek writer Diodorus tells us that he:

> …went across the Alpine mountains and eased the harshness of the track and its obstacles, so that it became possible to cross the pass with an army and its baggage. The barbarians dwelling in those mountains were accustomed to harass and pillage armies crossing over; he subjected them all and having killed the brigand-chiefs ensured the safety of those traveling that way.

But Heracles is most closely associated with the coast road between Italy and the Atlantic coast of Spain, the route of his mythological ten labors. If legend be construed as fact, he traveled through Gaul (France), putting down the practice of human sacrifice and pacifying the natives in the coastal region now known as the Riviera. Further west, in Iberia, Heracles killed a monster ruling over the local people. Legend then has him pushing apart the continents of Europe and Africa, planting massive rocks on either side of the strait to the Atlantic, thus forming the famous Pillars of Hercules: Ceuta and Gibraltar. Many classical leaders, including Alexander the Great, dreamed of emulating Heracles by winning control of the whole area between Italy and the western ocean. The Romans finally succeeded, and the Heraclean Way (Via Herculea) became their longest continuous route, stretching 1,700 miles from Rome to Gades (Cadiz) on the Atlantic.

The route is not easy. Along the curve of northern Italy (in early times considered part of Gaul), the Maritime Alps front the water; here there developed a prehistoric coastal track, sometimes following a rocky ledge along the sea-facing cliffs, sometimes traversing the crumpled contour slightly inland. Because this route was always arduous and often precipitous, an alternate route through the Alps was at times preferred, for the low Mont Genèvre Pass allowed a long, steady climb, instead of a succession of shorter, steep ones. From Genoa this alternate route fed north into the Alps and then west to Turin (Augusta Taurinorum) to the valley of the Durance (Druentis) River and down to the Rhône (Rhodanus), to rejoin the shore route. The shore route itself moved inland past modern Cannes, where cliffs gradually give way to a narrow coastal strip with many small bays and rocky harbors, and later lagoons; the primitive track moved further north to arc around the marshy Rhône delta, generally crossing the river at Arles (Arelate). Returning to the coast near Narbonne (Narbo Martius), the path crossed the Pyrenees by a pass called Le Perthus and moved halfway down the Mediterranean coast before cutting across the hilly inland

147

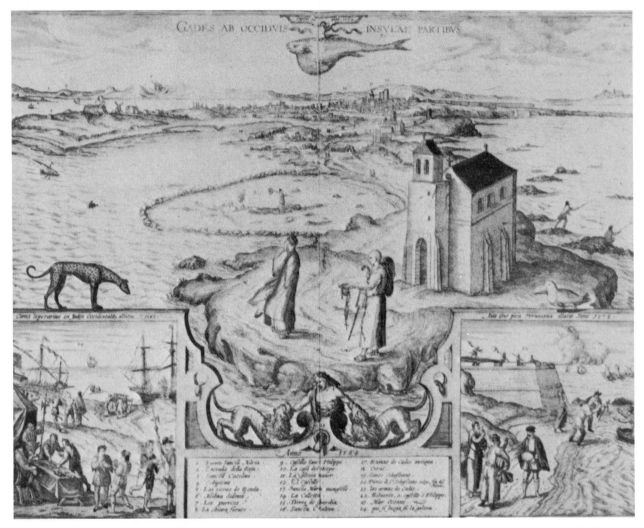

More than 2,000 years after it was founded, Cadiz (Gadir) was still a prominent port, graced by the distinctive rocky promontory shown in the foreground. (From G. Braun, Civitates Orbis Terrarum, *16th century)*

region to the valley of the Guadalquivir (Baetis) River and on down to the Atlantic Ocean.

The early peoples along the route were as varied as the terrain, being drawn from North Africa, Asia, and Europe. In the early second millennium B.C., the area south of the Pyrenees was populated by the Iberians, named after the River Iberus (Ebro); they were joined on the coastal strip by the Ligurians, Celtic peoples from Gaul and northern Italy. On the Italian peninsula, the native Italics were joined in about the 12th century B.C. by the Etruscans, who settled in the northwest between the Tiber and Arno rivers. During this period, the ancient land-track was primarily a local route or a long-distance migration route, not yet being used for regular trade and transportation. These western lands had no major role to play until the more advanced peoples of the east Mediterranean reached out for their plentiful resources, especially copper, tin, and silver.

At some point after 1100 B.C. (the traditional date,

though evidence indicates a later arrival), Phoenician traders crossed the length of the Mediterranean, passed through the Pillars of Heracles (Strait of Gibraltar) and founded a settlement they called Gadir (Enclosure), on the easily defended neck of land jutting out into the Atlantic and protecting a fine harbor. While sea routes were most important in the western Mediterranean in the mid-first millennium B.C., mariners were founding the main ports that would mark the Heraclean Way. The Phoenicians concentrated on southern Iberia, establishing mostly modest trading posts, not bases for conquest; after the fall of their homeland in the sixth century B.C., Phoenician traders from Carthage, in North Africa, increased their commitment to Iberia, making a major city of Gadir (Cadiz). Whether or not it was "the second city of the world," as the Greek geographer Strabo would later call it, Gadir (to the Romans, Gades) was a worthy terminus for the Heraclean Way. Meanwhile, the Greeks focused on northern Iberia and Gaul; from their main base at

Massalia (Marseilles) just east of the Rhône River delta, they founded many of the main ports along the Heraclean Way, including Emporiae (Ampurias) south of the Pyrenees, and—all east of Massalia—Antipolis (Antibes), Nicaea (Nice), and Heracles Monacus (Heracles Living-Alone, modern Monaco) on a rocky promontory, on the site of an earlier Phoenician landfall.

Pack horses were used to carry tin and other such loads on the Heraclean Way, and we hear of nomadic traders who sold their goods from wagons to the Ligurians near Massalia. Such trading apparently became rather standardized, for in the third century B.C., the Greek writer Pseudo-Aristotle noted:

> They say that from Italy as far as Celtica, in the territory of the Celtoligures and the Iberians, there is a road bearing the name of the Heraclean Way. Should a Greek or a local man venture along it, the inhabitants make sure that no harm befalls him, as they would bear the penalty.

People along the route collected tolls—often, in truth, "protection money"—from travelers, in return for promises of safety and for assistance at ferry crossings and portages.

The eastern sector of the Heraclean Way was, in the mid-first millennium B.C., shared by the Ligurians and the Etruscans, who briefly flexed their imperial muscles. They were overrun in the fourth century B.C. by another group of Celts moving southward, this time over the Alps and into Italy, overcoming the Etruscans and sacking the still-small city of Rome. But after the Latin League finally defeated the Celts, Rome emerged as the dominant power in the area, defeating all the peoples of Italy south of the Alps and making a virtual protectorate of the Greek coastal areas west to the river Iberus (Ebro). Rome and Carthage now shared the western Mediterranean—and the Heraclean Way—between them.

Unlike the previously dominant mariners, the Romans were landlubbers, and they made roads the lifelines of their empire. The Appian Way was the earliest of the major Roman roads, built to cement the union of the newly conquered tribes of Italy. But other roads came soon thereafter, with each section named for the person responsible for building it, and its distance measured from the Golden Milestone at the Forum in Rome. Construction on the Via Aurelia—the first section of the Heraclean Way out of Rome—was begun in 241 B.C., but reached only partway up the coast when it was halted by a series of conflicts with the Carthaginians.

Carthage had decided to develop its Iberian outposts into full-fledged colonies, founding a major new port on the east coast, called Carthago Nova (New Carthage, now Cartagena). They also widened and improved the trans-Iberian portion of the Heraclean Way. The Romans, suspicious of all this activity, apparently questioned the purpose of the road-building, but were lulled by reassurances that the Carthaginians were simply trying to move precious metals more efficiently. In fact, the Carthaginians under Hannibal were planning to attack Rome via the Heraclean Way.

From their stronghold at Carthago Nova, Hannibal and his army marched along the coast road; took the hilltop fort of Saguntum (Sagunto) from the Romans; and found the coast route open before them. Preparing his mercenary forces—including cavalry, infantry, slingers, and the famous North African elephants—over the winter, Hannibal Barca in the spring of 218 began to push northeastward around the coast, presumably crossing the Pyrenees through the traditional pass, Le Perthus. While he headed around the coast of Gaul toward the Rhodanus River, he was cheered by word of support by the Celts of the Maritime Alps and the Po Valley in northern Italia.

The Romans meanwhile had sent an army by ship (avoiding the troublesome Ligurians on the road) to Massalia (Marseilles) east of the marshy mouths of the Rhodanus River. There they awaited Hannibal, expecting him to follow the Heraclean Way to the usual crossing. But, forewarned by spies, Hannibal moved north along the west bank of the river, apparently planning to cross near Avignon. In the event, after buying up all the local rafts and boats, Hannibal found himself opposed by unfriendly Celtic tribes on the far shore, and so seems to have headed some miles further north, eventually crossing where an island divided the river, stationing some of the larger craft upstream to break the force of the fast-flowing Rhodanus. By a ruse, the Carthaginians were able to rout the Celts and, only then, deal with the difficult task of ferrying their elephants across the river. This was done by building a pier of a number of rafts tied together, using female elephants to lure the males out onto the rafts, then cutting the rafts loose to float them across the river. Most crossed this way safely, if with much anxiety, but some fell off into the water and were probably drowned (some Roman authors suggested that they walked across, holding their trunks above water, a most unlikely possibility).

While the Romans still waited near Massalia, Hannibal headed through the Alps with his Celtic allies by an unidentified route. Despite the treaties and bribes by which Hannibal had attempted to secure his route, Celtic tribes harassed the Carthaginian armies. (Their effectiveness was blunted by their ritual bragging of exploits, which exposed their positions to the Carthaginians, who then generally surprised them.) In one of the mountain defiles, where the army was strung out and the passage made difficult by the winter's snow, Hannibal's army was trapped temporarily, with Celts hurling boulders down on them from the precipices above. The pass itself was so high that some Carthaginian soldiers swore they could see Rome itself. That was either wishful thinking or wilful embroidery, for Rome was far away—but Italy was not. Five months after leaving Carthago Nova, Hannibal's army arrived at the Po Valley in northern Italia, crossing the Alps in a little over two weeks. Hannibal had the advantage of surprise, for the early Romans—more farmers than traders—knew none of the Alpine passes. For the next 15 years, the Carthaginians and Celts ravaged Italia.

But while Hannibal had been able to enter Italia unopposed, circling around the Roman army, the Romans were doing much the same thing. When some Roman legions left the Rhodanus to catch up to Hannibal, others sailed across the Ligurian Sea to the Greek port of Emporiae (Ampurias), just south of the Pyrenees; advancing down the coast road to Tarraco (Tarragona), they crossed the Iberus, eventually even taking the Iberian capital of Carthago Nova, cutting Hannibal's supply lines. In the end, they pushed the Carthaginians out of Iberia. Hannibal himself, after 15 years in Italia, was evacuated with some remnants of his army across the sea to Africa.

The years of fighting only reinforced the Roman belief in the importance of good roads; they moved quickly to build them on the new-won peninsula they called Hispania. In 206 B.C., working from both ends, they began to build a typically solid Roman road from Gades (their name for Gadir) to the Perthus Pass. This 980-mile section of the Heraclean Way, finished in 120 B.C., was at first called the Via Maxima, later the Via Augusta, and became the prime road in Hispania for the next six centuries of Roman rule. At the eastern end of the Heraclean Way, road-building did not resume so quickly. Even after the Carthaginians were out of Italy, their ships harassed Rome's coastal territory and the Greek territory under her protection; and these activities encouraged attacks from the north by the Gauls (as the Celts in that area were now known). The Greek colony of Massalia called for Roman assistance against these twin hazards in 154 B.C. and again in 125 B.C.; in return for their help, the Romans took a part of the coast for the building of a road to the important Iberian territory.

With the area secure, roadbuilding began in earnest. In 109 B.C. the Via Aurelia was extended up the coast past Pisae and Genoa, the new portion being named the Via Aemilia Scauri, though generally still called the Via Aurelia by travelers. A century later, the Via Julia Augusta, coming out of the Alps, extended the coast road to Forum Julii (Fréjus), passing through the hills of Monaco on the way. The Via Domitia completed the coast route to the Pyrenees, where it linked up with the Via Augusta. Even though these routes were not fully completed until 13–12 B.C., even the unfinished portions were so much improved by the Romans that, in 46 B.C., Julius Caesar was able to boast of having taken an army from Rome to Spain without getting their feet wet—quite a boast, considering the number of rivers and streams they had to cross.

These Roman roads were a major achievement. Instead of winding around obstacles, as the old dirt trail had done, Roman engineers often built up a section of road, or cut out a terrace, to keep the road as straight and level as possible, detouring only around major impediments. Laid on a bed of gravel, which provided good drainage and a proper base, the road surface was made of very large rocks, cut to fit together and provide a smooth, flat face for the roadbed. During this century and a half of building, the Heraclean Way employed a massive corps of workers; many of these were soldiers idled by temporary peace, sometimes building roads to their own new garrisons; others were local workers, some paid and some "impressed," or slaves captured or bought from other parts of the emerging Roman Empire. They built bridges, too, where only modest footbridges had been known before, such as the early one at Córdoba. Once completed, these structures would hold not only foot soldiers and light wagons, but the age's heaviest weapons of war. The Heraclean Way was well maintained, and sections of it were rebuilt, over the next six centuries; the number of Roman remains from this early period still existing in Spain attests to the solidity of their work.

The Romans brought many changes along the Heraclean Way. Continuing the process started by the Carthaginians, they encouraged the local inhabitants to lead a settled life by moving into the many cities they founded or adopting more extensive agriculture. The Iberian peninsula was divided into three provinces: Tarraconensis, with its capital at Tarraco (Tarragona); Lusitania, with its capital at Emerita Augusta (Mérida); and Baetica, with its capital at Corduba (Córdoba) and its major outlet at the mouth of the Baetis River at Gades. Products of the mines of Spain now found their way along the Via Heraclea; one feeder road brought so much silver along its path that it was named the Via Argenta (Road of Silver). Agricultural products, too, flowed along the roads, many to coastal seaports, becoming increasingly important as Rome expanded and became less self-sufficient at home. The products of Hispania were so valued that Rome forbade Alpine peoples to compete in cultivating grapes and olives. As befit her status as a cornerstone of the Roman Empire, Hispania played an important role in these early centuries. In the century before Christ, the civil war between Pompey and Caesar was partly fought on Iberian soil. Some of the finest Roman writers would come from Hispania, among them Martial, Lucan, and both Senecas; the peninsula even gave birth later to two emperors, Hadrian and Trajan.

Many changes came to the Gallic coast, too. Along with the main road, the Romans built a string of forts, most notable among them being Aquae Sextiae (Aix-en-Provence), on the main road north of Massilia (to use the Roman spelling) and Narbo Martius, at the end of the ancient Tin Route from Cornwall and Brittany to the Mediterranean. While the mountains above the coastal strip were still beyond Roman control, the coastal plain was made into a formal province of Rome, called Gallia Narbonensis or sometimes simply "Provincia," from which the area gets its modern name: Provence. The area became so settled and Romanized that Pliny the Elder said it was "more like Italy than a province." Cicero agreed, noting: "All Gaul is filled with traders and is full of Roman citizens." Even more traders and money-lenders moved in along the coast after Julius Caesar, in the sixth decade B.C., conquered the Gallic interior and brought it into the Roman fold. Colonies for disabled or retired veterans were also established along the clement coast, notably at Forum Julii, Arelate, and Aquae Sextiae. Gaul was, to many people, a kind of paradise, with minerals, grains, and animals in abundance. Although the minerals proved disappointing, being mined out quickly, the rest was true and provided even more goods for the traders—and new markets as well, for the Gauls were eager for luxuries introduced by the Romans, including wine from Hispania.

Throughout the early Roman period, the main traffic between Italy and Iberia went by sea or by the coast road. The truculent Celts held the mountain passes, and even threatened the Ligurian portion of the Heraclean Way. Not until the time of Caesar Augustus, in the decades just before the birth of Christ, were they subdued. Contemporary Greek geographer Strabo described the problem—and the solution:

The Salyes were the first of the Transalpine Celts to come under the domination of the Romans, who fought a long war against both this tribe and the Ligyes, for these two people barred the way that led to Iberia along the coast. They were indeed so successful with their brigandry on land and sea that this road was scarcely passable even to large armies. Finally, after 80 years of warfare, the Romans established with difficulty free transit over a width of 12 stadia for travellers on official business...
Indeed, Caesar Augustus finally suppressed brigandry through roadbuilding...

The road over the Mont Genèvre pass had been opened in 77 B.C. and improved by a native prince, Cottius, placed in charge by Augustus, in token of which the region was named the Cottian Alps. The road was far from easy, however. Even four centuries later soldier Ammianus Marcellinus complained that the road:

...follows the ridge that falls off with a sheer incline; terrible to look on because of the overhanging cliffs on every side. Especially in the season of spring, when the ice melts; then over precipitous ravines on either side and chasms rendered treacherous through the accumulations of ice, men and animals descending with hesitating step slide forward... wagons as well. They bind together a number of these vehicles with rope and hold them back from

behind with men and oxen and proceed at a snail's pace. But when the road is caked with ice...travelers ofttimes are swallowed up. They drive in stakes along the outer edge so that their line can guide the traveler.

By the first century A.D., wagons and people were pouring steadily along the Heraclean Way into Gallia Narbonensis and Hispania, necessitating extensive repairs over the whole road. The Romans were proud of having gained control of the whole of Heracles's route to the Atlantic, and the milestones posted all along the "Great Western Road" showed the mileage *ad oceanum* (to the ocean), so no one would forget that Rome controlled all the land to the edge of the world. Booksellers routinely sold itineraries for use by travelers. The 1,700-mile route from Rome to

A GADES		VSQVE	
ADPORTVM	XXIIII	VALENTIA	XX
HASTA	XVI	SAGTNTO	
VGIA	XXVII	ADNOVLAS	
ORIPPO	XXIIII	ILDVM	XXII
HISPALIM	IX	INTIBILI	
CARMONE	XXII	DERTOSA	
OBVCLA	XX	SVBSALTV	
ASTIGI	XV	TARRACONE	
ADARAS	XII	PALFVRIANA	
CORDVBA	XXIII	ANTISTIANA	XVI
ADDECVMO	X	ADFINES	
ADLVCOS	XVIII	ARRAGONE	XX
VCIESE	XVIII	PRAETORIO	
ADNDVLAS	XIII	SITERAS	
ADARAS	XIX	AQVISVOCON	
ADMORVM	XVIIII	GERVNDA	XII
ADSOLARIA	XVIIII	CILNIANA	X
MARIANA	XX	IVNCARIA	XV
MENTESA	XX	INPIRENEO	XVI
LIBISOSA	XXVIII	RVSCINNE	XXV
ARIETINIS	XXII	COMBVSTA	VI
SALTIGI	XVI	NARBONE	
ADPALEN	XXXII	BAETERRAS	XV
ADARAS	XXII	CESSERONE	XII
SAETABI	XXVIII	FORODOMITI	XVIII
SVCRONE	XV	SEXTANTIO	XV

SVMMA MILLIA

Silver itinerary goblets showed all the 106 stops between Gades (Cadiz) and Rome on the Heraclean Way, on the Mont Genèvre route. (From Konrad Miller, Itineraria Romana, *1916)*

151

Gades became so popular that silver mugs shaped like milestones were made, showing the itinerary city by city along the way; so famous was its destination, that the route was sometimes called the Via Gaditana. While the earliest of these mugs described the route via the coast road, later ones indicated the Alpine route from coastal Genoa via Augusta Taurinorum (Turin) to the Rhodanus. Early goblets also show the Rhodanus crossing at Arelate, where a permanent pontoon bridge was maintained. A later one shows the crossing at Traiectus Rhodani (Tarascon), a more direct connection between Aquae Sextiae and Nemausus (Nîmes).

For the great and ostentatious, travel was an opportunity to display wealth and status. Hundreds of two-wheeled chariots would be assembled and decorated with embossed metal plates; horses, mules, muleteers, and slaves would all be arrayed in traveling cloaks, often of bright red; sumptuous furniture would be packed for use on the road. Riding and driving were forbidden in Rome and most other cities except at night, since streets were overcrowded, so journeys generally started at the city gate. The traveler would be borne on a pillow-strewn litter by six to eight slaves to the assembly point, and would then transfer to a private chariot or coach, as would others of his retinue. Women travelers would often ride in a two- or four-wheeled closed carriage, while other servants would be conveyed in rougher wagons. En route, scouts were sent ahead to assess the condition of the road and arrange for repairs, if necessary. The truly extravagant, like the Emperor Gaius, known as Caligula, would sometimes require local inhabitants to sweep the roads and spray them with water to keep down the dust; others simply had to bear the dust and the heat. At night, such privileged travelers would stay with friends or would set up their own luxurious camps beside the road. The progress of an emperor seems often to have convulsed the countryside; Pliny, in praising Trajan's unpretentiousness, indicates the norm:

Now there is no disturbance over requisitioning vehicles, no haughtiness in receiving entertainment. The same food suffices for the emperor as for his suite. How different was the journeying of the other emperor [Domitian] in days not long past, if indeed that was a journey, not a devastation, when he carried off the goods of his hosts, when everything right and left was brought to rack and ruin, just as if those very barbarians from whom he was fleeing were falling upon the place.

While such travelers received much criticism from Roman moralists, they were a small minority on the Heraclean Way. The majority traveled more modestly. A closed four-wheeled coach was sometimes used to transport a whole family; such vehicles were also used as stage-coaches for individual travelers. Mules and horses were provided for changes along the way, with drivers and porters being under government supervision. Still other travelers preferred litters, even for long distances, being borne either by slaves or slung on poles carried by two mules, one fore, one aft. Such travelers were sheltered behind curtains, and could sleep, read, or write as they chose. Plutarch records the preferences of Julius Caesar, who made many trips on the Heraclean Way: "For the most part, Caesar slept in his chariot or in litters, so that he could still be active even though he was resting...He traveled with such speed that he needed no more than eight days to reach the Rhodanus from Rome." (Progress was slower in Spain.)

Someone whose tastes were simpler yet might drive his own chariot, or ride a horse or mule. Beyond these, there were, of course, many people on foot; indeed, many came from as far as Hispania to Rome, having heard of the prospects of charity from wealthy benefactors. For ordinary travelers—those not too particular about their company—inns were provided along the road, where food and lodging might be had. Many travelers were heading for a vacation to one of the resorts along the Gallic section of the Heraclean Way, prized even then for its salubrious climate.

In addition to these there were the couriers. Soon after Augustus pacified the Heraclean Way, he established an imperial post, with stations and changes of horses (veredi) provided. These were meant for use by imperial officials, who were provided with two folding tablets called a diploma, which was a passport good only for a certain time; such diplomas were occasionally issued to other privileged travelers. The army maintained its own system of couriers—some said spies—who traveled throughout the provinces; these were called peregrini, from which came the word pilgrim. Private persons employed riders or runners on their personal business; this, too, was often for show, and Seneca complained about "the rich coxcombs with their Numidian runners stirring up a cloud of dust." Merchants also traveled these roads, paying customs duties at each provincial border. For this reason alone, the sea route was often preferable to the land; but the shipping season ran only from late spring to early autumn, making the land route the main all-weather highway. So rough wagons hauling heavy cargo also joined the stream of traffic on the Heraclean Way. Those who traveled light and found no accommodation on the road would generally find shelter for the night under a pine tree or in the shadow of one of the many tombs that lined the main road, especially near cities.

When the Heraclean Way was the main lifeline of the Roman Empire, it was relatively secure for travelers. But as the empire expanded, and the armies were spread out to distant borders, highway robbers—often disenfranchised conquered peoples—attacked travelers boldly; in the third century, a band of over 2,000 preyed on the Heraclean coast road from their base in Albium Ingaunum (Albenga), between Genoa and Nicaea (Nice). Another force appeared on the road in the same period: Christianity. Spreading across the waters from the East and along the road from Rome, Christianity soon took strong hold, especially in the Rhodanus delta, centered on Arelate, which became an archbishopric. From there the new religion spread in all directions.

The Roman Empire itself was weakening, however, and its center shifting to the east. In the early fourth century, when Christianity was adopted as the state religion, a "new Rome" was founded on the Bosporus; called Constantinople after its founder, the Emperor Constantine, it became a focus for the pilgrims who began to make their way overland to Asia Minor and on to Jerusalem and soon eclipsed Rome itself. By the early fifth century, when the waves of Germanic invaders began pouring down toward

Along the Heraclean Way, in northern Italy, France, and here in Spain, were many health resorts, where Romans came to take the waters. (Authors' archives)

the Heraclean coast, Rome itself was left to be sacked; the government retired to Ravenna on the Adriatic coast and even the Roman fleet was nowhere to be seen in the west Mediterranean.

With this onslaught, the great early days of the Heraclean Way were over, and would not return for 1,400 years. Abandoned to their fate, the inhabitants of the shoreside towns began a long withdrawal to the hillside fastnesses where they could defend themselves from the Goths and Vandals who coursed through Gaul and Hispania. Pilgrims still made their way along Heracles's route, with difficulty and at great peril, but travel for pleasure was a thing of the past. Traders would continue to ply the route, as they had in prehistoric times, but working only at a rudimentary level, given the collapse of the Roman economic system. The road itself was left without any kind of maintenance—and indeed was often cannibalized by local residents for building purposes. As its condition became worse for use by carts and carriages, travelers turned increasingly to riding and walking, sometimes developing bridle or foot paths alongside the cracking and overgrown paved road.

In these dark centuries, the Heraclean Way became a divided route: the Visigoths controlled the Spanish portion and the coastal strip to the Rhône; the Franks held the short, but important midsection between Marseilles and the region of Nice; east of that was Lombardy, which stretched down the Italian coast to north of Rome. The final sector of the Heraclean Way was, for a time, part of the Eastern Roman Empire, but later was included in the Papal States centered on Rome, while the rest of Italy was divided up into duchies. No longer a main highway joining united lands, the Heraclean Way had little value except as a local road.

Conditions became even worse in the eighth century, when determined Moslem armies crossed from North Africa into Spain; they quickly took Iberia—which they called al-Andalus—and were stopped from proceeding much further only by the Franks, under Charles Martel, in 732. Although Moslem power was concentrated south of the Pyrenees, the Gallic midsection of the Heraclean Way was subjected to indiscriminate plundering and pillaging by Arab pirates, some of whom established their own bases along the Gallic coast. Destruction was so widespread that few records from this and earlier periods remain along the Provence coast.

In Spain itself, the Moslems had a very different impact. Many of the early Islamic invaders were only a few years removed from the desert; these people, many of them Berbers or Arabs from Yemen, were astounded by the amazing array of buildings, aqueducts, bridges, and roads which were "for the most part attributed to one of the ancient Kings of al-Andalus whose name was Hercules," according to Arab geographer al-Bakrì. But among these invaders were some of high culture, from Egypt and

Syria, bearing with them the learning of the East, especially of the Greeks, which they preserved and expanded, while Europe languished in ignorance. These Moslems— among whom were included many European converts— paid little heed to the roads of al-Andalus, using them as they found them. But they founded a high ecumenical culture, in which Moslems, Christians, and Jews lived together rather peaceably, intermarried, and even shared the houses of worship, their Sabbaths falling on different days of the week. With the decline of sea-trade along the western coast, the port of Gades—now called Cadiz— became less important, but some of the highest centers of Moslem culture were found along the old Heraclean Way, notably Córdoba and Seville.

Along the rest of the Heraclean Way, the ninth and tenth centuries saw some revival of the ports along the route, especially Pisa, Genoa, and Marseilles. The Crusaders, who streamed down from the north to these ports, and the traders who benefited from the Christian expansion to the east continued strengthening these ports—really city-states—over the centuries. But this had little effect on the coast road. Where it followed the coastal strip from the Pyrenees east, the road was generally rough but usable; but further east, in the region of the Maritime Alps, the lack of repair had left some sections barely usable as early as the eighth century. Even where roads were usable, bandits were a constant threat. This situation continued with little change for centuries, and travelers on the Heraclean Way often avoided the rocky coast by taking a boat, frequently from Marseilles or Frèjus to one of the Italian ports, like Genoa, Pisa, or Leghorn (Livorno).

The problem was not only the road, but the divisions between the petty kingdoms along the way—and the innumerable customs duties and tolls levied along the way. Regulations from tenth century Pavia, in the western Alps, noted that:

> All persons coming from beyond the mountains into Lombardy are obligated to pay the *decima* [ten percent tax] on horses, male and female slaves, woolen, linen, and hemp cloth, tin, and swords...But everything that [pilgrims] bound for Rome to Saint Peter's take with them for expenses is to be passed without payment of the *decima*.

In places where the borders zigzagged across the road, merchants might be subject to multiple tolls along a single section of coast, a practice certain to discourage trade. Squabbles between warring duchies also wrought trouble for travelers. In some periods, inland Florence harassed travelers who wanted to head into rivaling Pisa. Such arguments could lead to other problems along the road. The eighteenth-century English traveler Tobias Smollett noted the difficulty of crossing the Var River just west of Nice:

According to the report of a man still living, three bridges were thrown across the Var, and successively destroyed owing to the reciprocal jealousy between the kings of France and Sardinia. If there were only a bridge and a post road, I am quite sure the foreigners who cross the Alps would infinitely prefer this surer and more agreeable route. It would also be used by those who at present hire a felluca [an Arab-style sail-boat] from Marseilles to Antibes and thus expose themselves to the dangers and inconveniences of an open boat.

There was, indeed, some reason for bridges on the Heraclean Way to be dismantled, for the route served invaders in modern times as well as in classical, with the borders continually being adjusted between France and the many Italian states.

As for the road itself, it was little more than an eight-foot-wide dirt track, most difficult in the rocky section known as the Corniche, above Nice. As the French lady-in-waiting Madame de Genlis noted in 1780:

In many places the Corniche is so narrow that it is difficult for anyone to pass...at all the really dangerous places we dismounted and made the passer-by hold our hands.

Others, while aware of the hazards, were also attuned to the striking beauty of the coast road above Nice, like this French traveler in 1740:

On leaving Frèjus we did nothing but climb up and up and by very steep ascents. The side of the road was precipitous, which seemed to my companions a very bad arrangement. As for me, I thought this road the most beautiful in the whole world. It was, indeed, constructed with great care and lies through the most wonderful forests and trees.

At the turn of the 19th century, this road—and its Alpine alternate—attracted the attention of one who aspired to build a great empire in the tradition of Rome's, and who saw roadbuilding as an important part of the expansion process. Napoleon Bonaparte modernized the eastern part of the old Heraclean Way, still called *lu Camin Aurelian* by the locals in remembrance of its Roman heritage. He built the famous road called the Grande Corniche between Frèjus and Mentone (on the modern Italian border, east of Nice), running over the mountains 1,400 feet above the sea. In the same period, the Prince of Monaco built a coast road between Nice and Mentone, which is commonly known as the lower Corniche, or Route de Littoral. While these roads certainly facilitated communication between France and Italy, Napoleon's main route south was through the Alps; he preferred the Mont Cenis Pass, better placed for entry from the north,

but also improved the Mont Genèvre Pass connecting Italy and the Rhône via Grenoble and Briançon. Napoleon convulsed Europe for decades, but one of his most lasting monuments may have been the roads he built.

In the early 19th century, while northern European travelers were discovering the Mediterranean, some arrived on the shore of the Riviera. It was the British politician Lord Brougham who is credited with discerning the potential delights of Cannes, when in 1834 he was forced to stay in the small fishing village due to an outbreak of cholera in Nice. Travelers soon discovered what the Romans had known long ago: that the Riviera was as beautiful as it was healthful. A few decades later, in 1860, Nice opted to unite with France; Monaco remained independent, while Italy's many states united to form one nation. The borders between France and Italy assumed their modern position, just east of Mentone, and the eastern half of the Heraclean Way was split in two. The Italian Riviera, with Genoa at its center, sports several resorts, including Portofino and San Remo. The French Riviera, or Côte d'Azur, is graced by Mentone, Nice, Antibes, Cannes, and independent Monaco.

In the early 20th century, these resorts were the province of the rich and privileged, who made Nice "the Winter Capital of the World." International playboys with their new toys—automobiles—were naturally attracted to the Heraclean Way. At the time, the Corniches were probably the best roads in the world, for they were funded by tourist revenues; Monaco pioneered in the widespread use of tar on roads. It is not surprising that the 50-mile-an-hour speed record for automobiles was first broken at Nice in 1901. By that time, the historian of roads Hermann Schreiber estimates, the Grande Corniche saw about 500 automobiles, a like number of horse-drawn carriages, perhaps 200 motorcycles, and a few hundred rough carts daily. It was not the pleasurable sport of driving that alone attracted people, for the beauties of the landscape were soon widely known, figuring in innumerable novels and travel accounts.

The western half of the Heraclean Way followed its old route from the Rhône through the Pyrenees and partway down the coast before cutting inland. As Spain gradually passed from Moslem to Christian control over the centuries, its administrative centers were shifted from the south—especially from Seville and Córdoba—to the north. The Visigoths had made their capital in Toledo; Philip II in the 16th century decided to make a new capital at Madrid, in the middle of the country. The Portuguese, who occupied roughly the Roman province called Lusitania, made their major center Lisbon (Olisipo). The result of these moves was to pull the route of the Heraclean Way across the peninsula further north; the main road left the coast past Barcelona, crossed the Ebro River at Zaragoza (Saragossa, formerly Caesar Augusta), then angled across the central mountains to follow the course of the Tajo

(Tagus) River into Lisbon. Southern Spain lost its political power, though it surely retained the romance of its history, which in modern times draws increasing numbers of tourists. This was the main post route, the main invasion route, and the route later taken by the railroads, which also sent spurs south to the older cities.

Today the old Heraclean Way is a prime tourist route, traversed by modern travelers in their private automobiles. From Cadiz to the Spanish coast, through Le Perthus, along the Provence coast, around the Rhône delta they ride, following the road along the spectacularly beautiful Riviera through France and Italy to Rome, the ancient hub of the world. Indeed, so many tourists have come that a new route—the Middle Corniche—was built between Nice and Mentone just before World War II. There visitors follow the ancient way of Heracles on the cliff-face above the palace of Monaco and below the old hill route of the Caesars.

Selective Bibliography

Braudel, Fernand. *The Mediterranean and the Mediterranean World in the Age of Philip II* (2 vols.). Translated from the French by Siân Reynolds (New York: Harper & Row, 1972 and 1973). An unparalleled comprehensive work.

Charlesworth, Martin Percival. *Trade-Routes and Commerce of the Roman Empire* (London: Cambridge University Press, 1924). A classic, packing considerable detail into a small space.

Chevallier, Raymond. *Roman Roads*. Translated from the French by N. H. Field (Berkeley and Los Angeles: University of California Press, 1976). A detailed work, focusing on literary evidence and existing remains.

Devoluy, Pierre, and Pierre Borel. *The French Riviera* (London: The Medici Society Limited, 1924). A personal tour for travelers.

East, W. Gordon. *An Historical Geography of Europe,* third edition (London: Methuen, 1948). A very useful general work.

Leighton, Albert C. *Transport and Communication in Early Medieval Europe, A.D. 500–1100* (Newton Abbot: David Charles, 1972). A helpful overview.

Murray, A. H. Hallam, accompanied by Henry W. Nevinson and Montgomery Carmichael. *Sketches on the Old Road Through France to Florence* (New York: E. P. Dutton, 1927). A reprint of a 1904 travel work with many watercolor illustrations.

Rostovtzeff, M. *The Social and Economic History of the Roman Empire* (2 vols.); second edition revised by P. M. Fraser (Oxford: At the Clarendon Press, 1957). A full standard work; Volume II contains notes and indexes only.

Schreiber, Hermann. *The History of Roads: From Amber Route to Motorway.* Translated from the German by Stewart Thomson (London: Barrie and Rockliff, 1961). A general work, with several chapters treating the Roman roads, then and now.

Semple, Ellen Churchill. *The Geography of the Mediterranean Region: Its Relation to Ancient History* (New York: Holt, 1931). An exceptionally fine overview.

Sitwell, N. H. H. *Roman Roads of Europe* (New York: St. Martin's, 1981). A beautifully illustrated work with many useful detailed regional maps.

Skeel, Caroline A. J. *Travel in the First Century After Christ: With Special Reference to Asia Minor* (Cambridge: At the University Press, 1901). A brief gem, more general than the subtitle indicates.

Trend, J. B. *The Civilization of Spain* (London: Oxford University Press, 1944). A handy, well-written overview.

Von Hagen, Victor Wolfgang. *The Roads That Led To Rome* (Cleveland: World, 1967). A useful well-illustrated general survey of the Roman road system.

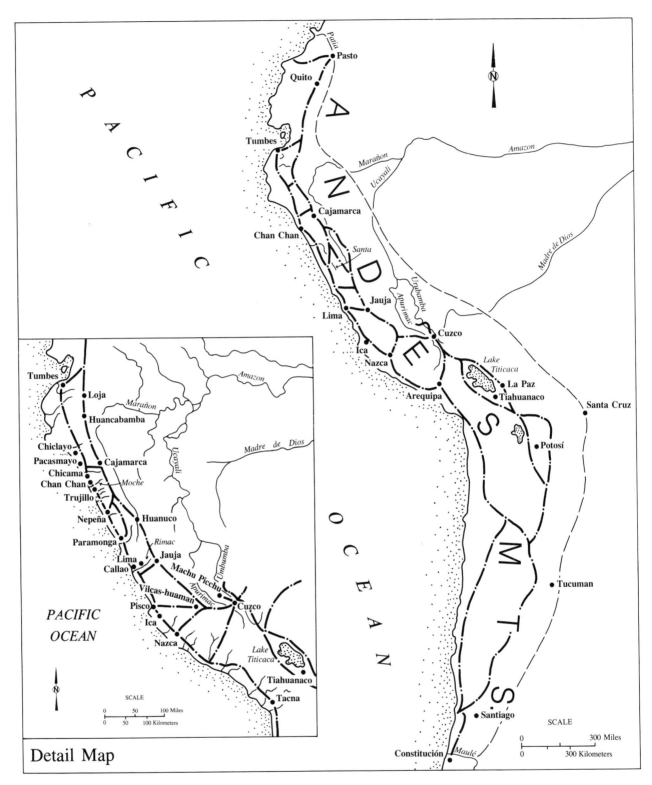

PACIFIC

OCEAN

Patia

Pasto

Quito

Tumbes

Marañon

Ucayali

Amazon

ANDES

Cajamarca

Chan Chan

Santa

Madre de Dios

Jauja

Lima

Urubamba

Apurimac

Cuzco

Ica

Nazca

Lake
Titicaca

La Paz

Arequipa

Tiahuanaco

Santa Cruz

Potosí

M

T

S

Tucuman

Santiago

SCALE

0   300 Miles

0   300 Kilometers

Constitución

Maulé

Detail Map

Tumbes

Loja

Amazon

Marañon

Huancabamba

Chiclayo

Pacasmayo

Cajamarca

Ucayali

Madre de Dios

Chicama

Moche

Chan Chan

Trujillo

Nepeña

Huanuco

Rimac

Paramonga

Umbumba

Lima

Jauja

Callao

Machu Picchu

Vilcas-huaman

Apurimac

Cuzco

Pisco

Ica

Nazca

PACIFIC
OCEAN

Lake
Titicaca

Tiahuanaco

Tacna

SCALE

0   50   100 Miles

0   50   100 Kilometers

The Inca Royal Road

—··—··— Main Inca Roads   ———— Approximate Borders of the
                                                    Inca Empire

158

The Inca Royal Road

When Spaniards arrived in South America, they were astonished to find an elaborate system of roads stretching for thousands of miles along the western coast and ranges of the continent. These early 16th century observers vied with each other in the exuberance of their admiration, more than one calling it "the longest and greatest" road system in the world. Hernando Pizarro affirmed: "Nothing equals the magnificence of this road across the sierra..." Scribe Pedro de Cieza de León noted: "Despite the great distance from Quito to Cuzco, which is more than the distance from Seville to Rome, the road is as busy as the one from Seville to Traiana, which is the most that can be said." Indeed it was, for that was the old Roman road, now over 1,000 years old and neglected, but still heavily used for transport of silver.

What occasioned all this praise is described by Cieza de León:

> ...this was a long road, over 1,100 leagues [about 3,300 miles] which went over rugged mountains and along precipices so sheer in many places that one could not see the bottom of the chasm, some of the sides of which were so sharp that the road-builders had to cut through the living rock to keep the level and maintain its proper width. In other places the road's incline was so steep that they had to build steps to ascend to the top, with platforms every so often so that the travelers could rest. In other places the road had to be forced through snow drifts and glaciers, which was the most dangerous. Yet through these drifts or through forests they built the roads level and, when necessary, well-paved with stone.

> Let those who read this and have been in Peru recall the road that goes from Pachacamac on the coast to Jauja, over the craggy mountains of Huarochiri and across the snow-bound peaks of Pariacá... Let them also recall the tunnels and the twisting step-road that runs down to the bridge at the Apurímac or how the road crosses the sierras of Paltas, Cajas and Ayabacas and other regions of this realm where the road is some fifteen feet wide...and in the time of the Incas clean of grass or any refuse (for they were always caring for it).

> ...In the memories of any other peoples I doubt that there is a record of another highway comparable to this.

The Incas themselves called the route *Capac Ñan*, or "Beautiful Road."

Spanning an empire approximately as long, though not nearly as large in area, as the Roman Empire at its peak, the Inca Royal Road system covered and united a land of extremes, from a coastal desert where rain might fall only a few times in a century, to some of the highest mountains in the world, to tropical jungle along the headwaters of the Amazon River. The central, and longest, portion of the road system ran over 3,000 miles — on the modern map from Quito, in northern Ecuador, to central Chile — along the ridges and across the deep gorges of the

Andes Mountains. The other main road in the Inca system ran along the coast for over 2,000 miles, being connected with the ridge route by a series of lateral roads that, like rungs of a ladder, followed the river valleys down to the coast. A shorter spur angled eastward from the ridge route into the Amazon Basin. But the Incas were only the last of many peoples to use this great road system, much of which existed before the Incas rose to power. Indeed, it was the road system that allowed the highland Incas to dominate such a vast empire—as it would later allow the Spanish to penetrate and conquer it in a matter of weeks, forever changing the life of the continent.

When the earliest inhabitants came to the region is a matter of considerable speculation and controversy. Certainly by 10,000 to 12,000 years ago immigrants had filtered across the Bering Strait and followed the main route down along the eastern slope of the mountains that form the backbone of the Western Hemisphere's continents. These early immigrants—who may have been joined by other immigrants who crossed the Pacific Ocean—settled in widely separated communities, isolated in oasislike river valleys amid uninhabitable coastal desert or in mountain pockets cut off by high peaks and deep river gorges impassable except during the dry season. The tribe that became the Incas was originally, and for most of history, more isolated than most, occupying a notch high in the Andes, between two of the furthest tributaries of the Amazon River, the roaring Apurimac (the Great Speaker) and the Urubamba.

Perhaps partly because of the difficulty of traveling in the mountains, advanced cultures appeared earliest in a 50- to 100-mile-wide strip of land on the Pacific coast. Although it borders an ocean, this coastal strip is one of the most arid areas on earth; the Peru, or Humboldt, Current carries icy Antarctic waters along the coast, keeping warm air aloft in a thermal inversion that brings fog but no rain. Habitable land was to be found only in the river valleys that drained the western face of the Andes range. As Cieza de León noted: "...between one valley and another...lie sand wastes and arid stretches of rocks where no living or growing thing is to be seen, neither grass nor trees." At first largely confined to these river oases, the coastal communities gradually coalesced into some distinct early cultures, bound together by trails along the desert strips between the various settlements. Along a northerly stretch of coast, the Mochica cultures emerged, some three centuries before the birth of Christ. Centered on the Moche and Chicama valleys, this culture produced a distinctive type of pottery, much of which has survived to this day; since the area had an almost total absence of rain, plastic mud from the river valleys was the main construction material, for both utensils and habitations. Further south, below modern Lima and centered in the area of Pisco, was the Paracas culture; south

of that, and somewhat later, was the Ica-Nazca culture. These cultures early developed an elaborate system of irrigation and terracing, to make the most of the limited water supply that reached them from the Andes.

The desert peoples were not completely self-sufficient, however. Gradually they established routes along the river valleys for trade with the mountain peoples, for each group had goods needed or desired by the other. The coastal peoples had salt and iodine-containing seaweed—both vital for health—as well as fish, decorative seashells, cotton, tobacco, cacao (the origin of chocolate), and possibly coca. The highlanders, for their part, offered wool and llamas, as well as minerals not available on the desert plain. The trade routes along the desert and the western slope of the Andes marked out the earliest portions of what would—over 1,000 years later—become the Inca Royal Road system, where the lateral river-valley trails intersected with the parallel coastal and highland trails. Only foot trails were necessary, for the wheel was unknown in the Americas before the arrival of Europeans. The roads did not require the smooth gradient needed for wheeled vehicles. Goods were backpacked by human carriers or loaded onto llamas, and steps were cut into the steep-sided mountains along the routes.

This network of trails sufficed for hundreds of years, during the height of the coastal cultures, and in approximately 1000 A.D. they provided invasion routes for the first of the empire-builders from the highlands. These were the Tiahuanaco peoples, who moved from their homeland near Lake Titicaca to conquer the coastal peoples, including the Nazca and the Mochica. Although the Tiahuanacos held the coastal strip for over two centuries, they had little lasting effect on the lowland cultures, and when their domination ended in the 14th century, the native cultures of the area re-emerged. The most significant of the resurgent cultures was the Chimu Empire, which developed out of the old Mochica culture. Extending beyond the old Mochica limits, the Kingdom of Chimor stretched for over 600 miles from Tumbes in modern Ecuador to within 100 miles of modern Lima, Peru. The Chimu Kingdom was roughly the size of early Egypt's at its height; its capital was at Chan Chan, a city estimated to have over 50,000 inhabitants, in the Moche Valley, near modern Trujillo.

The Chimus were great builders. Following the earlier lead of the Mochica, they developed an elaborate system of canals, which allowed them to extend agriculture and habitation out from the source of their water in the score of river valleys in their kingdom. (Some modern observers have suggested that the coastal inhabitants turned their land into desert by overfarming. However, more recent evidence indicates that over the centuries the coastal strip, forced upward by the action of geological plates, may have risen just enough to cut off the water sources for the Chimus' elaborate system of aqueducts

Along the route in the background, couriers brought fish from the coast to the Inca rulers at Cuzco, past the tampu *and storage bins in the foreground. (Victor W. Von Hagen)*

and irrigation ditches. The same phenomena may have occurred across the world on the Arabian peninsula.) In the larger settlements these activities supported, the Chimus built temples, forts, and other structures, all of large blocks of adobe brick. To protect these settlements from attacks by other peoples to the south, the Chimus elaborated, strengthened, and extended the "Great Wall of Peru" in the Santa Valley, rising up into the high sierra 90 miles from the coast. And to connect these more substantial habitations, the Chimus built more formal roads along the coast and river valleys.

The exact Chimu contribution to the great road system of western America is unclear; like that of the earlier peoples of the area, it is buried under the later Inca and modern constructions. But Chimu roads were probably very substantial, judging by the fact that Chan

Chan had regular streets and a 60-foot-wide promenade for formal processions, and by the various pyramids, administrative buildings, step roads, and forts that remain to show their influence.

The main roads in Chimor were approximately 20 feet wide and, where they passed through the shifting sand dunes called *medanos*, were edged by shoulder-high walls, made of adobe blocks bound together with mud as cement. Where the sand drifts were so deep that this kind of road was not feasible, the Chimus lined the route with long poles stuck into the sand as guideposts. Such roads required regular attention; as Cieza de León was later to note of the Incas: "...just as care was taken to keep the road clean and to repair the walls if they became worn or needed mending, so they were on the alert to replace any of the poles or piles in the sand if the wind blew them

161

Some of the many types of bridges devised for crossing deep mountain gorges are illustrated here. (From Juan and Ulloa, Voyage, *vol. I, Madrid, 1746)*

down." People on these roads traveled mainly on foot, some carrying 70 pounds or more of trade goods, but llamas were the main load-bearing animals. The pace was slow, with llamas moving about 10 miles a day. Carrying only about 100 pounds at full capacity—less than beasts of burden elsewhere in the world—llamas were, however, able to operate in both the extreme heat of the coast and the extreme cold and thin air of the mountains. Like other early civilizations, the Chimus continued to trade actively with the highlanders along the lateral routes, especially the route that ran along the Moche Valley, from Chan Chan into the mountains, and the heavily traveled route on Chimor's southern border, from Paramonga through the natural pass of the Rio Fortaleza Valley to the highlands road.

While the Chimus still ruled the coast, the highland peoples—including those speaking Quechua, who were later known as the Incas—remained relatively backward. With different languages and different gods, the tribes that lived in isolated gorges, on high plateaus, and along the terraced sides of steep mountains rivaled each other for power, but no one was dominant. In the 13th century, however, one dynasty emerged as the ruling family in the Cuzco Valley, high up in the mountains between the Apurimac and Urubamba rivers; they took the

name of Inca and set about subjugating their highland neighbors. They had some success until a tribe from the west, the Chancas, challenged them and in 1438 called for them to abandon their capital of Cuzco. While the Inca ruler withdrew, an Inca pretender—Yupanqui—refused to leave, instead going on the offensive and defeating the Chancas. As a result, the other Inca pretenders were set aside in favor of Yupanqui, who was given the name "Pachacuti," meaning "he transforms the earth."

It was Pachacuti who laid the foundations for the Inca Empire—and for the Incas' reputation as great builders. Under his rule, Cuzco was rebuilt as an imperial capital, largely constructed of the huge trapezoidal blocks of stone so characteristic of the Inca architecture. From then on, Cuzco was the center of the universe for the Incas; like Rome in Europe, all roads in western South America led to Cuzco. Pachacuti extended the Inca Empire in all directions, and each quarter was given a distinctive name. The Empire itself was called Tahuantinsuyu (the Four Quarters of the World). Under Pachacuti, it ran north to Cuzco along the highlands nearly to the level of the southern border of the Chimu Empire; west of Cuzco, it reached part way down the western slope of the Andes; and south of the capital it extended down along Lake Titicaca. These three quarters were largely treeless, although rain made the high valleys arable. The fourth quarter was quite different; it reached eastward toward the Amazon Basin, with dense forest above 8,000 feet and tropical jungle below. This area the Incas called the Antisuyu, from which later came the Hispanicized name "Andes."

The roads controlling each of these four quarters became administrative lifelines, as Pachacuti laid the basis for an Inca Empire. He established a pattern of resettlement and specialization, with tribal groups being moved within the empire at his direction to perform specific functions, often under the direction of imported resident governors. Where roads did not exist, Pachacuti had local residents build them. Cieza de León explained how it worked:

> ...Now, when an Inca decided to build one of these famous highways, no great provisions or levies were needed. An inspector went out ahead through the lands, laying out the route and assigning Indians each to their own section, for the building of the road....In this way, with each province responsible...for the building of the road, which it undertook at its own expense and with its own Indians, the road was built and laid out in a relatively short time. When the road came to a barren or unpopulated place, the Indians that lived nearest came with the necessary tools and victuals, and so all was done with sustained effort.

Roads were built straight wherever possible, but—arable land being precious to the Incas—new roads often skirted cultivated fields, going instead over less hospitable ground.

New roads required the building of bridges over rivers at key points throughout the Empire. Sometimes these were pontoon bridges, built on a base of reed boats and renewed after the floods each year. If the space was relatively narrow and shallow, a simple wooden bridge or some cantilevered stone slabs were used. But deep mountain gorges required different measures. Most important, if the Empire was to hold together, was a permanent, year-round crossing over the deep gorge of the Apurimac River, over which the road to the north had to pass. Before the Empire, local inhabitants had made do with baskets pulled across the gorge on tight ropes; but for heavier traffic, especially between November and May when the river was in flood, they had to detour hundreds of miles out of the way. Under Pachacuti, a tribe was assigned the task of building and maintaining a fiber-cable bridge for continuous use. This was the famous Apurimac Bridge, which astonished outsiders for centuries, as it hung suspended high above the river.

In this period, existing roads were also widened and expanded. Throughout the Empire, Pachacuti established a system of *tampus*, stone buildings built 12 to 20 miles apart (roughly one day's journey) to act as both administrative centers for the local area and as shelters for official travelers, and post houses, built one and a half to two miles apart, from which runners shuttled relaying messages. In these ways, Pachacuti laid the basis for his new empire and for its expansion.

And expand it did. Within 55 years, under Pachacuti and his successor, Tupa Inca, the Inca Empire expanded in all directions. South of Cuzco, it was extended to the Maulé River near modern Constitución, Chile, as well as inland to include the Bolivian high plateau (the Altiplano), as far as present-day Santa Cruz. The Incas also successfully defeated the Chimus, forcing the ancient kingdom into submission by cutting off its water supply. In addition to extending the Empire further east toward the Amazon, Tupa Inca reached north to Quito; his successor, Huayna Capac, completed the conquest of the eastern slope of the Andes, as well as pushing even farther north to Pasto on the Patia River in modern Ecuador. Starting from the small valley surrounding Cuzco, the Incas had in less than a century built an empire that extended over 3,000 miles, from north of the Equator to well south of the Tropic of Capricorn. The roads built before their emergence had eased their conquest, while the roads they blazed helped them consolidate victory.

But the Incas did not rest there. Using a system of periodic forced labor (rather than taxes), they set about building, rebuilding, expanding, and maintaining an all-weather road system throughout their empire. Following the old routes, they widened most roads to 20 feet or more, cutting into rockface where the route followed a cliff face or a sharp incline called for stairs. They provided drainage for low-lying roads or replaced them with raised causeways. Paving and curbing were laid on heavily traveled sections near large towns, and bridges were built over rivers and streams. And following the Chimu model for desert roads, they used high sidewalls to keep the route clear or lines of poles to mark the way across the sands. Distance markers were placed along the road, approximately every four miles. Piles of stones called *apachetas* often grew in high passes, where travelers who had just made the ascent tossed a stone onto the pile, as if to throw off their fatigue. Traffic along these roads was still by foot. Although the Inca family might be carried on litters by bearers, everyone else used their own two feet. Armies using these roads could reach any part of the Empire quickly, to assist local garrisons in difficulty. Professional couriers called *chasquis*—on call day and night—carried information recorded on *quipus* (string records, writing being unknown to the Incas), which supplemented memorized messages. Using relays, with each *chasqui* running only one and a half to two miles, this system could transmit information over the 1,250 miles between Cuzco and Quito in five to seven days—astonishing speed for a system relying solely on foot power. The roads were also used for transporting the luxuries and necessities that were produced by the Empire and stored in state warehouses for distribution among the population at imperial command. Controlling population movement within the Empire, the Incas allowed only local and official travelers on the roads.

So stood the Inca Empire, less than a century old, when the Spanish arrived in South America. When Francisco Pizarro's party arrived in Tumbes, the Empire's northernmost coastal town, they were much struck by the roads they found. The official recorder noted:

> We marched along a broad road made by manual labor and traversing the whole land. By the side of the road flow channels of water...at the end of each day's journey there is a *tampu* like an inn. Parts of the road are paved and bounded on each side by a wall.

He also noted some things that presaged changes on the Inca Royal Road: that "two carts could be driven abreast upon it," the wheel having arrived in South America with the Spaniards, and that six men on horseback could ride abreast on it. Horses, and the weapons carried by the horsemen, were equally new to the Incas, a term the Spanish came to apply to all native inhabitants.

Using this road system, the Spanish in 1532 went to the heart of the Inca Empire with astonishing speed. Francisco Pizarro and his men moved down the coast road for about 200 miles and then, in just two days, part of the force ascended a step road to Huancabamba, on the ridge road at 11,000 feet. Word of their arrival in Inca territory preceded them, as had word of their presence on the coast off Tumbes five years earlier. The new Inca ruler, Atahuallpa, was momentarily victorious in a civil war with his half-brother Huascar; after pillaging the holy city of Cuzco, Huascar's capital, he was returning to his own capital in Quito when word of the strangers arrived. Proceeding along the north road to Cajamarca to meet these "white men," Atahuallpa, with his army of 40,000 men, was so overconfident that he allowed himself to be captured by the Spanish force of less than 200 men. Then, in one of the most famous ransoms in history, the whole of the Inca Royal Road system was put into use ferrying gold to win the release of Atahuallpa. To win his freedom, he promised the Spaniards a roomful of gold. But in the interim, he had his rival, Huascar, put to death, an action the Spanish used as justification for their execution of Atahuallpa, even after the ransom was paid.

With the Inca nation in disarray, the Spanish took full control, setting up a puppet ruler. Their path of conquest was not always clear. When the Spanish headed toward Cuzco in the next year, they often found the road blocked with logs and rocks, with fields and villages burned ahead of them; and they were attacked in several of the narrow defiles through which the ridge road passed.

But it still took the Spanish only two months to move the 600 to 700 miles from Cajamarca to Cuzco, arriving there only a year after they had first entered Inca territory. The road system's contribution to the Spaniards' success was considerable; as Cieza de León noted regarding the army's approach across the marshy plain before Cuzco: "It would have been very difficult to cross this bog without the broad and solid causeway that the Incas ordered to be built." Francisco Pizarro agreed, noting: "After God, it was the Inca's roads that gave us victory."

A substantial portion of the population retreated to the wilds of the eastern Andes, under their chosen Inca, extending the Antisuyu Road ahead of them along mountain sides often too steep for farming without terracing. There in the forest and jungle they established new towns or expanded old ones, perhaps the most striking of them being Machu Picchu, on a mountain peak, and set up a new capital at Vilcabamba. For several decades continual wars raged between the Spanish and the Incas, and between the Spanish rulers themselves as they broke into factions, each wanting a bigger piece of the South American treasure. But in 1572 the last of the Incas was captured and beheaded, ending Inca control in any part of their old Empire.

From that point on, the Spanish were unchallenged. They had already begun to put their stamp on the area, founding their own towns, almost always on the site of old way stations (*tampus*). As early as 1535, Pizarro's followers founded Cuidad de los Reyes (City of the Kings) on the coast, near the mouth of the Rimac Valley. This city, which for a time was co-equal with Cuzco as a religious and administrative center, soon took dominance as the capital of the region, renamed Lima. Since the Spanish controlled this new colony primarily by sea, Lima's port of Callao became the terminus of the sea route between Peru and Central America. The old ridge and mountainside roads, which had suited the Inca imperial needs perfectly, were of little use to the Spanish, whose horses and mules could not traverse the steep trails as easily as llamas did, if at all. The balance in the region once again tipped toward the coastal portion of the road system, with the mountain roads degenerating.

Spain's greed and colonial policy had significant consequences for the later development of the road system. Spanish colonial policy restricted all trade in the Americas to just a few ports; all Peruvian business was to be conducted by sea from Lima to the Isthmus of Panama, shipped overland, and only then sent on to Spain. But worse than that, residents of the Rio de la Plata region, who had one of the best ports on the continent— Buenos Aires—were not allowed to use it, but were required to use the Panama Route instead. The Spanish crown's strict control over trade, with its resulting heavy costs, taxes, and duties, caused imports to sell for five to ten times as much as in Spain. It is no wonder that smugglers—Spanish, Portuguese, English, Dutch, and French— began to use Buenos Aires and bring their goods overland. Not only did they have goods from Europe to sell at attractive prices, but the discovery of some new, extremely rich silver mines in Bolivia provided valuable exports to smuggle out of the territory, without paying tribute to the Spanish crown. The result was the establishment of an active trading route; the southern road was extended over the Bolivian Altiplano through La Paz and the rich mining town of Potosí and down into the valley of the Rio de le Plata—aptly called the River of Silver— to Buenos Aires, a port specifically forbidden to traders. For the next three centuries, this route connecting the western coast with the Atlantic Ocean was an economic lifeline for the colonial settlers in Peru, who were otherwise being drained by their mother country, as the colonials were draining the survivors of the Inca Empire. Indeed, by undermining the authority of and ties with Spain in such early colonial times, this pervasive smuggling may have helped lay the basis for the independence movements that would arise in the 19th century.

Much of the Inca road system, meanwhile, lay fallow. The Spanish had to keep up the coastal roads, which otherwise would be swamped by sand dunes. But they had little inclination to build new roads or to maintain old ones; they may well have feared that good roads would

In marshy areas, some well-built causeways and the remains of walls still stand. (Victor W. Von Hagen)

make them easier prey to invaders, as the Incas had been laid open to Spanish attack. Whatever the reason, the Inca road system went untended, and its survival depended on the terrain. Except where the road was kept open by local usage, the eastern portions of the Antisuyu Road returned to the jungle. The mountain roads, too, remained in selective use. The bridge at the vital crossing over the Apurimac River, later made famous as the Bridge of San Luis Rey, was maintained and continued in use into the 19th century. Likewise, the pontoon bridge across Lake Titicaca's tributary continued to serve its purpose, being replaced each year by the local population. Some portions of the mountain route remained much as they had been in Inca times, having been carved out of rockface, but other parts fell into disuse, their routes no longer discernible.

During the Spanish period, the main land route was from Buenos Aires through Bolivia to the highlands around Lake Titicaca, down to and north along the coast. Along that route, illicit traders brought goods the colonials could not otherwise afford at inflated Spanish prices. Official imperial business went along that route, too, first to Panama, and later to the colonial center at Lima. And this route also served republican business, when in the 19th century, the Spanish colonials arose against their home country; as they pressed from east coast to west, leaders like Belgrano and Bolívar led their forces along this route, pushing the Spanish imperial forces to Lima and Callao, their last stronghold before final defeat in Spanish South America.

With the Spanish gone, republican South America entered into some decades of internal conflict over territories and borders. Inevitably, long-distance routes became part of the struggle and were disrupted by the strife. With Buenos Aires free to operate as a major port, traffic on the eastern portion of the overland route tended more in the direction of the Atlantic than the Pacific. But the Spanish transcontinental route between Buenos Aires and the Peruvian coast continued to be important. The earliest railroads in the region followed this route, although they did not join into a continuous route until the 20th century.

In more modern times this coastal and transcontinental route was chosen for the southern portion of the Pan-American Highway, built after World War II. Picking up the old Inca Road at Quito, the modern four-lane road moves along the coast, where it has obliterated most remaining traces of the old coast road from earlier centuries; at Arequipa, one branch continues down the coast to Santiago, Chile, near the old Inca southern border, while the other arcs up into the mountains of Bolivia and down the Rio de la Plata to Buenos Aires. These remain the main land routes in South America today.

In the last century, however, the highland portion of the old Inca road system has come alive again, not with conquerors but with explorers. Unlike the ancient Romans, the Incas left no written records of their roads. What we know of the road system comes from the reports of early Spanish travelers—and from the findings of modern archeologists. The 19th century passion for travel, exploration, and history brought the Inca Empire to world attention. Certainly much remained for visitors to see. Alexander von Humboldt, after whom the coastal current was named, in the early 19th century described his traveling difficulties on an Andean pass over 14,000 feet high, but he noted:

> Yet nearby our eyes were fixed on the magnificent remains of an Inca road, twenty feet wide and running for a distance of more than a league. The road had a solid foundation and was paved with well-cut dark-brown trap porphyry.

Such roads, many still in use, were particularly striking given the general lack of paved roads in supposedly more advanced Europe. As von Humboldt put it: "Nothing I have seen among the fine Roman roads of Italy, Spain or the south of France was more imposing than these works of the ancient Peruvians." In the late 19th century, even the Apurimac Bridge was still there; traveler-writer E. George Squier noted in 1869: "...the bridge could be seen swinging high in a graceful curve between the two precipices on either side, looking wonderfully fragile and gossamer-like."

Such descriptive writings encouraged many others to explore the remains of the old Inca roads, which composed perhaps 20 percent of the road system in use even as late as the mid-20th century. Thirty-four years after Squier's *Peru* was published, Macchu Picchu—long hidden in the jungles of the east Andes—was rediscovered by Hiram Bingham in 1911. Twenty years later, pioneer fliers Robert Shippee and Lt. Johnson rediscovered the remains of the Great Wall of Peru, using aerial photography. The sudden collapse in 1890 of the Apurimac Bridge, maintained and in use since Pachucuti had ordered it, was dramatized in Thornton Wilder's *The Bridge of San Luis Rey*, a novel that gained world attention. Since World War II, a more systematic study of the Inca Royal Road system has been undertaken, notably by Victor von Hagen, attempting to map out the exact routes followed. It was not until 1967 that Vilcabamba, the last Inca redoubt, was rediscovered; other villages from the Incas' "refugee" period are still lost in the jungle of the eastern Andes.

These explorers have, in turn, been followed by tourists from all over the world, who seem to agree with Hernando Pizarro's comments:

> The royal road over the mountains is a thing worthy of being seen, because the ground is so rugged. Such beautiful roads could not, in truth, be found anywhere in Christendom.

Selective Bibliography

McIntyre, Loren. *The Incredible Incas and Their Timeless Land.* (Washington, D. C.: National Geographic Society, 1975). A well-illustrated combination of history and contemporary journey.

Ubbelohde-Doering, Heinrich. *On the Royal Highways of the Inca: Archaeological Treasures of Ancient Peru.* (New York: Frederick A. Praeger, Publishers, 1967). Primarily photographs of ruins and artifacts, with expansive and useful captions.

Von Hagen, Victor W. *The Desert Kingdoms of Peru.* (Greenwich, Conn.: New York Graphic Society Publishers Ltd., 1965). Focuses on the pre-Inca Mochica and Chimu empires.

_____. *Highway of the Sun.* (New York: Duell, Sloan and Pearce; Boston and Toronto: Little, Brown, 1955). The story of the Inca Highway Expedition's exploration of the road system with many photographs.

_____. *The Royal Road of the Inca.* (London: Gordon Cremonesi, Ltd., 1976). On the road itself, and its four quarters; well-illustrated.

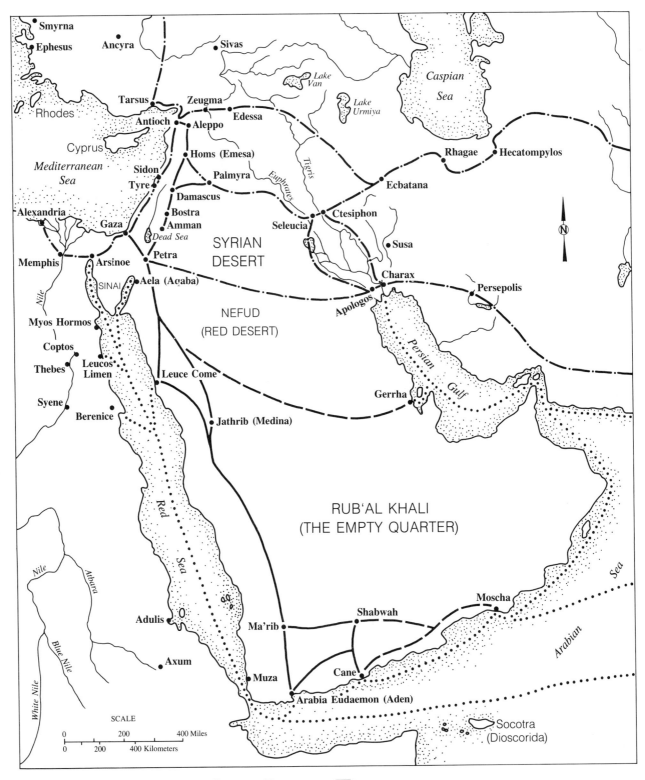

The Incense Road in Greco-Roman Times

——— Main Incense Road	—·—·— Main Connecting Land Routes
— · — · Secondary Incense Roads	·········· Spice Route

The Incense Road and the Pilgrimage Road

And when the queen of Sheba heard of the fame of Solomon...she came to Jerusalem with a very great train, with camels that bare spices, and very much gold, and precious stones...And she gave the king a hundred and twenty talents of gold, and of spices very great store, and precious stones; there came no more such abundance of spices as these which the queen of Sheba gave to king Solomon. (Kings I:10)

On her way to the land of Israel, the queen of Sheba followed the old Incense Road, which brought spices and other desired goods north to the great kingdoms along the Mediterranean Sea, like Egypt and Israel. The route ran from the Hadramaut, the southern coastal strip of the Arabian Peninsula, to Yemen, the southwest corner of Arabia, then up the west coast to the land of Jordan, a distance of about 1,600 miles. Emerging onto the great Fertile Crescent of the Middle East, it followed an inland route from Amman, Jordan, north through the ancient city of Damascus, and on to the crossroads city of Aleppo. There it met the Great Desert Route coming along the eastern horn of the Fertile Crescent from Mesopotamia. In Jordan itself, a branch of the Incense Road split off to the west, across the Sinai Desert to Egypt. The exact route of the Incense Road varied over time as different cities gained prominence, but generally it followed a course about 100 miles from the coast, except in Arabia where spurs occasionally dipped down to the sea, notably at the long-famous port of Arabia Eudaemon (Blessed Arabia, also called Arabia Felix, now Aden). This great inland highway is one of the oldest and most sacred routes in history, for it saw not only the rich trade famous in Biblical times, but also the rise of the great religions of the West, becoming in later times the Pilgrimage Road of the Moslems.

The beginnings of the Incense Road are lost in time. Trade along the route is thought to have originated in the seasonal migrations of the nomadic desert Arabs, who each spring moved with their herds from the Arabian Desert to the slightly better-watered Syrian Desert for the summer, and at some point began to load their animals with goods for trading along the way. From the northerly direction, herders and traders from ancient times moved around the Fertile Crescent from Mesopotamia into Syria and Palestine. In the early second millennium B.C., this was the route followed by Abraham as he obeyed his God's command to "go forth unto a land that I will show thee," the land of Canaan, across the Jordan River. Like earlier religious ideas, Abraham's belief in a single God percolated all along the route in his wake and even down the Incense Road into Arabia. Abraham's name is even traditionally associated with the Black Stone worshipped at Mecca for thousands of years (as were similar black stones elsewhere in the Near East); the Koran says that Abraham and his son Ishmael "raised the foundations" of the Ka'bah, the cube-like structure housing the Black Stone, which Moslems believe was given to Adam on his expulsion from Paradise so that he might gain forgiveness for his sins.

We do not know when Arabia began serious trading along the Incense Road; the Arabians' domestication of the single-humped camel by around 1800 B.C. was probably a vital step in the growth of formal trade. Southern Arabia produced the main early products on the Incense Road—frankincense, balsam, and myrrh—in a region warmer and moister than it is today. The low-lying southern coast, especially the main valley of the Hadramaut, seems to have been almost malarial. As late as the first century A.D., an anonymous Greek mariner noted in his guidebook, *Periplus of the Erythraean [Red] Sea:*

> The country is unhealthy in the extreme, pestilential even to those who sail along the coast, and mortal to the wretched sufferers employed in collecting the frankincense, who perish likewise as often by want (and neglect) as by the pernicious influence of the climate. The country inland is mountainous and difficult in access; the air is foggy, and loaded with vapors caused (it is supposed) by the noxious exhalations from the trees that bear the incense.

Semitropical it may have been, but others did not always agree that South Arabia was noisome. The second century B.C. Alexandrian writer Agatharchides felt quite the opposite about the Hadramaut coast:

> ...a heavenly and indescribable fragrance seems to strike and stir the senses of everyone. Even far out from the land as you sail past you do not miss a share in this enjoyment. For in the spring, whenever a wind arises from the land it happens that the fragrant odors blowing from the myrrh bushes and others of the kind reach the neighboring parts of the sea...

In Southern Arabia, the Incense Road also had an opening to the East. Indian sailors on the Spice Route reached the region in early times; by 2000 B.C. Egypt was already receiving supplies of cinnamon, grown only in the East and heavily used in embalming. But the Red Sea, the seemingly natural entree to Egypt, was plagued by contrary winds, dangerous reefs, and numerous pirates. As a result, at some point, Spice Route sailors began to bring their goods to the favored harbor of Arabia Eudaemon, selling their goods to Arabian middlemen, rather than hazarding the Red Sea. The Arabian traders would then transship the goods—notably spices and gems—in camel caravans north, snaking through the arid mountains, inland away from coastal attack and following the uplands for the best hope of water. By the time of Solomon, the southern caravans were primarily in the hands of the Sabaeans, who moved in from the north over several centuries to dominate the earlier Minnaeans. Indeed, many have speculated that the queen of Sheba—or Saba—had a specific mission in visiting Solomon: to try

The trading city of Petra was set in a rocky gorge, entered by narrow, easily defended passes through the barren hills. (From David Roberts, The Holy Land, *1829, Royal Geographical Society, London)*

to retain monopoly of the spice trade, at a time when Israelis and Phoenicians were launching ships on the Red Sea and bypassing the Sabaeans. In any case, the Arabians were not hurt by the competition. In the thousand years before the birth of Christ, almost every notice of the Arabians—the Sabaeans in the southwest, the Minnaeans in the midwest, the Nabataeans in the northwest, and the Gerrhaeans in the mideast—mentions their prosperity. The comments of Agatharchides are typical:

> ...no nation seems to be wealthier than the Sabaeans or Gerrhaeans, who are the agents for everything that falls under the name of transport from Asia and Europe. It is they who have made Ptolemaic Syria rich in gold, and who have provided profitable trade and thousands of other things to Phoenician enterprise.

At around the time of Christ, the Greek geographer Strabo agreed, noting that by their aromatic trade the Gerrhaeans (who brought spices across central Arabia to the Incense Road from their port of Gerrha on the Persian Gulf) and the Sabaeans were made

...the richest of all the tribes, and possess a great quantity of wrought articles in gold and silver, as couches, tripods, basins, drinking vessels, to which we must add the costly magnificence of their houses; for the doors, walls, and roofs are variegated with inlaid ivory, gold, silver, and precious stones.

Of the Incense Road itself, he noted:

Those tribes who live close to one another receive in continuous succession the load of aromatics and deliver them to their next neighbors as far as Syria and Mesopotamia.

Trade on the Incense Road made the fortunes of a number of cities along its route. In the Hadramaut, the chief center and effective southern terminus for the Incense Road was Shabwah, whose fame was known even in Rome, as Pliny reports:

Frankincense after being collected is conveyed to Sabota [Shabwah] on camels, one of the gates of the city being opened for its admission; the kings have made it a capital offence for camels so laden to turn aside from the high road. At Sabota a tithe estimated by measure and not by weight is taken...and the incense is not allowed to be put on the market until this has been done.

Clearly, the frankincense trade was highly controlled. Indeed, although many cities in the area, including Shabwah, have been swallowed up by the desert, the old route is marked by the remains of roads, some of them even paved; of graffiti-marked cliff-faces; and even of artificially constructed defiles, presumably for the purpose of having the caravan pass through single file, so taxes and tolls could be collected from all. Shabwah itself also received goods from the port of Cana 150 miles away; caravans carrying these goods, the Hadramaut frankincense, and loads of myrrh picked up on the way, headed west toward Ma'rib.

Ma'rib—the capital of Saba, inland from the port of Arabia Eudaemon—was itself a major city, which had an enormous dam for water storage and irrigation. The report of the 1951 Wendell Phillips archaeological expedition noted of Ma'rib: "The present Arab village occupied only a small portion of the ancient city area. Columns, walls, and pillars extended everywhere as far as our eyes could see..." To the north, midway up the coast, lay Jathrib (now Medina), also a crossroad of sorts, for a secondary caravan route ran down to the Red Sea port of Leuce Come (White Village), where goods were shipped across to Egypt in some periods. But one of the most famous caravan cities on the Incense Road was Petra, just east of the Sinai Desert, where the Incense Road forked to Egypt and Syria. At various places along the Incense

Road, Arabians had cut passes—and even stairs in especially steep areas—through mountain rock. Here they carved a whole city. In a rocky fastness entered by three deep gorges, the Nabataean merchants built Petra in a crater faced with sheer red-gold cliffs, into which they cut homes and later thousands of tombs and sanctuaries. While many other ancient cities are buried under layers of sand, Petra's facades remain open for all to see, astonishing even the most worldly traveler. What now remains only as a "necropolis, a fantastic city of the dead," was then the prime city on the Incense Road. The fame of the city even spread to China, where Petra was known as Li-kan. The trade of the Incense Road extended north along the inland route, through Amman, Damascus, and Emesa (Homs), to the crossroads of Aleppo, where it met the Great Desert Route from Mesopotamia and the Silk Road. Petraean merchants also established themselves in the north and in the Phoenician cities of Tyre and Sidon on the Mediterranean. (Later, with the rise of the Roman Empire, some even formed merchant colonies in Italy itself.)

But the very prosperity of the Arabian merchants drew envious intruders. In 800 B.C., the Assyrians had attempted to take control of the Incense Road; while they succeeded in extorting occasional tribute from the Arabian kingdoms, their main effect was to drive the Sabaeans south of the Minnaeans into Yemen. The Persian Darius and the Greek Alexander both had designs on the Arabian trade but were unable to fully carry them out. After Alexander's death, his heirs, Ptolemy and Seleucid, both eyed the rich Arabian trade routes. The Ptolemies in Egypt tried to cut out Petra, developing the Red Sea routes from the East and establishing the city of Naucratis (forerunner of Alexandria) near the mouth of the Nile to act as the main Mediterranean entrepôt. More than that, the Greeks began to Hellenize the region, founding new colonies, like Jerash (Gerasa), along the trade route and transforming older ones, like Amman, now renamed Philadelphia. Other Greeks attempted to divert the trade away from the inland route to the ancient Phoenician ports of Sidon and Tyre. But for all that, the Incense Road prospered. The Arabians were far from united in this period, often warring among themselves. The Minnaeans, in fact, often sent goods from their central portion of the coast directly to Egypt across the Red Sea or through Gaza, bypassing Nabataean Petra; and more than one temple remains dedicated to their god Athtar-Dhu-Gabdim in thanks for protecting their caravans from their rivals, the Sabaeans.

Under the Romans, conditions changed dramatically on the Incense Road. At first the Romans attempted to bypass the Arabians altogether. Employing Greek mariners, the Romans opened up full-scale trading on the Red Sea, sailing directly to India on the Spice Route; the port of Arabia Eudaemon was sacked and razed, reportedly by the Romans, but possibly by rival Arabs. This provoked an angry response from the Nabataeans, as Agatharchides reported:

> Of old, they earned a just livelihood, being satisfied with nourishment from their herds; but later, when the kings from Alexandria made the gulf navigable to merchants, they attacked shipwrecked persons, and building pirate ships plundered seafarers.

The Romans had grievances, for the Arabians wanted primarily gold for their trade goods. The Greek geographer Strabo was quite clear about the views of the Roman Emperor Augustus:

> The Arabs were also known from earliest times to be rich, as they traded their spices and precious stones against gold and silver and gave nothing back to strangers of what they received. For this reason he [Augustus] hoped either to exploit them as rich friends or to conquer them as rich enemies.

The Roman army took the latter course first, launching a campaign on the west coast of the Arabian peninsula. However, the soldiers landed too far north and stayed on the arid coast, rather than heading for the Incense Road; in any case, as Strabo reported, Arabian "merchants on camels with many people and animals can make their way safely and unimpeded amongst the hills and rocks, so that they have no need to fear even an army." The Roman army retired, after six months, defeated by the desert, not in battle.

The Romans had more success in treating the Arabs as "rich friends to be exploited." Gradually they took control of the whole Mediterranean strip, down through the region of Petra, which became the Roman province of Arabia Petraea. With their characteristic building fervor, the Romans developed roads throughout the empire, sometimes using old tracks, sometimes building roads where necessary, but throughout the desert regions sinking wells (every 28 miles, at least, unless a bountiful oasis was nearby) and building forts for their border guards. The main inland highway, which they named Strata Diocletiana in honor of the Roman emperor, ran from Aela (Aqaba) on the Red Sea through Petra and along the line of the old Incense Road through Damascus north over the Anatolian Plateau all the way to Trapezus (Trebizond, now Trabzon) on the Black Sea.

All of the cities along the route were geared for the caravan trade, with caravanserais being provided just inside the city gates, where weary merchants would find shops to supply their necessities, storerooms for their goods, marketplaces in which to sell them, and rooms for their stay in the city. Many cities on the Incense Road

This trail through a wadi, *trod by Petra merchants in biblical times, is still used by 20th century Bedouin.*

172

occupied easily defensible positions in a water-cut rocky gorge, or *wadi,* and had built necropolises into surrounding cliffs, although none was as spectacular as Petra's.

The region of the Jordan River and the Dead Sea, along the route that swung from Damascus southwest through Gaza to Egypt, was the main homeland of the Jews in Roman times. Abraham's God had attracted a still-small but fiercely loyal group of worshipers, while the rest of the population—which the Jews called Gentiles—continued to worship a wide variety of gods. Indeed, it was first the Greek and later the Roman policy to encircle Jewish cities with their own; the very name, Galilee, referred to the circle of Gentiles. Then at the height of the Roman power was born a male child named Jesus, proclaimed king of the Jews, a Messiah whose coming had been foretold in the Old Testament. Like Abraham before him, Jesus led a life thoroughly intertwined with the caravan roads north to Damascus and west to Egypt. His very birth occurred on the road, as Luke 2:1–7 tells us:

> And it came to pass in those days, that there went out a decree from Caesar Augustus, that all the world should be taxed...
>
> And all went to be taxed, every one into his own city.
>
> And Joseph also went up...to be taxed with Mary his espoused wife, being great with child.
>
> And so it was, that, while they were there [in Bethlehem], the days were accomplished that she should be delivered.
>
> And she brought forth her firstborn son, and wrapped him in swaddling clothes, and laid him in a manger; because there was no room for them in the inn.

Word spread quickly that the prophecy had been fulfilled, drawing "wise men from the east," who brought him treasures: gold, frankincense, and myrrh. The gifts were appropriate, for they were the most precious goods along the old Incense Road, the prime route of the region. The Romans, however, were not overjoyed to find in their midst a rival for the title "king." Attempts by King Herod to kill any such pretenders led Joseph to take his child into Egypt and return to Nazareth only after the danger had passed.

On his maturity, Jesus carried his ministry beyond his home city. Although his activities centered on the Jordan valley and west, his word was taken on the Incense Road by his disciples, most notably by Paul. This great missionary was converted to Christianity on his way from Antioch to Damascus (ironically on an assignment to arrest some Christians for the Roman authorities) and later proselytized all along the Incense Road, as far south as Petra. Thereafter, the monotheists in the region were split between the Christians, who believed that Jesus was the long-awaited Messiah, and the Jews, who did not. The

polytheistic Romans were hostile to both groups, making their lives increasingly difficult.

During Roman tenure, the northern part of the Incense Road—the Strata Diocletiana—thrived. In addition to goods from the southern Incense Road and from the Red Sea port of Aela, Petra also sometimes received goods normally destined for Mesopotamia, but diverted because of turbulence in the region; to reach that crossroads city, caravans followed difficult desert routes across the Arabian Peninsula, either from Gerrha or from Charax at the head of the Persian Gulf. In time, however, the very safety of the Roman province led to Petra's downfall, for it made the detour to its well-fortified stronghold unnecessary. Caravans on the Incense Road preferred to head straight for Bostra, which by the second century A.D. even became the new Nabataean capital. On the southern part of the Incense Road, the Sabaeans gradually gave way to a new power, the Himyarites, who maintained the old capital of Ma'rib. No seafarers, these Arabs gradually dropped out of sea trading—they were, in any case, being bypassed by Red Sea traders—and became dependent on others to bring them goods for trade on the Incense Road.

In later times, with the decline of the Roman Empire and its huge markets, the Incense Road fell on leaner days. Arabia was so weakened that in the fourth and later the sixth centuries Yemen was conquered by the Axumite (Abyssinian) kingdom from across the Red Sea, a Christian people of mixed Arab and African stock. Although the Axumites never fully controlled Yemen, Arabian attempts to expel them disrupted travel along the Incense Road; when they finally did so, the only result was that a Persian overlord replaced an Axumite one. Cities on the Incense Road suffered, and the old southern capital of Ma'rib was abandoned, being replaced by the city of San'a, which was better supplied with water in this drier period and safer from coastal attack.

Pilgrims and religious ideas continued to travel the Incense Road, as they had from the earliest times. As the Roman Empire disintegrated and its leaders stepped up persecution of Jews and non-orthodox Christians, like the Nestorians, religious refugees fled the turbulent Levant; many found shelter in Persia, but some found their way into the trading cities along the Incense Road, where they often formed segregated communities. Arabians at the time still worshiped various gods at shrines around the peninsula, but the Ka'bah in the city of Mecca had become a special object of pilgrimage along the old Incense Road, even in Roman times. We do not know when the Incense Road began to pass through the city of Mecca (the name itself possibly meaning sanctuary), but by the sixth century it was a flourishing trade center and pilgrimage destination. Like Petra and many other cities on the route, Mecca was set in a gorge in the inland mountains, which geographer R. Blanchard describes as "unbelievably bare, rocky crags with no scrap of soil, sharp, jagged, broken edges, sheer from top to bottom." So narrow was this gorge that the infrequent but violent rainstorms of the region sometimes flooded it, causing pilgrims to swim to the shrine—as still happens on rare occasions in modern times.

Into this setting was born in approximately 570 A.D. a boy who would change the history of the region: Mohammed. His ties with the Incense Road were extremely close. Before he was even born, his father had died returning to Mecca from the trading port of Gaza. By the time he was six, his mother had also died, leaving him a poor relation in the care of a rich merchant uncle. Tradition has it that this uncle took young Mohammed with him on a trip up the Incense Road to Syria; the Arabic writer Tabari chronicles the special recognition supposedly accorded Mohammed at this time:

When the company halted at Bostra in Syria, there was a monk named Bahira, who dwelt in a hermitage there and who was well-read in the learning of the Christians...This year, when the caravan halted near Bahira, he prepared much food for them. While he was in his hermitage, he had seen the Envoy of Allah among his companions; and a cloud covered him with its shadow...he questioned the Envoy of Allah about the things he felt when he was awake or asleep...Then he examined his [Mohammed's] back and found the seal of prophecy between his shoulders.

(Tabari also added: "Then Bahira said to his uncle, 'Go back then to your own land and keep him safe from the Jews. By Allah, if they see him and get to know what I know about him they will try to harm him.'" But this comment reflects a later attitude, for Mohammed often found refuge and support among Jews and Christians in his early years, and the physician charged with safeguarding his life was a Jew.)

Some scholars question whether or not the trip took place, but the story certainly indicates the importance the Arabs placed on the Incense Road and its connection with earlier religions. Mohammed made another trip to Syria somewhat later, and that one gained him a wife. While still poor, he had educated himself in many ways, including listening to "legends about the ancients" told by religious refugees in the land; and he had become a competent and trusted trader. A rich widow, 15 years older than he, first entrusted the 23-year-old Mohammed with her caravan to Syria, where he bought Byzantine goods for the Mecca market; in the end, she married him. With her backing, Mohammed became a citizen of some prominence in the community, so much so that when Mecca began rebuilding the Ka'bah housing the Black Stone, the 35-year-old Mohammed was chosen to supervise the moving of the sacred stone.

Then in 610 A.D., while meditating in a cave outside Mecca, near the end of the month of Ramadan, Mohammed received his first call, commanding him to bring to his people a new religion and a sacred book (for the Arabs—unlike the Christians and the Jews—had none at the time). While some of his family were early converts, most of their tribe resisted Mohammed, for they were made wealthy by the pilgrims visiting the Ka'bah. Some of Mohammed's persecuted followers fled across the Red Sea to Abyssinia (Ethiopia) in 615. They later returned when tensions eased somewhat, but in 622 Mohammed and his followers made their famous *Hegira* (migration) along the Incense Road to the city of Jathrib, thereafter renamed Medina, or al-Madinah (the City—of the prophet). With his followers increasing—both emigrants and new converts—Mohammed in 624 (also in the month of Ramadan) decided to attack a Mecca caravan south of Medina. Mohammed's 300 Moslems roundly defeated over 1,000 Meccans, who had come to the aid of their caravan. From then on, despite occasional losses, Mohammed's military successes drew increasing numbers of converts; in the process, he turned away from his Christian and Jewish connections, decreeing that ritual prayers were not to be said facing Jerusalem (as had been the early pattern for Moslems) but toward Mecca. He negotiated Moslem rights to visit Mecca in 628, but by 630 he was so strong that he took the city and himself destroyed the idols in the sanctuary. While Medina remained his political capital, he made Mecca the religious center, to which all Moslems should make pilgrimage, but in which no non-Moslems were allowed. In that same year, he even began to take his religion north into Syria, but his death in 632 temporarily stilled further expansion of Islam along the old Incense Road. Mecca being the center of the still-small but strong Islamic world, other regions were named with reference to it. The area around Mecca itself was called the Hejaz; the northern, or Syrian, portion of the Incense Road was called esh-Shem, for it was on the left hand of those who faced Mecca from the west; the southern portion of Arabia, formerly called Arabia Eudaemon by extension of its famous port's importance, came to be called Yemen, for it was on the right hand of Mecca.

After their leader's death, Moslems exploded north, east, and west, building an empire to rival Rome's in little more than a century. The territory around the Incense Road was conquered north past Aleppo in only a dozen years. In this newly united region, trade and travel flourished, especially the Mecca caravans that headed north every winter, when water and forage were most favorable. Such concerns were important, for these annual caravans often included 2,500–3,000 camels and 100–300 guards, depending on the turbulence of the times, along with the many merchants, camel drivers, servants, and overseers. Chief among these was the caravan leader, the *bashi*, who took sole responsibility for the caravan, in which almost every Mecca resident had some financial share, and who was obliged to make good any loss. Understandably, these leaders, upon whose judgment

Khans *or caravanserais like this one at Damascus gave shelter to traveling merchants and pilgrims for many centuries. (From Carruthers,* The Desert Route to India)

rested the welfare of the city, seldom delegated their responsibility but led the caravans personally, choosing the route; obtaining additional guards, as necessary, from local towns in areas liable to ambush; maintaining discipline within the caravan; and ensuring friendly, or at least neutral, relations with nomads en route.

Among the leader's assistants was the pilot, or *daleel,* who handled many of the details of the caravan's progress, such as how long to march, when to halt, and the precise path to take. Piloting was a hereditary calling, and many a *daleel* had trained as apprentice under a father or uncle before him. The decision of where and when to camp depended to a large extent on the local nomads in the region; while some were brigands requiring extra watch to be set, others were neutrals who welcomed the passage of the annual caravan and turned each halt into an impromptu fair. For communications, the caravans employed couriers, whose name and appearance varied with their purpose. When sent with bad news, they were called *nadeers,* and were distinguishable from a distance by their torn garments and reversed saddle, so that townspeople could send aid most quickly. When bearing good news,

they were called *basheers,* alerting the townspeople to begin beating the drum to herald the arrival of the caravan and the beginning of the annual fair. No firm schedule need be kept en route, for trading caravans carried non-perishable goods, like spices, perfumes, ivory, gold, and silver (the latter metals being mined at the time in the Hejaz); safety was paramount, and a caravan would always try to wait out danger if it could.

But the spread of Mohammedanism also called forth a different kind of traveler on the Incense Road: the pilgrim. While pilgrims had been journeying to Mecca for centuries, the Koran's injunction "the pilgrimage to the temple is a service due to Allah from those who are able to journey thither" began to draw thousands of people to Mecca every year. The object of the pilgrimage was the Ka'bah in the Beit Allah (House of God) in Mecca, which the pilgrim—wearing special dress—was to walk around and kiss. Most pilgrims also visited Mohammed's tomb in Medina, although it was not obligatory to do so. In the late seventh century, when the Umayyad Caliphs made the ancient city of Damascus their capital, pilgrims began to gather there, organizing into a large annual caravan whose departure date varied year by year, according to the rolling Islamic calendar. The Incense Road then came to be known as the Darb el-Hajj, or the Pilgrimage Road.

The Moslems were far from united. Disputes over the succession in the decades after Mohammed's death led to a schism that still exists today between the great majority of Sunni Moslems, who in the early decades gave their allegiance to the Umayyad Caliphs of Damascus, and the much smaller group of Shiites, or Shia (Party), predominantly from further east. The Shiites split off from the Sunnis in the middle of the eighth century B.C., establishing their own dynasty, the Abbasid, based in Baghdad, on the Tigris River in modern Iraq. But the Moslems all agreed on the importance of the pilgrimage, and, except when the parties were openly at war, Sunni and Shia pilgrims often shared—however uneasily—the same *hajj* caravan.

As Islam spread in all directions, pilgrims began to gather at other points for their journey. Those from Africa and the West Mediterranean congregated at Cairo in Egypt. In the early centuries, they often proceeded by boat from the ports of Aydhab or Qusa'ir to Mecca's port of Jiddah; but after the 13th century, the great caravan generally crossed the Sinai to take the Darb el-Hajj. Pilgrims from the East congregated either at Baghdad or at Basra, further south in Mesopotamia on the Euphrates River. These two caravans followed independent routes across the Syrian Desert, a region quite ill-suited for heavy traffic and usable for a *hajj* only because wells had been dug and fortified rest-places built all along the routes. Grateful pilgrims named the Baghdad route Darb el-Sitt (the Lady) Zubayda, after the wife of the Abbasid Sultan Harun el-Rashid, who had the route built in the late eighth century. As Islam spread even further north over the centuries, winning its fight against Christian Byzantium, pilgrims from Anatolia would congregate in smaller caravans at Damascus. All of the routes fed into the Darb el-Hajj as it wound down its ancient route. Likewise, pilgrims from the south would congregate in the main cities of Yemen and would follow the old Incense Road north to the holy cities.

The pilgrimage route varied over the centuries and was hardly a major highway in any time, even with the heavy pilgrimage traffic in addition to the continuing trading caravans. Indeed, it barely stood out from its surroundings after centuries of use; historian Christina Grant noted that much was simply empty desert, with a single beaten path generally emerging only where caravans had, for centuries, been forced into a defile. Elsewhere the route was marked by the "bleached bones and the skeletons of camels, horses, and mules," and the "little mounds of rock" that marked the graves of pilgrims who had died en route to Mecca.

Such deaths were not uncommon. Sick people were exempt from the obligation of the *hajj*, but many well travelers were ill-prepared to make the 900-mile trip from Damascus to Mecca in the 40 days and 40 nights dictated by the *bashi*. Some say the camel-owners and contractors first insisted on the 40-day trip to maximize their profits; others note that lack of water in the desert regions often necessitated a forced march, much of it at night, out of the day's heat. In any case, the 40 days became enshrined in tradition, and any pilgrim who could not keep up the pace was left behind. This would remain the pattern throughout the centuries of the camel caravan; in the 19th century, the British traveler Richard Burton observed a pilgrim whose stomach had been ripped open in a knife fight:

> On enquiring what had become of him, I was assured that he had been comfortably wrapped up in his shroud, and placed in a half-dug grave. This is the general practice in the case of the poor and solitary, whom illness and accident incapacitates from proceeding. It is impossible to contemplate such a fate without horror; the torturing thirst of a wound, the burning sun heating the brain to madness, and—worst of all, for they do not wait till death—the attacks of the jackal, the vulture, and the raven of the wild.

The pilgrims did not have to bear the burden of preparation for the *hajj* totally by themselves. The government became involved in support of the *hajj* from the early days of Islam. Like the Lady Zubayda, Moslem rulers often provided water and fortified shelter as necessary along the way; in especially arid areas, reservoirs were dug, to be filled by canals from a nearby *wadi* or by water-carriers who hauled in water from further away in dry years, in time for the caravan's arrival. A *hajj* fund, created and administered by the sultans, paid such water-carriers and soldiers to man the forts, as well as the costs involved in shipping necessary provisions to the forts, so pilgrims could replenish their supplies along the way. Rich Moslems who could not make the *hajj*, especially women who could not make the journey unescorted, also acted as benefactors for other pilgrims; the great Moslem traveler Ibn Battuta found that on the *hajj* in 1326:

> ...many draught camels [were provided] for supplying the poorer pilgrims with water, and other camels to carry the provisions issued as alms and the medicines, potions, and sugar required for any who fell ill. Whenever the caravan halted food was cooked in great brass cauldrons, and from these the needs of the poorer pilgrims and those who had no provisions were supplied. A number of spare camels accompanied it to carry those who were unable to walk. All those measures were due to the benefactions and generosity of the Sultan...

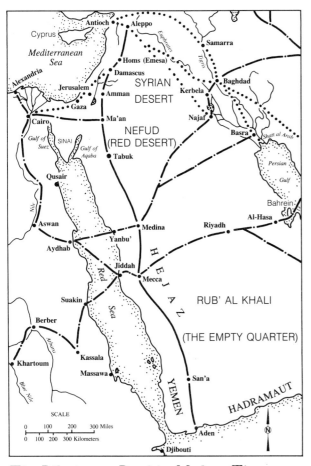

The Pilgrimage Road in Modern Times

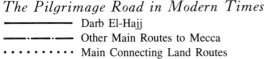

——————— Darb El-Hajj
—— · —— · —— Other Main Routes to Mecca
• • • • • • • • • • Main Connecting Land Routes

The *hajj* was not a purely religious exercise, however. Merchants took the opportunity of joining the caravans to sell their wares on the way to pilgrims and natives; and many pilgrims combined business with religion, a stance encouraged in Islam. Indeed, merchants often were given special protection; the Roman traveler Ludovicus Vertomannus, who accompanied a 16th century *hajj* caravan, noted that when they were under attack the camels were used as a bulwark, in the center of which were placed the merchants, "whyle the pilgrims fought manfully on every side."

The Incense Road, turned Pilgrimage Road, continued to serve other purposes, too. While the once-a-year *hajj* caravans included merchants, trading caravans continued to operate several times a year from the cities along the route, especially after the ninth century, as Moslems began to make themselves a power, with Aden their prime port. These roads served government purposes as well. While a *hajj* caravan, a virtual traveling city of thousands of people, might take 40 days from Damascus to Mecca, a fast-moving courier on horseback might make the trip

in only a few days. Following the pattern established by the Romans and Byzantines who had preceded them, the Umayyad caliphs re-established regular postal service, with riders shuttling along the Darb el-Hajj. This service was disrupted between the 11th and 13th centuries, as wars and revolutions shook the Arabic strongholds; under pressure from the Mongols, who sacked Baghdad in 1258, the Moslems moved their center of power to Cairo, then reintroduced the postal system. The couriers were essentially government messengers, bearing reports from the provinces twice a week in normal times, more often in emergencies – and sometimes even collecting taxes; but individuals could make special arrangements for·private messages to be carried. Each *berid* (courier) wore around his neck a silver plaque, identifying him as the sultan's messenger, and a yellow scarf on his back, which qualified him to obtain relays at post stations. Couriers on the Cairo-Damascus road generally took four days, with Aleppo being one day beyond. At convenient spots along the route, in the countryside or in a nearby town, *khans* or caravanserais were built to provide fresh mounts, water, food, and modest shelter for the couriers. These *khans* made travel on the Incense Road even easier and safer than it had been before.

The Mongol invasion of Syria in the 15th century disrupted the old *berid* system, and indeed travel along the Incense Road. Not until the middle of the 16th century, with the Ottoman Turks firmly in control of the Near East, was a courier system re-established, and then it was of a somewhat different type. The Turks established two sets of couriers, one for local service, and one for long-distance communication with their capital at Constantinople; large cities like Aleppo also had their own courier systems. These were all under the control of the local sheik, who set the service charges, depending on the season, the danger or difficulty, and the speed desired. The Ottoman government also employed special dispatch-bearers, called *tatars* (which European sometimes spelled *tartars*), who carried important missives or bullion throughout the empire. Another type of messenger also operated on the old Incense Road: the carrier pigeon. Following a practice begun in the eighth century in Baghdad, Moslems began using homing pigeons to carry messages in Syria and Egypt in the 12th century; with relays from specially constructed towers 50 miles apart, these birds were sometimes able to carry messages in a few hours that would otherwise take days.

A special *berid* system was employed by the *hajj* caravan. When the caravan left Damascus, a team of five couriers accompanied it; then at specified points on the route – at Ma'an, Mada'in, Medina, Mina (after completion of the pilgrimage rites), and Tabuk, on the homeward route – a courier would speed for home with letters from the pilgrims. So important was this post to the friends and relatives waiting at home that a cannon was fired thrice from the Damascus fort to signal that the *berid* had arrived with mail from the pilgrimage caravan.

While Damascus and Baghdad had in the early centuries been the prime pilgrimage centers, later—after the invasions of the Near East, especially the sacking of Baghdad—Cairo became the political capital of the Moslem world. While each major city had a *mahmil*—a specially decorated, untenanted litter—at the head of its caravan, Cairo's took precedence. Indeed, its first public appearance each pilgrimage season was a holiday, as the great 14th century Moslem traveler Ibn Battuta reported:

This is the day of the procession of the *mahmil* round [the city], a festival day...The four [officials]...are mounted, and along with them ride the principal jurists, the syndics of the heads of corporations, and the officers of state. They all proceed together to the gate of the citadel...where the *mahmil* comes out to meet them, borne on a camel, and preceded by the *amir* who has been designated for the journey to the Hijaz in that year. With him are his troops and a number of water-carriers mounted on their camels. All classes of the population, both men and women, assemble for this ceremony, then they go in procession with the *mahmil*...with the camel drivers singing to their camels in the lead...thereupon resolves are inflamed, desires are excited, and impulses are stirred up, and God Most High casts into the heart of whom He will of His servants the determination to set out upon the Pilgrimage, so they start to equip themselves and to make preparations for it.

To Cairo also fell *kiswa*, the honor of providing the new curtain each year for the Ka'bah.

Unlike the more barren Incense Road, this heavily used trade route from Cairo across the Sinai was well sup-plied with accommodations—and its borders were closely watched—as Ibn Battuta reports:

At each of these stations there is a hostelry *(funduq)*, which they call a *khan*, where travelers alight with their beasts, and outside each *khan* is a public watering-place and a shop at which the traveler may buy what he requires for himself and his beast. Amongst these stations is the well-known place called Qatya...where *zakat* (an alms tax) is collected from the merchants, their goods are examined, and their baggage most rigorously searched. There are government offices here, with officers, clerks, and notaries, and its daily revenue is a thousand gold dinars. No one may pass this place in the direction of Syria without a passport from Egypt, nor into Egypt without a passport from Syria, as a measure of protection for a person's property and of precaution against spies from Iraq. This road is under guarantee of the bedouins (that is to say, they have been made responsible for guarding it). At nightfall they smooth down the sand so that no mark is left on it, then the governor comes in the morning and examines the sand. If he finds any track on it he requires the Arabs to fetch the person who made it, and they set out in pursuit of him and never fail to catch him. They then bring him to the governor, who punishes him as he sees fit.

In the following centuries an occasional European began to appear on the Pilgrimage Road, giving a glimpse of this part of the world not often granted to "unbelievers." In 1503, Ludovicus Vertomannus, disguised as a "Mamaluchi renegado" so as not to arouse the wrath of the *hajji*, joined the Damascus caravan to Mecca, estimating its size at 40,000 men and 35,000 camels, with an escort of three score Mamelukes (Egyptian solders). More than once, the

Many of the supply forts that lined the Pilgrimage Road were later converted to railroad stations, after the Hejaz Railway was built. (By Jacob M. Landau, from The Hejaz Railway and the Muslim Pilgrimage, *reprinted by permission of Wayne State University Press)*

caravan had to fight off a like number of attackers. Nor was the caravan itself very peaceful, as he noted:

> Euery of these haue their proper bookes of factes and traditions...By this means are they marueylously diuided among themselues, and lyke beastes kyll themselues for such quarelles of dyuers opinions, and all false.

Mecca he found comparable to European cities, noting that "the citie is very fayre and well inhabited, and conteyneth in rounde fourme syx thousande houses, as well buylded as ours." The city itself had no walls, he found, but was "on euery syde fortified with mountains...About two furlongs from the citie is a mount, where the way is cutte out, whiche leadeth to a playne beneath."

Mecca was not, however, as rich as he expected, so he asked "where was the great aboundaunce of pearles, precious stones, spices, and other rich merchandies that the bruite went of to be in that citie." His Moslem informants blamed their relative poverty on the Portuguese, who had only a few years before arrived in the Indian Ocean, disrupting the Arabs' wealth-producing sea trade. The region itself had no resources, being made rich by the pilgrims; indeed, Vertomannus commented "ought you to consyder that, by the opinion of all men, this citie is greatly cursed of God, as appereth by the great barrennesse thereof, for it is destitute of all maner of fruites and corne [grain]." Provisions for the pilgrim hordes had to be shipped in from elsewhere, much of it from across the Red Sea, from Egypt and Ethiopia to the port of Jiddah, 40-odd miles west of Mecca, or on the Incense Road from Aden. With pilgrims arriving from all directions for the yearly sacred season, Vertomannus found a remarkable mix of people:

> Here we found a marueylous number of straungers and peregrynes, or pylgryms; of the whiche some came from Syria, some from Persia, and others from...the East Indiaes...I neuer sawe in anye place greater abundaunce and frequentation of peoples...These people resort thyther for diuers causes, as some for merchandies, some to obserue theyr vowe of pylgrymage, and others to haue pardon for theyr sinnes...

Pilgrims nearing Mecca, by land or sea, were instructed to put on the special religious garb, the *ihram*, at specified points. The men, after shaving their heads, cutting their nails, trimming their mustaches, and bathing themselves, dressed in two large cloths, one wrapped around the waist and extending to the ankles, the other draped over one shoulder and tied at the waist; head and instep were kept completely bare. Women pilgrims covered themselves from head to foot in white garments, and instead of the normal veil over the lower face, adopted a palm-leaf mask which totally obscured the face, leaving only two eye-holes. Special *dahleels* then guided them through the various parts of the pilgrimage. A young British sailor, Joseph Pitts, captured by Algerian pirates and forcibly converted to Islam, provides a rare view of the *hajj* in 1680, the activities centering around the Beit Allah, of which Pitts noted, "They say that Abraham built it; to which I give no credit." Here was housed the Ka'bah, and pilgrims were to circle around the Beit following a certain ritual, as Pitts explains:

> At one corner of the Beat, there is a black stone fastened and framed in with silver plate [later gold], and every time they come to that corner, they kiss the stone; and having gone round seven times they perform two...prayers.
> This place is so much frequented by people going round it, that the place of the *Towoaf, i.e.* the circuit which they take in going round it, is seldom void of people at any time of the day or night. Many have waited several weeks, nay months, for the opportunity of finding it so.

Following various other observances within the city, pilgrims then were led into the nearby mountains, to El Arafat, "the Mountain of Knowledge; for there, they say, Adam first found and knew his wife Eve," who was said to be buried at Jiddah. Later they went to another hill, called Mina, or Muna, where Abraham was said to have offered his son for sacrifice (Ishmael, according to the Moslems, not Isaac, as in the Judeo-Christian tradition). There the pilgrims pitched a tent city for three days, throwing stones at certain pillars to defy the devil, then proceeding to offer a sacrifice, as Pitts continues:

> ...after they have thrown the seven stones on the first day (the country people having brought great flocks of sheep to be sold), every one buys a sheep and sacrifices it; some of which they give to their friends, some to the poor which come out of Mecca and the country adjacent, very ragged poor, and the rest they eat themselves...

With this, they had completed their pilgrimage, returning to their ordinary clothes and commencing a great feast, in Pitts's time "rejoicing with abundance of illuminations all night, shooting of guns, and fireworks flying in the air; for they reckon that all their sins are now done away, and they shall, when they die, go directly to heaven, if they don't apostatize..."

The obligatory part of the pilgrimage over, the pilgrims headed for home, some directly and some with a stop at Medina to honor the prophet at his chosen place. The caravan formed up as on setting out, as Pitts describes:

Having hired camels of the carriers, we set out...If it happen that the camel dies by the way, the carrier is to supply us with another; and therefore, those carriers who come from Egypt to Mecca with the Caravan, bring with them several spare camels; for there is hardly a night passeth but many die upon the road...

The first day we set out from Mecca, it was without any order at all, all hurly burly; but the next day every one laboured to get forward; and...there was many time much quarrelling and fighting. But after every one had taken his place in the Caravan, they orderly and peaceably kept the same place till they came to Grand Cairo. They travel four camels in a breast, which are all tied one after the other, like as in teams. The whole body is called a Caravan, which is divided into several cottors, or companies, each of which hath its name, and consists, it may be, of several thousand camels; and they move one cotter after another, like distinct troops. In the head of each cottor is some great gentleman or officer, who is carried in a thing like a horse-litter, borne by two camels, one before and the other behind, which is covered all over with...cloth, and set forth very handsomely...In the head of every cottor there goes, likewise, a sumpter camel which carries his treasures, etc. This camel hath two bells, about the bigness of our marketbells, having one on each side, the sound of which may be heard a great way off. Some other of the camels have round bells about their necks, some about their legs...which together with the servants (who belong to the camels, and travel on foot) singing all night, make a pleasant noise, and the journey passes away delightfully. They say this musick makes the camels brisk and lively...

The organization of the caravan was especially important because the caravan traveled largely at night, as Pitts continues:

They have lights by night (which is the chief time of travelling, because of the exceeding heat of the sun by day), which are carried on the tops of high poles, to direct the Hagges on their march. They are somewhat like iron stoves, into which they put short dry wood, which some of the camels are loaded with...

These lamps were also carried by day, though unlit, because they carried information about each company, its size and camping place. The caravans normally pitched their tents in the morning for several hours, during which time the camels were unloaded and driven for water by their owners, while the other travelers rested and ate. The caravan would also rest for shorter periods on the road; the firing of a special gun normally signaled the halt or resumption of the march.

In the 17th century, the *hajj* route apparently bypassed any settlements, for in their 40 days' journey Pitts found "there is scarce any green thing to be met with, nor beast nor fowl to be seen or heard; nothing but sand and stones, excepting one place which we passed through by night; I suppose it was a village, where were some trees, and, we thought, gardens..." Arrangements were made to bring food to the caravans at various points along the route, sometimes the supply caravans being joined by greeting parties near the main caravan centers, as Pitts found:

When we had taken our leave of Medina...and travelled about ten days more, we were met by a great many Arabians, who brought abundance of fruit to us, particularly raisins; but from whence I cannot tell. When we came within fifteen days' journey of Grand Cairo, we were met by many people who came from thence, with their camels laden with presents for the Hagges, sent from their friends and relations, as sweetmeats, etc. But some of them came rather for profit, to sell fresh provisions to the Hagges, and trade with them...

When we came within seven days' journey of Cairo, we were met by abundance of people more, some hundreds, who came to welcome their friends and relations; but it being night, it was difficult to find those they wanted, and, therefore, as the Caravan past along they kept calling them aloud by their names, and by this means found them out. And when we were in three days' journey of it, we had many camel-loads of the water of the Nile brought us to drink. By the day and night before we came to Cairo, thousands came out to meet us with extraordinary rejoicing.

Over the centuries, the practice of Islam had changed somewhat from its origins, and in the mid-18th century a reform movement arose in central Arabia. Muhammad ibn 'Abd al-Wahhab, who had traveled to the Hejaz and in Syria and Iraq, became convinced that Moslems had strayed too far from orthodoxy; inspired by him, a group of followers called the Wahhabis, among them the Saudi family, created a puritan reform movement. It spread quickly, spurred by military action. At the beginning of the 19th century, the Wahhabis captured Mecca and Medina, destroying all that they thought smacked of idolatry; under Saudi leadership, the Wahhabis then pushed into Syria and Iraq, and east to Oman, until in 1818 they were stopped by the Ottoman Turks, whose empire they were encroaching upon. Although the Wahhabi movement was, at least for a time, crushed, their ideas spread throughout the Islamic world. These were years of great turmoil along the Incense and Pilgrimage Road, and 19th century travelers in the region all heard of the capture and purging of the holy cities.

With the collapse of Wahhabi activity and the sacking of their capital at Riyadh, on the route from eastern Arabia, the *hajj* resumed much as before. This being the age of the great European travelers, some non-Moslem intruders occasionally joined the great pilgrimage caravans; one such was the Englishman Charles M. Doughty, who describes the convulsions in Damascus as the city prepared for the annual event in the 1870's:

> There is every year a new stirring of this goodly Oriental city in the days before the Haj; so many strangers are passing in the bazaars, of outlandish speech and clothing from the far provinces...The town is moved in the departure of the great Pilgrimage of the Religion and again at the homecoming, which is made a public spectacle; almost every Moslem household has some one of their kindred in the caravan. In the markets there is much taking up in haste of wares for the road. The tent-makers are most busy in their street, overlooking and renewing the old canvas of hundreds of tents...and the curtains for litters; the curriers in their bazaar are selling apace the water-skins and leathern buckets and saddle-bottles...; the carpenters' craft are labouring in all haste for the Haj, the most of them mending litter-frames...the Haj caravan drivers...hold insolently their path through the narrow bazaars; commonly ferocious young men, whose mouths are full of horrible cursings...The *Mukowwems* or Haj camel-drivers...are sturdy, weathered men of the road, that can hold the mastery over their often mutinous crews; it is written in their hard faces that they are overcomers of the evil by the evil, and able to deal in the long desert way with the perfidy of the elvish Beduins. It is the custom of these caravan countries that all who are to set forth, meet together in some common place without the city. The assembling of the pilgrim multitude is always by the lake of Muzeyrib in the high steppes beyond Jordan, two journeys from Damascus. Here the hajjies who have taken the field are encamped, and lie a week or ten days in the desert before their long voyage. The Haj Pasha, his affairs despatched with the government in Damascus, arrives the third day before their departure, to discharge all first payments to the Beduw and to agree with the water-carriers, (which are Beduins), for the military service.
>
> The open ways of Damascus upon that side, lately encumbered with the daily passage of hundreds of litters, and all that, to our eyes, strange and motley train, of the Oriental pilgrimage, were again...silent...

For such a large number of people and animals — Doughty estimated that the *hajj* he accompanied included 6,000 people, more than half of them "serving men on foot," and 10,000 animals, mostly camels, but also mules and asses — the leavetaking was surprisingly orderly:

> The day risen, the tents were dismantled, the camels led in ready to their companies, and halted beside their loads. We waited to hear the cannon shot which should open that year's pilgrimage. It was near ten o'clock when we heard the signal gun fired, and then, without any disorder, litters were suddenly heaved and braced upon the bearing beasts, their charges laid upon the kneeling camels, and the thousands of riders, all born in the caravan countries, mounted in silence. As all is up the drivers are left standing upon their feet, or set to rest out the latest moment on their heels: they with other camp and tent servants must ride those three hundred leagues upon their bare soles, although they faint; and are to measure the ground again upward with their weary feet from the holy places. At the second gun, fired a few moments after, the Pasha's litter advances and after him goes the head of the caravan column: over fifteen or twenty minutes we, who have places in the rear, must halt, that is until the long train is unfolded before us; then we strike our camels and the great pilgrimage is moving. There go commonly three or four camels abreast and seldom five; the length of the slow-footed multitude of men and cattle is near two miles, and the width some hundred yards in the open plains...

The first day was generally a short one, neither pilgrims nor camels being inured to the hardships of the road. At the desert station that night, *hajji* found their tents already set up, as would be true throughout the trip, for the tent servants' train traveled ahead of the main body each day to prepare for the night's encampment. While the armed escort encircling the camp kept watch, pilgrims ate a repast cooked on a fire in a scooped-out hole, then relaxed, some with "drumbeating and soft fluting, and Arcadian sweetness of the Persians singing in the tents"; others chanting devotions by the light of a candle in a paper lantern.

From Muzeyrib, Doughty counted 26 marches to el-Medina, the prophet's city, and 40 marches to Mecca — the same 40 days as for centuries. The early part of the route he found "a waste plain of gravel and loam upon limestone, for ten or twelve days, and always rising, to Maan...near to Petra." There was no road as such, but "a beaten way over the wilderness, paved of old at the crossing of winter stream-beds for the safe passage of the Haj camels, which have no foothold in sliding ground; by some other are seen ruinous bridges — as all is now ruinous in the Ottoman Empire." Not only the bridges, but also the fortified stations and the towns themselves were often gone to ruin.

Unbelievers were still barred from Mecca, and outsiders were well-advised to disguise themselves as Moslems if they were venturing near the Moslem holy places. The famous 19th century traveler Richard F. Burton disguised himself as a Moslem Indian doctor and advised a similar approach to others. Burton approached the region first by sea, the Red Sea crossing being reopened in modern times; from Suez, he sailed to the port of Yanbu', then took a four-day journey by camel to Medina. Even so close to the holy places, the travelers were threatened by robbers, especially at an infamous gorge called Pilgrimage Pass, and several small caravans joined together in a united front through the defile.

En route to Mecca, traders and pilgrims passed many villages like Al-Suwayrkiyah, depicted above. (From Richard F. Burton, Personal Narrative of a Pilgrimage to Al-Madinah & Mecca Vol. I, *1893 ed.)*

It was in Medina that Burton's party awaited the great caravans from the north; from the house where he was staying, Burton awoke to find the Damascus caravan had arrived during the night:

...[The field] from a dusty waste dotted with a few Badawi [Bedouin] hair-tents, had assumed all the various shapes and the colours of a kaleidoscope...In one night had sprung up a town of tents of every size, colour, and shape; round, square, and oblong; open and closed,—from the shawl-lined and gilt-topped pavilion of the Pasha, with all the luxurious appurtenances of the Harim, to its neighbour the little dirty green "rowtie" of the tobacco-seller. They were pitched in admirable order: here ranged in a long line, where a street was required; there packed in dense masses, where thoroughfares were unnecessary. But how describe the utter confusion in the crowding, the bustling, and the vast variety and volume of sound? Huge white Syrian dromedaries, compared with which those of Al-Hijaz appeared mere pony-camels, jingling large bells, and bearing Shugdufs (litters) like miniature green tents, swaying and tossing upon their backs; gorgeous Takht-rawan, or litters carried between camels or mules with scarlet and brass trappings; Badawin bestriding naked-backed "Daluls" (dromedaries), and clinging like apes to the hairy humps...fainting Persian pilgrims, forcing their stubborn camels to kneel, or dismounted grumbling from jaded donkeys; Kahwa-jis, sherbet sellers, and ambulant tobacconists cry-ing their goods; country-people driving flocks of sheep and goats with infinite clamour through lines of horses fiercely snorting and biting and kicking and rearing; townspeople seeking their friends; returned travellers exchanging affectionate salutes...servants seeking their masters, and masters their tents, with vain cries of Ya Mohammed; grandees riding mules or stalking on foot, preceded by their crowd-beaters, shouting to clear the way...add a thick dust which blurs the outlines like a London fog, with a flaming sun that draws sparkles of fire from the burnished weapons of the crowd, and the brass balls of tent and litter...

To spend the maximum time in Medina, Burton had intended to take the *Kafilat al-Tayyarah* (Flying Caravan) which, being lightly laden and taking forced marches, would reach Mecca more quickly than the *hajj* caravan; an even faster dromedary caravan shuttled between the two cities, but each person was limited to what could be carried in his saddlebags. In the event, the rumor spread that the other caravans had been cancelled, so Burton joined the Damascus *hajj*. The caravan on the move was even more striking than the tent city Burton had seen on awakening:

The appearance of the Caravan was most striking, as it threaded its slow way over the smooth surface of the Khabt (low plain). To judge by the eye, the host was composed of at fewest seven thousand souls, on foot, on horseback, in litters, or bestriding the splendid camels of Syria. There were eight gradations of pilgrims. The lowest hobbled with heavy staves. Then came the riders of asses, of camels, and of mules. Respectable men, especially Arabs, were mounted on dromedaries, and the soldiers had horses: a led animal was saddled for every grandee, ready whenever he might wish to leave his litter. Women, children, and invalids of the poorer classes sat upon a "Haml Musattah,"—rugs and cloths spread over the two large boxes which form the camel's load. Many occupied Shibriyahs; a few, Shugdufs, and only the wealthy and the noble rode in Takht-rawan (litters), carried by camels or mules. The morning beams fell brightly upon the glancing arms which surrounded the stripped Mahmil and upon the scarlet and gilt conveyances of the grandee. Not the least beauty of the spectacle was its wondrous variety of detail: no man was dressed like his neighbour, no camel was caparisoned, no horse was clothed in uniform, as it were. And nothing stranger than the contrasts; a band of half-naked Takruri [Black African Moslems] marching with the Pasha's equipage, and long-capped bearded Persians conversing with Tarbush'd and shaven Turks...

On the route to Medina, the Damascus caravan was joined by the Baghdad *hajj;* in Burton's year, it included a num-

ber of Wahhabis, whom he found wild and pugnacious, but he was glad of their protection later, when robbers attacked the caravan in a pass just outside Mecca.

The *hajj* in the 19th century was little changed from the past; some of the saints' tombs and idols that had crept into the holy place over the centuries were gone, courtesy of the Wahhabi movement, but the elements of the pilgrimage remained the same. The caravans still combined religious and mercantile functions, providing the main source of income to the region and requiring supply increasingly through Jiddah but also through Aden. But that was destined to change. For the several centuries that Europeans had been in the Eastern oceans, Moslems had generally kept them out of the Red Sea, though they had several times tried to take Aden. But in the second half of the 19th century, the Europeans moved in to fill the vacuum left by the weakened Ottoman Turks. They established themselves in Egypt, Syria, and Palestine; more drastically, they cut through the Suez Isthmus to join the Mediterranean and Red seas with the greatest canal the world had yet seen. This brought Europeans into the region in force, for the Suez Canal became the world's main shipping artery.

European technology also reached inland. Between 1900 and 1908, the Turks (with German technical help) built the famous Hejaz Railway along the old Incense Road

In modern Arabia, camel caravans sometimes tread on paved highway, like this one on a Jiddah thoroughfare. (From Richard H. Sanger, The Arabian Peninsula, *Cornell University Press)*

from Damascus south to Medina, a distance of 800 miles. In the few years before World War I, pilgrims who once would have braved a 40-day trip from Damascus to Mecca piled onto railroad cars—many of them open wagons—for a four-day ride, sometimes as little as 72 hours; caravan relief stations were converted into train stations along the route. The only fear was of attack from the Bedouin, who were generally anti-Turkish, but more specifically anti-railroad, for much of their annual income had derived from rental of camels to pilgrims; indeed, they prevented the rail line from being extended all the way to Mecca. During World War I, Bedouin discontent found an outlet; it suited British interests to ally themselves with the resurgent Wahhabi movement against their Turkish enemies. The railroad, which served economic, political, and military interests for the Turks, was a prime target; southern portions of the line were destroyed by dissident Arabs, inspired by Lawrence of Arabia, on their way across the desolate and dangerous Nefud Desert to attack Aqaba, whose famous guns faced only out to sea. After the war, with Turkish control ended, the Saudis came to power, creating the modern state of Saudi Arabia. They were still against the railway, however, and demanded that other

Moslem nations help pay for the repair of the line—with the result that nothing was done, and the short-lived Hejaz Railway was never reopened below Ma'an, in modern Jordan. The great pilgrimage caravans never revived, however. Pilgrims increasingly turned to the sea routes, taking ships through the Suez Canal to Yanbu', the port of Medina, or Jiddah, the port of Mecca. Both Syria and northern Arabia, which for centuries had thrived on the pilgrimage trade, were bypassed, and the old Pilgrimage Road began to languish.

Outside influences brought even greater changes to the region later in the 20th century, for the British and, later, Americans carried out the early exploration for the oil that has made Arabia richer than incense or religion ever did. More recently the Saudis have found it necessary to build a 40-square-mile international airport near Jiddah, allowing the over two million annual visitors to fly over the fearsome deserts and over the borders that today divide the Moslem countries. Long-distance travel today is increasingly airborne, leaving now-macadamized roads to local traffic: the oil-supported automobiles and the age-old Arabian camel.

Selective Bibliography

Burton, Richard F. *Personal Narrative of a Pilgrimage to Al-Madinah & Meccah,* 2 vols. (New York: Dover, 1964; reprint of 1893 Memorial Edition published by Tylston and Edwards). A classic; includes selections from earlier first-hand accounts as well.

Doughty, Charles M. *Travels in the Arabia Desert* (Cambridge: At the University Press, 1888). A classic travel account.

Grant, Christina Phelps. *The Syrian Desert: Caravans, Travel and Exploration* (New York: Macmillan, 1938). Contains useful sections on the inland highway from Arabia.

Groom, Nigel. *Frankincense and Myrrh: A Study of the Arabian Incense Trade* (London: Longman, 1981). An extremely useful study of the early trade.

Hourani, George Fadlo. *Arab Seafaring: In the Indian Ocean in Ancient and Early Medieval Times* (New York: Octagon, 1975; reprint of 1951 edition of vol. 13 of Princeton Oriental Studies). Includes useful information about associated land routes.

Huzayyin, S. A. *Arabia and the Far East: Their Commercial and Cultural Relations in Graeco-Roman and Irano-Arabian Times* (Cairo: Publications de la Société Royale de Géographie D'Egypte, 1942). Includes coverage of the Incense Road as part of its wider treatment.

al-Munayyir, Muhammad 'Arif ibn Ahmad. *The Hejaz Railway and the Muslim Pilgrimage: A Case of Ottoman Political Propaganda.* Translated and edited by Jacob M. Landau (Detroit: Wayne State University Press, 1971). A commentary on the *hajj* at the time the railway was built.

Rostovtzeff, M. *Caravan Cities* (Oxford: Clarendon Press, 1932). Contains an historical survey of the caravan trade, plus accounts of modern visits to the ruined cities.

Sanger, Richard H. *The Arabian Peninsula* (Ithaca, New York: Cornell University Press, 1954). A view of the region in the 20th century.

Schreiber, Hermann. *The History of Roads: From Amber Route to Motorway* (London: Barrie & Rockliff, 1961). Translated from the German. Contains a chapter on the Incense and Pilgrimage Road.

Stark, Freya. *The Southern Gates of Arabia* (Los Angeles: J. P. Tarcher, 1976; reprint of 1936 edition). Memoirs of a European woman on the southern Incense Road in the 1930's.

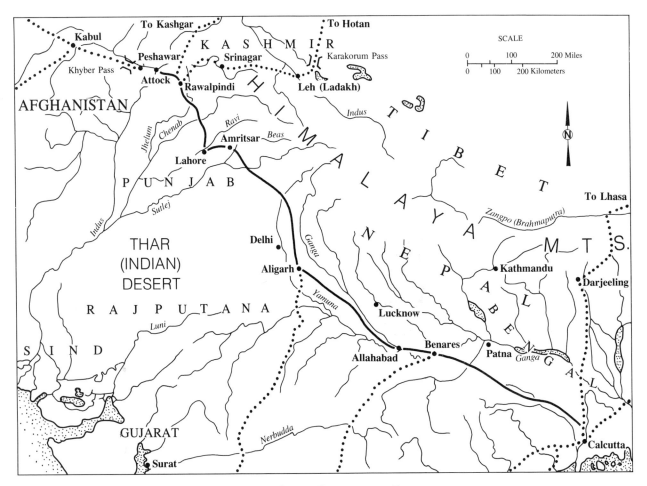

The Grand Trunk Road in 19th Century India

——— Grand Trunk Road · · · · · · Other Main Connecting Routes

The Indian Grand Road

When spring-time flushes the desert grass,
Our kafilas [caravans] wind through the Khyber
    Pass.
Lean are the camels but fat the frails [baskets],
Light are the purses but heavy the bales,
As the snowbound trade of the North comes
    down
To the market-square of Peshawur town.

In a turquoise twilight, crisp and chill,
A kafila camped at the foot of the hill.
Then blue smoke-haze of the cooking rose,
And tent-peg answered to hammer-nose;
And the picketed ponies, shag and wild,
Strained at their ropes as the feed was piled;
And the bubbling camels beside the load
Sprawled for a furlong adown the road;
And the Persian pussy-cats, brought for sale,
Spat at the dogs from the camel-bale;
And the tribesmen bellowed to hasten the food;
And the camp-fires twinkled by Fort Jumrood;
And there fled on the wings of the gathering
    dusk
A savour of camels and carpets of musk,
A murmur of voices, a reek of smoke,
To tell us the trade of the Khyber woke.

As Rudyard Kipling described it in "The Ballad of the King's Jest" (1890), so had the trade of northwestern India been for thousands of years. Although to the unknowing eye, the mountain passes guarding India might seem impenetrable—frigid and barren in winter, parched in the autumn—they have always come alive in the spring,

with the melting snow and rains bringing forage for the pack animals and water for all. Far from barring access to India, out of the northwestern passes there developed one of the world's major routes, the Indian Grand Road—a road not just for traders, but also for pilgrims, wandering players, students, horse traders, ever-present tourists, and always invaders. To the outside world, India's riches were always the stuff of legends; as the medieval Arab trader Hazrat Oman put it: "The Indian rivers are pearls, the mountains rubies, and trees perfumes." Religion also drew outsiders to India, her shrines attracting devout pilgrims for thousands of years. Dreams of conquest brought waves of invaders over the rugged mountain passes, among them Aryans, Persians, Greeks under Alexander the Great, Huns, Islamic Turks, and Mongols. All traveled the Indian Grand Route, from the northwest frontier across the dusty plains to the sacred Ganga River.

North India itself is a great plain bounded north and west by an arc of mountains and, in the east, by dense, matted jungle. The jungle has hindered the development of a major land route to Burma and China throughout history. An equally effective bar has been the great Himalayan range backed by the Tibetan Plateau, a system that includes the highest mountains in the world, Mt. Everest at over 29,000 feet and K2 at slightly less. Only the northwest has allowed ready access to India. There range after range of less formidable, but still rugged mountains lie between the Indian plain and Iranian plateau, gateway to the Silk Road beyond. These ranges were not easy to cross—one British soldier reportedly noted about the Afghan tableland: "Well, if it's a table, it is a table with all the legs uppermost!"—but over the millennia invaders have found their way through the Hindu Kush, the Pamirs, the Suleimans, and lesser ranges by a succession of passes. Mostly these are not the towering, snow-covered mountains that call forth rhapsodies from travelers—and that offer the *frisson* of danger to modern mountain climbers; indeed, more than one writer has called the route through these mountains the ugliest in the world. Indian historian Moti Chandra noted: "It lacks any trace of vegetation and the accumulation of ice does not enhance beauty, because there is scanty snowfall."

Of the Indian plains below the mountains, writers have been more kindly. These are shot through by two great river systems: the Indus (the Lion River), which cuts down from the Himalayan massif like "a gutter from the roof of the world," and the Ganga (the Peacock River), draining the southern flank of the Himalayas. Snaking through the plains as they run to the sea west and east of the Deccan Peninsula, these rivers dominate the scene, as the 17th century Jesuit missionary Pierre du Jarric describes:

The country is, for the most part, fruitful, producing the needs of life in abundance; for between the two famous rivers, the Indus and the Ganges, which wind over the greater portion of it, watering it like a garden, there are nine others which empty themselves into these two.

From the Bamyan Valley northwest of the Indian Grand Road, Afghan nomads file toward Kabul as of old. (Delia and Ferdinand Kuhn)

Prince Siddhartha, better known later as the Buddha, traveled to school in an ox-drawn chariot, common on the Indian Grand Road. (Victoria and Albert Museum)

In actuality, the picture was not quite so rosy as he painted it, for between the rivers the land was often desert. Of the heat in the Punjab—literally "five rivers," referring to the main Indus tributaries—the 20th century visitor Winston Churchill wrote: "You could lift the heat with your hands, it sat on your shoulders like a knapsack, it rested on your head like a nightmare."

For travelers from Mesopotamia or Persia—or those from China and Central Asia who circled around the Himalayas—the main gateway to India has always been through the northwest mountain passes, among them the

Kohat Pass from the south, the Malakand from the north, and the famous Khyber from the west. The various routes funnel into the Kabul River valley, the area where India's Grand Road traditionally began. Following the south bank of the Kabul to the Indus and crossing near Attock, the route proceeded to the market town of Taxila, where it was joined by routes from the more difficult passes—some 19,000 feet high—of Kashmir and the Karakorum (Black Gravel) Mountains just to the north. Descending from the mountains to the plains, the Grand Road cut southeast, crossed the rivers of the Punjab, then picked up the eastward-flowing network of rivers, crossing the Yamuna (Jumna) and then following the Ganga to the sea. (There it connected with two sometime routes to China, one over the Himalayas by way of Tibet, the other via Burma.) With occasional local shifts of the road, as different cities gained prominence along the route under India's many and varied rulers, the Grand Road has followed this main line throughout its history.

The earliest high Indian civilization seems to have developed along the lower Indus (Sindhu) River, especially in the cities of Mohenjodaro and Harappa; almost 5,000 years ago these peoples were trading with their contemporaries in Mesopotamia by land and sea along the Persian Gulf that ran between them. Declining for unknown reasons after its great period, this civilization succumbed to Aryan invaders from the northwest in the early second millennium B.C. Like their Greek and Celtic kin who migrated in the same general period, these Aryans originally came from the area north of the Black and Caspian seas; one group stayed in the Iranian plateau to found the Persian culture and the other moved on into India. Over several centuries, these nomadic Aryans moved across India, conquering and then settling and merging with the earlier inhabitants of the region, eventually forming a new high Indian civilization—and in the process developing a new religion: Hinduism.

It was this Vedic civilization that first developed India's Grand Road. These Indians found the region covered with dense forests, which sheltered robbers and wild beasts. Certainly they found the ancient tracks and trails unsatisfactory, for their early Sanskrit writings celebrate the *pathikrits* (pathfinders) who made new roads by cutting and burning their way through the forests and, further to the southeast, jungles. Nor were these roads left as rough tracks, for the main route was built up above the surrounding area, providing drainage and a firm base for chariots and bullock carts; dykes or causeways allowed for comfortable crossings in shallow, marshy areas, while small ferry boats operated at deeper water crossings. Rest-houses were provided for travelers, spaced at intervals and often at river-crossing points, and stones marked the way and distance along the route. The condition of the roads varied widely, however, especially since the area we know as India was, in the early first millennium B.C., made up of many competing states.

Nor was the Grand Road safe, even in the best of times. An old Vedic travelers' prayer goes: "God forbid that you should meet a robber on the way." Travelers often prayed to their special deity, Manibadra, to safeguard them from wolves and robbers who might take their goods and throw them into deep pits or hold some of the party for ransom. Given the dangers, people seldom traveled alone, but joined together in caravans under a chosen leader (*sārtha vāha*), often with paid locals acting as both guards and guides. Such local experts not only helped protect against robbers but also knew where to find water in the dry parts of the route and could advise on local plants, some of which were highly poisonous. Caravan masters urged their parties not to eat unknown leaves, fruits, and flowers without approval—and often had to treat their fellow travelers when they disobeyed and sampled the forbidden plants. No food being available on the road, caravans carried with them all the provisions needed for the journey and refilled their containers with water at every opportunity. The judgment of the caravan leader was very important in such matters, as innumerable stories show. In one such story, evil spirits tried to mislead travelers, saying that plenty of water was available up ahead. The foolish caravan leader paid heed to the evil spirits and failed to fill his water pots before crossing a desert, so his

Pilgrims, like these depicted in a Mathura stone mural, were frequent travelers on the Indian Grand Road. (State Museum, Lucknow, 2nd century A.D.)

whole party perished. But the wise *sārtha vāha*, leaving only a few days later, questioned the evil spirits' counsel, asking, "Has rain-laden wind reached us?" and "Has anybody heard thunder?"; he filled his water pots and his party survived. Camping spots also had to be chosen carefully; one caravan leader made the mistake of camping along an animal trail and, in the middle of the night, many of the party were trampled by a herd of wild elephants on their way to a water pool. Leaders taking caravans into desert country, either within India or on the Silk Road north of the Himalayas, sometimes received special training in nautical schools along the Indian coast, so they could navigate by the stars, like ships' pilots.

In the centuries before the birth of Christ, India and her Grand Road underwent great upheaval. In the sixth century B.C., Persian Aryans under Darius I moved through the northwest passes to the Indus and perhaps as far as the Beas, fourth of the Punjab's five rivers; instead of proceeding further on the Grand Road, however, they turned down the Indus to the sea (perhaps to protect their supply routes or because they thought, as did many others, that the Indus was the source of the Nile and a back door to the riches of Egypt). During their brief reign, the Persians provided special protection for the camel caravans between Persia and northern India, but they lost control of their Indian territories within decades. Of more lasting impact was the Buddha, born Siddhartha Gautama, who in the same century founded the religious reform movement of Buddhism; becoming a wandering ascetic in search of enlightenment, Buddha traveled all over the Indo-Gangetic Plain and up into the mountains of Kashmir, where tales of his passing were told for centuries after. As his influence grew, Buddha often found that local kings would ask him to delay his journey until they had had time to repair the route, as was often done for important travelers. In this period also the sixteen or so quarreling kingdoms that had made up India gradually were reduced to four.

Then another group of invaders arrived: the Greeks under Alexander the Great. In his desire to match Darius's exploits, Alexander in the mid-fourth century B.C. led his army on an eight-year march from the Mediterranean, across Mesopotamia and Persia, dipping south to the region of modern Kandahar, and then moving north in a series of spring campaigns to Bactra (where he married the Bactrian princess, Roxana) and Maracanda (later Samarkand). After all this he circled back and turned his attention toward India, source of fabled riches, exotic animals like elephants, apes, and peacocks, and—so he thought—of the Nile. Following difficult battles with the mountain peoples, Alexander crossed the Indus with relative ease on a bridge of boats he persuaded a local king to build for him. But only with difficulty could Alexander move his army further into India. At the River Beas the Greek soldiers balked, and Alexander was forced to turn

back and follow Darius's course down the Indus (learning in the process that it was *not* the source of the Nile) before heading homeward. Though his stay was brief and he died a few months later, Alexander's influence was lasting. Not only did his heirs establish kingdoms neighboring India, but the Greek art they brought, including the Greek coins with Alexander's head stamped on them, fascinated the Eastern world and played a significant role in shaping the Buddhist art that was later taken throughout Asia.

But northern India was to undergo an even more lasting change with the rise of a great leader of its own: Chandragupta Maurya. While Alexander was working his way toward the Indus (where he and Chandragupta are rumored to have met), Chandragupta was preparing to unite the area along India's Grand Road. Usurping the throne of the state of Magadha, centered in the Ganga basin, he took control of the important eastern portion of the Grand Road. His successors in the Mauryan dynasty expanded their control and influence until, by the time of the great king Aśoka in 250 B.C., the whole of the Grand Road was theirs.

Under the Mauryans, the Grand Road ran from the port of Tamralipti (where sailors traded across the Bay of Bengal for Eastern goods) up along the Ganga to their capital at Pataliputra; followed the Ganga through the ancient cities of Prayaga and Kanauj; crossed the salt desert to the Yamuna River at Mathura; and then cut northwest through the Punjab to Taxila, across the Indus, and on to the town of Kapisa, near modern Kabul. (An alternate midsection had once followed the Ganga north, later rejoining the main route, but by Mauryan times it extended only up to Hastināpura, the forest having reclaimed the rest.) Mauryan control stopped just short of the crossroads city of Kapisa, but the border was friendly, so much so that the Mauryan Empire exchanged diplomats with their Seleucid neighbors, heirs of Alexander. One Greek diplomat named Megasthenes praised Indian roadmakers in his reports and noted the provision of resthouses and itineraries outlining the route (perhaps modeled on Persia's earlier Royal Road). Indeed, the Mauryans did make the Grand Road safer and better maintained than ever before. A state official was charged with keeping the highway open and in good repair; with building and maintaining causeways and ferries; with putting up milestones and signposts all along the route; with digging wells where needed; with cutting down trees and breaking up rocks that blocked the road; and with planting trees on either side of the road for travelers' comfort in unforested arid areas where shade was precious. A special labor force seems to have been maintained to work on the roads, although armies and sometimes large caravans carried with them a separate group to make repairs and put up shelters as needed. Staging posts and guardhouses were also established for use by imperial messen-

This country scene from the 1st century B.C. includes a four-horse chariot that could only have been used on good roads. (From a terracotta plaque found near Allahabad)

gers along the approximately 2,600-mile route. Similar special care was taken with the main branch routes of the kingdom (which by the time of Aśoka extended far south toward the tip of India), especially the route from Mathura to the Gujarat port of Barygaza (Bharukachchha, or Broach) and the one down the west side of the Indus to the port of Barbaricon, both major ports on the developing Spice Route, in which Indian sailors played a central role.

Trade and travel flourished in India under these conditions, nowhere more than on the Grand Road. Merchants had always operated along the route, at first exchanging goods like cloth, leather, and animals for like goods by means of a simple barter system. But by Mauryan times traders had become far more sophisticated; although coin money was new to them—one reason why Greek and later Roman coins were so prized—traders sometimes carried their own balances to weigh out amounts of gold for use in barter. And the goods they traded became far more various, including hides, furs, and highly prized horses from Central Asia by way of the northwest passes; woven and embroidered shawls from the mountains of Kashmir and Nepal and from the Punjab; linens, silks, and cottons from the major cities of the Ganga Basin (some originating in China); precious stones and pearls, not only from India but also from Taprobane (Ceylon), Persia, Burma, and other places along the Spice Route; and aromatics, such as sandalwood, from various parts of Southeast Asia.

Some of the caravans on the Grand Road were so large—including elephants, horses, oxen, donkeys, camels, buffaloes, chariots, carts, litters, palanquins (covered sedan chairs for the rich, carried on the shoulders of porters), merchants backpacking trade goods, and walkers—that they seemed, so one poet said, "a moving ocean of men." Life on the road had a special camaraderie, too, for in the

Mahabharata a man commenting on the happy life said: "To those who go out on a journey, the caravan is a friend in the same way as wives are friends when they are residing in their homes."

Often joining these traders were pilgrims—generally not upper-class Hindus whose fear of contact with untouchables made travel extremely difficult, but Buddhists following the way of their master, either literally in his footsteps or more generally in ascetic wandering. After Aśoka converted to Buddhism in the mid-third century B.C., the religion became very widespread, and Buddhist pilgrims often traveled with itinerant peddlers or even became caravan leaders themselves.

The Jain religion, founded in the same century as Buddhism and popular among merchants and traders, also sent many travelers along India's Grand Road to visit Jain shrines and preach their religion. Jain monks and nuns were under special restrictions, however. They could only pass the night in a religious building or in a potter's or ironsmith's workshop, where they could sleep on a straw bed, or in extreme cases in a vacant house, a cemetery, or under a tree; they could not travel during the four rainy months of the year (generally June through September); they were obliged to avoid dangerous routes, where forests sheltered robbers or anarchy prevailed; and they had to follow strict dietary rules, begging for their food on the way, like most pilgrims. Jain nuns had to be even more careful in traveling; they were not allowed to stay in public rest-houses where their moral well-being might be affected by contact with prostitutes and other bad characters or where they might be exposed to ridicule when "answering a call of nature." While pilgrims sometimes traveled together as a separate group, they more often joined with caravans, some of which provided them with free food.

To these travelers were added students being sent into one of the main cities for their education; traveling performers—actors, dancers, jugglers, acrobats, and the like; groups of laborers in search of work; and young people who were taking their equivalent of a "Grand Tour" to complete their education. One such young man's adventures are described in Buddhist writings:

He wandered as a pedlar in Kalinga [south of the Ganga on the Bay of Bengal], and holding a staff he traversed uneven and difficult routes. He was often seen in the company of acrobats and sometimes he was seen trapping innocent animals. He often gambled and at times he spread his net to catch birds and sometimes he fought with a stick in the crowds.

Such activities did not always have the approval of the local population, as witnessed by the oft-told tale of the banker's son who fell in love with a female acrobat and ran away to join the troupe.

For the convenience of all, caravans were supposed to travel at a rate that could be undertaken easily by old men and children, breaking for midday meal and following the main route, where mendicants could beg for alms in the villages and animals could find proper grazing. Faced with hazards like robbers, floods, wild elephants, or tigers, caravans sometimes camped along the road to wait out the danger and to form a united front with other caravans. Wagons would often form a circle for defense, and most caravans carried fencing or thorny bushes which could be placed around the camp to ward off wild animals.

Whatever the type of traveler, all were highly regulated in Mauryan times. Passports were required of all persons, Indians or foreigners, for travel in the countryside; these were checked by "superintendents of meadows" who operated inspection houses at strategic points along the main roads. These people supervised the shelters and wells; used dogs and hunters to detect robbers or dangerous animals; and warned approaching travelers of danger by shouting and clanging bells or pans. Customs collectors also operated along the main roads, with customs houses located at the main gateways of each city. All travelers had to present their passports there, and merchants their goods. Merchants found making false declarations or forging seals paid eight times the normal duty; and those found to be carrying proscribed articles— such as weapons, precious stones or metals, certain grains and animals, and chariots, all of which were traded only under state monopoly—had their goods confiscated. Merchants also had to pay tolls to the local warden, to whom was delegated responsibility for the safety of goods passing through his region. Once through customs, the merchants could set out their goods for sale, but only in the shadow of the customs house flag, for the state also controlled prices. A Director of Trade fixed prices throughout the country and sometimes bought and sold on the king's behalf, evening out supply with demand and—far from incidentally—enriching the king's coffers. Other superintendents monitored the ports and ferry crossings; they set the ferryman's prices but did not ensure that he would be paid—for centuries ferrymen were cautioned to collect their fares *before* crossing or risk not getting them. At some major crossings, boat bridges were used during the winter season but dismantled before the spring and summer floods.

This highly organized and regulated system along the Grand Road fell apart somewhat after the death of Aśoka and the subsequent disintegration of the Mauryan Empire into two dozen smaller states. The next few centuries saw a series of invasions through the northwest passes, all backwashes of the major upheavals taking place among the nomadic peoples of Central Asia. The first was an invasion of Indo-Greeks from Bactria; in about 175 B.C. the heirs of the long-gone Alexander moved down the Grand Road to take northern India from the Indus to the

Hsüan-tsang was just one of many pilgrims who crossed Asia and circled the Himalayas onto the Indian Grand Road. (From Tōyō Bijutsu Taikan, *c. 800* A.D., *Toyko, British Museum)*

Ganga. Their direct control lasted only about 10 years, but many Indo-Greeks stayed behind, and their influence was felt for at least another century. A few decades later the Indo-Greek ruler from Bactra withdrew to Kapisa before a Scythian people called the Sakas. These Central Asian invaders circled to the southwest through Herat and Kandahar, attacking the Kabul River region and moving deep into India before being expelled.

The Sakas were followed by the even stronger Kushans, part of the powerful Yüeh-chih (Scythian) peoples from the region of the Oxus (Amu) River. Although centered around Bactra, the Kushans approached India by the lightly defended route from the north, over the rugged mountains of the eastern Hindu Kush. In the decades just before and after the birth of Christ, they took Taxila and moved along the Grand Road as far as Varanasi (Benares), perhaps even to Pataliputra. Under the Kushans, India became part of a vast empire that extended from the Persian Gulf north to the Jaxartes (Syr) River and east along the Silk Road to Hotan (Khotan), even pushing back the powerful Chinese Empire. For the first time, the route between the Ganga River and Central Asia was unified.

Keeping their main base deep into the continent, the Kushans established a new local capital at Peshawar (Purushapura, meaning "frontier town") on the Kabul River, establishing the Khyber Pass as the dominant northwest pass into India. Being in control of the western half of the Silk Road, they were also able to open, without impediment, subsidiary routes over the mountains. The most important of these were their original invasion route from Tashkurgan through the Hindu Kush to Peshawar; the route from Kashgar through Gilgit, which reached the Grand Road west of Taxila; and the route through the Karakorum Pass from Hotan through Leh (Ladakh) and Srinigar to Taxila. On these mountain routes travelers relied on pack animals, like camels and horses; carts were impossible to use in the narrow winding defiles. Indeed, the Indian name for such routes meant "tracks on which only goats could pass."

The Kushan Empire brought little that was new to India, mostly building on the remnants of the Mauryan Empire. The influence ran in the other direction, for the Grand Road and the subsidiary mountain routes brought Indian culture to the wider world of Asia. The greatest Kushan leader, Kanishka, a strong Buddhist, spread his religion throughout the Himalayas and into Central Asia, where it passed along the old Silk Road into China and on even to Korea and Japan. The impact of this Buddhist expansion would be felt for centuries, as it is even today, when the reign of the Kushans is largely forgotten.

While the Kushans reigned, the Roman and Chinese empires were at their height; international trade flourished, much of it by sea along the Spice Route, the rest by land, over the Silk Road and the Indian Grand Road—that portion of it under Kushan control. In Bengal, along the eastern section of the Grand Road, social and political upheavals drove many people, especially traders, to emigrate to Southeast Asia, where they hoped for gain in the spice trade. Along the rest of the Grand Road, trade continued and expanded. Indian traders dealt directly with their Chinese counterparts along the Silk Road, but trade between Rome and India was conducted by intermediaries, such as Armenians, Syrian Jews, Greeks, and Parthians. Indirect or no, the Romans were quite clear about whom they were dealing with; the geographer Ptolemy knew of the "road to India which goes through Palibothra [Pataliputra]." No matter the distances, for the Roman Pliny wrote: "India is brought near by lust for gain." This trade was so important that Kanishka even adopted Roman coins as the standard currency in his empire—and the Romans tried to limit the outflow of gold to India.

Kushans continued to reign in India until the fourth century A.D., when their weakness allowed the re-emergence of home rule in India. Under the Gupta dynasty, northern India was gradually reunited and the Grand Road was once again centrally administered. Gupta rulers continued active trade along the Grand Road and kept up close contact with the Indian colonists who had settled in the Hindu Kush and in Central Asia. Along the Gupta routes came many Chinese Buddhist pilgrims, seeking enlightenment in the homeland of the master and hoping to take back home with them copies of Buddhist texts unavailable in China. Many were warmly greeted by Buddhist communities along the way, some staying on for years to pray and learn. One such pilgrim, Fa-Hsien, traveling to India at the turn of the fifth century A.D., was struck by the extraordinary devotional images that Buddhists had made, many of which had become shrines in themselves. One artisan, transported three times to the heavens by "divine power" to "observe the height, complexion, and features" of the Buddha, had carved a wooden image "eighty feet in height, the folded legs of which measured eight feet across."

While some pilgrims followed the main route into India, many others wandered among the Buddhist aeries in the higher mountains, as Buddha himself had done. The existence of such communities in the towering Himalayas is as surprising today as it was then, given the conditions Fa-Hsien described:

> On these mountains there is snow in winter and summer alike. There are also venomous dragons, which, if provoked, spit forth poisonous winds, rain, snow, sand, and stones. Of those who encounter these dangers not one in ten thousand escapes....[We took] a difficult, precipitous, and dangerous road, the side of the mountain being like a stone wall ten thousand feet in height. On nearing the edge, the eye becomes confused; and wishing to advance, the foot finds no resting place. Below there is a river, named Indus...

In the northern, arid parts of the Indian Grand Road, travelers often rode the "ships of the desert." (By Henry Ainslie, 1852, India Office Library)

The plains of northern India were more congenial, and the people there—used to pilgrims—greeted them warmly. Fa-Hsien describes the usual welcome:

When traveling priests arrive, the old resident priests go out to welcome them and carry for them their clothes and alms-bowls, giving them water for washing and oil for anointing their feet, as well as the liquid food allowed out of hours.

Ironically, while many parts of Asia were sending Buddhist pilgrims to India, in India itself Buddhism was declining. The older Hindu religion in new guises was winning over the population, and Buddhist and Jain pilgrims on India's Grand Road were now often joined by Hindu pilgrims traveling to bathe themselves in the holy water of the Ganga.

This tendency increased over the following centuries, as the Gupta dynasty declined and India fell into an anarchic mosaic of states. In the mid-sixth century, yet another group of invaders pushed through the northwest frontier into India; these were the Hūnas, part of a Central Asian nomadic people better known to the West as the White Huns. Like their predecessors, they moved from Bactria down along the Grand Road to the Ganga plain, cruelly persecuting Buddhists throughout the area under their control. Northeastern India—the ancient core kingdom of Magadha, and Bengal to its east—stayed in Gupta hands, but war weakened it so that, even after the Hūnas were driven back into the high mountains, the Guptas were powerless. Unity along the old Grand Road was lost, and a series of petty states existed along its track, with the condition of the roads reflecting the collapse of control.

Visiting pilgrims reflected sadly on the state of the country and of their Buddhist religion. Hsüan-Tsang, a celebrated Chinese pilgrim visiting India in the mid-600's, told a mournful tale of the changes. From the great Buddhist city of Bactra—and from Bamyan, with its famous statues of Buddha, over 100 feet high, carved into a cliff—Hsüan-Tsang descended along the general line of the Grand Road. At Kapisa, once summer headquarters of the Buddhist prince Kanishka, he found the monastery dilapidated, and along the Kabul River, he found "there were few monks and...numerous stupas [shrines] were desolate and in ruins." Peshawar "held the ruins of its former greatness; its one thousand monasteries, deserted and in ruins, were overgrown with shrubs..." Elsewhere he noted: "Here again silence and desolation reigned where once nearly 20,000 monks studied and meditated and wrote." Further south, Hsüan-Tsang noted even further evidence of a great change when he came to Prayaga, where the Yamuna and Ganga Rivers join; there he saw devout Hindus committing ritual suicide by first starving and then drowning themselves in the holy river. Further along the Grand Road, the evidence of Buddhist decline and Hindu ascendancy was equally marked. In the city of Varanasi, Hsüan-Tsang noted: "Most of the people are Hindus; only a few follow the Law of Buddha." Likewise Rajagriha, capital of Magadha in Buddha's lifetime, and Magadha itself he saw as "a country whose glory had long since died."

The Grand Road itself suffered in these times. Safety on the road was very much an ad hoc affair, as Hsüan-Tsang (also called Tripitaka) found in the eastern Punjab. His biographer tells the story:

> Traversing a great forest, the party was stopped by a band of robbers, fifty sword-wielding desperados, who stripped them of their clothes and goods and then drove them at sword's point into a dried-up pond...enclosed by a wall of thickly matted, prickly vines...an ideal pen where the robbers could kill their victims...[some] forced their way through the barbed hedge, and once on the other side ran for help. They had to go almost a mile before they found a Brahman [Hindu] plowing his field. When he heard what had happened, he instantly unyoked his oxen and led them to the village, where he summoned the villagers by blowing on a conch and beating a drum. Eighty men answered the call. They grabbed whatever weapons they could and ran to the pond. The robbers, seeing so large a crowd, quickly dispersed and disappeared into the forest.

Pilgrims like Hsüan-Tsang were often helped by people of other religious faiths. After the robbery, in which Hsüan-Tsang lost all his clothes, the Brahman villagers supplied him with new clothes and travel necessaries. And non-Buddhist merchants and other travelers still joined forces with pilgrims, although most declined to follow Hsüan-Tsang when he angled into a dangerous forest to visit some largely abandoned Buddhist shrine. A king's protection was best, of course, and indeed, many kings welcomed the chance to have the various religions debate; in 642 A.D., the Buddhist King Harsha summoned to his capital of Kanauj thousands of monks—Buddhist, Hindu, and Jain—to do just that. Hsüan-Tsang was there:

> Each of these thousands of celebrated visitors was accompanied by a retinue of servants: some came on elephants, some in chariots, some were carried in palanquins, and some were distinguished by their show of standards and parasols.

Akbar is praying on the banks of the Indus, before heading up the river in 1572. (By Lal and Nand, Moghul artists, Victoria and Albert Museum)

The days of the wandering ascetics on India's Grand Road seemed rather far away.

The remaining Buddhist princes afforded foreign pilgrims special care, if they would accept it. Hsüan-Tsang himself, though not desirous of a comfortable journey, accepted from Harsha the gift of a great elephant, on which he could carry his precious manuscripts back to China, as well as "3,000 gold pieces and 10,000 pieces of silver given to defray his expenses along the way." Why so much money? Arthur Waley, in *The Real Tripitaka*, explains:

> A large elephant, like a big car, is expensive to run. This one consumed over forty bundles of hay a day and over twenty pounds of buns.

As with other important and valued travelers, King Harsha and other Buddhist princes also gave Hsüan-Tsang letters to other rulers along the route.

But natural hazards still remained. In crossing the Indus, Hsüan-Tsang "bravely forded it in the back of his elephant." But the ferry carrying his cargo was pitched about by a sudden storm, tossing some of the Buddhist manuscripts into the water. (These were replaced by a Buddhist prince along the way.) On the northern route through the Hindu Kush (which he called the Snowy Mountains), with each mountain higher and more difficult to climb than the last, snowstorms took their turn:

> ...when bitter cold had crusted the snow, they advanced up the ridge guided by a native riding a mountain camel. They floundered in deep snowdrifts and crossed crevasses trusting to snow bridges. Anyone who did not follow in the guide's footsteps would have fallen and perished. The entire party of seven monks, twenty porters, one elephant, ten asses, and four horses struggled up the pass...There was not a trace of vegetation, only a mass of crazily piled rock on rock and everywhere slender stone pinnacles looking like a forest of trees without leaves.

Passing through other midsummer snowstorms, Hsüan-Tsang returned safely to China with his Buddhist manuscripts; they helped form the basis for the independent Buddhist survival in East Asia, while in India Buddhism all but disappeared in the following centuries. After Hsüan-Tsang, the great age of Buddhist pilgrims came to an end. And with India itself in disarray, with the great Roman market gone, and with Central Asia carved into pieces, the international trade of India's Grand Road became negligible.

In this period, a new force was arising that would change the face of India. In the seventh and early eighth centuries, Islam spread, by sword and conversion, across Eurasia and Africa, until by 711 A.D. the Islamic world extended from Spain on the Atlantic Ocean to China's borders in Central Asia. Only India successfully resisted, the guardians of the northwest passes holding strong; although the lower Indus was taken by Islamic forces in 712, the rest of India held off invasion for almost 300 years. Indeed, India became truly vulnerable only after the Afghan peoples, who controlled the northwest passes, converted to Islam. Even so, while the Caliph of Baghdad ruled supreme, the region around Kabul was merely a backwater in a vast Islamic empire. But when that empire disintegrated into several caliphates, one centered on the southern route toward Kabul, India came under attack. The many warring Hindu kingdoms along the old Grand Road were ill-equipped to meet a threat from the northwest. In 991 A.D., Sultan Mahmud occupied Peshawar with his Islamic forces, then used that as a base for taking the Punjab. From there, he plundered and laid waste the great Hindu cities, among them Kanauj, Lahore, and Mathura, retiring some decades later to the Punjab. After that, Mahmud and his sucessors co-existed uneasily with their Hindu neighbors, with whom they shared the now-neglected Grand Road. The situation changed in 1191, when Mohammed Ghori moved eastward against

All along the Indian Grand Road and in the mountains to the north and west were sculptures of Buddha, like this Gandhara bas relief of his death. (Author's archives)

the temporarily united Hindu kings, taking the Ganga Valley and making the small town of Delhi (founded only two centuries before) his imperial capital. From there, the Sultans ruled (with one brief removal to an ill-fated new town) for the next three centuries over an empire that extended down into the Deccan Peninsula and sometimes included a recalcitrant Bengal.

Under the Sultanate, the Grand Road took on a new look. Safe and secure roads were vital to the new government, both for holding their new territory and for guarding their supply and retreat lines in case of uprisings. Indeed, armies often built and maintained roads for their own purposes alone, with some specially constructed boat-bridges unavailable for other travelers. But the roads became more important for everyone. Trade with the western Asian countries revived strongly, and immigrants arrived in India from throughout the Islamic world, from Persia, Africa, and Central Asia. These and other travelers—scholars, musicians, acrobats, clowns, beggars, artisans, political refugees, still-common pilgrims, and just plain adventurers—swelled the traffic on the Grand Road and the other routes of India. Not least among the travelers were the merchants; though regarded as lower-caste by the Brahman Hindus, they were highly regarded by the Moslems, the Prophet Mohammed himself commending merchants as "the couriers of the world and the trusty servants of God upon earth."

To make highway travel safe once again, the Sultanate took drastic measures. Amassing road crews of forced and hired labor, the government cut down the jungles and cleared the forests near main roads; robbers' dens were emptied and replaced by government forts—the robbers often having selected the most vulnerable spots along the road; more than that, in a masterly move, they converted the *dacoits*—semi-permanent robber bands—into the paid protectors of the roads. Indian writer Amir Khusrau described it this way:

> ...the very thieves who, before this, set villages on fire, now lit the lamps and guarded the highways; if a traveler lost a piece of thread, the people of the vicinity either found it or paid its price.

Ziau'ddin Barani echoed and expanded on his sentiment:

> ...the highwaymen, inspired by the fear of his (the Sultan's) sword, acted as sentinels and protectors of roads. Those who were confirmed and hereditary highwaymen now broke their weapons, sold their bows and shields, and took to ploughing and agriculture.

Such vigilance aided the Sultans in holding back potential rebellions, as well as in fighting off most incursions of Central Asian peoples from the north. The result was a revival in travel and trade along the Grand Road, with goods brought to India by sea from the East sometimes passing along the land route on its way to western and central Asia.

Travel itself was made easier and more convenient than ever before. Like the Mauryan rulers of centuries before, the Sultans provided rest-houses, wells, shade trees, and signposts. But the Sultans went far beyond this, providing also reservoirs, canals, and ponds so people and animals would not want for water on their journey—in the process encouraging the spread of population and cultivation along the road. The result was, some said, that people on the Grand Road might well imagine that they were "walking through a garden." Even more attractive were the changes made in the rest-houses themselves, which the Muslims called *sarais* or *caravansarais*. Shops in the *sarais* sold whatever items a traveler might need; rest-houses provided lodging, food, and water at short intervals along the route, so travelers no longer needed to carry tents, provisions, or water along the Grand Road; travelers could also change horses at the *sarais*. The

Soldiers exposed on the plains of Kabul were always at the mercy of Afghans on the heights. (Lithograph by Day and Haghe, 1842)

198

sarais—some public, some private—catered to other human needs as well; women of "bad repute" sometimes set up *sarais*, entertaining the travelers "in any manner they liked." As a 15th century Russian traveler named Nikitin noted:

> …it is the custom for foreign traders to stop at inns; there the food is cooked for the guests by the landlady, who also makes the bed and sleeps with strangers.

Islamic prohibitions generally operated, such as that against drinking or selling wine. At religious houses, called *khangahs,* travelers were also expected to respect the religious way of life and to join in prayers and were welcome to stay for three days free of charge.

The Grand Road was also put to more official purposes. To maintain communication within the empire, the Sultans operated an efficient courier relay system, modeled on the ancient Persian one. Stations were set about one-third of a mile apart for foot couriers (four miles apart for horse-couriers); the foot-courier carried the message or package (sometimes special fruits for the Sultan) in one hand and a bell-bedecked rod in the other; as the sound of the bells was heard at the next station, the fresh courier prepared, took the letter and rod from the arriving runner, and ran on to the next station. Using this system, news could reach Delhi from anywhere in the empire in just a few days—from Kanauj it took only three.

In the 14th century, the Moslem hold weakened, as some Hindu states revived. Then in 1398 came new invaders from the northwest. The Mongol leader Timur ("the lame," also called Tamerlane) pushed halfway down the Grand Road with almost no opposition, even plundering the imperial city of Delhi. Although Timur's forces withdrew to Central Asia, the Sultanate's weakness was exposed and various other states emerged along the Grand Route; one of these, under the Lodi dynasty, rivaled the Sultanate from its capital at Agra, further down the Ganga from Delhi. The situation changed completely only in the 16th century, with the arrival of Babur (also spelled Babar), descendant of both Timur and Genghis Khan and leader of a powerful Islamicized Mongol army. With the Afghan powers in disarray, Babur was able to take Kabul in 1503, using it as a base for his conquest of Delhi in 1526. Writer of poetry and lover of gardens—in both interests strongly influenced by the Persians—Babur always longed for his mountain homeland in Central Asia but is best known for establishing a new dynasty in India, the Mughal or Moghul Dynasty (both a corruption of "Mongol").

At Babur's death, however, that dynasty was tenuous. Babur's son Humayan, alternating indolence and energy, was forced to retreat for 15 years of exile in Persia. Babur's dynasty seemed at an end with the rise of a strong Afghan leader, Sher Khan Sur, who called himself Sher Shah. An extraordinary administrator, Sher Shah reorganized the north Indian government along Persian-inspired lines; it was he who laid out the course of the modern Grand Road, now more often called the Grand Trunk Road. From the city of Sonārgāon in Bengal, the road bypassed the lower Ganga Valley and the once-important cities of Kanauj and Patna (Pataliputra), reaching the river only at Varanasi (Benares); crossing there and recrossing at Allahabad (formerly Prayaga), the route followed the west side of the Ganga for a time before crossing the Yamuna to Delhi. Arcing east of the great Thar (Indian) Desert, the Grand Trunk Road then proceeded to cross the rivers of the Punjab, passing through Lahore and Rawalpindi—which had replaced Taxila as the main staging-post—before meeting the Indus at Attock.

Sher Shah revived and expanded the *caravansarai* system, which had fallen into disarray. He provided separate lodgings for Moslems and Hindus, with servants for each; food and water for travelers and their animals; often a small staffed mosque for Moslem travelers; and two post-horse riders to relay the royal mail. These *sarais* also acted as spy stations, giving Sher Shah up-to-date intelligence on activities throughout his domain, which he further protected by fortifying strategic sites. But his great abilities were to no avail. After only five years of power, Sher Shah died, and the Afghan alliance he had forged fell apart; Humayan was able to re-establish control in India.

It was Humayan's son Akbar, born en route to exile in Persia, who fully established the Mughal Dynasty when he took power in 1556. With his Moslem religion and Iranian education, Akbar set about forming a new union along the old Grand Road, adopting and expanding many of Sher Shah's plans in the process. Extending his empire along the Ganga, he relieved the Hindus of many oppressions imposed by previous Moslem rulers, such as taxes on pilgrimages; Akbar himself married a Hindu princess and brought many Hindus into responsible positions in the government. Recognizing the importance of the Grand Trunk Road, he substantially widened many sections, especially that leading to the Khyber Pass, and re-established regular ferries at main river crossings. Danger still remained, of course, especially during the summer when the waters were riding high; the Pathan poet Khushal Khan Khatak noted that all travelers:

> Must cross by the Attock ferry, trembling the while with fear,
> For Indus takes his tribute from pauper, and prince and peer.

To maintain full control of his empire, Akbar also expanded the string of forts at strategic points along the

Grand Trunk Road, most importantly at Attock. These forts were also intended to ensure safety for travelers along the road, for—despite all efforts to control them—*dacoits* still lurked in vulnerable places along the route. The Mughals' success in this respect was questionable, as some of the Europeans who arrived there in this period attested. An Azorean-Portuguese, Benedict Goes, joined a 500-man caravan at Lahore, but the 400 guards had to repulse so many attacks en route to the north that many merchants chose not to go beyond Kabul. (Later some of the early British East India agents would find the robbers no worse than the fort commanders, who extorted money from travelers supposedly under their protection.) The main means of transportation on the Grand Trunk Road still being bullock cart or camel pack-train, travel was also slow, taking approximately three months between Delhi and Bengal. For both safety and speed, travelers, especially merchants transporting bulk goods, often preferred to employ river boats on the Yamuna and the Ganga down to Bengal; a canal built between Delhi and the Yamuna made that even easier.

Many of Akbar's cultural reforms did not last, being dismantled by his successors, who reimposed special taxes on Hindus and destroyed many important Hindu temples, including those at Varanasi and Mathura; the Mughals also lost their base in Balkh (as Bactra was now called), retreating to borders near Kabul. But many Mughal building projects, among them the Taj Mahal in Agra and the great forts along the Grand Trunk Road, have lasted into modern times. More than that, the Persian influence they brought into India has remained, in literature, dress, and language.

The Europeans, who arrived in India by the Cape of Good Hope Route at about the same time as the Mughals, were the first successful conquerors to arrive from the sea, rather than through the northwest passes. The first of these were the Portuguese, under Vasco da Gama, who arrived on the Malabar Coast in 1498. They were followed by Dutch, French, Danish, and British traders, who began to set up trading centers all along the coasts of India; the port of Calcutta on the Hooghly River, near the mouth of the Ganga, was a main outpost of the British East India Company after 1690. As the Mughal empire began to disintegrate, these powers battled each other for supremacy, with the British emerging as dominant and expanding their territory rapidly, especially along the east coast and the Ganga Valley. By the turn of the 19th century, the Mughal dynasty was in a state of collapse, with various other groups—notably the Afghans, the Marathans of central India, and the Sikhs (a new religion that had arisen in the Punjab in the previous few centuries)—carrying on bloody battles all along the Indian Grand Road, each vainly seeking dominance over the region. The result was anarchy on the overland routes, along which British traders had expanded from the coast.

To protect their merchant interests, the British gradually took control—often directly, sometimes indirectly—of the entire region from Bengal to the Punjab and south. They also established an alliance with the Sikh Empire centered on Amritsar in the Punjab.

During this period the British applied to India many of the administrative and technical methods so characteristic of their own homeland. They established civil service training schools and reformed Indian laws to provide central and more "enlightened" administration. Along the Grand Trunk Road they made many significant changes. Most important, the British, sparked by Governor-General Dalhousie, modernized the Grand Trunk Road from Calcutta to Delhi, laying for the first time a "metalled" surface, made up of layers of broken stone, carefully graded from the coarsest to the finest on top. As British control was gradually extended to include the Punjab, Sind (the region of the lower Indus), and Kashmir, this process was applied to the whole of the Grand Trunk Road past Attock. More than that Dalhousie laid out a trunk railway line along roughly the same route, with branch routes to such main areas as Bombay on the west coast.

These were the days of military adventurism. While the British were pushing toward northwest India, the emerging Russian Empire was pushing down through Central Asia toward the all-important crossroads where the Indian Grand Road joined the Silk Road, while Persia was pressing from the southwest. Desiring a friendly buffer state in Afghanistan, the British ill-advisedly installed a puppet on the throne in Kabul, reaching that city by a relatively easy route from the south. With no experience of the area or its people, they were misled into thinking themselves secure. It was easy to do; Lieutenant Rattray of the occupying force described the scene:

Kabul...is well-built and handsome, and is one mass of bazaars...A fountain plays near; and here, in the heat of the day, loll the chiefs at ease, as they smoke their pipes to the sound of *sacringhi* or guitars.

Originally installed in the towering citadel, the Bala Hissar, they acceded to their "puppet's" desire to use that as a palace; the army, the wives and children who joined them, and the thousands of support staff all were moved to an open cantonment, with no defense to speak of. Unfortunately, when the British ceased paying subsidies to the local tribes for their support, these deceptively easy-going chieftains decided to throw out the occupiers. Ignoring early warning signs that might have let them retreat under better conditions, the whole camp—over 16,000 people in all, though only 4,500 in troops—was forced to leave Kabul on January 6, 1842. Midwinter conditions, lack of knowledge of the route or preparation for the journey, plus fierce Afghan fighters commanding defiles all along the route, spelled disaster. Worse, it proved impossible to separate troops from noncombatants; all suffered equally. After seven days of such action over the 110 miles from Kabul to Jalalabad, the nearest British garrison, the toll was such that on January 13th a lone horseman arrived in Jalalabad; as observer Sir John Kaye saw it:

> A shudder ran through the garrison. That solitary horseman looked like the messenger of death...he now reported his belief that he was the sole survivor of some sixteen thousand men.

There were, in fact, a few other survivors, who had been taken hostage and were released months later, but this was a catastrophe unprecedented in modern military history. The fort at Jalalabad held, and three months later a relief force was sent from India; these first British troops to enter the 30-mile-long Khyber Pass found the steep and narrow path above the gorge heavily fortified all along the way.

The British eventually returned to take Kabul and

had a series of wars with the Afghans, but for the rest of their tenure in India, their northwest border was generally at the Khyber Pass. Elsewhere along the Grand Trunk Road, they attempted to make the road secure for travel, although rebel attacks and mutinies kept the road in some turmoil, especially in the northwest. But the activities of the British army and their followers kept the Grand Trunk Road a central artery, along with the roughly parallel railroad line, which took increasing traffic. In *Kim,* a novel set largely along the Grand Trunk Road, Rudyard Kipling describes the scene by the mid-19th century:

> ...the Great Road...is the backbone of all Hind. For the most part it is shaded...with four lines of trees; the middle road—all hard—takes the quick traffic. In the days before rail-carriages the Sahibs travelled up and down here in hundreds. Now there are only country-carts and such-like. Left and right is the rougher road for the heavy carts—grain and cotton and timber, fodder, lime and hides. A man goes in safety here...The police are thieves and extortioners...but at least they do not suffer any rivals.

Crossing a river gorge on a bridge of ropes was one of the most harrowing experiences faced by travelers in the Himalayas. (By W. Simpson, 1860, Victoria and Albert Museum)

Idealized portraits of villages in the high Himalayas, like Leh (Ladakh) in Kashmir, laid the basis for tales of Shangri-La. (By W. Simpson, Victoria and Albert Museum)

All castes and kinds of men move here...Brahmins and chumars, bankers and tinkers, barbers and bunnias, pilgrims and potters – all the world going and coming. It is to me as a river from which I am withdrawn like a log after a flood...such a river of life as nowhere exists in the world.

With much of the long-distance traffic going by the railway, traffic along the Grand Trunk Road continued as in days of old, a medley of bullock carts, camels, and horses, all too often stampeded by royal elephants.

Along the roadside, the old *caravansarai* system continued to operate, with some modifications, as indicated by these 19th century regulations from a bureaucrat's guide called the *Sukraniti:*

The *sarais* or rest-houses for travelers are to be built strong and provided with tanks...[The *sarai*] is to be daily cleaned and well-governed...The master of the *sarai* is to ask the following questions of the travelers coming to it: Whence are you coming, and why? Whither are you going? Speak truly. Are you or are you not with attendants? Have you any arms in your possession and have you any conveyances with you? What is your caste? What are your family and name? Where is your permanent residence? After asking these questions, the master of the rest-house should note them down and in the evening, having taken the traveler's arms, should advise him: "Take sleep carefully." Having counted the number of men in the house and shut its gate, he should have it watched by the guards working for three hours each, and awaken the men in the morning. He should give back the arms, count the men, and then let them off by opening the gate and accompanying them up to the boundary line.

With the great powers pressing for advantage in Central Asia, information became vital, and many British explorers took to the Himalayas to explore the old mountain routes. Leaving the relative civilization of the Grand Trunk Road, they found a series of rough tracks too narrow and difficult for carts; with no forage along the road or *caravansarais* to provide for travelers, caravans in the mountains had to carry food for people and animals, often burying part of their stores for the return trip. Even so, the way was extremely difficult; as Diana Shipton noted in *The Antique Land:* "Never once until we reached the plains were we out of sight of skeletons. The continuous

202

lines of bones and bodies acted as a gruesome guide whenever we were uncertain of the route." But still the travelers came, men and women, too. One explorer, William Moorcroft, discovered that the Tibetan Lake Manasarowar (Mapam Yumco) was not, as had long been thought, the source of the Indus. Explorers often operated under special constraints, for secrecy was advisable as they approached foreign borders; disguised as traders or pilgrims, they surveyed the mountains. One particularly ingenious surveyor, dressed as a Buddhist monk, walked to Lhasa, Tibet, and back, counting his steps on a fake rosary of 100 beads (not the usual 108).

Some of these tracks were too difficult even for pack animals and could be traversed only by people on foot, often porters used as human beasts of burden. In *Where Three Empires Meet*, E. F. Knight described the trails:

On the so-called roads which penetrate these ravines one has to scale cliffsides by means of small wooden pegs let into the rocks, or swarm up a tree-trunk leading from one narrow ledge to another twenty feet above it...a fall of hundreds of feet being the consequence of a false step...Every now and again, in order to circumvent some impassable precipice overhanging the river, the road abruptly ascended six thousand feet or so, to descend again as steeply on the farther side of the obstacle.

Edging along such a route in his stocking feet, for his heavy shoes would not fit into the toeholes, H. L. Haughton, in *Sport and Folklore in the Himalaya* (sic) felt: "..all spread out like a beetle on a board, only far less secure for I had no pin through the middle of me to keep me there. I began almost to envy the beetle the luxury of a pin. Many hundreds of feet below rushed the Indus."

Most of these high mountain passes were open only in the summer, but even so, travelers crossing mountain rivers had to contend with icebergs continually breaking off the glaciers above. In *The Marches of Hindustan*, David Fraser described a typical crossing:

In the very first current, with the water up to my pony's belly, a lump of ice struck him square on the hocks...If I hadn't been frozen to the saddle by the cold I must have fallen off....It was impossible to cross at right angles owing to the depth and force of the water, and because of the ice. We therefore went down with the stream, edging across when opportunity offered, and returning upstream along the intermediate banks. The crossing occupied about an hour and at the end of it I had to take off my boots to see if my feet were alive.

The rare "bridges" were little better, as General Sir Ian Hamilton described in *Listening for the Drums:*

Whenever the footpath along the river ran up against sheer rock the traveller had to get across to the other bank to carry on and the way of it was this; there were two ropes, the upper one for the hands, the lower one for the feet—far above was the sky, far below ran the Indus. A tight-rope dancer would have been quite all right, I suppose, but these ropes were not tight; they were slack and sometimes my hands went one way and my feet the other. If I were to live to be a hundred these crossings will come back to me in nightmares.

With turmoil and competition in Afghanistan, Kashmir, and Central Asia, the Indian Grand Route was largely shorn of its international role in the 19th and 20th centuries. National enmities in the late 20th century went further than that; after the withdrawal of Britain in 1947, the route became primarily a series of quite separate sections, each within its own boundaries; today traffic seldom travels along the whole route and then only with difficulty. Kabul and the Hindu Kush and the routes west to Herat and southwest to Kandahar are in the hands of Afghanistan. After the Soviet invasion of Afghanistan in 1979, some traffic began to pass on the old route between Afghanistan and its northern neighbor, the Soviet Union, which controls the midsection of the old Silk Road. The Indus Valley is the province of largely Moslem Pakistan, which controls the Grand Trunk Road from the Khyber Pass through Peshawar and Rawalpindi to Lahore. The route is cut again in the middle Punjab by a national border between Lahore and Amritsar; at the time of independence and partition in 1947, many Moslems emigrated to Pakistan, while many Hindus and Sikhs from the western Punjab moved into Indian territory. The Grand Trunk Road border crossing, difficult at the best of times, was closed after the Indian-Pakistan War in 1965, forcing travelers to make a laborious detour to continue on the route. The Indian portion of the Grand Trunk Road is by far the longest, running from Amritsar through Delhi, Allahabad, and Varanasi to Calcutta. While India includes much of the Ganga River, the mouths of the Ganga, the region of Bengal, and the route east to Burma lie across yet another border, in what was first an eastern part of Pakistan, then the independent Moslem country of Bangladesh.

The mountain routes to the north were even more problematical. With Russia controlling the Pamirs and the main Silk Road connections, these routes through Kashmir became important enough to be the object of war between Pakistan and India in 1965. At the ceasefire, India was left in control of the Karakorum route to Hotan, winding from Amritsar around a bulge of Pakistani territory to Jamma, north to Srinagar, and east to Leh. There the route effectively stops, for—although Kashmir continues to attract tourists and mountain climbers—India has uneasy and sometimes openly hostile relations with China, which annexed Tibet. In a region of great political tension, however, alliances are also formed, and one of them resulted in the building of a new international road: the Karakorum Highway, built by Pakistan and China. From just west of Rawalpindi, this old route—opened by the Kushans almost 2,000 years ago—follows the Indus north to Gilgit, arcing through the western end of the Karakorum range to the old Silk Road city of Kashgar. Supposedly an all-weather route, the Karakorum Highway is still hazardous, often being blocked by avalanches in the unstable Himalayas.

Less glamorous in this century than the fabled mountain routes, the Indian Grand Trunk Road today serves more modest, local purposes. The road today reflects this less-than-international status and the extremes of life in the region. People on foot, camels, bullocks, horses, carts, bicycles, manpowered cycle rickshaws all share the road with buses, trucks, and cars—often ramshackle, but still more modern than their road compan-

ions. In many parts of the Grand Trunk Road, special provision is made for this wildly varied traffic. As in Kipling's day, the road in the Punjab generally consists of three broad swaths across the countryside; the paved, raised midsection is a double-lane highway for motorized traffic, while on either side are dusty lanes for less-modernized travelers. Southeast of Delhi, the paved road more often has simply a footpath for walkers and sometimes not even that, with slow carts uneasily jockeying with heavy buses and trucks, all settling into a hierarchy based on speed.

Walkers, drovers, carters, and truckers may spend the night at *sarais* (now sometimes called hostels), where they are still occasionally locked in overnight; in monasteries, which shelter pilgrims and other travelers who honor the religious customs of the house; or in one of the many campsites along the Grand Trunk Road, where the land is trampled hard from hundreds or even thousands of years of use. And up in the Khyber Pass, a dusty caravan track still parallels the motor highway and rail line through the narrow defile.

Selective Bibliography

Chandra, Moti. *Trade and Trade Routes in Ancient India* (New Delhi: Abhinav Publications, 1977). Contains much useful detail and paraphrases tales through the 11th century A.D.

Fairley, Jean. *The Lion River: The Indus* (New York: John Day, 1975). Follows the river from its source to the sea, with much interesting historical and anecdotal material.

Grousset, René. *In the Footsteps of the Buddha.* Translated from the French by J. A. Underwood (New York: Grossman Publishers, 1971). Classic work on the spread of Buddhism and the great pilgrimages.

Moreland, W. H., and Atul Chandra Chatterjee. *A Short History of India,* 4th edition (New York: McKay, 1967). A general survey.

Panikkar, K. M. *A Survey of Indian History,* 3rd edition (Bombay: Asia Publishing House, 1962). Provides a general overview.

Sabir, Mohammad Shafi. *Story of Khyber* (Peshawar: University Book Agency, 1966). A strongly Islamic history of the pass itself.

Spear, Percival. *A History of India,* 2 vols. (Baltimore: Penguin, 1965). Offers a useful overview.

Swinson, Arthur. *North-West Frontier: People and Events 1839-1947* (New York: Praeger, 1967). Covers British military activity on the frontier.

Verma, H. C. *Medieval Routes to India: Baghdad to Delhi: A Study of Trade and Military Routes* (Calcutta: Naya Prokash, 1978). Focuses on Islamic routes in pre-Mughal times.

Wiles, John. *The Grand Trunk Road: Khyber to Calcutta* (London: Elek, 1972). A modern walking tour on the old route.

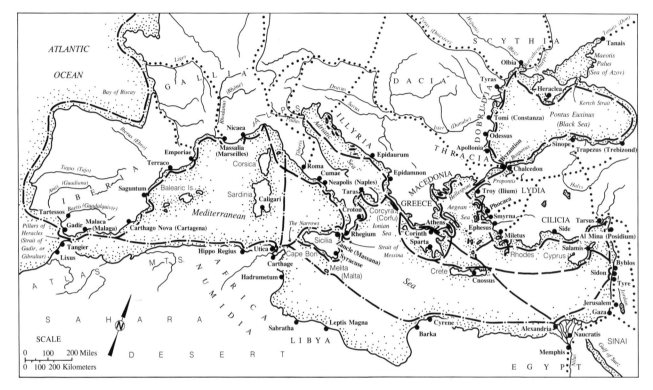

*The Mediterranean and Black Sea Routes
in Greek and Phoenician Times*

——·—— Main Phoenician Routes   ·········· Main Connecting Routes
——— — Main Greek Routes

The Mediterranean and Black Sea Routes

Thus we sailed up the straits, groaning in terror, for on the one side we had Scylla [the monster of the rocks], while on the other the mysterious Charybdis sucked down the salt sea water in her dreadful way. When she vomited it up, she was stirred to her depths and seethed over like a cauldron on a blazing fire; and the spray she flung on high rained down on the tops of the crags at either side. But when she swallowed the salt water down, the whole interior of her vortex was exposed, the rocks re-echoed to her fearful roar, and the dark sands of the sea bottom came into view.

My men turned pale with fear; and now, while all eyes were fixed on Charybdis and the quarter from which we looked for disaster, Scylla snatched out of my boat the six ablest hands I had on board. I swung round, to glance at the ship and run my eye over the crew, just in time to see the arms and legs of her victims dangled high in the air above my head. "Odysseus!" they called out to me in their agony. But it was the last time they used my name...Scylla had whisked my comrades up and swept them struggling to the rocks, where she devoured them at her own door, shrieking and stretching out their hands to me in their last desperate throes. In all I have gone through as I made my way across the seas, I have never had to witness a more pitiable sight than that.

So Homer described the dangers of the Mediterranean to the early Greek mariners, such as the rocks—personified by Scylla—against which so many were dashed, and the turbulent waters that sometimes threatened their frail craft. More specifically, Charybdis is thought to refer to the whirlpools of the Strait of Messina, between Italy and Sicily, where the waters of the eastern and western halves of the Mediterranean met and formed deadly currents and eddies that threatened ships even into modern times, although shifts in the seabed have made them less dangerous today. Despite the dangers, the Mediterranean and its smaller sister, the Black Sea, have been highways from the earliest periods of human civilization.

The Mediterranean itself is a young sea, formed only in late geological times when the Atlantic Ocean breached the isthmus between Europe's Rock of Gibraltar, and Africa's opposing Rock of Ceuta. The ocean's salt water flows throughout the Mediterranean and even into the Black Sea, but the lighter fresh water from the rivers that drain into the seas—notably the Ebro, the Rhône, the Po, the Drava and Sava, and the Danube—lies on top of the heavier saline layer. The differences in these levels and in the depths of the sea floor produce wide variations in the Mediterranean, which are sharpened because much of the sea is sectioned off by peninsulas and islands.

Most notably the Mediterranean is divided like a butterfly into two halves joined by a narrow waist. In the middle is the island of Sicily, which on its northeast side forms the Strait of Messina with nearby Italy and on its southwest side faces the 80-mile-wide passageway called The Narrows, looking across to Cape Bon in Tunisia. Ancient mariners certainly recognized the dividing line between the two seas; in describing the shipwreck of St. Paul on the island of Malta, just east of The Narrows, the Bible

Although Egypt traded with Palestine from very early times, she eventually withdrew from the Mediterranean and let others handle her sea trading. (By Manning de V. Lee, in Rupert Sargent Holland, Historic Ships, *1926)*

noted: "And falling into a place where two seas met, they ran the ship aground."

Within these two halves, the Mediterranean is almost a mosaic of smaller seas: the Balearic Sea, between the Iberian coast and the Balearic Islands; the Sardinian Sea between the Balearics and the large islands of Sardinia and Corsica; the Ligurian, facing the Riviera, north of Corsica; the Tyrrhenian, south of that, bounded by the Italian coast on the east and Sicily in the south; the long, narrow, windy Adriatic, between Italy and Yugoslavia; the Ionian, in the pocket formed by Greece, Italy, and Sicily; and the Aegean, the island-dotted region between eastern Greece, Turkey, and Crete, where sailors are rarely beyond sight of land. The wide waters between Africa's coast and the northern islands are known as the Mediterranean (literally, "in the Middle of Land"). Early peoples simply called it, in their various languages, "the sea"–or, more cosily, "our sea" (in Latin, *Mare Nostrum*). East of the Aegean, the mile-wide strait of the Dardanelles (Hellespont), formed by the thin peninsula of Gallipoli and the coast of Asia Minor, leads into the small Sea of Marmara (Propontis) and on through the Bosporus Strait to the kidney-shaped Black Sea, with the small Sea of Azov

(Maeotis Palus) attached in the northeast by the Kertch Strait (Cimmerian Bosporus).

Of these regions of the Mediterranean, the African coast is the most dangerous, exposed to great gales from the Atlantic and having few safe anchorages. But the other parts of the Mediterranean have their own hazards, for strong north winds blow out of Europe between October and April, especially at the mouth of the Rhône River in the Gulf of Lion, in the Adriatic, and on the Black Sea, where wintertime winds are sometimes so strong they send up waterspouts. The early Greek poet Hesiod warned, "Avoid the winter sea when the winds war loud," and most Mediterranean sailors have heeded him into modern times. The Mediterranean is truly a summer sea, presenting its kindest face to sailors from May through September. The Roman poet Horace suggested that "the sailing season begins in spring when the swallows build their mud nests under the eaves, when the meadows bloom, and the soft zephyrs blow over the unruffled sea." Of all the parts of the Mediterranean, the Ionian is the calmest, while the Aegean is the most favorable for sailing, with its relatively steady, predictable winds. Not surprisingly, it was here—in what Joseph Conrad called "that tideless basin freed from hidden shoals and treacherous currents"–that full-scale sailing on the Mediterranean seems to have developed.

We do not know when humans first ventured onto Mediterranean waters, nor what kind of craft they used. Certainly people very early moved out among the close-set islands of the Aegean; mariners arrived at Malta, less than 60 miles from Sicily, in the early fourth millennium B.C. The earliest vessels were probably dugout logs or reed rafts, these floats later being replaced by boats. Similarly, the earliest means of propulsion was probably paddling, but later rowing–with the back facing in the direction of movement, which gives more power–became dominant, continuing in use long after the development of sails. Sailing ships, developed on the Nile River and in the Persian Gulf, seem to have appeared in the Mediterranean by the early third millennium B.C.. The first written record of shipping on the Mediterranean dates from about 2650 B.C., in the reign of the Egyptian Pharaoh Snefru, with a scribal note about the "bringing of forty ships of one hundred cubits with cedar-wood from

Byblos." This was undoubtedly timber from the famous Cedars of Lebanon, for which Egyptians sent ships for thousands of years; indeed, the trade seems well-established by Snefru's time, some centuries into the Bronze Age. The Egyptians were not long-distance sailors, however, and their boats were simply expanded models of their river craft; they generally confined their trading to shuttling back and forth between Egypt and the coast of Palestine and Syria.

It was others who would develop long-distance trading on the Mediterranean, and their spur was the now-scorned, but then-precious tin, needed to alloy with copper in the making of bronze. It is hard to overestimate the importance of tin in the Bronze Age. It was as vital to these early civilizations as oil is to modern ones, for bronze weapons and tools were far superior to the copper and stone ones they replaced. It would eventually lead early mariners, many hundreds of years before the birth of Christ, to sail from the east Mediterranean as far as Britain and beyond; and many of the greatest ports in the Mediterranean–Marseilles, Carthage, and Cadiz (on the

This Phoenician merchant ship, with dolphins and other fish depicted in the water, appeared in bas-relief on the sarcophagus of a trader from Sidon. (Museum of Beirut)

209

Atlantic, just past the Strait of Gibraltar) among them—first came to prominence because of their position on the tin routes. Copper, by far the largest constituent of bronze, was available in plenty, both from the Anatolian highlands and from Cyprus, which shared its name with the metal that made it famous. Tin was the problem. At first, the early Bronze Age peoples mined the small deposits of the metal around the east Mediterranean, especially in Anatolia. But, those mostly exhausted, they were obliged to look elsewhere for their supply.

The earliest Mediterranean sailors to reach far outside the Egypt-Palestine orbit seem to have been voyagers from the Cycladic Islands, north of Crete in the Aegean; following the north Mediterranean coast for many weeks they may have reached Iberia by 2500 B.C. Historian A. R. Burn noted: "The way of a ship in the sea proverbially leaves no track, and overnight camps ashore scarcely more"; but similar settlements and artifacts from this period are found on both ends of the Mediterranean. The Cycladic traders were gradually eclipsed by the Minoans, who based their maritime empire at Cnossus on the well-placed, highly favored island of Crete. Cretans seem to have traded sporadically with Cyprus, the Levant, and perhaps directly with Egypt from as early as 3000 B.C.. By the end of the millennium, Minoan traders had established a regular route around the southeast Mediterranean, adding the island of Rhodes to their itinerary and extending their rule to some other islands in the Aegean. The rich palaces uncovered by archaeologists, housing finely worked objects of gems and precious metals from Egypt and the Levant, tell of the Minoans' prosperity. They also reached to the west, bringing home amber which had traveled overland from the Baltic and possibly carrying tin from Spain to the eastern Mediterranean.

Around 1900 B.C., an early wave of the Indo-European people we know as the Greeks began migrating out of their homeland north of the Black Sea and pushing down the Greek peninsula. By 1600 B.C., these Achaean Greeks had completed their conquest of the mainland; the Cretans traded with these rougher peoples, passing on some of their culture in the process. The Greeks themselves took to the sea, wresting some of the Egyptian and Syrian markets from Minoan control. Then in the 15th century B.C., they invaded Crete itself, conquering the Minoans, and forming a fused culture we know as Mycenaean. The Minoan cities, including Cnossus, were destroyed—some by the invaders, some by earthquakes—and dominance on the sea routes along the north Mediterranean coast passed to the Mycenaean Greeks on the mainland. These were the people of Homer's *Iliad*: of King Agamemnon, in the main city of Mycenae; of Menelaus, ruler of Sparta and husband of Helen, whose abduction sparked the Trojan War; of King Nestor of Pylus; and of the leaders of the lesser fortified towns, like Athens and Corinth, on the narrow isthmus that for centuries cried out for a canal.

In addition to taking over the old Minoan trade, and establishing their own trade across the Adriatic to southern Italy, the Mycenaeans vigorously expanded their contacts in western Asia. Greek traders established communities in the foreign quarters of main cities, notably in Tarsus in southern Anatolia and Ugarit (Ras Shamrah) on the Syrian coast. They soon moved beyond that to setting up trading posts or pirate bases which blossomed into colonies, on the islands of Rhodes and later Cyprus, and on the west and south coasts of Asia Minor, with their main settlement at Miletus. These colonies brought the Greeks into contact—and conflict—with the other inhabitants of Anatolia, especially the Hittites (some distantly related Indo-European kin) and other independent peoples, like the Trojans. The city of Troy (Ilium, now called Hissarlik) occupied a position commanding the important Hellespont, then the main crossing point into Europe, as well as the so-far-undeveloped water route to the Black Sea. More to the point, Troy had a fertile hinterland and access to the resources of interior Anatolia, including copper, which she traded with the peoples of the north Aegean. If Homer's tale of the great Greek siege of Troy has a foundation in fact, the conflict is likely to have been as much about trade routes as about a queen's abduction. The Troy Homer speaks of may have been destroyed by the Greeks around 1300–1200 B.C.—or it and Greece may have been plunged into a Dark Age by a new wave of Greeks—the Dorians—pouring down from the north. Breaching the fortified wall across the Isthmus of Corinth, the Dorians sacked and burned the main cities of Greece. Tradition has it that only Athens survived as a haven for refugees: certainly many fled across the Isthmus of Corinth to the region of Attica, driving yet another group of Greeks—the Ionians—out into the islands and across to the west coast of Asia Minor. While Mycenaean culture survived for some time in outlying colonies, its Mediterranean trading routes collapsed, and little is known of the region for some centuries.

With these invasions came the end of an era: The Bronze Age was over in the eastern Mediterranean. Iron had long been known in the Near East; indeed, it had been produced as a by-product of copper in Egypt and used for jewelry. But this wave of Indo-European invaders had brought with them iron weapons, which were stronger, cheaper, and easier to produce. Bronze was still used, of course, and tin would continue to be a magnet, but iron now became the common denominator of the civilized world.

The eastern Mediterranean also drew other invaders. Among the many Semitic peoples to settle in Syria and Palestine was one which would play a major role on the Mediterranean; these were the Phoenicians, so-named by the Greeks for the famous purple dye they manufactured and traded. (So valued was this dye that only the richest and most powerful people could have clothing of the "royal purple.") With the collapse of the Greek trading routes,

The Dardanelles (Hellespont), here defended by heavy cannons on one side and a fortified city on the other, long hindered early sailors. (From Montecuculli, Commentarii Bellici, *1788, MS. suppl. turc 226 f. 14v. Bibliothèque Nationale)*

the Phoenicians moved out from their port of Byblos into the Mediterranean in force, in strong, well-made boats, crafted from Lebanese cedar at the shipbuilding center of Gebāl, making Sidon and island-fortified Tyre their chief ports. For three centuries, between 1200 and 900 B.C., these Phoenicians—a confederation of city-states sharing a common language and commitment to trade—were masters of the Mediterranean. As quintessential middlemen, they brought raw materials from the West—especially wheat, oil, wine, and the still-important tin—and traded them to the higher cultures of the East, along with their own products: timber, dye, and expertly made glassware.

At first, the Phoenicians (also called Canaanites) concentrated on the east Mediterranean, in the 11th century B.C. setting up their own colonies on Cyprus and Rhodes, from which they traded into the Aegean and Asia Minor. But, not content with island-hopping and coastal sailing like the early Aegean mariners, the Phoenicians soon headed straight out across the more open seas of the Mediterranean; nor were they confined to daytime, fair-weather sailing, for they had developed the art of sailing by the stars, especially the North Star. (The Greeks, who later learned the technique from them, called this the

Phoenician Star.) Perhaps on advice of Mycenaeans, they headed toward tin-rich Iberia.

Tradition has it that they founded the city of Gadir (now Cadiz) on the Atlantic coast of Iberia in 1200 B.C. Certainly this was both a prime Phoenician port and entryway to the mines of Iberia, but Phoenicia's earliest actual colonies seem to have been on the North African coast. Utica, astride The Narrows, was founded around 1100 B.C., with the more easterly Hadrumetum and Leptis Magna settled in the same period. Over the next few centuries Phoenicians spread the length of the Mediterranean, founding trading posts and some full-fledged colonies along the north African coast, including Tangier on the Strait of Gadir (now Gibraltar Strait); in southern Spain, including Malaca (Malaga); on the Balearic Islands; on southern Sardinia; on Malta; and on western Sicily. In the end they controlled all the key points on their route through the southern Mediterranean between Tyre and Gades. In about 814 B.C. they also founded, just east of Utica, a daughter city, Carthage, which would eventually outshine Tyre. Virgil's *Aeneid* tells the story of Dido (literally, "the Fugitive") who, with a number of other disaffected Tyrians, went, via Cyprus, to found Carthage; according to the tale, she fell in love with Aeneas, refugee from fallen

In early galleys like this one, the Greeks explored all the way from the Black Sea to the Pillars of Heracles (Strait of Gibraltar). (By Manning de V. Lee, in Rupert Sargent Holland, Historic Ships, *1926)*

Troy, who was shipwrecked in Carthage on his way to Italy, where his descendants founded Rome.

Dido was, in fact, a historical figure named Elissa, niece of the royal couple Jezebel of Tyre and Ahab of Israel. This union is indicative of the relations between Phoenicia and Israel, which had long been close. From at least the 10th century B.C., Israelis had conducted joint commercial ventures in Phoenician ships. Some of these brought back silver, iron, gold, and lead from the port of Tarshish, possibly Tarsus, on the coast of Asia Minor, but more likely Tartessus, a mart on an island in the Baetis (Guadalquivir) River in Iberia, near modern Seville, which had all those metals in abundance. Whatever the identification for the elusive Tarshish, the Phoenicians were clearly the pre-eminent sailors of the age.

Early Phoenician sailors used two main types of boats on the Mediterranean, both biremes, with two banks of oars and a deck above, on which were displayed the shields of the occupants. The "long" ship used for warfare had a pointed prow that doubled as a ram; a convex stern with a steering oar; and a sail on a central mast, although the craft was mainly powered by rowing. The "round" ships used by traders were smaller, had no sails, and were convex at both prow and stern. Much smaller craft, designed to be paddled rather than rowed, were used in rivers or near the coast, for fishing or as harbor lighters. Phoenicians (like other early peoples) conducted most of their trade by barter; where no common language existed between the two parties, the barter was silent or dumb. Herodotus describes how the Phoenicians—in this case Carthaginians, whom he called Carchedonians—went about their trade on the Atlantic coast of what is now Morocco:

Another story too is told by the Carchedonians. There is a place in Libya [Africa], they say, where men dwell beyond the Pillars of Heracles [Strait of Gadir, or Gibraltar]; to this they come and unload their cargo; then having laid it orderly along the beach they go aboard their ships and light a smoking fire. The people of the country see the smoke, and coming to the sea they lay down gold to pay for the cargo and withdraw away from the wares. Then the Carchedonians disembark and examine the gold; if it seems to them a fair price for their cargo, they take it and go their ways; but if not, they go aboard again and wait, and the people come back and add more gold till the shipmen are satisfied.

Herein neither party (it is said) defrauds the other; the Carchedonians do not lay hands on the gold till it matches the value of their cargo, nor do the people touch the cargo till the shipmen have taken the gold.

While a fair amount of trust must have existed between the parties for such a trade to operate, elsewhere the Phoenicians were considered untrustworthy. The works ascribed to Homer, the *Iliad* and the *Odyssey*, accuse the Phoenicians of stealing women and children. Telling his tale to Odysseus, Eumaeus related how his nurse was seduced by the Phoenicians to come aboard with gold and bring him, as a young child, for sale as a slave; their preparations before putting their plans into action give us some idea of how they operated, as Eumaeus explained:

The traders stayed with us for a whole year, during which they bought and took on board a vast store of goods. When the hold was full and their ship ready for sea, they sent up a messenger to pass the word to the woman.

By the eighth century B.C., the Greeks were beginning to revive as a trading people, so their picture of the Phoenicians may be colored by commercial rivalry. The Phoenicians in this period withdrew from direct trading in the Aegean, surrendering that to the Greeks themselves; but they retained their dominance all along the southern strip of the Mediterranean.

While accusing the Phoenicians of brigandage, the Greeks themselves engaged in piracy, as did peoples all around the Mediterranean. In those times of coastal sailing, pirates often waited in river mouths or on the far side of promontories ready to swarm toward unwary ships in their easily hidden light boats or rafts. Others acted as wreckers, using false signals to lure ships onto rocks, where they could be readily plundered. When carried out by a people *en masse*, piracy became very close to warfare, and in any case was often considered an acceptable means of production, especially for people living along infertile, rocky coasts; Aristotle, for example, classed brigands under the category of hunters. The fifth century B.C. Greek historian Thucydides describes the norm:

For the Grecians in old time, and of the barbarians both those on the continent who lived near the sea, and all who inhabited islands, after they began to cross over more commonly to one another in ships, turned to piracy, under the conduct of their most powerful men, with a view both to their own gain, and to maintenance for the needy, and falling upon towns that were unfortified, and inhabited like villages, they rifled them, and made most of their livelihood by this means; as this employment did not yet involve any disgrace, but rather brought with it somewhat of glory.

While strong states were sometimes able to bring piracy under some control, freebooters continued to be a hazard throughout the history of the Mediterranean, even into the 20th century. It was for good reason that many early coastal dwellers established their cities high on rocky points, often far from the shore, and had elaborate systems of beacon fires and flares to warn of unidentified ships approaching.

Another smaller group, the Etruscans, penetrated into the Mediterranean in the early first millennium B.C. While few in number, they had superior weapons and tactics, forming a distinct and sophisticated culture in northwestern Italy, in which they were the aristocracy and the Italians the workers. They soon established trade with both the Greeks and the Phoenicians, and by the seventh century B.C. began to expand outward, controlling the lands around the Tyrrhenian Sea, founding some outposts in northern Spain, and possibly even trading directly south with Carthage. But the established strength of the Phoenicians and the emerging presence of the Greeks kept the Etruscans from moving much beyond this orbit.

Throughout this period there seems to have been little activity on the Black Sea. While the main early sailing peoples—the Minoans of Crete, the Mycenaeans of the mainland, and the Phoenicians—may have had some dealings in the Propontis (Fore-Sea) they did not seem

Ulysses is tied to the mast so he can hear the sirens' song without danger; his sailors have had their ears plugged for safety. (British Museum)

to have penetrated the Black Sea on any regular basis. The strait leading eastward from the Aegean was the initial formidable obstacle. Indeed the current running in the Hellespont (Dardanelles) was so swift that boats propelled by muscle-power had great difficulty passing between the peninsula of Gallipoli and the headland of Troy into the Propontis. As a result cities on both sides of the strait exacted tribute from mariners passing through; and, more often than not in the early days, traders would unload their goods at a port in the northwest Aegean and portage through Trojan territory to the Propontis—chafing all the way at the required payment of tolls to Troy.

During the Aegean Dark Age, some Semitic traders from Asia Minor entered the Black Sea, setting up some modest settlements along the north and west coasts. These Carians made little lasting impact on the sea, however, and indeed helped spread its bad reputation; the unfriendly nature of both its people and its north winds led to the sea being named Pontus Axeinus (the Inhospitable Sea). The entryway to the sea itself shared the infamy. Although the name Bosporus means, literally, "Ox-Ford"—and was enshrined in myth as the crossing-place taken by the goddess Io between Europe and Asia—the Bosporus was described by the Greek playwright Aeschylus as "the jagged jaw, evil host of mariners." Only later would the eastern sea be fully explored and settled.

Adopting the Phoenicians' alphabetic system of transcribing sounds with letters, the Greeks in this period began to write down their great oral stories—memories of past adventures mingled with imaginative myths foretelling future greatness—giving us not only the *Iliad* (probably transcribed in the eighth century B.C.) and the *Odyssey* (a century later) but also many other tales of gods and godlike humans. These Greeks were once again fanning out over the seas, replacing the Phoenicians as the main traders in the Aegean and expanding westward toward Italy and eastward into the Black Sea. Many of the tales and myths from this period award the seas a major role; the *Odyssey* is thought by most people to be a portrayal of the Greeks' wandering across the Mediterranean (though some say the Aegean or Black Sea), while the story of Jason and the Argonauts in search of the Golden Fleece is thought to reflect the early explorations of the Black Sea. Many of these tales reflect real hazards faced by fledgling Greek sailors entering unknown waters—but they may also have taken some of their color from the horror tales spread by both the Phoenicians and the Carians to dissuade others from venturing into their territory.

Apparently the earliest of the sea tales is that of Jason and the Argonauts; it was not fixed in a single written form for many centuries, however, so it changed as Greek seafaring developed and as the story was molded by different hands over the years. The oldest references to the Argonauts, in the tales ascribed to Homer, make no mention of either the Pontus Axeinus or the Golden Fleece, being a simple story of a young mariner's adventures far from home. But over the centuries both became central to the story; and with familiarity, the sea's name was changed by the Greeks to Pontus Euxinus (the Hospitable Sea). Setting out from Thessaly, Jason's *Argo*—in one version of the story called "the most excellent of all ships that have made trial of the seas with oars"—headed eastward into the unknown, with 50 legendary heroes on board, including Heracles for his strength and Orpheus for his music. Passing through the Hellespont (so-named for here Jason's niece, Helle, was drowned), they reached

This Spartan warship, depicted on an ivory relief once probably decorated with amber in the holes, is about to set sail on the Mediterranean. (Museum, Sparta)

the old Carian settlement of Salmydessus near the Bosporus. There they helped the local king subdue the vicious birds called the Harpies, with the aid of the sons of the North Wind, Boreas (the north winds of the region are still called *boras*). They also were given the secret of passing through the "clashing rocks" at the head of the Bosporus. Historian W. W. Hyde explains:

> A dove was first sent between them and had its tail clipped by the closing rocks; when they opened again, the *Argo*, heartened by Orpheus' lyre, slipped through unscathed, and thereafter the rocks remained forever fixed in place.

After passing by the groaning Prometheus in the Caucasus, on the eastern shore of the Pontus Euxinus, Jason had to perform three set tasks in order to obtain the Golden Fleece (possibly referring to the ancient practice of placing sheepskins in a streambed to catch alluvial gold particles). Then, after a stop at Tomi (now Constanza) at the mouth of the Danube, the *Argo* proceeded on its great wandering voyages before arriving home in Greece.

The homeward route taken by the *Argo* varied widely from version to version; some had her sailing up one of the European rivers to the northern seas, and back around Europe to the Mediterranean. Others had her sailing up past the Crimean peninsula and eastward to the Indian Ocean and back around Africa, at one point carrying their boats across the Libyan desert before returning to the Mediterranean. Still others had her sailing into European rivers and westward until she emerged at the mouth of the Rhône in the western Mediterranean. All these versions were a mixture of the real and the fantastical, for in the centuries during which the Jason story developed, the Greeks were wandering in all these directions, although often with uncertain geography.

Unlike their Phoenician rivals, the Greeks were fiercely independent; although regarding themselves as Hellenes, they gave their main allegiance to their city-state, be it Athens or Sparta in mainland Hellas or one of the many Greek colonies in Asia Minor. The various city-states established their own spheres of influence, as they spread in all directions between the eighth and sixth centuries before Christ.

The Pontus Euxinus became the special province of the city-state of Miletus, near the southwest corner of Asia Minor. Taking their woolen goods to trade for grain (mostly wheat), metals, wood, fish, and slaves, they were the first Greeks to fully explore the eastern sea and to establish major towns along its shores. Their Euxine center was established at Sinope, a point of land jutting into the midsection of the southern coast. From here, Milesians also set up commercial depots along the other coasts, notably at Trapezus (Trebizond) in the southeast corner; at Tanais on the Tanais (Don) River; at Panticapaeum

(Kerch) on the Strait of Kerch; and at the former Carian town of Odessus. No city existed on the site of modern Istanbul until the Greeks founded a settlement called Byzantion in the mid-seventh century B.C. Indeed, the Greeks' oracle at Delphi reportedly called the native city on the Asian side of the Bosporus "the city of the blind" for their failure to recognize the magnificent site on the European side of the strait. Panticapaeum later became the center of Sparta's Kingdom of the Bosporus, with an active grain trade. While the Greek language and ways were adopted in many of these coastal areas, Greeks in the Pontus Euxinus seem to have been more interested in commerce than in culture.

The case was quite different with the Greeks in the western Mediterranean, for many of the brightest lights of Hellene culture would come from the far-flung daughter-states of Greece. Corinth was dominant in the Ionian Sea, colonizing the island of Corcyra (Corfu) in 753 B.C., and moving north along the coast of Illyria (Albania) as far as Epidamnon (later, as Apollonia, terminus of the Egnatian Way.) But the pirates of the Adriatic were notoriously as fierce as the winds (which even today cause inhabitants of some northern Adriatic cities to cling to guide ropes on the main streets in winter), discouraging regular trade further north. In the same period, Greeks from several city-states—including the islands of Euboea, Chalcis, and Corinth—had established entrepôts in the Levant, the most important being Al Mina (later known as Posidium) in northern Syria (now Turkey).

Southern Italy and Sicily attracted several groups of Greeks—especially Achaeans from the mainland, Dorians from Asia Minor, and Euboeans; these fertile and then-forested lands, for many centuries a main granary of the Mediterranean, were known as Magna Graecia (Greater Greece). The oldest Greek colony in the west is thought to be Cumae in southwestern Italy, founded in 750 B.C. north of the now-more-famous Greek colony of Neapolis (New Town, now Naples). Western Sicily, of course, was very much Phoenician territory, but they made little attempt to stop the Greeks from founding new colonies in eastern Sicily, or from taking over older colonies from native Sicels, especially their city of Zancle, which the Greeks renamed Messana (later Messina), overlooking the strait to Italy. Rhegium (Reggio) across the strait dates from this period, as do Taras (Taranto) and Croton—on the heel and instep, respectively, of Italy's boot—and the splendidly situated port of Syracuse on the southwestern side of Sicily. Like the Phoenicians before them, the Greeks used their colonies in the mid-section of the Mediterranean as staging points for their sailing routes westward to Spain.

The greatest sailors among these Greek emigrants were the peoples of Phocaea, on the mid-west coast of Asia Minor. It was the Phocaeans who found and settled what may be the best port of the Mediterranean: Massalia (later

Early Greeks used "liquid fire" to repel invaders, as the later Byzantines do here against Vikings from Northern Russia. (Bibliothèque Nationale)

Massilia, now Marseilles), just east of the muddy delta of the Rhône River. Soon after their arrival in 600 B.C., the Phocaeans began to challenge the Phoenicians as long-distance traders; although the Phoenicians blockaded the Strait of Gadir (to Greco-Romans, Gades) for most of two centuries, between the late sixth and late fourth centuries B.C., Phocaeans occasionally managed to slip through, including one Pytheas, who apparently sailed north to Britain and beyond. For much of this period, however, the Phoenicians controlled Iberia, and the Phocaeans had to content themselves with overland trading, founding subsidiary trading colonies along the Gallic coast, like Emporiae (Ampurias) in the west and Nicaea (Nice) and Heracles Monacus (Monaco) in the east. Although Phoenicians had had some early contacts with the Gallic peoples at these sites, they left the northern Mediterranean routes primarily in the hands of the Greeks.

While the Greeks were exporting their culture around the Mediterranean, the Phoenicians were very much on the wane. Although the island fortress of Tyre resisted capture, Phoenicia (roughly modern-day Lebanon) gradually lost its independence; her fleets still sailed the east Mediterranean as of old, but now in the service of other peoples. Phoenicia's western outposts gradually became far stronger than the mother cities, Carthage (New Town) above all; and the west Mediterranean traders (who still called themselves Canaanites) came to be known as

Carthaginians. Strong in its own right, Carthage controlled the southwest Mediterranean, and even allied herself with the Etruscans to prevent further expansion by the Greeks.

The Greeks proved too strong, however. Off Cumae in 474 B.C., they destroyed the Etruscan fleet, and with it their claim to control the Tyrrhenian Sea. With the decline of Phoenicia, the Greeks also moved to the northeast coast of Africa. There they found the surprisingly fertile land of Libya, traditional home of the Lotus-eaters of the *Odyssey*, of which Homer says: "...there neither lord nor shepherd lacketh aught of cheese or flesh or sweet milk, but ever the flocks yield a continual store of milk." Their main port here was Cyrene, but they also founded a port called Naucratis on one of the many arms of the marshy Nile delta, trading directly with the ancient land of Egypt.

The Persians—who had taken Phoenicia, along with the rest of western Asia—also threatened the Greeks. Crossing the Hellespont on a bridge of boats in 513 B.C., the Persians succeeded in taking control of the region between Macedonia and the Black Sea; 20 years later—with their mostly Phoenician fleet only too happy for the chance to punish their former rivals—they crushed the Greek fleet in the Aegean. Herodotus tells all too plainly the fate of many Greek cities in Asia Minor and on the Aegean islands: "...the best-looking boys were chosen for castration and made into eunuchs; the handsomest girls were…sent to Darius' court. Meanwhile the towns themselves…were burnt to the ground."

Mainland Greece was still free, however. In 491 B.C., the Persian fleet headed toward Hellas, but—like the Spanish Armada off England a millennium later—was dashed against the rocky north shore of the Aegean by a sudden storm. A year later, after assembling "the largest fleet the world has ever seen," Darius once again headed toward Greece, his sailors now including not only Phoenicians but also Ionian Greeks—and using specially designed landing craft to carry horses for the Persian cavalry. When the Athenians heard of their landing on the coastal plain of the Bay of Marathon, they sent a courier to call Sparta to battle. (A later run by Pheidippides is still commemorated in the marathon races of today.) In the event, Sparta refused immediate help because it was a religious week for them (which the Persians may well have known). The soldiers of Athens and a few smaller allies alone faced the Persian force that outnumbered them by four or five to one and defeated them.

But the threat from the Persians was not over. In the feverish years that followed, each side pressed ahead with preparations for the confrontation to come. The Greeks, for their part, developed a stunning new ship, a triple-banked trireme, the like of which had never been seen on the Mediterranean before. The Persians, meanwhile, had their engineers working to prepare crossing points for their armies. Bridges were thrown across the smaller rivers on the European side, while the Hellespont was spanned by a double bridge formed by almost 700 boats. Herodotus noted that these boats:

> …were moored head-on to the current—and consequently at right angles to the actual bridges they supported—in order to lessen the strain on the cables. Specially heavy anchors were laid out both upstream and downstream—those to the eastward to hold the vessels against winds blowing down the straits from the direction of the Black Sea, those on the other side, to the westward and towards the Aegean, to take the strain when it blew from the west and south. Gaps were left in three places to allow any boats that might wish to do so to pass in or out of the Black Sea.

After wintering at Sardes, western end of the Persian Royal Road in Asia Minor, the Persian forces—now under Xerxes, son of Darius—headed toward Greece by both land and sea. Forced into union by the Persians, the Greeks were steadily pushed back, making a famous sacrificial stand at the narrow pass of Thermopylae (Hot Springs); the Persians found their victory here so costly that they thereafter decided to pursue their campaign by sea—always a difficult choice in hostile waters, with no land support. In the end, the Greeks withdrew to the island of Salamis,

off the coast of Athens, and lured the Persian fleet into a trap, decimating it. The Greek playwright Aeschylus, later telling the tale from the Persian point of view, described the scene this way:

> …the Greek ships, handled most skillfully, circled around us and kept striking in towards the center until you could not see the sea itself for blood and broken ships. On every beach and every reef there lolled the bodies of the dead. All the ships of all our Persian fleet strove hard to get away. But still the Greeks, like men who circle round gaffing tunny or other great shoals of fish, stabbed and killed with oars and other lumps of wood, while cries and screams echoed across the sea—until the night came down.

In the end Xerxes turned for Persia, and the land forces he left behind suffered a final defeat the following year; the Persians would no more threaten the Greek mainland, although the Greek colonies in Asia Minor were left in a kind of limbo.

Taking advantage of the Greeks' preoccupation with the Persians, the Carthaginians and Etruscans combined to deal with rising Greek power in the west. Greece had pushed the Etruscans out of southern Italy and had taken all of Sicily except the far west, the Carthaginians retaining Panormus (Palermo) and Motya—with its sailors' landmark, the temple to Astarte, patron goddess of mariners—on the route from Carthage to Sardinia and Etruscan Corsica. In 479 B.C. (tradition has it on the same day as the Greek victory at Salamis), the Greeks—led by Syracuse, which had become the pre-eminent city in the west—defeated their rivals in northern Sicily. Although both the Carthaginians and the Etruscans were beginning a long decline, their power roughly balanced that of the Greeks, and the result was a seesaw series of battles over the next two centuries.

Nor was there peace in the eastern Mediterranean. No sooner had the Persian threat been removed than the Greeks once again fragmented into bickering city-states, forming into shifting groups of alliances. The main two groups—Athens and her Delian League, and Sparta and her Spartan Confederacy—eventually entered into the Peloponnesian Wars, which would last for decades, from 431 B.C. on. These were the great days of classical Greece, the days of Socrates, Pericles, Herodotus, and Euripides, the days when Greece laid the rational foundations for some of the best aspects of European civilization. Yet the great fifth century B.C. was filled with the irrational destruction of Greek fighting Greek; Athens itself, in the midst of its golden period, was sequestered behind two walls, one on land, the other a wall of ships on the sea. While war was conducted only during the favorable summer, and was suspended for the essential harvest, the city-states of Greece braced themselves for the annual invasions that convulsed the eastern Mediterranean. War was also carried further afield. Athens extended its rivalry with Sparta into an internecine battle in Sicily, and was badly defeated when she threatened Syracuse's might. Meanwhile, Sparta and her Syracusan allies attempted to cut Athens's route to the vital grain supplies of the Pontus Euxinus. The remnants of the once-great Athenian fleet were finally destroyed in the Hellespont in 406 B.C., and the walls of the city razed.

In the end, Greece would be united by an outsider, Philip of Macedon, who took mainland Greece in 338 B.C.; focusing Greek aggression on the Persian enemy, he dreamed of conquests in the East. These dreams came to fruition through his son, Alexander the Great. In 334 B.C.—after stopping to pay homage at the tomb of Achilles in Troy, Alexander swept through the Near East, breaking Persian power in a series of battles. He was stopped only by the island city of Tyre; while all of Phoenicia had fallen to other powers, Tyre had withstood all sieges over the centuries. But Alexander would not be denied. Although it took him most of the year 332 to do so, he finally conquered Tyre, building a causeway from the mainland (the remains of which still exist) and attacking from the sea as well. In desperation, Tyre asked for help from Carthage, but in the end went to defeat alone. The great empire of Phoenicia had ended. From there, Alexander swept on south and west across the Gaza strip into Egypt, where he directed that a new port be founded on one of the western arms of the Nile; it would be named Alexandria. Alexander himself then passed out of Mediterranean history, pursuing a land empire in the East until his death a few years later. But his empire, divided among his lieutenants, remained and was the basis of a *Pax Hellenica* in the east Mediterranean, after long years of turbulence.

Where Greek ships were once pulled across the isthmus on rollers, the Corinth Canal would be opened in the 1880's. (From Frank G. Carpenter, The Alps, the Danube, and the Near East)

Nurtured in the frozen fjords of Norway, the Norse Vikings were well-suited to open the northerly route across the Atlantic. (By Manning de V. Lee, from Rupert Sargent Holland, Historic Ships, *1926)*

Controlling the portage route across Jutland, Hamburg and Lübeck were the most powerful ports in the Hanseatic League. (From Bilderhandschrift des Hamburgischer Stadtrechts, *1497, Staatsarchiv, Hamburg)*

Travelers on the Great Desert Route passed through many small villages, where people barely outnumbered poultry and live-stock. (From al-Harīrī, Maqāmāt, *1237, MS. ar. 1847 f. 138r, Bibliothèque Nationale*

After the Battle of Lepanto, oared Turkish ships, like those shown attacking the Venetian flagship, were largely abandoned for sailing ships. (By Manning de V. Lee, from Rupert Sargent Holland, Historic Ships, *1926)*

East India ships left the Netherlands with their flags flying in the great days of the Cape of Good Hope Route. (By Hendrick Cornelisz. Vroom, Rijksmuseum, Amsterdam)

In recent centuries, travelers have found largely ruins—fallen or pulled down—along the Appian Way. (By Jakob Wilhelm Mechau, Goethe-Museum, Düsseldorf)

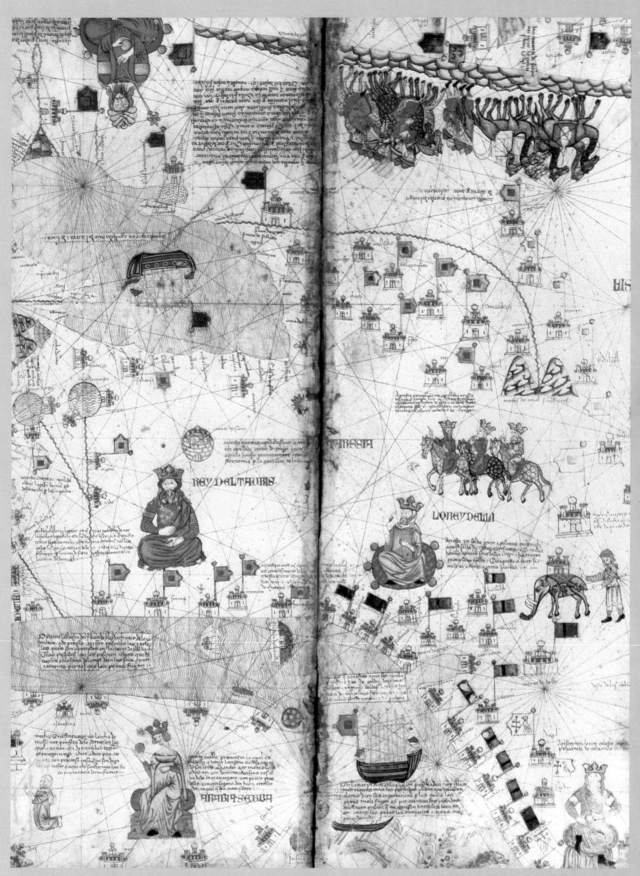

This was one of many maps drawn of Eurasia after European traders began to travel eastward. (From Atlas Catalan, *1375, Bibliothèque Nationale)*

Day and night the Conestoga wagons thundered along the National Road in Pennsylvania in the 1830's. (By C. W. Jefferys, from Archer B. Hulbert, The Paths of Inland Commerce, *1921)*

Pilgrims bound for Mecca set off from Baghdad and other cities with great show and celebration. (13th century, Bibliothèque Nationale)

In 1521 the Ottoman Turks drove the Knights of St. John
Hospitallers from their fortress at Rhodes to the sanctuary of
Malta. (From Sulaymān-nāma, 1557, H. 1517 f. 149r, Topkapi
Saray Library, Istanbul)

Many Moslem romances featured a pilgrimage to Mecca and the
Ka'bah. (From Niza, Khamseh, 1442, MS. Add. 25900 f. 114v,
British Library)

An old-style Chinese junk and a modern ship share the waters off Hong Kong. (Willie K. Friar, Panama Canal Commission)

Once steamboats of shallow draft had been developed, the upper Mississippi and the Missouri were opened for travel and trade. (By Ferdinand Reichardt, 1857, Minnesota Historical Society)

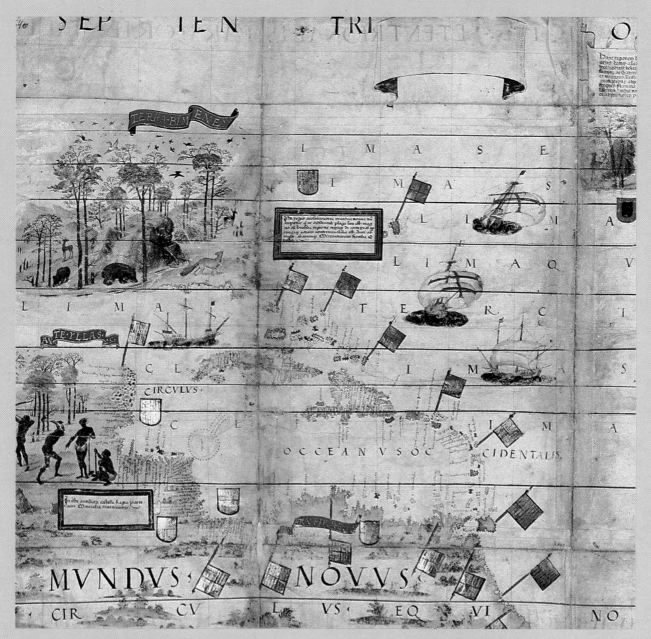

Within decades of Columbus's arrival in the Caribbean, cartographers were producing maps of the Mundus Novus *(New World).*
(Attributed to Lopo Homem, 1525, Bibliothèque Nationale)

Long after Venice's great days as a world power, it remains famous as a uniquely beautiful city, shot through with canals. (By A. H. Hallam Murray, in Sketches on the Old Road Through France to Florence, *1904)*

This rather unflattering portrait of Hsüan-tsang, complete with sandals and backpack, was found in the Cave of the Thousand Buddhas in Dunhuang. (Stein Collection, British Museum)

On the great liners, first-class passengers—but not steerage emigrants—were treated to sumptuous feasts. (Deutsche Staatsbibliothek, Kartenabteilung, Berlin)

Complete with passengers, slaves, and crew, this 12th century Arab ship sails the Persian Gulf. (Bibliothèque Nationale)

The canal from the Mediterranean port of Narbonne followed the line of the old Tin Route as it headed toward the Atlantic. (By A. H. Hallam Murray, in Sketches on the Old Road Through France to Florence, *1904)*

The sack of Baghdad by the Mongols in 1258 was as shocking to the Islamic world as the sack of Rome was to Europe. (From Rashīd ad-Dīn, Universal History, *late 14th century, MS. suppl. pers. 1113 f. 180v-181r, Bibliothèque Nationale)*

The road on the cliff below Cannes is in direct line from the Heraclean Way, which skirted the Mediterranean in Roman times. (By A. H. Hallam Murray, in Sketches on the Old Road Through France to Florence, 1904)

The Cathedral of St. Etienne at Toulouse was one of the shrines usually visited by pilgrims bound for Santiago de Compostela. (By A. H. Hallam Murray, in Sketches on the Old Road Through France to Florence, 1904)

Operating for centuries to keep invaders out and Chinese in, the Great Wall has now become a tourist attraction in itself. (Willie K. Friar, Panama Canal Commission)

Even when the port was frozen, activity in Archangel proceded on foot or on sleds pulled by reindeer. (By B. Peeters, National Maritime Museum)

Modern travelers to Rome have often deserted the coast road for the inland route past Pisa, with its famous leaning tower. (By A. H. Hallam Murray, in Sketches on the Old Road Through France to Florence, *1904)*

When the Moslems controlled the Spice Route, Yemen was a main slave-trading center. (From al-Harīrī, Maqāmāt, *1237, MS. ar. 1847 f. 105, Bibliothèque Nationale)*

Near the ruins of ancient Carthage, at the Narrows of the Mediterranean, sprang up the modern city of Tunis. (By Benton Fletcher, from Norma Lorimer, By the Waters of Carthage, *1906)*

A caravan leaves the bustle of daily life in Ankara on a trading journey to distant lands. (Detail from The Bazaar at Ankara, *by J. B. Van Mour, Rijksmuseum, Amsterdam)*

From Verona, the old Amber Route leads north through the Alps via the gentle Brenner Pass. (By A. H. Hallam Murray, in Sketches on the Old Road Through France to Florence, *1904)*

In modern times, Antibes and other Riviera towns have become health and pleasure resorts, as in Roman times. (By A. H. Hallam Murray, in Sketches on the Old Road Through France to Florence, *1904)*

Supposedly depicting Jacob's journey into Egypt, this painting actually gives a picture of privileged 14th century travelers. (From Weltchronik des Rudolf von Ems*)*

With Marco Polo testing the product, laborers pick the famous pepper from the Malabar coast. (Bibliothèque Nationale)

This view of Marco Polo in Venice also depicts the famous horses of St. Mark's, in the upper left-hand corner, taken as booty from Constantinople. (The Bodleian)

And yet the world had changed. For the first time, the peoples of the Mediterranean were looking beyond their home sea. Alexander reached the great markets of the East by land; his heirs also reached out by sea to Arabia and India, funneling the luxuries of the Orient back to the Mediterranean. Such goods had long reached Egypt and the Levant; now they were being shipped to people around the Mediterranean, increasingly through the new port of Alexandria. Designed especially as a refining and distribution center for the Greek-controlled Mediterranean world, Alexandria had an enviable double harbor, with capacious warehouses. Its great lighthouse on Pharos Island was considered one of the Seven Wonders of the World; rising over 400 feet in the air and shining a light—fire reflected with mirrors—many miles out to sea, it was a beacon to all mariners, marking the port entrance on a low coast devoid of the rocky landmarks of the north Mediterranean. Drawing on the best of three continents, Alexandria also became a great cultural center, attracting scholars and scientists from throughout the Greek world, replacing mainland Greece and Asia Minor as the center of learning and culture.

But while the east Mediterranean was reaping the benefits of peace, the central and west Mediterranean were about to undergo a great convulsion, with the rise of a new power: the Romans. Originally a land power, Rome was strong enough by the third century B.C. to contest with Carthage over control of the important Messina Strait, forcing the Carthaginians to withdraw. From this small incident grew the great series of conflicts known as the Punic Wars, because the Romans knew the Carthaginians as *Poeni* (Phoenicians).

At first, the Romans were at a disadvantage. Their soldiers were highly disciplined, and much more effective than the Carthaginian mercenaries, but they had no experience of the sea. They were, however, quick to learn. Legend has it that the Romans captured a Carthaginian ship and had their shipbuilders use it as a prototype for their own fleet. But they did not simply copy; they also improved. While the previous battle tactic on the Mediterranean had been to ram the opponent's ship with a hard, pointed prow, attempting to sink it, the Romans developed a gangplank that could be lowered to the opponent's ship and stuck into its deck with a spike, allowing soldiers to board the enemy's craft. This allowed the Romans to convert sea warfare, previously largely a matter of battering, into hand-to-hand combat, at which they excelled. With advantage of this device, called a *corvus*, the Romans won a stunning victory in 260 B.C. against the newly allied forces of Carthage and Syracuse; they even erected a column to commemorate the event, decorated with the rams, or "beaks," from the prows of the ships they had taken. By the end of the First Punic War, Rome controlled Sicily, Sardinia, Corsica, and the vital Tyrrhenian Sea. The Carthaginians withdrew to North Africa, and the western

Greeks began to be absorbed into the Roman world—providing much of the cultural base for the empire to come.

With their loss of control in the central Mediterranean, the Carthaginians looked west. They had always traded with Spain and beyond, but now they established true colonies in the west Mediterranean, among them Carthago Nova (New Carthage, now Cartagena). But while the Carthaginians continued to be active traders, they were no longer a great sea empire. Indeed, the Second Punic War, during which Hannibal crossed the Alps into Italy, was almost entirely a land war.

After losing this second bout, Carthage hung on, still trading with the Atlantic and expanding into the hinterland of northern Africa. But in 149 B.C. the Romans moved to finish off the remains of the once-great empire. Withdrawing into the citadel of Carthage, protected by a triple wall across its peninsula, the Carthaginians held out against the Romans' siege. In the end, they were starved out, the people slaughtered or sold into slavery, the city razed and burned—the site smouldering for days—and then plowed and sown with salt. So ended the Punic civilization.

Well-embarked on the course of empire, the Romans then turned to the east Mediterranean, for both Greeks and Syrians had allied themselves with Carthage. Even during the Punic Wars, the Romans had moved across the Adriatic, taking the island of Corcyra, which they charged was a base for Illyrian pirates, and then against Macedon and Syria. The same year that Carthage was razed, Corinth was taken, as was Athens soon after. Rome continued to expand, taking north Africa eastward from Carthage to the Red Sea, and also moving deep into Asia Minor and to the Black Sea. As Rome turned eastward, the Aegean became a battleground, suffering both retribution for revolts and depradations during the century of civil war, notably between Pompey and Caesar, in the first century B.C. A Roman traveler in 45 B.C., writing to his friend, the orator Cicero, was dismayed at the result:

> As I was returning from Asia, I looked at the coastlines about me. The island of Aegine lay astern, and Megara before me. On my right was Piraeus [port of Athens], and on my left was Corinth. These were all once prosperous, highly populated cities—but now they lay before my eyes ruined and devastated.

So was the greatness of Greece turned to ruin.

From the beginning of sailing on the Mediterranean, the routes had been relatively simple. The Greeks followed the east-west route along the north shore of the sea, from Iberia around Gaul and down the west coast of Italy to the Ionian Sea; rather than swinging all the way south around Greece, they often took a shortcut into the Gulf of Corinth and across the four-mile-wide isthmus, portaging their boats on a roller tramway, the tolls for which made Corinth's fortune. Once into the Aegean, the Greek route forked, with one branch arcing northeast into the Black Sea, and the other heading via Crete, Rhodes, and Cyprus to the Levant and Egypt. The Phoenicians, later Carthaginians, had a simple, straight east-west route from the Levant past Malta and Carthage to the Strait of Gadir (Gibraltar). In the central Mediterranean, a north-south route ran between Carthage and Etruria, in northwest Italy, with subsidiary routes running to the major islands.

But with the coming of the Romans, that changed. They were the first and only rulers to unite the whole Mediterranean; they also changed its focus. Not only all roads, but all sea routes led to Rome. As Rome grew from a small republic to a major empire, and her towns grew into massive cities, she drew on the resources of the entire region; from the granaries of the Black Sea, Spain, and North Africa came food and other products vital to an urban society. The great multi-banked ships developed in the Punic Wars were still built, but were used mostly for show; they had been found less serviceable than the old bireme, which became the mainstay of the Roman merchant fleet. In some ways little had changed, however. The Romans were still not sailors. The people who built and manned the Roman ships—both in commerce and war—were the same mariners as before: Greeks, Carthaginians, and other conquered peoples.

Rome itself was called "a city without a harbor," for she lay over 15 miles up the muddy Tiber River. In early times, great convoys brought grain to the port of Puteoli, near Naples, which was then transported by road to the capital. The annual ships from Egypt were most eagerly awaited, and at the first sight of the convoy's flags, Puteolians poured into the harbor to greet them. Civil wars occasionally disrupted the flow of grain from around the empire, and when Caesar Augustus established peace at the beginning of the empire, the people of Puteoli thanked him "for life itself, for liberty of trade, for freedom and fortune." Weather also occasionally played havoc with these vital ships; in a story about one of these ships being blown off course to Athens, the second century writer Lucian imagines the surprise of the Greeks on seeing her:

> What a big ship she is, a hundred and twenty cubits long...And then how huge the mast is, and what a great yard-arm and what forestays! To see the stern curving up gently like a goose's neck, and the prow stretching out so far, with the image on both sides of Isis, after whom the ship is named! Then the decoration, the paintings and the bright-colored topsail, the anchors and capstans and windlasses and the cabins aft—all this seemed to me simply wonderful. Why, you might compare the number aboard to an army, and enough corn [grain] was there, I am told, to feed the whole of Attica for a year.

Ships headed directly for Rome generally had to anchor in open water at Ostia, while their cargo was unloaded onto barges and towed upriver to Rome. Later, in the first century A.D., Emperor Claudius built a massive harbor at Ostia, backed by over a mile of warehouses and refineries, to handle the traffic, largely replacing Puteoli.

But beyond necessities, Rome desired luxuries. From Egypt, she sent Greek mariners to develop direct trade with India and the East, bypassing Arabian middlemen. Goods came overland, too, as the products of distant China began to find their way across Central Asia into Syria for the hungry Roman markets. Some of these goods came directly across the desert, through the caravan city of Palmyra, to the east Mediterranean ports, like Tyre or Alexandria-in-Syria (now Alexandretta or Iskanderun), port of Antioch. Most funneled through Rome's perfectly situated base at Alexandria on the Nile—even some goods from overland in Asia were shipped around Arabia into the Red Sea to this major refining and distribution center. As a result, Alexandria became the second focus of the Mediterranean sea routes—and shared in the opulence and glamor of the luxuries she handled. Not for her beauty alone was Cleopatra, last queen of the Ptolemaic line in Egypt, the focus of attention for powerful men like Julius Caesar and Mark Anthony.

Though there were great risks in the Mediterranean trade, still there were great fortunes to be made. In his *Satyricon*, the Roman writer Petronius tells of an ex-slave, Trimalchio, who converted an inheritance from his former master into a true fortune—but not without some dificulty along the way:

> ...I built five ships, loaded them with wines, which at that time were as dear as gold, and sent them to Rome...All my ships foundered at sea, that's the truth, no story; Neptune swallowed up on one day three hundred thousand...Do you think I broke upon it? No. The loss was but a flea-bite, for, as if there had been no such thing, I built others, larger and better than the former, so that everyone called me a man of courage...I loaded them with wine, bacon, beans, perfumes, slaves. And here Fortunata [his wife] showed her affection; for she sold what she had, nay, her very clothes and jewels, and put a round sum in my pocket...What the Gods will is quickly done; I got a hundred thousand by the voyage...[then] whatever I went about gathered like a snowball. But when I grew richer than all the country besides, I resolved to give up trading...

Nouveau riche merchants like Trimalchio were a well-known type on the Mediterranean of early Rome.

During the civil wars that rocked the Roman Empire in the mid-first century B.C., Mediterranean trade was badly disrupted—and subjected to blatant attacks from pirates. Julius Caesar himself was captured and forced to ransom his freedom. The grain ships from Egypt, which

In the 1st century A.D., Ostia became Rome's main port, replacing Puteoli on the Bay of Naples. (Museo Torlonia, Rome)

supplied much of Rome's food, were threatened so serious-ly that Pompey was, in 67 B.C., detailed to sweep the Mediterranean clear of pirates. He destroyed hundreds of vessels, captured hundreds more, and killed—or resettled—thousands of pirates. These internecine wars, involving Julius Caesar and his successors, came to an end in 31 B.C. in the Battle of Actium off northwest Greece, when the combined naval forces of Mark Antony and Cleopatra were defeated by those of Octavian, who adopted the new name Augustus.

With the accession of Caesar Augustus, a *Pax Romana* descended on the Mediterranean, protected by a fleet spread around the sea. From the Gallic coast, from the Bay of Naples, from Ravenna on the Adriatic coast of Italy, from the naval base and repair center at Malta, from various parts of the east Mediterranean, troops could be shipped on short notice to wherever they might be needed, to put down a revolt or push back a frontier—on occasion braving the winter storms, when the needs of empire dictated it. While the bireme remained the stand-ard ship, some 30 other specialized ships were used, in-cluding a spy ship completely painted blue so it would not show up against the sea waters.

One people that did not lie easy under Roman op-pression was the Jews. Roman troops were brought in time and again to put down revolts in Judea; and, indeed, many Jews had left their homeland over the centuries to settle around the Mediterranean—they formed perhaps 40 per-cent of the cosmopolitan population of Alexandria. But in 70 A.D., the Romans laid siege to Jerusalem and razed it; many Jews were enslaved and sent throughout the Mediterranean, in an acceleration of the dispersal known as the *Diaspora*. The same century also saw the rise of Christianity along the same coast. Missionaries carried the new religion throughout the region; St. Paul alone traveled throughout the east Mediterranean, to Asia Minor, Greece, southern Italy, Sicily, and even Malta. Christianity won a large number of converts in Alexan-dria, and from there many sailors and traders disseminated it throughout the Mediterranean.

By the third century A.D., however, the Roman Em-pire began to weaken, torn by strife between rival armies and increasingly pressed by peoples from the north. In the following century the emperor Constantine decided to build a New Rome on the site of the old Byzantion (to the Romans, Byzantium). This came to be known as Constantinople, the capital of the Eastern Roman Empire, as the empire split in two. Meanwhile the situation in the west Mediterranean deteriorated. By the fifth century, when Germanic invaders swept in full force down into Italy and Gaul and sacked Rome itself, no Roman fleet was left in the west Mediterranean, and even the government had left the capital; both had withdrawn to Ravenna, a coastal city of canals with houses on stilts, south of the Po River, safe from attack by the landbound invaders.

Under these circumstances, piracy reasserted itself in the west Mediterranean, and traditional trade and travel was disrupted. The Vandals, one of the many invaders from the north, took an unwary merchant fleet in 425 and swept eastward across to North Africa. Only a few walled cities held out for some time against the Vandals, among them Carthage, rebuilt by the Romans on its superb site a century after its razing. When Carthage finally fell in 439 A.D., the Vandals—recognizing its importance in controlling the east-west sea lanes—made it their capital. They also took Sicily, Sardinia, and Corsica, cutting off the Italian mainland and contributing to the final collapse of the Western Roman Empire. They were not traders,

however, but plunderers. For at least a century, piracy reigned in the west Mediterranean and much of the east; only in the Aegean and most of the Black Sea, still controlled by the Byzantine fleet, was any semblance of normalcy retained.

Then in the seventh century a new power arose on the Mediterranean: the Moslems. While not originally a seagoing people, they soon became so, drawing on the Greek learning acquired in Syria and later Alexandria—and on contacts with the Spice Route to the East. Like the Romans, the Arabs used native seamen from the ports of Egypt, Palestine, and Syria to control the southeast Mediterranean; after they captured Cyprus and later Crete they not only penetrated the Aegean but also bedeviled Byzantine ships en route past Greece to the west Mediterranean.

Constantinople itself was attacked more than once; in the late seventh century it was reprieved by a rift in the Moslem world, but in the eighth century it received a full-scale assault. Situated behind heavy walls on a peninsula overlooking the magnificent harbor called the Golden Horn, Byzantium was well-protected, not only by a heavy

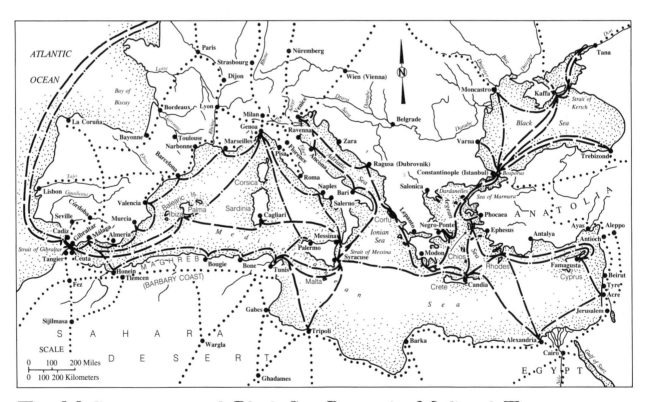

The Mediterranean and Black Sea Routes in Medieval Times

———·—— Main Genoan Routes   ·········· Main Connecting Routes

——— Main Venetian Routes

chain strung across the entrance to the harbor, preventing access, but also by a secret weapon: Greek fire, flammable liquid known to earlier Greeks, but refined in the seventh century. A later Russian opponent was appalled at the "liquid fire," which was "shot out upon our ships from long tubes placed in the parapets," noting: "The Greeks have a fire like lightning from the skies. They cast it against us and burned us so that we could not conquer them." This substance was also delivered from ships; an Italian captain from some centuries later described how the Byzantine ships:

> ...had at their prow the head of a lion or other land animal, made of brass or iron, with the mouth open, and all gilded so that the very aspect was terrifying. The fire which he directed against the enemy was passed through tubes set in the mouths of these beasts, so that it seemed as if the lions and other monsters were vomiting fire.

Not surprisingly, the secret of this Greek fire was jealously guarded. It was called Greek for Byzantium was increasingly Hellenic, being not only the repository of Christianity but also of Greek culture—even the main language of the so-called Eastern Roman Empire was Greek. While Byzantium repulsed this eighth century Arab threat, at times it had little more than its faith, its harbor defenses, and its Greek fire to ensure its survival.

Although thwarted in the Aegean, the Arabs moved into a vacuum in the west Mediterranean. Sweeping across North Africa, they handily won control of the strait to the Atlantic, marked by the opposing great rocks known to the Greeks as the Pillars of Heracles (Hercules, to the Romans). The rock on the European side of the strait came in this period to be called Jebel-al-Tariq (Rock of Tariq) after its conqueror, a name ultimately transformed to Gibraltar. Throughout the Mediterranean, the Arabs spread the arts and crafts of the East, among them some major contributions to navigation: the magnetic compass (probably originally from China); an improved technique for calculating latitude (a skill long-neglected in the Mediterranean, since coastal voyages were still the norm); and the triangular lateen sail, which made possible sailing in adverse winds—and which laid the basis for the development, centuries later, of the great ocean-going sailing ships of the West. But most of the Arab sailing was done on the Spice Route; the Mediterranean was to some extent a backwater to these early Moslems, who were as much pirates as traders in the Mediterranean.

Other raiders—the Vikings—also invaded the Mediterranean. From the east, Vikings came down through Russia to the Black Sea; there they traded with the Byzantine Greeks and later various Moslems (and some remained to form a personal bodyguard for the Byzantine emperor). In the ninth and tenth centuries, their plundering western kin swept through the Strait of Gibraltar to raid for over a century in the west and central Mediterranean from bases in the south of France, occasionally penetrating the east, possibly as far as Alexandria. While their presence disrupted trade on the Mediterranean, it had little long-term effect.

The main battle continued to be between the Moslem Arabs and the Christian Byzantines. Although the Byzantines beat back Arab raids into the Black Sea, the Arabs boxed in Byzantium and used Crete as a major pirate base for raiding into the Aegean and as a slave market for selling unlucky captives. In the ninth century the Arabs also took most of Sicily; from there and Barcelona, they attacked and sacked almost every major port in the west, from Marseilles and Genoa to Nice and Ostia; only the north Adriatic, where some vestiges of the old Roman sea power remained, and the north Aegean and Black seas were proof against their raids.

In this period, the Black Sea became Byzantium's main trading artery. At the fertile Crimean peninsula and at the port of Tana on the Don, she traded with Swedish Vikings called the Rus, who operated the only active route across Europe in the ninth and tenth centuries. Byzantine traders also reached the Silk Road and its eastern markets through the port of Trebizond (once Trapezus). Another trading partner through Tana was the Jewish kingdom of the Khazars, in the Caucasus. The 10th century Jewish traveler Chisdai Abu-Yusuf was told of this kingdom "fifteen days' distant" from which came ships "bringing fish, skins, and wares of every kind." Unfortunately, he was unable to visit it because he was told that "the peoples through whom he must pass were engaged in warfare, that the sea was stormy and could not be navigated except at a certain time," clearly a reference to the Black Sea's less hospitable aspect.

Gradually the Arab and Christian antagonists settled down to an uneasy truce, trading with each other relatively peaceably, although pirates still threatened the seas. Italian trading cities began to revive. Pisa, which had escaped the worst depredations of the Arabs, had the initial advantage, making trade treaties throughout the Mediterranean, in Spain, North Africa, Syria, and Egypt. But peace would favor Genoa, whose port was far superior (especially after Genoese sailors dumped a shipload of boulders in Pisa's harbor, causing it to silt up).

The status quo between Moslem and Christian was changed in the mid-11th century by the appearance of two new groups of outsiders: the Normans and the Seljuk Turks. The Normans, a branch of the Vikings who had lived in France for some centuries, were drawn southward not simply as plunderers, like their forbears, but also as conquerors, out to win lands for Christianity, as well as themselves. Concentrating on the Strait of Messina, they soon made themselves masters of southern Italy, Sicily, and Malta—in the process threatening to cut Moslem east-west sea lanes.

The rock on the right—Jebel-al-Tariq, or Gibraltar—has long guarded the strait between the Mediterranean and the Atlantic. (Library of Congress)

At the same time the Seljuk Turks appeared from Central Asia, taking Syria and Palestine and cutting pilgrimage routes to Jerusalem. Byzantium called to Europe for help in regaining the Holy Land, especially Jerusalem, and reopening the pilgrimage routes. The result was the Crusades.

The first Crusaders generally followed the old overland route to Constantinople, where the Byzantines transported them across the Bosporus to face the Turks. Recovering much of the coastline of Asia Minor, which they returned to Byzantium, the Crusaders moved victoriously on to the Levant, where they set up a number of Crusader States along the east Mediterranean coast. With the Syrian and Palestinian ports secure in Christian hands, and with the Christian Normans controlling the central Mediterranean sea passages, the sea routes became preferable for traders, pilgrims, and later Crusaders coming to defend the new-won land.

Well-placed to take over this trade were the Italian city-states: Genoa on the Riviera at the head of the Ligurian Sea, serving Western Europe; Pisa, further south on the Italian west coast; and Venice, city of islands and canals near the head of the Adriatic, terminus of the main overland routes from Central and Eastern Europe. Over the coming centuries, these marine city-states would transport not just knights and pilgrims from the West but goods and culture from the East, setting the stage for the Renaissance to come in Europe. In doing so, they became rich and powerful in their own right, and began to bind the Mediterranean together once again.

The transportation of pilgrims to the Holy Land was highly organized, and nowhere more so than in Venice. Some hospices were reserved solely for Jerusalem-bound travelers, and ship captains vied with each other for contracts with these early tour groups. The 15th century pilgrim Brother Felix Fabri describes how the system operated:

In this square, before the great door of St. Mark's Church, there stood two costly banners, raised aloft on tall spears, white, and ensigned with a red cross...By these banners we understood that two galleys had been appointed for the transport of pilgrims; for when the lords of Venice beheld a number of pilgrims flocking together there, they chose two nobles...and entrusted the care of the pilgrims to them...The servants of these two noblemen stood beside the banners, and each invited the pilgrims to sail with their master, and endeavored to lead the pilgrims (to one or the other)...

The captains even offered free food and drink to win the pilgrims' favor. In the end, each pilgrim group worked out a contract with the ship's captain, specifying timing, payment, and other such details, generally with part paid in Venice and the balance in Palestine.

Genoa and Venice soon came to dominate the Mediterranean routes, with Genoa strongest in the west and Venice on the Adriatic (replacing Ravenna, whose port had silted up) more powerful in the east. Both traded in The Narrows and the Strait of Messina in the center, and at Alexandria, Cyprus, and Constantinople. And both reached for more distant markets in the Black Sea, replacing Greek traders from Byzantium, which still nominally controlled the Aegean and Black seas. Constantinople was still a great city, but primarily as a meeting place for other traders, as the 12th century traveler Rabbi Benjamin ben Jonah found:

All sorts of merchants come here from the land of Babylon...from Persia, Media, and all the sovereignty of the land of Egypt, from the land at Canaan and the Empire of Russia, from Hungaria, Patzinakia [Rumania], Khozaria, and the land of Lombardy and Sepharad [Spain]. It is a busy city, and merchants come to it from every country by sea or land, and there is none like it in the world except Bagdad, the great city of Islam...

But the city was declining. Constantinople may have survived with European help, but its strength and will were gone; by the 13th century, notes Greek historian Nicetas, the Byzantine admiral "had sold the anchors, sails, and everything else belonging to the Byzantine navy that could possibly be turned into money." Its defensive walls, too, had been allowed to fall into disrepair.

Constantinople, ready to fall to any invader, proved irresistible to the increasingly powerful Venetians. By applying some far-from-genteel pressure, they convinced the knights of the Fourth Crusade to attack not the Moslems but their fellow Christians in Constantinople. The result was a disgraceful sacking of the once-great capital, which so shocked Europeans that the perpetrators were excommunicated. The knights and their Venetian partners parceled out the loot among themselves, including the famous horses that thereafter graced the cathedral of St. Mark in Venice; these beautifully wrought works did much to spark the Renaissance in northern Italy. A rump of the Byzantine Empire survived for another two and a half centuries, its leaders sometimes Latin and sometimes Greek, under the sway of either Venice or Genoa. But Byzantium's great days were over.

Meanwhile, the Moslems in the east Mediterranean were reviving in the late 12th century under the Egyptian leader Saladin. Over the course of the 13th century, the Moslems gradually drove the Christians out of all their strongholds in Antioch, Acre, and other Crusaders' states. While some of the crusading orders retired to Europe, others stayed in the Mediterranean, the best known being the Knights of St. John Hospitallers. Combining crusading and nursing, this powerful order—recipients of enormous donations from European benefactors over the years—removed first to Cyprus, which for a time became the main meeting place for Christian and Moslem traders. When that became untenable, they removed (at papal suggestion and with Genoa's help) to Rhodes just off Asia Minor. There they became Christian corsairs, protecting Christian shipping routes in the east Mediterranean and raiding the Moslem coast. As late as the 15th century, the Jewish traveler Meshullah ben R. Menahem, traveling along the coast road disguised as a Moslem, noted of his stay at a town four miles from the sea:

> ...the Moslems keep guard there because of the corsaires of Rhodes who come mostly to levy booty from the travelers there.

During the summer months, their light, fast galleys lay alongside Rhodes, in the words of Ernle Bradford, "ready to swoop out like hawks upon the fat migrant birds of eastern Merchantmen." On the island itself, the Hospitallers built heavy defenses; the 15th century Jewish traveler Obadiah da Bertinoro noted of this island fortress: "No one who has not seen Rhodes, with its high and strong walls, its firm gates and battlements, has ever seen a fortress."

As the Middle Ages began to shade into the Renaissance period, Venice became even more dominant in the Mediterranean—where she acquired the main islands, including Crete—and in the Black Sea. (In addition to the desired products of the East, ships along these routes brought home the Black Death, the plague that devastated much of Europe in the mid-14th century.) More interested in trade than in religion or war, Venice had quickly made trade agreements with the Moslems after the expulsion of the Christians, and so traded actively with the Levant and Egypt. The great Venetian galleys—made more powerful with the advent of guns in naval warfare in the 14th century—were a model for the rest of the Mediterranean. Genoa was still in the running, disputing with Venice over control of Cyprus and the important island of Chios off Asia Minor. Their rivalry broke out in open warfare and, in a naval battle fought north of Sicily in 1373, Venice emerged victorious. Genoese ships continued to ply the Mediterranean, but she increasingly came under the influence of other states, leaving Venice to rule the Mediterranean.

Venice's success is all the more remarkable because of the navigational hazards of the Adriatic, which had rightly daunted earlier sailors. The late 15th century traveler Rabbi Meshullam ben R. Menahem noted of the passage in the north Adriatic to Venice:

> ...[it] is very dangerous because of the numerous rocks, and there are also places where the sea is very shallow, and any one not acquainted with the place can come to grief with his ship or his vessel by grounding or striking the rocks...

Ships often had a slow passage north, putting in at various ports on the way, such as Ragusa (now Dubrovnik) on the east coast.

The dreaded north winds blasting out of Europe made the Adriatic corridor even more difficult. Rabbi Menahem describes his passage north in October 1481:

> ...we were in a canal...and some of the sailors wished to hoist the big sail and other sailors said that this is not the time to hoist because the wind is strengthening; and there was a dispute between them, and finally they decided to hoist the sail, but they could not, and [it] was torn...the mast was almost shifted, and all the sailors and we and all the pilgrims took hold of the mast but were not able to keep it upright, and we were in very great danger...
> On the same day, at night, there was thunder and lightning and heavy clouds on the mountains, and rain pouring on the ground with a deafening east wind like I have never seen in my life, and a sea came upon us...and we were nearly stranded...I swear that I heard the sailors say that never since they had been at sea had they seen so powerful and evil a wind as that, for the waves passed over all sides and every corner of the ship, and it went under water and then came out; but God saved us from that tempest...

225

Though many were saved, many yet were lost. It is no accident that Shakespeare begins his *Merchant of Venice* with laments on the anxieties of waiting to learn of a ship's fate. When blowing on his broth to cool it, the merchant Salarino gets himself into a fever thinking: "What harm a wind too great at sea might do." The anxious Venetian cannot even go to church:

> ...And see the holy edifice of stone,
> And not bethink me straight of dangerous rocks,
> Which touching but my gentle vessel's side
> Would scatter all her spices on the stream,
> Enrobe the roaring waters with my silks...

Like capitalists the world over, they tried to spread their risk by employing several ships, that one might arrive safely even though others might fail.

For a time Venice ruled supreme on the Mediterranean—but not for long. Hoping to enter the rich trade themselves, Spain and Portugal imported Italian sailors, especially from declining Genoa. With this expert help, Portugal began a series of exploratory voyages that would, by the end of the 15th century, lead to the opening of the Cape of Good Hope Route around Africa to the fabled markets of the East. In the following century, the Portuguese cut Venice almost completely out of the spice trade. Later, when the Portuguese were unable to handle all the trade along the great Spice Route, some goods from the East gradually began flowing into the Mediterranean again, but Venice never fully recovered. At the same time, Spain, too, sent Genoese sailors into the unknown, discovering America and beginning an active trade across the Atlantic. With their attention focused elsewhere, Europeans in the coming centuries sometimes called the Mediterranean "the Forsaken Ocean." While in truth far from that, she was a backwater on the world stage. In the vacuum that developed, pirates once again began to flourish.

Then, in the 15th century, the Ottoman Turks gave a new face to the Mediterranean. Newly converted Moslems, it was they who finally brought Islam to Constantinople in 1453. While signs of the city's former greatness were there for all to see, the present was desolate; even in the 14th century, the Arab geographer Abulfeda noted: "There are sown fields within its walls and a great many ruined houses." Arriving on the coast, the Turks immediately emerged as a sea power, beginning to clear pirates from the Aegean and forcing Venice to pay annual tribute for trading privileges. It was the Turks who gave the Pontus Euxinus its modern name—the Black Sea—and who came to know Constantinople as Istanbul (popularly, Stamboul), adopted as the official name centuries later.

In the early 16th century the Turks, having extended their holdings to include Greece, moved across the sea to Tunis (ancient Carthage). In the same period the Spanish expelled from their peninsula at least 300,000 Moriscos, Moors who had accepted Christian baptism, but whose conversion was insufficient to please the fanatic inquisitors. The combination of the two turned the western and central Mediterranean into a battlefield. Plundering Turks, Moriscos eager for revenge, and Christian and Jewish renegades all became pirates on the Barbary Coast, between Tunis and Ceuta. Indeed, these Barbary corsairs moved beyond the Strait of Gibraltar to attack the great Spanish galleons bringing silver and gold from America. Goods from around the world—gold, silver, amber, spices, pearls, silks—were seized by these pirates and carried to their home ports; the corsairs called one of the main bases, Algiers, "our India, our Mexico, our Peru." Most famous of the corsairs was the Algerian leader, a young Turk named Khizr, better known to Moslems as Kheir-ed-Din (Protector of the Faith) and to Christians as Barbarossa (Red Beard).

It was not to be expected that the Turks would long tolerate the presence of Christian corsairs on Rhodes; in 1522, they expelled the Knights of St. John Hospitallers. With the help of the Spanish, the Hospitallers established themselves in the "navel of the Mediterranean," the island of Malta; their tribute of one falcon a year to their patron sparked the popular modern mystery, *The Maltese Falcon.* The knights themselves became so identified with the island that they were often known afterwards as the Knights of Malta.

In this period, a major shift took place in the manning of Mediterranean ships. In the past, ships had generally been manned by free men; though perhaps subject peoples, they were both oarsmen and warriors, often sharing equally in any booty gained by naval action. But in this period, with Moslem and Christian antagonisms reaching a peak, it became common to use slaves, often prisoners-of-war, to row the great galleys. Christian galleys were often manned by Turkish slaves (along with civil criminals and debtors, later), while the Turkish galleys were manned by Christian captives. Malta itself became a major slave market, where the Knights of St. John sold captives from their raids on the Moslems. The hardships preserved in the still-used phrase "to work like a galley slave" would not change until modern times; they are described by a later French naval officer, Barras de la Penne:

> Many of the galley-slaves had no room to sleep at full length, for they put seven men on one bench; that is to say, on a space about ten feet long by four broad...The creaking of the blocks and cordage, the loud cries of the sailors, the horrible maledictions of the galley slaves, and the groaning of the timbers are mingled with the clank of chains. Calm itself has its inconveniences [because of] the evil smells which arise from the galley.

With ships like these, Christian knights carried on running sea battles with their Moslem opponents. (By Manning de V. Lee, in Rupert Sargent Holland, Historic Ships, *1926)*

Sailing ships were developing space in this period, drawing on experience with the world's windy oceans; but oared ships were still used because the occasional failure of winds in the Mediterranean could easily becalm a ship relying on sails alone.

Recalled from Algiers to take over the Turkish navy, Barbarossa set about taking the remaining Venetian possessions in the Aegean. Aiming to end the Turkish threat, the Venetians, Genoese, and Spanish decided to join forces in 1538, under the experienced Genoese admiral Andrea Doria. Meeting the Turks at Preveza in the Ionian Sea, near where Antony and Cleopatra went down to defeat, the Europeans were hampered by an awkward mix of sailing ships and rowed galleys; but their defeat was sealed by Barbarossa's use of a new technique: the broadside. Rather than ramming and boarding, which had been the main fighting techniques since early times, the Turks eschewed individual targets for the pattern of shooting cannons straight across the water at the enemy's ships.

Despite their victory at the Battle of Preveza, the Turks were bedeviled by the Knights of St. John at Malta, astride the main east-west route. In 1565, the Turks threw perhaps 40,000 men at the tiny fortress, and lost over half of them in a failed siege that gave heart to the Europeans. The Turks extended their empire no further west, although Barbary corsairs thrived for centuries more. The Europeans once again united, meeting at the port of Messina and facing the Turks off the Ionian coast of Greece, this time at Lepanto in 1571. This time the Europeans were victorious, shattering the Turkish fleet. The Battle of Lepanto did see one permanent change; oared galleys gave way to sailing ships, increasingly armored with metals or hardwoods, as protection both against broadsides and the slower, more insidious *teredo* worm.

The Barbary corsairs were not the only predators on the Mediterranean in these times. The Aegean, in particular, gave shelter to pirates of all nationalities. As always, these brigands used islands and capes to their own advantage, following a seasonal routine, as described by an Englishman named Roberts who, in 1692, was taken by a corsair ship and put into service as a gunner. As Aegean sailors had for centuries, these pirates wintered in island refuges until the March winds were favorable for the beginning of their round:

> And then they go for the Furnoes [Fourni Islands], and lie there under the high Land hid, having a watch on the Hill with a little Flag, whereby they make a Signal, if they see any Sail: they slip out and lie athwart the Boak of Samos, and take their Prize; They lie in the same nature under...[other islands] in the Spring, and forepart of the Summer; Then for the middle of the Summer, they ply on the Coast of Cyprus; and if they hear the least noise of any Algerines and Grand Turks ships at Rhodes, away they scour for the Coast of Alexandria...being shole Water, well knowing the Turks will not follow them thither. The latter part of the Summer they come stealing on the Coast of Syria, where they do most mischief with their Feleucca, which commonly Rows with 12 Oars, and carries 6 Sitters: For at Night they leave the Ship, and get under the shoar before Day, and go ashoar, where they way-lay the Turks...From hence towards the Autumn they come lurking in about the Islands, to and fro...until they put in also to lie up in the Winter.

In the following centuries, English, Dutch, and Scandinavian sailors became increasingly active in the Mediterranean, not only for trading in the sea itself, but as a shortcut to the East. Because the Cape of Good Hope Route often required two years for a round trip to India, Europeans—especially the British, following the lead of the Portuguese before them—increasingly sent couriers through the Mediterranean to India, either crossing at Suez and shipping down the Red Sea, or debarking at Alexandretta, port of Antioch, and taking the Great Desert Route overland to the Persian Gulf. Britain signaled permanent interest in the region by claiming the Rock of Gibraltar for itself. The British also established a base at Naples, controlling the north-south route in the central Mediterranean. In this period the great northern European sailing ships abandoned finally the old pattern of coastal voyages, which had persisted in the Mediterranean since the beginning. Some of the British ships were equipped to go for as long as four months before putting into port. For the first time scurvy—never before a problem in the Mediterranean, for sailors had fresh produce in every port—afflicted sailors, until the practice developed of supplying them with lemons from Sicily. The British and other Europeans reached an accommodation with the Barbary corsairs, who accepted tribute rather than fighting, and supplied paying customers with passes to ensure their safety.

It was the French who finally drove the Knights of St. John from Malta and took Alexandria, now in sad dis-

repair, but by the end of the Napoleonic Wars, the British were firmly established at Gibraltar and at Malta. The rapid development of British interests in the East meant that messengers, traders, and adventurers increasingly took the overland routes from the Levant or Egypt to the Indian Ocean. American ships also began to make their appearance in the Mediterranean; but they refused to follow the European practice of paying tribute to the Barbary pirates. From 1803 on, American expeditions took action against pirate bases, starting with Tripoli in Libya; by 1830, when the French took Algiers, the Barbary corsairs were effectively finished. By 1827 a British-dominated European fleet had devastated the Turkish fleet, breaking her hold on the routes into the Black Sea. Greece regained her independence and Britain and France took some of the former possessions of Venice, which had fallen almost without notice in 1797.

In the resulting Pax Britannica, English emerged as the common trading language on the Mediterranean. British officials and that new breed—the tourist—began to appear in the eastern Mediterranean. Everyone who was anyone in Britain showed up in the Mediterranean sooner or later, and scenes from these travels were transformed and incorporated into many a romantic novel. The British also brought modern technology to the Mediterranean, most notably the steamship—ideally suited to the Mediterranean, for it avoided the becalming that threatened sailing ships. While the west Mediterranean was still relatively backward and untouched, except along the coast, the prosperity of the central and eastern Mediterranean was evident. William Makepeace Thackery described Valetta, the main harbor of Malta, in the mid-19th century:

> ...the entrance to the harbour...is one of the most stately and agreeable scenes ever admired by sea-sick traveller. The small basin was busy with a hundred ships, from the huge guardship, which lies there a city in itself; merchantmen loading and crews cheering, under all the flags of the world flaunting in the sunshine; a half-score of busy black steamers perpetually coming and going, coaling and painting, and puffing and hissing in and out of the harbour; slim men-of-war's barges shooting to and fro, with long shining oars flashing like wings over the water; hundreds of painted town-boats, with high heads and white awnings...Round this busy blue water rise rocks, blazing in sunshine, and covered with every imaginable device of fortification...

In the vacuum created by the decline of Turkey, both the Russians and the Western Europeans saw potential advantages, leading to their conflict in the Crimean Peninsula in the 1860's; Russia, which had aspired to control routes into the Mediterranean, was forced to allow neutralization of the Black Sea, leaving it open for all nations.

More important in the long term, the 1860's saw

the building of the Suez Canal, initially under French auspices, but later dominated by the British. The Cape of Good Hope Route, which had led to the decline of the Mediterranean in the 16th century, was itself eclipsed; the route from the Far East through the Red Sea and the Suez into the Mediterranean became the main sea artery in the world. With coaling stations at Gibraltar, Malta, and Port Said, the Mediterranean revived, not as an enclosed inland sea, but as the mid-section of a seaway spanning a quarter of the world. The balance shifted west, as Marseilles became one of the major ports, along with Toulon (home of the French fleet), a revitalized Genoa, Messina, and Algiers, increasingly important as the French settled the interior of North Africa. Venice did not share in the prosperity, except as the focus of romantic tourists, but Italy in this period was united—for the first time since the Roman Empire—into a single nation.

Modern technology reached Greece, as well. At Corinth, where ships had once been dragged across the isthmus on rollers, a canal was cut through in 1893. Although never large enough for full-size steamships, it was a boon to the many fishermen and sailors operating small merchant ships between the Aegean and the Ionian, saving over 50 miles.

In the late 19th and early 20th centuries, Europeans also built lighthouses all around the Mediterranean, for the steamships—no longer crawling along the coast, but speeding across the seas—needed guidance to the harbors and hazards of the Mediterranean. The dark, menacing promontories, behind which might lurk pirates, gave way to a succession of powerful sea lights. In the words of Ernle Bradford:

From Alexandria...to the distant, cloud-broomed Rock of Gibraltar, a necklace of lights was laid upon the sea. Along the southern coast of France, with its many ports and harbours, they sparkled like a *rivière* of diamonds...

The coasts, which had been largely abandoned since the advent of the Barbary corsairs, were repopulated by people coming down from their hilltop retreats and by foreigners who were increasingly attracted by the Mediterranean's shores.

During World War I, the main battles were fought on land, not at sea. But the British bases at Gibraltar, Malta, and Alexandria guarded the sea routes which brought expeditionary forces to Gallipoli (aiming for Constantinople), Salonika (aiming for the Balkans), and the Levant. By the end of the war, the Ottoman Empire was no more, being replaced by a new Turkish government. The Greeks—allied with the many ethnic Greeks who still populated Turkey's Aegean shores—attempted a revolt against the Turks. In response, the Turks devastated the port of Smyrna, and hundreds of thousands of Greeks fled to mainland Greece and the Aegean Islands. While Greece was attempting to assimilate these many immigrants, Italy—under Benito Mussolini—was attempting to revive the Roman dream of the Mediterranean as Mare Nostrum (Our Sea) by reaching across to Africa. In these turbulent times many people from southern and eastern Europe also chose to emigrate to the Americas, and the great passenger liners of the first half of the 20th century carried millions of people westward from Marseilles, Naples, and Piraeus (the port of Athens). While rumbles of a second world

By the 19th century, Alexandria had long since passed its prime, and its great lighthouse had fallen into ruin. (From Description de l'Egypte, *1820)*

war were heard in the distance, tourists flocked in increasing numbers to the Mediterranean, no longer just the rich, but also many middle-class travelers and impoverished artists, drawn by the climate and the aura of the great classical cultures.

When war finally broke out, and France fell to Germany, the Mediterranean became a main battlefield between the Allies and the Axis. While Italy took Rhodes and Germany Crete, the British held their positions in Gibraltar, Malta, and Alexandria, controlling the main east-west routes and threatening supply routes between Italy and North Africa. While the main desert campaign was aimed at Alexandria, it was Malta that provided the key to Allied victory. In November 1940, a new type of ship—the aircraft carrier—based there made a crippling air attack on the Italian southern base at Taranto (an attack that may have served as a model later for Pearl Harbor). Thereafter, although Malta's position was so difficult she could sometimes be supplied only by submarines, Allied forces there continued to disrupt Axis supply lines, most of all the vital oil needed to power the land armies. And it was from Malta that the Allied invasion of Sicily was launched.

The years after the war brought yet another set of changes to the Mediterranean. The Suez Canal gained increasing importance as the world depended more and more on oil from the Middle East, and great tankers crossed the wine-dark sea to the main ports of the Mediterranean

and beyond. But as Britain relinquished its empire in the Far East, the Mediterranean lands pressed for the same treatment. In 1956 the Egyptians broke free, nationalizing the Suez Canal over British resistance. Then in 1967, a dispute between Israel and Egypt—which would allow no Israeli ships to use the canal—erupted in war, closing the canal for some years. Although it would later reopen, the oil-rich countries had in the meantime built supertankers too large for the canal, reviving the old Cape of Good Hope Route around Africa. Britain gradually gave up other possessions in the Mediterranean, including Malta and Cyprus (which resulted in a civil war and de facto division of the island between Turks and Greeks), but keeping Gibraltar. With British power gone, the United States and Russia—the main powers in the world—jockeyed for influence in the sea, with the Russians pushing out from the Black Sea into the Mediterranean.

In the late 20th century, the great passenger liners that had once passed through the sea on their way east gradually lost ground to airlines. But the Mediterranean itself proved to be a magnet, and cruise ships—many of them owned by Greeks—carry passengers flown in from around the world. And sailing ships, too, which had been replaced by steam-powered craft, once again roam the sea—but now more for recreation than commerce. These pleasure craft, however, are eqipped with motors, for the uncertain winds of the Mediterranean can still becalm a mariner relying on sails alone.

Selective Bibliography

Bradford, Ernle. *Mediterranean: Portrait of a Sea* (New York: Harcourt, Brace, Jovanovich, 1971). A useful and readable history.

Braudel, Fernand. *The Mediterranean and the Mediterranean World in the Age of Philip II,* in 2 vols. Translated from the French by Siân Reynolds (New York: Harper & Row, 1972 and 1973). An unparalleled comprehensive work.

Casson, Lionel. *The Ancient Mariners: Seafarers and Sea Fighters of the Mediterranean in Ancient Times* (New York: Macmillan, 1959). A general work extending beyond the Mediterranean.

Connolly, Peter. *Greece and Rome at War* (Englewood Cliffs, New Jersey: Prentice-Hall, 1981). A useful detailing supplemented by many maps and illustrations.

Cornell, Tim, and John Matthews. *Atlas of the Roman World* (New York: Facts On File, 1982). A well-illustrated guide to places, roads, and history.

Grant, Michael. *The Ancient Mediterranean* (London; Weidenfeld and Nicolson, 1969). Focuses on the land more than the sea.

Harden, Donald. *The Phoenicians* (New York: Praeger, 1962). Part of the Ancient Peoples and Places series. A useful review of the culture and its accomplishments.

Hoskins, Halford Lancaster. *British Routes to India* (New York: Octagon Books, 1966; reprint of 1928 Longman Green edition). Some chapters focus on the Mediterranean part of the routes.

Hourani, George Fadlo. *Arab Seafaring: In the Indian Ocean in Ancient and Early Medieval Times* (New York: Octagon, 1975; reprint of 1951 edition). Volume 13 of Princeton Oriental Studies. Includes a chapter on Arab sailors in the Mediterranean.

Hyde, Walter Woodburn. *Ancient Greek Mariners* (New York: Oxford University Press, 1947). A wide-ranging survey of early navigation, featuring the Greeks.

Levi, Peter. *Atlas of the Greek World* (New York: Facts On File, 1980). A beautifully illustrated guide to sites and culture.

Lewis, Archibald R. *Naval Power and Trade in the Mediterranean, A.D. 500–1100* (Princeton: Princeton University Press, 1951). A detailed account.

Lopez, Robert S., and Irving W. Raymond. *Medieval Trade in the Mediterranean World: Illustrative Documents Translated with Introductions and Notes* (New York: Norton, no date; reprint of earlier Columbia University Press edition). Focuses on the commercial transactions.

Ludwig, Emil. *The Mediterranean: Saga of a Sea.* Translated from the German by Barrows Mussey (New York: Whittlesey House, McGraw-Hill, 1942). A popular history.

Morand, Paul. *The Road to India* (London: Hodder and Stoughton, 1937). Part Two focuses on the Mediterranean portion of the route to the East.

Ormerod, Henry A. *Piracy in the Ancient World: An Essay in Mediterranean History* (Totowa, New Jersey: Rowman and Littlefield, 1978; reprint of 1924 edition). A useful review.

Semple, Ellen Churchill. *The Geography of the Mediterranean Region: Its Relation to Ancient History* (New York: Holt, 1931). An exceptionally fine overview.

Tavernier, Bruno. *Great Maritime Routes: An Illustrated History.* Translated from the French. (London: Macdonald, 1972). Three sections focus on the Mediterranean.

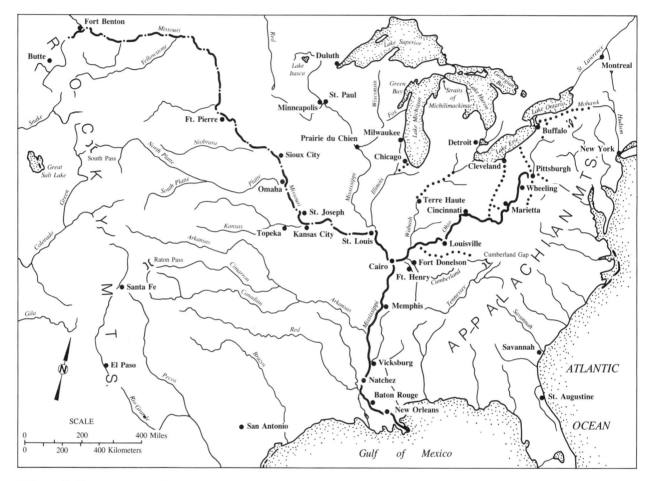

The Mississippi Route in the 1840's

———————— Main Mississippi Route · · · · · · · · Main Canal Connections

—·—·—·— Main Missouri Route

The Mississippi Route

...the great Mississippi, the majestic, the magnificent Mississippi, rolling its mile-wide tide along, shining in the sun...

This mighty river, as seen by Mark Twain (Samuel Clemens) in his *Life on the Mississippi*, was surely well-suited to occupy center stage in North America. Its very name means "Great River."

Coming from the East, from Europe, North America opens a swift, relatively easy water route to its heartland in only two places. The first starts at the Strait of Belle Isle and courses through the St. Lawrence and the Great Lakes, linking up with the Mississippi in the north via a short overland connection, well over a thousand miles into the continent. This is the long voyage into North America started by Jacques Cartier in 1541, finally taking the French out to the Mississippi beyond the lakes 130 years later. The other is through the mouth of the Mississippi at the Gulf of Mexico, a far easier way to enter the North American heartland, involving as it does a direct water route, by sea to the mouth of the river and then up the valley of the Mississippi.

The same year that Cartier entered the Strait of Belle Isle, Hernando De Soto "discovered" the Mississippi. He and his party crossed it near what is now Memphis, Tennessee, coming overland from Florida, in the third year of a four-year journey that took them all the way to what is now Texas. De Soto was to fall sick and die somewhere on the lower Mississippi, a year later. De Soto and his party were seeking gold; they found none and went away, quite unaware that they were leaving behind what might have been the key to a continent. Here is how Mark Twain saw it, in *Life on the Mississippi:*

De Soto merely glimpsed the river, then died and was buried in it by his priests and soldiers. One would expect the priests and the soldiers to multiply the river's dimensions by ten—the Spanish custom of the day—and thus move other adventurers to go at once and explore it. On the contrary, their narratives, when they reached home, did not excite that amount of curiosity. The Mississippi was left unvisited by whites during a term of years which seems incredible in our energetic days. One may "sense" the interval to his mind, after a fashion, by dividing it up in this way: after De Soto glimpsed the river, a fraction short of a quarter of a century elapsed, and then Shakespeare was born; lived a trifle more than half a century, then died; and when he had been in his grave considerably more than half a century, the *second* white man saw the Mississippi. In our day we don't allow a hundred and thirty years to elapse between glimpses of a marvel...

Like other contemporary Europeans, the Spanish were seeking a passage to Cathay and the Spice Islands, but they concentrated on central America, leaving the Mississippi to be developed by others, starting with the French. Seeking the always-elusive Northwest Passage to the Far East—as well as riches from the fur trade—Cartier,

For 130 years after De Soto visited the Mississippi, Europeans left the great river unexplored. (Engraving after painting by W. H. Powell, New-York Historical Society)

Champlain, La Salle, Jolliet, Marquette, and the other great French explorers moved step by step across North America during the 130 long years between Cartier's entry into the St. Lawrence and La Salle's journey to the mouth of the Mississippi.

The French may have been the first Europeans to explore and trade on the Mississippi, but they were scarcely the first traders on the river. Substantial Native American cultures were farming, trading, and creating artworks on the Mississippi a thousand years before Christ was born, when most of the cultures of Northern Europe were no further advanced than the cultures of the North American heartland. Trade on the Mississippi, the Missouri, the Ohio, and many of the other streams and rivers that make up the huge Mississippi Basin had probably gone on for many years before that. We encounter it first in a highly developed form, as a network of trading activities that span the continent from at least the Appalachians and southern Atlantic coast to the Rockies and from the Gulf of Mexico to the Great Lakes and the high northern plains. As early as the first century B.C., at the time of Rome and the great Han culture of East Asia, the

Hopewell culture (named after the modern owner of the land containing one of their burial sites in Ohio) arose in the valleys of the Ohio, the Illinois, and the lower Mississippi. The huge mounded burial sites they left behind show that these Native American farmers and hunters were also the great North American traders of their day, using the waterways of the Mississippi Basin—and beyond—to acquire such things as grizzly bear teeth from the Rockies, conch shells from the Gulf of Mexico, mica from the southern Appalachians, and copper from the Great Lakes.

The Hopewell culture was superseded by other Native American cultures in the period 500–700 A.D., but the pattern of widespread trading continued. The earliest French and Basque fishermen to follow John Cabot to the shores of the New World after 1497 found ready trading partners on shore, and the trade of European tools and other goods for furs was well-established even before Cartier entered the Gulf of St. Lawrence in 1534. The French traded for furs for over 70 years before starting west from Montreal, following the well-worn trail of the fur brigades of the Ottawas, one of the great trading tribes of eastern

Canada. Again and again in the history of North American exploration and trade, the invading Europeans followed the paths of Native American hunters, trappers, traders, and middlemen, paths that had existed for hundreds and, in some instances, thousands of years before the Europeans came.

The Mississippi River system occupies the heart of North America. It includes the Mississippi itself, flowing from Lake Itasca, northwest of Duluth, Minnesota, almost 2,400 miles to the Gulf of Mexico; the Missouri, flowing from Grand Forks, Montana, almost 2,500 miles to its junction with the Mississippi, a little north of St. Louis; the Ohio, flowing almost 1,000 miles west to its junction with the Mississippi at Cairo, Illinois; and scores of other tributaries, all joined together in a single interconnected system with well over 15,000 miles of navigable waterways. From the north, it provides easy passage from the St. Lawrence and Great Lakes to the Gulf of Mexico. It also provides easy water passage from east of Pittsburgh on the Ohio all the way out on the Missouri to western Montana, and an easy linkup there with the Columbia river system. (It was this Missouri-Columbia route out to the Pacific that the Lewis and Clark party took in the first decade of the 19th century.) The Mississippi's tributaries provided most of the main routes west, either

directly or indirectly by use of the river valleys they created. In the East, the Ohio, Tennessee, and Cumberland Rivers provided routes through and beyond the Appalachians; west of the Mississippi, explorers, trappers, traders, and then settlers followed the Missouri, Platte, Kansas, Arkansas, and Red (Colorado) Rivers across the plains to the Rockies, and beyond to the Pacific.

The first of the French explorers to reach the Mississippi were Louis Jolliet and Father Jacques Marquette, in 1673. Twenty-nine years earlier, in 1634, Jean Nicolet had explored the Great Lakes country as far west as Green Bay, on the western shore of Lake Michigan, not realizing how close he then was to the great river. Now Jolliet and Marquette went further: traveling west from the French outpost at Michilimackinac, at the western end of Lake Huron, they entered Lake Michigan and followed Nicolet's route to Green Bay. Continuing west on the Fox River, they were then guided by local Native Americans on the old and well-used portage between the Fox and Wisconsin rivers. Once on the Wisconsin, they had entered the Mississippi River system and were able to take the Wisconsin directly into the Mississippi, which they entered on June 17, 1673, near what is now Prairie du Chien.

The Jolliet and Marquette party, traveling in two

On the site of small Fort Harmar, in 1790, grew the settlement of Marietta, jumping-off point for many settlers heading down the Ohio. (From The American Pioneer, *1842, New York Public Library)*

These Mandan women, descendants of the great Mississippi Valley cultures, are gathering driftwood from the river, to be taken up to their river-bluff village for fuel. (After Charles Bodmer, from Maximilian, Prince of Wied Neu-Wied, Travels, *New York Public Library)*

birchbark canoes, then followed the Mississippi south for almost a thousand miles, passing the mouths of both the Missouri and Ohio; they turned back after reaching the mouth of the Arkansas River, at a point only about 400 miles from the mouth of the mighty system. Father Claude Dablon describes the first sighting—probably as related by Marquette—of the mouth of the Missouri, later to be known to many generations of Americans as "The Big Muddy":

...sailing quietly in clear and calm water, we heard the noise of a rapid, into which we were about to run. I have seen nothing more dreadful. An accumulation of large and entire trees, branches, and floating islands, was issuing from the mouth of the river Pekitanoui [Missouri], with such impetuousity that we could not without great danger risk passing through it. So great was the agitation that the water was very muddy, and could not become clear.

Pekitanoui is a river of considerable size, coming from the northwest, from a great distance, and it discharges into the Mississippi. There are many villages of savages along this river, and I hope by its means to discover the vermillion or California sea.

Judging from the direction of the course of the Mississippi, if it continues the same way, we think that it discharges into the Mexican Gulf. It would be a great advantage to find the river leading to the southern sea, toward California; and, as I have said, this is what I hope to do by means of the Pekitanoui, according to the reports made to me by the savages. From them I have learned that, by

ascending this river for 5 or 6 days, one reaches a fine prairie, 20 or 30 leagues long. This must be crossed in a northwesterly direction, and it terminates at another small river, on which one may embark, for it is not very difficult to transport canoes through so fine a country as that prairie. This second river flows toward the southwest for 10 or 15 leagues, after which it enters a lake, small and deep, which flows toward the west, where it falls into the sea. I have hardly any doubt that it is the Vermillion Sea, and I do not despair of discovering it some day.

Aside from a misunderstanding of the distances involved, that is a sound description of the course of the route from the Missouri, across the Continental Divide, to the Columbia River system, and down to the Pacific. That is not surprising; Native Americans living on the Mississippi had, by then, been traveling that route at least since the time of Christ. Some research indicates that many of the Native American tribes of the Mississippi Valley during the period of French exploration were in direct line from the people of the Hopewell culture and the Mississippian Culture that followed, which had been decimated by the plagues that accompanied the European conquest of the Americas.

Nine years later, in 1692, La Salle completed the long French journey from the Gulf of St. Lawrence to the mouth of the Mississippi. His was the pursuit of empire; he claimed the Mississippi and its adjacent lands for France, and hoped to return to begin building a French presence in the continental heartland. It was not to be, either for La Salle or for France. He was killed by mutineers during his second expedition to the Mississippi, in 1687. And the French hold on the Mississippi Valley would not survive British victory over the French in the struggle for North America. The territory that La Salle had named Louisiana, after his patron, Louis XIV of France, was French for only a short time. After 1763, Great Britain took control of the land east of the Mississippi, while Spain held the land west of the Mississippi and the Mississippi delta itself, all still called Louisiana.

After La Salle, French travel and trade on the Mississippi began to develop, but slowly. In 1699, French coming south from the Great Lakes established the outpost of Cahokia, across the river from what would later be St. Louis. Notably, Cahokia had also been the largest center of the Native American Mississippian culture, containing the largest of their burial mounds. A year later, in 1700, Pierre le Moyne, Sieur d'Iberville, coming in from the gulf, established the first French colony near the mouth of the Mississippi, and the European settlement of the lower Mississippi began.

New Orleans was founded in 1718, plantations were established upriver, and both French settlers and slaves were by mid-century on the river in considerable numbers. By 1770, there were an estimated 13,500 French in Louisiana, and substantial numbers of black slaves and Native Americans. By then, considerable traffic had begun on the river, with such goods as cotton and furs moving down

the river by pirogue (dugout canoe), keelboat (covered flat-bottomed boat), and flatboat (open barge). There would also be sugar cane, molasses, and rum by the end of the 18th century. Travelers and trade goods went downstream easily, for they were running with the current; return trips upstream were more difficult, calling for considerable muscle power in hauling or poling boats against the current, especially with bulk cargo. As a result, the Mississippi reached its full potential as a water route only later.

By 1812, three events had occurred which together were to make the Mississippi, Ohio, Missouri, and the other inland waterways of the Mississippi basin tremendously active avenues of travel and trade: the United States became an independent nation, the cotton gin was invented, and the steamboat arrived on the Mississippi. The impact of these three events was enormous.

After the American Revolution (or War of the Rebellion, depending on which side is describing the war), the former British lands became part of the United States, with the Mississippi River itself the new country's western border. The new Americans abrogated the British-Native American treaties, which had kept settlers pinned to the east coast. The Mississippi delta continued to be Spanish until 1800, when it went back to France for three years; but after 1803, with the Louisiana Purchase, the Mississippi itself and much of the basin to the west was added to the United States. The explosion westward from Atlantic to Pacific began.

As early as the late 1780's tens of thousands of

Steamboat pilots on the Mississippi and its tributaries had to watch sharp for natural hazards, like tree trunks that were washed downstream and collected on snags in the river. (After E. de Girardin, from Le Tour du Monde, *1864)*

Americans were going west by raft, flatboat, and keelboat on the Ohio, Tennessee, and Cumberland rivers, and thousands more by land on the Wilderness Road. In 1788–89, 800–900 boats went west past Fort Harmar (Marietta) on the Ohio, carrying 20,000 people, 7,000 horses, 3,000 cows, 900 sheep, and 600 wagons. By 1790, there were over 45,000 people in Ohio; ten years later the population had jumped to 230,000, and by 1820 was more than double that. By 1860, Ohio had almost 2.5 million people, and the states of the Mississippi basin held over 12.5 million people, almost 40 percent of the population of the United States.

In the Mississippi basin itself, the invention of the cotton gin in 1793 greatly accelerated the development of cotton planting on the Mississippi—and built up demand for more economical trade alternatives on the river.

The demand was met by the use of newly invented steamboats on the Ohio and lower Mississippi in the second decade of the 19th century, and of later adaptations for use on the shallow waters of the middle and upper Mississippi and the Missouri. Whoever held them— Native Americans, French, Spanish, British, or the new Americans—the waterways of the Mississippi basin had continued to be the main travel and trade routes of the American heartland. But now—with farmers, fur traders, and planters in desperate need of an outlet to the sea— the rivers became enormous and busy highways, with steampower providing a sure, economical journey back upstream.

The first steamboat on the river was the *New Orleans,* a two-masted sidewheeler, launched at Pittsburgh in March 1811 by Nicholas Roosevelt, Robert Fulton, and Robert Livingston as principals of the Ohio Steamship Navigation Company. Nicholas Roosevelt and his wife took the *New Orleans* the length of the Ohio and lower Mississippi. Just after running the extraordinarily difficult Falls of the Ohio, near Louisville, they were caught in the New Madrid earthquake, the most violent North American earthquake of its time. Yet they and the *New Orleans* survived, at Natchez even taking on the first load of cotton to be carried by steamboat on the Mississippi. Arriving at New Orleans on January 12, 1812, they had inaugurated a new era of travel and trade in the Mississippi basin.

Yet the *New Orleans* was not the kind of shallow-draft steamboat needed to traverse much of the basin. It needed too deep a stream to consistently be able to go from Pittsburgh to New Orleans and back; as a practical matter, such boats were limited to the deeper navigation channel of the lower Mississippi, south of Natchez. But in 1816 Henry Shreve invented and put into service the first shallow-draft steamboat, the *Washington,* flat-bottomed, with engine and boilers on deck, a second deck for cargo and people, and a pilothouse and two smokestacks high above all the rest. This was the profile of all the Missis-

sippi basin steamboats that were to follow. With it in use, the Ohio, Mississippi, and Missouri became emigrant highways, opening up the continent.

This was when the great era of Mississippi basin steamboating began. Now substantial shallow-draft steamboats could carry large numbers of people and enormous amounts of cargo on the Ohio and Mississippi. Smaller, even shallower-draft steamboats could open up navigation on the Missouri all the way to Fort Benton, in northern Montana, to the Yellowstone country, and to the mouth of the Little Big Horn. The small northern river steamboats took supplies, settlers, traders, and soldiers north and brought back furs, lead, soldiers, and in some periods, large quantities of gold and silver from the West.

The rivers were not easy, though. There were always new hazards on the rivers: tree trunks to avoid, rockfalls, snags, and obstacles of all kinds. And the river itself shifted; had someone attempted to follow La Salle's route down the Mississippi two centuries later, most of the voyage would have been a walk on dry land. Here is Mark Twain, who was a Mississippi river pilot in the 1850's, relating some of what his master-pilot teacher taught him when he was an apprentice:

You see, this has got to be learned; there isn't any getting around it. A clear star-light night throws such heavy shadows that, if you don't know the shape of a shore perfectly, you would claw away from every bunch of timber, because you would take the black shadow of it for a solid cape; and you see you would be getting scared to death every fifteen minutes by the watch. You would be fifty yards from shore all the time when you ought to be within fifty feet of it. You can't see a snag in one of those shadows, but you know exactly where it is, and the shape of the river tells you when you are coming to it. Then there's your pitch-dark night; the river is a very different shape on a pitch-dark night from what it is on a star-light night. All shores seem to be straight lines, then, and mighty dim ones, too; and you'd better *run* them for straight lines, only you know better. You boldly drive your boat right into what seems to be a solid, straight wall (you knowing very well that in reality there is a curve there), and that wall falls back and makes way for you. Then there's your gray mist. You take a night when there's one of these grisly, drizzly, gray mists, and then there isn't *any* particular shape to a shore. A gray mist would tangle the head of the oldest man that ever lived. Well, then, different kinds of *moonlight* change the shape of the river in different ways. You see—...you only learn the shape of the river; and you learn it with such absolute certainty that you can always steer by the shape that's *in your head,* and never mind the one that's before your eyes.

It was in this period—and largely thanks to Mark Twain himself—that the Mississippi began to occupy a unique position as a source of American folklore. Here is Twain on Marquette and the legendary Mississippi catfish:

A big catfish collided with Marquette's canoe, and startled him; and reasonably enough, for he had been warned by the Indians that he was on a fool-hardy journey, and even a fatal one, for the river contained a demon "whose roar could be heard at a great distance, and who would engulf them in the abyss where he dwelt." I have seen a Mississippi catfish that was more than six feet long, and weighed two hundred and fifty pounds; and if Marquette's fish was the fellow to that one, he had a fair right to think the river's roaring demon was come.

During the American Civil War, the Mississippi became less an avenue of travel and trade than a battlefield. The Union sought to take the river, all the way to the Gulf, thereby splitting the Confederacy. The Confederacy sought to hold the river, while concentrating its main efforts on the eastern seaboard. In a series of major battles during 1862, Union forces advancing from the north and south took control of the entire river, effectively splitting the trans-Mississippi states from the Confederacy and laying much of the basis for the winning of the war. A Union fleet under the command of David G. Farragut took New Orleans in April 1862. Union forces under the command of Ulysses S. Grant successively took Fort Henry, on the Cumberland; Fort Donelson, on the Tennessee; Memphis, Tennessee; and cleared the Mississippi in series of battles ending with the successful siege of Vicksburg.

The great days of Mississippi steamboating ended with the coming of the railroads. In the East, railroads began to cut into river traffic along the Ohio and the other eastern tributaries of the Mississippi even before the Civil War. After the war, as the huge American transcontinental railroad network grew, travel and trade on the rivers declined. In the early 1880's, there was still considerable travel and trade on the Mississippi and Missouri; but the last steamboat left Fort Benton in 1890, and by the early 1890's, the steamboating era was over throughout the Mississippi basin.

There is still substantial commercial shipping on the Mississippi, the Ohio, the Missouri, and some of their tributaries. Such materials as coal, steel, iron ore, and lead can often be more economically shipped by water than by truck or railroad. And some passenger ships have returned to the rivers, too, often in the form of reconditioned steamboats from the last century, serving those for whom a steamboat trip on the Mississippi is a nostalgic and satisfying journey into a time and style that will not come again.

Steamboat trade on the Mississippi made New Orleans a major world port. (After A. R. Waud, authors' archives)

Selective Bibliography

Banta, R. E. *The Ohio* (New York: Rinehart, 1949). Part of the Rivers of America series. A detailed anecdotal work on the Ohio River.

Billington, Ray Allen. *The Westward Movement in the United States* (New York: Van Nostrand Reinhold, 1959). A concise, useful, general history of American westward movement from sea to sea.

Carter, Hodding. *The Lower Mississippi* (New York: Farrar & Rinehart, 1942). Part of the Rivers of America series. A comprehensive work on the history of the lower Mississippi River and its surrounding area.

Caruso, John Anthony. *The Mississippi Valley Frontier* (New York: Bobbs-Merrill, 1966). A comprehensive, detailed history of the exploration and settlement of the Mississippi Valley by the French.

Clemens, Samuel (Mark Twain). *Life on the Mississippi* (H. O. Houghton, 1874). A classic work on the Mississippi and Missouri, with brief historical introduction, and main focus on life during the great era of steamboating.

Cummings, W. P., et al. *The Exploration of North America* (New York: Putnam's, 1974). A large, heavily illustrated work, containing a good deal of material quoted from early explorers, accompanied by editorial commentary.

De Voto, Bernard. *The Course of Empire* (Boston: Houghton Mifflin, 1952). A substantial, anecdotal history of the exploration and conquest of North America.

Donovan, Frank. *River Boats of America* (New York: Crowell, 1966). A good, detailed, anecdotal survey of American river boats and boating.

Drago, Harry Sinclair. *Roads To Empire: The Dramatic Conquest of the American West* (New York: Dodd Mead, 1968). A brief history of most of the main American western trails; includes a section on steamboating on the Missouri.

Eifert, Virginia S. *Of Men and Rivers* (New York: Dodd Mead, 1966). A substantial work on the history of United States rivers, focusing upon the steamboating era.

Hulbert, Archer B. *The Paths of Inland Commerce* (New Haven: Yale, 1921). A classic short work on American trails, roads, and waterways.

Josephy, Alvin M. *The Indian Heritage of America* (New York: Knopf, 1969). An excellent, comprehensive general work on the history and culture of the Native Americans of the North Americas.

Merk, Frederick. *History of the Westward Movement* (New York: Knopf, 1978). A comprehensive, detailed history of the entire American expansion, including the modern period.

Parkman, Francis. *La Salle and the Discovery of the Great West* (Boston: Little, Brown, 1897). Parkman's classic work on La Salle, his explorations, and those with whom he was associated.

Semple, Ellen Churchill. *American History and Its Geographic Conditions* (Boston and New York: Houghton, Mifflin, 1903). A classic, comprehensive work on the influence of geography upon patterns of development and settlement in the United States, with excellent maps.

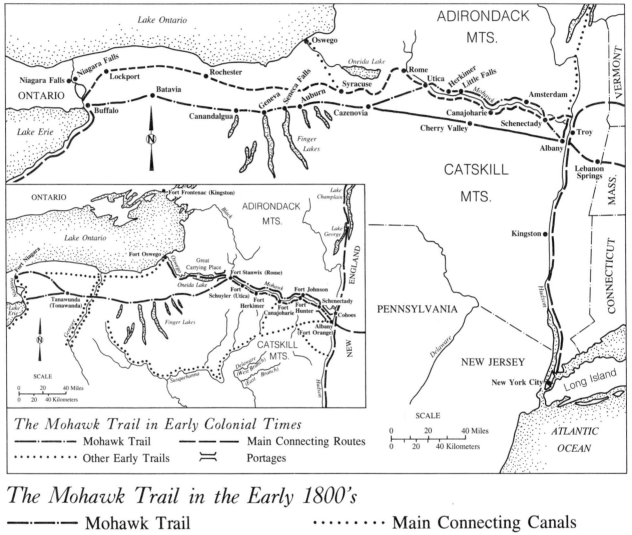

ADIRONDACK MTS.

Lake Ontario

Oswego

Oneida Lake

Rome
Utica
Herkimer
Little Falls

Niagara Falls
Niagara Falls
Lockport
Rochester

Batavia

ONTARIO

Buffalo

Lake Erie

Canandalgua

Geneva
Seneca Falls
Auburn
Syracuse

Cazenovia

Mohawk
Amsterdam

Canajoharie

Cherry Valley

Schenectady

Troy

Finger Lakes

Albany

CATSKILL MTS.

VERMONT

Lebanon Springs

MASS.

Kingston

CONNECTICUT

Hudson

Fort Frontenac (Kingston)

Lake Champlain

ONTARIO

ADIRONDACK MTS.

Black

Lake George

Lake Ontario

Fort Niagara

Fort Oswego

Great Carrying Place

Oswego

Fort Stanwix (Rome)

Oneida Lake

Mohawk

Fort Schuyler (Utica)

Fort Herkimer

Fort Johnson

Fort Canajoharie

Fort Hunter

Schenectady

Cohoes

NEW ENGLAND

Tanawunda (Tonawanda)

Genesee

Lake Erie

Finger Lakes

Albany (Fort Orange)

PENNSYLVANIA

CATSKILL MTS.

Delaware (West Branch)
(East Branch)

Susquehanna

Hudson

NEW

Delaware

NEW JERSEY

New York City

Long Island

ATLANTIC OCEAN

SCALE

0   20   40 Miles
0   20   40 Kilometers

SCALE

0   20   40 Miles
0   20   40 Kilometers

The Mohawk Trail in Early Colonial Times

—·—·— Mohawk Trail   — — — Main Connecting Routes

·········· Other Early Trails   ⫤ Portages

The Mohawk Trail in the Early 1800's

—·—·— Mohawk Trail   ·········· Main Connecting Canals

———— Great Western Turnpike   — — — Main Connecting Roads

-------- Erie Canal

The Mohawk Trail

In 1777, the British Army had a master plan for defeating the rebels in North America. In a three-pronged attack, they would send one army south from Montreal through the Champlain Valley, one north from New York City through the Hudson Valley, and one east from Lake Ontario, through the Oswego River and Oneida Lake, along the Mohawk Trail. The three armies were to converge on Albany, splitting the Revolutionary forces and—perhaps more importantly—presenting them with British forces at their rear. But at Fort Stanwix (now Rome) near the northward curve of the Mohawk River, the rebels—looking like ragtag farmers, although many had fought for the British in the French and Indian War—held off what they called "a banditti of robbers, murderers, and traitors, composed of savages of America, and more savage Britons." Even so, the cost of the Battle of Oriskany (near Stanwix) was so great that the Mohawk Valley revolutionary forces might have collapsed had it not been for an ingenious ploy by their regional commander-in-chief, Benedict Arnold. Arnold sent into the British camp an Iroquois-raised boy named Hon Yost Schuyler; considered crazy by the Iroquois, Schuyler was easily able to convince them that Arnold's forces numbered as many as the leaves on the trees, a "fact" supported by a specially composed letter on his person stating that Arnold's forces numbered 15,000. The result was that the British and their Iroquois allies beat a hasty retreat.

Although the execution failed, the conception was

brilliant, for British strategists well knew the importance of controlling the Mohawk Trail and the vital crossroads at Albany; they had learned well from the Iroquois, French, and Dutch before them.

The Mohawk Trail was the gateway to the heartland of North America. Stretching from mid-Georgia to Canada, the Appalachian Mountains divide the east coast of North America from the rest of the continent, cut by only one easy, level land route to the western lands. This is the great human pathway that came to be known as the Mohawk Trail—migration route, battleground, economic lifeline, key to North America, and spur for the development of New York City into a world capital.

The original Mohawk Trail, also called the Iroquois Trail, ran along the well-drained banks on both sides of the Mohawk River Valley, from Albany to Rome; it then turned directly westward along the Ontario Plain, touching the tops of the Finger Lakes, passing through Tanawunda (the Great Hearing Place, near modern Batavia, where the distant Niagara Falls could be heard in the wilderness quiet) to the eastern end of Lake Erie. This natural passage separating the Catskill and Adirondack mountains—the native Americans called the Mohawk "Te-non-an-at-che" (the River Flowing Through Mountains)—links New England and the Hudson River Valley with the Great Lakes and the Western Plains. In the early history of the land, the Mohawk Trail was the main route of native Americans pushing east and colonists pushing west to open up the continent to European settlement—and to send back the riches of the Midwest. As such it was for several centuries the subject and site of battles between many peoples, for control of the Mohawk Trail meant control of Northern America.

The trail itself was originally a footpath, in part probably following game trails, beaten down by the Algonquins who moved into the eastern lands 3,000 to 5,000 years ago, or perhaps even earlier. Tamped down several inches below normal ground level, the trail was narrow—only a foot or so wide, just enough to accommodate walkers single file—and winding, as it detoured around natural obstacles left in place. It was also generally dark, dank, and muddy, for most of its route was through dense forest of mature hardwoods and pines; when the trees were in leaf, they formed a canopy shutting out almost all light and warmth from above.

However unsatisfactory, such trails formed the basic travel and communications network for the native Americans. The Mohawk Trail was the main link between many other routes, among them the north-south Genesee Valley Trails; the Catskill Trail, which ran southeast from the Genesee River to the Susquehanna near Binghamton and then northeast back up to Canajoharie and Albany; the north-south Hudson River and Champlain Valley Trails; the various eastward trails from Albany toward Massachusetts and Connecticut; and routes to the north and west, through the Great Lakes and the Ohio and St. Lawrence valleys.

Given the difficulty of land travel, early native Americans and later colonists often preferred to travel by water where they could, portaging—that is, carrying their canoes—around rapids and falls or from one body of water to another. The Mohawk River itself acted as such a water route. Travelers from Lake Ontario passed up the Oswego River to Oneida Lake and up the small Wood Creek to "The Great Carrying Place," the portage to the head of navigation on the Mohawk, near modern Rome. From there they were able to travel down the river, with occasional portages, until progress was barred by rapids and falls, especially the Cohoes Falls, described by early Dutch observer Johannes Megapolensis as flowing between two high rocky banks where the Mohawk joins the Hudson and "falling from a height equal to that of a church, with such a noise...that we could hardly hear one another." Debarking before the falls at Schenectady, water travelers joined the land trail on the 16-mile portage to Albany on the Hudson River.

In the early 17th century, the Iroquois—who had been moving eastward from the Mississippi Valley since the 13th century—took control of the Mohawk Trail, pushing the formerly dominant Algonquins to the east and south of Albany. From their commanding position astride the trail, the Iroquois collected tribute from surrounding tribes in every direction. Unlike the Algonquins, who were only loosely united, the Iroquois formed a tight confederation known as the "Brotherhood of Five Nations" or the "Brotherhood of the Long House," after their communal buildings. The easternmost of the Iroquois tribes were the Mohawks, who were called the Keepers of the Eastern Door of the Long House, by token of their position on the Trail. (It was their enemies who named them "Mohawks," meaning "Eaters of Living Creatures," an indication of their ferocity that some early Europeans took to mean cannibalism.) The other tribes of the confederation were, heading westward along the Mohawk Trail, the Oneidas, the Onondagas, the Cayugas, and the Senecas, later joined by a sixth, the Tuscaroras. By the mid-17th century, the Iroquois were firmly in control of the trail and had established a network of runners along the main route and its subsidiary links, providing constant and rapid communication among the brother nations.

French explorers, fur traders, and missionaries were the first Europeans to penetrate the region of the Mohawk Trail; in the early years of the 17th century they moved from the St. Lawrence Valley and the Great Lakes to the Niagara River, which runs between Lakes Ontario and Erie, with a portage around the famous Falls, and along the Oswego River route to the Mohawk River. Not long behind were the Dutch, who began fur trading along the eastern end of the trail in 1614, only five years after Henry Hudson's exploratory trip up the river that bears his name; in 1624 they founded Fort Orange (now Albany) just south of the junction of the Hudson and Mohawk rivers. From there the West India Company carried on an active trade with the Iroquois, exchanging cloth, sewan, and wampum (beads used for decoration and trade), axes, kettles, and other iron goods for fur skins, to be shipped down the Hudson through the port of New Amsterdam (New York) to Europe.

Concerned about French incursions on fur trade at the eastern end of the trail, the West India Company in 1634 sent a party of three Dutchmen and five Mohawk guides to negotiate with the Iroquois. It was Herman Meyndertz van dan Bogaert, company surgeon and leader of the party, who left us the first written record of a trip along the trail. Traveling by foot and carrying backpacks, the party followed the trail from Fort Orange northwest to the Mohawk River and then along the south bank. Since it was mid-December, the trip was especially difficult, "because it snowed very often up to the height of a man." Combinations of snow and rain also swelled the streams they had to cross, making the trip doubly hard, as Bogaert described:

> This stream ran very fast; besides, big cakes of ice came drifting along, for the heavy rainfall...had set the ice drifting. We were in great danger, for if one of us had lost his footing it had cost us our lives; but God the Lord preserved us, and we came through safely. We were wet up to above the waist...

With the Mohawk River in the background, this Mohawk village has cabins and tents but no longhouses in view inside its wooden palisade. *(New York Public Library)*

Once on the other side, it often happened that their "shoes and stockings in a very short time were frozen as hard as armor."

Fortunately, they had little problem with accommodations; Iroquois villages, called castles, dotted the route and welcomed the travelers. In one castle they stayed with the chief, who personally cooked their meal of beans and maize and took them to hunt turkeys when they were unable to proceed "because all the footpaths had disappeared under the heavy snowfalls." One "famous hunter" named Sickarus wanted so much for them to stay with him that he "offered to carry our goods and to let us sleep and remain in his house as long as we liked."

In these castles, Bogaert saw some of the famous "long houses," buildings 80 to 100 paces long. While some castles, such as Canagere (modern Canajoharie), were "built on a hill, without any palisades or any defense," others were heavily defended with three rows of palisades. Nor did the party always reach accommodations; at one point the road became so difficult "that some of the savages had to stop in the forest and sleep in the snow. We went on, however, and reached a little cabin, where we slept." Like the cabin, not all the castles were inhabited; some were testimony to the battles that preceded the Europeans' arrival, as Bogaert noted:

...the savages pointed to a high mountain where their castle stood nine years before. They had been driven out by the Mahicans [sic], and after that time they did not want to live there.

In January 1635, the party finally arrived at the Oneida Castle, which lay south of the portage route between Oneida Lake and the Mohawk River. As Bogaert describes it:

...the savages showed me the branch of the river that passes by Fort Orange...This road was mostly full of birches and beautiful flat land for sowing...And we saw...a large river [the Mohawk] and on the other side thereof tremendously high land that seemed to lie in the clouds.

In the castle itself, their welcome was not all they might have hoped for, since the French had whetted the Oneidas' appetite for gifts:

...one of the council came to me, asking the reason for our coming into his land, and what we brought for him as a present. I told him that we did not bring any present, but that we only paid him a visit. He told us we were not worth anything, because we did not bring him a present...

By the 1790's a wide road extended on the north side of the Mohawk River, and much of the fertile valley land was under cultivation. (From New York Magazine, *March 1793)*

The same council member was dissatisfied with the prices offered by the Dutch traders, saying they were "scoundrels" because they did not pay enough for their beaver skins. At the end, however, they achieved their goal: an exclusive trading agreement between the eastern Iroquois—the Mohawks and the Oneidas—and the Dutch. The French meanwhile maintained a monopoly on fur trading on the western half of the trail.

A series of trading wars was thereby set in motion that was to affect the history of the Mohawk Trail for the next 150 years. The Iroquois, finding that the Dutch offered more favorable trading terms than did the French, expanded their supply of trade goods by exacting further tribute—in the form of furs—from the weaker tribes around them. At the same time, the Europeans moved into the first stage of a long-term battle, with the French in the north and west opposing first the Dutch in the south and east, and later the English, who in 1664 took over the territory and renamed Fort Orange as Albany and New Amsterdam as New York. Problems in the area were increased when the Europeans began to supply their valuable Iroquois allies with guns. The French were not without allies among the Iroquois, however, especially the "praying Indians" they had converted to Catholicism. While more than one French trader or missionary lost his life in Iroquois territory during this period, the

French and their allies also inflicted damage; in 1690, they penetrated almost to the eastern end of the Mohawk Trail, burning Schenectady.

During the following decades of alternating war and uneasy peace, most of the Mohawk Trail stayed in Iroquois hands. To ensure the continuation of their trade alliance with the Iroquois—which blossomed into a military alliance—the English confined their settlement to the eastern portion of the trail, leaving the western two-thirds of the trail to the Brotherhood of the Long House, who continued some fur trading with the French, especially at Forts Niagara and Oswego. Few outsiders passed through this territory in the early 18th century. One who did, Philadelphia naturalist John Bartram, noted in 1743 that the route was "fine level rich land most of the way and tall timber oak, birch, beech, ash, spruce, linden, elm...and maidenhair in abundance." Oswego he called "an infant settlement," where the whole navigation in the region was "carried on by the Indians themselves in bark canoes." Interlopers were viewed with suspicion, Swedish botanist Peter Kahn found when he went to view the "Great Falls at Niagara"; as he wrote to Bartram in 1750:

...The French there [at Fort Niagara] seemed much perplexed at my first coming, imagining I was an English officer who, under pretext of seeing Niagara Falls, came with some other view; but as soon as I shew'd them my passports they chang'd their behavior and received me with the greatest civility.

In the eastern portion of the trail—in the Mohawk Valley itself—European settlement began to change the face of the land. Palatine German and Scotch-Irish immigrants, along with Dutch and English smallholders, not content to work as tenant farmers for the large Hudson River landowners, started clearing and working small farms along the Mohawk and its main tributary, the Schoharie. The Mohawk Trail, once tamped only by moccasined feet, became firmer and wider under the impact of hobnailed boots and the hooves of cattle and horses. Gradually this part of the trail was widened to accommodate more traffic; for the first time, wheels began to cut ruts into the dirt path, as the farmers added food to the mix of goods traded along the trail. But even in the fertile Mohawk Valley settlement was sparse, for the area was the main battleground between the English and

French for control of the Mohawk Trail and of North America. By the last of these wars, the French and Indian War, the English soldiers had penetrated to the western end of the trail, all the way to Fort Niagara, and had effectively ended French trading south of the St. Lawrence Valley and the Great Lakes. The treaty ending the wars left the western part of the trail in Iroquois hands; indeed, the British "proclamation line of 1763" forbade settlement west of Fort Stanwix (now Rome). But in truth, the Mohawk Trail had come under English control, and with it the key to the continent.

By 1760, when the fighting ended, a thin line of European settlements had extended to Fort Stanwix, and the Mohawk Trail had become known as the King's Highway. Property owners were obliged to contribute time and labor to keep up the roads in their local areas; even Sir William Johnson, baronet of the Mohawk region, was assessed on the tax rolls for 10 days' work on the road, as his share of the maintenance. Much of the work involved clearing away each year's encroachment of underbrush; cutting back trees from the side, to widen the road; and "corduroying" swampy sections, which involved

Many of the early turnpikes were straight cuts, carved out of the mature forest, like this one with farmland beside it. (From Weld's Travels Through the States of North America...1795, 1796, and 1797, *London, 1800)*

247

placing 10- to 12-foot logs close together to provide a firmer, though often slippery, footing for people and animals. Large trees and other natural obstacles were usually left in place, and few bridges were built, although poles might be thrown across a stream or banks near fording places might be cut through and graded for easier crossing. During the short interval of peace, towns also began to develop, generally on the north side of the Mohawk, and by the 1770's some portions of the trail were made wide and straight enough for horse races to be held. But while the eastern portion of the trail was being improved, in the wilderness west of the European settlements narrow footpaths still prevailed. So stood the Mohawk Trail at the time of the American Revolution.

The Mohawk Valley was a dangerous place to live during the Revolution. The settlers who supported the Revolution were exposed on the northwestern frontier, in the early years far from any hope of support from their army. Aside from acting as the "breadbasket to the Revolution," their main contribution was to keep British forces (including their allies, the four easternmost Iroquois tribes) from passing eastward along the Mohawk Trail, in August of 1777 in the Battle of Oriskany, 10 miles east of Fort Stanwix.

Thereafter, while the armies were fighting the main battles elsewhere, Revolutionary supporters all along the frontier were subjected to heavy attacks by the Iroquois and by British sympathizers. The Iroquois attacks became so worrisome that in 1779 Washington sent some of his troops on the offensive along the Mohawk Trail, to aid Revolutionary supporters and to protect vital food supplies. These troops vigorously carried their attacks deep into Iroquois territory; by the time the war ended, they had broken Iroquois power. Many Iroquois followed their Loyalist allies north into Canada after their defeat; the rest were powerless against the political and economic moves made against them by the new Americans now in control of the Mohawk Trail.

The whole western portion of New York, centered on the trail, was opened to settlement at the end of the Revolutionary War. The remaining Iroquois were forced to sell or cede almost all of their land to the new governments and to retire to small reservations. Of the 18 million acres of land thus accumulated, a Military Tract of over 1.5 million acres was set aside in the Finger Lakes area for war veterans, who had been promised free land for their services. Some families moved into the area immediately, not waiting for legal arrangements to be completed; many more waited until 1790, when the surveying, demarcation, and naming of townships—many with classical names like Syracuse and Utica—were completed and lots were awarded to veterans or to those who had bought veterans' rights. After resolution of a title dispute between New York and Massachusetts, the rest of the land westward from the Finger Lakes to Lake Erie was also opened up for settlement, much of it being bought by financial investment companies, among them the Holland Land Company, which bought up the fertile Genesee Valley. One New England veteran, Eliphalet Stark, who in 1787 moved to the "Oneida Woods" on the frontier near Fort Stanwix, described the western New York wilderness at the time:

> ...it seemed like walking forever through an empty dark world of trees where the sun stopped in the upper branches, where the lakes were cold as Nantuckett [sic] water and as big as a Massachusetts county.

He noted that "if they ever got roads beyond the frontier at the carrying place at Fort Stanwix all of New England would be over to settle." How right he was.

The result of opening the Mohawk Trail was a migration the like of which had never been seen by this young country. From the Hudson Valley, from New Jersey, Pennsylvania and Maryland, but most of all from New England came veterans, farmers seeking better soil and fewer stones, young people after their own land, pioneers seeking "elbow room." The exodus from New England was so great that the name "Mohawk Trail" was extended to cover several of the routes that led from the Atlantic to Albany, routes that themselves were old native American trails, now taken over by the Europeans. Emigrants from Massachusetts took the Old Bay Path from Boston west through Worcester to Springfield, where they were joined by southern New Englanders who took the Connecticut Path which ran up the Connecticut River Valley; together they crossed the Berkshire Hills going northwest through Lebanon Springs to join the old Mohawk Trail at Albany. Others from northern New England crossed in southern Vermont, on what is now U.S. Route 2, to the Hudson Valley at Troy. Between 1790 and 1800, over 60,000 people moved along the trail to settle the lands between Rome, at the old demarcation line, and Buffalo; by 1810, nearly 200,000 had moved in. On a single February day in 1795, one observer counted over 500 sleighs passing through Albany on their way west.

Eliphalet Stark was wrong about one thing, though; he thought "...it will be a hundred years before they ever got roads to the [Great] Lakes through these forests." He underestimated his countrymen. In the 50 years after Stark arrived along the Mohawk, almost one million people moved into the western New York lands, building roads as they went. With the Mohawk Trail open, many other pioneers pushed straight on, past New York, moving westward along the strip of plain on the southern rim of Lake Erie and on out into the Great Plains of the Midwest. In the early days of this great migration, many people preferred to travel in winter; a frozen path, or even a frozen river surface, was much preferable to a muddy trail. Farmers, idled in the winter anyway, would arrive in time for spring planting, sometimes sending for the other family members only then. But the impulse to migrate was soon too strong to be bound by the seasons.

With long-distance traffic along the Mohawk Trail, roads became a public and commercial matter; local citizens could no longer maintain roads fit to handle such volume. To meet the needs of people traveling west, and the increasing volume of freight being shipped back east and down the Hudson, New Yorkers turned to other methods of building and maintaining roads. From 1790 on, New York State directly compensated those who built roads or bridges on what was then still state land. Lotteries were also used to raise money for road building, most successfully in 1797 to build the Great Genesee Road, a log and gravel road 64 feet wide running along the route of the old Mohawk Trail for 100 miles from Utica west to Geneva.

But most long-distance roadbuilding in this period was carried on by the turnpike method, in which stock companies financed the building of wider, firmer roads. Maintenance—and company profits, if any—came from tolls paid by travelers using the route; tollgates blocked the road at intervals, usually every 10 miles, and were opened to allow travelers through after payment of a toll. (Local travelers and worshippers on Sunday were exempt.) The first turnpike along the Mohawk Trail was established in 1797 between Schenectady and Albany; this 16-mile stretch of road was especially important because across it traveled freight from both the road and water routes, over the ancient portage between the Mohawk and the Hudson. Completed in 1805, it was soon followed by other turnpikes: the Mohawk Turnpike from Schenectady to Utica; the Rensselaer and Columbia Turnpike from Albany to Springfield, Massachusetts; and after the Great Genesee Road was converted to a turnpike, the extension of the road westward, first to Canandaigua and then all the way to Lake Erie, shortly after the War of 1812. These turnpikes were so heavily used that a shortcut was made, running south of the Mohawk River more sharply westward from Albany through Cherry Valley and Cazenovia, linking up with the main turnpike south of Oneida Lake. In most cases these highways followed the line of the old trails, although if the surveyors and engineers could remove a natural obstacle or cut through a shorter, straighter route, they had the power to do so. To meet the needs of wheeled traffic, entrepreneurs also found it profitable to place toll ferries at strategic water crossings, and wooden bridges, some of them covered, began to be built.

With the turnpike system in place, full access and communications were opened up along the whole route of the Mohawk Trail. Over these roads traveled hundreds of thousands of emigrants, many from the New England states but many others fresh from Europe, journeying from the port of New York over the easiest route to the west—the Mohawk Trail. Regular stagecoach lines followed—and sometimes even preceded the completion of—the turnpikes. The first weekly stage along the trail began in 1793 between Albany and Schenectady, and no sooner did the Great Genesee Road open than a stagecoach line was set up, delivering its passengers from Utica to the new Geneva Hotel in just three days. The stagecoaches carried not only passengers, but also mail, newspapers, and other important matter, such as banknotes and business documents, to the townspeople along the line. Sharing the road with stagecoaches, emigrant wagons, and local farm carts were teamsters and drovers, transporting goods and livestock along the line, mostly eastward for shipment down the Hudson. The wagoners, or teamsters, drove large canvas-covered wagons pulled by teams of four to eight horses; a wagoner would sometimes ride a horse near the wagon wheel, but more often would walk alongside the team, holding a line to the lead horse and guiding the team with a whip—and incidentally wearing footpaths by the side of the turnpike. Drovers, too, operated along the turnpikes, buying up animals along the route eastward and assembling a herd—often of cattle, hogs, even turkeys—to be sold at a market near the Hudson River.

To provide food and shelter for all these travelers, taverns, or "ordinaries," were set up all along the line; some places, such as near the crossroads at Albany, averaged as many as one tavern per mile. Each tavern tended to cater to a particular group of travelers; wagoners and drovers, who did not mix well, generally congregated at their own taverns, as did the more affluent travelers, such as those who could afford to charter a private coach. Many poorer emigrants camped alongside the road; the wagoners and drovers often carried oilcloths to provide rough cover for themselves and their horses, when taverns were overcrowded. Along the main routes, towns sprang up seemingly overnight and, as settlers spread out in all directions, feeder roads and auxiliary turnpikes were built. Drovers often preferred these less-traveled, softer-surfaced roads, since the harder-surfaced turnpikes tended to lame their animals. The turnpikes themselves were subjected to increasing use by heavily loaded wagons, which cut apart the road with their narrow wheels; some turnpike companies even offered toll-free passage to wagons with wide wheels, which would serve to roll down rather than carve up the roads. When turnpikes fell too far behind in maintenance, government inspectors forced them to suspend collection of tolls until the road was repaired. As settlement increased in western New York, the flow of people and supplies west began to be equaled by the flow of goods back east—grain, fruit, animals, lumber, and other produce—along the trail and down the Hudson to New York.

With canals and trains taking much of the traffic, taverns like Chauncey Jerome's on the Mohawk Turnpike in 1897 relied on local trade, if they survived at all. (By R. A. Grider)

Meanwhile, the water routes through the Mohawk cut were also being improved. Through the Revolutionary War period, the largest waterborne vehicles in the area were bateaux—flat, bargelike boats, poled or pulled from towpaths by eight to ten men—which could carry only one to two tons of freight. These loaded bateaux had to be pulled, like sledges, along the shore across portages and around falls and rapids on the Mohawk River; in 1797, Eliphalet Stark reported that it took 10 days for his wife and baby and furniture to travel from Albany to Old Fort Schuyler (Utica), and that "it took six yokes of oxen to get their bateau around the carry at Little Falls." He also reported "...if they ever get a canal around Little Falls and one across the carrying place at Fort Stanwix, these Mohawk Dutch will begin to see things happen along the river that will make their eyes pop." Stark was right again. Starting in the early 1790's, short stretches of canal were built to circumvent problem areas, and by 1796 the Mohawk water route was open from Schenectady west to Seneca Falls to flat-bottomed Durham boats, which could carry 15 to 16 tons and were large enough to have decks and sails. But while they cut the cost of shipping along the River, overland shipping costs for the farmers of western New York were still excessive. The cost of shipping a ton of grain from Buffalo to New York was $100 a ton, for example, while from Buffalo to Montreal the cost was only $30 a ton. These western New York farmers, and those of Ohio and the Midwest as well, began to try other routes for their produce—down the Ohio and Mississippi to New Orleans; up the Great Lakes-St. Lawrence Route to Montreal; or on turnpikes through the mountains to other ports, such as Baltimore or Pittsburgh.

At this point, New Yorkers made a crucial decision: to build an inland water route through the Mohawk cut, joining the Great Lakes with the Hudson and the Atlantic. Such a connection had been proposed as early as 1783, first by Irish-American engineer Christopher Colles, but the Erie Canal became a reality only through the efforts of some determined men, primarily DeWitt Clinton, later Governor of New York. Many people derided the project, calling it "Clinton's Ditch"; ironically, New York City's representatives were united in opposition to the project, which was to make their city the preeminent port of the country. The first Erie Canal was not an attempt to harness the rivers and lakes of the State, but rather was an independent cut and series of locks, running parallel with the Mohawk River for part of its course and rising 564 feet from Albany to Buffalo. While the eastern portion ran mostly on the south side of the Mohawk River (it was later rerouted to the north side), the western portion of the canal route was built somewhat north of the original Trail, passing through, and making the fortunes of, cities like Syracuse and Rochester. Construction of the Erie Canal, begun in 1817, was completed in 1825 with the ceremonial "Marriage of the Waters," when De Witt Clinton poured a bucket of Lake Erie water into the Atlantic Ocean off

New York City. Passengers immediately flocked to the canal, temporarily almost bankrupting the fledgling turnpike system, and the cost of shipping grain from Buffalo to Albany dropped from $100 a ton to $6. As a result, virtually all produce from the upper Mississippi and Ohio valleys was funneled through the Erie Canal to New York City, which then supplied the whole East Coast and Europe. New York had won a decisive victory over its rivals; by exploiting its control over the Mohawk cut, it had become "the Empire State."

On the new canal, the old bateaux and Durham boats were outclassed by heavy freight boats and passenger packets that carried 30 tons and, after 1830, up to 75 tons. Along with the freight came a flood of new immigrants from all over northern Europe, among them numerous Irish workers who helped to build the canal and stayed to settle along its route. Many of them went west singing songs about "Low bridge, everybody down," the warning to passengers who rode on the cabin roofs on sunny days; other songs recalled the animals on the towpaths, like the "mule named Sal," who pulled the boats along the canal. Emigrants of the time may have been packed in crowded boats—"like two mice in a mitten" one described it—but all the way to the "Far West" of Illinois, Indiana, Wisconsin, Minnesota, and Michigan they sang of the people who "dug a mighty ditch" to let them "...sail upon the waters to Mich-i-gan-i-ay..." With the steady flow of immigrants, and the plentiful supply of raw materials and water power, industry also began to build up along the canal, especially as the advent of the steamboat further increased the canal's carrying capacity. The popularity of the canal did not cause the turnpike system to collapse, however, for there was soon traffic enough for both. Indeed, the Erie Canal rapidly became so crowded with freight that most passengers, except for the long-distance emigrants seeking cheap transportation, preferred the faster stagecoach lines, which had also continued to carry the mail. More importantly, the canal was closed by ice four to five months a year, while in winter the stagecoach lines set speed records, sometimes over frozen roads, but more often along the hard ice surface of the Mohawk River, the Erie Canal, and even, moving their route north for the season, along the frozen southern edge of Lake Ontario. But soon both road and canal had a new rival: the railroad.

The first railroad built along the Mohawk Trail was between Albany and Schenectady in 1831, a train of stagecoaches linked together, running on wooden tracks laid over granite blocks. Originally conceived as supplementing water routes, many short, unconnected railroad lines, often built to different specifications, were established along the trail in the 1830's. As they began to threaten the dominance of the state-controlled canal, railroads were placed under heavy restrictions. However, the freight passing through the Mohawk Trail soon be-

came more than the Erie Canal could handle, even after expansion and improvements in the 1830's and 1840's, and by 1851 railroads were able to operate freely. The short railroad lines began to join together; along the Mohawk cut they formed the New York Central, advertised as "the only water level route to the West," which ran close to the route of the Erie Canal. With the Erie Canal and the New York Central Railroad in place, a very high proportion of the long-distance freight from the expanding West moved through the Mohawk cut, and New York consolidated an indisputable position as the trade and financial center of the nation.

With the arrival of the railroad, the turnpike system was finished. Even the best of the turnpike companies had paid only small dividends to their stockholders, and many had from the beginning hovered near bankruptcy, because of the cost of maintaining the roads. They made one last bid for life: in the 1840's, Russian-style plank roads began to be built in the timber-rich country along much of the Mohawk Trail. Planks eight feet long were placed horizontally over beams buried lengthwise in the earth; usually only the more heavily traveled side of the turnpike was planked, sometimes being relocated to provide easier grades than did the original turnpikes. Planked roads could carry heavier loads and were passable no matter what the weather; unfortunately, the planks decayed quickly and the resulting roads became dangerous. Both plank roads and ordinary turnpikes thereafter fell into disrepair, and were surrendered to the state government by the bankrupt companies. By 1871 only the easternmost 10 miles of the Great Western Turnpike leading into Albany was still operating as an independent company. Many taverns along the way were converted into private homes, and the few surviving stagecoach lines moved to run connecting lines between rural towns and the railroads and canals, a purpose they served for several decades until automobiles became common. Towns along the turnpikes became backwater villages, except for those few that had established themselves as resorts, especially those along the Finger Lakes or those with mineral springs, which attracted vacationers from New England and southern New York.

The railroad's impact on the Mohawk Trail was even greater, however, for once engineers had the ability to cross mountains with ease, the route through the Appalachians lost some of its natural advantage. Goods and people, including millions of immigrants from northern and later southern and eastern Europe, continued to pass through the Mohawk cut on the New York Central Railroad; luxury express trains like the Twentieth Century Limited and the Empire State Express set speed records along the level route from New York to Chicago. But other east-west routes through the mountains, even though they could not match the New York Central's speed, began to take an increasingly larger share of the traffic. The Erie Canal, too, lost its predominance in the face of this double shift to the railroad and away from the Mohawk route. New York State revived the canal in the early 20th century by almost doubling its width and partly rerouting it, in the east canalizing the north side of the Mohawk River itself, and in the west passing north of Syracuse, before rejoining the old route. Completed in 1918 and made part of the State's Barge Canal System, the revamped canal could take ships large enough to carry 2,500-ton loads from distant Great Lakes ports through to New York without reloading. Even so, it gradually lost ground to other routes. While it continued state-subsidized operations, carrying mostly grain and petroleum products, by mid-century it had ceased to be a major factor in the nation's economy, especially after the opening of the St. Lawrence Seaway in 1959.

The advent of the automobile and the substantial improvement in engineering methods in the early 20th century continued the diversion of traffic through artificial cuts in the Appalachians, rather than through the one natural cut along the Mohawk. While New York City retained its importance as a financial center, it was as the crossroads of many routes, not the terminus of just one. Upstate New York was, to a large extent, bypassed by the rest of the country. But the highway system that was revived in the automobile era—now serving more local than national needs—often still followed the old routes. Modern travelers on the Massachusetts Turnpike (Interstate 90) or riding the rail line from Boston to Albany roughly follow the route taken by early New Englanders

moving west along the Mohawk Trail. Commuters on New York State Route 5 (State Street) between Albany and Schenectady are tracing the route of the old portage that was part of virtually every passage along the Mohawk, before the Erie Canal cut a direct connection to the Hudson. Riders taking that route—the old Mohawk Turnpike—through the heavily industrialized area on the north bank of the Mohawk River are following one leg of the original Mohawk Trail, while the New York State Thruway (Interstate 90) for a stretch follows the general line of the other leg, running south of the river before crossing short of the old fording place at Utica, and then following the canal and railroad routes. Most tourists along U.S. Route 20, with its beautiful views along the escarpment that edges the wide Mohawk Valley, would probably be surprised to learn that they are taking the shortcut route of the Great Western Turnpike, later joined by State Route 5 along the Great Genesee Road, which continues to Buffalo and south of Lake Erie out to Chicago. Peter Wilson, Chief of the Cayugas, probably put it best in an 1847 speech before the New-York Historical Society:

The Empire State, as you love to call it, was once laced by our trails from Albany to Buffalo; trails that we have trod for centuries; trails worn so deep by the feet of the Iroquois that they became your roads of travel, as your possessions gradually ate into those of my people. Your roads still traverse those same lines of communication which bound one part of the Long House to the other.

New Yorkers had good reason for celebrating the opening of the Erie Canal, for it would make their city a world metropolis. (Museum of the City of New York)

Selective Bibliography

Flick, Alexander C., ed. *History of the State of New York,* 10 vol. (New York: Columbia University Press, 1933–1935). An excellent resource, especially Volume V, which includes a short history of transportation in New York State.

Freedgood, Seymour, and the Editors of Time-Life Books. *The Gateway States: New Jersey, New York.* (New York: Times, Inc., 1967). Part of the Time-Life Library of America. A handy historical overview of the area, with useful maps of the trails and routes at various stages.

Hislop, Codman. *The Mohawk.* (New York: Rinehart & Co., Inc., 1948). Part of the Rivers of America Series. An informal, popularly written history of the trails and waterways of the Mohawk Valley, with much colorful detail.

Hulbert, Archer B. *Historic Highways of America,* 17 vol. (Cleveland, Ohio: Arthur H. Clark Co., 1902–1905). Described by the author as "a collection of monographs of varying quality written with youthful enthusiasm by the author, who traversed in good part the main pioneer roads and canals of the eastern portion of the United States."

————. *The Paths of Inland Commerce: A Chronicle of Trail, Road, and Waterway.* (New Haven: Yale University Press, 1920). An attractively written overview of the development of human pathways in the eastern United States.

Jameson, J. F., ed. and trans. *Narratives of New Netherland.* (New York: 1909). A collection of early accounts.

Wright, Louis B., and Elaine W. Fowler, eds. *The Moving Frontier.* (New York: Delacorte Press, 1972). "North America Seen Through the Eyes of Its Pioneer Discoverers."

Writer's Program of the Works Project Administration in the State of New York. *New York: A Guide to the Empire State.* (New York: Oxford University Press, 1940). Part of the American Guide Series. Unparalleled compilation of interesting historical detail for travelers.

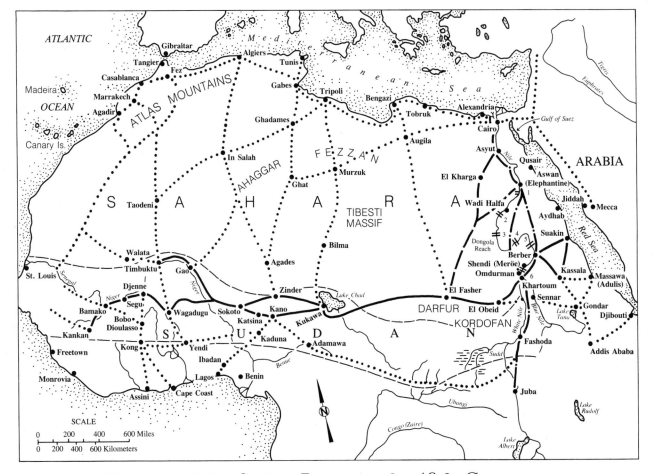

The Nile Route and the Sudan Route in the 19th Century

———— Main Sudan Routes

– – – – Derib el Arba'in (Track of the 40 Days)

– · – · – ·

········ Main Connecting Routes

– – – – – Sahel Corridor

= Cataracts

The Nile Route and the Sudan Route

In January of 1885 the famous British general Charles George Gordon—loved and even revered by many for his efforts to end slavery in the eastern Sudan a decade earlier—lost his life in the great city of Khartoum. Ordered to evacuate the city, he sent some people down the Nile with repeated requests for reinforcements. Besieged by the Sudanese forces, including the fierce fighters the British called Dervishes, Gordon learned in a personal note from their leader, the Mahdi, that his ship did not pass through:

> To Gordon Pasha of Khartoum: may God guide him into the path of virtue, amen!
>
> Know that your small steamer, named *Abbas*—which you sent with the intention of forwarding your news to Cairo, by way of Dongola...has been captured by the will of God.
>
> Those who believed in us as Mahdi, and surrendered, have been delivered; and those who did not were destroyed...

Those who had stayed with Gordon died with him when the city fell, for the British relief expedition, sent in reluctant response to Gordon's urgent pleas, arrived just two days too late to help their allies and compatriots.

The importance of Khartoum lay in its location. Occupying a triangle of land just above the juncture of the Blue Nile (Bahr el Azraq) and the White Nile (Bahr el Abiad) it lay in the path of two of the most ancient routes in human history. The routes of the Sudan and the Nile form a lopsided cross. The Nile forms the main north-south axis in East Africa. From its many-armed Mediterranean delta, it cuts south, at first directly and then in a succession of curves both small and large, its progress interrupted by six cataracts. The White Nile—with its main tributaries, the Atbara and the Blue Nile, both draining the Ethiopian highlands—winds its way past the great papyrus marshes called the Sudd into the Kenya highlands and far beyond Lake Victoria to its source over 4,150 miles from the Mediterranean. The Nile is easily navigable only up to the First Cataract; south of that the river is forced into an often-narrow course between sandstone palisades, with boat passage made difficult by rocks and shoals, except for one long, readily navigable stretch called the Dongola Reach, between the Third and Fourth Cataracts. As a result, travelers often followed land routes along the banks of the Nile, or cut across the deserts, avoiding the lengthy loops of the great river.

The other main axis of travel in East Africa runs east-west, following the Sahel Corridor, a strip of mixed savannah and grassland that runs along the southern fringe of the Sahara Desert from West Africa eastward, skirting the Ethiopian highlands and the coastal hills to the shores of Eritrea on the Red Sea. This region—generally called the Sudan (orginally Bilad al-Sudan, or Land of the Blacks)—has been a major human passageway for millennia.

Another main land route cuts from the Nile, near

This model of a Nile riverboat dates from around 4,000 years ago. (Science Museum, London)

where it begins its great S-curve, to the El Kharga Oasis and then arcs gently southwestward across the Sahara to the ancient Sudanese crossroads of El Fasher, in the region called Darfur. This trail is the famous Derib el Arba'in – the Track of the Forty Days.

The Sudan and Nile routes are two of the oldest pathways in the world, for human beings seem to have evolved in the savannahs of east-central Africa, notably in the region of the great Rift Valleys, roughly 30-mile-wide divides in the Earth's crust, where East Africa is

slowly being ripped away from the rest of the continent. Over the eons of human evolution in Africa, these were main routes of migration, as human beings spread throughout the continents and across land bridges to the rest of the world.

By about 10,000 years ago, the peoples of the world had differentiated into many races, several of them in Africa. South of the Sudan and Nile lived dark-skinned Negroid peoples, while the Blue and White Nile regions around modern Khartoum were occupied by Nilo-

Saharans, also dark-skinned but generally taller and thinner. The rest of habitable Africa was occupied by peoples who originated in the Arabian Peninsula: Berbers along the coastal strip of northern Africa and Cushites in the Ethiopian highlands. The Egyptians of the lower Nile were a mixture of these last two. While humans remained primarily hunters and food-gatherers, they occupied forests and grasslands that supported them; but from about 5000 B.C. new practices of cultivating grains and domesticating animals began to produce radical changes in the way of life along the Sudan and Nile Valley routes.

The Sahel Corridor was superbly adapted to the nomadic way of life, in which humans led their herds to different seasonal pastures. The practice of herding spread into the Sudan by around 3000 B.C., and both the Cushites and the Nilo-Saharans adopted the pastoral way of life, as did the Negroes somewhat later. Nomadic movement within the Sahel Corridor was generally north-south, with herds grazing near the Sahara's edge in winter and moving south toward the moister equatorial forests in summer. The Sudan Route saw no regular flow of traffic along its east-west axis, in these times being primarily a migration route.

In Egypt, the nomadic life was less appropriate and attractive than the sedentary agricultural life. While the Nile Valley offered only a narrow fertile strip—which some have called a 15-mile-wide oasis in the Sahara Desert—the seasonal flooding of the Nile brought both rich silt and irrigation to these early farmers. Egyptians were enabled to adopt a settled life, building permanent, sometimes walled villages which gradually grew into cities. In approximately 3000 B.C., Upper (southern) and Lower (the delta) Egypt were combined under Menes, the river being the center of the kingdom's existence. The kingdom's boundary was set at the First Cataract, just south of Elephantine Island (near modern Aswan), but its range of contact extended much further.

From the people of Nubia, the region between the First and Second Cataracts, the Egyptians secured hardwood and ivory, and later granite for the great tombs that characterize Egypt in the period of the Old Kingdom. They also sent occasional military expeditions south along the Nile, exacting tribute while, in the process, spreading Egyptian culture and skills. The Pharaoh Snefru, of the pyramid-building Fourth Dynasty in the 28th century B.C., boasted of his campaign to Nubia: "I brought back

The famous Egyptian pyramids dominated the lower Nile from very early times. (From Clara Erskine Clement's Egypt, *1903)*

seven thousand prisoners, and two hundred thousand cat-tle, large and small." In these early times, goods from the south were often collected at the entrepôt of Elephantine—called "The Door to the South"—and then shipped down the Nile to Thebes and Memphis.

The earliest boats on the Nile seem to have been built of papyrus, designed to be rowed, poled, towed from the riverbank, or sailed upstream with the prevailing northerly winds of the region. Rowing and sailing were—and would remain until modern times—the dominant modes of Nile travel between the delta and the First Cataract. But the cataract region required more control than sailing could provide, so rowing and towing were in order, though both were difficult in either low water or flood times. Later Nile boats were fashioned of Nubian hardwood, the better to carry the massive blocks of granite needed for the pharaoh's pyramids. By about 2300 B.C., the Egyptians had even built a canal around the First Cataract to enable heavily laden boats to pass downriver more freely.

During these early times, trade goods were also reaching Egypt from the Land of Punt on the Red Sea coast, despite the obstacles of the Red Sea hills and the Ethiopian highlands. By 2800 B.C., when the Egyptians decided to try reaching Punt by sea, this trade route was already ancient, for early records describe how Punt was "heard of from mouth to mouth by hearsay of the ancestors. The marvels brought thence...were brought from one to another...as a return for many payments." These included not only gold from the Red Sea hills, but spices from the East, including Arabia and at some early point also India. During some periods the Egyptians opened a canal between one of the easterly arms of the Nile and the Gulf of Suez, allowing ships to sail down to Punt and return directly by water. But more often goods were brought overland by donkey caravan from various Red Sea ports to Coptos, just north of Thebes, and then fer-ried up or down river. This trade, too, was under the supervision of the lords of Elephantine.

The Egyptians sent other expeditions southwest-ward into the Sudan. The tombs at Aswan include those of caravan leaders whose exploits make their epitaphs. One such leader, named Harkhuf, made four exploratory ex-peditions to the land of Yam, apparently somewhere in the Sudan, the round trips each taking as long as eight months. At least one of these expeditions left "by the Elephantine Road," and is thought to have angled westward through smaller oases, including Selima, to meet with the Derib el Arba'in (the Track of the Forty Days, which may already have been in use) to Darfur. He may even have proceeded further west, for on his third journey, Harkhuf found that the king of Yam had gone "to smite Temeh [his enemy] as far as the western corner of heaven." Harkhuf followed, and on his return brought incense, ebony, ivory, and leopard-skins. His fourth expedition

yielded a dancing dwarf (possibly a Pygmy) who greatly delighted Pharaoh Pepi II. Camels and horses being un-known in Egypt and undomesticated anywhere at this time, the caravans' pack animals were donkeys; on Harkhuf's third trip they included 300 donkeys, 100 car-rying trade goods, 100 food, and 100 water.

But soon after Harkhuf's journeys, Egyptian unity collapsed with the death of the last pharaoh of the Old Kingdom. Nubians and Sudanese who had once served in Egyptian armies, notably against desert nomads attack-ing trade routes, now themselves attacked Egypt. The great cities of ancient Egypt—the political capital of Memphis near the delta and Thebes further upriver, near which were built the great pyramids of the Valley of the Kings—declined as trade with the outer world was cut off. The resulting chaos is clear in the Ipuwer Papyrus:

> The Palace has been overthrown. Princes are starv-ing, the masses triumphant; noble ladies go hungry; owners of fine clothes are in rags. Plunder and squalor are universal. Great and small say: "I wish I were dead." The harvester is robbed of his posses-sions. The storehouses are empty and their keepers lie dead upon the ground. There have been terrible scenes. The peasant goes out to plough weapon in hand. Men are forced to eat food that used to be given to poultry and pigs. No skilled laborers are working, for these enemies of their country have ruined their crafts. People's faces are blanched with terror for the criminals are at large. Laughter has died out of the land. The songs of the musicians have turned to a dirge. All is in ruins.

During these Dark Ages of Egypt, new nomadic peoples moved into Nubia from somewhere along the Sahel Corridor.

After a century or more of decline, Egypt was reunited in the Middle Kingdom under a new dynasty based in Thebes. The Theban princes quickly moved to re-establish trade with, and then dominion over, the peo-ple of the Middle Nile. Soldiers drove up the Nile, establishing a series of 14 forts beyond Elephantine, with most concentrated in the difficult stretch before and after the Second Cataract. At Iken, just past Wadi Halfa, cargo was probably shifted into the smaller boats needed to negotiate the rocky waters of the upper Nile, while the frontier was guarded by a final fort at Semna, 25 miles beyond the Second Cataract. These forts protected river traffic and associated caravan routes from the depredations of nomads in the most vulnerable parts of the route and allowed Egyptian traders to trade directly with the more friendly people of Kush. At the Kush capital of Kerma, just beyond the Third Cataract and at the beginning of the Dongola Reach, the Egyptians built a trading post on an island in the river. Although fortified, Kerma seems to have been a welcome—or at least accepted—part of the Kush community. Egyptian artisans of all kinds—potters,

Travelers on the Track of the Forty Days or crossing the desert loops of the Nile were always vulnerable to violent sandstorms. (From Clara Erskine Clement's Egypt, *1903)*

jewelers, metalworkers, cabinetmakers, and the like—settled in increasing numbers as the Kush culture became increasingly Egyptianized.

This trade route was broken in the 18th century B.C., when Egypt was invaded by peoples from western Asia; these invaders, the Hyksos, are noted primarily for bringing Egypt the horse and chariot, as well as new bronze weapons, superior to Egypt's copper ones. When the Theban princes revived a century later, their forces of the "New Kingdom" were strengthened by new weapons.

Pressing southward, Egypt this time went well past Nubia and Kush to the Dongola Reach and beyond the Fifth Cataract. She may even have spread her dominion to Meroë (near modern Shendi), between the Fifth and Sixth Cataracts. Trade certainly extended even further; Egyptian beads from this period have been found even beyond Juba, far up the Nile, well south of the Sudd. Egyptian traders themselves probably did not penetrate so deep into Africa, however, operating instead through middlemen. For the first time the Egyptians had reached far enough south to encounter large numbers of Negroes, who increasingly figure in Egyptian art of the period. Tuthmosis I in the 16th century B.C. had no doubt about his achievements in the New Kingdom, boasting that he had "penetrated valleys which the royal ancestors knew not, which the wearers of the double diadem had not seen...his name had penetrated the whole earth."

Despite occasional rebellion, a relative peace settled on the Nile. Egypt reoccupied the old forts in Nubia and cleared the canal at the First Cataract, conducting periodic punitive expeditions against desert nomads who threatened the flow of traffic along the Nile. Most desired of the goods from the south was the "gold of the mountains of Kush" lauded in many Egyptian inscriptions. But Nubian-built boats also brought to Egypt a wide variety of other items, ranging from ebony and ivory to ostrich feathers and fly-whisks made from giraffe tails, plus perfumes, oils, and some raw materials. A few hundred slaves a year, obtained by raiding Negro villages further to the south, completed the annual tribute sent north on the Nile, probably transferred to larger ships at Iken. Trade goods were still arriving by various overland caravan routes from the Red Sea; and in the 15th century B.C. Queen Hatshepsut resumed sea trade with the Land of Punt. Large numbers of Egyptian administrators were sent south, and indeed the region was sufficiently peaceful that the market towns and administrative centers became more important than the forts built to guard the Nile.

But by the 13th century B.C., Egypt's central government began to rely to an ever-greater extent on Nubian mercenaries and lapsed into civil war. At some point in this period, Kush moved its capital further north to the region of Napata, just beyond Dongola Reach and the Fourth Cataract, although Meroë remained its southern capital; the two being separated by a great bend in the

Nile, communication was maintained by a caravan route across the great arid bulge of land. By the 10th century B.C., Kush was effectively independent, regarding herself as the protector of all that was best in the Egyptian civilization, and expanding into Egypt itself. During the eighth century, the kings of Napata pushed north to the delta, bringing the royal line of Kush to Egypt itself.

But the Kushite reign was ended within a century by Assyrians from the East, who overwhelmed the people of the Nile with their new iron-tipped weapons. Stopped temporarily from entering Egypt in 701 B.C. by a plague in Palestine, the Assyrians swarmed into the Nile Valley in 671 B.C., devastating Thebes. The shock of that sacking was felt throughout the ancient world; 50 years later, foretelling doom for the Assyrians themselves, the prophet Nahum asked:

Art thou better than Ne-Amen [Thebes] that was situate among the canals, and that had the Nile round about it for a rampart and a wall? Kush and Egypt were her strength...Yet she was carried away, she went into captivity: her young children were dashed in pieces at the top of all the streets: and they cast lots for her honorable men, and all her great men were bound in chains.

It was in these campaigns that camels seem to have made their first appearance in Egypt; they did not, however, become widely used in these early centuries, for they did not breed well in the Nile Valley. When the over-extended Assyrians withdrew their garrison, the Egyptians recaptured the royal line for themselves, driving south, sacking Napata, and establishing a permanent southern frontier against Kush at the Second Cataract.

Although defeated by the Egyptians, the kingdom of Kush was far from ended. Shifting its capital back to Meroë, it based its revival in large part on the iron technology learned from the Assyrians. Meroë, with its ready access to both iron ore and wood for the smelting process (at first a closely guarded royal secret), became the ironworking center for East Africa; its slag heaps are still in evidence today. In this period Kush extended westward into the Sudan, at least as far as the region of Kordofan, between Darfur and the Nile. Caravan routes through the Ethiopian highlands also brought Meroë into contact with international traders on the Spice Route. Indeed, Kush became so prosperous that its huge herds of cattle, sheep, and especially goats apparently overgrazed the region, over the centuries turning the once-fertile banks of the Dongola Reach into unproductive desert.

The days of Egypt's greatness were gone, and a succession of weak dynasties made her prey to the great empire-builders from Eurasia, first the Persians, then the Greeks. In 332 B.C. Alexander the Great marched into Egypt almost unopposed—preceded, it is true, by reports

of his astonishing success against the far-more-numerous Persian forces in the East. With extraordinary prescience, he chose the site of an obscure fishing village on a western arm of the Nile's delta as the site for his Egyptian capital and main seaport, soon named Alexandria. After Alexander's death in the East, Egypt fell to the Greek general Ptolemy. Under the Ptolemaic dynasty, Alexandria grew into a true capital, not just of Egypt but of the Western world, attracting some of the best and brightest thinkers as well as traders from all directions—to whom the 600-foot-high lighthouse, on the island of Pharos, marking Alexandria's harbor, was one of the world's Seven Wonders.

In Ptolemaic Egypt, the Nile and Sudan were almost a backwater. Europeans were far more interested in the Spice Route, which began on the Red Sea, than in the tarnished wonders of the Nile. To be sure, some Greeks traded on the Nile, but the region south of the Second Cataract held few charms. The kings of Meroë had long since withdrawn from Napata, and the nomads of the Sudan raided the middle reaches of the Nile freely.

The same was initially true of the Romans, who added Egypt to their growing empire near the beginning of the first century B.C. But the Kushites brought themselves to Rome's attention by raiding Aswan (Elephantine) and nearby Philae—and wrecking statues of Caesar Augustus—while the local garrison was on a mission in Arabia. The Romans responded with a punitive expedition south, razing Napata and fortifying the region above Dongola Reach. In the middle of the first century A.D., the Roman emperor Nero sent a scouting party up the Nile, to assess if the Sudan was worth conquering; their report was that it was too poor to bother with. In this period, Kush was also oriented mainly toward the East. Overland routes from the port of Adulis (modern Massawa) on the Red Sea coast to the east and from the inland city of Axum connected Meroë with the Spice Route, opening it to Greek, Arabian, and Indian influences. The kingdom of Axum also traded with the peoples of the Ethiopian hills, conducting silent barter of cattle, salt, and iron for precious gold nuggets.

The middle Nile, between Meroë and Roman Egypt was, for a time, a kind of no-man's land, with nomadic marauders discouraging long-distance trade. Egypt, drained by heavy grain tribute to Rome, was also entering a steep decline; villages became depopulated, irrigation systems were abandoned, riots were common in the main cities, and Upper Egypt itself became fair game for desert brigands—among whom were counted numerous dispossessed Nile Valley farmers. Even the great city of Alexandria was besieged and sacked. In this period, especially between 250 and 350 A.D., Christianity spread in Egypt—indeed, many Christians, attempting to avoid the havoc of those turbulent times, chose to retire to the desert, adopting the monk's life.

In the third century A.D., the Romans attempted to calm the region—not by demanding tribute, but by paying subsidies to border nomads in return for promises of peace. Although tribute was paid for some time, little tranquility resulted. In the mid-fifth century, a Roman army even marched up the Nile Valley against these nomads—and was roundly defeated. In the mid-sixth century, when Rome itself had fallen and Egypt was under the Eastern (Byzantine) Roman Empire, these unruly outlanders were gradually converted to Christianity, at least to some extent. Indeed, Christian items from Byzantine Egypt found their way, via the hand-to-hand tribal trading of the Sudan Route, all the way to West Africa; Europeans, arriving by sea centuries later, found copies made by bronzeworkers in what later came to be called the Gold Coast.

The Kushite kingdom of Meroë, meanwhile, had ceased to exist. We have no store of written records like those from earlier times to tell us the tale, but an inscription from northern Abyssinia relates that the king of Axum sacked Meroë and destroyed the kingdom, complaining of the Kushites:

Twice and thrice they had broken their solemn oaths, and had killed their neighbors without mercy, and they had stripped our deputies and messengers whom I sent to enquire into their raids, and had stolen their weapons and belongings. And as I had warned them, and they would not listen but refused to cease from their evil deeds and betook themselves to flight, I made war on them...They fled without making a stand, and I pursued them for 23 days, killing some and capturing others...I burnt their towns, both those built of bricks and those built of reeds, and my army carried off their food and copper and iron...and destroyed the statues in their temples, their granaries, and cotton trees and cast them into the the river Seda [Nile].

Pushed into the Sudan, the Kushites seem to have settled in Kordofan (a part of their territory for many centuries since) and Darfur. They may also have penetrated further west in the Sudan, to the regions of Tibesti and Lake Chad, where later nations, notably Bornu, tell of their links with peoples from the East.

While Egypt proper languished under Byzantine rule and the middle Nile saw an ever-changing array of nominally Christian petty kingdoms along its banks, a new power was approaching the land, which would change the face of the Nile and the Sudan: the religion of Islam. Only eight years after the death of the Prophet Mohammed in 632 A.D., Arab conquerors under his banner carried Islam into Egypt. They also quickly moved across the Red Sea to take the main Axum ports, in the process isolating the Christian kingdoms of Abyssinia and the upper Nile. Over the next two years, the Moslem Arabs invaded Nubia; apparently the Christian nations united against them, for the Arab general—after besieging the city of Old Dongola with catapults—made a treaty with the Nubian king, whose territory was described as reaching "from the frontier of Aswan to the frontier of Alwa [near modern Khartoum]." Under the terms of the peace treaty, the Nubians were to send 400 slaves annually to Aswan, while the Arabs in return gave the Nubians horses, cloth, and grains such as wheat, barley, and lentils. Trade and traffic resumed on the Nile, and lasted under the terms of this treaty for the next six centuries, with occasional interruptions. Other treaties required the peoples of the Middle Nile to provide the Egyptians with camels; camels were provided by the Sudan for many centuries, with some camel-breeding

Despite the severe heat and dryness of the area, the crossroads of the Nile and Sudan routes have always held a trading center, such as Sennar, shown here in the 19th century. (By Linant de Bellefonds, Ashmolean Museum)

Although it looks impregnable, the Cairo Citadel fell easily to Europeans. (From Description de l'Egypte, *1822)*

centers of the central Sudan, notably Agades, later sending a yearly caravan of many thousands of camels to serve Egypt's needs.

Like Christianity, early Islam was characterized by a wide variety of major and minor sects; Egypt and the Sudan supplied an attractive home to many religious refugees over the centuries. In the mid-eighth century some crossed the Red Sea from Arabia and settled in the region of Sennar, on the Blue Nile. Others moved overland into Egypt and then up the Nile, settling in the southern lands and converting many local settlers, whose Christianity was, in any case, lightly rooted. By the 10th century, a large number of these Moslems had colonized Nubian lands; one administrator, called the Lord of the Mountain, was even authorized to control the traffic at the Egyptian border at the Second Cataract. South of the border, where once the kings of Kush had reigned, there existed only a rude barter economy, based on slaves, cattle, camels, iron, and grain. Moslem control in the region expanded gradually, reaching part-way along the Sudan Route to Darfur by the 12th century. The remaining Christians were mostly pushed westward in the Sudan — or isolated in the mountain kingdom of Abyssinia. (It was word of these Christian remnants that gave credence to the medieval myth of a Christian kingdom ruled by one Prester John.)

In the same period, Islam was advancing along the Sudan Route from the west, introduced by traders and migrants who had followed the ancient caravan routes across the Sahara. Many of these converts had even made the many-months-long *hajj*, the prescribed pilgrimage to Mecca; but rather than following the geographically natural route across the Sahel Corridor — which would have

taken them through disordered infidel countries — they grouped together in caravans to cross the Sahara to North Africa and took the coast route eastward to Cairo and then on to Arabia. The Sudan Route had yet to be adopted as a main east-west corridor.

This pattern was soon to be changed by events in the Sudan, in Cairo, and in Baghdad. To ensure their control over unruly nobles, Islamic caliphs had long employed a personal military corps of warrior-slaves, mostly Mongols or Turks; but by 1250 these Mamelukes (Slaves) were strong enough to take control of Egypt in their own right. Less than a decade later the great Moslem center of Baghdad was sacked by Mongol invaders from the East. The result of these two convulsions in the Moslem world sent waves of refugees — many of them skilled or learned people — fleeing into the Sudan. Most of the remaining Christian kingdoms in the Sahel Corridor fell to the Moslems within a century, while the tiny kingdom of Alwa, centered near modern Khartoum, lasted somewhat longer, and only mountain-fast Abyssinia survived the Moslem flood. A 16th century visitor reported of the Alwa region only the remains of the Christian affiliation:

> ...there are in it a hundred and fifty churches which still contain crucifixes and effigies of Our Lady, and other effigies painted on the walls, and all old... These churches are all in old ancient castles which are throughout the country; and as many castles there are, so many churches...

The Moslem groups were far from united, operating in the region in a free-for-all way. One 13th century leader, named Afram, who was operating "thirty-three marches south of Dongola," reported that "the Moslem forces had brought fear and consternation to all tribes of the land of the blacks. For they had penetrated districts where no army had even been before, unless it were that of Alexander the Great." By the late 14th century, Arab emigrants had extended their power westward to Lake Chad, where they were a decisive factor in the formation of a new dynasty in the kingdom of Bornu (Kanem). The Bornuese—who had been converted to Islam long before and whose sovereignty had extended from West Africa eastward almost to Darfur—sent a written complaint to the Mameluke ruler in Cairo, accusing the Arabs of pillaging the region and selling captives as slaves. The clash of these two Moslem groups, of differing traditions, prevented the Sahel Corridor from developing into a settled trade route, and most Sudanese trade continued to be conducted with the north across the Sahara. Even in the mid-14th century, the great Moslem traveler Ibn Battuta, who had crossed the Sahara to Timbuktu, in West Africa, chose to return north across the eastern Sahara, rather than on the Sudan Route.

But if the upper Nile and the Sahel Corridor were not flourishing highways in this period, the lower Nile certainly was. Ibn Battuta reported that:

...in Cairo there are twelve thousand water-carriers who transport water on camels, and thirty thousand hirers of mules and donkeys, and that on its Nile there are thirty-six thousand vessels belonging to the Sultan and his subjects, which sail upstream to Upper Egypt and downstream to Alexandria and Damietta, laden with goods and commodities of all kinds.

Cairo itself was in this period one of the greatest of all the Moslem cities. Ibn Battuta certainly felt that way about the city he knew as Misr, calling it:

...mother of cities and seat of the Pharaoh the tyrant, mistress of broad provinces and fruitful lands, boundless in multitude of buildings, peerless in beauty and splendor, the meeting-place of comer and goer, the stopping-place of feeble and strong. Therein is what you will of learned and simple, grave and gay, prudent and foolish, base and noble, of high estate and low estate, unknown and famous; she surges as the waves of the sea with her throngs of folk and can scarce contain them for all the capacity of her situation and sustaining power... She has as her peculiar possession the majestic Nile, which dispenses her district from the need of entreating the distillation [of rain].

Cairo had always been a focus for the Moslem pilgrims of Africa, who generally headed for this great city on their way to Mecca. From the Sudan, even from

the west coast of Africa, they made their way across the desolate Sahara to intermediate staging cities like Fez, Marrakech, Sijilmasa, and Tripoli; this Maghribi caravan then followed the coast road through Aujila and the Siwa Oasis to Cairo. From the arrival of Islam in Egypt, the main hajj route from Cairo had taken pilgrims up the Nile and then by camel caravan overland to the Red Sea ports of either Qusa'ir or the more southerly Aydhab, where they embarked on boats for Mecca's port of Jiddah, across the water. But in the 13th century, that pattern changed; Ibn Battuta was a witness to the problem:

On reaching Aydhab we found that...the sultan...was engaged in hostilities with the Turks, that he had sunk the ships, and the Turks had fled before him. It was impossible for us to make the sea-crossing, so we sold the provisions that we had made ready, and returning to Upper Egypt with the Arabs from whom we had hired the camels, arrived back at the town...We sailed thence down the Nile (it was the flood season) and after a passage of eight nights from Qus arrived at Cairo.

From the 14th century on, the land route across the Sinai was preferred by pilgrims, and each year until 1883 the great hajj caravan formed in Cairo with much fanfare and headed across the Sinai to join the Damascus, Baghdad, and Basra caravans on the Pilgrimage Road to Mecca. This land route was, of course, an ancient trade connection and had long been the route taken by the very poor African pilgrims who could not afford the boat fare across the Red Sea. In the early 16th century the Turks who had threatened the seagoing hajj routes annexed Egypt into their empire, although the Mamelukes still ruled in the region, and Cairo retained her special role in the hajj.

Gradually, unity of religion in the Sudan encouraged the establishment of at least some tenuous long-distance contact across the continent. As tribal raiding made caravan routes across the Sahara occasionally hazardous, routes through the Sudan became more attractive—at least in those periods when the local kingdoms were not at war. Routes from the central Sudan varied. From Hausaland, and its main cities of Katsina and Kano, one route arced down to Adamawa on the Benue River, then headed east to pass south of the Sudd and then down the White Nile, generally crossing to the caravan center of Sennar on the Blue Nile. But when peace obtained in Darfur, the preferred route was to head eastward, from Adamawa or from Lake Chad, to El Fasher. From there, both traders and pilgrims took the Derib el Arba'in on a 40-day trek north to Asyut on the Nile, following the ancient desert route that had been used, off and on, since the time of the Old Kingdom. Some traders might prefer to continue east from Darfur to Sennar, calling at the emerging town of Omdurman, just west of the juncture of the White and Blue Niles, before heading downriver.

But the Sudan Route did not become the preferred choice of the pilgrim until after the 16th century. The strongly Islamic Funj Empire arose along the Middle Nile; the Funj leader, Shaykh 'Abjib al-Kafuta, made the pilgrimage to Mecca, in the process opening up a new *hajj* route, swinging northwest through the lower ranges of the Red Sea hills to the Red Sea and across to Jiddah. As Islamic holy men from Funj spread further into the Sudan, they inspired many more Muslims to make the *hajj*, and often guided the caravans themselves, bringing increasing numbers of pilgrims on the Sudan Route and then across to the Red Sea. From El Fasher to the Islamic center of El Obeid, they crossed north to the Funj city of Omdurman, then cut northwest to Shendi, crossing the Atbara to Berber; from there, they either threaded through the arid hills to Suakin or followed the Atbara Valley southeast before cutting northeast, on a longer, but easier route to the same port. An alternate route—sometimes the main route, when trouble threatened Suakin—headed eastward from El Obeid across the White Nile to the Blue at Sennar, then on to Gondar in the heart of the Ethiopian hills, near the source of the Blue Nile, to the port of Massawa (formerly Adulis). This route, though never favored, was possible because the Christian Ethiopians had, over the centuries, reached an accommodation with the Islamic Arabs who held the Red Sea coast.

The Sudan Route had one signal advantage over the Sahara routes pilgrims had previously favored: Because the land was less hostile, pilgrims were not obliged to travel in large groups and make elaborate preparations, as were required for desert crossings. Pilgrimages became more common, with some people returning to Mecca several times; one Bornuese leader, Mai Ali b. 'Umar, reportedly made the *hajj* four times, and local tradition noted: "The journey to Mecca was to him as a night ride." While some earlier West African kings, using the Sahara routes, had been accompanied by thousands of servants and fellow *hajji*, later kings using the Sudan Route might take less than 100, a fact which caused one Timbuktu judge to lament "surely the world is fast deteriorating." Many of these pilgrims headed north on the Derib el Arba'in, a route open only to those with cash, as the Swiss traveler John L. Burckhardt noted even in the early 19th century:

> Pilgrims from the most western countries meet at Darfur after which such as can afford to travel with the Darfur caravan, (which requires capital sufficient to buy camels and provisions for the journey through the desert) repair to Siout [Asyut] from whence they proceed to Djidda [Jiddah], by way of Kossair [Qusa'ir].

With the Sudan routes there also arose large numbers of trekker-pilgrims, individuals with no money and few possessions, often religious zealots, who traveled eastward, living on whatever alms and earnings they could garner on the way. Not having the cash to pay for the sea crossing, nor for the desert route, most of these foot pilgrims worked their way along the banks of the Nile, finally to join the great caravan at Cairo. Burckhardt describes these trekker-pilgrims as they appeared on the Nile:

> The greater part of them are quite destitute, and find their way to Mecca, and back to their own country, by begging and by what they can earn by their manual labour on the road. The equipments of all these pilgrims are exactly alike and consist of a few rags tied around the waist, a white woolen bonnet, a leather provision sack, carried on a long stick over the shoulder, a leather pouch containing a book of prayer, or a copy of a few chapters of the Koran, a wooden tablet, one foot in length by six inches in breadth, upon which they write charms, or prayers for themselves or others to learn by heart, an inkstand formed of a small gourd, a bowl to drink out of, or to collect victuals in from the charitable, a small earthen pot for ablution, and a long string of beads hanging in many turns around the neck.

Some few of these foot pilgrims even made the desert crossing, relying on the charity of the caravaners for their food and water.

While the Sudan Route and the Darib el Arba'in were developing, new empire-builders began to eye Egypt. Like their Greek and Roman predecessors, they were at first mostly interested in Egypt as a land bridge. After the early Portuguese attempts to enter the Red Sea, most Europeans were kept east of the Strait of Bab al-Mandab. But as Europeans developed large empires in the East, they searched for alternatives to the long Cape of Good Hope Route around Africa; the Isthmus of Suez was by far the shortest. In the early summer of 1798, a French fleet under Napoleon Bonaparte, still flushed with his European victories, arrived in Egypt, determined to take control of this key link between the Mediterranean and the Spice Route. Horatio Nelson, equally determined to prevent French control, arrived in Alexandria first, asking for anchorage and supplies, and warning of the French threat. The Egyptian officials responded with astonishment and disbelief, clearly suspicious of British intentions, for (as they rationally asked): "Why should you English want to fight the French in Egyptian waters when you have the whole of the Mediterranean in which to settle your differences?" But barely had the British departed than the French arrived, with a fleet so large observers said it "had no beginning and no end." Government couriers, using relays of horses, raced up and down both sides of the Nile warning of the impending invasion. Landing at the now-grubby mud-hut village of Alexandria, the French quickly moved upstream on the west side of the Nile, while the Egyptian army assembled to meet them, watched by

British soldiers filing into the Ethiopian hills followed the old trade route toward the Red Sea. (From Illustrated London News, *July 4, 1868)*

the great pyramids in the desert and the unfortunate Cairenes on their city walls. The outcome of the Battle of the Pyramids was never seriously in doubt. However unprepared the French soldiers may have been for the steamy mosquito-ridden banks of the Nile, they were a modern army, while the Egyptian military was still living in the days of the Crusades. Within a day, Napoleon had succeeded in "freeing the Egyptians of Turkish tyranny."

In the end, however, the French could not hold Egypt. Within three years, they were gone, beaten by Egyptian intractability—and British force. But this brief period changed the course of the region irrevocably. With the Europeans gone, an Albanian Muslim soldier, Muhammed Ali, sent to fight in Egypt for the Turkish service, assumed power. Ending the reign of the Mamelukes, he eventually forced the Turks to name him their viceroy and set about modernizing Egypt.

While European governments were mostly looking from Egypt's delta to the empires of the East, the region of the upper Nile called out to travelers from around the world. Geographical ignorance was rife. Many Africans,

much less Europeans, were unaware that the Nile was a double river—the long White Nile and the shorter but much more powerful Blue Nile. Indeed, due to confusions perpetrated by early writings, there was a widespread belief that the Niger, the great river of West Africa, flowed underground and was actually the source of the Nile. The lure was irresistible, and many of the great explorers and adventurers of the modern period were drawn to the region. One of the earliest of these was Englishman James Bruce, who in 1769 landed at Massawa, seeking the source of the Nile. Following the old Ethiopian route with his party of 20—and with great daring and bravado—he moved inland to the ancient city of Axum and up into the hills of Gondar. Circling Lake Tana, and thereby visiting the source of the Blue Nile, he then headed overland—choosing not to follow the Nile as it wound far south through its narrow, impassable gorge—to the Funj center of Sennar.

In the process, he passed from one clime and way of life to another, of which the difference in religion was only a reflection. The horses and donkeys used for hauling from Massawa had to be exchanged for camels, as the

In the 19th century, European travelers, especially English men and women like Mr. and Mrs. Samuel Baker, headed up the Nile and into the Sudan. (By Samuel Baker)

party moved from the high mountains into the miasma of the Nile. While he had found backward infighting tribes in the Ethiopian Mountains, the shock of Sennar—in some decline with the rise of Shendi further north—was palpable:

> No horse, mule, ass, or any beast of burden, will breed, or even live at Sennar, or many miles around it. Poultry does not live there. Neither dog nor cat, sheep nor bullock, can be preserved a season there... Two greyhounds which I brought from Atbara, and the mules which I had brought from Abyssinia, lived only a few weeks after I arrived.

Even allowing for exaggeration, and the trauma of the change, Bruce's description of the heat in Sennar carries considerable force:

> I call it *hot*, when a man sweats at rest, and excessively on moderate motion. I call it *very hot*, when a man, with thin or little clothing, sweats much, though at rest. I call it *excessively hot*, when a man in his shirt, at rest, sweats excessively, when all motion is painful, and the knees feel feeble as if after a fever, I call it *extreme hot*, when the strength fails, a disposition to faint comes on, a straitness is found round the temples, as if a small cord was drawn round the head, the voice impaired, the skin dry,

and the head seems more than ordinary large and light. This, I apprehend, denotes death at hand...

Bruce experienced nearly all of these stages on his own journey down the Nile. From Sennar he proceeded by camel caravan, with the remains of his party, to Shendi, where he found a flourishing caravan center close by "heaps of broken pedestals and pieces of obelisks" which he rightly took to be the site of ancient Meroë. After following the caravan routes along the riverbank, he decided to commit himself to the desert, when the river began its great winding loop southwest. Buying fresh camels at Berber, he and his eight remaining companions headed on the 400-mile crossing to Aswan. Aside from the heat—apparently excessive even for the region, for it drove one of his fellow travelers mad—and the hot sandstorms called *simooms*, Bruce was stunned by the desert itself: "Silence, and a desperate kind of indifference about life, were the immediate effect upon us." In the end, all of the camels died, the baggage was left behind in the desert (though later retrieved), and after 18 days the party stumbled into Aswan. Yet this was one of the main routes north along the axis of the Nile, the other straightening the western loop of the Nile, swinging north from Omdurman and Khartoum across the Nile and the Nubian Desert to Aswan.

James Bruce's claim to have found the source of the Nile did not satisfy rival explorers, however. After a hiatus of some decades, others focused their attentions on the White Nile, which Bruce had studiously ignored. Most—Richard Burton, John Speke, and others—entered East Africa at Zanzibar and headed toward the great lakes of the western Rift Valley, producing various claimants for the source of the White Nile. More to the point, the Egyptians were themselves intrigued with the source of the Nile—and with gaining access to the supplies of slaves and gold that had been pouring out of the Sudan for millennia. In 1820 Muhammad Ali sent an expedition up the Nile, of which he later wrote: "You are aware that the end of all our effort and this expense is to procure negroes." His motley army of mercenaries—ranging from Turks in flashy pantaloons and slippers to Arabs in ankle-length robes—was disorganized, but their rifle-power swept before them a people who had had little contact with such modern technology. Wiping out the remnants of the Mamelukes along Dongola Reach, the Egyptian forces marched along the river to the sound of kettledrums and quickly took Shendi and then Sennar—sending back the ears of their slaughtered opponents to Cairo for bounty payments. Succeeding armies expanded Egyptian rule into Kordofan, Darfur, and the great papyrus swamp of the Sudd. The surprised Egyptians found, however, that the gold mines were nearly exhausted, and that many slaves—sometimes half the total—died on the trip north to Cairo. Nor did the Egyptians find rule of the region easy; many Sudanese migrated out of administrative reach, but others revolted, killing the provincial governor at Shendi in 1822. The eastern Sudan went through the convulsions of revolt and devastation, until the Egyptians finally established control, with their all-powerful governor established at Khartoum, from 1825 on.

Unsatisfied with the wasted Sudan, the Egyptians—for the first time in the modern period—extended into the Sudd and the upper Nile. Cut off by hills, swamps, and equatorial forests, the people of the upper Nile had led a sheltered existence, secure in their unorganized nomadic ways. At first, traders from the outside were greeted with some awe, but no dismay, their beads purchasing abundant quantities of cattle and ivory. Ivory soon became the favored product, drawing European traders and, increasingly, Arab merchants from the Sudan, especially from Darfur. As readily available ivory dwindled, great elephant hunts were organized to meet the demand of the outside world. Slaving, too, came under the control of Arab traders, who established themselves in riverbank trading posts, playing tribe against tribe for their own advantage.

Change also came to the Sudan Route. Like other parts of the Arab world in the 19th century, Sudan was gripped by evangelical and millenarian reform movements. In the central Sudan, where animist religions still flourished, there arose a number of *jihad* states, which vowed

war on infidels—in the process establishing new empires. Throughout the Sudan, holy men called *sufis* were believed to partake of God's powers and were accorded mystical devotion. In the eastern Sudan there was the belief in a Second Coming, in which a Mahdi would appear in the East. Many people from the central and western Sudan shared in this belief, and were advised by some holy men that the *hajj* was no longer necessary. Wise man Muhammad Bello, for example, thought that many pilgrims incurred unnecessary difficulties on the *hajj*, noting: "...you find them dead and strewn along the roads. They have acted against God's order by punishing themselves." Instead, many Moslems were advised that the *jihad* (holy war against infidels) was a proper substitute; as Bello noted: "...*jihad* once is better than making four hundred accepted pilgrimages." Many Moslems chose to head toward the eastern Sudan, there to await the promised Mahdi. The result was a great migration across the Sahel Corridor.

During the 19th century, the Egyptians had become increasingly Westernized; although at first French influence dominated, through the building of the Suez Canal in 1869, the British came to have increasing weight. Because Britain had abolished slave trading in its dominions, Egypt tried to follow suit, naturally employing British aid. At first the explorer Samuel Baker was assigned to end the slave trade, but only with the arrival of General Charles Gordon (via the overland route from Suakin in a record 21 days) did the campaign have some success. Ruling as governor-general of the province of Equatoria, from his capital at Khartoum, he brought the ivory trade under government monopoly and drove the Arab traders largely out of the slave business. Gordon even pushed up the Nile, forcing his way well past Juba, on occasion dismantling his boat for portaging around some falls and reassembling it on the far side. While his predecessors had waxed enthusiastic about the region, Gordon was less sanguine:

A more dreary, weary set of marches you cannot conceive. The country is quite uninhabited—a vast undulating prairie of jungle grass and scrub-trees...Everything relating to this country has been much exaggerated.

From the upper Nile and the western tributaries the Arab merchants were driven back into the Sudan, notably into Kordofan and Darfur. With the Mahdist fervor approaching its peak, the two cultures were on a collision course.

It is not surprising that the 37-year-old man who in the summer of 1881 declared himself to be the long-awaited Mahdi came from a family of dispossessed slave-and-ivory merchants. Muhammad Ahmad, the Mahdi, had begun to collect a following among the people along the upper Nile 20 years before, as a highly regarded *sufi*, drawing both on religious fervor and economic discontent. When Egypt was riven by army revolts in 1881–82, resulting in direct British occupation of the lower Nile, the Mahdi made his move. He first took El Obeid, astride the Sudan Route, and then demolished a British expeditionary force sent to retake the surrounding province of Kordofan. After that, he spread to Darfur, to the western tributaries of the Nile, and along the pilgrims' route through the Red Sea hills, to just short of Suakin. General Gordon was recalled from England to Khartoum to evacuate the Egyptians and British.

Canadian voyageurs sent to aid Gordon in 1884 met the same problems the Nile had posed for thousands of years, as they tried to move upstream through cataract country:

> The Nile boat...is from 30 to 32 feet long, 6 or 7 in beam. From 8 to 12 soldiers were told off [assigned] to each boat, and one voyageur...
>
> As a usual thing six men pulled. The voyageur took the rudder, sometimes the bow. When the boat came to a strong current, the men would pull their best, and with a good way on would get up, but if they failed and were carried back, I have seen them make the attempt a second and third time, straining every nerve, and then succeed. If it was impossible to row up, all the crew but the bowman and the man at the rudder would disembark, get out their tracking line, put it over their shoulders, and walk along the bank, tracking the boat, until they reached smooth water again. When they came to a bad rapid, instead of having one crew on the rope, 3, 4, or 5 crews, according to the rush of water, would be put on. This was avoided as much as possible, as it took 5 times as long. When it became necessary to place 30 or 40 men on the line it was generally necessary also to unload the arms, and perhaps part of the load. Great care had to be exercised to see that there should not be any slack rope, so that on the Nile you would hear the words from morning until night, "Pull up the slack," "Haul away." When the men were on the line and when all was ready the word would be given, "Shove off." If there was too much slack rope, the current would catch the boat, running her out into the stream broadside on, and sometimes filling the boat. She would turn over, throwing the voyageurs into the water, unless they were smart enough to climb over one side as she went under at the other, and then cling to the bottom, until taken off.

Clearly, shipping on the Nile south of the First Cataract continued to be difficult, even with the advent of modern steam-powered boats.

The peoples of the Nubian Nile rose up against the oppressing infidels, and annihilated them. When the Mahdi died, only a few months later, his successors attempted to establish a reform state, with its capital at Omdurman. They even tried to carry their *jihad* into Egypt itself, striking north of Wadi Halfa in 1889. But in 1898,

a large British force moved up the Nile to finally crush the Mahdist troops—and encountered French forces moving eastward from the center of Africa. Bringing their technology to bear, the British, led by General H. H. Kitchener, built a railroad, first down the west bank of the Nile and then the east, through Aswan and Wadi Halfa, then across the Nubian Desert and down the Nile again, through Berber and Atbara to Khartoum. Further extensions followed the old caravan routes, with one passing through Sennar, then angling south up the White Nile to the trading post of Juba and on into Kenya. The other cut from Khartoum across the Nile to Omdurman and then to El Obeid and west.

This was the period of the partition of Africa, with the French taking most of the Sahara and western Africa, except for Nigeria, and the British dominant in the east, including Egypt and the eastern Sudan. For the Europeans the main axis of travel continued to be north-south. But for many Moslems, the east-west Sudan Route continued to be the main corridor, regardless of imperial dictates. Despite the death of the Mahdi, people continued to look to the East. Some simply made pilgrimages along the route to the Red Sea, but many migrated wholesale. One observer, Captain Boyd Alexander, wrote in 1907 of a migration caravan:

> The caravan which now comes into my story had originally started from Timbuctu, and increasing its following as it went along from all countries on the way now numbered 700 souls and a 1000 head of sheep and cattle. Its leaders were Hausa and Fulani Mallams, who saw to the feeding of the pilgrims and were responsible for law and order in the caravan...It was a wonderful organisation, this slowly moving community, with its population of varied races, and cattle and sheep, forming a column that stretched for miles along the way. Whole families were there, carrying all their belongings...perched upon the backs of oxen were little children, some of whom had been brought forth on the road...It was a strange, picturesque pilgrimage; in the throng there travelled pale faced Fulanis, Hausa from Sokoto, handsome dark-skinned people from Melle and Timbuctu...and many Mallams turbaned and clothed in white, walked calm and heedless of all danger, incessantly telling their beads.

Famines, like that in 1913, sometimes swelled their number, as people wished to be near Mecca if they were to die. Many of these pilgrims did, in fact, complete their pilgrimage. But others settled along the upper Nile, participating in the more prosperous culture based on technology which filtered up the Nile, as of old. Indeed, some industries, notably cotton, took advantage of the supply of labor offered by the West African migrants. Railroads in the Sudan followed the old routes, too, from Kano in Nigeria to Ndjamena in Chad, El Fasher in

Darfur, and El Obeid and on across, via Khartoum, to the Red Sea ports of Suakin and Massawa. In the 20th century, the region gradually assumed its modern shape. Chad was formed in the central Sudan, and to the east were Ethiopia, with its new capital of Addis Ababa, and various contested Red Sea lands.

The Nile itself was divided along its natural boundary lines. When the British withdrew after World War II, the line between Egypt and the Sudan was drawn just north of the Second Cataract, above Wadi Halfa. Modern technology is most striking there, too, for the early, modest dam placed at Aswan in 1906 was in the 1960's replaced by the great Aswan High Dam, which created the huge Lake Nasser, extending across the border into Sudan. The old canals that allowed sometime shipping through the lower cataracts are now long gone, flooded by the dammed-up waters of the Nile. But the older caravan routes, only replaced by automobile highways in the more prosperous regions, still follow the line of the Nile as it cuts into the heart of Africa.

Selective Bibliography

Arkell, A. J. *A History of the Sudan: From the Earliest Times to 1821.* Second Edition (London: University of London, The Athlone Press, 1961). A valuable review with an archaeological emphasis.

Baines, John, and Jaromir Malek. *Atlas of Ancient Egypt* (New York: Facts On File, 1980). A beautifully illustrated detailing of the Egyptian sites.

Ibn Battuta. *Travels, A.D. 1325–1354* (3 vols.). Translated by H.A.R. Gibb (Cambridge: Cambridge University Press, 1958–71). Hakluyt Society Publications, Second Series. A fine edition, with helpful maps.

Bruce, James. *Travels to Discover the Source of the Nile.* Selected and edited by C. F. Beckingham (New York: Horizon Press, 1964). An abridgment of the 1804 Second Edition; first published in 1790.

Fairservis, Walter A., Jr. *The Ancient Kingdoms of the Nile and the Doomed Monuments of Nubia* (New York: Thomas Y. Crowell, 1962). An overview, incorporating quotations from modern travelers.

Jarvis, H. Wood. *Pharaoh to Farouk* (New York: Macmillan, 1955). A popular history focusing on the modern period.

July, Robert W. *A History of the African People.* Second Edition (New York: Scribner's 1974). A useful general history.

Ludwig, Emil. *The Nile: The Life-Story of a River.* Translated by Mary H. Lindsay (New York: Viking, 1937). A popular and personal work.

Moorehead, Alan. *The Blue Nile* (New York: Harper & Row, 1962). Western explorations from 1798 through the 19th century.

———. *The White Nile* (New York: Harper & Row, 1960). Western explorations from the 1850's to 1900.

Al-Naqar, 'Umar. *The Pilgrimage Tradition in West Africa: An Historical Study with Special Reference to the Nineteenth Century* (Khartoum: Khartoum University Press, 1972). A specialist work drawing on many first-hand accounts.

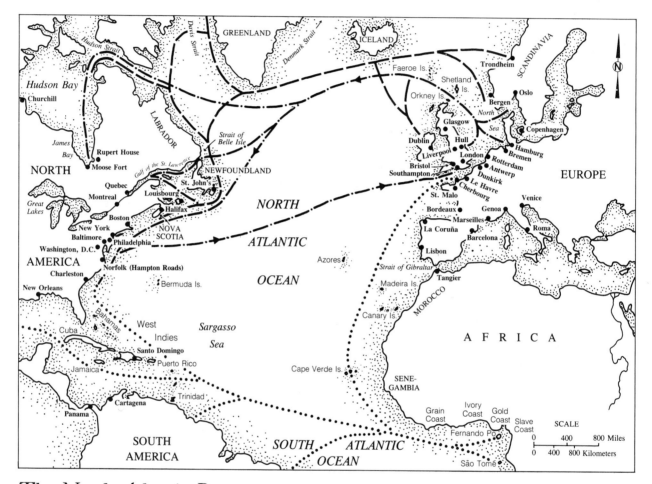

The North Atlantic Route

— — — Early Exploratory Routes ⋯⋯⋯ Slave Trade Routes
—·—·— Later Main Sailing Routes

The North Atlantic Route

...Come my friends,
'Tis not too late to seek a newer world.
Push off, and sitting well in order smite
The sounding furrows; for my purpose holds
To sail beyond the sunset, and the baths
Of all the western stars...

Although Tennyson was speaking of the Greeks in the Mediterranean in these words from *Ulysses*, he was writing when the North Atlantic Route was at its height and clearly reflected the attitude of northern Europeans toward the opening of the New World of North America.

The great sea highway of the North Atlantic Route has, since the beginning of the modern era, linked the most populous and industrially advanced parts of the Old World and the New. From the beginning of the 16th century to the present day, an ever-increasing tide of vessels has moved along the sea lanes of the North Atlantic, carrying fishers, traders, explorers, soldiers, officials, clerics, and a vast flow of emigrants from Europe to North America. The North Atlantic Route carried the main thrust of the European exploration and conquest of North America—and still binds together modern North America and Europe. Today, the North Atlantic is by far the most heavily traveled sea route in the world; but it was not always so. For most of human history it was a seemingly impassable barrier that led nowhere.

The North Atlantic is one of the world's stormiest seas, and the route across it is extremely vulnerable to changes in climate. The most natural sailing route westward is a northerly one. Starting from the North Sea, which links with the main nations of northwest Europe, the route feeds northwest on either side of the Shetland Islands, from along the Norwegian coast or past the Orkney Islands just off northern Scotland; there it is joined by a branch from the Irish Sea. Swinging past the Faeroe Islands further out into the ocean, the North Atlantic Route passes Iceland, crosses the Denmark Strait and cuts south of Greenland, then arcs southward to follow the coast of North America. Some ships leave the North Atlantic Route at this point to follow the St. Lawrence-Great Lakes Route into the heart of the continent.

But the main North Atlantic Route continues with the favorable coastal current down past Newfoundland and its port of St. John's, past Nova Scotia with its prime fortress-harbors at Louisbourg and Halifax, to the main ports of the United States: Boston, New York, Philadelphia, Baltimore, Norfolk, Charleston, later New Orleans, and in modern times Hampton Roads in the capacious Chesapeake Bay. This northerly, island-hopping sailing route, with its easterly winds, made crossing the North Atlantic relatively easy—but only when the climate was good. During the winter and during centuries when the prevailing temperatures were cool, this route was precluded because of the amount of drift ice there. The fate of the *Titanic*, the largest and supposedly one of the safest ships of its day, serves as a reminder of what a brief encounter with subsurface ice can do to the hull of even a steel ship.

Viking longships doubled as tents on exploratory trips, until permanent settlements were made. (Library of Congress, Prints and Photographs Division)

The eastbound course of the North Atlantic posed no such problems for sailors, for they were able to take advantage of the warmer and more southerly Gulf Stream, with its favorable winds and currents, to cross the ocean at the latitude of New England, swinging only slightly northward on the approach to Europe, entering either the Irish Sea, with its prime ports of Bristol, Liverpool, and Dublin, or the English Channel, along which lay some of the most important ports of Europe, including Cherbourg, Le Havre, London, Bremen, and Hamburg.

The Gulf Stream itself is just one half of a huge circulatory system. From the British Isles, a large branch of the Gulf Stream flows south past Spain and West Africa as the Canary Current, then swings westward to the Caribbean, exiting through the Strait of Florida, between Florida and the Bahamas, as the Gulf Stream, to once again cross the Atlantic. But the very strength of the Gulf Stream's westerlies weighed against the North Atlantic in harsh, icy periods, for westbound ships forced out of their northerly course by drift ice were hard-pressed to make headway against the Gulf Stream's heavy winds and currents. In this is something of an explanation of the North Atlantic Route's late arrival on the world scene.

Almost 2,500 years ago, the Pythagoreans and Aristotle, among others, believed that the earth was round, but there was no systematic exploration westward to test this theory until almost 2,000 years later in the time of Columbus, who, indeed, followed the great circulatory system that includes the Gulf Stream.

Who first explored the North Atlantic is a very controversial question. Some evidence suggests that Phoenician (Carthaginian) sailors, perhaps engaged in trading north for Cornish tin, went westward, island-hopping across the North Atlantic as early as the fourth century B.C. The climate would have allowed it in that period, as it would not for many centuries thereafter, for it soon turned colder, and the northern sea lanes would have been mainly blocked by ice until the fourth century A.D.

The Roman historian Pliny tells of another possible voyage on the North Atlantic. In the fourth century B.C., a Greek mariner named Pytheas sailed from Massalia (Marseilles) in the Mediterranean through the Pillars of Hercules (Strait of Gibraltar) into the open Atlantic and followed the coast of Europe north, at least as far as northern Britain, and probably further—though whether to Scandinavia or west to the Atlantic islands is not clear. Pytheas called the most distant land he reached Thule; Pliny and many later historians often called it Ultima Thule, the furthest land ever reached by humanity. Here is Pliny's description:

The outermost of all known lands is Thule. At the time of the solstice, when the sun passes through the sign of the crab, there are no nights there. In winter the days last only a short time, whereas the nights are very long...

A finding of Roman coins in Iceland also suggests that Iceland may have been visited in Roman times, but there is no very substantial evidence to this effect.

It is quite clear, though, that Celtic sea rovers and anchorites visited and settled the nearer Atlantic islands before the seventh century A.D., and may have traveled a good deal further in these warmer centuries. As early as the sixth century A.D., St. Brendan seems to describe a huge volcanic island in eruption; if so, that could be no-

where else in the North Atlantic but Iceland. There apparently were Irish settlements in Iceland in the seventh and eighth centuries. More concretely, the Irish monk Dicuil, in 825 A.D., writes about the Faeroes and the Shetlands:

All round our island of Hibernia there are islands...Off the coast of the island of Britain are many islands, some big, some small, some middling; some lie in the sea to the south of Britain, some to the west; but they are most numerous in the northwestern sphere and the north. On some of these islands I have lived, on others set foot, of some had a sight, of others read...

It is now thirty years since clerics who lived in that island from the first day of February to the first day of August told me that not only at the summer solstice, but in the days on either side of it, the setting sun hides itself at the evening hour as if behind a little hill, so that no darkness occurs during that very brief period of time, but whatever task a man wishes to perform, even to picking the lice out of his shirt, he can manage it precisely as in broad daylight. And had they been on a high mountain, the sun would at no time have been hidden from them...

These Irish settlers were still there when the Norse arrived on the North Atlantic Route, as the later excellent Norse records clearly show.

It was the Norse—Vikings from Norway—who first developed the North Atlantic Route. As climatic conditions continued to improve—some contemporary accounts seem to indicate that they were, by then, very nearly ice-free—Norse sea-rovers and settlers began to move out across the Atlantic from island to island. This northerly, island-hopping course is an easy one, for it is only about 200 miles from Bergen, Norway, to the Shetlands; 200 more from the Shetlands to the Faeroes; 400 more to Iceland; and only 200 beyond that to Greenland. The route was probably opened by a combination of accident and intent. Certainly the sagas speak of ships being blown off course and coming upon unknown islands, but these were then deliberately explored by the venturesome Norse. By late in the seventh century A.D., Norse emigrants had settled in the Shetlands and Faeroes, as well as in northern Scotland and Ireland. By the middle of the eighth century, Norse raiders had repeatedly raided these islands, with new emigrants from Norway following the raiders to occupy islands in the middle of the North Atlantic.

Norse ships began to appear off Iceland in the middle of the ninth century. The first of what would become a substantial wave of emigrants traveled to Iceland in the 870's, to be followed very soon by hundreds and then thousands of settlers from the 880's on. By 900 A.D., the Norse population of Iceland was an estimated 20,000; by 930, it was 40,000. Half a century after that, the Norse were in Greenland.

In the infamous "triangle trade," Europeans brought slaves from Africa to the Americas, then followed the Gulf Stream home with colonial goods. (From Anonymous, La Commerce de Amerique par Marseilles, *1764)*

There is considerable evidence that Eric the Red, who had come to Iceland with his father Thorvald while still in his teens, completed the Norse journey across the North Atlantic from Iceland to Greenland, arriving in Greenland in the early 980's. Many Icelanders had probably sighted Greenland earlier, and some may even have made landfall there. But Eric the Red landed and explored, returning to Iceland three years later to lead a group of settlers back to build the Eastern Settlement, on the southeastern coast of Greenland. The Icelandic *Saga of Eric the Red* tells us that he called the place Greenland, because "men would be all the more drawn to go there if the land had an attractive name."

Eric's son, Leif, and many other Greenlanders and Icelanders explored south and west from Greenland after the founding of this new colony. The way was far from easy, and many a ship came to grief on the way. The *Saga of Eric the Red* tells of one expedition:

> They were in high spirits and were pleased with their prospects. But they ran into prolonged difficulties and were unable to reach the seas they wanted. At one time they were within sight of Iceland; at another they observed birds off Ireland. Their ship was driven back and forth across the Ocean. In the autumn they turned back…worn out by exposure and toil.

It was in this period that the Norse may have reached the mainland of North America. The evidence on the question is scant, and speculation endless, but the powerful thrust toward exploration and settlement that had taken the Norse clear across the Atlantic, coupled with the excellent weather of the period, would probably have led the Norse to explore further down the coast and probably some distance into the North American continent.

In any case, the Norse had for the first time opened a sea route across the North Atlantic, most of which continued in use for a thousand years, and is in use today. Only the last 200 miles or so, from Iceland to Greenland, fell into complete disuse, as the northern climate worsened during the 13th and 14th centuries, deteriorating into the "Little Ice Age" of the 15th century. By then, even the routes between Iceland and Norway were often blocked by ice, leaving the Icelandic population to rely on dried cod from English fishing boats operating off Iceland for part of their food supply.

The Greenland settlements fell on especially hard times as the climate worsened. At their height, the Norse Greenland settlements had had a population of 5,000–10,000 people. By 1350, the settlements on the western shore of Greenland had been abandoned; those on the eastern shore may have lasted until as late as the middle of the 16th century—half a century after Columbus had "discovered" the New World, and well after the early North Atlantic voyages of the great age of European exploration.

In this harsh, icy time, ships coming from Europe could take advantage of the northern islands and the prevailing easterly winds only in the very brief summer; at most times of the year, they had to swing south, traveling against the prevailing westerly winds. But still they came. Acting largely in ignorance of the Norse activity on the western end of the North Atlantic Route, the Europeans who headed out over this uncharted ocean in the late 15th and early 16th centuries acted from quite different motives. While the Norse sailors and settlers of the eighth and ninth centuries had sought new lands to settle and freedom from oppression in their homeland (as would many later emigrants across the North Atlantic), these newcomers were seeking a new route to the riches of the East—a route that now seemed possible, given the revival of the theory that the earth was round.

Not surprisingly in the frigid 15th century, the main activity was in the mid-Atlantic, on the southern half of the ocean's circulatory system. Columbus and his successors used this in their crossings to the Americas. The Portuguese also used it to swing out around the bulge of Africa almost to South America, before cutting back to South Africa, on the Cape of Good Hope Route to the East. Columbus was also the first to understand and use the prevailing westerlies for his return trip, swinging north from the Caribbean to about the latitude of Bermuda and proceeding eastward very easily to the mid-ocean island group called the Azores and then home to Europe.

Northern Europeans—now generally Dutch, British, and French—soon joined in the exploration, especially as the climate moderated. But whether they were looking for a new route to Cathay or for the fabled seven cities of Cibola, supposed to have been founded centuries before on an ocean island by refugee Christian bishops from Moorish Spain, Columbus's westward route was ill-suited for their purposes. It was far longer and more circuitous than the more direct—although more difficult—northern route.

A look at the map makes that difficult northern choice even easier to understand. Bristol, the main British port of departure for explorers west, is at about the same latitude as the Strait of Belle Isle, far north between Newfoundland and Labrador, which was the main entry point into the Gulf of St. Lawrence and the interior of North America. Liverpool, the main point of departure in later centuries, is even further north. Brittany and the northern coast of France, site of the great port of Le Havre, are across the English Channel, at the same latitude as Newfoundland. Even Lisbon, far south in Europe, is at about the latitude of New York and Philadelphia. (That these European coastlands are not just temperate, but often downright warm, is due to the Gulf Stream, which flows directly toward the continental land mass, warming all of

Fires and wrecks took a fearful toll in the North Atlantic; this 1873 liner ran aground off Nova Scotia, and 562 of 952 people were lost (Library of Congress, Prints and Photographs Division)

western Europe. It does not do the same to North America only because it flows too far off the coast.) Given these distances, the early northern sailors naturally chose the northerly course of the North Atlantic Route westward, as did the main body of the tremendous trans-Atlantic sailing trade that was to follow.

As western Europeans began the exploration, conquest, and settlement of North America, traffic began to grow on the sea lanes of the North Atlantic. There may have been Portuguese fishing boats on the Grand Banks, off Newfoundland, even before John Cabot landed on the American mainland in 1497. Certainly substantial

numbers of Portuguese, Basque, Breton, and British boats were fishing the Banks only ten years later, drying their cod on shore, trading with the local Native Americans for furs, and beginning the immense trade in fish and furs that was to flow across the North Atlantic from then on. (The main body of the fur trade would end in the 19th century; but the fish trade across the North Atlantic continues to this day.)

Cabot and his successors had always to deal with the hazards of the North Atlantic, not the least of which was the fog. The French sailor Marc Lescarbot, traveling off Newfoundland in 1601, noted that from St. John's they:

...fell to the fogs again, which (afar off) we might perceive to come and wrap us about, holding us continually prisoners three whole days for two days of fair weather they permitted us...Yea, even divers times we have seen ourselves a whole sennight [week] continually in thick fogs, twice without any show of sun.

To the fog add rocky outcroppings, and you can easily see why so many capes along the North Atlantic coast have earned the name "Graveyard of Ships."

But still the exploration continued, as sailors from Bristol in western England and from Brittany, especially St.-Malo and Dieppe, led the way west across the ocean. John Davis, England's first great Arctic explorer, visited Greenland in 1587, coming across the Atlantic south of Iceland. By then, there were no more Norse in Greenland, the main European exploration of North America was in progress, and the outlines of what would be the modern North Atlantic sailing ships route had begun to emerge.

The fishers and explorers who had kept open the North Atlantic Route in the early 16th century were gradually joined by settlers, as the climate moderated—and as religious persecution led Europeans to seek freedom across the Atlantic, as the Norse had centuries before. Then began the flow of people from Europe to North America that was to culminate in the Great Migration of the 19th and early 20th centuries.

At first, it was only a trickle; in 1600, a full century after Cabot's landfall in the New World, there were still only a few hundred French settlers and traders in Canada, and the British had not even made their first settlements in Virginia. But by 1650, the flow of British settlers across the North Atlantic had started in earnest, with 20,000 people in Virginia and 30,000 more in New England, although Canada was still very lightly populated. And by 1700, the population of British North America had reached 280,000, of whom 100,000 had come across the Atlantic, 10,000 as slaves. The balance were North American-born. The flow of emigrants westward across the North Atlantic continued throughout the 18th century, with relatively heavy Scotch, Irish, and Palatine German emigration in mid-century swelling the population of the 13 British colonies, along with the importation of slaves, which continued into the early part of the 19th century. The westward passage northern route across the Atlantic was especially difficult, for sailing ships took twice as long to travel from northwestern Europe to northeastern North America as to travel eastbound back to Europe. That was to mean enormous hardship for millions of emigrants from Europe to America, packed into the holds of sailing ships bound for America.

Ships in the North Atlantic trade carried an enormous quantity of goods, as well as people, the growth in trade paralleling the expansion of the United States and its later growth into the world's single most powerful industrial country. The infamous "triangle trade" took advantage of the circulatory currents of the Atlantic, thereby avoiding the northern routes and making increased profits. Ships took goods from America to Europe using the prevailing westerlies, then sailed south with the wind and the Canary Current to West Africa. There they picked up "cargoes" of slaves, and sailed with the favorable wind and current westward to the Caribbean and the American South, where they would sell slaves and pick up new cargo, in later years mostly the cotton produced by the very slaves they had sold.

But traffic always continued heavy on the northerly westbound route. As the English North American colonies grew, so did a substantial trans-Atlantic trade, in the standard colonial way, with raw materials flowing from North America to Britain and manufactured goods flowing from Britain to America. Even long after American independence, until the American Civil War, that kind of unbalanced trading pattern continued. It accelerated after Eli Whitney's invention of the cotton gin, in 1793, for then American planters, using slave labor, enormously expanded cotton production and extended the plantation system into the new southwestern lands acquired from France, far out into the Mississippi basin. This was the time of Britain's Industrial Revolution, which preceded that of the rest of the world, and British mills used all the cotton the Americans could supply. By the time of the Civil War, Americans supplied half of Britain's cotton, while the United States had become a very large market for British finished cotton goods and other manufactures of all kinds.

Until the 1820's, the North Atlantic trade depended on sailing ships. Larger and larger ships, to be sure, but nonetheless ships that had to fight the stormy North Atlantic and go against wind and current from Europe to America. Poor emigrants from Liverpool and other European ports could expect to spend two months in "steerage," the upper hold of a pitching, heaving sailing ship; seasick, lice-infested, poorly fed, and without adequate care, they faced every conceivable kind of infectious disease. On many ships, typhus and cholera raged unchecked; in 1847, 15,330 of the 89,738 who left Liverpool bound for Quebec died, either en route or shortly afterward in Canadian hospitals. Here is one emigrant's description of the voyage in steerage from Liverpool in that year:

Before the emigrant has been a week at sea he is an altered man. How can it be otherwise? Hundreds of poor people, men, women, and children of all ages, from the drivelling idiot of ninety to the babe just born, huddled together without light, without air, wallowing in filth and breathing a fetid atmosphere, sick in body, dispirited in heart, the fever patients lying between the sound, in sleeping places so narrow as almost to deny them the power of indulging, by a change of position, the natural restlessness of the disease; by their ravings disturbing those around, and predisposing them, through the effects of the imagination, to imbibe the contagion; living without food or medicine, except as administered by the hand of casual charity, dying without the voice of spiritual consolation, and buried in the deep without the rites of the Church.

The food is generally ill-selected and seldom sufficiently cooked, in consequence of the insufficiency and bad construction of the cooking places. The supply of water, hardly enough for cooking and drinking, does not allow washing. In many ships the filthy beds, teeming with all abominations, are never required to be brought on deck and aired; the narrow space between the sleeping berths and the piles of boxes is never washed or scraped, but breathes up a damp and fetid stench...

The meat was of the worst quality. The supply of water shipped on board was abundant, but the quantity served out to the passengers was so scanty that they were frequently obliged to throw overboard their salt provisions and rice...because they had not water enough for the necessary cooking and the satisfying of their raging thirst afterwards. They could only afford water for washing by withdrawing it from the cooking of their food. I have known persons to remain for days together in their dark, close berths because they thus suffered less from hunger...

The sailing ships of the North Atlantic trade were generally called "packets," whether they were the large square-rigged ships of the 19th century, or the much smaller barks, barkentines, brigs, and brigantines of earlier times. These were all true ocean-going sailing ships, as distinct from the oar-assisted longships of the earlier Norse, Irish, Greek, and Carthaginian voyagers. And these packets were far from the big New England clipper ships of the China trade, which had their heyday in the mid-19th century. They were workhorses, strong, square-rigged ships capable of withstanding the pounding of the North Atlantic, and making their way across the ocean fully loaded against the prevailing westerlies and often in the teeth of a gale.

In the early years, the packets ran when they would, waiting for mail, passengers, and cargo in port until their owners gave them sailing orders. But in 1818, many packets on the North Atlantic became "liners," or units in shipping "lines," which ran scheduled sailings from specified port to port. Among these mostly American lines, the Black Ball Line was the best known; some others were the Black Star, Red Star, and Black X. These ships and lines then became the main carriers in the North Atlantic. Traveling west, their typically thousand-ton packets carried luxury passengers on their upper decks, with emigrants jammed into their upper holds, also known as " 'tween decks" or "steerage"; cargo was stowed further below. Traveling east, they carried cargo instead of emigrants in their upper holds. Mid-19th century packets made considerably better time across the North Atlantic than had earlier sailing ships; now the average time going west was 36 days, and going east 24 days.

But in the course of the 19th century all that

Past Ellis Island (far right), the Statue of Liberty (upper left) and Castle Garden (lower left), this liner is steaming back to Europe for more immigrants. (Library of Congress, Prints and Photographs Division)

Bristol, shown here in 1673, was the home port of many early British maritime explorers. (City Archives of Bristol)

and seven years later before Samuel Cunard's British and North American Royal Mail Steamship Company instituted the swift, regular service that was to quickly supplant sailing ships on the North Atlantic. Several small steamships crossed between 1833 and 1840, and the *Great Western* made several commerical runs. But it was the Cunard line's *Britannia*, first of four ships built with British government subsidy for the Liverpool-North America run, that really inaugurated the age of the steam on the North Atlantic and the other oceans of the world. Ten years later, America's Collins Line, also with the help of government subsidies, provided competition for Cunard, but the withdrawal of American subsidies doomed the line, leaving the North Atlantic trade substantially in British hands for most of the rest of the 19th century.

Charles Dickens, who crossed on the *Britannia* in 1842, two years after it had been put in service, described his sleeping accommodations as "...an inaccessible shelf they called a sleeping berth [with] a very thin quilt covering an equally thin and very flat mattress, utterly impractical and quite preposterous, which I thought at first was merely a cheerful jest on the part of the ship's owners and captain." Not so; he should have seen what steerage accommodations were like. For the fact was that the early steamships crossing the Atlantic were not much larger than modern ocean-going tugs, being in the same thousand-ton class as most of the sailing ships in the packet lines.

But after a few years, the steamships were able to make the vital east-to-west run, against the wind and current, faster and more surely than could the sailing ships. By the 1850's the Collins and Cunard ships, joined for a time by the ships of the Inman line, were routinely making the east-west run in 10–12 days. The steamships began to be larger, as well, and thereby became able to carry more people far more comfortably, both above deck and in steerage, than in earlier times. These capacious vessels also carried more goods. Steerage was still far from comfortable, and it took a great deal of government regulation and enforcement on both sides of the Atlantic to contain the rapacity of some shipowners, but larger and faster ships made the trip far more bearable. By the late 1850's, fast, reliable steamships in the 3,000–4,000-ton range were being built, and the days of the packet ships were done. Sailing ships remained in service, certainly, carrying cargo, and sometimes passengers as well. Some sailing ships were in profitable use on some Australian-American intercontinental runs as late as the 1940's, and experimental sailing ships carrying substantial amounts of cargo are back in use today. But on the North Atlantic, with its special needs, the age of steam came quickly.

With the age of steam came traffic, the kind of traffic that had never before been seen across any of the world's oceans. And with that traffic came the enormously enhanced danger of collisions. In response, the great early American oceanographer, Lieutenant Matthew Fontaine

changed. The American westward expansion—an explosion, really—beyond the Appalachian Mountains, coupled with the coming of the age of steam to the North Atlantic, resulted in a huge European migration to America. The first experimental crossing using steam was made by the *Savannah* in 1818; within a few decades, huge steamships would be sailing from every major port in Europe to every major North American port, far more swiftly and efficiently than had sailing ships. From the early 1840's through the early 1920's, when United States immigration restrictions virtually ended the flow, well over 35,000,000 Europeans came across the Atlantic to North America in what has aptly been called the Great Migration.

The *Savannah* was a steam-assisted sailing ship, and very much ahead of its time on the North Atlantic. For, while steam came to dominate the inland waterways of North America, sailing packets continued to dominate the North Atlantic trade. It was another 15 years before the age of steam was really introduced on the North Atlantic,

Maury, working out of the Department of Charts and Instruments in Washington, D. C. (later the Hydrographic Office of the United States Navy), charted parallel tracks across the Atlantic for eastbound and westbound ships, supplying different tracks for different seasons. Now, for the first time, there were truly sea lanes across the North Atlantic. They were not fully agreed upon until 1924, but Maury's work laid the basis for all that followed. For this and much else, Maury was known as "The Pathfinder of the Seas."

The ships were becoming much bigger and faster in the same period. By the late 1870's, there were 8,000-tonners in service, capable of making the crossing in seven days. And by 1897, Germany's 14,350-ton *Kaiser Wilhelm der Grosse*, then the largest liner in the world, made the westbound crossing from Southampton, England, to Sandy Hook in New York harbor in 5 days, 22 hours; it then made the eastbound crossing in 5 days, 15 hours, and 10 minutes. And this was less than 60 years since Cunard had inaugurated the age of steam on the North Atlantic. Rapid development, indeed, as was much of the pace of change in the 19th century; but in the 20th century the pace of change accelerated even more, as it has throughout the history of the modern world.

In 1906, the *Mauretania* and *Lusitania* were launched; these were 30,000-ton superliners capable of crossing the Atlantic in just under five days. They were soon joined by many even larger liners, built by many nations, such as the 45,000-ton *Titanic*, all launched in the years immediately preceding World War I. Each was in turn designed to set new standards of speed, safety, and luxury. Even steerage passengers on some of these ships enjoyed a somewhat more comfortable and stable journey than had their predecessors.

With steam, the crossing was easier; but it was still a very hard, crowded, miserable journey for tens of millions of emigrants from Europe to America, even though they were now carried from every major port in Europe in ships that could steam swiftly against the wind. For those who had never before traveled on the open sea, a crossing in steerage on the stormy North Atlantic, in a wholly alien environment, was often remembered like this:

It was so rough! Oh God, it was so rough! I didn't see a thing. A lot of time you just lay in your bed when you don't feel so good. You don't get up and go because if you do you get dizzy and then you get worse sick, because the water was so rough. That was rough weather—in November, winter starts. Oh, the waves! Oh God! I thought the ship would turn over, but it didn't...

That was a Ukrainian named Mary Zuk describing her trip across the North Atlantic in 1912, not in a 2,000-tonner, but in a far more stable 20,000-tonner. Yet her fears were not entirely without cause, for only six months earlier, the "unsinkable" *Titanic* had hit an iceberg and sunk with a loss of over 1,500 lives, in the sea lanes of the North Atlantic.

During the First World War—as in the Second, a generation later—the North Atlantic continued to be the main highway between Europe and North America. In both wars, people and goods continued to flow across the North Atlantic, but now there were soldiers, rather than emigrants, and war materials, rather than peacetime goods. The North Atlantic was a major theater in both World Wars, in which hundreds of thousands of people, thousands of surface ships, and hundreds of submarines were lost.

After each war, more and faster superliners were built for the trans-Atlantic passenger trade, and hundreds of cargo ships continued to carry goods between Europe and North America. This was the era of the greatest—and last—trans-Atlantic superliners. In the 1920's and 1930's, dozens of superliners regularly made the crossing, and some of them were huge by any previous standard. The 79,300-ton *Normandie*, launched in 1935, the 80,750-ton *Queen Mary*, launched in 1938, were the great passenger ships of their day, and together ended an era. A few other major ships were built after World War II, such as the *United States* and the *Queen Elizabeth II*. But with the coming of regular trans-Atlantic air flight, the great days of the superliners were over.

No longer the great routes of the northern explorers or hardy emigrants, the sea lanes of the North Atlantic still thrive, but now primarily as commercial routes, with massive shiploads of cargo flowing both ways across the Atlantic. The Viking longships are gone, as are the sail-borne packet ships and most of the liners that once plied the stormy northern seas. Only a few travelers—drawn more by the romance of the great liners than by the speed of flight—keep alive the North Atlantic's reputation as one of the great passenger routes of history.

Selective Bibliography

Armstrong, Warren. *Atlantic Highway* (New York: John Day, 1962). A detailed history of the ships and entrepreneurs engaged in the North Atlantic passenger trade during the age of steam, from the 1830's.

Briggs, Peter. *Rivers in the Sea* (New York: Weybright and Talley, 1969). A good, brief study of the main currents in the world's oceans; useful in helping understand the impact of the Gulf Stream on Europe and North America.

Brownstone, David M., Irene M. Franck, and Douglass L. Brownstone. *Island of Hope, Island of Tears* (New York: Rawson, Wade, 1979). Useful for its treatment of emigration across the North Atlantic in the late 19th and early 20th centuries.

Denison, A.D. *America's Maritime History* (New York: Putnam's, 1944). A brief, useful introduction to the history of ships and shipping, focusing on the United States, but with larger world backgrounds explored.

Fiske, John. *The Discovery of America*, in 2 vols. (Boston: Houghton, 1892). An excellent, comprehensive, classic work on the history of North America and of Europe, ultimately focusing on the European exploration, invasion, and conquest of the Americas.

Jones, Gwyn. *The Norse Atlantic Saga* (London: Oxford, 1964). An excellent, scholarly work on the Norse voyages of exploration and settlement of Iceland, Greenland, and America.

Jones, Maldwyn A. *Destination America* (New York: Holt, Rinehart and Winston, 1976). Useful for its treatment of emigration across the North Atlantic in the mid-19th century.

Leip, Hans. *Rivers in the Sea* (New York: Putnam's, 1958). An anecdotal history of exploration in the North Atlantic, focusing on the influence of the Gulf Stream.

Maxtone-Graham, John. *The Only Way To Cross* (New York: Macmillan, 1972). A well-written, detailed, anecdotal discussion of the great era of the North Atlantic super-liners.

McCutchan, Philip. *Tall Ships* (New York: Crown, 1976). A well-illustrated work, which deals in part with the North Atlantic and the ships traversing it.

Morison, Samuel Eliot. *The European Discovery of America: The Northern Voyages* (New York: Oxford, 1971). A comprehensive work on early European voyages of exploration in North America.

Mowat, Farley. *Westviking* (Boston: Little, Brown, 1965). An excellent, though somewhat speculative work on early Norse exploration in North America.

Parry, J. H. *The Age of Reconnaissance* (New York: Praeger, 1969). An excellent, comprehensive, scholarly work on European exploration, trade, and settlement of much of the rest of the world in the period 1450–1650.

_____. *The Discovery of the Sea* (New York: Dial, 1974). A heavily illustrated, excellent work on the worldwide European sea exploration of the 15th and 16th centuries.

_____. *Europe and the Wider World, 1415–1715* (London: Hutchinson, 1949). A brief, excellent scholarly work on the early European exploration and conquest of much of the rest of the world.

_____. *Trade and Dominion* (New York: Praeger, 1971). An excellent, comprehensive, scholarly work on the European overseas empires in the 18th century.

Penrose, Boies. *Travel and Discovery in the Renaissance, 1420–1620* (New York: Atheneum, 1975). An excellent, scholarly work on the European exploration and early colonization of the Americas.

Silverberg, Robert. *The Challenge of Climate* (New York: Meredith, 1969). A useful work on climate as relating to humans and their environment, with good treatment of the impact of the Little Ice Age on the Norse North Atlantic settlements.

Villiers, Alan. *Wild Ocean* (New York: McGraw-Hill, 1957). A history of the North Atlantic and of the people and ships who sailed it; especially useful for its treatment of ships, sailors, and the sea.

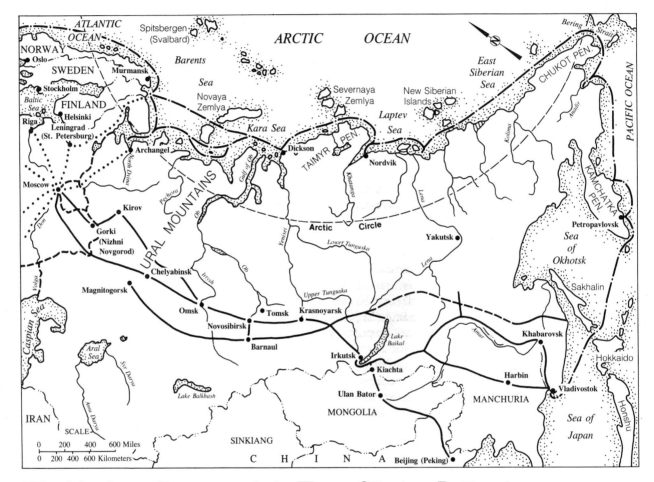

The Northeast Passage and the Trans-Siberian Railroad

—·—·— Northeast Passage

·········· Connecting Railroads

———— Trans-Siberian Railroad

------- Main Canal-River Connections

- - - - - Under Construction

The Northeast Passage

On the 18th of September, 1553, the flagship of the first English expedition to explore the Northeast Passage, under the command of Sir Hugh Willoughby, pulled into a haven, as the captain describes:

...wherein were very many seal fishes and other great fishes, and...we saw bears, great deer, foxes, with divers strange beasts...which to us were unknown, and also wonderful. Thus remaining in this haven the space of a week, and seeing the year far spent, and also very evil weather, as frost, snow, and hail, as though it had been the deep of winter, we thought best to winter there. Wherefore we sent out three men south-southwest, to search if they could find people, who went three days' journey, but could find none. After that, we sent other three westward four days' journey, which also returned without finding any people. Then sent we three men southeast three days' journey, who in like sort returned without finding of people, or any similitude of habitation.
Here endeth Sir Hugh Willoughbie [sic] his note, which was written with his owne hand.

These are the last official words we have from Willoughby and his crew, excepting a will dated January 1554, for all died; their frozen bodies were found by Russian fishermen the following year. They were the first, but far from the last, to lose their lives in the search for a Northeast Passage to the East.

The Northeast Passage is the world's most unikely sea route. That it exists at all is testimony to the European desire for Asian markets, to the Russian drive toward the Pacific, and to modern technology. So difficult is this route linking the Atlantic and Pacific "across the top of the world" that only since World War II has it been open for substantial use. Following a course for many thousands of miles above the Arctic Circle, the Northeast Passage runs from the North Cape of the Scandinavian Peninsula along the coast of Siberian Asia, across several gulfs of the Arctic Ocean, on through the Bering Strait that separates Asia and America, around the great peninsula of Kamchatka, to the ports of the northern Pacific. Despite the hazards of a route through this frozen world, its importance to Russia's navy and to its development of Siberia's enormous resources has made it one of the major sea routes of the modern world.

Surprisingly, the impetus for exploring the Northeast Passage came not from the Russians but from other Europeans, notably the English, Dutch, and Scandinavians. The early Russians were not a seagoing people, even though the modern nation was founded in the ninth century by Vikings from Sweden, called Varangians. The local Slavs called them Rus, from which came the name Russia. Some later Vikings, in the 12th century, sailed northeast of Scandinavia and discovered a "great river" – probably the North Dvina, which flows into the White Sea near modern Archangel – but no regular sea trade developed. In the mid-15th century, when western European explorers were venturing onto great oceans, Russia was simply a small landlocked duchy centered on Moscow. By the mid-16th century, it had pushed westward to the Gulf of Finland, the tongue of the Baltic Sea, but that did it little good, for the Baltic trade was under the rigid control of the German-based Hanseatic League. More to the point, it pushed north to the White Sea and neighboring Arctic waters. But Russia had neither the vision nor the skill at that time to capitalize on her opening to the sea.

The English had both. They were inspired by Portuguese and Spanish voyages to the south and west, all seeking a sea route to Asia. And they had been developing practical skills, for their sailors had seen service in the navies of various European governments and their merchants had worked as commercial agents in such cities as Seville, home base for the West Indies trade. Since the Portuguese controlled the Cape of Good Hope Route south around Africa, the Spanish the Panama Route across the Atlantic, and the Moslems the routes to the East, the English decided that they should look to the north for a route to Cathay, which might also provide them with markets for their woolen goods. In their charter, the Company of Merchants-Adventurers put the situation this way: "...there is left but one way to discover, which is into the North, for...of the four partes of the worlde, it seemeth three parts are discovered by other Princes." The search for a North*west* Passage (which has never resulted in a practical route) served to open up North America, while the thrust toward the Northeast Passage opened up Siberia; many of the same merchant-adventurers were involved in early explorations in both directions. Notable among them was Sebastian Cabot, who formed the joint stock Company of Merchant-Adventurers in London to fund an expedition to the northeast around Asia. Such a route had long been believed possible; Marco Polo reported that he had sailed from Cathay northeast to a land named Anian, "always finding the seas open before him." English geographer John Dee, relying on Arab geographers, assured the expedition that, once past the North Cape of Scandinavia, the shoreline of Asia would slope sharply to the southeast, meaning their route would run mostly through temperate waters.

This was far from the actual truth. The first of the English voyages to the northeast took place in 1553. The three ships in the fleet were immediately separated by storms off Norway, in which one ship was lost. The flagship, under Sir Hugh Willoughby, passed the North Cape and proceeded across Arctic waters to the large double island called Novaya Zemlya (New Land) and into the Kara Sea. Blocked from crossing the sea by the coming of winter in late August, the crew turned back and set up winter quarters on the mainland; but before the long Arctic midnight ended with the arrival of spring, all had died. The third ship, commanded by Richard Chancellor, was more fortunate. After rounding the North Cape, it crossed the relatively protected White Sea to arrive at a small

fishing village (modern Archangel), where Chancellor found the natives "amazed with the strange greatness of his ship (for in those parts before that time they had never seen the like.)" Although these fishermen first fled from him in awe, Chancellor overtook them and learned that he had arrived at a country called Russia, or Muscovy, ruled by Ivan (known to history as "The Terrible"). With his letters of introduction, Chancellor arranged to be taken south to Ivan's court—over 600 miles—by sled, noting:

> ...the people almost not knowing any other manner of carriage. The cause whereof is the exceeding hardness of the ground congealed in the wintertime by the force of the cold, which in those places is very extreme and horrible...

In Moscow he was cordially welcomed, so much so that when he returned home the following year he took back the first Russian ambassador ever to appear at an English court, as well as mutually beneficial trade agreements. Cabot's Company of Merchant-Adventurers was renamed the Muscovy Company, and a regular trade was established between London and Archangel. Despite the fact that Archangel (in Russian, Arkhangelsk) was icebound for four months of the year, it operated as Russia's major northern port for over a century.

In the next 30 years, English sailors periodically attempted to find the elusive Northeast Passage, but none was able to pass from the White Sea into the Kara Sea, because it was blocked by ice in the Kara Straits, the narrow waters on either side of Vaigach Island, which lies between Novaya Zemlya and the Siberian mainland. Nor was ice the only hazard. Those ships that had looked so large to the Russian fishermen were still only small, frail craft, and whales posed a real threat. Master Steven Burroughs, traveling west of the Kara Straits in 1556, related a terrifying experience:

> On Saint James his day...there was a monstrous whale aboard of us, so near to our side that we might have thrust a sword or any other weapon in him, which we durst not do for fear he should have overthrown our ship. And then I called my company together, and all of us shouted, and with the cry that we made he departed from us...and at his falling down he made such a terrible noise in the water that a man would greatly have marveled, except he had known the cause of it. But God be thanked, we were quietly delivered of him.

In 1584 an English party did penetrate the Kara Straits and crossed the normally ice-clogged Kara Sea to the mouth of the great Ob River, but at that point they turned back, never having found the mythical Cape Tabin, where the coast was supposed to turn southeasterly

Using implements like those lying on the ice, Barents's crewmen attempted to chop a passageway through the ice before the ship was caught fast. (Authors' archives)

into warmer waters. This was the extent of the English attempts.

The Dutch, too, were interested in trade through the Northeast Passage. By 1577, they joined in the sea-going trade through the White Sea, with Dutch ships coming to outnumber English. Some traders journeyed from Archangel eastward into Siberia, but the Ural Mountains made an overland passage difficult; others took coastal voyages during warm weather across to the Ob River. In this they were following the local inhabitants, who fished the coast and had a modest trade between river mouths during the long, warm days of summer.

The Dutch also made more ambitious attempts, notably under the great explorer William Barents between 1594 and 1596. During his first voyage, Barents circumnavigated Novaya Zemlya and then passed on across the Kara Sea to the Ob River; but on his second voyage, the following year, the Kara Straits were packed with ice, barring the way completely. On his third voyage, Barents headed not northeast, but across the sea later named after him toward the North Pole, in the process discovering Spitzbergen, a large island in the latitude of northern

Greenland. Unfortunately, although it was only the 26th of August, they were unable to return, as Barents noted:

> ...the ice began to drive with such force that we were enclosed round about therewith, and yet we sought all the means we could to get out, but it was all in vain....The same day in the evening we got to the west side of the Ice Haven, where we were forced, in great cold, poverty, misery, and grief, to stay all that winter.

Ferrying driftwood on rough sledges from four miles away, they built winter quarters, as their ships were slowly crushed by the ice, something "most fearful both to see and hear, and made all the hair of our heads to rise upright with fear." This second party of modern explorers to winter north of the Arctic Circle was more fortunate than Willoughby's had been. Although Barents himself died, most of the crew survived and, after the spring thaw, made a near-miraculous voyage back to the mainland in the open boats they had salvaged from their ships.

In the next few years, a few other exploratory voyages were made, among them one by Henry Hudson, but by the end of the 17th century, both the English and Dutch had generally given up hope of finding a Northeast Passage, believing the way to be perpetually barred by ice. Trade continued through Archangel, although it declined somewhat after 1620, when foreign trade was restricted, and even more after 1703, when St. Petersburg, on the Baltic, became Russia's prime northern port. Many English merchants continued to prefer the port of Archangel, however, regarding their Russian counterparts there as "most honest and intelligent," more than other Russians—probably a reflection of the fact that, through trade with the English, many of them could read, write, and keep accounts, rare skills in those times.

In the 17th century, much more activity was seen on the eastern end of what would later become the Northeast Passage. The Cossacks, a mixed group of peoples living north of the Black and Caspian seas, moved eastward across Siberia to the Pacific coast, taking land in the name of the Russian government. A semiautonomous group (their name comes from the Turkish *kazak*, meaning "adventurer" or "free man"), they spread throughout the vast land, following the network of great rivers that lace Siberia. In that period, the prime resource exploited from the region was furs, which the Cossacks took in plenty. Following the fur-bearing animals along the north-flowing Siberian rivers—especially the Ob, the Yenesei, the Lena, and the Kolima—the Cossacks reached north to the "Cold Ocean," the Arctic, and east to the "Great Southern Ocean," the Pacific. Still following their prey, these fur hunters explored the Chukot peninsula, whose projection reaches across almost to North America, and the peninsula of Kamchatka, which extends down into the north Pacific, around the rim of the Pacific Ocean itself. The Cossacks were not sailors, however; in their small boats, they set no course and kept no direction—one group even ended up on the North American coast thinking it was just another island. Of more immediate and permanent benefit to Russia, the Cossacks moved down the Amur River, a major east-flowing waterway that later acted as a border between Russia and China, to the Sea of Okhotsk and, south of that, to the Sea of Japan, both gulfs of the Pacific Ocean.

A century after Vitus Bering had established a shipbuilding center there, Petropavlovsk on Kamchatka Peninsula was still a very quiet port. (Lithograph by Kittlibt, from Voyage of Lutke, 1826–9)

Such a vast territory with an extensive shoreline made it imperative that Russia become a sea power and, if possible, open the Northeast Passage. Peter the Great, Czar of Russia, recognized this need, although most of his countrymen did not. The Czar himself went to Archangel to study English and Dutch ships (and was almost drowned crossing the White Sea), visited Europe to study industrial methods, and even worked for a time, in disguise, as a ship's carpenter in the Netherlands. He also sent Russians to western European ports to learn the shipbuilding art and commissioned various expeditions to explore the Siberian coast, for little specific information was available. One main unanswered question was: are Asia and North America separate continents, or is the "Strait of Anian" simply an inlet to a great bay formed by a continuous land mass? When several Russian expeditions failed to provide Peter with a definitive answer, he brought in outside experts, under the direction of Danish navigator Vitus Bering. At Peter's direction, Bering built on Kamchatka Peninsula a shipbuilding installation, a naval academy, and an ironworking plant to provide the necessary metal fittings and anchors. The improvements must have been significant, for an 18th century observer (W. Coxe, in *An Account of Russian Discoveries Between Asia and America*) had noted that Russian ships in the Pacific area were "commonly built without iron, and in general so badly constructed, that it is wonderful how they can weather so stormy a sea." Using a primarily western European crew, in 1728 Bering moved northeast along the coast, through the strait that now bears his name, and then west, reaching the Kolima River on the Arctic Ocean, where he was blocked by ice; though he could go no further, he concluded that Asia and North America were, indeed, separate land masses.

The more Siberia became developed, and the more trade went by a tortuous river-and-portage route across Siberia to China, the more important finding a Northeast Passage became. Catherine the Great continued efforts to open the Northeast Passage from both west and east, with expeditions often undertaken in sections, between Archangel and the Ob River, between the Ob and the Yenesei, between the Yenesei and the Taimir Peninsula (the northernmost point in mainland Asia and the most difficult section of the projected route), and between the Lena River and Anadir Bay, south of the Bering Strait. By the mid-18th century most of the Northeast Passage had been traveled and surveyed, but no one had yet traveled continuously along the whole route. With the knowledge gained from these explorations and with ships larger than those of the first venturers on the Northeast Passage, merchant-sailors gradually extended regular trading routes from Archangel first to the Ob and then to the Yenesei. By the second half of the 19th century, ships from western Europe had penetrated hundreds of miles along these great rivers into the heart of Siberia and come out with

profitable cargo, such as grain and tallow. All of this activity laid the basis for the first continuous trip along the Northeast Passage.

Like many other major explorations along the route, this journey was made not by a Russian but by a western European, the Swedish Baron Nils Nordenskiöld. Having participated in several commercial trips to the Siberian rivers, Nordenskiöld realized that these rivers brought warmer waters from the south to the Arctic Ocean, and timed his trip to take advantage of this moderating influence. Leaving from Karlskröna in southern Sweden, he rather easily crossed the Kara Sea and, at the mouth of the Yenesei River, made his first valuable discovery: a fine harbor on an island just off the mainland. Naming the harbor Port Dickson, after one of his sponsors, Nordenskiöld showed some prescience in predicting that it "will certainly in the future be of great importance for the foreign commerce of Siberia...I am convinced that the day will come when great warehouses and many dwellings inhabited all the year round will be found at Port Dickson. Now the region is entirely uninhabited."

Moving steadily along the coast, Nordenskiöld rounded the great Taimir Peninsula and arrived at its tip, Cape Chelyuskin (named for the Russian who had explored it). For Nordenskiöld this was a major event:

> We had now reached a great goal, which for centuries had been the object of unsuccessful struggles. For the first time a vessel lay at anchor off the northernmost cape of the Old World. No wonder then that the occurrence was celebrated by a display of flags and the firing of salutes, and when we returned from our excursion on land, by festivities on board, by wine and toasts...

Past Cape Chelyuskin, Nordenskiöld attempted to move out to sea, intending to visit the New Siberian Islands; but finding the seas clogged with ice, he returned to the relatively ice-free waters along the coast. This confirmed his theory that the coastal route allowed the best chance of success along the Northeast Passage. He then worked his way through floating ice for nearly 2,000 miles, across a sea fed by the great Lena River (a sea for a time named after him, but now called the Laptev Sea), through another strait, and into the East Siberian Sea.

From the time they entered the Kara Sea, Nordenskiöld had seen "neither men nor human habitations, if I except the old uninhabited hut between Cape Chelyuskin and the Khatanga River." It was with great excitement, then, that the party spotted two boats off Cape Shelagsky on the Chukot Peninsula.

> Every man, with the exception of the cook, who could be induced by no catastrophe to leave his pots and pans and who had circumnavigated Asia and Europe perhaps without having been once on land, rushed on deck.

Since the parties shared no common language, they used sign language. (Oddly, none of the mainlanders knew Russian, but one young boy could count to 10 in English, indicating that American whalers had probably been there before them; the same was true for some other Chukchi villages farther east.) Sign language proved very successful, however, along with presents of tobacco and Dutch clay pipes.

On the 28th of September 1878, Nordenskiöld lay offshore at Kolyuchin Bay, near the tip of the Chukot Peninsula. In the morning he found that the night's frost had so firmly bound together the drift ice that his ship, the *Vega*, could not move. At first, Nordenskiöld was not uneasy about the delay, for he knew that many American whalers had stayed in the area until mid-October, and after all, the ship needed only "a few hours' southerly wind...sufficient to break up the belt of ice," scarcely a Swedish mile (6.64 English miles) in breadth. But he gradually came to realize that the wind would not be arriving. Like his predecessors, Nordenskiöld was forced to winter north of the Arctic circle, but he had the benefit of their experience. With the ship not in danger of being crushed (though he had a cache of vital items stored on shore just in case), the crew survived astonishingly well on board. While scurvy was a problem, there was not even a serious case of frostbite. As Nordenskiöld reported:

> On board the vessel in our cabins and collection rooms it was...by no means so cold as many would suppose....Much greater inconvenience than from cold did we in the cabins suffer from the excessive heat and the fumes which firing in large cast-iron stoves is wont to cause in small close rooms.

Perhaps worse was the knowledge that the wintering could have been avoided if they had arrived even a few hours earlier. Throughout the next 10 months, there were plenty of "if only's" uttered: "The *Vega* did not require to stay so long at Port Dickson, we might have saved a day at Taimir...and so on." It was perhaps sharpest just a few days after they were iced in:

> A southerly wind after some days brought the open-water channel so near the vessel that it was possible to walk to it in a few hours. It then swarmed with seals—an indication that it was in connection with a sea that was constantly open.

But it was not until July 18th of the following year that the sea released Nordenskiöld's ship.

By 11 A.M. on the following morning the journey was complete:

> ...we were in the middle of the sound which united the North Polar Sea with the Pacific, and from this point the *Vega* greeted the Old and New Worlds by a display of flags and the firing of a Swedish salute...Now for the first time, after the lapse of three hundred and twenty-six years, and when most men experienced in sea matters had declared the undertaking impossible, was the Northeast Passage at last achieved.

Nordenskiöld was rightly proud of his achievement, completed "without the sacrifice of a single human life." He was, however, overoptimistic about the future of the route, saying "the same thing may be done again in most, perhaps in all, years in the course of a few weeks." In truth, great difficulties remained. The next person to hazard the passage, in 1900, died in the attempt. But the Russian government was spurred to continue developing the Siberian route, and other governments were eager for the commercial opportunities. In 1896, an English company was given special terms for establishing trade with the west Siberian rivers; by 1905, a fleet of 22 ships was sailing to the Yenesei River. Archangel, which had declined with the rise of St. Petersburg on the Baltic Sea, began to revive as a major northern port. Sea trade developed on the other end of the route, too. The Russians had established a prime port, Vladivostok, on the Sea of Japan; although it was icebound for three months of the year, it became the home port of a fleet of steamships that in the warmer months sailed through the Bering Strait to the Kolima River. (For a short time, the Russians had an ice-free harbor at Port Arthur, but they lost that in 1905, in the Russo-Japanese War.)

The Russians also organized a series of expeditions to obtain even better information about their Arctic territories, the expeditions gaining considerably from technical advances of the age. Not only did the Russians now have much more accurate surveying equipment, they also had the wireless to improve communications between exploring parties and—perhaps most important—they had specially reinforced ships to act as icebreakers. These icebreakers were generally converted whaling ships, all foreign-built, generally by the British. With this equipment, the Russians moved to explore more thoroughly the islands in the Arctic Ocean that they regarded as theirs. Some of these islands had been discovered by British, American, or Canadian explorers, but Russia moved to stake its claim to them. (In like manner, the Russians had long since abandoned most of their fur-trading settlements along the west coast of North America, which had reached south nearly to San Francisco; land explored by Cossack fur hunters or by expeditions under Russian-sponsored explorers like Bering had now become part of the United States or Canada, with the territory of Alaska being sold to the United States in 1867.)

The Russians increasingly realized the importance of a Northeast Passage—no longer to reach Cathay but now to protect and develop their own extensive territory.

Such a route became increasingly important in case of war, which could cut Russia's access to Europe's large inland seas—the Baltic, Black, and Mediterranean—or which could require the passage of ships from Europe to East Asia, via a long route through the Suez Canal, around Africa, or later through the Panama Canal. The Northeast passage had demonstrated its immediate utility in the 1890's, when metal for the Trans-Siberian Railway was shipped across the Arctic and inland along the Yenesei River. Norway, too, was interested in such ventures; in 1912 the Norwegians established a steamship company to operate between Oslo and the Yenesei. In World War I, the Allies were anxious to receive food supplies from Siberia, especially from the Yenesei wheatlands, along the relatively secure passage the Russians call the Northern Sea Route. Britain built four icebreakers for Russia, and sent five others from Canada, to ensure the flow of supplies between Archangel and western Europe.

But in 1917, the Revolution came to Russia. Foreign ships and supplies were taken over by the new Soviet government, and civil war disrupted traffic throughout the region. Still the Northern Sea Route had a role to play. (Indeed, Lenin had originally planned to return to Russia from exile by going around the North Cape to Mur-

mansk, a small settlement east of the North Cape; instead his route took him through Sweden and Finland to Petrograd on the Baltic.) Allied Forces—notably the British, who had had close ties with the Russian royal family for centuries—landed in both Archangel and Murmansk; they penetrated some distance inland but finally had to give up their attempt to rout the Bolsheviks. When the Soviet government reasserted its control over the region, it found food supplies desperately short, especially in Archangel; to ease the famine, supplies of grain were brought in from northern Siberia through the Kara Sea, in a series of expeditions over several years.

During this period, development of the Northeast Passage slowed but did not stop completely. Two complete trips from Vladivostok to Archangel were made, one in 1914 by the Russian Boris Vilkitski and one in 1918 by Norwegian Roald Amundsen (the first man to complete the North*west* Passage); in both cases, the parties had to winter en route, taking two seasons to complete the journey. Meanwhile technical advances continued to be applied to the problem of making the route feasible. Good information on temperature and ice conditions was essential for navigators, who had only a two- to three-month season of relatively open water in the most difficult parts

The sailing ship Vega, *accompanied by the* Lena, *celebrates her arrival off the northernmost point in Asia, Cape Chelyuskin, in 1878. (Anonymous engraving from* The Voyage of the Vega, *by M. Kiold)*

of the route. Meteorological stations were set up around the Arctic; five were in place before the 1917 Revolution, and almost 70 more were set up by the late 1930's, including one at the North Pole. Airplanes (and later helicopters) were brought in to perform a variety of functions. They could fly ahead of a ship to scout the best route through the floating ice; they could supply distant observation stations around the Arctic; and they could perform rescue missions. This latter function allowed scientists to set up temporary stations on ice floes, drifting with the ice, to chart speed, direction, and behavior; then, when the ice floe became too small for safety, the scientists would signal for a plane to pick them up and transfer them to a ship.

Emphasis on technology had the desired effect: in 1932, a ship made the first trip through the Northeast Passage in a single season. The trip was so difficult that the ice broke every blade on the propeller; in order to replace the blades, the crew had to shift hundreds of tons of coal into the bow, to raise the stern; then when the propeller itself was lost, the ship used sails to pass through the Bering Strait, only days before the ice closed in. The success of this ship, the *Sibiriakov*, did not make the trip easier, however. The following year a scientific expedition in a more heavily reinforced ship, the *Chelyuskin*, attempted the same voyage, but it became locked in an ice field when winter arrived early, drifted toward Alaska and then north, and finally sank; thanks to modern technology, the crew were rescued, after radioing for a plane to come in on a landing strip they had built on the ice.

Clearly, if the Northeast Passage was to become a practical route between the east and west coasts, heavier icebreakers were needed. One Russian official put it this way: "The aeroplane is the eye; the radio station is the ear; and the icebreaker is the fist in this work of ours." The few icebreakers in use in the mid-1930's were old and makeshift; the *Sibiriakov*, for example, was an ex-whaler built over 20 years earlier on Scotland's River Clyde. They were also relatively small ships, of only 1,000 to 4,000 tons. In 1932 the Russians established a special Northern Sea Route Administration to develop shipping along the route. They began to build their own icebreakers (the first being produced only in 1937), larger vessels of 10,000 to 12,000 tons. Unlike earlier icebreakers, which rammed the ice, more modern versions were designed to climb onto the edge of the ice and crush it; some were built with tanks to take on extra water for more weight and with heavy-duty engines to help push the broken ice aside. Newer icebreakers were also sometimes equipped with small seaplanes, launched by catapults.

Progress was not continual. Indeed, after a successful shipping season in 1936, 26 ships were stranded in the ice as winter closed in the following year; they were rescued, although that did not save the leaders of the Northern Sea Route Administration from being purged for their failure. Only in 1939 did the Russians come to have what they regarded as their "first year of normal commercial exploitation" along the Northeast Passage. By this time Nordenskiöld's prophecy was beginning to come true. Port Dickson had the wharves and warehouses he had predicted, and a population of 3,000 to 4,000 during the navigation season, being described as one of the "liveliest points in the Arctic."

The Russians also modified the route itself. Taking a lead from the Allied Expeditionary Forces' landing choice in 1918, Stalin shifted the western terminus to Murmansk, it being near enough to the Gulf Stream to remain ice-free year-round. Archangel became a back-up port, relieving the strain on Murmansk in the warmer months. They also linked the Northern Sea Route with inland waterways in western Russia. The White Sea Canal was built to connect the Baltic and White seas. For the first time, Russian ships from the Baltic fleet could sail directly north to Siberia and—in theory, at least—to the Pacific, without passing through areas controlled by other countries. Other inland waterways linked the Black and Caspian seas in the same network, through the Don and Volga rivers, with canals all joining in Moscow.

But Russia had only a short time to enjoy the rewards of these inter-sea connections. In 1941, it was attacked by Germany, its former ally; Murmansk was cut off, and Finnish soldiers destroyed the White Sea Canal. Russia's developing Siberian hinterland once again supplied the White Sea region with food, fuel, and vital resources. Fully aware of the importance of the Northern Sea Route, the Germans took Norway partly to control access to it, trying to keep Anglo-American aid from reaching Russia. The Germans sent ships (among them the formidable *Tirpitz*), airplanes, and submarines to harass Allied supply ships at the Atlantic entrance to the Northeast Passage. But Anglo-American convoys continued to supply Russia's White Sea ports, sending 739 ships in three and a half years, with nine out of ten reaching their destinations. Sailors on these icy voyages constantly had to remove ice forming on the exposed decks, so it would not make the ships top-heavy; and submarine crews continually had to grease the hatch with gelatin so the vessel could at a moment's notice dive underwater to remove ice.

On the eastern end of the passage, Lend-Lease ships brought supplies from North American ports like Seattle to Russian ports between the Bering Strait and the Taimir Peninsula. These ships were less vulnerable, the Siberian Sea being unfamiliar territory to enemy ships. As a World War II Russian captain put it: "You see, the ice is our friend. We can hide in the ice, if nothing else. There isn't a warship commander who would dare follow us in." In the midsection of the Northern Sea Route, Russian ships continued to ply back and forth, ferrying supplies and building up more experience for the development of the

Modern travelers wintering in the Arctic carry portable shelters and can be rescued by air, unlike Barents's crew, pictured here in their winter quarters. (Authors' archives)

regular commercial route that would come.

Russia still had few icebreakers, and some of them were Lend-Lease ships that had to be returned to the United States within a few years after World War II. Those that were in use had heavy fuel needs and often had to detour for additional coal at refueling stations set up along the route, losing valuable time. But in the years after the war, coal-burning icebreakers were largely replaced by oil-fueled and some atomic-powered ships, such as the massive *Lenin*, launched in 1959, king of the Northern Sea Route and the second icebreaker to bear the name.

Acting singly or in groups, icebreakers are able to double the time that the complete route is open, to four months of the year or more, providing much more flexibility and turnaround time for the hundreds of Russian ships operating there. Based in Murmansk, modern icebreaker convoys carve a route that varies with the ice conditions; from the White Sea, the route might be on either side of Vaigach Island or—more common in recent decades—through the Strait of Matochkin between the two halves of Novaya Zemlya. From there they may open

routes for convoys down the Ob or the Yenesei; or they may go on past Cape Chelyuskin to the Lena, deep in the Siberian heartland; or they may proceed all the way around the great bulge of land that forms the Bering Strait to Kamchatka's ports or to the main Pacific port of Vladivostok. During the colder months of the year, the icebreakers generally ply between local points, keeping shipping lanes open on sections of the Arctic coast or along the Siberian rivers.

Although the route remains difficult for the sailors who follow it, the rewards are great and the Russians have the full benefit of them, since they control the route completely. With the Northeast Passage a reality, and their inland waterways restored, they are able to move their ships—military or cargo—from ocean to ocean, and sea to sea, without interference from any other country. Even when interference is not in question, the saving in distance is extraordinary; before the Northeast Passage was open, ships traveling between Murmansk and Vladivostok often went through the Panama Canal or around the Cape of Good Hope, either way a distance of about 14,000 miles. But the Northern Sea Route between the two points is only 6,000 miles. How important the Northeast Passage remains depends to some extent on the climate; for much of the 20th century, the Arctic has been warmer than in previous centuries, especially the "Little Ice Age" that prevailed when Europeans made their first attempts to open the route. Even if the Arctic does become colder, however, technology may keep the route open. In any case, the most significant benefit of the route to Russia will remain the ability to develop the great Asian empire that it built in the centuries during which the Northeast Passage was sought. Those who dreamed of the easy route through temperate waters to the riches of Cathay would have been surprised by the riches that lay hidden in the frozen land of Siberia.

Selective Bibliography

Armstrong, Terence E. *The Northern Sea Route: Soviet Exploitation of the North East Passage*. (Cambridge: Cambridge University Press, 1952). A sound treatment, focusing on the modern development and administration of the route; published for the Scott Polar Research Institute.

Krypton, Constantine. *The Northern Sea Route: Its Place in Russian Economic History Before 1917*. (New York: Research Program on the U.S.S.R., 1953). A pamphlet.

_____.*The Northern Sea Route* and *The Economy of the Soviet North*. (New York: Praeger, 1956; published for the Research Program on the U.S.S.R). Both focus on the modern economic and political development of the White Sea-to-Bering Strait section.

Mitchell, Mairin. *The Maritime History of Russia, 848-1948*.

(London: Sidgwick and Jackson, 1949; New York: Macmillan, 1949). A prime book, covering both sea and river travel, with much fascinating detail.

Penrose, Boies. *Travel and Discovery in the Renaissance, 1420–1620*. (New York: Atheneum, 1975; reprint of the 1952 Harvard University edition). Excellent; one chapter focuses on the search for northern passages.

Stefansson, Vilhjalmur, ed. *Great Adventures and Explorations: From the Earliest Times to the Present as Told by the Explorers Themselves*, revised edition. (New York: Dial Press, 1952). One section focuses on the Northeast Passage explorations.

Tavernier, Bruno. *Great Maritime Routes: An Illustrated History*. (New York: Viking, 1972). Translated from the French; one chapter is on the Russian routes of the Far North.

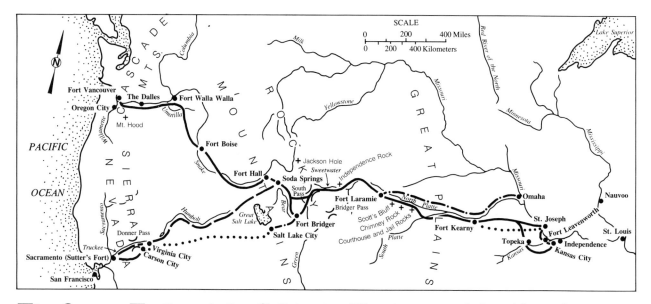

The Oregon Trail and the California Trail in the Mid-19th Century

——————— Oregon Trail   —·—·— Mormon Trail

— — — California Trail   ········· Pony Express Route

The Oregon Trail and the California Trail

The roads were rocky and often very steep... Sometimes to keep the wagons from pressing upon the animals in going down grade young pine trees were cut down and after stripping them of all but the top branches they were tied to the front and under the rear axle. The branches dragging upon the ground, or often solid rock, formed a reliable brake. Then again a rope or a chain would be tied to the rear of the wagon and everyone, man, woman and child would be pressed into service to hold the wagon back. At other times a chain or rope would be fastened to the front axle and we climbed up impossible bowlders and pulled with might and main while the men pushed with herculanian strength to get the loaded wagons over some barrier.

And oh, such pulling, tugging it was! I used to pity the drivers as well as the oxen and horses — and the rest of us.

This was the experience of Catherine Haun, crossing the mountains on the Oregon-California Trail at the height of the rush westward, in the spring and summer of 1849.

It was a long and difficult journey: a thousand-mile walk over prairie and high plains, followed by another thousand miles of mountain, desert, and white-water river country. It was not impossibly difficult, though; the overwhelming majority of those who traversed the trails to Oregon and California reached their destinations, completing the long trek west that had started at Plymouth Rock and Jamestown over two centuries earlier and ultimately closing the American frontier.

Many had traveled west before, earlier in their lifetimes, with the hundreds of thousands of settlers who had poured through the Mohawk Valley and out through the Cumberland Gap into the great forest beyond the Appalachian Mountains in the half century after the American Revolution; on the way they had taken the land all the way west to the Mississippi, expelling the Native Americans who had lived there to new treaty lands beyond. There they paused, but only for a few years, for they never stopped looking west, beyond the forest and the central prairies and out into the main body of the continent beyond.

In the 1840's these settlers began to move again, out into the Oregon country, over a body of routes that were to become known as the Oregon Trail and the California Trail. They have also been called the Oregon Trace, the Emigrant Road, and the Platte, or Great Platte Trail. Some portions of the route have been called the Overland Trail, the California Overland Trail, and the Mormon Trail. The Native American name for the wagon road created by the passage of the emigrants was the Great Medicine Road. Francis Parkman called it the Oregon Trail, and it is this name by which the route is best known, although most of those who traveled it went to California rather than into the northwest. All of the country west of the Rockies and north of California was known as Oregon before 1846, so emigrants had been traveling through Oregon for hundreds of miles before they branched off on the trail to California.

The Missouri River drains much of the northeastern

slope of the American Rockies, flowing eastward through Montana, southeast through the Dakotas, Nebraska, and Kansas, and then eastward again, across Missouri to join the Mississippi River at St. Louis. There, in the towns at the bend of the river on the Kansas-Missouri border, westward-bound emigrants gathered every spring, starting in 1841, to set off together toward Oregon and California. Their starting places were Independence, Kansas City, Liberty, Fort Leavenworth, and St. Joseph, with most emigrants gathering at Independence, generally considered the start of the trail.

Starting in 1847, the Mormon emigration from Illinois to Salt Lake City also joined the Oregon Trail, with large bodies of Mormon emigrants setting out from further north on the Missouri River, at Florence, Nebraska, now part of Omaha. These emigrants traveled westward parallel to the main Oregon-California migration trail for some distance and then joined the main trail for some hundreds of miles before branching off to the Salt Lake country.

Coming west out of Independence, travelers were initially not on a separate Oregon-bound trail but rather on the Santa Fe Trail, which ran from St. Louis to Santa Fe. Nine miles out of Independence, they crossed the Missouri state line into what was then treaty-granted Indian Country (later Kansas), still on the Santa Fe Trail. Forty-one miles out, the road branched, and the separate Oregon-California Trail began; in the early days this was signaled by a small hand-lettered sign that read "Road to Oregon."

For the next 60 miles, the trail went almost due west, to the Kansas River. Ferries were available at several places along the Kansas, some of them maintained by displaced Shawnees and Delawares; the main crossing in the later years was at the Topeka ferry.

Crossing the Kansas, the emigrant trains turned northwest, traveling across the prairie to the South Fork of the Platte River, a distance of a little over 200 miles. This was always a spring crossing; the main bulk of the wagons set out from Independence in May, for they had to move across the Cascades, 2,000 miles away, before the snow closed the mountain passes that autumn. In the spring the flowering prairie was beautiful and relatively easy to traverse. The more difficult portions of the trail were still far ahead. Of the river and prairie, missionary Father Pierre-Jean De Smet said:

> ...nothing can be more pleasing than the perspective which it presents to the eye...[The river islands] have the appearance of a labyrinth of groves floating on the water. Their extraordinary position gives an air of youth and beauty to the whole scene. If to this be added the undulations of the river, the waving of the verdure, the alternations of light and

"Crossing the Platte, Mouth of Deer Creek." (By F. R. Grist from Howard Stansbury, Exploration and Survey of the Valley of the Great Salt Lake, 1852)

Before the great days of emigration on the Oregon and California trails, Fort Laramie was a small, primitive wooden stockade. (From Frémont report in 27th Congress, 3rd Session, Senate Doc. 243, Serial 416, National Archives)

shade, the succession of these islands varying in form and beauty, and the purity of the atmosphere, some idea may be formed of the pleasing sensations which the traveler experiences on beholding a scene that seems to have started into existence fresh from the hands of the creator.

At the Platte River, the trail turned westward, following the south bank of the river 450 miles across the Great Plains and into the Rocky Mountains. It was a climb of several thousand feet as well, but spread out over so long a distance as to be almost imperceptible; what was felt and seen was that the land and climate changed. As the days and weeks went by, forest and river valley gave way to lush grasslands; along the Platte, grassland gave way to treeless prairie and then to the arid scrub and windswept rock that characterizes the high plains.

Here the emigrants began to see and hunt buffalo. An early migrant, traveling in 1841, recalled the huge herds of buffalo:

I have seen the plain black with them for several days' journey as far as the eye could reach. They seemed to be coming northward continually from the distant plains to the Platte to get water, and would plunge in and swim across by thousands— so numerous were they that they changed not only the color of the water, but its taste, until it was unfit to drink; but we had to use it.

They also began to use buffalo dung, which they called "chips," as their main source of fuel. Along the Platte, traversing most of present-day Nebraska and part of Wyoming, they entered the American West.

The Oregon-California Trail followed the south bank of the Platte and—past the forking of the river into North and South branches—the South Platte for well over a hundred miles. Then, at one of several possible fords, the emigrants crossed the South Platte and cut across country to meet the North Platte, following it westward almost 200 miles more to Fort Laramie. This was high plains country, where the altitude made work and walking much more difficult and where the land was much less hospitable. Halfway to Fort Laramie on the North Platte, they began to encounter notable rock formations, such as Courthouse and Jail Rocks, and the even more extraordinary Chimney Rock, visible from many miles away across the plains. Further on, they found the huge rock formations at Scott's Bluff, now a national monument.

In his classic account of the Oregon-bound migration of 1843, Jesse Applegate gives a vivid picture of life on the prairie portion of the route:

It is 4 o'clock A.M.; the sentinels on duty have discharged their rifles—the signal that the hours of sleep are over—and every wagon and tent is pouring forth its night tenants, and slow-kindling smokes begin largely to rise and float away in the morning

297

air. Sixty men start from the corral, spreading as they make [their way] through the vast herd of cattle and horses that make a semicircle around the encampment, the most distant perhaps two miles away.

The herders pass to the extreme verge and carefully examine for trails beyond, to see that none of the animals have strayed or been stolen during the night. This morning no trails led beyond the outside animals in sight, and by 5 o'clock the herders begin to contract the great moving circle...

From 6 to 7 o'clock is a busy time; breakfast is to be eaten, the tents struck, the wagons loaded and the teams yoked and brought up in readiness to be attached to their respective wagons. All know when, at 7 o'clock, the signal to march sounds, that those not ready to take their proper places in the line of march must fall into the dusty rear for the day...

It is on the stroke of seven; the rush to and fro, the cracking of whips, the loud command to oxen, and what seemed to be the inextricable confusion of the last ten minutes has ceased. Fortunately every one has been found and every teamster is at his post. The clear notes of a trumpet sound in the front; the pilot and his guards mount their horses; the leading divisions of the wagon move out of the encampment, and take up the line of march; the rest fall into their places with the precision of clock work, until the spot so lately full of life sinks back into that solitude that seems to reign over the broad plain and rushing river as the caravan draws its lazy length towards the distant El Dorado.

At Fort Laramie, over 600 miles from the Missouri, most emigrant trains rested for a few days and then continued northwest along the North Platte, fording to its north bank well over a hundred miles further on, in the vicinity of what is now Casper, Wyoming. This main final crossing of the North Fork of the Platte was extremely difficult until the establishment of Mormon's Ferry in 1847.

The Mormon Church, a major 19th century dissident Christian sect, had by that year been persecuted and expelled from several locations in the eastern and midwestern United States. In 1846, they were expelled from their center at Nauvoo, then the largest city in Illinois, with a population of 25,000. In the spring of 1847, they were on the Missouri River, north of the Platte and of the Oregon-California Trail gathering points. That spring, an advance party led by Brigham Young set out west, crossing the Missouri, going south to meet the Platte, and then following the Platte and the North Platte west and northwest. The route on the north side of the Platte as far as Laramie became known as the first portion of the Mormon Trail, which extended from Omaha to what was to become Salt Lake City, a distance of a little over a thousand miles.

Brigham Young's party—and the Mormon Trail—crossed the North Platte to its south bank at Fort Laramie, there joining the main route of the Oregon-California Trail. At the North Fork crossing near Casper, the Mor-

mons used the boat they had brought along—the *Revenue Cutter*—to ford the river. Because the river was, at that time, nearly at flood stage, emigrant trains coming behind them could not ford the river without boats or ferries. The Mormons provided both—for a fee. The boat took people and goods, and a ferry they had quickly built on the spot took wagons. The Mormon party continued on, traveling the main trail, but left their ferry and people to run it in place until the river was bridged two decades later.

After this final crossing of the Platte, the westward trail headed away from the river across 50 miles of arid country to the Sweetwater River valley. Near the beginning of the valley was Independence Rock, called by many the Great Register of the Oregon, California, and Mormon trails. Here, with 900 miles of grassland and high plains behind, and well over a thousand miles of mountains, deserts, and rivers ahead, tens of thousands of people stopped to place their names on the huge gray granite rocks, just as the solitary trappers who had preceded them into those mountains had done. Then they headed into the formidable Rockies.

The valley of the Sweetwater ran clear and level for 100 miles through otherwise extremely difficult terrain up through South Pass, a 20-mile-wide, easily traversed cut through the mountains. Although the pass was almost 7,500 feet above sea level, the approach to it was so gradual and easy that many emigrants did not even know when they had reached the top of the pass and were beginning to descend—although at that point those bound for Oregon and California were halfway to their destination and were generally considered to have entered Oregon.

Twenty miles west of South Pass, travelers had to make some route decisions. This was relatively open country, and emigrant parties made many different choices, depending on their knowledge of the land and the condition of their animals and people.

The main body of those bound for California and Oregon took the most direct route west, called Sublette's Cutoff, after the fur trader who had first used and recommended it as a way west. This was 110 miles of mostly desert country; a long, straight haul across entirely inhospitable, almost waterless country to the Green River. Smaller groups went further south by a somewhat longer route, by way of Fort Bridger, a small trading post founded by mountain man and trapper Jim Bridger and his partner, Louis Vasquez. This route, which rejoined the main trail at the Green River, was a little easier on animals and people, though it was 70 to 80 miles longer. Mormon emigrants went from the Little Sandy River to Fort Bridger but did not then turn west toward the Green River; instead they fought their way over 120 miles of extremely difficult terrain to what was to become Salt Lake City.

Most emigrants bound for California and Oregon continued from the Green River along the main trail

"First View of the Great Salt Lake Valley, from a Mountain Pass." (From Stansbury report in 32nd Congress, Special Session, March, 1851, Senate Executive Doc. 3, Serial 1608, National Archives)

toward Fort Hall, 125 miles further northwest, up the Bear River, and close to where the trail picked up the Snake River. Fort Hall had been built by New Englander Nathaniel Wyeth in 1834, during the days of the fur trade, and later was taken over by the Hudson's Bay Company. For those on the Oregon-California Trail, it was a resting place, and for many a place to make the final choice between California and Oregon. Forty miles southwest of Fort Hall, when travelers reached the Raft River, the two trails parted. Out of Fort Hall, the main trail followed the southern bank of the Snake. Those bound for Oregon continued along the Snake after passing the Raft River; those bound for California turned south along the Raft. This portion of the trail also held the highest crossing on the main California and Oregon trails: the 8,000-foot pass over the divide at the eastern end of the Bear River valley. Like South Pass, however, it was an easy ascent.

Emigrants following the Oregon Trail now faced the hardest part of the journey: 300 miles of desert following the deep cut that was the impassable and often-unreachable valley of the Snake, followed by a very difficult climb over the Blue Mountains into Oregon. This stretch of the trail followed the Snake to Fort Boise and left the Snake to follow the valley of the Powder River up and over the Blue Mountains into the Grande Ronde Valley. Most early emigrants swung north to the Walla Walla River, meeting the Columbia River at Fort Walla Walla, a favorite resting place. But by 1844, most emigrants were bypassing Fort

Walla Walla in favor of the shorter, more southerly route that went by way of the Umatilla River and into the Columbia.

Then it was a slow overland road down the Columbia almost 200 miles to a settlement called The Dalles, followed in the early years by an extraordinarily difficult final 60 miles by boat or raft down the Columbia itself. Livestock were driven over a narrow mountain trail south of Mount Hood, while emigrants faced a long portage past the Cascades 40 miles from Fort Vancouver. By 1846, however, the Barlow Road had been built, bypassing the final 60 miles down the river and providing a usable wagon road from The Dallas to Oregon City, in the Willamette Valley. Once in the Willamette Valley the emigrants had traversed the 2,000-mile-long Oregon Trail.

While the Oregon Trail headed northwest, the California Trail headed more directly westward. Emigrants to California had several alternative routes heading west beyond South Pass. Some bound for California turned west before Fort Hall, cutting across rather inhospitable country 70 miles up the Bear River to near Soda Springs, so named because of the mineral springs in the area. After 1847, when Salt Lake City was established, increasing numbers of California-bound travelers followed the last section of the Mormon Trail to Salt Lake City rather than turning north and west again from Fort Bridger. The Salt Lake City Route, although somewhat longer than the more northerly Fort Hall route, allowed emigrants to rest and refit before moving on across the desert and mountains to California. But whether they went south and west via Soda Springs, came around by way of Salt Lake City, or took the main route through Fort Hall and then split off from the Oregon Trail at the Raft River, they all joined each other again further west at the Humboldt River, then the main way west to California.

On the main California route, it was 150 miles south and west along the Raft River and then Goose Creek to the Humboldt, in what is now northeastern Nevada. From there it was over 350 miles along the Humboldt—a long but relatively easy section, with water and grass all the way, unlike the Snake to the north. Then, after the Humboldt literally sank out of sight into the desert and marsh area called the Humboldt Sink, it was a little over 50 miles of very difficult, waterless, desert travel to the Truckee River, a stretch that included that bane to all California-bound travelers, the 40-Mile Desert. For several hundred miles, from what is now Wells, Nevada, all the way across desert and mountains into California's Sacramento Valley, U.S. routes 40 and 80 roughly parallel this earliest California Trail route.

Once at the Truckee River, it was 100 miles more along the river valley, up over the Sierra Nevada mountains and down into the Bear Valley of northern California. This is the road over the Donner Pass, named after the ill-fated Donner emigrant train of 1846. Coming late through the pass that year, the party was unable to make it through because of snow, and ultimately lost 47 of its 87 people, with some of the living cannibalizing the dead to survive. It was a high, difficult pass; but scores of thousands of other emigrants made it over the pass safely.

After 1848, a second, somewhat easier route across the mountains was found. This was the Carson Route, opened that year by the Mormon Battalion, going "home" from California to Salt Lake City, where most of them had never been. This was a battalion of 500 men, recruited by the United States government while the Mormons were still on the Missouri, to fight in the Mexican War. In return for the Mormon supply of the battalion, the government assented to the Mormon move west to Salt Lake City. The Carson Route, named after the Carson River, runs about 25 miles south of the Truckee or Donner route, cuts west along the Carson River, then arcs over and through the mountains to Lake Tahoe. From the crest of the Sierra Nevada, coming by either the Donner or Carson Route, it is less than 100 miles, mostly downhill and then across the level Sacramento Valley, to Sutter's Fort, now Sacramento, the terminus of the California Trail.

Whether to Sutter's Fort in California or to Fort Vancouver on the Willamette, it was a long trail; 2,000 miles of high plains, mountain range, desert, and mountain range again, with the worst mountain pass on each trail at the western end, when all were exhausted and a heavy early snow blocking the mountain pass could be life-threatening. At best, emigrants could reasonably hope to be safely over the last pass into Oregon or California after three-and-a-half to four months on the trail, in late August or early September. At worst, late-starting or misfortune-plagued parties might find themselves struggling through the western mountains in late October or even early November. The Donner party reached the last pass late on October 31, 1846, and found it blocked by early snow; a week earlier, they would have made it through without undue difficulty.

The wagons were the main problem. These were not the huge horse-drawn Conestoga wagons encountered in Western films, with drivers riding on them as if they were stagecoaches. The overwhelming majority were oxen-drawn covered farm wagons, with drivers walking alongside. Indeed, most emigrants walked to California, with only some children and the infirm riding most of the way; wagons were for hauling vitally needed food and water, as well as possessions. And the more strongly built and lightly loaded the wagon, the better chance it, its goods, and its people had of getting through. And most of those who emigrated to Oregon, California, and Salt Lake City did get through, although many had to abandon goods, animals, and vehicles along the way. (Indeed, many more of the Donner party might have survived if they had just left their wagons bogged down in the snow and walked out of the mountains.) In all, well over a quarter of a million emigrants traveled west between the early 1840's and the late 1860's, when the railroads began to take a large share of the westward bound traffic.

Like so many other great human enterprises, it had all started as an idea in the minds of a few visionaries. For in the largest sense, the search for and development of the Oregon Trail was part of the search for a passage west to the Indies and Cathay that had led all the seafaring peoples of western Europe to the Americas in the 15th and 16th centuries. For the English and French, encountering the main body of North America, the search continued for three centuries as a quest for a Northwest Passage, a northern route through to the Pacific. John Cabot and his son, Sebastian, sought it, as did Jacques Cartier after them. Sebastian Cabot thought he had found it in 1509, when he sailed through to Hudson Bay, as did Henry Hudson a century later, in 1610, when he thoroughly explored the huge body of water that was to bear his name. A little further south, Champlain, La Salle, Jolliet, and Marquette, reaching west down the St. Lawrence and out through the Great Lakes to the Mississippi, were both exploring the huge North American heartland and searching for a passage to the Pacific. This was the main entrance into North America from Europe, cutting behind the Appalachian Mountains, essentially unobstructed for thousands of miles. Alexander Mackenzie thought he had found it when he made a round trip of 3,000 miles from Lake Athabasca in western Canada out

In the snow-covered Sierra Nevada, the survivors from the Donner party were finally rescued by a relief party from California. (Bancroft Library)

to the Arctic Ocean in the summer of 1789, on what was to be named the Mackenzie River. Mackenzie became the first of the European explorers to actually find a way through western Canada to the Pacific four years later, in the summer of 1793.

The year before, in 1792, Thomas Jefferson had proposed to the American Philosophical Society a northwest expedition by way of the Missouri and Columbia (then the Oregon) rivers. It did not happen then, but Jefferson's continuing interest in the Northwest eventuated in the Lewis and Clark expedition, which started up the Missouri on May 14, 1804, a little over two months after the purchase of the upper Louisiana Territory by the United States from France. Lewis and Clark found the main water route west, going north and then west on the Missouri, over the Continental Divide in what is now northern Montana, and then into the tributaries of the Columbia River system, finding their way to the Snake, into the Columbia itself, and then down to the sea. This was, for the Americans, the real opening of the Northwest, and their Northwest Passage to the Pacific, pointing the way toward the Oregon Trail that was to follow.

That the later Oregon Trail did not follow the Lewis and Clark route was partly a matter of distance, but at least as much a matter of power. From the 1820's through the early years of the Oregon-California migration, the powerful Blackfoot Confederation effectively blocked the upper Missouri route, while the route along the Platte had no such strong Native American opposition. Nor could an American military presence clear the way before 1846, years after the start of the Oregon migration. From 1818 to 1846, the Oregon country, the lands beyond the South Pass, was disputed territory, subject to an uneasy and ambiguous joint British-American administration. After 1846, when the Oregon territory was divided between Great Britain and the United States, the Missouri-Columbia route might have been opened for emigrants to Oregon, but by then emigration patterns were well established and the old route of the Oregon Trail prevailed.

California, too, was not available for mass American overland migration before 1846. A few Americans had come overland via the Southwest in earlier years, and a few hundred more reached California in the early 1840's, especially after the Frémont expeditions of 1843–1846 had mapped and popularized some of the northern and southern approaches to California. But California was part of Mexico; the huge area from west Texas to the Pacific and from Oregon to the Rio Grande was not American until it was seized by the United States during the United States-Mexican War of 1846–1848.

After the Lewis and Clark expedition, American trappers and traders began to explore the country between the Missouri and the Pacific, moving up into the Jackson Hole and Yellowstone country and establishing a fort at the mouth of the Big Horn River. In 1811, John Jacob Astor's Pacific Fur Company sent an overland party from the Missouri to the mouth of the Columbia and built Fort Astoria there, but the company was forced to sell it under wartime pressure to the British Northwest Company in 1813. During the next decade, there was little American activity in the Oregon country, but much independent trapping and trading activity along the upper Missouri. Then, in the 1820's, with the organization of the Rocky Mountain Fur Company, American trappers moved out from the Missouri River into the West, taking large quantities of furs, competing with the Northwest Company and later with Astor's American Fur Company, and in the process traversing the old Native American trails up the Platte and out through the western mountains. These trappers and traders, among them Jim Bridger, Kit Carson, William Sublette, and Tom Fitzpatrick, were to be the early trailblazers and guides along the Oregon, California, and Mormon trails.

The first two parties of emigrants to the Oregon country were led by Nathaniel Wyeth in 1832 and 1833. These parties established the general route of the Oregon Trail, going generally northwest up the Platte and the Sweetwater, through South Pass to the Snake, and out to the Columbia and the Willamette Valley. The first expedition in 1832—with trapper William Sublette acting as guide—went by way of the annual trappers' rendezvous, that year at Pierre's Hole, a little to the north of what would become Fort Hall, and then swung south to and west to the Snake. Later, following the old Native American trail out to the Columbia, Sublette's group left the Snake to go north to Fort Walla Walla, there meeting the Columbia. The second expedition went through South Pass and swung south to what was in 1841 to become Fort Bridger; moving northwest again, they built Fort Hall, leaving some of the party there to hold the fort, and then moved on to Oregon, again by way of the old water routes—taken by Native Americans and then trappers—through the mountains. This expedition took the shorter Umatilla River into the Columbia, bypassing Fort Walla Walla. These were the routes, with minor variations, that were to be used by hundreds of thousands of emigrants west for the next half-century.

A few other small emigrant parties reached Oregon in the 1830's, overland and by sea, some including missionaries. A trickle of Americans also went into Spanish California by the southern land route and by sea. In all, there were no more than a few hundred Americans in Cali-

At night, wagon trains formed a circle not only for defense but also to keep livestock like these unbridled horses from straying. (Denver Public Library, Western History Department)

fornia by 1840, and perhaps 500 Americans in Oregon's Willamette Valley. But they wrote back home about huge new landholdings and the richness and promise of the new land; and their letters were widely publicized throughout the country by editors, politicians, and clergy. Throughout the 1830's, "Oregon fever," "Oregon societies," and "California societies" began to grow. There was precedent for this; many chains of immigration from northern Europe in this period grew in exactly the same fashion, with the "American letters" of Scandinavian immigrants playing a particularly important role in the development of the Scandinavian emigration to the United States.

There was also Senator Thomas Hart Benton of Missouri, a tireless advocate of American westward expansion. Quite properly, his large open-air statue in St. Louis faces and points west, and is inscribed "There is the East. There is the Road to India." For 30 years, from 1821 to 1851, he fostered exploration of and expansion into the West. His greatest coup was the government sponsorship and financing of the westward surveying and mapping expedition of his son-in-law, John C. Frémont, in 1842. The expedition itself made little or no contribution to the mapping of the West, mainly traversing quite well-worn and well-known Native American, trapper, and emigrant paths, but was a massive publicity victory. Frémont's reports were very widely circulated, greatly fanning the Oregon fever of the time and stirring a major increase in the emigration to Oregon. In 1840, fewer than a score of emigrants went overland to Oregon. In 1841, fewer than 100 emigrants traveled from the Missouri out to California and Oregon, the Bartleson Party of 1841 being the first American emigrant party to go overland through to northern California. In 1842, a little over 100 went overland to Oregon and none to California. But in 1843, after the publicity surrounding the Frémont expedition, almost 1,000 emigrants went all the way from the Missouri to the Willamette; it was from then on known as the year of the "Great Emigration" to Oregon. It was the year of decisive breakthrough, with emigration to Oregon continuing at those and greater levels, decisively changing the balance of population and power in Oregon and paving the way for American sovereignty over what is now the American Pacific Northwest by treaty with Great Britain in 1846.

The California migration grew simultaneously, but much less swiftly—until the discovery of gold at Sutter's Fort and the California Gold Rush of 1849. In 1848, about 400 Americans emigrated overland via the California Trail; by 1849 the number had risen to about 25,000, and in 1850, the best estimate is about 44,000. By this time Americans were also entering California in large numbers via sea and more southerly land routes, as well, the land drawing settlers as well as prospectors.

The years of 1849 and 1850 were extraordinarily hard for most travelers on the California and Oregon Trails. Large numbers of them were gold-seekers, ill-prepared and ill-equipped for the 2,000-mile trek to California. Cholera was epidemic; grass was used up by the earliest of the tens of thousands of settlers in the caravans that stretched for miles; game was scarce to nonexistent; and many parties ran completely out of water on the desert. The trails were intrinsically no more difficult to traverse in those years—indeed, there were well-organized ferries, the first bridge across the Platte, and a set of trails to follow that had been beaten down by thousands of wagons—but hardship was enormous in those years, and death commonplace.

In 1849, cholera struck the huge emigrant trains pouring west, many emigrants bringing it with them to the marshaling points on the Missouri. F. A. Chenoweth, who traveled in that year, reported that:

> Very soon after the assembled throng took up its march over the plains the terrible wave of cholera struck them in a way to carry the utmost terror and dismay into all parts of the moving mass... This terrible malady seemed to spend its most deadly force on the flat prairie...and about Fort Laramie

Another traveler, backed up at a river crossing in midsummer, reported that:

> ...here at this time are two or three hundred wagons with their accompanying teams of men, and the ground is covered with a coat of light dust two inches in depth, which the wind is constantly carrying to and from, whilst the sun is pouring down his hottest rays upon us, and the wonder is that some of us only and not all of us are sick.

The California emigration slowed to a trickle in 1851, as hardship stories and impoverished people drifted back east. Even the Oregon migration slowed a little that year, although over 3,500 did emigrate to Oregon as compared with only a little over 1,000 to California. But then, emigration grew again—now the steadier emigration of large numbers of farmers and tradespeople flowing through the high plains and over the western mountains to settle northern California and the Pacific Northwest. In only 11 years, from 1849 through 1860, well over 200,000 emigrants went west overland on the California Trail, almost 55,000 more to the Willamette Valley on the Oregon Trail, and almost 45,000 more to the Salt Lake City country on the Mormon Trail, a total of about 300,000 in all.

The American Civil War and related Native American wars greatly slowed travel west of the Missouri, but only for a few years. By 1865, and every year thereafter until the railroads took over most of the traffic, tens of thousands of emigrant wagons went west on the Oregon, California, and Mormon trails. Now, however, many were

In narrow valleys, westbound travelers often had to criss-cross from side to side to find a trail fit for wagons. (National Archives)

not going all the way through to the Pacific states, but were settling and mining the high plains and mountain states. Now there was no longer only one main trail with three branches going northwest, but also a body of trails and then roads serving growing local populations.

The trails themselves had also changed considerably by then, with many more bridges, ferries, and toll roads, and many new cutoffs across the mountains into California and Oregon. By the late 1850's, even federal and local governments, which had done little to improve these main routes until then, had begun building roads and bridges on the trails. By 1853, both the Laramie and the Platte had been bridged. By 1859, even the main route across South Pass had been relocated, the new road being called the Landers Cutoff, after the engineer who had recommended the new route to the federal government.

Now, too, there were new gold finds, and silver besides. In 1859, a small gold strike near Denver, which was soon exhausted, triggered a gold rush that took many thousands of gold-seekers out along the trail to Colorado, their slogan being "Pike's Peak or Bust." In the same year, a massive gold strike—the Comstock Lode—was made east of the Sierra Nevada near Lake Tahoe, and thousands of gold-seekers traveled both east and west on the California trail to settle the Carson City-Virginia City area.

As the whole region between the Missouri and the Pacific became settled, overland commerce and then coast-to-coast mail service grew. Emigrants on the overland trails were, by the 1860's, joined by thousands of large freight wagons and tens of thousands of oxen, transporting both military and civilian goods throughout the West. One company alone—the Central Overland California and Pike's Peak Express Company, headquartered in Leavenworth, Kansas—at its fullest extension operated over 6,000 wagons and 75,000 oxen, carrying freight on the Oregon, California, and Mormon trails, as well as all over the northern mountains and plains year-round, subject only to the closing of many of the mountain passes in winter.

This was also the company that initiated and ran the first fast transcontinental overland mail route—the Pony Express—from its inception on April 3, 1860, to its demise on completion of the first transcontinental telegraph line, on October 24, 1861. Starting from St. Joseph, a little east of the Missouri and north of Independence, the Pony Express route paralleled the main line of the Oregon Trail to Fort Kearny, there joining the main trail and traveling with it all the way up the Platte and the Clearwater to Fort Bridger. There it took the road to Salt Lake City and then went south of and parallel to the Humboldt River section of the California Trail, to Carson City, Virginia City, and across the mountains south of Lake Tahoe to Placerville, Sacramento, and San Francisco. It was a very short-lived enterprise, mainly notable for the enormous pride with which it was regarded in the United States of its time and for the great romantic interest it holds to this day.

Daily overland stage and mail service from Missouri to California started in July 1861. For the first year, it followed the main Oregon Trail to Fort Bridger and then went through Salt Lake City and across to Carson City and Sacramento. After that, it followed the Oregon Trail only as far as Julesburg, Colorado, on the Platte, about 100 miles west of Fort Kearny. There it joined part of the Cherokee Trail, also known as the Overland or Central Overland Trail, which from 1849 had run from Fort Smith, Arkansas, to Fort Bridger, there joining the Oregon, California, and Mormon trails. The stage line ran to Denver, across the mountains to Fort Bridger, then to Salt Lake City and west to California, generally following the same route as did the Pony Express.

After the Civil War, the railroads came west, and use of the old trails declined. There were emigrant wagons on the Oregon Trail as late as the 1890's, and freight wagons even later than that. But the main emigrant and freight traffic began to shift to the railroads soon after they were built, for reasons of speed, economy, and convenience.

Construction of the first transcontinental railroad started in 1863, the Central Pacific starting east that year from California. In 1865, the Union Pacific started building west from Omaha. The two lines met on May 10, 1869, signaling the beginning of the end of what had been the main wagon trails west. Along the Platte and Humboldt, the railroad to some extent followed the old Oregon and California trails, as did the later Union Pacific line northwest to Walla Walla and the Oregon Short line from Walla Walla to Portland.

Today, the trails are gone, replaced by cities, towns, farms, and hydroelectric projects that dam rivers and build huge lakes where the old trails ran a century and more before. Some highways roughly parallel sections of the three trails, such as U.S. routes 80 and 26 along the Platte, and routes 30 and 84 northwest out across Idaho and Oregon, paralleling the Snake and the Columbia. Further south, U.S. routes 40 and 95 take the old Truckee and Donner Pass route through Reno, Nevada, and over the mountains to Sacramento, while U.S. Route 50 takes the more southerly Carson River route through Carson City and Virginia City to the south shore of Lake Tahoe and then to Sacramento.

All the way from Missouri to the Pacific and from the Canadian border deep into the American Southwest, there are markers, monuments, museums, and festivals commemorating the old Oregon, California, and Mormon trails, and all the subsidiary trails that fed them. These were the main roads west and opened the last American frontier; they are well remembered.

Selective Bibliography

Billington, Ray Allen. *The Far Western Frontier, 1830–1860* (New York: Harper and Row, 1962; reprint of the 1956 edition). A good general history of the Western frontier of the period, with a chapter on backgrounds and on the Oregon, California, and Mormon Trails.

———. *The Westward Movement in the United States* (New York: Van Nostrand Reinhold, 1959). A concise, useful, general history of the American westward movement from sea to sea.

Chapman, Arthur. *The Pony Express: The Record of a Romantic Venture in Business* (New York: Cooper Square, 1971). A popularly written, adequately detailed history of the Pony Express.

Drago, Harry Sinclair. *Roads to Empire: The Dramatic Conquest of the American West* (New York: Dodd, Mead, 1968). A brief history of most of the main American western trails, with a detailed treatment of the Mormon Trail.

Federal Writers' Project. *Oregon Trail* (New York: Hastings House, 1939). A brief history and motor road guide circa 1939, with a considerable body of illuminating detail, location by location, along main roads paralleling the old trail.

Ghent, W. J. *Road to Oregon* (New York: Longman, 1929). A comprehensive, detailed treatment of the Oregon, California, and Mormon Trails.

Holbrook, Stewart H. *Rivers of America: The Columbia* (New York: Rinehart, 1956). A popularly written history of the Columbia River basin, with chapters on the Oregon Trail.

Josephy, Alvin M. *The Indian Heritage of America* (New York: Knopf, 1969). An excellent, comprehensive general work on the history and culture of the Native Americans of the Americas.

Lavender, David S. *Westward Vision: Oregon Trail* (New York: McGraw-Hill, 1963). A comprehensive history of the background and early years of the Oregon Trail.

Merk, Frederick. *History of the Westward Movement* (New York: Knopf, 1978). A comprehensive history of the entire American westward movement from sea to sea, up into the modern period.

Moody, Ralph. *The Old Trails West* (New York: Crowell, 1963). A brief history of each of the main western trails; includes chapters on the Oregon and California Trails, with excellent maps.

Parkman, Francis. *The Oregon Trail: Sketches of Prairie and Rocky Mountain Life.* 8th edition, revised (Boston: Little, Brown, 1890). Impressions of life on the Oregon Trail by the noted North American historian.

Schlissel, Lillian. *Women's Diaries of the Westward Journey* (New York: Schocken, 1982). Includes good first-hand accounts of the trip west on the Oregon and California Trails.

Semple, Ellen Churchill. *American History and its Geographic Conditions* (Boston and New York: Houghton, Mifflin, 1903). A classic comprehensive work on the influence of geography upon patterns of development and settlement in the United States, with excellent maps.

Stewart, George R. *The California Trail* (New York: McGraw-Hill, 1962). A useful, fully detailed treatment of the California Trail, with good maps.

Unruh, John D., Jr. *The Plains Across: The Overland Emigrants and the Trans-Mississippi West, 1840–60* (Urbana, Illinois: University of Illinois Press, 1982; reprint of 1979 edition). An excellent history of the overland emigration movement of the period.

Winthur, Oscar Osborn. *The Great Northwest: A History* (New York: Knopf, 1947). A comprehensive history of the Pacific Northwest, with chapters on the fur trade and the Oregon Trail.

———. *The Transportation Frontier: Trans-Mississippi West, 1865–1890* (New York: Holt, Rinehart, 1964). A comprehensive history of the development of trails, freighting, and railroads in the American West, with excellent maps.

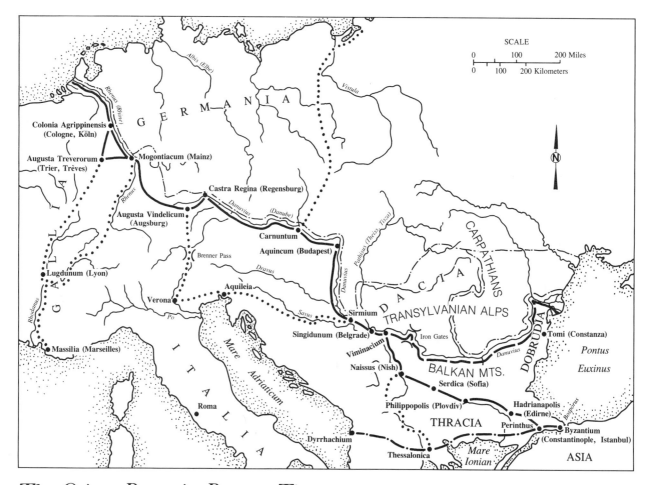

The Orient Route in Roman Times

——————— Main Road   — — —· River Route   —·——·—· Roman Frontier

—·——·—· Egnatian Way   ·········· Connecting Routes

The Orient Route

*I*n the spring of 1096, tens of thousands of Christian pilgrims began massing in France and Germany, inspired by the pope and by wandering preachers like Peter the Hermit and Walter the Penniless, to make a crusade against the Turkish Moslem infidels who were barring Christian access to the holy city of Jerusalem. These rough, undisciplined bands did not wait to meet the Turks, however. In the grip of a religious fervor—often shouting their motto *Deus volt!* (God wills it)—many began attacking "God's enemies" in Europe, as they headed eastward. The German groups were particularly virulent, attacking Jews in cities like Cologne and Mainz all along the Rhine and in Bohemia, most violently in Prague. By the time this People's Crusade came together on the upper Danube near Regensburg, they had a well-earned reputation as marauders—a reputation only confirmed as the "army," now perhaps 100,000 strong, headed toward the Orient.

In truth, the difficulties were legion. The pilgrims were supplied with some funds from benefactors, but there was little enough food to be had in Bohemia, Hungary, and the Balkans even for the small local population, much less for these hordes. Anger at the inflated prices asked for the scant food available brought the Crusaders into armed conflict with Christian inhabitants along the way; their assault on the citizens of Belgrade brought a full-scale retaliation from the king of Hungary, in which thousands were killed. Many Crusaders fell by the wayside, too, to accidents, starvation, or sheer exhaustion from walk-

ing for over four months through the rugged hill country of the Balkans. Even so, when they reached the plain before Constantinople, Anna Comnena, daughter of the Byzantine emperor, saw them as "a countless people...more numerous than the sands of the sea..." Those who survived their trek on the Orient Route were no more fortunate—and no more kindly to strangers. Although ostensibly allied with the Byzantines, the People's Crusaders ravaged Christian communities around Constantinople until, without waiting for the knights who constituted the only professional soldiers on this First Crusade, they were shipped across the Bosporus into Asia Minor. There they continued their depredations against the local Christians—apparently regarding all Asians as heretics—until they met with the Turks, who cut them to pieces. Those who were not killed were enslaved, with few, if any, ever reaching their goal: Jerusalem.

The People's Crusade was one of the largest groups to travel along the Orient Route until modern times. Although the route follows a natural pathway into Central Europe, the section from Istanbul to the upper Danube has always been so exposed to invaders that for long periods, the Orient Route has not been a major highway at all. At other times, as under the Romans, the main highways have run diagonal to, rather than with, the route. During a few times in history—as during the early Crusades—the Orient Route did become a well-used pathway; but only in modern times, with relative peace, did it become a major international highway, the route

Trajan's column in Rome celebrates not only great battles but also more homely events like the crossing of the Danube from a fortified city. (Forum Traiani, Rome)

chosen by the most romantic and exotic of all railroads: the Orient Express.

The Orient Route itself is more a land route than a waterway. Certainly boats had, from the earliest times, been used on the Danube River, but natural hazards—like the great frothing rapids at the narrow gorge called the Iron Gates, near Orsova—often required that boats be unloaded and their goods portaged to the next navigable portion of the river, a procedure both costly and dangerous when robbers were abroad. As a result the Danube has always seen heavy boat traffic in sections, but has rarely operated as a main through water route. In addition, the Danube near its mouth angles eastward to the Black Sea, while most travelers have always aimed for Byzantium (later Constantinople, now Istanbul), gateway to Asia Minor. As a result, the land route has predominated, although it follows the axis of the Danube and its main cities lie on the river.

From Istanbul, on the Bosporus Strait between Europe and Asia, the Orient Route followed the coast of the Sea of Marmara to Perinthus and then began a long angle northwest across Thrace, reaching the Danube River near Belgrade (Singidunum), at the junction of the Danube and Sava rivers. From Belgrade, the route generally avoided the Danube's deep right angle by cutting northwest to the twin cities of Buda and Pest, then followed the Danube Valley west to Bratislava (Pressburg) and Vienna.

Routes from around northern Europe funneled into the Orient Route. One main branch followed the Rhine on its northward arc through Frankfurt-on-Main and Cologne, to the North Sea; another headed across southern Germany toward Paris via Munich and Strasbourg. An important connecting route has always headed westward from Belgrade along the Sava River (and sometimes the parallel Drava River) to the head of the Adriatic Sea, in Roman times to the port of Aquileia, in later times to Venice and Trieste. The Orient Route, traced by early traders, laid down by the Romans, and trod by medieval pilgrims, only in modern times became a true international highway, bridging political boundaries.

Through much of human prehistory, the lower part of the Orient Route held the highest civilizations in Europe. New techniques developed in the Middle East—of stone-working, farming, metal-working, herding—quickly spread from Asia Minor across the Bosporus and the Dardanelles into Thrace. From there up to the Iron Gates, which acted as something of a natural barrier, the Danubian civilization developed, among the Indo-Europeans who—as Greeks, Celts, Gauls, Germans, and a host of other groups—would come to dominate Europe and much of western Asia. From the third to the first millennium B.C., this civilization was relatively stable; by 2000 B.C., wandering traders were traversing the region in their four-wheeled wagons and two-wheeled chariots, inventions adopted from the East. But the development of mounted warfare by the nomads of the Eurasian Steppe made the Danube Valley prey to a succession of invaders, who swept down the Black Sea's coastal strip, the Dobrudja, toward the fertile loess plains of Hungary. With the arrival of nomadic Scythians in 700 B.C., trade and travel were disrupted, and did not redevelop on the Orient Route until the Greeks entered the picture.

Moving into the Black Sea around the same time as the Scythians, Greeks began trading up the Danube River, at first only up to the Iron Gates, but later to the region of Belgrade, as well as west on the Sava River to the Adriatic. How far their trade actually extended is not quite clear. Some early Greeks thought that Europe was an island, cut off from the mainland by a great strait formed by the Danube and Rhine rivers. (They were not far wrong, for the upper reaches of these two mighty waterways approach within less than 50 miles of each other in the Black Forest of Germany.) Most likely the confusion resulted because the Celts, the Greeks' trading partners, laid their main paths along the Rhine-Danube axis. It was the Greeks who founded the southern terminus of the Orient Route, establishing a trading post they called Byzantion on the European side of the Bosporus in the seventh century B.C. The Orient Route between Byzantion and the region of Belgrade was only a secondary route at this time, however; the main route between Europe and Asia in those early days crossed at the Dardanelles (Hellespont), from Troy (Ilium) to the Gallipoli Peninsula and headed westward into Thrace and toward Greece. The development of the route awaited the Romans.

But even the Romans paid little heed to the Orient Route in the early days. Being occupied with their western territories, they were at first content to hold only the coast of the Adriatic Sea, with its port of Aquileia, and the corridor of the Egnatian Way from Albania through Macedonia and Thrace to Byzantium. Only two centuries later, when these territories were being harassed by unruly tribes from the east, did the Romans turn their attention toward the Danube Valley. Having long since established a fortified frontier, the *limes,* along the Rhine River, the Roman legions began converging on the Danube from either end in the first century A.D. Soldiers who had once won their laurels against the tribes of Germania now had to deal with the equally fierce tribes of Eastern Europe, most notably the Dacians, in what is now Rumania and eastern Hungary. The first Roman legions to cross the Danube—using a wooden bridge they built for the purpose—were massacred by the hard-fighting Dacians; it took the great emperor-general, Trajan, to carry the attack successfully in the region. More to the point, it was Trajan who saw to the consolidation of the Danube *limes,* ensuring its strength by building a road along the frontier. That road laid the basis of the Orient Route.

Although the many gorges on the Danube offered

On its way southeast across Europe to Istanbul, the Orient Express route would later follow the left bank of this gorge 200 miles south of Belgrade. (Yugoslav National Tourist Office)

little natural footing for a highway, Trajan's engineers carved a wagon-wide road out of sheer rock, sometimes extending the road out over the river on wooden balconies hung from specially prepared bores in the rock. Until a modern dam and canal project covered it with water, the channel carved out of rock could still be seen; the Romans, who set up plaques and monuments to celebrate both their engineering prowess and their triumph over the Dacians, were justly proud. With this road, soldiers could travel quickly to any point on the Danube or Rhine, with supplies and even heavy siege engines able to follow them.

Trajan and his successors also founded, rebuilt, or renamed many of the main cities along the Orient Route: Hadrianapolis (now Edirne), renamed for the Emperor Hadrian in 125 A.D.; Philoppopolis (now Plovdiv), originally named for Philip II of Macedonia, and resistant to Roman attempts at renaming; Serdica (now Sofia), settled 2,000 years earlier and named for the local Serdi tribe; Naissus (now Nish), at the junction with the main south road to Thessalonica, on the Aegean Sea; Viminiacium, at the mouth of the Morava River, where the Orient Route meets the Danube; Singidunum (now

Belgrade), both names referring to the city's status as a fortress, at the junction of the Danube and Sava rivers; Aquincum (now Buda and Pest), near where the Danube changes direction from north to west; Carnuntum, near modern Bratislava, where the Vistula Amber Route cut across the Orient Route on its way from Poland to the Adriatic Sea; and Castra Regina (now Regensburg), on the upper Danube. These fortress cities formed the main line of the Orient Route, as their successors do today. During Roman times the route dipped down from Castra Regina to Augusta Vindelicum (Augsburg) and then gently curved northwest to Mogantiacum (Mainz), at the junction of the Main and Rhine rivers, and headed on to Colonia Agrippinensis (Cologne, or Köln), main fortified terminus of the Roman frontier, which stretched 1,800 miles. On the Danube itself, Trajan also built a branch road to follow the lower river from Tomi (now Constanza) on the Black Sea along the south bank of the river to where it joined the Orient Route.

In addition to the road, Trajan built bridges across the river, some pontoon bridges on which soldiers and wagons could cross, but others quite permanent structures

312

with stone piers, most notably across the quarter-mile-wide Iron Gates. Although the Emperor Hadrian destroyed the bridge within decades, so it could not be used by Rome's enemies, later observers found even the ruins impressive: Dio Cassius in the late second century noted:

> Brilliant as were Trajan's other achievements this stone bridge surpassed them all. Although the bridge is of no use today, for merely the piers are standing...they seem to have been erected for the sole purpose of demonstrating that there is nothing which human ingenuity cannot accomplish.

Under the Romans, the Orient Route was primarily a military road. The first rough tracks were hewn out by construction specialists accompanying legions as they moved into the district; later these sappers and the soldiers themselves were pressed into work to build the permanent roads that would form the lifeline of their frontier existence. But, unlike other Roman roads, the Orient Route saw few pleasure travelers. Even traders frequented primarily the lower portion of the route, between Byzantium and Singidunum, preferring to head more directly toward the settled lands of Italy via the Sava River.

The eastern parts of the Roman Empire became increasingly important in later times; several emperors were born in the East, some along the Orient Route itself, and many spent large parts of their careers defending the frontier marked by this highway. This shift was marked by the establishment of a second Roman capital on an old site; in the early fourth century, the still-small city of Byzantion—Byzantium, to the Romans—was rebuilt and renamed Constantinople, after the Emperor Constantine who in the same period adopted Christianity as the state religion. The Bosporus had already begun to supplant the Dardanelles as the main crossing point between Asia and Europe; from this time on, Constantinople would clearly be the gateway between the two continents, the city itself always being considered more part of Asia than of Europe.

But Rome was in decline, and new waves of nomads were beginning to sweep in from the Eurasian Steppe Route. First they filtered, then they poured through the once-secure Roman *limes*—whole communities of them, complete with herds and covered wagons. Rome tried to bring into the imperial fold some of the Germanic peoples who came in the fourth century, resettling them along the frontier; but with the arrival of the Huns in the fifth century, the frontiers burst, no longer shielding the core of the empire. For the Orient Route, the effect was disastrous. The main cities on the route were destroyed, some of them not to be rebuilt until modern times. Worse than that, many inhabitants fled before the invaders, who swarmed into the Hungarian plain. This basin proved a magnet for successive invaders over the coming centuries—Huns, Goths, Slavs, Avars, Magyars—each time emerging from

With trade on the Orient Route disrupted, cities like Vienna were often served by merchants from Italy or Germany, like these from Berlin. (From Toggenburger Bibel, *mid-16th century, Kupferstichkabinett und Sammlung der Zeichnungen, Berlin)*

313

the onslaught poorer and less populated than before. Large sections of farmland were taken out of cultivation and returned to pastureland for the nomads' herds.

In these early Middle Ages, the Orient Route effectively ceased to exist. Trade and traffic from the northern seas reached the Black Sea not by the Rhine-Danube axis, but by the Russian River Routes opened by the Slavs and later the Swedish Vikings much further to the east. Historical geographer W. Gordon East put the case quite simply: "...the middle Danube lands were as yet so uncivilized and so disorganized politically as to exclude commercial intercourse."

The picture only began to change in the 10th century. Unlike other nomadic invaders, who had eventually retreated back to the steppes, the Magyars elected to stay in the Hungarian plain. Adopting Christianity, they were increasingly drawn into the European circle. At a time when the urge to travel and seek religious forgiveness was giving rise to widespread pilgrimages, Hungary opened the old Orient Route to Constantinople for those going to Jerusalem. The prime mover in this change was King Stephen of Hungary (later St. Stephen), whose contribution was noted in chronicles of the time:

> ...he made the way very safe for all and thus allowed by his benevolence a countless multitude both of noble and common people to start for Jerusalem.

Pilgrimages to the Holy Land had started in the fourth century, after Emperor Constantine's conversion and his rebuilding of Jerusalem and other shrines in the region. The relatively few early pilgrims generally made their way eastward along the Egnatian Way or by the Mediterranean. But by the 10th century, when the pilgrimage movement began to take hold, many would-be pilgrims lived in northern Europe, so the Orient Route was far more suitable for them as a route to Asia Minor. This overland route through Constantinople to Palestine took Christian pilgrims into Moslem territory; but the Near Eastern Moslems had, for some centuries, allowed pilgrimages, if only for the additional income to be gained from these medieval tourists.

Then, in the 11th century, the Seljuk Turks arrived in the Near East. Newly converted to Islam, these zealots cut off pilgrimage routes to Jerusalem and harassed Christian residents in the region. Byzantine Emperor Alexius Comnenus called on the Roman Catholic pope for a joint effort of Christians to free the Holy Land; the result was the Crusades. Quite naturally, many of the earliest Crusaders took the Orient Route winding along the Danube and across the Balkan Peninsula to Constantinople. Though the People's Crusaders were ill-prepared and ill-fated, the Christian knights who followed them were not. The contingent from Flanders and Lorraine under Godfrey of Bouillon took the Orient Route, meeting other knights at Constantinople; crossing Asia Minor they met and defeated the Seljuk Turks and succeeded in carving out a series of Christian states in the Near East.

Knights on the Second Crusade also took the Orient Route, gathering at various points in northern Europe and assembling into one large host at Regensburg on the upper Danube. The horde was certainly varied, ranging from royal leaders, like Louis VII of France and his wife, Eleanor of Aquitaine, to "gallows birds recalled for this enterprise from the gates of hell," as one contemporary put it. They made quite a show, as the *Gestes de Louis VII* records:

> Anyone seeing these cohorts with their helmets and bucklets shining in the sun, with their banners streaming in the breeze, would have been certain that they were about to triumph over all the enemies of the cross and reduce to submission all the countries of the Orient. And this they would doubtless have done if the pilgrimage had been pleasing to God.

Baggage wains preceded the main body of the Crusaders, who followed on foot at 10–20 miles a day, taking about three months to travel from the lower Rhine to Constantinople. Nor was this an all male army. In addition to Eleanor (later Henry II's queen of England and mother of Richard the Lionheart), many other women joined the Crusades, despite the fact that prostitutes and camp followers were expressly forbidden by the church to take part in the affair. The Byzantine historian Nicetas notes:

> ...there were in the army women dressed as men, mounted on horses and armed with lance and battle axe. They kept a martial mien, bold as Amazons. At the head of these was one [Eleanor] in particular, richly dressed, that went by the name of the "lady of the golden boot." The elegance of her bearing and the freedom of her movements recalled the celebrated leader of the Amazons.

But the crossing of Asia Minor was difficult, even without Turkish opposition, and as Christians began to regain control of the Mediterranean from the Moslems, the sea routes to Jerusalem came to be preferred by pilgrims, traders, and Crusaders, although some supply trains might go by the Orient Route. With travelers heading across Europe toward the Italian ports, especially Venice, the Orient Route was bypassed once again, after its brief moment on the world stage. Even the cities of the upper Danube—Ratisbon, still-small Vienna, and Ulm, normal head of navigation on the river—were supplied not via the Orient Route but over the Alps by traders along the Brenner Pass Amber Route.

The Orient Route and the Danube River once again

The swift currents of the Danube's Iron Gates still cause difficulties to boats headed upstream. (Yugoslav National Tourist Office)

came to serve primarily local purposes, and the various principalities that lay along them did not make travel or trade easy for foreigners. Although foreign traders, like Greeks or Italians, were occasionally permitted to trade along the Orient Route, the many towns and principalities all charged duties, demanded the right to handle all transport, and sometimes conducted outright extortion. In these times, then, the Orient Route had little possibility of developing into a through highway.

Political conditions also conspired against the use of the Orient Route. In the late 11th century, other invaders renewed the pressure from the Eurasian Steppe, aiming toward the Hungarian plain. The Pechenegs (Patzinaks), Cumans, and Bulgars successively pushed a wedge between Hungary and the now-shrinking Byzantine Empire, thoroughly dividing the Orient Route. Hungary itself received heavy attacks from the Mongols in the 13th century. Constantinople—weakened by attacks from the Fourth Crusaders—was gradually reduced to a shell, little more than a vassal for the Italian city-states, at different times Genoa or Venice. By the late 14th century, when the Ottoman Turks began to push from Asia Minor into Europe, little effective resistance remained; the Byzantine Empire consisted of only a few small holdings by the time Constantinople finally fell to the Turks in 1453.

The fall was more than symbolic, however. The Ottoman Turks shifted their base from Asia Minor to Constantinople and easily overcame other peoples on the lower Orient Route. The Ottoman Sultanate now faced Christian Europe on its own ground, and the two groups would battle over the Orient Route for some centuries. At first, Belgrade took the brunt of the attack. The Turks had already pushed along the Orient Route to beyond Sofia before they took Constantinople; within decades they were

The plush cars of the Compagnie Internationale des Wagons-Lits figured in innumerable tales of the Orient Express. (Authors' archives)

threatening Belgrade. The city finally fell to the Turks in 1521, leaving the rising city of Vienna—seat of the Hapsburgs since the late 13th century—open to siege. The battle raged on the Orient Route between those two cities for the next two centuries; the Austrians twice took back Belgrade, though only briefly, while Vienna was able to stave off Turkish advances only with substantial help from other European nations.

Along the lower Orient Route, the Moslem Turks ruled over the predominantly Christian population, and over the Gypsies, a nomadic people who had been pushed into the region all the way from the Indo-Iranian plateau ahead of the Turks. The various religious and ethnic groups in the region rarely mixed, falling into an uneasy accommodation with each other. Greeks who had long ruled in the region became the bankers, merchants, and administrators of the new order; Bulgarians generally operated as carriers handling camel or horse trains along the Orient Route, especially bringing foodstuffs from Hungary and Rumania for Constantinople; Gypsies operated along the route as nomadic tinkers, musicians, and horse traders. The peoples along the Orient Route made a different kind of contribution to their rulers, as well; young Christian boys were taken from youth to be trained as an elite celibate military corps called the Janissaries, who formed the special guard for the sultanate for several centuries.

In the 15th and 16th centuries, travel was not totally disrupted on the Orient Route. During periods of temporary peace, the Turks even made occasional trade agreements with their Christian neighbors. But travel, whether on land or on the river, was exceedingly dangerous. On the Danube, the Turkish grain ships were heavily armed, as were the occasional ships of other nationals, like the French, which were allowed on the lower Danube. Land conditions were even worse, with armed robbers awaiting travelers at every vulnerable point, especially at the shaky wooden bridges or fords across streams and rivers en route. Travelers often settled for an unsatisfactory combination of land and water routes, as did Austrian ambassador Count Busbecq in 1554. Traveling by coach with his family and goods from Vienna to Buda, he then switched to river travel, with the whole party—including horses and coaches—being taken downstream on the Danube in two small boats hauled by a 24-oar-power tug. The windings of the river, obstruction by trees and water-mills, and heavy rainstorms all conspired to make the five days' continual travel slow and tiresome—but even so it was faster than the normal 12-day land time to Belgrade, and considerably safer. At Belgrade Count Busbecq and his family reluctantly returned to the overland route. Only in the southern portion of the route, on the plains leading to Constantinople, was travel relatively trouble free, enough so to impress an anonymous French visitor, who noted in 1528:

"...the country is safe and there are no reports of brigands or highwaymen...The Emperor does not tolerate highwaymen or robbers."

For some centuries the Turks seemed unbeatable, and indeed the Christians were much drained by fierce religious wars between Catholics and Protestants. But in the early 18th century, the Austrians rallied sufficiently to push the now-weakened Turks back to Belgrade, which they would hold for yet another 150 years. Downstream traffic on the Danube was begun between Ulm and Pressburg (Bratislava), though upstream traffic was uneconomical, being against the strong current. Under Austria, the roads, too, were improved; no longer needing temporary wooden bridges that could be dismantled rapidly at the approach of an enemy army, the Orient Route north of Belgrade shared in the general improvement of European roads in the period. While the Austrians tried to open the middle Danube for long-distance trade, the local Hungarian nobility resisted the attempt, sabotaging tow-path construction along the river. Only in the late 18th century were the Austrians able to open traffic the length of the Danube, by agreement with the Turks. Even so, the river's utility for upstream commerce was marginal, at best; eight boatmen, forty horses, and thirty drivers were needed to bring a single load of grain upstream from Pest to Vienna–a trip that took a whole month. Because cataracts in the river still hindered navigation, ships also often had to be unloaded to lighten their draft, while the cargo was shipped overland past the obstruction, as had been true for centuries. The hauling and trans-shipment called for such heavy labor that much of the work was carried on by convicts.

As with other great rivers around the world, the Danube's fortunes were changed by the advent of the steamboat, which in the 1830's for the first time made upstream traffic economical and timely. At first operating on the upper Danube, between Vienna and Pressburg, steamship service gradually extended downriver, past the many water mills of Hungary, through the bridge of boats that connected Buda and Pest, past Belgrade (then sometimes described as a "city of the dead"), and on down river to Constanza, port on the Black Sea. The cataracts of the middle river, especially at the Iron Gates, still posed a problem, however; overland passage was still needed in parts. Even in times of high water, when the narrows were more passable, smaller steamboats were required, and passengers and cargo had to be transferred to larger ones below the Iron Gates. This problem was partly solved by the blasting of new and deeper channels in the gorges. At the Danube delta, where sandbars also posed problems for larger vessels, sailors generally adopted the simple Turkish stratagem of trailing a rake behind the ship, to flatten sediment disturbed by the ship's passage. As the Danube began to fulfill its promise as a major waterway, the powers of Europe increasingly moved to interna-tionalize the river for free use by all.

While the Danube developed, the land route languished. But modern technology would soon have its effect there, too, as the railroad began to make its appearance in Europe. At first these were primarily local lines, but a Belgian financier and train-fancier, Georges Nagelmackers, dreamt of a railroad that would cross the many cultures and countries of Europe. His first plan, for a train from Paris to Berlin, was foiled in 1870 when the Franco-Prussian War broke out. His alternative was, as a neutral, to drive a railroad from Belgium's port of Ostend on the English Channel across France, Switzer-land, and Austria; through the Brenner Pass in the eastern Alps into Italy; and then down the Italian peninsula to Brindisi, ancient terminus of the Appian Way, reviving that city as a port for sea travelers heading eastward. But when, a few years later, the French blasted a tunnel through the Mont Cenis Pass in the western Alps and built a shorter, faster route to Brindisi, Nagelmackers' line folded. Indeed, his company almost went bankrupt, but was saved by some outside support, reviving as the Com-pagnie Internationale des Wagons-Lits et des Grands Express Européens.

Nagelmackers envisioned an international route, one that would cross the main boundaries of Europe. He began to put together a luxury railroad line, at first just on various short runs between Paris and the main cities of Western Europe, using opulently appointed sleeping and restaurant cars modeled on American prototypes by George Pullman. From the beginning, Nagelmackers had royal support (if only because King Leopold II of Belgium owed him money); he needed such influential friends in negotiating contracts with eight different railroad lines in half a dozen countries, and a shipping line besides. There were not just political enmities to consider, such as that between France and Germany, but also the unsettled state of the Balkan region, devastated by recent wars between Turkey and Russia, with new states emerging and others attempting to break free.

Because of such problems, the transcontinental railroad developed by Nagelmackers never followed a single line; its route varied with political conditions. The first route of the Orient Express–dubbed so by the reporters who covered it–was from Paris through Munich, Salz-burg, Vienna, and Budapest; up to that point, the route followed the main Orient Route of old. But because the Balkans were so unsettled at the time, Nagelmackers chose to swing his line east from Budapest through Rumania to Bucharest and then to the river town of Giurgiu, where passengers were ferried across the Danube to the Bulgarian city of Ruschuk (Ruse). Their fine luxury cars left behind on the Rumanian side of the Danube, passengers boarded a Bulgarian train to continue their trip eastward to the port of Varna, on the Black Sea; there they boarded a ship for the 18-hour voyage to Constantinople. Passengers on the inaugural journey of the Orient Express in October of 1883 received red carpet treatment all the way. Royalty greeted them at every stop, often with dinners and entertainments; not all of these were entirely unalloyed pleasures, since in Rumania passengers were obliged to walk in the rain on a muddy road to the king's castle. Balanced against that was the Gypsy band that played and danced for the passengers on a 70-mile portion of the journey through Rumania. Most of the passengers—all men, except two women who joined the party at Vienna—stayed with the train on its round-trip; most seem to have agreed with French writer Edmond About, who pronounced it "eleven wonderful days of a unique and historic journey."

The Orient Express, on its first journey and on most of its trips thereafter, was on schedule; the weak link, of course, was the Black Sea portion of the route, where sea conditions were unpredictable. More to the point, Nagelmackers wanted his own trains to take passengers

the complete, direct route to Constantinople—or, as the Turks had come to call the city, Stamboul. Even after agreement was reached with the Turkish government, through trains could not make the trip, for the Balkan region, much impoverished under long Turkish rule, was quite isolated. Nagelmackers' solution was to build a link between the Turkish railroads in the south and the Orient Express lines to the north. Beginning in 1885, he began service on the main old line of the Orient Route, from Budapest down through Belgrade to Nish, where intrepid passengers had to leave their comfortable train for the dubious joys of a "flying coach." On good roads, these diligences might have made 10–12 miles an hour with a fast team of horses, but on the rutted muddy tracks of the Balkans, three to four miles an hour was more often the rule, with baggage wagons going much slower than that. One passenger noted of the vehicle: "The interior was small with tiny windows, the latter for reasons of safety from brigands' bullets." Robbers were, indeed, a prob-

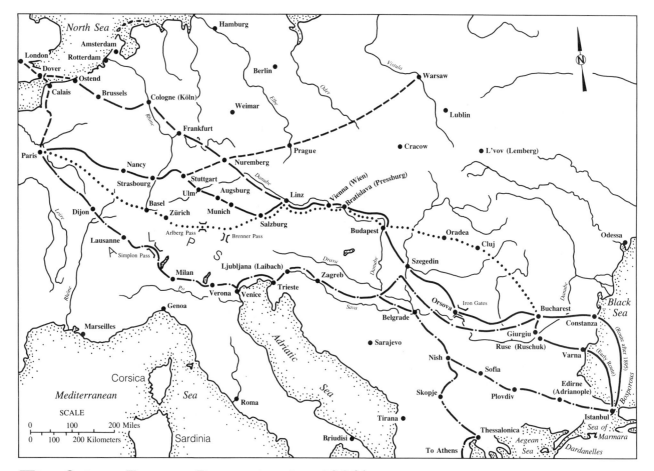

The Orient Express Routes in the 1920's

———— Orient Express

—·—·— Simplon Orient Express

············ Arlberg Orient Express

——— — Ostend Orient Express

-------- Main Connecting Routes

lem, and the Wagons-Lits company paid for armed guards to escort passengers on the two-to-three day journey to the beginning of the Turkish rail lines beyond Sofia. This arrangement continued until 1889, when the connection was completed and passengers were, for the first time, able to ride directly across the continent from Paris to Constantinople without leaving their Wagon-Lits cars. (The other routes, to the Black Sea, continued to run for several years afterward.)

The Orient Express was a great success. To Nagel-mackers' surprise, the passengers on the celebrated train included not just royalty, government officials, and business travelers—though there were plenty of all those—but also tourists, who were drawn by the striking scenery of the Alps, the Danube, the Balkans, and exotic Constantinople. Indeed, this city became so famous that the train was known by some as the Stamboul Express.

The western part of the Orient Express route was, of course, the most traveled, for Western Europe was far more settled and developed. After initial service twice weekly, the Orient Express began to travel daily between Paris and Vienna, and twice a week on to the Bosporus. By 1900, two trains a week traveled between Paris and Constantinople via Belgrade, and two via Constanza, the Black Sea port that replaced Varna after the building of a rail connection through Bulgaria. French writer Paul Morand gave a picture of the Orient Express in the days before World War I, when the old ways still prevailed in Europe:

> Prior to 1914 the passengers were a microcosm of our world...Turkey was retreating from Europe, but the Orient Express still remained the umbilical cord which attached her...and in the corridors one could still encounter...[Turks who] kept their veiled wives, guarded by eunuchs, firmly locked in their compartments, to which not even the train's *contrôleur* was admitted.

Mixed with these were Austrian aristocrats; ubiquitous British hunters and explorers; Eastern European nobility (some hiding in bathrooms for fear of assassins) heading for Vienna or Paris, centers of high fashion and culture; French tutors for the aristocratic sons of the Danube; Americans, "their portmanteaux stuffed with gold coins for bribes in exchange for some new oil concession"; the occasional Indian maharaja; "mysterious financiers on some errand to fix yet another loan for the Tsar of Russia"; and diplomats "travelling to and from one of the sixty-nine conferences somewhere in Europe to confer about the status-quo and to postpone some war."

It was a world passing quickly. The Compagnie Internationale des Wagons-Lits added a new transcontinental route, with the opening of the Simplon Tunnel through the Swiss Alps in 1906. From Paris, this more

These 13th century Mongols were simply part of a long line of invaders irrupting onto the Hungarian plain. (New York Public Library)

southerly route carved its way through the Alps via Lausanne and Milan to Venice, being extended to Trieste, at the head of the Adriatic Sea, in 1912. The outbreak of World War I disrupted this service, but at the end of the war, this route emerged as the main route of the Orient Express, since it avoided the territories of Germany, Austria, and Hungary, all of whom were hostile to the foreign train. Reopened in 1919, the Simplon Orient Express followed its former route to Venice and Trieste and then was extended eastward along the line taken by the Romans centuries before. Angling through Ljubljana and Zagreb, it followed the Sava River to the rail link of Vinkovci; there the line forked, with one branch heading east toward Bucharest, and the other heading south. In these postwar years, the southern route to Thessalonica and Athens became increasingly important, but Constantinople—which officially became Istanbul in 1930—remained inextricably linked in the popular mind with the Orient Express.

Another route was opened in these postwar years, too, similarly circling south of German territory; from Paris, it swung through Basle and Zurich and the spectacular Swiss Alps via the newly opened Arlberg Tunnel to Innsbruck, Salzburg, Linz, Vienna, and Budapest, then carving a new route through inner Rumania to Bucharest. By 1932 the original Orient Express Route was also restored, and passengers could, via one or another of these routes, leave Paris for Constantinople any day of the week.

This was the heyday of the Orient Express, the time when crowned heads and tourists rubbed elbows with spies and diplomats on the fabled train, and novelists and moviemakers eagerly traded on the glamor of the transcontinental link with the mysterious East. But these days did not last long. Germany was always reluctant to have the Orient Express cross its territory, and when the Nazis came to power they sabotaged the Wagons-Lits trains at every opportunity; when in 1938 they took Austria, the original Orient Express and the Arlberg Orient Express were both cut off. The Simplon Orient Express continued to run until 1940, when Hitler pressured Mussolini to stop traffic on the route. After the war, the Compagnie attempted to reopen the routes as before, but political problems continued to hamper them. Running battles between Yugoslavia and Greece, between Turkey and Bulgaria, between various Eastern European countries and their Russian occupiers, all threatened the revival of the Orient Express.

These trains—which had, for the first and only time, made the Orient Route a true international highway—also faced a different kind of competition from automobiles and airplanes. In Western Europe, speedy highways increasingly took passengers from the trains; in Eastern Europe, where good roads were far less common, travelers often preferred to fly over the borders of countries, rather than face the interminable checks of visas and papers. The Orient Express trains continued to run toward the East for decades, though they gradually lost all pretense to luxury; the last Wagons-Lits trains had not even a restaurant car, leaving travelers to the tender mercies of station restaurants that took only local currency.

But if international through trains no longer cross from Paris to Istanbul, train-lovers can still—with some determination—follow the old Orient route, changing trains from one country to another, riding along the Danube, past the magnificent gorges of the Iron Gates, the striking scenery of the Balkans, and the verdant plains before Istanbul. Others, who have chosen style over substance, ride restored Wagons-Lits trains on tourist runs in Western Europe, trying to recapture the flavor of the Orient Express, without the difficulties of passing through the tangled lands of Eastern Europe on the old Orient Route.

Selective Bibliography

Chevallier, Raymond. *Roman Roads*. Translated by N. H. Field (Berkeley and Los Angeles: University of California Press, 1976). A useful review of archaeological and literary information on the construction and life of the roads.

Clark, J. G. D. *Prehistoric Europe: The Economic Basis* (London: Methuen, 1974; reprint of 1952 edition). An invaluable work, with many illustrations of archaeological artifacts.

Cookridge, E. H. *Orient Express: The Life and Times of the World's Most Famous Train* (New York: Random House, 1978). A popular work for train-fanciers.

East, W. Gordon. *An Historical Geography of Europe*, Third Edition (London: Methuen, 1948). Part of the Dutton Advanced Geographies series. A very useful overview, with a separate chapter on the Danube Route-Way.

Heichelheim, Fritz M. *An Ancient Economic History: From the Palaeolithic Age to the Migrations of the Germanic, Slavic, and Arabic Nations*, in 3 vols. Translated into English by Joyce Stevens. (Leyden: A. W. Sijthoff, Vols. 1 & 2 1968, Vol. 3 1970). A comprehensive work with much fascinating detail.

Kendall, Alan. *Medieval Pilgrims* (New York: Putnam, 1970). Part of the Putnam Documentary History series. An interesting brief review, with selections from many first-hand accounts.

Lengyel, Emil. *The Danube* (New York: Random House, 1939). A popular history focusing on modern times.

Lessner, Erwin, with Ann M. Lingg Lessner. *The Danube: The Dramatic History of the Great River and the People Touched by Its Flow* (Garden City, New York: Doubleday, 1961). A popular history from Roman times.

Obolensky, Dimitri. *The Byzantine Commonwealth: Eastern Europe 500–1453* (New York: Praeger, 1971). A sound general history.

Piggott, Stuart. *Ancient Europe: From the Beginnings of Agriculture to Classical Antiquity* (Chicago: Aldine, 1965). A fine standard review.

Tihany, Leslie C. *A History of Middle Europe: From the Earliest Times to the Age of the World Wars* (New Brunswick, New Jersey: Rutgers University Press, 1976). A useful overview.

Von Hagen, Victor W. *The Roads That Led to Rome* (Cleveland and New York: World, 1967). A well-illustrated, readable work by the director of the Roman Road Expedition.

Wechsberg, Joseph, and the Editors of Newsweek Books. *The Danube: 2,000 Years of History, Myth, and Legend* (New York: Newsweek Books, 1979). A well-illustrated work focusing on modern times.

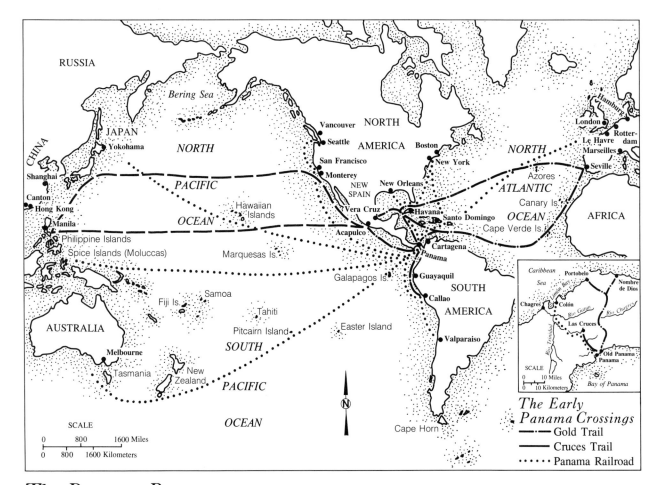

The Early
Panama Crossings
—·—·— Gold Trail
——— Cruces Trail
·········· Panama Railroad

The Panama Route

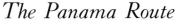

—·—·— Early Panama Routes   ·········· Main Modern Panama Routes

——— Manila Galleon Route

The Panama Route

To convey the depth of his feelings in "On First Looking into Chapman's Homer," John Keats turned quite naturally to the events at Darien, on the Isthmus of Panama, in 1513:

> Then felt I like some watcher of the skies
> When a new planet swims into his ken;
> Or like stout Cortez when with eagle eyes
> He stared at the Pacific—and all his men
> Look'd at each other with wild surmise—
> Silent, upon a peak in Darien.

Keats's history was wrong—it was Balboa, not Cortés—but he had the feeling right, for the Europeans' first sight of the Pacific Ocean from the Americas certainly ranks as one of the major experiences in that great age of European discovery. But more extraordinary than the sighting itself was the vision that led these Europeans to plan a route across unknown waters and, when they found the way blocked by the Isthmus of Panama, to plan a route across it.

The Panama Route was, indeed, a European invention. The native Americans who had made their way from Asia down the spine of the Americas over thousands of years had no ocean-going vessels and no need for east-west trade. The little trade they had in Central America was local and generally north-south, both trail and coastal balsa-raft trade. But the Europeans had grand ideas. They envisioned a western sea route to Asia and they eventu-

ally created just that, even though they found two vast continents, joined by a narrow neck of land, barring their way. Even before a canal was built across the Panama Isthmus, the Europeans—primarily the Spanish—carried on an active trade more than halfway around the world, from Cadiz to Cathay. And in modern times, the Panama Route, with the Panama Canal as its centerpiece, has become the prime sea route in the world, as important as the Mediterranean or Suez routes ever were.

The 15th century Europeans were mesmerized by thoughts of a sea route to Cathay (China) and Cipango (Japan). The fracturing of the overland Asian routes by Turkish conquests in the Near East, and the resulting decline of the Mediterranean sea trade, had led many sailors, especially Italians, to congregate on the Iberian sea coast. Many of these migrant mariners sailed in the service of Portugal, the rising sea power of the time, and explored a sea route to the south, along the coast of Africa. Indeed, the Portuguese—with their great naval academy at Sagres, where Henry the Navigator had brought together technical advances, new geographical ideas, and practical seagoing experience—were the logical people for the young Christopher Columbus to contact about his idea of exploring a westward sea route to Asia. But the Portuguese turned him down. The Spanish, however, were just completing their reconquest of the Iberian peninsula from the Moslems, and they were ripe for expansion. Though not experienced mariners themselves, they were ready to listen to and support this adventurer, who reasoned that,

Columbus's arrival in "India" is fancifully depicted here by an artist a century later. (From Theodor de Bry, Collectiones peregrinationum in Indiam orientalem et occidentalem, *Frankfurt-on-Main, 1590–1634)*

if the earth was a sphere of the size he calculated, he needed only to sail about 3,500 miles west on the 28th parallel to reach Asia.

Leaving from the small port of Palos (the ancient main port of Cadiz being clogged with ships carrying Jews deported by Spain), Columbus began his voyage under the Spanish flag on August 3, 1492, with two small caravels, the *Niña* and the *Pinta*, and a larger flagship, the *Santa Maria*. Following the well-established Portuguese route, they moved south to the Canary Islands for reprovisioning and repairs; then after several weeks they headed west, pushed by the known trade winds that blew from the northeast in that latitude, as well as by an unexpected westward current. Had Columbus held his course across the Atlantic, he would likely have landed in Florida but, confused by the Sargasso Sea—a becalmed, seaweed-

clogged region in the mid-Atlantic—and misled by sightings of birds, he turned south. His confusion is not surprising, as Columbus later described:

> ...I found all the [Sargasso] sea full of vegetation of a kind which resembles pine branches and very full of fruit like that of the mastic tree. And it is so dense that...I thought that it was a shallow and that the ships would run aground, and until this line was reached not a single branch was found.

Thirty-three days after the fleet's last sight of land—the volcanic cone of Tenerife in the Canaries—the lookout shouted "Tierra! Tierra!"

Believing that he had reached the outlands of Asia, Columbus landed on an island in the Caribbean, one of the Bahamian islands, which he named San Salvador (later Watling's Island). Proceeding from island to island — "to each one I gave a new name" — he searched for the mainland; at Isla Juana (now Cuba) he thought he had found it:

> When I reached Juana, I followed its coast to the westward, and I found it to be so extensive that I thought that it must be the mainland, the province of Cathay.

Finding "only small hamlets" on the shore, he followed the coast looking in vain for great cities or towns; then he tried a different tack:

> ...I sent two men inland to learn if there were a king or great cities. They traveled three days' journey and found an infinity of small hamlets and people without number, but nothing of importance.

Although this search was fruitless, Columbus persisted in believing that the islands — including that of Española (Hispaniola) — lay off the coast of Asia, calling them Las Ylas Indias (The Indian Islands), which soon were shortened to "the Indies."

Cities or no, the first description of the New World was a glowing one, in Columbus's first letter to his "most illustrious King and Queen":

> ...all the [islands] are very fertile to a limitless degree....In it [Hispaniola] there are many harbors on the coast of the sea, beyond comparison with others which I know in Christendom, and many rivers, good and large, which is marvelous. Its lands are high, and there are in it very many sierras and very lofty mountains, beyond comparison with the island of Tenerife. All are most beautiful, of a thousand shapes...and filled with trees of a thousand kinds...they seem to touch the sky...the plains and arable lands and pastures, are so lovely and rich for planting and sowing, for breeding cattle of every kind, for building towns and villages...

More ominously for the people who lived there, he noted that most of the rivers contained gold, and that great gold mines were to be found on the island. Indeed, gold was so common there that sailors were able to exchange pieces of broken crockery or glass for their weight or more in gold. More ominous still was his seizure by force of some of the island's inhabitants; while these early hostages were primarily taken as guides — and shouted to each new village "Come! Come to see the people from Heaven!" — Columbus's act foreshadowed the future slave trade.

Having completed his preliminary exploration of these several islands, and having lost his flagship, the *Santa Maria*, off Hispaniola, Columbus faced a problem.

He was not the first to have entered the uncharted waters of the mid-Atlantic. Others had preceded him, accidentally or intentionally; in earlier times, probably Phoenicians and Egyptians, and in his own time, Portuguese. But before Columbus no one venturing across the mid-Atlantic had returned to tell the tale — and that was now Columbus's problem. The westward currents and winds barred a return by his original route, so he finally — and fortunately — sailed north to find an eastward wind and current, discovering what we now know as the Gulf Stream, that great warm river-in-the-sea that flows northeastward out of the Gulf of Mexico toward Europe. These took him back across the Atlantic, although dangerous hurricanes caused him to shelter at the Azores and at Lisbon (where the Portuguese now would have appreciated his intelligence), before he finally arrived at his home port. Although he never got to use his letter of introduction to the Great Khan, Columbus had established the eastern half of the sea route that would later reach from Europe to China. The route that he took was to be the standard one followed by sailing ships for centuries; the only significant change was that later captains went farther south of the Canaries, sometimes to the Cape Verde Islands, to find steadier and more reliable winds, before turning westward. As one captain put it: "South till the butter melts, and then due west."

In the next decade the Spanish sent eight other expeditions to the new lands, three more under Columbus. Searching for the desired passage to Asia, they found almost all of the major islands of the Carribean and explored the coast from Honduras down to the easternmost bulge of present-day Brazil — what would later be called "the Spanish Main," or mainland. Columbus himself explored the coast of the Panama area, for native Americans had told him of a narrow place between two seas, and of a people who collected much gold, who lived in a land that was "very lofty but not at a distance" (possibly the first reference to the Incas). Arriving at the Isthmus, and naming as he went, Columbus charted the Bay of Ships (now Limón Bay) and two harbors, Puerto Bello (Beautiful Port) and Nombre de Dios (Name of God). Columbus was also the first European to visit the river that later would form the basis for the Panama Canal, the Rio Chagres, which he called the "River of Crocodiles." Because it was the rainy season and floods threatened, he decided not to travel inland, even for the promised view of a great sea on the other side. Eventually, however, he had to turn back, admitting his failure to find the westward passage. While Columbus still felt that he had reached Asia, others were not so sure; one early voyager who openly stated that this was not Asia but a new land was rewarded by having his name refer to the whole hemisphere: Amerigo Vespucci gave his name to America.

The Spanish moved quickly to explore, conquer, and consolidate their new American territories. With their center at Santo Domingo, on the island of Hispaniola, the Spanish sent settlers, farmers, and skilled artisans as well as soldiers and friars, to set up colonies, to supply riches to be shipped back to Spain, and to explore the new lands. Only a decade after Columbus's discovery, the Spanish set up a colonial office and a department of commerce called Casa de Contratación (House of Trade), that would administer colonial activity from Seville for hundreds of years. Among the earliest settlement licenses granted were one for the Isthmus of Panama and another for the northeast coast of New Granada (Colombia); although the settlements there had grave difficulties, a leader emerged from them, a stowaway tolerated because of his experience in an earlier voyage: Vasco Núñuz de Balboa.

By skillful dealings with the local tribes, in 1513 Balboa became the first among his countrymen to penetrate the jungles of the isthmus, climbing over the continent-dividing mountain range, to find the great sea on the other side. He was drawn not only by the ocean, but also by tales of gold. Balboa's biographer, Alonso de Ovalle, notes that the native Americans had contempt for the Europeans' love for gold and taunted them: "Is it possible you should value so much a thing that so little deserves your esteem?...Have some shame, Christians, and do not value these things..." Nevertheless, they pointed the way:

> ...they should see...another sea, when they had passed over certain high mountains, where they should see other people who could go with sails and oars as they did: and...passing that sea, they should meet with vast quantities of gold...

Following his native American guides, Balboa walked for over three weeks before approaching the continental divide, as de Ovalle reported:

> A little before they were at the highest, Vasco Núñez de Balboa caused a halt to be made, desir-

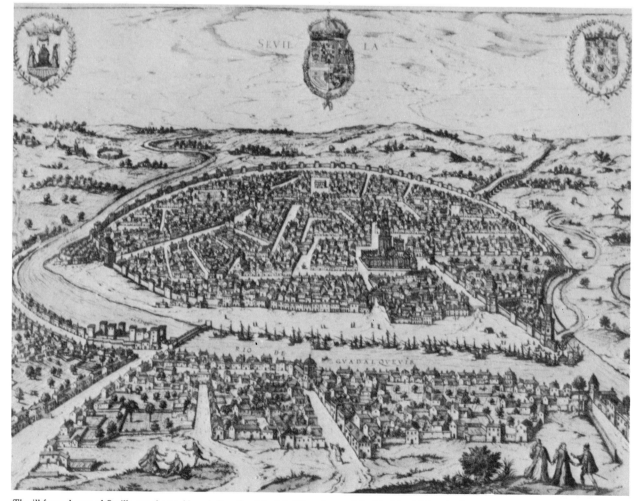

The ill-favored port of Seville, up the muddy, winding Guadalquivir River, is crowded with ships joining the flota *to the Indies. (From G. Braun,* Civitates Orbis Terrarum, *16th century)*

326

ing to have the glory of having himself been the first man that ever saw the South Sea, and so it was. He goes alone, discovers that vast ocean, and the large bays of the South Sea called Pacific...He made a sign after this to his companions to come up, and so they all run in haste, pushing one another on. And when they were on the top, where there is a full prospect of the sea, 'tis not to be imagined the content they all received in admiring that vast and smooth liquid crystal, which, not being animated, did not on its side give leaps of joy nor go out of its bed to the tops of the mountains, to welcome those who came to deliver it from the tyranny the Devil exercised over it...with the breath of idolatry...

Bemused as they were about the foreigners' love of gold, the native Americans were even more "in great amaze" at the ceremony that followed. After cutting down trees and making great crosses on which he carved the names of his sovereigns, Ferdinand and Isabella, Balboa descended to the coast and, in full armor, went:

...into the sea up to the mid-leg with a naked sword in his hand, said that he took possession of it, and all the coasts and bays of it, for the crowns of Castile and Leon...

On this expedition, Balboa also discovered something of more immediate use: gold was in plentiful supply among the west coast tribes. As this gold began to be shipped back to the Atlantic coast, the isthmus took on its alternate name of Castilla del Oro (Castle of Gold), for the abundance of that precious metal in the region.

It was Balboa who first had the idea of a canal across the Isthmus of Panama, but he did not wait for it to be built. In 1516, only three years after he first saw the Pacific, Balboa dismantled four ships on the Atlantic side, carried them across the isthmus, and reassembled them on the other side, where he launched them and sailed to the pearl-rich Perlas Islands just off the coast. Balboa himself was beheaded in 1517, as the result of a factional dispute among colonial leaders, but his ideas took hold. In 1519, Spain's King Ferdinand ordered the establishment of a wagon road between Nombre de Dios on the Atlantic and the new settlement of Panama on the Pacific. The workers who hacked the trail out of tropical jungle were the first of many to experience the dangers of the disease-ridden Panama Isthmus. After the Spanish conquered the Inca Empire on the west coast of South America in the 1530's, most of the gold and silver stripped from that land passed by mule train over this winding, muddy path. These metals were soon joined by other products from the west coast, including pearls, wool, dyes, tobacco, and woods, especially mahogany. Later work was done on the Rio Chagres to improve navigation; during the rainy periods, when the gold road was at its worst, goods were taken by boat up the river to Las Cruces (The Crossing) and then by a shorter land route to Panama. By the late 1530's, the isthmus became so important in Spanish colonial thinking that a second administrative district was set up, in addition to that of Santo Domingo. This new district, centered on Panama, at first included all South American territory from Nicaragua southward. All shipping, whether products or post, had to travel along the Panamanian route, even though that meant some goods had to travel overland across half the continent before reaching Lima's port of Callao, there to be loaded onto one of the few galleons that plied between Callao and Panama.

The Spanish still had their eyes on the Far East, however. Between 1519 and 1522, Ferdinand Magellan's expedition circumnavigated the globe, discovering in the process the full extent of South America and the Pacific Ocean, and staking Spain's first claims in the western Pacific. The distance and difficulties of the journey were daunting, however, and explorers were urged to continue looking for the imaginary strait through the Americas; in 1523, the Spanish King Charles V urged the conquistador Hernando Cortés to search carefully "for the passage which would connect the eastern and western shores of the New World and shorten by two-thirds the route from Cadiz to Cathay." As it gradually became clear that such a strait did not exist, the idea of a canal gained attention, with Spanish engineers proposing a canal across the Isthmus of Panama in 1528. By this time, Cortés was in agreement, stating: "We have not found as yet a passage from Iberia to Cathay, but we must cut it. At no matter what cost, we must build a canal at Panama."

The Isthmus of Panama was not the only candidate for such a canal. One isthmus at Nicaragua was longer in miles, but much of the distance was taken up by navigable lakes and rivers, which had a plentiful water supply. Cortés discovered an old route across the Tehuantepec Isthmus in New Spain (Mexico), which partly followed the Coatzacoalcos River, but that was both longer and dryer. Another possible crossing point was Balboa's route south of Panama, near the Gulf of Darien; Balboa himself had rejected it as too difficult, although the colonials did transport some disassembled ships along this route to the west coast. However, the idea of a canal was soon lost in a series of squabbles between those who insisted that a canal was impossible and others who insisted that it was both possible and vital—but could not agree on the proper route. Among the religious, including Charles V, there were even fears of God's vengeance, should they tamper with the face of the earth; others more worldly thought a canal would make the rich west coast colonies more vulnerable to invasion.

Meanwhile, trans-isthmian traffic continued to cross by the Panama Route. Even as South America's coasts began to be known and settled, no direct trade was permitted between any South American port (except for Cartagena on the north coast) and Spain; all shipping had to pass across the Panama Isthmus. The Casa de Contratación in Seville only gradually and grudgingly allowed a modest travel to develop on the west coast of the Americas, but even then it was limited to three legal ports: Panama, Callao, and Acapulco, New Spain. On the east coast, too, Indies trading was strictly limited to a few legal ports. At first the main port was Santo Domingo. Then, as it became clear that the tail was wagging the dog, ports on the mainland became dominant, especially Vera Cruz (a port established on the coast east of Mexico City) and Nombre de Dios at the Panama Isthmus. And, since the Spanish claimed all of the Americas as theirs, trading was—by direction of the Casa—restricted to Spanish ships.

Such restrictions might have been enforceable if the Spanish had had exclusive control of the seas, but in the real world they faced strong competition. As early as the 1520's, French privateers—some of them only small fishing boats from the Newfoundland waters—began to waylay homebound Spanish ships, drawn not only by the great stores of gold carried by these ships but also by the precious maps that would guide others into the waters of the new American lands. The English, too, wanted their share of these central American riches and conducted raids in the Caribbean and on the Atlantic return route. At various times in the 16th century, Spain found its route, or even the whole Iberian coastline, blockaded by European competitors. The Spanish response was, first, to increase the size of the trans-Atlantic ships, so they could be more heavily armed and also take more goods. Spanish ships sailing to the Caribbean went from a minimum of 80 tons in 1522 to 600 tons or more by the end of the 16th century. Smaller ships, generally food carriers less attractive to pirates, were allowed to continue operations on the Atlantic only between the Canary Islands and the Caribbean.

But as piracy continued, the Spanish gradually adopted a convoy system of shipping, in which ships were allowed to travel only in groups, or *flotas*, between Spain and the Caribbean. By 1543, a minimum of 10 ships was required for a sailing to the Indies; not incidentally, the convoys of ships had the advantage of requiring fewer expert navigators, who were in short supply, given the great demands of the Atlantic traffic. By the 1550's the Spanish had developed a large, heavily armed fighting ship called the galleon, which was designed to escort convoys and keep the Spanish sea lanes open. From the 1560's on, the *flota* followed a regular routine, leaving Seville in late summer and returning early the following summer. Generally the *flotas* consisted of two contingents, one heading for Vera Cruz, the other for the Isthmus of Panama. Once in the Caribbean, the New Spain *flota* (which sometimes left earlier in the year) headed south of Cuba and Hispaniola

for Vera Cruz, while the Panama *flota* headed for Nombre de Dios. Both these cities were unhealthy spots, being located in swampy, tropical lowlands, and so were deserted for most of the year. But when the *flotas* were in port, they came alive with fairs that brought traders and other colonials from throughout the region, all seeking a chance at the scarce and precious goods from Europe.

These harbors were unprotected, however, so after trading was completed, the *flotas* retired to fortified harbors, the Panama *flota* to Cartagena, the New Spain *flota* to Havana. Many ships never made the return trip. Some obsolete or worn-out ships were used for local coastal shipping. Others, damaged beyond repair by the worms infesting the tropical waters, were broken up in port; indeed, many buildings in ports like Nombre de Dios were built of wood from broken-up ships. Shipbreakers transported the iron and brass fittings overland, often to Guayaquil on the coast of Ecuador, where new ships were being built of mahogany for use in Pacific waters; such fittings were so much in demand that a captain unable to find an adequate return load would sometimes find it profitable to sell a seaworthy ship to the shipbreakers. After the turn of the year, those ships that were returning made their way north—sometimes stopping at Santo Domingo to complete their load with bulky goods like hides and sugar—to well-fortified Havana, Cuba; there the *flotas* rendezvoused and prepared for their late spring return through the Florida Channel, a favorite haunt of pirates. The *flota* system certainly did not rid the sea of pirates, but it did make Spanish ships somewhat less vulnerable to them.

In the same period, the Spanish were trying to develop the Pacific leg of their route to Asia. In the four decades after Magellan's voyage across the Pacific, several expeditions left the west coast of the Americas for the Far East—but none found a return route. Finding themselves unwelcome by the Portuguese, who regarded the Far East as their territory, these expeditions disintegrated, with the various ships and crews dispersing. Not until 1564 was the return route found, by an expedition under Miguel Lopez de Legazpi. Leaving from Navidad on the west coast of New Spain, Legazpi easily made the westward run to the Philippine Islands, named by the Spanish after their King Philip II. To return, the Spanish had to move very far north, struggling for many weeks through an area of variable winds and frequent typhoons, to the latitude of Japan, before picking up a westerly wind to take them east to North America. The journey was still not easy, for they had to struggle against adverse winds down the coast of California to reach New Spain. Even later, when the route was well-established, the westward leg took eight to ten weeks, but the eastward leg took four to seven months. As historian J. H. Parry noted: "...on the longer passages hunger, thirst and scurvy could reduce a ship to a floating cemetery." Indeed, the early 17th century exploration of California was triggered largely by the desire to find a safe harbor for the Manila galleons. Only the Spanish desire to fulfill their vision would have justified the opening of such a difficult route.

There were rewards to be had, however. They were not immediately evident in the Philippines, which had little to offer directly. But Manila, where the Spanish established themselves after a few years, had one of the best harbors in the world and was well-placed to receive goods from throughout the Far East. The gold and silver that the Spanish had in quantity was extremely attractive to the Chinese, who soon started bringing their junks, loaded with silk goods, porcelain, and delicate metalwork, across the China Sea to Manila. Spices from the whole region and cotton from Moghul India were added to the mix later, along with tea, various drugs, and even rugs from Persia. While gold, silver, and pearls were the main Spanish offerings, the Spanish-Americans later traded other items, including chocolate from Guayaquil, and some imported goods from Europe, such as Flemish lace, shipped overland by mule train from Vera Cruz to Acapulco before being loaded onto the Manila galleons, also called China ships. For over 200 years, the Spanish carried on this trade with Manila, leaving Acapulco early in the year and returning during the summer; during these years they controlled the Pacific Ocean so completely that it was sometimes called "the Spanish Sea." Oddly, even after the decline of Portuguese power, they did not seriously attempt to establish direct trade between the Philippines and Europe on the Cape of Good Hope Route around Africa; until the late 18th century all Spanish trading was carried on through the Americas. The Far East trade sometimes acted to the detriment of merchants in Spain; they periodically called for a halting of the Manila trade, since the American markets were often glutted with silks, leaving few buyers for Spanish textiles. The trade continued despite such protests, but the Casa did restrict the Manila trade to two galleons a year—built in the Philippines of the finest teak.

The Spanish trade was much more at risk on the Atlantic side of the great Panama Route. In the early 16th century, Spanish-American colonies were heavily dependent on Spain for subsidy and support, requiring shipments of basic materials. Despite convoy protection, piracy at all times and privateering in wartime often cut the supply line; as a result the *flotas* sometimes failed to appear for several years. Even when the *flotas* were operating normally, the Casa's restrictions created significant difficulties. Seville, an administrative center 70 miles up the muddy, winding Guadalquivir River, was not suitable as a major port for large ships. The largest ships fully loaded could not even cross the sand bar at the mouth of the river; they completed their loading and took on passengers at San Lúcar de Barremeda, or at the ancient port of Cadiz, which was also ill-suited for such heavy traffic, being on a rocky peninsula. When *flotas* numbered

50 to 100 galleons, which was not unusual in the late 16th century, the whole 70-mile stretch of river became Seville's harbor, with goods loaded and unloaded by smaller craft from shore. As the Spanish administrators swarmed over this whole area, trying to record everything and ensure that all appropriate duties and fees were paid to the king, delays and costs mounted. The irregularity and cost of shipments often left the Spanish-Americans in need of essentials and in great desire of luxuries their silver would buy.

Other Europeans began to fill these needs and desires. In the early decades of the 16th century, of course, all non-Spanish Europeans were regarded as pirates—and piracy certainly continued. In 1595, Francis Drake landed at Nombre de Dios, ambushed the silver train on the trail between Las Cruces and Panama, and returned with his booty to Nombre de Dios and then to England. The Spanish in response selected the more easily fortified Puerto Bello as their port of entry. But between 1668 and 1670, the pirate Henry Morgan twice attacked Puerto Bello and even crossed the Isthmus to take and destroy Panama itself. Gradually, however, more Europeans began appearing as smugglers rather than pirates. English, French, Dutch, Portuguese, and even Spanish traders all conspired to circumvent the Spanish Casa's restrictions. Some used unauthorized ports in the Caribbean, while others sold their wares in the main ports, like Cartagena and Puerto Bello, stopping there under the pretense of taking on fresh water and provisions. Some even came into these ports legally, acting under a contract with the Spanish to bring slaves from Africa, and surreptitiously bringing others goods to sell as well. So much illicit trade was carried on that, by the 17th century, officially authorized *flotas* often could not sell their goods, the colonists' needs already having been supplied—and more cheaply—by others. The *flotas* continued, though with fewer ships, into the 18th century; the last annual *flota* sailed in 1735, and in the next few decades Spain gradually bowed to the inevitable, opening its American ports to all traders in 1778. By that time, several other European countries had established bases in the Caribbean, and much of the shipping in the region was being carried on by the British, from such ports as Southampton and London to bases in Jamaica, Bermuda, the Bahamas, and elsewhere in the Caribbean.

The Manila trade continued for somewhat longer. The Spanish ships in the Pacific were still relatively insulated from the rest of the world. In the 16th century the English had penetrated the area; Drake had taken booty from a ship bearing Chinese goods from Acapulco to Callao, had come away with maps of the Manila routes, and even claimed northern California as New Albion, (New England). But being far from friendly ports, the British did not become active in the Pacific until the 18th century; surprisingly, it was they who in 1778 discovered the Sandwich Islands (Hawaiian Islands), which had all the while lain between the eastbound and westbound routes of the Manila galleons. It was not the direct intrusions of others that ended Spain's domination of the Pacific. Rather it was, first, loss of markets to European traders in the Caribbean, and then loss of New Spain. In the early days of the Pacific trade, the arrival of the Manila galleon in Acapulco had brought people along the "China Road" to the Acapulco fair from throughout New Spain, especially from Mexico City. By 1804, however, three Manila galleons sat in Acapulco harbor, having been unable to unload their goods for more than a year. More than that, Spain began to lose its American colonies. When the Mexicans began their fight for independence in 1811, one of their earliest moves was to take back the silver already loaded onto a galleon headed for Manila. The last "China ship" left Acapulco for Manila in 1815, ending Spanish control over the Pacific.

Change came rapidly to the Panama Route in the 19th century, for the political situation in the Americas was in flux. As the former colonials of the United States of America had done before them, the Central and South American colonials severed themselves from Europe and set up independent states. With Spain's power broken, the British—with their fast, light clipper ships—became dominant on the Atlantic route, although the Dutch, the French, the Portuguese, and the Spanish continued to be active; they were soon joined by the emerging North Americans. The Pacific, virtually abandoned by Spain and its former colonies, soon attracted them as well. The British and Americans began to explore, fish, and set up routes across the Pacific, primarily using the Cape Horn Route south of the Americas, to trade with China and Japan, which were brought out of their self-imposed isolation. American and British action in the Pacific coincided with their westward push in North America. Before the building of railroads, overland routes through mountain and desert could not adequately supply frontier territories; the Mississippi and Missouri might supply the center of the country, but not the far West. Indeed, New England traders, calling at California cities like San Diego, San Francisco, and Monterey, the capital, laid the basis for California's annexation by the United States, as the Santa Fe trade had done for New Mexico's. Faced with the problem of supplying the West Coast, and with the great distance and difficulties of the Cape Horn Route, North Americans began to eye possible canal routes over the Central American isthmus.

Certainly the 19th century was the age of canals. The north of Scotland was in 1822 cut across by a series of locks in the Caledonian Canal; in 1825, the Erie Canal opened the heart of North America to water-borne trade; and in 1869, the Suez was bridged by a sea-level canal. Voices throughout Europe and America called for a Central American canal—even Thomas Jefferson and Benja-

min Franklin had expressed interest in the idea. The same four alternatives existed—Panama, Nicaragua, Tehuantepec, and Darien—along with one or two other latecomers to the race, but opinion was divided as to which was preferable. Worse than that, with the practical canal experience of the 19th century, had come a new choice: should the canal be cut through the land at sea level, like the Suez, or should a series of locks be built to lift ships up over the heights and then down the other side? While scientists and engineers argued—and did remarkably little to examine the alternatives—events took over.

In January 1848 gold was discovered in California; as the news spread, the rush was on, and people started to move from East Coast to West, any way they could. They had three ways to go: "the Plains across, the Horn around, or the Isthmus over." The Plains were still largely uncharted, hostile territory at this time; the trip around the Horn cost a good deal of money; and both took at least three months. An isthmus route was faster and more accessible, and people flooded to all the crossing points Central America afforded. Voting with their feet, the majority chose Panama, cutting 8,000 miles off the 13,000

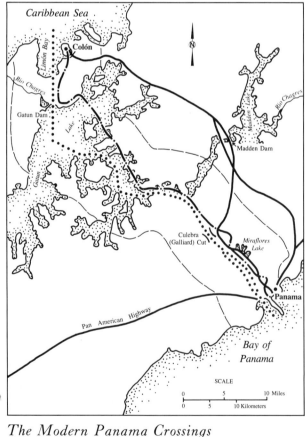

The Modern Panama Crossings

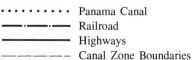

· · · · · · · · · Panama Canal

———·——— Railroad

———— Highways

— — — — — Canal Zone Boundaries

While the inhabitants flee inland, French privateers raid this small Spanish settlement in the Caribbean. (From de Bry, Grands Voyages*)*

mile trip between New York and San Francisco. Oddly, because of the geographical twists of Central America, they were actually traveling eastward, Panama City on the Pacific being farther east than the Atlantic end of the route. Ships of all shapes and descriptions were pressed into service to take eager would-be prospectors down the East Coast to Panama, while others operated on the West Coast between Panama City and San Francisco. The land routes on the Panama Isthmus were in sorry shape. The old gold road had shrunk to a jungle path scarcely three feet wide; the more heavily used Cruces Trail, connecting the Rio Chagres with Panama City, was little better. Forty-niners generally hired canoes at exorbitant prices to take them up the Chagres to Las Cruces, and then traveled by mule or foot to the Pacific side. One U.S. Army unit (including the future General and President

Ulysses S. Grant) was temporarily stranded in Las Cruces because the baggage mules they had hired at 11 cents a pound were instead rented to civilians willing to pay up to 20 cents a pound; the medical officer with the unit complained:

We had the vexation of seeing hundreds of citizens forwarded, with scarcely an hour's detention, while our men were kept at the most unhealthy place on the isthmus....[I] recommended that the whole detachment should be furnished with mules, lest the fatigue of marching over so desperate a road should excite the disease in men predisposed to it, and they should perish. This was done, but notwithstanding every precaution on our part, three fatal cases did occur on the road.

The forty-niners were fortunate in one respect, though: the Pacific Mail Steamship Company had just established a passenger service and federally subsidized mail delivery service between the East and West Coasts of the United States across the Panama Isthmus; they were in a position to provide sea-going transport to travelers, some of whom might otherwise have been stranded in Panama City.

With the land crossing still extremely difficult, railroad speculators moved into the isthmus, with concessions purchased from New Granada, now Colombia, which ruled the area. Rejecting both the old Spanish port of Nombre de Dios and its successor, Portobelo (as it came to be spelled), the engineers chose to place their terminus on Manzanilla Island in Limón Bay, discovered centuries before by Columbus; they called their settlement Aspinwall, after one of the railroad company owners, but others called it Colón, the Spanish word for Columbus, and that name stuck. At its completion in 1855, the railroad was the most expensive in the world—both in cost per foot and in human lives, lost to disease, primarily yellow fever, malaria, and sometimes cholera. Although the railroad company kept no accurate records, some thousands of laborers, many imported from China and Ireland, are thought to have died in constructing the railroad—one for every tie on the Panama Railroad, many people said. Nor were the transcontinental travelers immune; many became ill and died while making the crossing, or on the ship to California. But still they came, and the desire to cross as quickly as possible made the railroad a great success immediately. After only the eight-mile section between Colón and the Chagres was completed, travelers clamored to take that, to shorten the canoe part of the voyage. As a result the railroad was a money-making venture long before it was finished. With the railroad half-completed, travelers could theoretically cross the isthmus in one day, although most took the journey in two, bedding down at Las Cruces; after the five-year construction was finished, the 47-mile trip took just four hours. In this period, before overland stage routes and transcontinental railroads crossed North America, the Panama Route was not only used by most travelers, it was also the official mail route between the U.S. coasts, as Panama had once been between Peru and Spain.

The importance of the Isthmus Route did not go unrecognized, especially by the United States; President Ulysses S. Grant expressed it plainly: "To Europeans the benefits of and advantages of the proposed canal are great; to Americans they are incalculable." It was Grant who authorized the first serious explorations of the possible canal sites, with seven expeditions between 1870 and 1875. With the horror stories of the Panama crossings clearly in mind, the United States favored a lock canal at Nicaragua, with Darien often the second choice over Panama. A French speculator named Lucien Napoleon Bonaparte Wyse, however, obtained from the Republic of Colombia the rights to build a canal at Panama, and enlisted Ferdinand de Lesseps, great builder of the Suez Canal, to take charge of the operation. While the Americans were still considering a Nicaragua canal, this French corporation moved to start a canal at Panama. De Lesseps was extremely optimistic, proclaiming: "Panama will be easier to build, easier to finish, and easier to maintain than the Suez Canal." Unfortunately, he had seriously misunderstood the geological problems of the area, not to mention underestimating the medical difficulties, and opted for a sea-level canal, which meant a straight cut across the isthmus from sea to sea. Geographical explorations had located a gap in the mountains only 275 feet above sea level, 200 feet less than previous estimates, so this seemed feasible; but the hills at the Culebra Gap were covered with clay tens of feet thick, which, when the rains came, simply slid back into the diggings. Indeed, the work crews made the ground more unstable by digging in the area, and in some periods they lost ground to the mudslides. An even more serious problem was disease, which took the lives of many thousands of workers during the eight-year effort. Apart from that, de Lesseps apparently had not solved the problem of dealing with the Rio Chagres, which at times had 40-foot floods. Finally in 1889 the canal corporation collapsed, with charges of corruption causing a great scandal in France. The failure was so complete that Panama was, for a time, almost dropped from consideration as a transcontinental canal route. A successor corporation kept a few people digging to maintain the canal rights, but most of the route was simply abandoned to the jungle.

The failure of the de Lesseps canal at Panama reinforced the U.S. government's preference for the Nicaraguan route. And events elsewhere in the world made a canal even more important to the United States. As Americans had come to regard the taking of the North American continent as their "manifest destiny," their trading activities had led them to extend that thinking to the Pacific. Thomas O. Selfridge, leader of Grant's Darien expedition, put it bluntly: "The Pacific is naturally our domain." In the late 19th century, the United States built a bridge of island bases across the Pacific, taking Hawaii and winning others from Spain in the Spanish-American War (which also brought them Caribbean possessions). A canal had now become vital. Most Americans still favored Nicaragua, but the French corporation, which had hired an American lawyer, had Panama rights to sell, and a French engineer—a survivor of the de Lesseps debacle—had an obsession with Panama. While the Americans were exploring the Panama alternative, Colombia decided to try renegotiating the basic terms of the franchise; at that point, the Frenchman, Phillippe Bunau-Varilla, made a series of complex and somewhat bizarre moves, arranging for the Panamanians to secede from Colombia and to

The harbor of Acapulco, with its famous cliffs in the foreground, was home port for Spain's Manila galleons. (From François Valentijn, Oud en Nieuw Oost Indien, *Amsterdam, 1721-26)*

grant the canal rights to the United States. In the end, a volcanic eruption along the proposed Nicaraguan route swung the Americans, and Bunau-Varilla, who had had himself appointed as Panama's representative to the United States, drew up the treaty declaring a 10-mile-wide Panama Zone sovereign territory of the United States. At the same time, the United States took over the remaining assets of the French canal company and the Panama Railroad as well, which proved invaluable in transporting supplies during the building of the canal.

The Americans were more fortunate than the French. By the time American engineers started work, in 1904, the causes of malaria and yellow fever had been discovered, and prevention and treatment plans dramatically cut the risk of disease. They were able to learn from de Lesseps's mistakes; they opted for a lock canal, which was all the more preferable because of the rapidly increasing size of steamships, which were replacing the 19th century clipper ships. They also solved the problem of the Rio Chagres, by building two dams, with the benefit of recent technological advances. A dam across the Chagres

at Gatun, the point where the railroad had reached the river from the Atlantic, created a huge lake that allowed engineers to control water levels; a much smaller dam did the same in the misnamed Rio Grande Valley on the Pacific side. The route chosen by the canal engineers roughly followed that of the railroad, whose original track was largely submerged; the Atlantic entry point was shifted somewhat to the new port of Cristóbal (Hispanic for Christopher), which became a main repair facility for ships. The Culebra Cut—renamed the Galliard Cut, for the engineer who supervised the work—still caused great trouble, of course, but the use of locks helped support and stabilize the hills on either side of the canal. The canal project was under the direction of several engineers before President Theodore Roosevelt assigned the job to army engineers headed by Colonel George W. Goethals. The process took 10 years; unfortunately, because of differing engineering choices, virtually none of the French work was usable; much of it was submerged by the new artificial lakes.

Oddly, the opening of the Panama Canal was almost anticlimactic. When the United States finally succeeded in breaching the land barrier between the world's two great oceans and opening the long-desired route from Cadiz to Cathay, the world's attention was elsewhere. On August 3, 1914, the day the first ship passed through the Panama Canal, Germany declared war on France. By the time the canal opened officially, the guns of August were booming, as World War I began. But despite a momentary lack of attention from the world, the Panama Canal introduced a major shift in world sea routes. Ships that formerly would have had to work their way laboriously around Cape Horn passed through the canal in a mere eight hours, guided by powerful tugboats. Goods that would have had to be unloaded, trans-shipped across

Panama by rail, and then reloaded on another craft could now remain on one ship for the whole route. The United States and Canada were immediate beneficiaries of the new canal, being able to ship easily from coast to coast; industrial products from the East could more readily be exchanged with produce from the West, in a pattern that continues today.

Europe's shipping patterns changed, too. During the 19th century, Great Britain had established dominance over world shipping, primarily through the Suez Route, with London becoming the world's entrepôt. Even goods from the north coast of South America were often shipped to London, and only then back to the United States. The dangers posed by German U-boats during World War I broke this pattern, however, and sped the shift to the

Steaming through the infamous Culebra Cut in 1915, the battleship Ohio's *journey from Atlantic to Pacific was at least 7,000 miles shorter than it would have been the year before. (Library of Congress)*

Panama Canal Route – and to U. S. ships. Freed from the necessity of following favorable winds and currents, steamships on the Panama Route from Europe no longer swung down to the Canaries and across; instead they followed the North Atlantic Route, running against the Gulf Stream, from northern Europe westward, turned southwest near Newfoundland, and then either headed straight for the canal or stopped at major east coast ports along the way. On the Pacific side, the Panama Route now split into two branches. One moved up the west coast of North America, often stopping at ports like San Francisco, then headed west via the Hawaiian Islands to Japan and China. The other headed across the old "South Sea" to Australia and New Zealand, which increasingly supplied produce to Europe. The Panama Canal came to occupy such a central position among the world's sea routes that, before the Northeast Passage was opened for commercial shipping through the Siberian Sea in the 1940's, ships from Russia's northern European port of Murmansk sometimes passed through the Panama Canal to reach its Pacific port of Vladivostok. As ships have grown even larger in the 20th century, the canal has been widened to accommodate greater tonnage, taking all but the very largest aircraft carriers and supertankers in its two-directional locks. In the decades after World War II, increased trade with the Far East, especially Japan, and greater reliance on imported fuel, has made the Panama Route more active than ever before.

Apart from its economic importance, the Panama Canal has also rightly been regarded as a wonder of the modern world, attracting tourists in the great age of round-the-world cruises. Even today, when most travelers prefer airplanes for long-distance trips, cruises take tourists on the old routes followed by colonists, traders, and pirates. On the isthmus itself, few traces of the old world remain. Nombre de Dios and Portobelo are now collections of hovels, with an occasional Spanish ruin or collapsed gun emplacement; the old gold road and Cruces Trail are barely traceable through the tangled jungle; Las Cruces itself lies under the waters of Gatun Lake; and the old Panama was never rebuilt in the same spot after being sacked by Morgan. In their places are the newer, more modern cities of Colón, Cristóbal, and Panama City. Near these cities, the Panama Zone itself is crowded with suburban housing, in some places fenced off from the poorer Panamanians, but scheduled to be turned over gradually to Panama by the end of the 20th century. Beyond, in the jungle, rusting, vine-covered machinery can be seen in de Lesseps's abandoned diggings, testimony to the price that was paid to bring alive the Europeans' dream of a westward sea route to the riches of Asia.

Selective Bibliography

Bishop, Joseph Bucklin. *The Panama Gateway.* (New York: Charles Scribner's Sons, 1913). Focuses on construction of the U.S. Canal, by the Secretary of the Isthmian Canal Commission.

Chapman, Charles Edward. *Colonial Hispanic America: A History.* (New York: Macmillan, 1933).

_____.*Republican Hispanic America: A History.* (New York: Macmillan, 1937). Together they make a sound history of Spanish America.

Du Val, Miles P., Jr. *Cadiz to Cathay: The Story of the Long Struggle for a Waterway Across the American Isthmus.* (Stanford, California: Stanford University Press, 1940). Focuses on the political history of the canal, especially in modern times, with interesting detail.

Haring, Clarence H. *The Spanish Empire in America.* (New York: Oxford University Press, 1947). A useful general history, with one chapter focusing on the commercial trade routes.

_____. *Trade and Navigation Between Spain and the Indies, in the Time of the Hapsburgs.* Detailed account of the Spanish Indies trade.

Howarth, David. *Panama: Four Hundred Years of Dreams and Cruelty.* (New York: McGraw-Hill, 1966). A balanced account of the history of the Panama Isthmus.

McCullough, David. *The Path Between the Seas: The Creation of the Panama Canal, 1870–1914.* (New York: Simon & Schuster, 1977). Focuses on the actual construction, French and American.

Morison, Samuel Eliot. *The European Discovery of America: The Southern Voyages A.D. 1492–1616.* (New York: Oxford University Press, 1974). A closely detailed account of the early explorations.

Parry, J. H. *The Age of Reconnaissance: Discovery, Exploration and Settlement, 1450 to 1650.* (New York: Praeger, 1969).

_____. *Trade and Dominion: The European Overseas Empires in the Eighteenth Century.* (New York: Praeger, 1971). Together provide excellent detail and overall context for trade and travel in the period.

_____. *The Spanish Seaborne Empire.* (New York: Knopf, 1966). A fascinating account; especially good on seafaring detail.

Penrose, Boies. *Travel and Discovery in the Renaissance, 1420–1620.* (New York: Atheneum, 1975; reprint of the 1952 Harvard University Press edition). Very useful on the early explorations.

Schott, Joseph L. *Rails Across Panama: The Story of the Building of the Panama Railroad, 1848–1855.* (Indianapolis: Bobbs-Merrill, 1967). A useful, detailed account.

Schurz, William Lytle. *The Manila Galleon.* (New York: Dutton, 1939). Comprehensive account of the Spanish trade with Manila.

Tavernier, Bruno. *Great Maritime Routes: An Illustrated History.* (New York: Viking, 1972). Translated from the French; contains chapters on the Spanish gold and silver routes and the Panama route.

Wiltsee, Ernest A. *Gold Rush Steamers of the Pacific.* (Lawrence, Mass.: Quarterman Publications, 1976; reprint of 1938 ed. of Grabhorn Press, San Francisco). Filled with buff-pleasing detail.

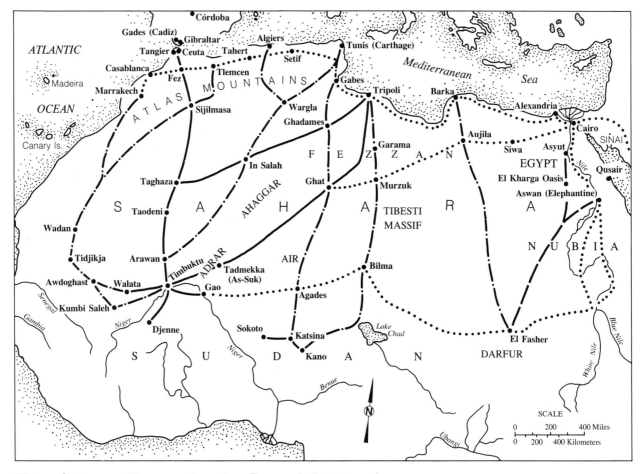

The Sahara Routes in the Late Middle Ages

―――――― Main Gold and Slave Routes

―・―・― Other Main Trans-Sahara Routes

― ― ― Derib El Arba'in (Track of the 40 Days)

・・・・・・・ Main Connecting Routes

The Sahara Routes

In 1559, the Spanish Moor Al Hassan ibn Mohammed Alwazan, better known in Europe as Leo Africanus, published an account of a town he had seen on his Saharan travels. He said of Timbuktu:

Here are many shops of artificers and merchants, and especially of such as weave linnen and cotton cloth. And hither do the Barbarie merchants bring cloth of Europe. All the women of this region except maid-servants go with their faces covered...The inhabitants, and especially strangers there residing, are exceedingly rich, insomuch that the king that now is, married both his daughters unto two rich merchants. Here are many wels containing most sweete water; and so often as the river Niger overfloweth they conveigh the water there-of by certain sluces into the towne. Corne, cattle, milke and butter this region yeeldeth in great abundance; but salt is scarce heere, for it is brought hither by land from Tegaza [Taghaza] which is five hundred miles distant. When I myself was here, I saw one camells loade of salt sold for 80 ducates.

The Europeans had long heard of the "golden trade of the Moors" across the Sahara to the Sudan. They listened most eagerly to Leo Africanus's description of one building in Timbuktu: "...there is a most stately temple to be seene, the wals where-of are made of stone and lime; and a princely palace also built by a most excellent workeman of Granada." And they gave a ready ear to his account of the royal court's magnificence: "The rich king...hath many plates and scepters of gold, some whereof weigh 1,300 poundes: and he keepes a magnificent and well furnished court."

From these descriptions, and from stories of fabulously rich Moslem African princes who had journeyed to Mecca, Europeans built up an image of Timbuktu as a place of grandeur greater than that of India. In doing so, they quite ignored the rest of Africanus's depiction; he himself had expected a more gracious city, noting: "...all the houses where-of are now changed into cottages built of chalke and covered with thatch" which was much in danger of fire. If the city did not live up to its romantic image, it was indeed a major caravan center and a cultural center as well, for he noted:

Here are great store of doctors, judges, priests, and other learned men, that are bountifully maintained at the king's cost and charges. And hither are brought divers manuscripts or written books out of Barbarie, which are sold for more money than any other merchandise.

The source of Timbuktu's strength was its position on the main caravan routes, which connected the steppe and bush of the south with the coast of the north, across the waste of the Sahara.

Like a national flag, northern Africa west of the Nile is composed of four horizontal strips. Facing the Mediter-

Sandstorms were always a major hazard in the Sahara, against which travelers protected their faces. (From James Richardson, Travels in the Great Desert of the Sahara, *1848)*

ranean, the first strip is hospitable, undulating country, backed by semi-arid uplands, including the Atlas Mountains; the western portion, which pushes out into the sea to within 14 miles of Spain, is called variously Barbary, Mauretania, or the Maghreb. Second comes the broad, inhospitable swath of the Sahara, the largest desert mass in the world. South of that is the Sudan (originally Bilad al-Sudan, meaning Land of the Blacks); this transitional belt—also called the Sahel Corridor—is composed of semi-arid steppe shading into savannah and then parkland. A tropical jungle strip completes the great bulge of Africa, running from the Atlantic eastward; the great Niger River courses through it, arising in the southwest, arcing northeastward up into the Sudan, and then swinging down to the ocean.

The immense Sahara, which dominates north Africa, is not a uniform desert, however. The vast expanse—over 3,000 miles wide from the Atlantic to the Red Sea, and 800–1,200 miles deep—is itself made up of various parts. The great regions of sand and sand dunes, called *ergs,* which can move dangerously in the wind, and which are so prominent in the popular imagination, occupy much less than half of the Sahara's territory. The Sahara also includes mountains, some 8,000 feet high and occasionally capped with snow; two of the most notable mountain groups are the Tibesti Massif in the east-central Sahara, and the Ahaggar Mountains in the west-central

region. Other parts of the Sahara, called *reg,* are hard-packed ground covered with loose gravel; while some—the *hammada*—are almost uncrossable regions of blackened rocks and boulders. Slicing through these are the deep-cut *wadis,* water channels given to flash floods—sometimes so suddenly as to drown people halted in the streambed, who were unaware of a storm some miles away. This enormous desert, covering over 3,000,000 square miles, is watered by only a few dozen main oases; many of these are clustered in the north-central region known as the Fezzan, while "deserts within the desert," like the central gravel pan, may go years with less than an inch of rain. The desert's very name means "wilderness" (in Arabic, *sahrá*). As much as any area in the world, the geography of this region has determined its history.

But the region has not always been as it is today. Although the Sahara is now one of the most desolate places in the world, there are scattered throughout the desert evidences of a different kind of life. Fishhooks and bone harpoon points are found in some profusion in the whole southwest quadrant of the present-day Sahara. More than that, life-size rock carvings in the central and northern Sahara depict animals who could no longer survive there, including the elephant, rhinoceros, and hippopotamus. Later rock carvings show domestic cattle; still later, horse-drawn chariots are seen in over 300 drawings in the northern Sahara; then the chariots disappear, to be replaced by lancers on horseback, and then by men on camels. The drawings themselves are difficult to date, but may have been begun as early as 5000 B.C. The distribution of the drawings seems to describe some main routes across the desert; some archaeologists, indeed, believe that the chariot drawings indicate various stations along ancient routes through the then-moister Sahara. From the region of modern Tripoli, early gateway to the Sahara, a route fed down into the oasis-studded Fezzan and swung west to the northernmost curve of the Niger, in the region of Timbuktu. The other route fed through the Atlas Mountains, making a wide swing southwest to the region between the Senegal River and the Upper Niger, then eastward to Timbuktu.

Then, sometimes between 3000 and 1500 B.C., came a change in the climate that had allowed the Sahara to support so many fishers, hunters, and herders. Lakes and swamps that had once existed were no more. And those people remaining gradually decimated both animal and plant life, causing many animals to become extinct in the Sahara and destroying the forests that had grown in some regions in earlier times. All of this only increased the size and severity of the Sahara, a process that is still going on today. By the time Mesopotamians and Europeans, with their written records, arrived on the scene, the Sahara was much as it is today, in character if not in size, although the Maghreb was more lush and full of animals, including many elephants, lions, leopards, and ostriches. The fifth century B.C. Greek historian Herodotus was very clear on that point:

> Libya [Africa] is full of wild beasts, while beyond the wild beast region there is a tract which is wholly sand, very scant of water, and utterly and entirely a desert.

We know very little about travel across the Sahara in early times. Most likely it was, in its general character, much as it has been into modern times: in the warm season, desert nomads would leave their quickly depleted wells and pastures and head out of the desert with their herds, either north to the Atlas Mountains or the uplands of Algeria and Tunisia, or south to the Sudan, especially to the Niger Valley and Lake Chad for more temperate climes. As they traveled with their oxen and donkeys (camels arrived only later), they would carry modest goods for barter. Gold and slaves from the interior would later be the staples of the trans-Sahara trade, but we do not know when they first began to be traded. One of the earliest chroniclers of the region, Herodotus, did note that "the Garamantes hunt the Ethiopian hole-men, or troglodytes, in four-horse chariots, for these troglodytes are exceedingly swift of foot." Some have identified the Garamantes as inhabitants of the Fezzan and the troglodytes as potential slaves from the Tibesti Massif to the southeast.

Between the southern Sahara and the Sudan was a different kind of trade. The barren Sahara had one product needed desperately by the people of the Sudan: salt. In turn, the Sudan offered gold, from its bountiful mines, and later slaves. We do not know when salt caravans began crossing the Sahara from the Sudan. The earliest routes through the Sahara had apparently followed streambeds or run alongside hills where water and vegetation were most likely to be found; this was particularly important when oxen and horses were the main pack animals. But at some point the caravan routes began to angle toward the main salt mines: in the west to the old mines at Taghaza, north of Timbuktu; in the east to Bilma, north of Lake Chad.

We also do not know whether any traffic went all the way across the Sahara. Herodotus does tell of five young men who, as an adventure, set out across the desert and came to a fertile plain with fruit-laden trees; there they were captured by Negroes and taken to a crocodile-infested river, running from west to east, before being allowed to return home. Some believe the story partly supported by evidence from the rock-drawings, suggesting that the young men may have reached the Niger; others are skeptical of the ingenuous and highly imaginative Herodotus.

Even in these early times, the peoples of the Sahara were quite diverse, but there were two main groups. One was a dark-skinned or negroid group, descendants of immigrants who had begun pushing north from the Sudan into the Sahara as early as the third millennium B.C.; these were generally known to Europeans as Ethiopians (in Greek meaning "with burnt faces") and were said to occupy all the land south of Libya. The other main group was the light-skinned peoples who dominated North Africa and the west and central Sahara. The Greeks called these Libyans, but the Romans called them *barbari* (barbarians), from which came the regional name Barbary. (Later, Europeans called these people Berbers.)

The arrival of foreign colonists in Barbary changed the mix but little, for their numbers were small; they did, however, introduce widespread cultural changes. In the first millennium B.C., Phoenicians began to establish colonies in Barbary, from the Gulf of Syrtis—with its prime port of Leptis (Lepcis) Magna, near modern Tripoli—to the Atlantic. By 500 B.C., these colonies had become an independent empire with its capital at Carthage (now Tunis), guarding the Narrows of the Mediterranean. Leptis Magna was important not only as a fine seaport but also because it was the end of the Garamantes road from the Fezzan (then called Phazania). What goods were carried along this road we do not know, though they may include skins, timber, ivory, ostrich feathers, gold from the Fezzan, or slaves—all later products. The only specific product mentioned by several classical writers is the carbuncle, an unknown kind of stone; according to some highly speculative hypotheses, carbuncles were beads of chalcedony originating on the west coast of Africa. If so, they might have been the earliest items to be shipped routinely all the way across the Sahara to foreign traders.

In the time of Christ, the Romans took over the Barbary colonies. Like their predecessors, the Romans made their headquarters near Carthage, calling the area Provincia Africa—a name later applied to the whole continent. Unlike the Phoenicians, who had lived essentially in isolated coastal enclaves, the Romans attempted to establish a firm frontier along the hills of North Africa; unfortunately, that brought them into direct conflict with the nomads of the north Sahara, who moved their herds into the hills in the summer. Attempting to hold back the nomadic guerrillas whose enmity they had gained, the Romans established garrisons at oases on the main routes leading into the north Sahara. With no group did they have more difficulty than the Garamantes of the Fezzan. The Romans responded by sending an expeditionary army into the heart of the Fezzan; with surprise on its side, the Roman force readily captured the main Fezzan oases, including Cydamus (Ghadames) and the capital, Garama (Germa). The effective subjugation was only temporary, however; soon the Roman army had to withdraw to its defensive line, retracing its 30-day march over almost waterless desert. The Garamantians, shocked by the invasion of territory they had thought secure, took action to prevent a recurrence, as the Roman writer Pliny tells us: "It has been impossible to open up the road to the Garamantes country, because brigands of that race fill up the wells with sand."

What changed the situation was the introduction of domesticated camels into the Maghreb. Camels had reached Egypt as early as the sixth century B.C. and the eastern Sudan before the time of Christ, but apparently reached the Maghreb only around the Christian era, either imported by Romans or brought by Zenata (Berber) nomads who were pushing along the coastal strip from the west. By the second century A.D., camels had become common enough to be depicted in local sculptures of agricultural activities; and by 363 A.D. the officials of Leptis Magna, the main Roman port, were asking the Romans to send them 4,000 camels for use in dealing with a local uprising. During these centuries, camels seem to have begun transforming travel and political relations in the region. We find the Garamantes and the Romans becoming allies, and the Romans discovering "new roads" in the region—presumably cross-desert routes that were unusable before, because they had too little water for the usual pack animals. Camels, as their reputation attests, could last far longer without water, and could also travel faster over this terrain than many other bearing beasts— although some areas were too barren even for them.

In this period, Romans and their native allies traveled further than ever before. Around 100 A.D., a Roman party traveled south of the Fezzan for three months, which would have brought them into the Sudan, although we know nothing of their actual terminus. Shortly after that, the Roman writer Ptolemy records:

> Julius Maternus, setting out from Leptis Magna and Garama with the King of the Garamantes, who was beginning an expedition against the Ethiopians, by bearing continuously southward came within four months to Agisymba, the country of the Ethiopians where the rhinoceros is to be found...

Agisymba is unidentified, but many have suggested that it was in the Tibesti Massif, a group of mountains, to the southeast of Tripoli in the Sahara.

Some other expeditions may have been more spontaneous, among them those by Jewish settlers. Jews had been living in North Africa for many centuries. Some apparently arrived with Phoenician settlers in the early first millennium B.C.; others settled further east, in Cyrene, in the sixth century B.C., where they apparently converted a large number of Berbers to Judaism. In 115 A.D., these Cyrene Jews revolted against the Romans and lost, fleeing westward. While most seem to have established themselves in oases in the northern Sahara, some moved deep into the desert; a few may even have reached West Africa, for oral tradition in the region says that the early kings of Ghana were white, and other kings in the region are said to have been from Yemen (meaning Arabia) "on the road to Mecca." Be that as it may, Europeans and Asians seem to have reached some distance into and possibly across the Sahara in the late Roman period.

Roman domination brought other changes as well. Some were destructive, most notably the hunting and capturing near to extinction of the many animals that had blessed Libya, especially the small North African elephant made famous by Hannibal and now extinct, and the lions that were shipped by the hundreds from Leptis Magna to Ostia, port of Rome, for the infamous and bloody bouts with gladiators. Like the Carthaginians before them, the Romans used local peoples in their armies; but they apparently took few as slaves, being well supplied in that department from Europe and Asia, and from prisoners-of-war. The Romans also, however, had strong constructive influences on the region. Most importantly, their technology helped the North Africans make the most of the precious water they received. Springs were tapped from afar and brought to the Roman outposts by great aqueducts; one brought water to Carthage from nearly 90 miles away. Closer to home, the Roman engineers built dams across *wadis*, so that the occasional rainfall could be collected in reservoirs; smaller amounts of water were collected in cisterns, in the hills and even on the roofs of private houses. These supplies of water allowed the peoples of Roman Africa not only to keep back the Sahara, which always threatened to encroach upon any oasis, but also to expand, using irrigation to convert arid desert into cultivated land. (The depletion of wild animals may have been an inadvertent boon to farming.) Even when Roman power fell, Roman engineering allowed the towns and northern desert oases to flourish for many centuries.

Throughout this period, the Romans and their successors had focused their attention in the eastern Maghreb. Builders that they were, they had constructed roads eight to twenty-two feet wide, primarily along the Mediterranean coast, from the Atlantic to Egypt, but also in the region inland from Carthage, especially to the market towns like Cirta (now Constantine), frequented by nomads. But beyond the Roman roads were the caravan trails. Many of these were established by the Zeneta Berbers who, with the advantage offered by camel transport, moved into the Sahara from the East over several centuries, conquering many oases and mountain regions, subjugating earlier negroid peoples, and reaching as far as the Niger River. By the time the Arab Moslems arrived in the seventh century, the line of the main caravan trails had been set—a line partly determined by the location of vital salt mines. In the western Sahara, the main route ran north from the great bend of the Niger to the salt mines of Taghaza and then on to the Atlas Mountains. Further east, the main route went north from Lake Chad to the salt mines of Bilma and then to Murzuk, through the Fezzan, and on to Tripolitania. No other routes at the time passed between these, for travelers would have had to traverse barren and almost waterless terrain.

In the late seventh century, the Arabs arrived from the East bearing the new religion of Islam—destined to change the character of the Sahara. Unlike the Europeans, who had focused on Libya and Tunisia, the Arabs moved on across the Maghreb to the Atlantic, converting many Berbers, and headed across the Strait of Gibraltar to take Spain. Settling in the fertile, well-watered land of the western Maghreb, these newcomers created a lively, flourishing culture, drawing on the learning and skills of the great Mediterranean civilizations, and on a flow of settlers, ranging from farmers to scholars, many of them from Spain. The mix of peoples was sometimes uneasy, especially in the early years. The city of Fez, for example, was founded in the ninth century by 2,000 families from Kairouan, in Tunisia; 8,000 families expelled from Córdoba joined them a few years later, but lived on the opposite bank, remaining for a long time separate, even while the city was becoming the cultural center of the region.

The Arabs transformed the rudimentary trade of the Sahara. In the eighth century, the kingdom of Ghana, west of the Niger, monopolized the gold trade of the region and was the salt distribution center for the western Sudan; a trade route ran between Ghana's capital of Kumbi and the Berber-controlled salt mines at Taghaza, 20 days' march north. Long a commercial people, the Arabs quickly moved to expand the trade, building an entrepôt at Sijilmasa, an oasis in the fertile *wadi* Tafilalt, just south of the Atlas Mountains. Arabic writers were quite clear that Sijilmasa's fortune was based on gold; the 10th century writer Ibn Haukal, noting that the city cannot be entered "but by way of the desert, which the sand renders difficult," talked of the "most pure and excellent gold" to be found in the gold mines of the south, even though "the way to them is dangerous and troublesome." An anonymous 12th century Moslem author noted of this trade that:

> ...in the sands of that country is gold, and merchants trade with salt for it, taking the salt on camels from the salt mines. They start from a town called Sijilmasa...and travel in the desert as it were upon the sea, having guides to pilot them by the stars or rocks in the deserts. They take provisions for six months, and when they reach Ghana they weigh their salt and sell it against a certain unit of weight of gold, and sometimes against double or more of the gold unit, according to the market and the supply.

Ghana herself did not produce the gold, however; that came from a country called Wangara, whose location was a closely guarded secret. Cupidity drew Arabs to attack Ghana in the mid-eighth century, but the expedition failed, although descendants of the Arab soldiers were found in Ghana in the 11th century. To the west of Ghana was a rival kingdom of Sanhaja Berbers, who had pushed south out of the Sahara. (Their name was corrupted centuries later by Europeans and applied to the river that watered their land: the Senegal.) The Sanhaja set up a rival market at Awdoghast, 15 days' march west of Kumbi Saleh. Both Kumbi and Awdoghast housed Arab merchants, who generally lived apart from the local residents.

Despite the rivalry between the various peoples, and the restlessness of tribes under their dominion, trade generally continued on the caravan route north to Sijilmasa. Indeed, in northern Africa trade often continued regardless of any military action taking place, with a truce being called so that a mutually beneficial market could open. Trade was so brisk that Ibn Haukal mentions a Sijilmasa man who owed 40,000 gold *dinars* to an Awdoghast merchant. The trade itself was somewhat unusual. Arab traders from Sijilmasa would leave bearing cheap goods like coral beads, picking up salt on the way through Taghaza; in Kumbi they were joined by Ghanaian agents, who took them 20 days' march southwest to the Senegal, where they beat drums to announce their arrival. The Arab merchants spread out their goods on the river bank and then left; only then would the natives come out of the "holes" (presumably gold mines) in which they lived. The natives placed on the river-bank an amount of gold they thought equal to the value of the goods, and themselves left the scene. If the merchants thought the trade was fair, they would take the gold and retire, beating the drums to signal their acceptance. Despite many attempts by outsiders to discover the source of gold, it remained secret and this silent trade, or dumb barter, continued for many centuries. Arabs on the trans-Sahara routes did not seek only gold, however. Merchants from new cities, like Fez, also sought slaves; Ghana supplied them, raiding the equatorial forest bordering the Sudan.

However active the trade, however, the Sahara remained dangerous for travelers. Any trip across the wasteland was like a new throw of the dice, dependent on each well having its supply of precious fluid. Even as late as 1805, lack of water cost the lives of all 2,000 men and 1,800 camels of a caravan en route home to Fez from Timbuktu. The too-rare oases, sometimes a week apart, were spots of green in the wasteland, which would come to life only briefly, when a caravan arrived. Writing in the 19th century, René Caillié might have been describing the arrival of a caravan at a desert well a thousand years before:

> In the midst of this vast desert, the wells of Mourat, surrounded by fourteen hundred camels and by the four hundred men of our caravan, who were crowded round them, presented the moving picture of a populous town; it was a perfect turmoil of men and beasts. On the one side were camels laden with ivory, and bales of goods of all sorts; on the other, camels carrying on their backs negroes, men, women and children, who were on their way to be sold at the Morocco markets; further on, men prostrate on the ground, invoking the Prophet.

Arabs also settled further east in the Maghreb, in the region once favored by the Carthaginians and Romans, often intermarrying with Jewish settlers who had survived in the oases. Like their western counterparts, they reached the Sudan and joined in the slave trade. While some crossed from their center at Wargla to join in the slave trade at Ghana, others preferred the eastern route from the Fezzan to Lake Chad, which later became a main slave route. On both routes, slaves were driven north, some destined for killing work in the salt mines, others for labor in irrigated fields around oases, the rest for sale in the coastal cities. Many did not survive the march across the desert, their bones and the skeletons of camels acting as deadly signposts for other travelers on the routes.

Trade with the north brought other changes to the region as well. Islam percolated into the Senegal region; the Tucolor of the kingdom of Tukrar, were the earliest Black converts. Being the first West African pilgrims to make the *hajj*, or pilgrimage to Mecca, their name—corrupted to Takarir—was for centuries applied by Arabian Moslems to any Black pilgrims from the region. Pilgrims began to make their way to Mecca; but, unlike other Moslem countries, the West African peoples did not organize annual caravans. Instead, members of the royal families would go on pilgrimages, some more than once,

and some hundreds of thousands of their people would join the party. Others who chose to make the long journey without such royal protection had to make up small *ad hoc* caravans or join merchant caravans to cross the Sahara. Pilgrims from the west would head for one of the main staging areas of the Maghreb—Sijilmasa, Fez, or Marrakech; pilgrimage caravans from there would head for Tripoli, to which came pilgrims from the central Sahara. From there all would continue on the old coast road to join with the great pilgrimage caravan from Cairo, either taking a ship from Aydhab or Quasir to Jiddah or, more commonly after the 13th century, crossing the Sinai Desert to head down the old Incense Road to Mecca. The journey was long. Crossing the Sahara alone took two months, and pilgrims from far away normally spent the fasting month of Ramadan in or near Mecca, so they could be in the holy city to complete their obligatory duties on the prescribed dates. It was also expensive—both in cash and in lost earning power—and extremely difficult. As a result, the *hajj* was performed by only a small portion of the Moslem population in West Africa in these early centuries, and indeed local scholars in the region judged that, because of the difficulty, the *hajj* could not reasonably be required of all Moslems.

The royal, wealthy, or learned who did choose to make the pilgrimage, however, often visited other renowned Moslem cities along the way, bringing back with them cultural influences from abroad. One group of Sanhaja Moslems, the Almoravids, became so strong that they assaulted the Maghreb with an army of 30,000 men, capturing Fez, founding Marrakech (whose name, corrupted to Morocco, was later applied to the whole region), and taking Moslem Spain, even fighting the Iberian Christians. In the south they turned against still-pagan Ghana, in 1076 capturing Kumbi, massacring its citizens, and imposing Islam on the region. While the Almoravids remained strong in the north, they soon weakened in the south, leaving the remnants of the kingdom of Ghana at war with each other. The resulting disruption caused the Arabs to establish their own southern entrepôt in the early 13th century, about 100 miles north of the now-bypassed Kumbi, at an old camping ground called Walata. Awdoghast also suffered by the establishment of Walata as a caravan center, especially as the gold fields of the nearby Senegal River were being outproduced by those of the upper Niger, nearer to Walata.

But Walata itself was soon replaced as the main southern entrepôt for the western Sahara route. Traders began to frequent a camping ground just a few miles from the Niger River but in easy reach of the desert; there both river and desert people could barter grain, kola nuts, and gold dust for goods from the north, especially dates and the precious salt. By 1100, this camping ground, called Timbuktu, had become a small village of grass huts, which themselves soon gave way to a town of sun-dried-brick buildings. After the disintegration of the kingdom of Ghana, the kingdom of Mali became the main trading nation in the area, making Timbuktu its trading and cultural center.

In the early 14th century, Mali caught the attention of the world when its king, Mansa Musa, made a pilgrimage to Mecca in 1324. It was not the distance of the pilgrimage that was unusual—though that and the difficulty were great—but his spectacular display of wealth. Accompanied by 500 slaves, each carrying a staff of gold, he rode on horseback, showering gold and extravagant gifts wherever he went and in Cairo joined the annual pilgrims's caravan to Mecca itself. Tales of Mansa Musa spread throughout the world. Indeed, he seems to have been faced with none of the prejudice normally accorded to Negroes by Moslems of the time—a result that some attribute to his rather light skin, and others to the 80–100 camel-loads of gold he carried (so much that the gold market collapsed in Egypt for a time). On his return home, Mansa Musa turned aside to visit the town of Gao, capital of the Songhai people of the middle Niger, which Mali had recently captured. At Gao, he commissioned the building of a mosque by a poet-architect named as-Sahili, who had accompanied him back from Mecca; built of burnt bricks, a technique before then unknown in the region, the mosque stood for 300 years, its foundations into the 20th century. The kingdom of Mali eventually extended from the Atlantic coast, including the Senegal and Gambia rivers, eastward to include Walata; the desert market of Tadmekka (also called as-Suk, the Market), north of Gao; and the upper and middle Niger. Only Djenne, crossroads of the upper Niger, remained independent, perhaps because its surrounding network of waterways shielded it from attack.

Being on the border between desert and river, Timbuktu was the main crossroads for the Sahara trade. From there some of the salt was sent further south, to be used in the silent trade, which still continued. In forested country, where camels could not travel, the salt was often transferred to human porters. A Portuguese sea captain

René Caillié's sketch of Timbuktu makes clear how barren its setting was. (From Journal d'un Voyage à Temboctou et à Jenne dans l'Afrique Centrale, *1830)*

recorded how the natives described the transfer of salt and the "dumb barter" in the 15th century; slabs of salt are broken into pieces, one per man:

> and thus they form a great army of men on foot, who transport it a great distance...until they reach certain waters...Having reached these waters with the salt, they proceed in this fashion: all those who have the salt pile it in rows, each marking his own. Having made these piles, the whole caravan retires half a day's journey. Then there come another race of blacks who do not wish to be seen or to speak. They arrive in large boats, from which it appears that they come from islands, and disembark. Seeing the salt, they place a quantity of gold opposite each pile, and then turn back, leaving salt and gold...

As they had for hundreds of years, these traders would adjust the piles, if necessary, to reach a settlement judged fair by both, and then would take the desired goods and depart. The actual source of the gold—known as the country of Wangara—was still secret, attracting both Arab and European explorers in turn. In truth, there seem to have been several goldfields that fed the Sahara trade at various times, and it now seems most likely that Wangara was not a specific place, but a region.

While Timbuktu and the kingdom of Mali were rising in the south, the peoples of the north were being subjected to new rulers from outside. In the 11th century the Bani Hilal, a group of Bedouin Arabs, swept into the Maghreb, destroying as they went. Aqueducts, dams, and cisterns, which had kept many northern towns green and productive since Roman times, were smashed; buildings and bridges, too, were demolished. Land went out of cultivation and, worse than that, the herds that accompanied the invading nomads made terrible inroads on the remaining forests and scrub of the region. The desert began to win, and the Maghreb has never quite recovered from the blow; today some of the great cities of early times—even seaports like Leptis Magna or nearby Sabratha—are now buried by sand. The newly arrived Arabs tended to stay in the lowlands, along with some Berbers, but other Berbers took to the highlands, remaining somewhat apart for many centuries. Most Berbers later adopted Islam—although of a widely varying, often unorthodox sort. Some, among them the Moors of West Sahara, also came to adopt the Arab language and ways. But others retained their Berber language and customs; most notably, the Taureg—the most distinctive surviving Berber group—retain a face veil for men (adopted some time between 600 and 1000 A.D.) but has none for women, unlike other Moslems. The Taureg in this period became dominant in the Sahara itself, from its main oases of Ghadames and In Salah south to the Niger, especially in the massifs of Ahaggar, Air, and Adrar; from there, they terrorized

caravans for centuries, supplementing their lean desert pickings with not-so-genteel blackmail.

But while the Arab invasion destroyed much in the north, it also opened a far wider door to the East—and inaugurated a great age of travel. While West African kings had formerly made a great show of a *hajj*, travel was increasingly taken up by the ordinary Moslem. One of the most striking of these Moslem travelers was Ibn Battuta, a Tangier native who traveled so widely that when he was in Sijilmasa, he met the brother of a man he had met in China. Like most other travelers headed for the Sudan, Ibn Battuta joined with a caravan forming in Sijilmasa, then proceeded to Taghaza. This he found:

> . . .an unattractive village, with the curious feature that its houses and mosques are built of blocks of salt, roofed with camel skins. There are no trees there, nothing but sand. In the sand is a salt mine; they dig for the salt, and find it in thick slabs...No one lives at Taghaza except the slaves of the Mesufa tribe, who dig for the salt: they subsist on dates imported from Dra'a and Sijilmasa, camel's flesh, and millet imported from the Negrolands. The negroes come up from their country and take away the salt from there. At Walata a load of salt brings eight to ten *mithgals* [1 equals about ⅛ ounce of gold]; in the town of Mali it sells for twenty to thirty, and sometimes as much as forty. The negroes use salt as a medium of exchange, just as gold and silver is used [elsewhere]; they cut it up into pieces and buy and sell with it. The business done at Taghaza, for all its meanness, amounts to an enormous figure in terms of hundredweights of gold-dust.

Leo Africanus, writing over a century later concurred, adding:

> Neither have the said diggers of salt any victuals but such as the merchants bring unto them; for they are distant from all inhabited places almost twenty days' journey, insomuch that oftentimes they perish for lack of food, whenas the merchants come not in due time unto them. Moreover, the southeast wind doth so often blind them, that they cannot live here without great peril. I myself continued three days amongst them, all which time I was constrained to drink salt-water drawn out of certain wells not far from the salt-pits.

After leaving Taghaza, Ibn Battuta's caravan stopped at an unidentified waterhole for a few days, as was the common practice when an appropriate place was found, to rest the animals and themselves and to mend the all-important water-skins that had to supply them between wells. Under way again, the caravan sent a special messenger called a *takshif* ahead to Walata, to arrange for water to be carried out to the caravan, for without this aid, some might not survive to reach the city. This, too, was common practice, for a lone rider on a fast mount could always make far better time than a caravan of weary loaded camels, grazing as they traveled at the rate of about two miles an hour. Astonishingly, sometimes the head *takshif*, who piloted the caravan, was blind, or nearly so; that was the case for both Ibn Battuta and Leo Africanus, who noted that the guide, who rode "foremost on his camel, commanded some sand to be given him at every mile's end, by the smell whereof he declared the situation of the place." Caravans crossing in the heat of summer would often travel by night to avoid the worst of the sun's effects, as they lurched from oasis to oasis. The trip between Sijilmasa and Walata took Ibn Battuta's party two months. From there, he went on to some of the main cities of the kingdom of Mali, including Timbuktu and Gao. None except the latter seemed to have impressed him much, but he was hampered by a prejudice against Negroes, whom he had known before only as slaves.

The fame of the gold-rich kingdoms attracted the interest of many. Written accounts, like those of Leo Africanus and Ibn Battuta, were supplemented by maps drawn by Jewish cartographers in the late 14th century, based on information from Jewish merchants traveling on the Saharan caravan routes. These maps, rudimentary though they were, showed the cities of Timbuktu, Gao, and Mali, among others, and included annotations such as: "Through this place pass the merchants who travel to the land of the negroes of Guinea, which place they call the valley of the Dra'a," referring to one of the main passes through the Atlas Mountains.

Some European merchants did try to explore inland for the source of the gold; a Genoese merchant in the mid-15th century reached as far as Tuat, the region of the central Sahara crossroads of In Salah; but he sent back the discouraging report that he had talked to a sheik with much experience of the Sudan, who had said: "I spent fourteen years in the Negro country and never heard of, or saw, a man who could say of certain knowledge 'This is what I saw, this is how they find and collect the gold.' Also it is to be presumed that it comes from afar, and, in my opinion, from a very circumscribed area." A Florentine named Benedeto Dei apparently managed to penetrate to Timbuktu in 1470, but had to say only: "I have been to Timbuktu, a place situated beyond Barbary in very arid country. Much business is done therein selling coarse cloth, serge, and fabrics like those made in Lombardy." The land routes were held tightly by the Barbary merchants, who wanted no competitors for the gold of Sudan.

A surprising number of Christian Europeans had lived in North Africa for some centuries; ever since the days when knighthood was in flower, thousands of Christian knights—from as far away as Italy, France, Germany, and even England—had served as the Sultan's personal elite corps. These mercenaries—collectively known as Franks or *Frendji*—do not seem to have penetrated into

The camel-driver was always an important figure in the Sahara, for he ran the caravans that linked the Maghreb with distant Sudan. (Garrigues, Tunis, from Norma Lorimer, By the Waters of Carthage, *1906)*

the interior regions. But in the 15th century, religious differences between Moslems and Christians were sharpening; both took to persecuting heretics within their own ranks. The remaining Christians in North Africa were submerged by the Moslem tide. Jews, meanwhile, suffered at the hands of both, and many were massacred in the northern Sahara oases some had called home for a millennium or more. In this situation, land routes were effectively closed to Christians.

But sea routes were open. While the Moors were gradually being pushed out of Spain, the Portuguese began looking for a route to the East—and, not incidentally, for a back door to the goldfields of West Africa. As they worked their way around the bulge of Africa, these early expeditions concentrated on slave-trading; they sent some envoys inland, however, vainly searching for the gold country called Wangara. These had little success, and their slave-hunting activities made them unwelcome in the coastal regions. They also encountered the diseases, insects, and serpents that all threatened death to Europeans. As a result, they set up no real trade routes into the interior. The Europeans' desire for gold and slaves pumped an increasing amount of European goods into the region, however, so the Sahara trade flourished as much as before, if not more.

In the Sudan itself, change was also taking place. The kingdom of Mali was in decline, threatened by the Taureg nomads from the Sahara and the rising kingdom of Songhai on the middle Niger to the east, which had regained its capital of Gao. In 1468 the Songhai army seized Timbuktu and killed many of its citizens; a few years later they took Djenne, which became increasingly important in the European trade. The Mandingos of Mali even asked the newly arrived Portuguese for assistance against the Songhai, but in vain. Walata, too, was added to the Songhai Empire, which eventually extended to the west coast around the Gambia River; north to include the salt mines of Taghaza; northeast to take in the Air Mountains, and the nearby market town of Agades; and down the Niger and southeast to encompass the Hausa peoples. Timbuktu continued as a major market town and cultural center, home of scholars from the Maghreb. Songhai rulers eagerly adopted the Mali mantle; echoing Mansa Musa's journey, the Songhai ruler who called himself Askia the Great took a pilgrimage to Mecca with 500 cavalry, 1,000 infantry, and 300,000 pieces of gold. Under the Songhai the main route across the Sahara continued to be that between Timbuktu and Sijilmasa; the Tauregs—driven out into the desert by the Songhai—continually fought to regain their lands in Agades and the Air Mountains, attacking passing caravans.

The Europeans were not the only ones eyeing West African gold. The Moors had long desired to reach the gold sources directly, bypassing Sudanese middlemen, but had not wished to disturb the fragile network of trade that stretched across the Sahara; indeed, it was widely believed that the Sudan could not be invaded from across the desert. But in the second half of the 16th century, the Moroccan ruler, al-Mansur, emboldened by newly acquired firearms, decided to risk the attempt. He first focused on the salt mines of Taghaza, key to the gold trade; when the Songhai refused to cede Taghaza to him, he marched out to take it—and found only an empty shell. Forewarned, the local nomads and their Negro slaves had decamped, and were forbidden by the Songhai to return; without them, the mines could not be worked, so al-Mansur had gained nothing. In fact, this move spelled death to the Taghaza mines. Taureg nomads, who had been attacked by the Moors, told the Songhai of another large salt deposit about 100 miles to the south, at Taodeni; the Songhai developed these mines, which were closer to the surface and therefore easier to work, with the result that the Taodeni mines are still being worked today, while the Taghaza mines were never reopened.

After this worthless victory, al-Mansur resolved to attack the Sudan itself, overcoming the universal opposition of his advisers and merchants with this argument, recorded by chronicler al-Ifrani:

You talk of the dangerous desert we have to cross, of the fatal solitudes, barren of water and pasture, but you forget the defenseless and ill-equipped merchants who, mounted or on foot, regularly cross these wastes which caravans have never ceased to traverse. I, who am so much better equipped than they, can surely do the same with an army which inspires terror wherever it goes...Our predecessors would have found great difficulty if they had tried to do what I now propose, for their armies were composed only of horsemen armed with spears and of bowmen; gunpowder was unknown to them, and so were firearms and their terrifying effect. Today the

By the mid-19th century, Kano had long since replaced Timbuktu as the main trading center on the Sahara caravan routes. (New York Public Library)

Sudanese have only spears and swords, weapons which will be useless against modern arms. It will therefore be easy for us to wage a successful war against these people and prevail over them.

Winning over his counselors, al-Mansur began to prepare. This was no easy matter, for the wells that barely provided enough water for relatively small caravans across the Sahara would be totally inadequate to supply sustenance for many thousands. Most food and water for the 1,500-mile journey would have to be carried on pack animals, which in the end included 8,000 camels (along with 1,000 drivers) and 1,000 pack horses. The soldiers themselves were drawn from far afield, Morocco not being a heavily populated area. Of the 4,000-man force assembled, 1,500 were a light cavalry composed of Moors; but the balance—2,000 infantry and 500 cavalry, all armed with arquebuses—were either Spanish Moors exiled from their former home or European Christians, who were renegades or prisoners from the various religious wars. The leader of the expedition was himself Andalusian, a blue-eyed eunuch named Judar, born in Granada and raised in Marrakech. Accompanying all these were 600 sappers, who specialized in constructing—and demolishing—military fortifications. The store of supplies gathered was enormous, ranging from 31,000 pounds of gunpowder to 3,000 yards of English cloth "for lining the tents of the arquebusiers of the victorious army."

Leaving at the most favorable time, mid-October, the army wisely followed the ancient route along the foothills of the Atlas southeast for as long as they could, to be nearest fertile land and water; in the valley of the Dra'a they assembled the pack animals, food, and water needed for the journey. Then, their route forced by the location of oases, they headed east into the desert to pick up the main caravan route through Taghaza. We have no account of their march, but Leo Africanus, who traveled the route earlier in the century, describes what this army faced:

In the way which leadeth from Fez to Timbuktu are certain pits environed with the hides or bones of camels. Neither do the merchants in summer pass that way without great danger of their lives: for oftentimes it falleth out, when the south wind bloweth, that all these pits are stopped up with sand. And so the merchants, when they can find neither those pits, nor any mention thereof, must needs perish with extreme thirst: whose carcases are afterwards found lying scattered here and there, and scorched with the heat of the sun. One remedy they have in this case, which is very strange: for when they are so grievously oppressed with thirst, they kill forthwith some one of their camels, out of whose bowels they wring and express some quantity of water, which water they drink and carry with them, till they have either found some pit of water, or till they pine away for thirst.

Others talked of—in the desperation of thirst—drinking urine caught from the camels. But still many died. The toll for al-Mansur's army was apparently heavy, for only 1,000 men are thought to have taken the field in the first battle with the Songhai, although some others may have been too weak to fight then, but later recovered. Even so, they had had a narrow escape. The Songhai, warned that the Moorish army was coming, had sent out messengers to order all wells stopped with sand—the old desert trick—but by chance the messengers had been taken by Taureg marauders.

Al-Mansur was right in his assessment of the efficacy of gunpowder against the Sudanese. Although outnumbered by over twenty to one, the Moors easily overcame the Songhai army. But this victory, too, was hollow. Both Gao and Timbuktu were very far from the magnificent cities they had expected—the mud-and-thatch buildings surely looked squalid to eyes accustomed to the magnificence of Moorish architecture. Nor was there much gold to be found for the source of the precious metal remained secret, and the Sudanese had buried most of their personal gold in caches outside the main cities. Beyond that, there was the difficulty of controlling the country once it had been won. War continued in the region for some years, with the Songhai assembling armies of allies from the surrounding regions, and the Moors being bolstered by reinforcements from across the Sahara; the Moors were ordained to win, but the network of alliances and trading arrangements that had been developed over the centuries was badly damaged. Nor, in the end, did the Moors get much for their investment. In mid-1599 Judar returned to Morocco with 30 camel-loads of unrefined gold (which an English merchant then living in Marrakech valued at £604,800), plus loads of other goods and many slaves. Tribute continued to be sent for some years to Morocco, but with the death of al-Mansur and the subsequent civil war, the remains of the Moorish army were left on their own in the Sudan. The Mandingo and other subject tribes revolted, but the Moors, merging with the local population, established a mulatto aristocracy called the Arma, which ruled in the region for two centuries, until it was absorbed into the general population. Trade resumed as before, and Morocco and the Sudan retained some tenuous ties. Moroccan rulers in the 17th century even came to rely on Negro troops, many of them descendants of the slaves brought back to Marrakech by Judar, and even as late as 1958, King Muhammed V of Morocco averred that his country stretched across the Sahara to include Timbuktu.

These were the centuries when northern Europe's star was rising, and southern Europe's falling. Portugal, which had long controlled the foreign trade of West Africa, was gradually replaced by Britain, from the time that Queen Elizabeth I made a mutually beneficial deal to sell arms to the Moroccans in return for saltpeter. The more energetic northern Europeans also moved in on the many slaving ports of the Portuguese—first the Dutch and Danish, then the British and French. Gradually they diverted trade from the Sahara, as they began to supply salt from Europe. In the north the Ottoman Turks extended their empire westward as far as Algiers. Gradually the focus of the Sahara began to shift eastward again, for the first time since the arrival of the Moslems in the seventh century.

The ancient Timbuktu-to-Fez route, the fabled gold trail which had been the best-known and most-used Sahara route over the centuries, began to lose its dominance and its route as well. Sijilmasa, long the northern terminus where caravans were fitted out and equipped, went into decay, and was finally destroyed in the late 1700's. No one city replaced her, and traffic from the northern end of the Taghaza route dispersed in several different directions. The ancient caravan center of Walata also was bypassed, with traffic from Taodeni heading almost due south through Arawan to Timbuktu. Two routes from the northeast—one from Tunis via Wargla, the other from Tripoli via Ghadames—met at In Salah and crossed the Sahara to Arawan as well.

The image of Timbuktu still enthralled foreigners and, in this age of exploration, northern Europeans headed for the fabled city. Prizes were even offered to the first modern European traveler who could visit Timbuktu and return to tell the tale. More than one died trying. In the early 1800's, a British explorer, Alexander Gordon Laing, succeeded in reaching Timbuktu, but on his return trip was murdered, and all his journals burnt. A few years later, a young Frenchman, René Caillié, succeeded in making the round trip, though his face was horribly disfigured from scurvy and he suffered from a spine injury received when thrown from a camel. But Timbuktu was already in its decline, and although Caillié was properly fêted on his return to Europe, his comments on seeing Timbuktu reflect the difference between image and reality:

> I had formed a totally different idea of the grandeur and wealth of Timbuktu. The city presented, at first view, nothing but a mass of ill-looking houses, built of earth.

Trade had been its only life-blood, as Caillié demonstrates:

> From the tower I had an extensive view of an immense plain of white sand, on which nothing grows except a few stunted shrubs, and where the uniformity of the picture is only broken here and there by some scattered hills or banks of sand. I could not help contemplating with astonishment the extraordinary city before me, created solely by the wants of commerce and destitute of every resource except what its accidental position as a place of exchange affords.

To the east, two other routes became increasingly important in these centuries. One extended down from Tunis (ancient Carthage) or Tripoli through Ghadames and Ghat, past the Ahaggar Mountains to Agades and then on to Katsina or to Kano, a city that came to have some importance as the main metropolis of the Hausa people. This route was perhaps as old as the Taghaza route; Sahara historian E. L. Bovill commented: "Where it passes over rocky ground the deeply worn tracks prove its antiquity and the great weight of traffic it carried. Its route seems never to have varied." The track apparently always skirted Agades, whose terrain was unsuitable for heavily laden camels; in addition to being the main southern entrepôt in the region, before the rise of the Hausa in the 17th century, Agades was most important as a camel-grazing ground. Here, every autumn, many thousands of camels were assembled for the annual trip eastward to Bilma for salt; as late as 1908, a caravan of 20,000 camels was gathered for this purpose. In modern times, Kano became a great trading city—far outdistancing Timbuktu—with a resident colony of 30,000 Arabs from Tripoli in the 19th century. Unlike Timbuktu, which survived on trade alone, neither spinning nor sowing, Kano included not only farmers but also fine weavers and dyers. The 19th century explorer Henry Barth noted:

> The great advantage of Kano is that commerce and manufactures go hand in hand, and that almost every family has its share in them. There is really something grand in this kind of industry, which spreads to the north as far as Murzuk, Ghat, and even Tripoli; to the west, not only to Timbuktu, but in some degree even as far as the shores of the Atlantic, the very inhabitants of Arguin dressing in the cloth woven and dyed in Kano...

In return, the people of Kano received goods as diverse as silk from France and glass beads from Venice.

The other main north-south route ran from Tripoli through Fezzan's capital of Murzuk south through Bilma to the land of the Bornu around Lake Chad. While this is, in many ways, the easiest of the trans-Sahara routes, it has—for whatever reason—not had long and continuous use. Certainly it was always subject to raids, especially from the Tebu of the Tibesti Massif and the Taureg of Air. It was in use by the ninth century, at least, but became a major route only with the rise of the Bornu in the 17th century. The increasing demand for slaves also led to this route's prominence, for it was—more than anything else—a slave route. As horrified European explorers recounted in gruesome detail, the route was lined with human skeletons, mostly of young women and girls, often clustered near wells which they had died trying to reach. While slaves from the West African ports often were headed for the Americas, these slaves—many of them highly prized Hausa, carried off by the Bornu in bloody raids—were

The eastern Sudan was a prime center for the slave trade, until the British ended it. (From The Pictorial Edition of the Life and Discoveries of David Livingston, *by J. E. Ritchie)*

destined for the Moslem world, primarily Turkey, Egypt, or the Barbary States. Many of the young men were castrated—in a crude operation only one in ten is estimated to have survived—for service in the harems of the sultans, who often employed hundreds of such eunuchs. In the early 19th century, the British and later other European countries outlawed slavery, ending a great injustice in western Africa—and, incidentally, ending all but the most modest trade on the Fez-to-Timbuktu route. But slave-trading continued for longer in the central Sahara; on one route between Wadai in the south and Benghazi in the north, the slave caravans were still being marched across the Sahara in 1911, until the Italians arrived in Cyrenaica and ended the open trade, though some illicit slave-trading apparently continued even beyond that.

In the late 19th century's scramble for Africa, France took most of West Africa, and its presence brought about substantial changes in the Sahara. The nomads of the desert—increasingly poor as the trans-Sahara trade declined and there were fewer caravans, whose booty might enrich their minimal existence—were gradually brought under governmental control. Indeed, former desert marauders made up the backbone of the Sahara Camel Corps, founded in 1902 to pacify the desert peoples, especially the Tauregs of the Ahaggar. The French Foreign Legion also served the same purposes, continuing the long tradition of European mercenaries fighting in the lands of the Sahara.

But more than anything else, it was the automobile that transformed the Sahara in modern times. With speed,

humans were no longer dependent on the well-lined routes of old; cars allowed them to make their own, often shorter routes, and to carry water as needed. Not only that, but the flat, waterless gravel plains so deadly to caravans on foot provided a perfect base for modern automobiles. As a result, under French influence, new routes were carved across the Sahara. The main French base being (until 1962) in Algeria, the main modern roads to "Les Territoires du Sud" run in the desolate region between the old main routes. From the city of Algiers, one runs south to In Salah—receiving tributary routes from Tunis, Constantine, and Wargla to the east—and then south and slightly east to Agades and finally Kano. The other route, a bit to the west, runs south from the port of Oran, being joined by routes from Morocco, across the otherwise uncrossable central Sahara to Gao on the Niger. These have been, in modern times, the main highways to the south; that statement should, however, be qualified, for as geographer Benjamin E. Thomas points out: "A traffic flow of only one vehicle per day over a road in northern Algeria would indicate an insignificant rural route, but in the southern Sahara it would indicate a surprisingly well-traveled 'main-highway'." Automobiles have changed the region in other ways, as well. The need for fuel spurred a search for oil, which was successful in many areas of the north Sahara, including Libya. As a result of modern intervention, many of the now-impoverished nomads left their desert homes for the roustabout's life in the oil settlements—and the oases they once tended are increasingly being swallowed up by the growing Sahara Desert.

Selective Bibliography

Ibn Battuta, *Travels A.D.1325–1354* (3 vols). Hakluyt Society Publications, 2nd Series. Translated by H. A. R. Gibb (Cambridge: At the University Press 1958–71). An extraordinary memoir of travels in the 14th century Islamic world.

Bovill, E. W. *The Golden Trade of the Moors,* 2nd edition (London: Oxford University Press, 1968). The standard history; an updating of the earlier *Caravans of the Old Sahara.*

Brown, Slater. *World of the Desert* (Indianapolis: Bobbs-Merrill, 1963). A generalized discussion.

Gautier, E. F. *Sahara: The Great Desert.* Translated from the 2nd French edition by Dorothy Ford Mayhew (New York: Octagon, 1970; reprint of 1935 Columbia University Press edition). A classic account of the desert and its life.

July, Robert W. *A History of the African People,* 2nd edition (New York: Scribner's, 1974). A very useful general history.

Ross, Michael. *Cross the Great Desert* (London: Gordon & Cremonesi, 1977). A retelling of the experiences of explorer René Caillié.

Thomas, Benjamin E. *Trade Routes of Algeria and the Sahara*; University of California Publications in Geography, Volume 8, No. 3, pp. 165–288 (Berkeley: University of California Press, 1957). A useful review, with emphasis on the modern period.

Wellard, James. *The Great Sahara* (New York: Dutton, 1965). A personalized history, stressing modern exploration.

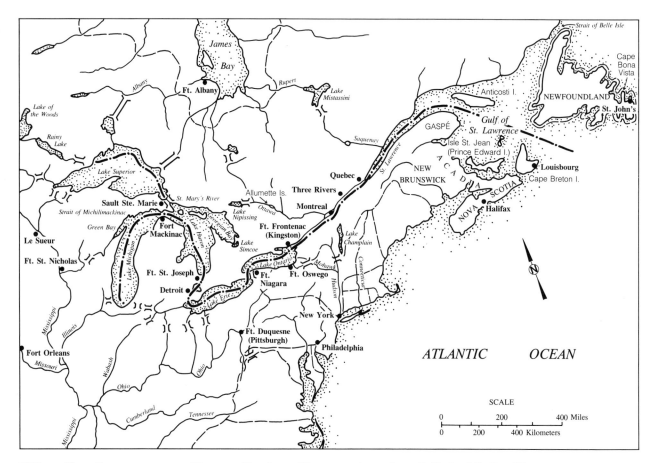

The St. Lawrence-Great Lakes Route in the Mid-18th Century

—·—·— Main St. Lawrence-Great Lakes ————— Boundaries of English
Route   Settlements

⊃⊂ Main Portages

The St. Lawrence-Great Lakes Route

The Sieur de Champlain undertakes to discover the South Sea passage to China, to the East Indies, by way of the river St. Lawrence...which issues from a lake about 300 leagues in length, from which lake flows a river that empties into the said South Sea.

So wrote Samuel de Champlain to his king, Henry IV of France, in 1618. The belief that the mighty St. Lawrence River and its associated inland seas formed a gateway to the East would lure Europeans for centuries. Champlain, John Cabot, Jacques Cartier, Henry Hudson, and the other great early northern explorers sought the Northwest Passage to Cathay and the riches to be obtained therefrom; instead, they found, explored, and laid the basis for the European conquest of North America—and with it riches incalculably greater than those that might have been obtained in the Far East.

First the Vikings had come, the great seafarers of northern Europe from the ninth to the twelfth centuries after Christ, stepping island by island across the North Atlantic, until finally they crossed what is now called Denmark Strait, from Iceland to Greenland. Then, hundreds of years later, the earlier Greenland settlements abandoned or at least unknown to them, came the European seafarers of the great age of exploration and conquest—the Spanish and Portuguese to the south, the French, English, and Dutch to the north—all seeking the passage to the Indies, to Cathay, to the Spice Islands.

The Bristol merchants who in 1497 financed John Cabot (born in Venice as Giovanni Caboto) thought it quite likely that they were funding a passage to Cathay 2,000 leagues (6,000 miles) shorter than the Cape of Good Hope Route around Africa, with great riches flowing from the Orient directly back to England. Henry VII of England granted Cabot a royal commission to:

...saile to all parts, countries and seas of the East, of the West and of the North...to seeke out, discover and finde whatsoever isles, countries, regions or proviinces of the heathen and infidels, in what part of the world so ever they be, which before this time have been unknowne to all Christians.

So, too, with Jacques Cartier, sailing out of St.-Malo, Brittany, in the spring of 1534. The first European of this period to explore the Gulf of St. Lawrence and enter the river itself, he—like the others—sought a passage to the East. His first royal commission was to:

...make the voyage from this kingdom to the new lands, to discover certain isles and countries where there is said to be found a vast quantity of gold and other rich things.

His second royal commission, issued a year later, while he was still exploring the Gulf of St. Lawrence, enjoined him "to discover beyond the new lands," and "to discover certain far-away countries."

What Cartier found and began to explore is the great water route into the heart of North America. It is entered from the northeast by ships using the shortest and still the best way across the Atlantic from northern Europe; cuts through the rugged north-south mountain ranges that otherwise block access to the main body of the continent; opens out into the five linked inland seas that are the Great Lakes; and provides easy entry into the huge Mississippi-Missouri river system. The French, using it first, were able to reach, explore, and claim the whole center of the continent while the English were still penned into the narrow space between the Atlantic and the Appalachian Mountains.

There was one other water level cut through the mountains—up the Hudson and west through the Mohawk Valley—but that way was barred by British treaties with the greatest Native American power in eastern North America, the Iroquois. Only after the British-Iroquois defeat in the American Revolution did large numbers of Europeans pour west on the Mohawk Trail.

For well over 200 years, the main routes west were the French routes up the St. Lawrence past Quebec City and Montreal and west, either on the St. Lawrence into the Great Lakes or on the main Trans-Canada canoe route north of the lakes. The Trans-Canada Route led either into the Mississippi-Missouri system or further west through Lake Winnipeg and out beyond the Rockies to the Pacific, as well as north to Hudson Bay and the Arctic. The southern route from the St. Lawrence led out through the Great Lakes to an easy linkup with the Mississippi Route.

The route itself is clear; its very early history is not, at least not yet. Some speculation indicates that Phoenician (Carthaginian) and Greek sailors exploring the northern coast of Europe visited Iceland and perhaps went beyond as early as 330 B.C. Some speculation, joined by suggestive evidence, indicates that Celtic sailors were visiting Iceland as early as 300 A.D. There is considerable evidence that Celtic settlements existed in Iceland by 750–800 A.D. and were there when the Vikings arrived about 100 years later.

What is very clear is that a substantial Scandinavian emigration to Iceland began in the period 850–875 A.D. and that Iceland has been continually occupied by Scandinavians since then. A little over 100 years later, about 980–990 A.D., a substantial Icelandic emigration to Greenland began, probably led by the Icelandic navigator and explorer Eric the Red. There were Icelandic settlements, with populations numbering in the thousands, until at least the end of the 14th century, 300 years later. After that, most settlements were abandoned; explorers like Cabot saw only their ruins, although some settlements

Not until the 19th century did canals like this one around the Long Sault Rapids begin to tame the St. Lawrence (Public Archives of Canada)

may have survived into the mid-16th century.

What is not at all clear—and is the source of enormous and continuing controversy—is whether or not the Norse settlers of Greenland went further during those centuries, exploring the coast of North America and entering the interior of the continent. There were two ways they might have done so: into the Gulf of St. Lawrence and up the river itself, or into Hudson Bay, which pushes deep into the continent north of what is now Minnesota. There was little to prevent either course of exploration; the climate was much the same as it is in the modern era, and there was ample time to go either way, starting from Greenland, even in the short northern summers. The urge to speculate in this direction is well-nigh irresistible; it is very hard to believe that the great Norse seafarers stopped at Greenland, with all of North America and both main water routes open before them. Beyond logic, there are artifacts and the remains of structures in eastern North America, thought by many to be Norse. But the Norse of that period had no such motive as the quest for the Northwest Passage; nor did they have the military technology of the later European explorers and conquerors. The question of which Europeans first penetrated the North American heartland awaits further evidence and insight.

Whether or not the Norse came first, it was the French who in the 16th century entered the Gulf of St. Lawrence and proceeded to open up the main body of the continent from the northeast. Jacques Cartier in 1534 sighted Cape Bonavista, on the southeastern shore of Newfoundland, sailed north along the shore, and penetrated the Gulf of St. Lawrence through the Strait of Belle Isle, between Newfoundland and the Quebec mainland. That summer, he sailed along the northern shore of the gulf and partway around Anticosti Island; landed on the Gaspé Peninsula, on the coast of New Brunswick, and on Isle St. Jean (Prince Edward Island); and then sailed back along the Newfoundland coast, through the same strait, and back to France.

The next year, guided by two Native American captives he had taken on the first voyage, he came back through the Strait of Belle Isle, but this time sailed past Anticosti and into the St. Lawrence past the Saguenay River and up the river to the Native American village of Stadacona, later to be Quebec City, and on to Hochelaga, later to be Montreal. At Hochelaga-Montreal, he climbed Mount Royal (to the French, Mont Réal), saw the Lachine Rapids, and understood for the first time that he would be unable to sail through on the St. Lawrence to Cathay and the Indies. Instead, the French portion of the invasion of North America had begun.

For the French, the St. Lawrence was more than a gateway to the continent; it became the main center of French population and power in North America. It was itself also a local road—for well over 100 years the only real road available to the traders and colonists who began to come from France in small numbers after Cartier's voyages of discovery. In the mid-1660's, 130 years after Cartier's voyages, the few thousand French settlers were mostly sprinkled along the St. Lawrence River, especially in and near Quebec, occupying long riverfront farms, with the river as the only available route for travel. A massive colonization effort was started in 1663, with the land being cleared and settled along the river all the way from Quebec to Montreal; only then did settlement and road-building begin in areas a little back from the river.

In the meantime, the exploration of the St. Lawrence and the Great Lakes continued with Champlain, Louis, Comte de Frontenac, Etienne Brûlé, and others pushing west in pursuit of furs and trade, as well as in continuing pursuit of the Northwest Passage. To a considerable extent, the history of the French penetration of the continent is also the history of the fur trade, for the French, the British, and then the Americans trapped and traded for beaver and other furs for three centuries in North America, following the disappearing beaver all the way from the St. Lawrence over the mountains and to the Pacific.

That exploration was greatly advanced by French adoption of the light, very durable birchbark canoe, which Canada's Native Americans had used to great advantage to travel the shallow, swift rivers west. A canoe 20–25 feet long was light enough for two men to carry overland on portages: yet it could carry a substantial number of travelers and much cargo and be entirely maneuverable on a stream that would be impossible for a heavier craft.

In 1670, Father René Galinée described these canoes and what they meant to the early French voyageurs and explorers:

Navigation above Montreal is quite different from that below. The latter is made in ships, barks, launches, and boats, because the River St. Lawrence is very deep, as far up as Montreal, a distance of 200 leagues; but immediately above Montreal one is confronted with a rapid or waterfall amidst numerous large rocks, that will not allow a boat to go through, so that canoes only can be used. These are little birchbark canoes, about twenty feet long and two feet wide, strengthened inside with cedar floors and gunwales, very thin, so that one man carries it with ease, although the boat is capable of carrying four men and eight or nine hundred pounds' weight of baggage. There are some made that carry as many as ten or twelve men with their outfit, but it requires two or three men to carry them. This style of canoe affords the most convenient and the commonest mode of navigation in this country, although it is a true saying that when a person is in one of these vessels he is always, not a finger's breadth, but the thickness of five or six sheets of paper, from death... It is only the Algonkin-speaking tribes that build these canoes well...

Before canals were built at Sault Ste. Marie, Michigan, goods and even whole boats were carried over the neck of land, in the 1850's on a horsepowered railroad. (Great Lakes Historical Society)

The convenience of these canoes is great in these streams, full of cataracts and waterfalls, and rapids through which it is impossible to take any boat. When you reach them you load canoe and baggage upon your shoulders and go overland until the navigation is good; and then you put your canoe back in the water, and embark again.

In the spring of 1613, three-quarters of a century after Cartier had explored the St. Lawrence as far as Montreal, Samuel de Champlain began the historic series of explorations that were to open up the North American heartland. Bypassing Lakes Ontario and Erie—as well as the homelands of the powerful and hostile Iroquois nation—he followed the most direct water route west, taking the Ottawa River past the Long Sault Rapids and the site of modern Ottawa, and went as far as Allumette Island, about 70 miles further on into what is now Ontario. Two years later, in 1615, he went much further, up the Ottawa all the way to Lake Nipissing, and then on French River into Georgian Bay and Lake Huron. On this trip, traveling with a Huron war party, he went south by way of Lake Simcoe to Lake Ontario, participating in an attack on an Onondaga village south of Ontario, at Lake Oneida. He did not complete the circuit back to Montreal by way of Ontario and the St. Lawrence, however; instead he returned north with the defeated Hurons, going back to Quebec the way he had come.

Etienne Brûlé traveled with Champlain as far as Lake Simcoe in 1615. There they parted, with Brûlé traveling south. The evidence is scanty, but he is thought to have then traveled to the western end of Lake Ontario and perhaps from there via the Niagara River to and along the south shore of Lake Erie. In the next five years, he is thought to have explored Georgian Bay, the north shore of Lake Huron, and on up the St. Mary's River to Lake Superior. If so, he was the first of the French explorers to reach Erie and Superior. Jean Nicolet, who had also traveled with Champlain, in 1634 went all the way to the western end of Lake Huron, and to the Strait of Michilimackinac, then on along the north shore of Lake Michigan to Green Bay.

After Cartier, the most notable explorer of the St. Lawrence and the Great Lakes was Robert La Salle. In 1668, he traveled up the St. Lawrence and on to the far western end of Lake Ontario. Eleven years later, in 1679, he made an extraordinary voyage, up the St. Lawrence, traversing four of the five Great Lakes from end to end, missing only Lake Superior. Ultimately he linked up with the Mississippi, following it all the way out to the Gulf of Mexico, and in the process opening up the continent as no European had done before.

Starting west from Fort Frontenac (now Kingston), on the north shore of Lake Ontario, he went past the mouth of the Niagara River, where he built a fort, and past Niagara Falls to the vicinity of what is now Buffalo,

New York. Other Europeans had, by then, seen Niagara Falls, but Father Louis Hennepin, who accompanied La Salle, gives us a vivid description of the striking cascade:

> Betwixt the Lakes of Ontario and Erie, there is a vast and prodigious Cadence of Water which falls down after a surprising and astonishing manner, insomuch that the Universe does not afford its Parallel. 'Tis true, Italy and Suedeland boast of some such Things; but we may well say they are but sorry Patterns, when compar'd to this of which we now speak. At the foot of this horrible Precipice, we meet with the River Niagara, which is not above half a quarter of a League broad, but is wonderfully deep in some places. It is so rapid above this Descent, that it violently hurries down the wild Beasts while endeavouring to pass it to feed on the other side, they not being able to withstand the force of its Current, which inevitably casts them down headlong above Six hundred foot.
>
> This wonderful Downfall is compounded of two great Cross-streams of Water, and two Falls, with an Isle sloping along the middle of it. The Waters which fall from this vast height, do foam and boil after the most hideous manner imaginable, making on outrageous Noise, more terrible than that of Thunder; for when the Wind blows from off the South, their roaring may be heard above fifteen Leagues off.

At Buffalo, La Salle built a ship of about 30 tons, the *Griffin*, the first vessel other than a canoe to sail the Great Lakes – unless the Norse had done so half a millennium earlier. With 34 men aboard, the *Griffin* proceeded up the Niagara and sailed the length of Lake Erie to the Detroit River, passing up the river into Lake St. Clair and into the St. Clair River, which lead into Lake Huron. La Salle's party sailed north the full length of Lake Huron to Father Marquette's mission at Michilimackinac, and from there across Lake Michigan to Green Bay. At Green Bay, La Salle sent the *Griffin* back with a cargo of furs and headed southward on Lake Michigan by canoe. But the *Griffin* never reached the fort at Niagara; it was lost without a trace and has never been found.

La Salle himself went south to the foot of Lake Michigan, passing what is now Chicago, and then link-

The taking of Quebec, in the Battle of the Plains of Abraham, was a crucial event in the establishment of English domination in Canada. (Public Archives of Canada)

To avoid the rapids on the left, this 15-man birchbark canoe is being put ashore; some goods are already being transported on the portage in the right background. (By W. H. Bartlett, from N. P. Willis, Canadian Scenery, *1842, New York Public Library)*

ing up with the Mississippi system via the St. Joseph River. Marquette and Jolliet had reached the Mississippi six years before, in 1673, taking the canoe route on the Ottawa and over to Sault St. Marie and then across to the Mississippi along the north shore of Lake Michigan. But La Salle set the pattern for the modern St. Lawrence-Great Lakes Route that would be followed, after the opening of the St. Lawrence Seaway, from the heart of North America out to the Atlantic.

The largest of the Great Lakes remained: Lake Superior. It was explored mainly by the French moving west along the Ottawa and Lake Huron canoe trails, probably beginning with Brûlé in about 1620 and coming to completion with Daniel Duluth's exploration of the western end of Superior in 1678–79. This route—the beginning of what would become the Trans-Canada Route—was north of the Iroquois country; here exploration and the establishment of missions and trading posts went together, while south of the lakes the hostile and powerful Iroquois did not welcome the French.

Starting in the early 1640's, Jesuit missionaries began to come into the Lake Superior country. Fathers Isaac Jogues and Charles Raymbault were the earliest, in 1641. Father Jerome Lalemant describes their first trip to Sault St. Marie that year:

They started from our house of St. Marie, about the end of September, and after seventeen days of navigation on the great Lake or fresh-water sea that bathes the land of the Hurons, they reached the Sault, where they found about two thousand Souls, and obtained information about a great many other sedentary Nations, who have never seen Europeans and have never heard of God,—among others, of a certain nation, the Nadouessis [the Sioux], situated to the Northwest or west of the Sault, eighteen days journey farther away. The first nine days are occupied in crossing another great Lake that commences above the Sault [Lake Superior].

By the 1660's, missions had been established on the south shore of the lake. Father Marquette established a mission at Sault St. Marie in 1668; five years later, he and Jolliet were to explore the Mississippi. Pierre Radisson trapped along and explored the northwestern shores of the lake in the early 1660's.

By the end of the 17th century, the main outlines

of what was, by then, becoming the St. Lawrence-Great Lakes Route had emerged. But there were considerable obstacles to the development of this route, most of them political. The unfriendly Iroquois still barred full development of trade along the south shore of the lakes, especially in the east. More to the point, the British and French were engaging in an increasingly bitter struggle for control of North America—which, to a large extent, meant control of the St. Lawrence River and the Great Lakes. It is no accident that the key battles in this war were fought along this route: at Fort Niagara; at Louisbourg, the Nova Scotia fortress that guarded one of the access routes from the North Atlantic into the Gulf of the St. Lawrence; at Quebec, in the famous battle on the Plains of Abraham; and finally at Montreal itself, which surrendered to the British in 1760.

With the French loss in North America, the character of the St. Lawrence-Great Lakes Route changed markedly. The population of the river, from Montreal east, was still largely French—as it is to this day—but the British influence increasingly dominated. Names of many old French towns or forts became Anglicized or were changed altogether; Fort Frontenac, for instance, became Kingston (for a time the British capital). Under the English, the route also lost its predominance as an exploratory avenue; British westward explorers tended to use the Trans-Canada Route westward from Ottawa, rather than the longer, more circuitous passage through the troubled waters of the Great Lakes. This became increasingly true in the decades that followed, as the American nation split off to the south and the Americans and British faced each other across the St. Lawrence and Great Lakes in hostile action during the War of 1812.

Other obstacles to full development of the St. Lawrence-Great Lakes Route were primarily physical. They could not be seriously addressed until westward expansion and new technology brought on the great era of canal-building that started early in the 19th century—and laid the basis for the international cooperation needed to build the St. Lawrence Seaway.

During the 18th century, the lower St. Lawrence, between Montreal and the sea, continued to be the great highway of New France, later English Canada. Then, as now, the St. Lawrence was a wide, easily navigable river, hospitable to ocean-going ships for almost 1,200 miles, from the Strait of Belle Isle to Montreal. But the almost-200-mile passage between Montreal and the eastern end of Lake Ontario was quite another matter and was to be so for all but very small craft until early in the 19th century, and for large ocean-going craft until the middle of the 20th century. There were other bottlenecks, as well, further on into the lakes. The Niagara portage, made necessary by Niagara Falls, was one major obstacle, as it had been for Champlain and all the explorers and traders that followed. The neck of land separating Lakes Huron and

Superior at Sault St. Marie was another.

Despite the political and physical obstacles, the fur trade and the supply of competing French and British forts and armies had led to the development of substantial lake traffic between shore towns during the 18th century. By 1800, there was substantial traffic on all the Great Lakes, and the portage roads past all the main bottlenecks from Montreal onward were heavily used. As early as 1797, a canal and lock were built at Sault St. Marie by Canada's Northwest Company, but it did not survive the War of 1812.

The 19th century saw the true beginning of the era of canal-building so vital to the modern development of the St. Lawrence-Great Lakes Route. Of great significance was the Erie Canal, finished in 1825, between Lake Erie and the Mohawk River. Although not part of the St. Lawrence-Great Lakes system, it brought so much immigration and commerce to Buffalo and Lake Erie that it created powerful new incentives on the American side of the lakes to engage in waterway development projects.

A series of canals completed during the 19th century made it possible for ships of small draft to navigate the difficult stretch from Montreal to Lake Ontario. The first Lachine Canal, bypassing Montreal's Lachine Rapids—the same rapids that had barred Cartier coming in from the sea—was completed in 1825; a series of other Lachine canals during the rest of the century deepened and improved the passage. And in the 1840's, there were similar relatively shallow draft canals built at Cornwall and Williamsburg along the upper St. Lawrence, making the passage from Ontario to Montreal more feasible. In 1832, the 126-mile-long Rideau Canal, from Ottawa to Kingston, on Lake Ontario, was completed. It bypassed the most difficult portions of the St. Lawrence entirely, for ships of small draft. This was more a political than a commercial necessity for Canada; the War of 1812 had shown Canadians how vulnerable their St. Lawrence shipping was to United States attack, and the Rideau Canal bypass was thought far easier to protect in the event of another war.

Further on into the lake system, two major bottlenecks needed elimination so that lake shipping in deep-draft vessels could develop. The first was at the Niagara River. That was bypassed in 1829 by the 26-mile-long Welland Canal, running a few miles west of the Niagara River and connecting Lakes Ontario and Erie. It was rebuilt later, in 1932, to accommodate the much larger modern ships.

There was also the mile-long portage between Lakes Huron and Superior. Here, by the 1840's, an enormous bottleneck had developed. From 1840 to 1855, starting with the schooner *Algonquin*, ships had been hauled over the portage on greased rollers; the need for a canal was quite evident. The first American Sault St. Marie Canal was completed in 1855; the first Canadian Sault St. Marie

Canal was completed in 1895. Together these toll-free pass-ageways form one of the busiest canals in the world.

By the end of the 19th century, it was possible for large ocean-going vessels to move freely up the St. Lawrence as far as Montreal, and for lake vessels to move freely between all the Great Lakes ports. But only with the completion of the St. Lawrence Seaway in 1959 did it become possible for ocean-going ships to sail from the industrial heartland of North America—from places like Duluth, Chicago, and Detroit—all the way to the Atlantic, a distance of 2,300 miles. The St. Lawrence Seaway itself—extending from the eastern end of Lake Ontario out to the Gulf of St. Lawrence—became one of the most heavily traveled inland waterway routes on earth.

And so Cartier's voyage was completed—not to Cathay and the Spice Islands, but to the much richer land at the far end of the inland seas. From beginning to end, the St. Lawrence-Great Lakes Route has been primarily a commercial waterway, in both ambition and fact. If it lacks the glamor of some of the world's more exotic routes, the triumph of modern technology has its own excitement, with tourists from around the world being drawn to see ocean-going ships passing through the massive locks of the St. Lawrence-Great Lakes Seaway.

Selective Bibliography

Barry, James P. *Ships of the Great Lakes* (Berkeley: Howell-North, 1973). A substantial history of Great Lakes shipping, with many good ship photos.

Browne, George Waldo. *The St. Lawrence River* (New York: Putnam's, 1905). A substantial history and turn-of-the-century description of the St. Lawrence, from the Gulf of St. Lawrence to Kingston, Ontario.

Burpee, Lawrence J. *An Historical Atlas of Canada* (Toronto: Nelson, 1927). An excellent historical atlas, with notes relating to maps, historical population statistics, useful chronologies, place-name changes, and bibliography.

————.*The Discovery of Canada* (Toronto: Macmillan, 1944). A brief, simply written, useful history of Canadian exploration, written primarily for young people but worthwhile for adult nonspecialist readers, as well.

Creighton, Donald. *A History of Canada* (Boston: Houghton Mifflin, 1954). A good standard general history of Canada.

Cumming, W. P., et al. *The Exploration of North America* (New York: Putnam's, 1974). A large, heavily illustrated work, containing a good deal of material quoted from early explorers, accompanied by editorial commentary.

Curwood, James Oliver. *The Great Lakes* (New York: Putnam's, 1909). An early, substantial, anecdotal history of the Great Lakes, with many excellent photos.

Glazebrook, G. P. de T. *A History of Transportation in Canada* (New York: Greenwood, 1969; reprint of the 1938 edition). A detailed, comprehensive, useful work covering the entire history of land and water transport in Canada, from French Canadian beginnings through the mid-1930's.

Guillet, Edwin C. *The Story of Canadian Roads* (Toronto: University of Toronto Press, 1966). A comprehensive, well-illustrated history of major Canadian roads.

Hatcher, Harlan. *The Great Lakes* (London: Oxford, 1944). A substantial but concise history of the Great Lakes region.

Hatcher, Harlan, and Erich A. Walter. *A Pictorial History of the Great Lakes* (New York: American Legacy Press, 1963). A large, heavily illustrated book, notable for illustrations rather than for text.

Hills, T. L. *The St. Lawrence Seaway* (New York: Praeger, 1959). A brief, useful history and description of the St. Lawrence Seaway.

Josephy, Alvin M. *The Indian Heritage of America* (New York: Knopf, 1969). An excellent, comprehensive general work on the history and culture of the Native Americans.

Malkus, Alida. *Blue-Water Boundary* (New York: Hastings House, 1960). A comprehensive, concise history of the St. Lawrence and the Great Lakes, mainly focusing on the Great Lakes.

Mansfield, J. B. *History of the Great Lakes,* 2 vols. (Chicago: J. H. Beers, 1899). Volume 1 contains a large, detailed history of the Great Lakes to 1898, plus a 200-page chronology and list of lake vessels. Volume 2 is a biographical dictionary of people prominent on the lakes, especially during the latter portion of the 19th century.

Morison, Samuel Eliot. *The European Discovery of America: The Northern Voyages* (New York: Oxford, 1971). A comprehensive work on early European voyages of exploration in North America.

Mowat, Farley. *Westviking* (Boston: Little, Brown, 1965). An excellent though somewhat speculative work on early Norse exploration in North America.

Munro, William Bennett. *Crusaders of New France*, vol. 4 in the Chronicles of America series (New Haven: Yale University Press, 1918). A good, now standard work on early French exploration in North America.

Parkman, Francis. *France and England in North America*. Edited by Samuel Eliot Morison (London: Faber & Faber, 1954). A substantial selection from Parkman's works, covering the history of early French exploration of the St. Lawrence and Canada through the end of the British-French contest for North America.

————.*La Salle and the Discovery of the Great West* (Boston: Little, Brown, 1897). Parkman's classic work on La Salle, his explorations, and those with whom he was associated.

Wrong, George M. *The Conquest of New France*, vol. 10 in the Chronicles of America series (New Haven: Yale University Press, 1918). A good, now standard work on the British-French struggle for North America.

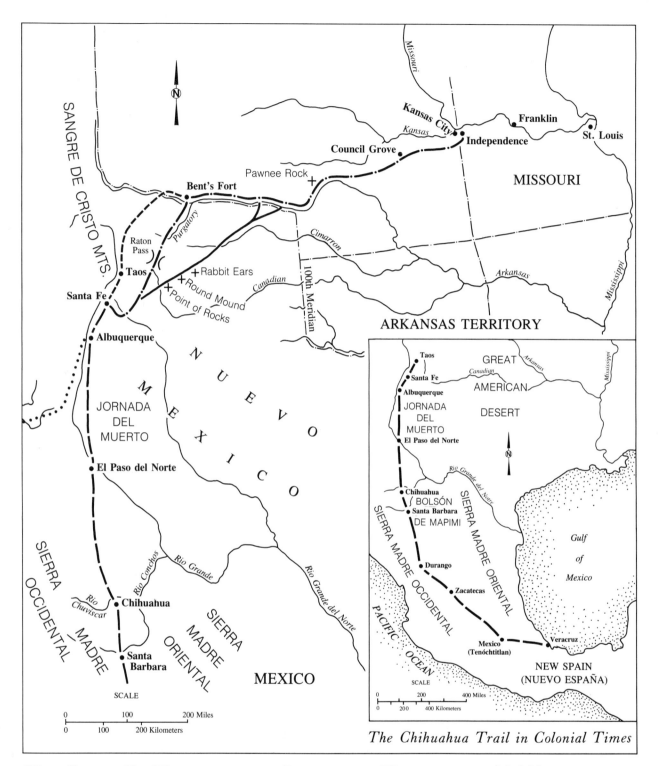

The Chihuahua Trail in Colonial Times

The Santa Fe Trail and the Chihuahua Trail in the 1830's

— · — · — Santa Fe Trail (Raton Pass Route)

- - - - Chihuahua Trail

· · · · · · · Gila Trail

- - - - - - Taos Trail

——— Cimarron Cutoff

— · · — · · — Territorial Boundaries

The Santa Fe Trail and the Chihuahua Trail

*I*n early 19th century Santa Fe, the arrival of a caravan from Missouri was a great event. Josiah Gregg, himself a Santa Fe trader, described the scene in his classic chronicle *Commerce of the Prairies:*

> To judge from the clamorous rejoicings of the men, and the state of agreeable excitement which the muleteers seemed to be laboring under, the spectacle must have been as new to them as it had been to me. It was truly a scene for the artist's pencil to revel in. Even the animals seemed to participate in the humor of their riders, who grew more and more merry and obstreperous as they descended towards the City. I doubt, in short, whether the first sight of the walls of Jerusalem were beheld by the crusaders with much more tumultuous and soul-enrapturing joy.
>
> The arrival produced a great deal of bustle and excitement among the natives. *"Los Americanos!"– "Los carros!"– "La entrada de la caravana!"* were to be heard in every direction; and crowds... flocked around to see the new-comers...

Caravans were not new to Santa Fe–they had been traveling north from Mexico through Chihuahua for over 200 years, on what was known as the Chihuahua Trail. What was new was the Americans, and the affordable goods they brought. Santa Fe had long been a neglected frontier outpost of New Spain (now Mexico), drained of what little value it had and cut off from the world. But to the Americans Santa Fe was an oasis in the "Great American Desert" of the Southwest. The Santa Fe Trail grew and the Chihuahua Trail flourished out of the mutual desire of Nuevo Mexicans and Americans for contact and trade.

Like two halves of an arch, the Santa Fe and Chihuahua trails reached out to each other, bridging the open spaces between the Spanish colonies of the old Southwest and the settlements east of the Mississippi River. The Chihuahua Trail cut north through central Mexico between the western and eastern mountain ranges–the Sierra Madre Occidental and Oriental–crossing a dry, rugged plateau and skirting along the west side of a 500-mile-wide desert, the Bolsón de Mapimi, which pushes up to the Big Bend of the Great River of the North, the Rio Grande del Norte. Meeting the river where it turns due north, the route crossed at the narrow ford named El Paso del Norte. From there it followed the river bank until just past present-day Albuquerque, where it left the river valley and climbed northeast into the foothills of the Sangre de Cristo Mountains, part of the continent-dividing Rocky Mountain chain, toward the site of Santa Fe. The Santa Fe Trail then dipped southeastward around a tongue of mountains and went north again through Raton Pass to the north side of the Arkansas River (an alternate route crossed the Cimarron Desert to the Arkansas) and across the plains to the juncture of the Kansas and Missouri rivers.

These routes passed through some of the longest-

Even expert Mexican muleteers sometimes had difficulty controlling their beasts of burden. (From C. Nebel, Voyage pittoresque et archéologique dans la partie la plus intéressante de Mexique n.d.)

settled country in the Western Hemisphere. Migrants from Asia had come to this area over 10,000 years ago, as they followed the Great North Trail along the eastern slope of the mountainous backbone of the Americas, which includes the Rockies. Some of the highest cultures of the northern continent flourished here, most notably the Pueblo (Village) cultures in New Mexico. From a few centuries after the birth of Christ to the 14th and early 15th centuries, these cultures thrived, before suddenly collapsing for reasons that are unclear, perhaps because of a climatic change. Some of the Pueblo peoples vanished, possibly moving south to the Chihuahua area and contributing to the Aztec culture, as Aztec legend indicates. Other village-dwelling people also moved southward, being pushed by nomadic newcomers from the north. These interlopers called the cliff- and village-dwelling peoples Anasazi (The Old Ones); the Anasazi called these nomadic raiders Apache (The Enemies). Some of the newcomers stayed enemies of the Pueblo peoples, notably the Apache

and the Comanche, who continued their raiding for centuries, but others, such as the Navajos, intermarried with them and adopted a settled life. By the time the European settlers arrived, the southerly line of the Chihuahua Trail was part of Aztec territory, with the arid middle section sparsely populated by various tribes; the area north of El Paso was occupied by Pueblo tribes, with the Apaches and Comanches dominating what would become The Santa Fe Trail. These cultures (none of which possessed the wheel) established foot trails in some areas, especially in the mountains, which formed the basis for later European routes.

The modern history of these routes starts in the south. Less than 30 years after Columbus discovered this New World, the Spanish landed at the site of modern Vera Cruz, moved over 200 miles inland to take the Aztec capital of Tenóchtitlan, later renamed Mexico, and swiftly occupied the arid plateau to the north, which they found to be studded with silver mines. By 1580 the colony of

Nuevo España (New Spain) extended 850 miles north of Mexico City, to the Valle de San Bartolomé, stopping short at the arid Bolsón de Mapimi. In this wild territory, widely dispersed Spanish miners, soldiers, ranchers, and missionaries found travel unwise and unsafe except in large groups with military escort. Despite a web of traces crisscrossing the countryside, most travelers stuck to one north-south road that ran from Mexico City through Durango to the then-northernmost town of Santa Barbara. This was the first and most important of the Mexican roads to be called El Camino Real (the Royal Road).

Tales of gold to be gathered and heathens to be converted led explorers and missionaries to try various routes to the farther north; to be sure of water, they detoured hundreds of miles out of the way, following a network of rivers, and even going so far west that they reached the Rio Grande by way of the Gila River Valley (today part of Arizona). These expeditions created only antagonisms between the Spanish and the Pueblo peoples; no permanent benefits, settlements, or routes resulted. Not until 1598 was the main direct route to the north found, by Don Juan de Oñate, son of a wealthy silver miner. He led not a military or missionary expedition but a full-fledged, royally approved, emigrant caravan of approximately 200 people, half as many wooden-wheeled vehicles, and 7,000 head of livestock. Dressed in the latest European styles, according to their stations, these emigrants heading for unknown country hardly fit the image of the plainly dressed, sparsely furnished pioneer. One aristocrat in the party, for example, carried several suits, including some of satin, Italian velvet, and Chinese silk, all with appropriate trimmings; 14 pairs of French linen breeches; 40 pairs of boots and shoes; and much else ill-suited to his new home.

Traveling beyond the last settlement on El Camino Real, Oñate's caravan followed the edge of the Bolsón de Mapimi and then camped at the last sure water source, the Rio Chuviscar. From there they headed directly north across the arid wasteland, following a trail blazed by an advance party. Although later travelers would have more difficulty, this first caravan was lucky enough to experience a rare cloudburst, which left them with plenty of water; they also wisely dropped some wagons along the way to spare the load-bearing animals. Through the rugged country, they wound past mountain spurs and skirted a large area of shifting sand dunes, called the Médanos, before reaching the Rio Grande just south of El Paso (the Pass).

After over two months on the road, Oñate held an official ceremony in which he took possession of the Rio Grande and the surrounding area as its governor. The emigrant train then proceeded up the west bank of the river through the narrow gorge to cross at El Paso; this rough part of the trail, especially difficult for wagons to negotiate, was completed under the guidance of local

tribesmen, who told them that some ill-fated earlier explorers had crossed there from the northwest some years before. The caravan then followed the east bank of the river to Robledo, named for one of their number who died and was buried there. At this point the river—earning its alternate name, Rio Bravo del Norte (Rapid River of the North)—bends into a channel too narrow for wagons or even pack horses, forcing the route across a 90-mile desert. Recent rain allowed Oñate's party to cross the desert without incident, detouring to springs in nearby mountains for water. But later travelers, who were forced to make the crossing in three night marches to avoid the heat of the day, called the desert the Jornada del Muerto (Day's Journey of the Dead Man) after someone who died trying to cross it in one day. Once across this desert the caravan again followed a tortuous trail along the east bank of the Rio Grande, reprovisioning from local Pueblos along the way. Oñate's journey ended at a site he called Santo Domingo, five months and over 700 miles from the Rio Chuviscar. Oñate's trail became, with only a few minor deviations, Mexico's central Camino Real, the northern part of which was later famous as the Chihuahua Trail.

Once at the end of their journey, the emigrants dispersed, the missionaries to convert the native Americans, the soldiers to explore the surrounding area, and the settlers to work ranches established with some justified trepidation in the river valley, where they were joined by some other emigrant parties in the next few years. Unfortunately for Oñate, he did not find rich mines desired by the Spanish government, nor was he an effective governor; he was recalled from the post within a decade. Indeed, the whole route would have been abandoned had it not been for the Franciscan friars, who pleaded that the crown support their missionary work. They got their wish. A new governor was appointed who, at the turn of the year 1609-10, founded a new capital called Santa Fe (Holy Faith) in a 7,000-foot-high valley in the Sangre de Cristo (Blood of Christ) Mountains, 25 miles northeast of Oñate's original headquarters. Of Santa Fe, Josiah Gregg noted:

> Like most of the towns in this section of country it occupies the site of an ancient Pueblo or Indian village, whose race has been extinct for a great many years. Its situation is...at the western base of a snow-clad mountain, upon a beautiful stream of small mill-power size, which ripples down in icy cascades...

For the next 70 years, the settlers in Santa Fe and along the upper Rio Grande depended on a caravan service from Mexico City to provide goods they could not supply themselves. Although scheduled to make one round trip every three years, allowing six months on the road each way and six months for distributing supplies and loading return goods, the caravan sometimes did not reappear for six or seven years. No wonder that the settlers of Nuevo Mexico were so happy to see the arrival of the iron-wheeled wagons, with royal banners flying. The route north was so hazardous that people traveling to the area for any reason generally waited for the caravan, and over the decades the wagon train evolved into a public conveyance for everything from mail and prisoners to commercial goods. Although specifically forbidden by the king of Spain to do so, government officials routinely used the caravans to haul goods for their private trading; indeed, trade goods sometimes crowded out the intended cargo of mission supplies.

Spanish colonial policies caused difficulty in the area, however. As would be true until Spanish rule ceased, all of New Spain's trade was controlled out of Mexico City, with the only official ports of entry and exit at Vera Cruz and, to a much lesser extent, Acapulco on the west coast. With their monopoly on trade, the Spanish continually drained resources from the outlying provinces, with settlers' products bought cheap and supplies sold dear. Hardship among the Spanish settlers led to even further hardship for the native American populations, whom they had subjugated and virtually enslaved; this, coupled with harsh punishment for converts who reverted to native religions, led to a revolt of the Pueblo peoples in 1680. Four hundred Spaniards were killed and the remaining 2,200 settlers retreated, mostly on foot, 330 miles back across the flood-swollen river at El Paso del Norte, surviving largely on emergency supplies from a special caravan that reached them before they had to cross the Jornada del Muerto. Many of the settlers chose to stay in the area, forming a town on both sides of the river at El Paso. The northern part of the trail remained closed to the Spanish for a dozen years until the native Americans were again subjugated by a new governor, operating from the site later called Albuquerque. In 1693 some of the settlers from El Paso returned north, driving their herds before them to trample down the brush and scrub that had grown over the trail. They were soon joined by new emigrants from central Mexico, who re-established European domination of the area, this time for good.

In the same period, another important settlement was founded. Near the Rio Chuviscar, where Oñate's caravan had camped, a mission called Nombre de Dios (Name of God) was founded in 1697; as Spanish settlers moved northward in the colony of New Spain, many congregated in this strategic area and, after 20 years and several name changes, the site came to be known as Chihuahua. In later decades, Chihuahua would emerge as the focal point of northern New Spain, becoming a chartered city, a rich mining town, a military command headquarters, and a major commercial center.

In the early part of the 18th century, however, control of these functions still rested with Mexico City. With the re-establishment of the province of Nuevo Mexico, north of El Paso, the still-irregular caravan service was resumed. In the absence of a fixed schedule, the caravan's arrival and departure were announced in Santa Fe (once again the capital) several days in advance by a town crier accompanied by drum and bugle. But as the northern population and the commercial importance of the caravan service grew, its schedule became more regular. An authorized trade fair held in the old pueblo of Taos, in the hills 70 miles north of Santa Fe, provided a fixed point of contact between Spanish merchants and the many tribes of the region; the caravan gradually adopted a schedule that brought merchants to Santa Fe in time for the Taos Fair, in July or August. The caravan service—by mid-century no longer even nominally a missionary supply operation but a government one—was also sometimes supplemented by unscheduled special purpose caravans as traffic on the Chihuahua Trail increased.

Travel on the Chihuahua Trail was far from safe, however. Caravans, regular or special, always included military escort, and regular troops were established at *presidios*, or forts, in the main towns along the way, including Chihuahua, El Paso del Norte, Albuquerque, and Santa Fe. For protection against the hostile native population, ranchers often drove their herds along with the regular caravan and some even hired special guards to accompany them on their seasonal herd migrations. All male travelers with the caravans were expected to be armed, and their firearms were inspected before departure.

Nor was Nuevo Mexico a place where a settler was likely to get rich, for the Spanish policy of draining the provinces continued. That made the Nuevo Mexicans particularly interested in the new trade goods that began to reach their region from the east in the early 1700's. In previous centuries, when the Spanish were establishing royal roads in the Southwest, the English and French had only small, tentative colonies in North America. The English settlements were strung out along the east coast of the continent, with westward movement blocked by the Appalachian Mountains, as well as by strong and active native American tribes. The French settlements were concentrated in the far northeast of the continent, but the St. Lawrence brought them by a water route north of the Appalachians to the Great Lakes; from here, and from their other settlements at the mouth of the Mississippi River, they came into the heart of the country. In the early 18th century, it was goods from French traders that arrived in Nuevo Mexico, at first indirectly, the goods having been traded in Louisiana to some Pawnees, who traded them to some Comanches, who brought them to the Taos Fair. When two French traders, Paul and Pierre Mallet, followed in person in 1739, they were at first greeted warmly and their arrival announced by the town crier, especially since their goods were many times cheaper than comparable goods from the south. But when the viceroy in Mexico City forbade commercial relations with the French, these first traders were sent home; later traders were interned, some even being sent as prisoners to Mexico City and held for years.

As long as the Spanish policy remained unchanged, there was no incentive to carve out a route to Santa Fe. But after 1762, when the province of Louisiana was transferred from France to Spain, the governor of Nuevo Mexico authorized a French trader to survey the route from Santa Fe to the Mississippi. Aside from the exploitative Spanish colonial policy, the cost of shipping goods overland 1,600 miles from Mexico City to Santa Fe alone made many items prohibitively expensive. The Rio Grande was navigable only by small boats, and it was often too shallow or even too dry for that, so there was no shortening the overland route to the south, even had the Spanish permitted it. The Nuevo Mexicans saw potential advantage in goods being brought by water to the Mississippi and shipped the shorter distance overland from some point such as St. Louis or Natchitoches. A survey was made in 1792-93, marking out on paper the general route later known as the Santa Fe Trail, but the Spanish authorities refused to allow development of the route. In 1800 Louisiana was returned to France and in 1803 was sold to the United States; American traders,

some of French descent, began to trickle along the trail to Santa Fe, but they met with the same treatment—arrest and internment—that had faced earlier traders. One such venturer duly taken in charge by the Nuevo Mexicans was Zebulon Pike. His captors attempted to keep him from making astronomical and geographical observations while they escorted him to Chihuahua and then on to Texas. But Pike, possibly on a secret mission to explore Santa Fe and the trade possibilities of the Chihuahua Trail, outwitted them. After being warned not to take notes, he "made a pretext to halt—established my boy as a vedette [lookout], and sat down peaceably under a bush and made my notes, &c. This course I pursued ever after, not without some very considerable degree of trouble to separate myself from the party." Pike's notes formed the basis for a widely circulated report that whetted the appetite of American traders.

The picture did not change until 1821, when the Mexicans won their independence from Spain and, on their own for the first time, welcomed trade with a prosperous neighbor who could supply needed goods. Traders from various points in Missouri headed for Santa Fe with their pack trains that year, the first being William Becknell; some, like Becknell, followed native American river and mountain trails they had come to know as Indian

Many fords on the Sante Fe Trail were level and easy, like this one on the Smoky Hill River, northeast of the Arkansas's great bend. (Kansas State Historical Society, Topeka)

traders. These trips were successful enough for certain traders to return the following year; indeed, several trappers and traders crossing the plains toward Missouri in the summer of 1822 were astonished to see wagon tracks on the plains, the first these southwestern prairies had ever known. These were made by wagons belonging to Becknell, who on his return to Missouri had blazed a trail across the Cimarron Desert, an arid basin drained by the Cimarron River, which lay between the Canadian and Arkansas rivers. On the desert crossing, water was the main problem, as Becknell's party found; their scanty canteen supply running out in two days, Josiah Gregg reports:

> ...the sufferings of both men and beasts had driven them almost to distraction. The forlorn band were at last reduced to the cruel necessity of killing their dogs, and cutting off the ears of their mules, in the vain hope of assuaging their burning thirst with the hot blood. This only served to irritate the parched palates, and madden the senses of the sufferers.

In desperation, the party scattered in search of water, "frequently led astray by the deceptive glimmer of the mirage, or false ponds,...those treacherous oases of the desert." They survived only because they found a buffalo "with a stomach distended with water," which had just come from the Cimarron River (nearby, but unknown to them). Gregg continues:

> The hapless intruder was immediately dispatched, and an invigorating draught procured from its stomach. I have since heard one of the parties to that expedition declare, that nothing ever passed his lips which gave him such exquisite delight as his first draught of that filthy beverage.

Despite the difficulties, trade was so brisk that, by 1824, some Missouri traders found Santa Fe short of money for buying wares; having been systematically bled by the Spanish, the inhabitants of that small town had little of value to trade. But to the south lay a much larger city, the center of northern Mexico—and perhaps more importantly—a mining town with its own mint: Chihuahua. Many of the Missouri trade goods soon found their way there, some being brought directly by Missouri traders who extended their journeys down the Chihuahua Trail; other goods arrived in Chihuahua indirectly. In the early days, most Eastern traders—anxious to return home, often to pay home property mortgages that had provided their capital—sold their goods to Nuevo Mexican traders, who in turn sold them in Chihuahua. At prices one-third the inflated cost of goods available through Vera Cruz and Mexico City, these Missouri goods soon won the northern Mexican market. Some Nuevo Mexican traders even began

to buy goods at the source; one caravan returning to Missouri in 1825 brought with it two Mexican traders, the first known to have traveled eastward along the Santa Fe Trail.

The Americans were not slow to recognize opportunity. In the spring of 1825, the U.S. Congress passed a bill, sponsored by Missouri's Senator Thomas Hart Benton, calling for funds to lay out a road between Missouri and Santa Fe and to negotiate safe passage for caravans from the native Americans along the route; the governor of Nuevo Mexico concurred, sending an envoy to Missouri for the same purpose in 1825. In the next year a commission surveyed and marked a 750-mile road from Missouri to Taos. Its activity was largely symbolic, however, for the Western traders preferred to make their own routes. In practice, there was no single Santa Fe Trail. Instead, many tracks crossed the flat, almost featureless plains Josiah Gregg called "the prairie ocean." In the absence of landmarks, and with continual concern for water, many traders tended to follow one of the many east-flowing rivers on their way from Missouri to Santa Fe. But some general routes did emerge.

The eastern part of the Santa Fe Trail began just west of the Mississippi River. Travelers from the northeast often approached along the Ohio River, here changing their mode of travel from canoes and barges along navigable streams to wagons and pack trains along dry prairie; as a result St. Louis had early been established as an outfitting center. As Western travel increased, other outfitting towns and trading posts were established along the eastern portion of the Missouri and Kansas rivers, among them Franklin and Independence and later Westport and Kansas City. In the early days of the Santa Fe trade, large trading caravans generally started out from the area near Independence, Missouri, but small groups would gather about 150 miles farther along the route at Council Grove, until they had formed a large enough group for safe crossing. Of this stand of timber on a small creek, Josiah Gregg, chronicler of the early Missouri trade, warned:

> Lest this imposing title [Council Grove] suggest to the reader a snug and thriving village, it should be observed, that on the day of our departure from Independence, we passed the last human abode upon our route; therefore, from the borders of Missouri to those of New Mexico not even an Indian settlement greeted our eyes.

At Council Grove, the ad hoc caravan would select its captain and organize its travel arrangements. The caravan itself was grouped into divisions, usually four, from each of which was drawn a lieutenant. These lieutenants formed an advance party which scouted the route ahead of the main caravan, choosing the best crossings and pre-

Travelers sometimes detoured to the top of Round Mound to watch the caravan heading toward Santa Fe. (From Josiah Gregg, Commerce of the Prairies, *1844)*

paring them by cutting brush, digging ramps out of the steep sides of creeks and ravines, marking the ford with sticks to avoid occasional patches of quicksand, and sometimes making temporary bridges of willow branches, grasses, and earth. Once underway, the caravan crossed the headwaters of several streams and rivers, from the south side of the Kansas River to the great bend of the Arkansas River. One of the few outstanding landmarks on this part of the prairie crossing was Pawnee Rock, on which many early travelers carved their names.

Once past the Arkansas River's great bend, travelers took a variety of crossing points. The clearest and earliest route continued along the north side of the Arkansas to the Purgatory (Purgatoire) River, where the trail—now determined by the terrain—led south through the Raton Pass, a difficult, precipitous route. Travelers taking the Cimarron Cutoff blazed by Becknell forded the Arkansas River just past the great bend and struck out southwest across the desert. In the early years, wise travelers did not make this trip unguided, for the prairie was far from trackless; although no Santa Fe Trail was marked, buffalo paths crisscrossed the desert and could easily lead greenhorns astray. As Josiah Gregg described it, these buffalo paths had "...all the appearance of immense highways, over which entire armies would seem to have frequently passed." Not until 1834 was a permanent Santa Fe Trail

cut across the desert; the ruts cut by the wagons of the large annual caravan crossing the prairie in the spring rains that year were followed for decades thereafter, and are still visible today. On the other side of the desert, broken hills heralded the approach of the Rocky Mountains, some springs refreshed the thirsty traders and several landmarks came into view: two twin towers of rock called Rabbit Ears; a rocky dome called Round Mound, which travelers often climbed for a view of the country-side; and an outcropping called Point of Rocks. After crossing the headwaters of the Canadian River, the Cimarron Cutoff rejoined the Raton Pass Route and turned south toward Santa Fe.

An alternative route to Santa Fe, the Taos Trail, was open only to pack trains, being impassable by wagon. Travelers taking this route followed the Arkansas River past the Raton Pass turnoff and on into the Sangre de Cristo Mountains to Taos, and then down to Santa Fe. Other travelers occasionally followed more southerly rivers westward from the Mississippi, such as the Canadian River (then often called the Rio Colorado), but these routes were preferred only for late autumn starts, since they lacked a major provisioning center like St. Louis.

Approaching Santa Fe, caravans were often cheered by the arrival of runners from that city, who greeted them up to 200 miles from their destination. These *avant-couriers*, who traveled at night for safety, arranged for provisions for the Missouri traders and, more importantly, returned to Santa Fe as their agents, authorized to arrange for storage space and customs inspection with the Nuevo Mexican authorities. Santa Fe itself was a surprise. Josiah Gregg thought he saw "brick-kilns scattered in every direction" in the midst of cornfields, and was chagrined to find that he was looking, not at the suburbs, but at the city itself. Zebulon Pike had noted in 1806 that the city's one-story adobe houses looked from a distance "like a fleet of flatboats" of the type he had seen on the Ohio River. But it was to the buildings around the public square, where the governor's administration, the guards, and the clergy were housed, that the traders were headed. Here they negotiated duties with the customs house officials, who commonly took a large part of the amount as their personal share. At Santa Fe, the various routes from the east and north joined the much older Chihuahua Trail to form a continuous connection between the two still-fledgling nations: Mexico and the United States.

Although the Chihuahua Trail had been in use for well over a century, it was no more a road in the modern sense than was the Santa Fe Trail, and traveling conditions were much the same on both. Where the route was not determined by a crucial pass or ford, caravans often preferred to spread out on the plains; that gave the livestock fresh grazing and did not oblige travelers to eat someone else's dust or, more troublesome, to become mired in someone else's mud. No public inns existed along the route; traders and teamsters alike camped out in the open, often even in the towns, except for the lucky few who were invited to stay with well-to-do local families. In the early 1800's, travel was still such an event that the arrival of a trading caravan in a town was often announced by a town crier and celebrated with a lively ball called a *fandango*.

No bridges or ferries existed, so in periods of high water, caravans had to ride through the water at the best available ford or, in extreme cases, float the wagons across on makeshift rafts. After such a crossing, it was necessary to spread goods out on the far side to dry, before the traders repacked and moved on. In low-water times, caravans sometimes traveled on or crisscrossed over dry riverbeds, detouring off the main route for fresh water.

Either way, travel was hard on the wagons, whether they were primitive wooden-wheeled carts, such as many Mexicans used, or Conestoga wagons, the well-known canvas-hooded "prairie schooners," made in Pittsburgh, and sported by many Missouri traders. On the high, dry southwestern plateaus, the Missouri wagons shrank, and often the iron tires had to be refitted to the smaller wheel, occasionally being tied on with rawhide. On the other hand, immersion in water made the wood swell and stick. Wagoneers were well-supplied with such lubricants as resin and tallow to ease movement and cut down on the squeaking of wood on wood. Extra wood for repairs was carried slung under the wagon body, for no usable wood

After two decades of the Santa Fe trade, the city still looked to some eyes like "brick-kilns scattered among cornfields." (From W. H. Emory, Notes of a Military Reconaissance, *1846–7)*

existed along the route. The wagons themselves were usually pulled by oxen or mules. Horses were sometimes used and were ridden by some travelers and traders (as well as by the native Americans of the plains, who had bought or stolen them or picked up strays over the previous centuries), but they could not compare with oxen and mules as haulers.

Because wagons were vulnerable in a variety of ways, and could not negotiate certain mountainous routes, such as the Taos Trail, the pack train remained a standard type of caravan on the Chihuahua and Santa Fe trails. Traveling in trains of 50 to 200, feeding on free prairie grass, and carrying as much as 400 pounds each, mules provided an economical alternative to wagon-freighting. *Arrieros,* or muleteers, each handling eight or nine animals, were highly respected men on the trail—so much so that the U.S. Army adopted their techniques in the transport division later formed in the Southwest.

Travel on the Santa Fe and Chihuahua trails was no more safe than it was easy. The native Americans of the high plains and plateaus did not take kindly to intrusion on their territory. In the early years of the Santa Fe trade, they posed more threat than actual danger to the caravans; in general, they preferred accepting goods and making off with livestock to fighting the armed traders. Traders alone or in small parties were more vulnerable, however; after two advance scouts of a caravan were killed in 1828, violence on both sides escalated quickly, and traders took other measures for their defense. Although the Kansas River area was relatively safe, wagons still rode in a double column, in order to form a defensive circle more easily. Once past Pawnee Rock, caravans generally tightened their formation to four abreast, as they moved into Pawnee and Comanche territory. Mounted on horses, the native Americans were expert light cavalry; as they gradually armed themselves with guns—bought or stolen—they posed a substantial hazard to wagon trains. Traders asked for and received military escort from the U.S. Army, but the inexperienced infantry at first provided was no match for the danger. In any case, protection could be supplied only up to the territorial limit of the 100th meridian, just past Pawnee Rock, where the greatest danger began. The Mexican government sent escorts out from Santa Fe to meet major caravans, but they also did not go into the most hazardous area, being mainly concerned with catching smugglers who might wish to avoid customs duties payable at Santa Fe.

Between the somewhat protected areas on either end of the Santa Fe Trail, travelers were on their own. They were especially exposed on the Cimarron Cutoff, far from the aid of anyone. The Raton Pass Route, though over 100 miles longer, came to have significant advantages for travelers. Hunters and trappers, "mountain men" who had moved in the region for decades, came to the aid of trading caravans, at first unofficially and later as paid armed

escorts of considerable effectiveness; the most famous such group was the Carson men, led by Kit Carson, who guarded many caravans along the Santa Fe Trail. Some of these men even left their mountain pursuits and joined in the Santa Fe trade. Most notable among them was a trio of Americans from St. Louis: William and Charles Bent, sons of a judge, and Céran St. Vrain, from a French fur-trading family. As Bent, St. Vrain & Company, they built a trading fortress on the north side of the Arkansas River, just past the Purgatory River, near the junction of the Raton Pass Route and the Taos Trail. At the same time, they widened the Raton Pass Route for use by wagon caravans; it soon became the preferred route for all but the largest, best-protected caravans, which still hazarded the Cimarron crossing.

Between Santa Fe and Chihuahua, the trail was little safer. The native American population had by no means been subdued by the Spanish-Americans. Added to that was the danger from bandits, who lay in wait for traders; they knew when and where to wait because travel permits required for the trip between Santa Fe and Chihuahua specified the contents and schedules of the trading caravans—information available to robbers from the customs officials for a modest bride. The travel situation was made even more difficult when, in 1836, Texas broke away from the Republic of Mexico. Believing (not without justification) that the United States had not only encouraged Texas's move for independence but also planned to do the same in Nuevo Mexico, Mexico further decreased its modest protection of the traders, while increasing tariffs on trade (and, incidentally, corruption in the customs houses). Texans complicated matters even more by attacking Nuevo Mexican traders, and any Americans who happened to be with them. Emboldened by these attacks against the Mexican government, and by internal political divisions in the country, the native American tribes in northern Mexico became far more hostile, so much so that many of the smaller villages between Santa Fe and Chihuahua were abandoned at this time, their occupants moving to the better-protected larger towns.

Despite the difficulties, trading flourished. From an estimated $15,000 worth of trade in 1822, the traffic grew to approximately $1 million in 1846. Missouri traders came to make Chihuahua their destination, with Santa Fe being merely a customs point and city of entry. Once in Chihuahua, traders would rent a shop or market stall from which to sell their goods, with the most successful traders later renting permanent space, and some—like Céran St. Vrain—even taking Mexican citizenship and marrying into local families. So hungry were the Mexicans for goods that traders sometimes sold the whole train, teams and wagons and all, the Conestoga wagons being highly prized in Mexico, even battered and worn after a 1,300 to 1,400 mile trip. Loaded with silver, such traders sometimes continued on down the Chihuahua Trail

Ruts on the Santa Fe Trail, like these just west of Dodge City, Kansas, were cut so deep they can still be seen in some places. (Kansas State Historical Society, Topeka)

to Mexico City and Vera Cruz, taking a ship back across the Gulf of Mexico to the Mississippi River and home. Others traded some of their cash for Mexican mules, which, even after a grueling drive across the plains, brought a handsome price in Missouri and Illinois. The rest of the traders made their way back to Missouri in much lighter, smaller, faster caravans. The silver they brought back with them had a significant impact on the Midwestern economy. By 1828, the Mexican peso was more common in the Midwest than the American silver dollar (which had slightly less silver content). By 1831, the peso was the main currency not only in Missouri but in most other Western states, allowing these states to weather rather well the panic and depression that hit the rest of the country in 1837.

But the heyday of the Santa Fe-Chihuahua Trail was brief. Once Chihuahua became established as a main terminus of the route, traders wishing to avoid the duties at Santa Fe (payable again at each city the caravan passed through) established new, more direct paths through Texas to Chihuahua, draining trade away from the old main route. More importantly, Mexican-U.S. relations deteriorated into war in 1846, when the U. S. Army—now cavalry—moved down the Santa Fe Trail and took Santa Fe without bloodshed (a feat possibly arranged by a well-known Santa Fe trader, James Wiley Magoffin). With the immediate area under U.S. control, traders poured into Santa Fe, swamping the market, which had too little silver to pay for the goods. The traders then attempted to move southward toward Chihuahua, but their advance party was arrested at El Paso, and the balance of the large trading caravan was stranded for some months in a camp just north of the Jornada del Muerto. Facing starvation with the onset of winter and bankruptcy with the inabil-

ity to sell their goods, the merchants asked for military support, which eventually was granted. On Christmas Day in 1846, a column of U.S. troops met a Mexican force over twice its size at Rancho del Bracito; after a brief skirmish, the Mexican force retreated down the Chihuahua Trail, followed by U.S. troops and traders who had accompanied the column. Some traders bypassed the armies and headed for Chihuahua, but the rest—traders and teamsters handling over 300 wagons—were impressed into military service. Early in 1847, at Sacramento, 20 miles north of Chihuahua, U.S. troops defeated the Mexican forces there and then moved in to occupy Chihuahua. Susan Shelby Magoffin, who had lost her baby on the trail at Bent's Fort, arrived with her trader-husband shortly after the takeover and described the scene:

> …the good citizens of Chihuahua had never dreamed I dare say that their loved homes would be turned into quarters for common soldiers, their fine houses many of them turned into stables, the rooves made kitchens of, their public *pila* [drinking fountain] used as a bathing trough, the fine trees of their beautiful *alamador* [public walk] barked and forever spoiled.

For the next two months, the northern traders desperately tried to unload their goods; then when the U.S. Army returned to El Paso, most traders returned with them, except those who had chosen Mexico as their permanent home.

Traders and settlers along the old Chihuahua and Santa Fe trails played important roles in this turbulent period—and had difficult personal choices to make. Certainly, the Nuevo Mexicans felt strong ties to the U.S.

traders who had brought them relative wealth and stability. Even Mexico itself had strong ties to the traders, for the caravans with their expert guards had made the Chihuahua Trail safer than it had been in previous times, and had even been entrusted with the Mexican government's mail and payroll shipments. Considering this history, it is not surprising that the governor of the Territory of New Mexico, now under U.S. control, was a trader, Charles Bent, of Bent, St. Vrain & Company. The war with Mexico continued until 1848, with Chihuahua being occupied temporarily for a second time. Then, after some discussion of whether or not the whole territory should become part of Texas, Nuevo Mexico became the Territory of New Mexico, in 1850, with Santa Fe as its capital.

The Santa Fe and Chihuahua trails were never the same after that. Trade with Mexico continued, but it now followed many routes, most entering Mexico from the northeast at El Paso, which had become the westernmost point in the state of Texas. (The part of the city on the Mexican side of the border was called Ciudad Juarez.) Perhaps more importantly, the attention of the United States had turned westward. Drawn by tales of traders, mountain men, and California gold, people moved across the Mississippi by the thousands to create that very special brief experience known as "The Old West." Along the Santa Fe Trail, Kansas City became the dominant starting point, and Dodge City sprang up where the Raton Pass Route and the Cimarron Cutoff diverged. Along the Chihuahua Trail, cowboys bragged of being the "fastest gun west of the Pecos," which was the river running southeastward from Santa Fe toward the Gulf of Mexico.

But the Santa Fe Trail played a relatively minor part in the movement to the West. Prospectors and settlers heading for California and Oregon generally took the northerly Oregon and California trails. Settlers heading for the Southwest sometimes followed the old Santa Fe and Chihuahua trails south past Albuquerque, and then west along the Gila Valley, but most came to favor a more southerly route, running through San Antonio and El Paso toward southern California. All these routes were vulnerable to attack, by free-lancing bandits, or by native Americans and Mexicans, who protested for decades against the U.S. government's annexation of the territory. (During one such uprising, New Mexico's territorial governor, Charles Bent, was killed.) To protect traders and travelers in the western territory, the U.S. cavalry established forts; among those on the old Santa Fe Trail were Fort Union, built at the point were the Raton Pass Route and the Cimarron Cutoff rejoined going west, and a new Bent's Fort, built downstream from the site of the old one, which had been blown up by William Bent in 1849. Enterprising traders soon found as much profit in supplying the forts with goods as in trading down the long trail to Santa Fe and Chihuahua, and some settled down in the towns that grew up along the route, making and selling goods to soldiers and other new settlers.

With the increase in traffic, stage lines were established along the old Santa Fe and Chihuahua trails, but the main stage and mail route became the southern route to California, the Butterfield Southern Overland Mail Route. Without Chihuahua as its main partner, Santa Fe – the oldest colonial settlement in the area – gradually lost its unique position. When railroads were being planned for the Southwest, in the 1850's and 1860's, the city was still important enough to be the planned terminus of the Atchison, Topeka, and Santa Fe Railroad. During the building of this railroad, the owners had to fight another railroad company for the route through the Raton Pass, which could accommodate only one railroad. But in the decades following, trade along the Santa Fe Trail, which had peaked with the many new settlers and traders traveling westward, dropped sharply. By 1879, Santa Fe's importance had so diminished that it was bypassed by the railroad that bore its name, the board of directors considering it not worthwhile to swing the line 30 miles northward to link up with the city; instead, the railroad continued on westward across New Mexico, although a link to Santa Fe was built in 1880.

With the completion of the railroad, the old Santa Fe trade – merchant caravans of prairie schooners pushing across dry, dangerous deserts – came abruptly to an end. The Texas routes to Chihuahua were also soon replaced by railroads, and in 1882 the Mexican government completed a railroad along the old Chihuahua Trail, up to El Paso, to which the Atchison, Topeka, and Santa Fe Railroad laid a connecting line. Mexicans tested the border several times in the second half of the 19th century, once during the American Civil War (sparking a strong native American revolt at the same time); again at the turn of the century; and finally in 1916, before accepting the current boundaries. In the same period, the United States closed the Indian Wars, and the remaining native Americans in the area were deported or sequestered in reservations. In these same decades, the ranchers who first opened the lands of the "Great American Desert" to the cattle herds and cowboys began to be replaced in many areas by farmers, who turned the seeming desert into fertile cropland.

Although they have long since lost their dominance over the travel and trade of the area, the Santa Fe and Chihuahua trails still form a main route between Mexico and the central prairies of the United States. The Mexican Central Railroad (Ferrocarril Nacional) roughly follows the old route from Chihuahua to Ciudad Juarez, opposite El Paso, Texas, as does Camino 45, the old Camino Real from Mexico City to the Rio Grande. U.S. Route 25 continues the route north to Santa Fe and on through the Raton Pass, where, at Trinidad, Colorado, a lesser route swings northwest along the old trail to La

Junta, near the site of Bent's Fort. The trail is completed by U.S. Route 50 following the Arkansas River through Dodge City, Kansas, around the great bend, to Kansas City, whose size and importance owe no small debt to the Santa Fe and Chihuahua trails. U.S. Route 56 from Dodge City across to Springer, New Mexico approximates the old Cimarron Cutoff. In all of these routes, modern engineering and nature's changes have caused a shift in the roadbed from one side of a riverbank to the other, or through the now more stable Médanos sand dunes, rather than around them. But the main course of the Santa Fe and Chihuahua trails remains the same, these trails that carry their history with them. It was the Santa Fe trade that gave the northern Mexican province of Chihuahua much of its historical importance and stability, while the Santa Fe trade gave to the United States the whole Southwest. To both it gave a common background. As historical geographer Ellen Churchill Semple put it:

> ...every wagon-track and mule-trail across the plains marked the passing of the shuttle weaving northern Mexico and the American Republic into one fabric.

Selective Bibliography

Cleland, Robert Glass. *This Reckless Breed of Men: The Trappers and Fur Traders of the Southwest.* (New York: Knopf, 1963). Focuses on activities on the mountain trails.

Connor, Seymour V. and Jimmy M. Skaggs. *Broadcloth and Britches: The Santa Fe Trade.* (College Station and London: Texas A & M University Press, 1977). A detailed, lively account of the trade between Santa Fe and Missouri.

Garrard, Lewis H. *Wah-To-Yah and the Taos Trail*, ed. by Ralph P. Bieber. (Glendale, California: Arthur H. Clark Company, 1938). A firsthand account of a young tourist traveling with Céran St. Vrain's caravan in 1846–47.

Gregg, Josiah. *Commerce of the Prairies*, ed. by Max L. Moorhead. (Norman, Oklahoma: University of Oklahoma Press, 1954; reprint of a 19th century edition). A classic account of the Santa Fe-Chihuahua trade by one of the main traders along the route.

Magoffin, Susan Shelby. *Down the Santa Fe Trail and Into Mexico: The Diary of Susan Shelby Magoffin, 1846–47,* ed. by Stella M. Drumm. (New Haven: Yale University Press, 1926). The journal of a young bride traveling with her husband, one of the Magoffin trading family.

Moorhead, Max L. *New Mexico's Royal Road: Trade and Travel on the Chihuahua Trail.* (Norman, Oklahoma: University of Oklahoma Press, 1958). A prime historical treatment of the route between Chihuahua and Santa Fe.

Perrigo, Lynn I. *Our Spanish Southwest.* (Dallas: Banks Upshaw and Co., 1960). A strong overview with much detail.

Semple, Ellen Churchill. *American History and its Geographic Conditions.* (Boston and New York: Houghton Mifflin, 1903). An excellent account of how the land shaped human settlement.

Vestal, Stanley. *Old Santa Fe Trail.* (Boston: Houghton Mifflin, 1939). An evocative attempt at recreation; not a history.

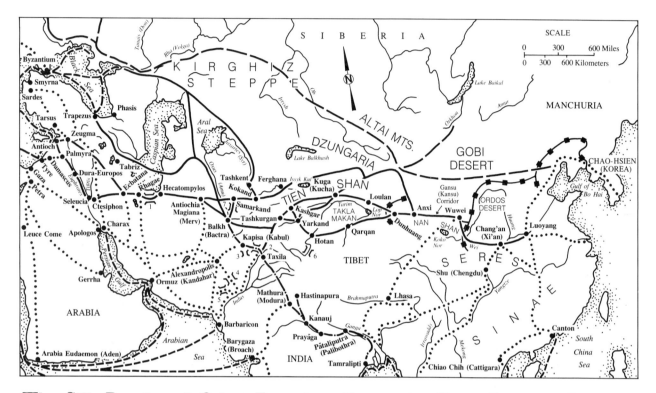

The Silk Road and Other Eurasian Routes in Greco-Roman Times

———————— Main Silk Routes

—·—·—·— Indian Grand Road

— — — — Eurasian Steppe Route

· · · · · · · Main Connecting Land Routes

- - - - - - Main Connecting Sea Routes

■—■—■ Fortified Wall

⹀ Passes:

1. Caspian Gates
2. Khyber Pass
3. Kurram Pass
4. Bolan Pass
5. Mula Pass
6. Karakorum Pass
7. Iron Gates

The Silk Road

In the late winter of 1907, the Anglo-Hungarian explorer Marc Aurel Stein arrived in the settlement of Dunhuang (Tunhuang), just inside the Great Wall of China. He had walked over 3,000 miles, across frozen mountains and deserts, on a trek so arduous that a later, similar trip would cost him five toes from frostbite. But it was not the length of the journey that was so remarkable; the people of Central Asia had walked such distances routinely for thousands of years. Nor was the sight of a town noteworthy; on his journey he had seen the remains of many once-thriving communities, their croplands gone to desert, their buildings in ruin and partly buried by the drifting sand. Nor was the town unique in its hive of caves carved out of the soft loess cliffs; although Dunhuang was well known for its mile-wide temple called the "Cave of the Thousand Buddhas," other towns along the way had been graced by similar cave clusters, as well as by some statues a hundred feet high. What made Dunhuang worthy of special attention was the rumor that, in a sealed room guarded by a lone self-appointed monk, were books centuries old, records of former days of greatness along the route Stein had taken—the old Silk Road.

It took some time for Stein to convince the monk to open the storeroom, whose contents and even existence had apparently been forgotten for almost 1,000 years. What they found surely surpassed all expectations, for among the Chinese governmental records and the irreplaceable translations and transcriptions of early Buddhist texts, some dating from the fifth century and many of them brought back from India along the Silk Road, was the oldest known printed work—a copy of the Diamond Sutra, a Buddhist text—dating from 868 A.D., over five centuries before Gutenberg produced his printed Bible in Europe.

Dunhuang and its treasures were striking proof of the vitality of China and, indeed, all of Central Asia during the many centuries when the Silk Road stretched 5,000 miles from East Asia to the Mediterranean. Along this road came silk to conquer the West, Buddhism to conquer the East. Along this way, Alexander the Great marched to the East and the Chinese approached the West. Later, during the one brief century when the Silk Road was united under a single power, the Mongols, Marco Polo—perhaps the most famous traveler of all time—passed along this route, bringing back tales of its wonders to an astonished West.

The Silk Road began in the home of Chinese culture: where the Huang He (Yellow River) makes its great northward loop, and the Wei He, its main tributary, continues straight west, to almost complete a loop with the Huang. The eastern terminus of the Silk Road varied over the centuries; in early times it was generally either Chang'an (near modern Xi'an) in the Wei Valley or Luoyang (Loyang) further east on the Huang; in later times, the Silk Road extended to the more modern capital of Beijing (Peking), north of Luoyang. From the fertile Wei Valley the route headed westward across the Huang,

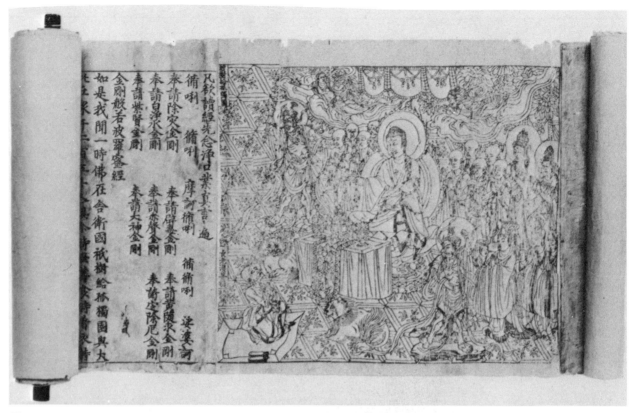

The earliest known printed work, a Buddhist text produced in 868 A.D., was found in the Cave of the Thousand Buddhas at Dunhuang. (Stein Collection, British Museum)

for much of its history guarded to the north by China's famous fortified wall. Swinging slightly northwest, the Silk Road followed the Gansu (Kansu) Corridor between the Gobi Desert to the north and the Nan Shan (Southern Mountains), outposts of the great Kunlun mountain range, itself backed by the Tibetan Plateau and the Himalayas. Passing through Anxi (Anhsi) and Dunhuang, the route left the wall's protection through Yumen, better known as the Jade Gate.

Debouching onto the salt-encrusted flats surrounding the wandering lake called the Lop Nor, the main route of the Silk Road divided, forking around the Takla Makan, one of the most desolate, uninhabited regions in the world. Composed of vast waves of shifting dunes that could, in sudden storms, bury a town or a caravan, this desert struck proper terror into the hearts of travelers for thousands of years. Newcomers were always cautioned against straying from the main path, whether through carelessness, fatigue, or fear of robbers—or because of the mirages and illusory sounds of the desert, which often seemed to beckon the unwary into the dunes. The Silk Road steered clear of the worst part of the desert. The Southern Way followed the foothills of the Kunlun through the oases of Qarqan (Char-chan, now Qiemo) and Hotan (Khotan) to Yarkand (Schache) on the far side of the Takla Makan. The Northern Way followed the fringe of the Tien Shan (Celestial Mountains) through the oases of Loulan and Kuga

(Kucha) and then either to Kashgar (Kashi) or Yarkand, where it linked with the Southern Way. The Southern Way was the earlier route, favored by Hotan's jade market, but it was very dry, with little food or forage along the way. The Northern Way was watered by streams from the Tien Shan, notably the Tarim River, so it had more grazing for animals and better hope of provisions for humans; it had little trade of its own, however, and was open to raids from the nomads of the vast Mongolian steppes just to the north.

At Yarkand and Kashgar, travelers faced the Pamirs, a high, crumpled plateau that stretched 300 miles to the west. This region posed its own difficulties, for many of the passes were narrow and dangerous, while the thin air of the heights caused dizziness, headaches, and ringing ears. The Chinese knew the Pamirs as the Onion Mountains, apparently because they thought these symptoms were caused by the onions growing there. The Persians called this rugged country the Roof of the World; but the name Pamir actually refers to the many valleys that lie "at the Foot of Mountain Peaks." The name is appropriate, for it was by its extraordinary tangle of river valleys that the Silk Road made its way west; the exact route varied over time, but the terminus on the far side was throughout history the favored city of Bactra (Balkh). This city, roughly halfway on the route, was called by many "paradise on earth" for its beautiful and fertile valley and for its bazaars, which drew traders from throughout Eurasia. This prime crossroads city not only stood astride the Silk Road but lay at the head of India's Grand Road from the south, while also drawing traders from the Eurasian steppes, who came south along the valley of the Oxus River (Amu Darya).

Passing from Bactra over the Iranian Plateau, the Silk Road headed west through Antiochia Margiana (Merv) and Hecatompylos (near modern Mashhad) along the Elburz Mountains through a pass called the Caspian Gates, at the foot of that sea, to Rhagae (Rayy, near modern Tehran) and Ecbatana (Hamadan). Descending from the Iranian Plateau through a gap in the Zagros Mountains, the Silk Road emerged onto the river plains of Mesopotamia, heading for the place where the Tigris and Euphrates approach each other closely; there a series of cities acted as entrepôts for trade with the East—Babylon, Seleucia, Ctesiphon, and Baghdad among them. From there the Silk Road turned northwest along the Euphrates to Antioch, traditional main western terminus of the Silk Road. From here Eastern goods were fed either down the coast for refining or directly across the Mediterranean through one of Syria's ports.

Not surprisingly, such a lengthy and tenuous route was easily cut. In many periods, political, commercial, or climatic reasons forced the Silk Road traffic to follow one of the secondary spurs that fed in either direction all along its route. The first and most important of these routes left through the Great Wall at Anxi and headed north and then west via the Turfan Depression to pass north of the Tien Shan and the Issyk Kul (Warm Lake); crossing the Talas River, the route then turned south again to Tashkent on the Jaxartes River (Syr Darya) or continued directly to Samarkand (Maracanda). Although this route was wide open to the steppe nomads, it was a popular route in peaceful times, for it not only ran over hospitable ground, but, by swinging north, avoided the Pamirs—no small advantage. From Samarkand, travelers could cut through a pass called the Iron Gate to Bactra; that would be the choice of those headed directly toward India or to southern Mesopotamia. But most travelers would continue westward from Samarkand through Bukhara and across the Oxus to join the main road at Merv. Those who wished to avoid Mesopotamia, however, had other choices. They could follow the Oxus north, circling around the Caspian Sea to cross the Volga and Don rivers and emerge at the north side of the Black Sea. Or they could leave the Oxus short of its mouth at the Aral Sea, and cut west across the Caspian Sea and the Armenian plateau to the port of Trapezus (Trebizond, or Trabzon) in the southeast corner of the Black Sea. In some periods, travelers followed the main Silk Road to Rhagae and then cut north overland through Tabriz to Trapezus.

From the main Silk Road, spurs also cut off to the south. Near Lanzhou (Lanchow) and the lake called the Koko Nor (Qinghai Hu), a route fed up onto the Tibetan Plateau and across that high wasteland to Lhasa. Descending the front range of the Himalayas by various difficult tracks, it led down into the valley of the Ganga River. While never suited to be a main trading route, this alternative kept up modest connection across the Himalayas and was often used by Buddhist pilgrims. Pilgrims also favored a daring route further west. From between Hotan and Yarkand, this route forced its way into the high mountains through the formidable Karakorum Pass to Leh (Ladakh), near the headwaters of the Indus River. Crossing the northern reaches of the Indus and its tributaries, it passed through Srinigar to connect with India's Grand Road near Kabul.

Movement and contact along the vast distances of the Silk Road seem to have begun with the nomadic peoples of Central Asia, who migrated to higher elevations in summer and back to the lower levels in winter. In their wanderings, they took with them portable items of value, which they traded with each other. So it was that at a very early period, Mesopotamia was receiving gold, tin, and turquoise from the Iranian plateau; lapis lazuli and rubies from Afghanistan; and cotton cloth from India. The peoples of Central Asia early tamed horses and the two-humped Bactrian camel for use in this lucrative trade. China also benefited from contact with nomadic traders. To the Wei and Huang valleys came goods from far across the continent: Iranian turquoise, Afghan lapis lazuli, gold from Siberia, and—most attractive of all—jade from Hotan. Other less tangible influences also percolated in from the West, including the wheel and the chariot; techniques of metalworking; and probably at least the idea of writing. Between 1500 and 500 B.C., chariot warfare gave way to mounted cavalry in Central Asia, making the Iranians (Indo-European immigrants from the Eurasian Steppe) and their nomadic neighbors forces to be reckoned with. The practice of mounted warfare spread quickly to both China and the West.

Of the nomadic peoples who were the intermediaries in this early trade, we know little. The higher civilizations on either end of the Silk Road looked down on their unsettled brethren, failing to distinguish clearly among the many different groups that always swirled around the heart of Asia. To make matters worse, the various cultures—Mesopotamian, Iranian, Chinese, and Indian—each had their own names for these nomads who rode the wind, so it is difficult to tell when they are describing the same group. In addition, the "land of the two rivers" and the "yellow kingdom" were so far apart that they existed for each other as—at most—fanciful rumor; for most of the first millennium B.C., it was clear only that trade goods and techniques had come to each from very far away.

Here, surely, was reason for penetrating into the lands of Central Asia. Who did so first, bypassing the tenuous chain of middlemen, is an open question. The

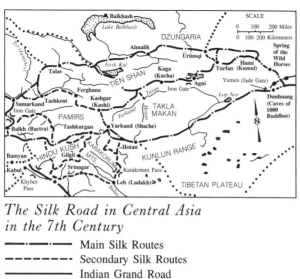

The Silk Road in Central Asia in the 7th Century

———·——— Main Silk Routes
——————— Secondary Silk Routes
————————— Indian Grand Road
··············· Main Connecting Routes
—■—■—■— Fortified Wall

Chinese had a legend of a mythical princess, Hsi Wang Mu, who supposedly lived in the West and, in about 1000 B.C., was visited by their Emperor Mu-Wang. Mu-Wang's travel memoirs tell of how the "God of the River" showed him "the precious articles of the Ch'un Mountain," including gems and valuable jades, and "the beautiful palaces of Kunlun." It is tempting to speculate that Chinese travelers had reached toward Hotan in these early centuries, though we have no real evidence of their having done so.

Word of the Chinese seems to have reached the West through the Scythians, north of the Black Sea, by the mid-first millennium B.C. Drawn by tales of the East, none other than Alexander the Great penetrated along the Silk Road. After defeating his ancient Persian rivals, this young prince headed eastward on the main route from Ecbatana through the Caspian Gates and past Hecatompylos; then he looped southward, founding several cities named Alexandria, among them those on the sites of modern Herat, Kandahar, and Ghazni. Arriving in Bactra, he cemented his local position by marrying an Iranian princess, Roxana. From his Bactrian base, he pushed in several directions, northward across the Oxus and up to the Jaxartes, eastward into the formidable Hindu Kush, southeastward into the Indus Valley. In the East Alexander was faced with *terra incognita,* with little hint of the great country that lay across the Central Asian wastes; India was nearer and better known. In the end, however, the army resisted going beyond the Indus River; forced to desist, Alexander returned to Persia, where he died. When his empire was divided among his lieutenents, the eastern portion went to Seleucus who, for a time, ruled the whole western half of the Silk Road from the Jaxartes and the Indus west all

the way to Syria. Under the Seleucid governors, the city of Seleucia, on the Tigris, became the main entrepôt for trade with Iran and India, replacing the once-great Mesopotamian city of Babylon nearby.

In the East, China was also reaching outward. In later centuries China would often wait like a queen bee for others to come to her, but in this early period she was young and expansive—and in need of help. From its original home on the Huang, the Ch'in dynasty had unified much of China under a central government. But she was continually being harassed by nomads from the desert steppes to the north and west. As a result, she mobilized her always-substantial labor force to build a series of fortified lines against these invaders; by the third century B.C., these fortifications had been joined and extended to form a Great Wall. Not yet the "long stone serpent" some have called her, this largely earth-and-wattle wall stretched from Chao-Hsien (Chosen, or Korea) around the Gulf of Bo Hai, across to the northernmost curve of the Huang and down the western side of its loop; another early section of wall crossed diagonally inside the loop, along the edge of cultivation. Soldiers, often deported criminals sent for frontier service, manned the walls, lighting signal fires at the first sign of invaders. This protection worked rather well for a time, but by the third century B.C. it had ceased to be effective, as the army grew lax and as the Chinese faced a serious threat from the steppes: the Hsiung-nu. Better known to Europeans as the Huns, these nomads had pushed westward an earlier threat, the Yüeh-chih (Scythians). The Chinese reasonably thought that the Yüeh-chih might welcome an alliance against the Hsiung-nu; under the Han Emperor Wu-Ti, who was leading China into a golden age, an expedition was launched to propose such a partnership.

In 138 B.C., a party of 100 men left for the West, led by an extraordinary leader, Chang Ch'ien. Once past the Gansu Corridor, which was by this time also partly protected by a fortified wall, the Chinese were in alien territory—and were almost immediately captured by the Hsiung-nu. There they stayed for 10 years, during which Chang Ch'ien married and had a child; he always kept with him the yak's tail that signified his office, however, and finally escaped with some of his men. Following a line of oases through the jade country of Hotan, Chang Ch'ien arrived on the far side of the Takla Makan in the land of Ferghana (Ta-yüan) along the upper reaches of the Jaxartes River. The Chinese historian Ssu-ma Ch'ien, writing some decades later, noted that the king of Ta-yüan "had heard of the wealth of the Han empire and wished to establish communication with it, though as yet he had been unable to do so." He readily provided guides and interpreters for Chang Ch'ien's trip to the Yüeh-Chih.

The Yüeh-Chih, who had emigrated westward roughly along the route north of the Issyk Kul, had finally come to rest in the region between the Jaxartes and the

Oxus. Alexander had reached this region called Sogdiana two centuries earlier, but the Greek kingdoms he had left behind were now gone, and Bactria was under the domination of the Yüeh-Chih. Secure and successful in their new homeland, the Yüeh-Chih were uninterested in Chang Ch'ien's proposals for an alliance. After a year of being ignored, Chang Ch'ien returned home; captured by the Hsiung-nu once again, he escaped and arrived in 126 B.C. with his wife and a servant, but only two of his original party. Although the mission had failed, Chang Ch'ien's trip was still a success. He had found that the eager traders of Ferghana had powerful horses "which sweat blood; their forebears are supposed to have been foaled from heavenly horses." These were far better suited than small Chinese ponies for mounted warfare, especially since their hard hooves resisted wearing down, no small consideration in the days before shoeing. (The parasites which are thought to have caused bleeding sores on their skin apparently did not affect their performance significantly.) Chang Ch'ien also found that there were "many precious stones in the region" west of the Lop Nor.

More than that, Chang Ch'ien brought back word of countries beyond Ta-Hsia (Bactria). First there was An-hsi (Persia), which in this period was ruled by a group known as the Parthians. West of that was T'iao-chih "near the western sea" (the Mediterranean); presumably this referred to Syria (now the only territory left to the Seleucids) and perhaps Asia Minor as well. According to Chang Ch'ien's report, the "old men of An-hsi" said that the mythical princess Hsi Wang Mu lived in T'iao-chih, though they had never seen her—an intriguing survival of an ancient legend. Chang Ch'ien also noted that "to the north of An-hsi there lies a country called Li-chien"; although he knew nothing but the name, this may have been the first reference to the Roman Empire, which would soon be China's main trading partner. On this trip the Chinese also first learned of a land they called Shen-tu (India); indeed, they were surprised to learn that Shen-tu traders brought to Bactra bamboo and cloth from Sichuan (Szechuan). Realizing that this region—southwest of the Huang and not yet part of China's empire—must have a direct route to Shen-tu, Chang Ch'ien later recommended that the Chinese try to reach this new country through the jungles south of the Yangtze River or over

To get battle horses like this one, the Chinese drove halfway across Asia. (T'ang bas-relief, University Museum, Pennsylvania)

The mirages and strange sounds of the Takla Makan desert have lured unwary travelers to their deaths for many centuries. (By Aurel Stein, Royal Geographic Society)

the Tibetan plateau; that was easier said then done, however, and China's main attention continued to be focused toward the West.

Less than a decade after his return, Chang Ch'ien was off again to the region of the Issyk Kul, this time to propose an alliance with the Wu-sun, a people of whom he had heard when he lived with the Huns. The expedition this time was larger and somewhat more elaborate, as Ssu-ma Ch'ien reported:

> The emperor...put [Chang Ch'ien] in charge of a party of three hundred men, each of which was provided with two horses. In addition the party took along tens of thousands of cattle and sheep and carried gold and silk goods worth a hundred billion cash. Many of the men in the party were given the imperial credentials making them assistant envoys so that they could be sent to neighboring states along the way.

Such a train was not only for show, but was necessary to provide food in the infertile lands through which they traveled. Like the Yüeh-chih, the Wu-sun feared the Hsiung-nu and thought China too distant to be an effective ally; after some of their envoys saw China itself, however, they were eager to trade, supplying some large horses for the Chinese cavalry. Ssu-ma Ch'ien describes the end result of this expedition:

> A year or so later the envoys whom Chang Ch'ien had sent to Ta-hsia and the other states of the west all returned, accompanied by envoys from those states, and for the first time relations were established between the lands of the northwest and the Han. It was Chang Ch'ien, however, who opened

the way for this move, and all the envoys who journeyed to the lands in later times relied upon his reputation to gain them a hearing. As a result of his efforts, the foreign states trusted the Han envoys...

The continuation and safety of these contacts was assured when the Chinese finally defeated the Hsiung-nu; although these nomads remained just on the far side of the Great Wall, the Chinese drove them well north of the Issyk Kul in Central Asia. In short order the Chinese had extended their influence all the way to the Jaxartes River. It was in this period that the east-west route first came to deserve the name "Silk Road," for the main gifts sent with the Chinese envoys were silk—for good reason, since in China itself silk was the main form of currency, in which even taxes were paid. They also sent weapons, notably armor, to the Western countries; in return they brought back mostly horses, for "the Son of Heaven [the emperor] loved the horses of Kokand," which were even more powerful than the Wu-sun breeds.

Relations between China and its trading partners were not always smooth, however. The Chinese were dependent on others to supply their needs over the long route, and others were not always disposed to comply— nor to send China all that she wanted. The Chinese so desired the horses from one village near Kokand that they sent "a great quantity of silver and a horse made of solid gold" for them. But the Kokand rulers had a surfeit of Chinese objects and refused; clearly they felt they could do so with impunity, saying (as Ssu-ma Ch'ien reported):

> China is far off and the road is long; travelers lack both fodder and water; in the north they run the

risk of being attacked by the Hsiung-nu; in the south there is neither water nor grass. Moreover, as the country along the road is but thinly populated, the travelers themselves are often short of food. The Chinese ambassadors bring with them a suite of several hundred men, and they are always so short of food that about half of them die of starvation. How could an army ever reach us? China can do nothing to harm us.

But they reckoned without China's will. Assembling tens of thousands of men and great stores of supplies, the Chinese crossed Central Asia to lay siege to Kokand, winning its capitulation when they diverted its city's water supply. (Kokand asked too late for help from the engineers of Ta-Ch'in—which would have been China's first contact with the Roman Empire.) Only one-sixth of the Chinese army returned, but they brought with them 1,000 horses (2,000 having been lost on the way); through judicious horse-breeding, the Chinese soon made these their standard war-horses. Though they would continue to import some horses from the western territories, thereafter they wanted little but precious metals and gems from the outside world.

Among the ambassadors following Chang Ch'ien's lead was one to Parthia (Persia). Met at the border by a 20,000-horse escort, the Chinese ambassador was whisked to the capital, passing through "some dozens of towns" and noting that "The population covers the land almost without a break." On his return to China, the Chinese envoy brought with him an ambassador, who presented to the Chinese court "an ostrich egg and some conjurors from Li-chien (the Roman Empire)," both of which gave the Son of Heaven great pleasure. Chinese and Persian trade and diplomatic relations date from this exchange, in about 115–105 B.C. Soon afterward, Chinese goods, especially silk, began reaching further west. In 53 B.C. the Romans faced the Parthians at Carrhae near the Euphrates River; at a crucial point in the battle the Parthians unfurled their brilliantly colored, iridescent banners in the face of the exhausted Roman legions. The battle turned into a rout—but the Romans took home with them in defeat the memory of those dazzling standards, their first sight of the new cloth. The Greeks had before then talked of an Eastern people they called the Seres, for their cloth called *ser;* the Romans now called this fabric *sericum,* later known as silk. But while the Romans were still embroiled

The great caravans of the Silk Road once traveled through the great arch of Ctesiphon in Parthia, on their way from China to the Mediterranean. (Iraq Petroleum Company)

in civil war, they did not attempt to reach Eastern markets.

Meanwhile the Chinese were integrating the new Central Asian territories into their empire. Setting up provinces guarded by strategically placed forts, they populated the new territories primarily with convicts and exiles; these served both as military guards on the routes and farmers to supply food for travelers. By the middle of the first century A.D., the Chinese were fully in control of the Silk Road west to the Jaxartes.

Throughout this period, Chinese goods were being transported from Bactra down into India, for its own use and for trading at its seaports with Western sailors. China attempted to open more direct trade with a country it called Chi-Pin, probably along India's Grand Road toward the upper Indus Valley. The Chinese history *Thung Chien Kang Mu* reported that Chi-Pin "refused to submit, considering that the soldiers of Han could never reach there. Its king even put to death several Chinese envoys." After a change of heart, Chi-Pin sent embassies to the East; then it was China that raised objections, notably one of its main advisers, Tu Chhin, who said:

Passing into the mountains, Silk Road traders generally exchanged their camels for mules, like these in the Himalayas. (Delia and Ferdinand Kuhn).

> Friendly intercourse with barbarian nations is advisable only where communications are reasonably easy. The Hsientu passes will always be an obstacle to relations with Chi-Pin...
> ...[To reach Chi-Pin] our envoys would have to traverse four or five countries, each of which is full of robbers. Then one must cross the Greater and the Lesser Headache Mountains, chains of naked and burning rocks, so named because they cause headache, dizziness, and vomiting. Then comes the San-Chhih-Phan gorge, thirty *li* long [a *li* equals approximately one-third of a mile], where the path is only 16 or 17 inches wide, on the edge of a precipice, and where the travelers have to be tied together with ropes. From here through Hsientu it is 3000 *li* and more, on a road full of dangers.

The exact route referred to here is unknown, though the "Greater Headache Mountains" might well be the Hindu Kush, one of the highest ranges in the world. In the end, the Chinese declined further direct contact, leaving middlemen to handle most of the exchanges between the two cultures.

Meanwhile in the West, Caesar Augustus had imposed peace on the Roman Empire and had reached a stalemate with Parthia. With each recognizing the power of the other, they established an agreed-upon border in Mesopotamia. The Parthians would permit no foreigners to pass through their territories, reserving for themselves roles as middlemen. The Romans chafed at this, attempting without success to open up a northern route around the Parthians and developing the Spice Route by sea. But in the end most silk reached Rome by the Silk Road through Parthia. Chinese, Bactrian, Indian, and Parthian traders met to exchange goods at a place called the Stone

Tower; many places in Bactria and Ferghana are or were named Tashkurgan (Stone Tower), but which of these was the well-known meeting place is a matter of heated controversy. Once in the hands of the Parthians, silk was brought down to Mesopotamia through the Parthian winter capital of Ctesiphon, opposite Seleucia, to the Parthian frontier-town of Dura-Europos, on the Euphrates. From there it passed into other hands, either directly to the Romans at Antioch or, more commonly, through the semi-independent buffer city of Palmyra, in the Syrian Desert. The raw silk then went to one of the seashore towns, where it was dyed, generally with the Phoenician purple, which was actually a whole range of colors from red to blue-violet, so deep it was almost black. The dyeing required freshly killed shellfish, so it was done only in seashore towns during autumn and winter. Initially the silk was so expensive and rare that it was worn only in patches or strips on basic white togas or tunics, with gold and purple the preferred colors. In early times purple had been allowed only for priests or royalty, and under some later rulers, it was a capital offense for anyone other than the emperor to wear certain shades.

Barely had the Romans become accustomed to the luxurious silk, however, than China was plunged into turmoil; during much of the first century A.D., it left its western provinces to fend for themselves. The fifth century historian Fan Yeh explains what happened then:

> The Western territories were roused to indignation; they broke their bonds of vassalage, put an end to their relations with the Central Empire [China], and submitted once more to the Hsiung-nu...

During this period silk became extremely rare in the West. Some did reach the Romans via India on the Spice Route, for traders were bringing silk, among other goods, by sea from southern China. By late in the first century A.D., the Chinese had restored order and reopened their lines to the West — to find that they had been joined by another power in Central Asia: the Kushans. This new kingdom, formed of Yüeh-Chih (Scythians) and Indo-Greeks (survivors of Alexander's influence in the region), formed a vital new force on the Silk Road, stretching from the western oases of the Takla Makan, including Hotan, southward into the Indus Valley and northward to the Aral Sea, with their heartland in Sogdiana, between the Oxus and Jaxartes rivers. Indeed the Kushans were so strong that it took one of China's greatest generals, Pan Ch'ao, to restore Chinese control over the eastern Tarim basin.

With the four great powers — the Chinese, the Kushans, the Parthians, and the Romans — in place across the 5,000-mile route, the Silk Road entered into its first great period. The route itself was divided into sections, with goods being carried by Chinese, Kushan, Parthian, and Roman caravans successively. Such an arrangement satisfied no one absolutely, except perhaps the Parthians, and the powers tried various strategies and alliances over the years to circumvent each other along the route. In 97 A.D. Chinese general Pan-Ch'ao sent an ambassador named Kan Ying to Ta-Ch'in (the Roman Empire). The *Hou-Han-shu* (History of the Later Han) written three centuries later, describes what happened:

> When he reached T'iao-chih, near the great sea, Kan Ying wanted to press on still farther. The captains of the ships at the western frontier of An-hsi told him that the sea was very extensive and that the return voyage would take three months with favorable winds and as much as two years if they were unfavorable. For this reason people who embarked on that sea took supplies of grain for three years...and it was not unusual for some to die of [homesickness].

If Kan Ying was in Mesopotamia, his informers may have been describing a sea leg of the Silk Route which fed around the Arabian Peninsula rather than crossing the desert to the Mediterranean; in addition, the Parthians were probably trying to discourage him from making direct contact with the Romans and perhaps arranging for direct trade. In any case, Kan Ying gave up the attempt. A century later the Romans sent an envoy via the Spice Route to southern China, which they called the land of the Sinae. (Europeans would for centuries distinguish between the Sinae, reached by sea, and the Seres, reached overland in the north; the distinction was not unwarranted, for the people of the south only became fully sinicized in medieval times.) But nothing came of that, either. Although barred from crossing Parthian territory, a few Mesopotamian traders seem to have reached China, but no regular direct trade resulted. As far as we know, no Chinese and Romans ever met via the overland route, except possibly some Roman soldiers who were taken prisoners by the Parthians and apparently resettled in Central Asia.

In the end, the Silk Road settled into relative stability, with its four main powers keeping the way secure. From Chang'an (which the westerners called Sera Metropolis) and Luoyang (Sinae Metropolis), caravans made their way west through the Jade Gate, on the three-to-four-week trip to Lop Nor, an inhospitable region of dry salt swamps, where wild camels could be as frightening as the Hsiung-nu or the Tibetans who threatened from either side. The caravans would make their way — traveling with all due speed — past the red-gold drifting dunes of the Takla Makan toward the main oasis of Hotan.

In some parts of the Tibetan Himalayas, between Central Asia and India, human porters were and still are often the main "beasts of burden." (Delia and Ferdinand Kuhn)

On the way the main problems were finding drinkable water and keeping to the trail, which could sometimes be covered by a sudden sand storm. In summer, the heat was so severe that caravans would often travel by night; some caravan pilots trained at a marine school in India so they could navigate by the stars, like ships' pilots. Mostly these caravan travelers camped out in the open, with just tents to shield them from the cold night air—or from the heat of the sun. But when they arrived at a garrison community they would often take a few days or even weeks to rest themselves and their animals, repair their equipment, and barter some of their goods for local products, which they would sell further on their way. At these oases were also found courtesans, musicians, and dancers who provided entertainment for the long-deprived caravaners.

For safety, caravans joined together in convoys, sometimes reaching as many as 1,000 camels, and hired troops of archers as escorts. Chinese traders sometimes journeyed all the way to the Parthian border, but Kushans provided many of the professional caravaners on the route. It was they who took the caravans through the threatening river gorges, precipitous defiles, and high pasturelands of the Pamirs, where both humans and animals were afflicted with mountain sickness. Horses and camels were the main beasts of burden on the eastern portion of the route, but mules and yaks were preferred in some rougher mountain sections. These animals often gave warning of danger, which wise guides heeded; the Chinese chronicle *Pei Shih* notes how they would sometimes alert travelers of a dangerous sandstorm in the Takla Makan:

> When such a wind is about to arrive, only the old camels have advance knowledge of it, and they immediately stand snarling together, and bury their mouths in the sand. The men always take this as a sign, and they too immediately cover their noses and mouths by wrapping them in felt. This wind moves swiftly, and passes in a moment, and is gone, but if they did not so protect themselves, they would be in danger of sudden death.

Loads were transferred to appropriate draft animals at caravan centers on the way; the local inhabitants made a tidy profit from the constant exchange, fattening up the surviving animals for a few months before selling them to another caravan. Whichever animals bore the trade goods, they were spared the added load of human passengers, who generally walked. Indeed, sometimes the traders themselves would carry a large share of the load in particularly difficult passes.

Once across the Pamirs, the caravans made their way to the Stone Tower, probably somewhere on the Yarkand River, where traders of many cultures gathered. The Roman writer Pliny, reporting secondhand in the first century A.D., described the trade:

> The goods carried thither [to the Stone Tower] are deposited on the further side of a certain river beside what the Seres have for sale, and the latter, if content with the bargain, carry them off...

Others later repeated the tale of such "dumb barter" or "silent trade," but it seems more likely that traders soon employed interpreters, as they did for their long-standing diplomatic contacts. (Indeed, Pliny's word is quite questionable, for he describes the Seres as "surpassing the ordinary stature of mankind, as having red hair, blue eyes, hoarse voices, and no common language to communicate by." His informants may have been referring to Bactrian or Kushan traders, not Chinese.) However the trade was conducted, the goods then dispersed in various directions, some to the north, more through Bactra to India in the south, and most through Parthia to Mesopotamia. There, Parthian traders yielded their goods to the Greek, Syrian, and Jewish merchants who carried on Rome's trade on the Great Desert Route, where one-humped Arabian camels assumed the burden.

To justify being carried over these thousands of miles, goods had to be lightweight, portable, and extremely valuable. Silk certainly filled the bill for the West. Sent as woven cloth or skeins of yarn, silk passed first through the hands of the expert weavers and dyers of the eastern Mediterranean, being shipped as finished products to Rome. So much silk was brought into increasingly profligate Rome that in the first century A.D. Tiberius even passed a law forbidding men to wear silk, fearing that the luxury would soften and feminize the Romans; many writers complained of the waste, as gold drawn from around the Roman Empire was sent eastward for bolts of the wispy fabric. For its part, China was most interested in gold but was also attracted by perfumes and cosmetics from Egypt, Arabia, and Persia, and by jewelry and colored glass from the fine artisans of Syria and Mesopotamia. Furs and slaves, often obtained from the north from the Eurasian Steppe nomads—who also had a taste for silk and other luxuries—joined in the mix along the great Silk Road.

Initially, most long-distance travelers on the Silk Road were traders, soldiers, or diplomats. But in the first century A.D., during the time of the Kushans, these were joined by missionaries from India, people much influenced by the Greek art of Bactria and carrying the centuries-old religion of Buddha to new territories. Following in the footsteps of Buddha and his early disciples, these missionaries made their way not just on main roads but on the inaccessible tracks and trails of the high Himalayas. Filtering through the Karakorum Mountains, they opened a secondary route through the Karakorum Pass to Hotan, which became a major Buddhist center. Following the Silk Road into China, Buddhism quickly spread through the main trading centers with large foreign populations, notably Dunhuang, Chang'an, and Luoyang. From there it spread not only north to the Hsiung-nu and south below the Yangtze, but also around the coast of Korea and across the sea to Japan. By the mid-second century A.D., Luoyang had become a prime center for translating into Chinese the few Buddhist manuscripts brought east by the missionaries.

By the third century A.D., the balance of power along the Silk Road began to shift. In the Mediterranean, the Western Roman Empire had begun its decline, with the gold drain being no small contributor to it. The Eastern Roman Empire soon emerged as the new center of gravity, and Byzantium (later Constantinople, now Istanbul) and Antioch became the main termini for the Silk Road. Parthia was transformed into Persia, with an aggressive new dynasty, the Sassanids, annexing large portions of Kushan territory. Both the Kushans and Chinese were also assaulted by fresh waves of invaders from the northern steppes. In China itself, the Han dynasty disintegrated, being replaced by successive, relatively im-

potent dynasties. In the end the Hsiung-nu pushed so far south that they cut the Silk Road for a time, stopping the flow of great caravans. This was a sore blow to both the Roman Empire and China, which – in the absence of contact – would accumulate a host of outlandish myths about each other as the centuries went by. Sassanid Persia was less upset at the loss of the Silk Road, for it now controlled the sea route to the East, trading with southern China, which was dominant in this period. Jealous of its monopoly, Persia resisted full-scale trading over the overland route long after traffic resumed on the Silk Road.

This was the end of an era in more ways than one on the Silk Road. The invaders were destroyers, burning cities, including Luoyang, and making settled agriculture impossible in many of the Central Asian oases where Chinese garrisons had once farmed to provide food for travelers. Many fields that went out of cultivation never again felt the plow, for the Tarim basin was becoming increasingly arid. When trade once again revived among the

Within the mountains, local trade has always focused on the caravan stops, where goods are exchanged, here rice for wool. (Delia and Ferdinand Kuhn)

many petty states of Central Asia, the Northern Way around Loulan had become so arid that it was abandoned; instead the route left the Wall at Anxi and arced through Turfan before rejoining the old route through Kuga. That this was a more attractive route than the salt flats around Loulan is indicated by the Chinese name for the route: Road Through the Willows. When political conditions allowed, travelers often preferred the even more northerly route; at Hami (Kumul), they would head around the Tien Shan through the centers of Urumqi and Almalik west, skirting the Dzungarian Basin and the Kirghiz Steppes, toward Tashkent or the Sogdian stronghold of Samarkand. Central Asian traders tried various routes to Constantinople, for the Byzantines were continually trying to break Persia's monopoly on silk, which became increasingly rare and more expensive, while demand was rising, not least in the Christian churches. The Persians, through spies throughout their territory, tried equally hard to keep control of the profitable silk trade.

Through all these centuries, China had held tight the secret of silk-making. Then in the fifth century the technique began to leak out; exactly how is unclear. Many tell of a Chinese princess who brought to her bridegroom, the king of Hotan, the precious silkworms, carrying them inside her false wig. Because all Chinese women, including the nobility, were responsible for producing silk, she would have known the necessary techniques; somehow Hotan acquired the mulberry trees necessary for feeding the worms. A century later, Byzantium received the secret, reportedly when some monks carried westward some silkworms, hidden in a hollow cane. Persia gained the secret in the same period. But these people all produced inferior silk for many centuries, and China's silk continued in some demand.

The main traders on the Silk Road in these centuries were the Sogdians, whose language provided the common commercial argot of Central Asia. The Turks, a rising mixed group of northern nomads, were extending their control into Central Asia; but they were satisfied with tribute, leaving the Sogdians and the Bactrians to handle the silk trade. Going beyond simple trading, many Sogdians emigrated along the Silk Road to the East, bringing with them some innovations from the West. They built many underground canals in the eastern Tarim basin, which brought mountain water to irrigate dry lands while avoiding evaporation in the desert air. Such canals later fell into disrepair in Persia, but are still in use along the old Silk Road, making the Turfan Depression—one of the naturally dryest places in the world—a market garden for luscious fruits like melons and grapes. From the Sogdians, the Chinese learned the technique of making the special colored glass they so prized from the West; in the early seventh century they also learned to make the true porcelain for which they are rightly praised. As a result, they lost interest in Western glass and pottery. The Sogdians

also became famous as armorers, fusing Persian techniques with Turkish metalworking skills, becoming the main source of supply for the nomadic warriors to the north and bringing new styles of armor to China.

Throughout the turbulent centuries after the fall of the Han dynasty, China lay back within its shrunken borders, behind its fortified wall, which—not for the first time, or the last—served as much to keep Chinese people in as invaders out. Few Chinese ventured—or were allowed to travel—westward in these centuries. The exceptions were the intrepid Buddhist pilgrims who made their way—often on foot and alone—across Central Asia into India, there to find and bring back copies of religious texts, for the Chinese felt sorely the loss of contact with Indian Buddhists. Many pilgrims took years on their journeys, returning eventually either by sea, on the Spice Route ships, or overland, often detouring into the inaccessible mountains, as they followed the footsteps of Buddha. Pilgrims stopped at monasteries along the way, for months or years, to learn or study. In honor of their presence, religious convocations were often assembled for the sharing and celebration of the faith, as a Chinese pilgrim named Fa-Hsien found when he arrived in Kashgar in the fifth century A.D.:

> ...[the King] invites Shamans [Buddhists] from all quarters, and these collect together like clouds. The place where the priests are to sit is splendidly adorned beforehand with streaming pennants and canopies of silk; silk, embroidered with lotus flowers in gold and silver, is also laid over the backs of the seats. When all is in order, the king and his ministers make their offerings according to rite...[making] a vow to hand over those things as alms.

One of the best known of these Chinese Buddhist pilgrims is Hsüan-Tsang, who in the early seventh century decided to "travel in the countries of the west in order to question the wise men on the points that were troubling his mind." Defying the ban against travel, Hsüan-Tsang stole past the watchtowers that guarded the exits to the west, playing on the Buddhist sympathies of his captors to win his release when he was caught. Bereft of companions and guide, he set out alone with only vague directions for the nearest waterhole—and almost immediately dropped his water bag, spilling all of its precious contents. From there, he stumbled on, little knowing where he was going, as his biographer tells us:

> ...the trail being extremely circuitous he no longer knew which direction to follow. Looking around him in every direction, he could see only a limitless plain with no traces of either men or horses. During the night evil spirits shone torches as numerous as the stars; during the day terrible winds lifted the sand and scattered it like torrents of rain.

In the end, it was his horse who saved him, sniffing green pastures on the breeze and leading them both to water. From there they reached the first main oasis, Hami, and then proceeded to Turfan. To secure safe passage from the Turkish leader, Hsüan-Tsang threaded his way through the Tien Shan, where, he said:

> From the beginning of the world the snow has accumulated...and has turned into blocks of ice, which melt neither in springtime nor in summer. They roll away in boundless sheets of hard, gleaming white, losing themselves in the clouds...

Having gained his passport, he headed west, crossing the Talas and Jaxartes Rivers, and arriving in the Kizil Kum (Red Sand) desert of Sogdiana; this is how he found it:

> The road stretches as far as the eye can see and it is impossible to discern its limits. Only the sight of some high mountains in the distance and the discovery of some abandoned skeleton will show the direction to be taken and indicate the road one must follow...

Passing south he arrived at the more hospitable region of Samarkand, which possessed "vast quantities of rare and precious merchandise." The oasis was especially attractive after his passage through the desert.

> The soil is rich and fertile; all types of seed grow there in abundance, the forests are magnificent in their vegetation, and prodigious quantities of flowers and fruit are to be found in the country...

Samarkand was, at this time, a center of the Zoroastrian religion, which had arisen many centuries before in Bactria and Persia; but the Sogdians were hospitable to Buddhists, with whom they traded, and guided Hsüan-Tsang on his way.

While Silk Road traders would generally travel west from Samarkand, Hsüan-Tsang's destination lay to the south, along one of the minor routes through the Pamirs,

In the high, arid valleys east of Balkh, camel caravans still follow the line of the old Silk Road. (Delia and Ferdinand Kuhn)

389

through a pass called the Iron Gate—for once literally, not figuratively, as his biographer relates:

> The paths through these mountains are deep and dangerous. Once engaged upon them the traveler finds neither water nor vegetation. After a journey of three hundred *li* through the middle of these mountains he enters the Gates of Iron. These are the gorges between two mountain masses which rise to right and left to a prodigious height. They are separated only by a path which besides being extremely narrow is fraught with precipices. On either side of these, mountains form huge walls of rock the color of iron. The rocks in fact contain iron ore. At the entrance a double door has been erected and above are hung a multitude of little bells of cast or wrought iron. And because the passage is difficult and well defended it received the name which it still has to this day. This is the barrier against the advance of the Turks.

In truth, however, the Turks had already extended their influence to the south, for Hsüan-Tsang brought greetings from the north to the Turkish leader of Balkh (as Bactra was now known). Built on a "magnificent plateau," Balkh was "truly a privileged land," for he found "the plains and adjacent valleys are quite exceptionally fertile."

There followed a 15-year sojourn, in which Hsüan-Tsang criss-crossed the holy trails of India before heading homeward once again. Rather than returning through Bactra, he chose to cross the fearsome Hindu Kush, which he called the Snowy Mountains. The way was indeed tortuous. Of the highest mountain on the route, he noted: "So high was this peak that the frozen clouds and the wind-driven snow did not even reach its peak." Even in these ranges and the Pamirs that followed, Hsüan-Tsang and the small caravan of traders he had joined were not free from attack by robbers; in the end, they came through safely, however, and arrived at Yarkand, proposing to return to China by the Southern Way. Still a prime source for jade, Hotan most impressed Hsüan-Tsang as a Buddhist center. Leaving Hotan, he found the route affected by the increasing aridity of the Takla Makan:

> Going east from...[Hotan] we enter a great drifting sand desert. These sands extend like a drifting flood for a great distance, piled up or scattered according to the wind. There is no trace left behind by travelers, and oftentimes the way is lost, and so they wander hither and thither quite bewildered, without any guide or direction. So travelers pile up the bones of animals as beacons. There is neither water nor herbage to be found, and hot winds frequently blow. When these winds rise, then both men and beasts become confused and forgetful, and then they remain perfectly disabled. At times sad and plaintive notes are heard and piteous cries, so that between the sights and sounds of the desert men get confused and know not whither they go. Hence there are so many who perish in the journey.

Hsüan-Tsang reached Qarqan without incident, however, and then proceeded to Dunhuang. There he waited to see if he would be welcomed—or arrested for contravening the travel ban. Luckily, in the 16 years that had passed, the emperor's anger had abated; indeed, word of his great trip spread throughout the capital of Chang'an and when he arrived he found "the rumor of his arrival had spread like lightning and the streets were filled with an immense multitude of people eager to set eyes on him."

Hsüan-Tsang recorded a world of change. Buddhism, which had been dominant in Central and East Asia for centuries, was beginning to decline, especially in its homeland, India; soon it would be under heavy attack from either end of the Silk Road. He also traveled the Silk Road as China was recovering from several centuries of disorder and confusion. Within Hsüan-Tsang's lifetime, China had united under the new T'ang dynasty, ushering in a golden age that would last for three centuries, while Turkish control of Central Asia collapsed. Emboldened, China once again spread beyond its walls; by the eighth century, it had spread north past the Issyk Kul to Lake Balkhash and west to the Talas and Jaxartes Rivers, where the powerful Ferghana horses still roamed. It was in this period that Central Asia began to be called Sinkiang (New Dominion), signifying China's revival. Its influence extended even further. Kings of Samarkand ascended their thrones only with Chinese approval, and the always troublesome Tibetans, who had long since accepted Buddhism from India, acknowledged China's power by accepting a Chinese princess as a bride for their king.

Under the T'angs, China was open to the world. Jugglers, singers, acrobats, dancers, actors, and magicians from Syria, Bactria, and India made their way across the Silk Road to entertain the Chinese (as a few of their counterparts had done centuries before in Roman times). Scholars and monks, who came from the West to study the ways of the East, found there cosmopolitan intellectual communities, including Koreans, Japanese, Tibetans, and Annamese (Vietnamese), as well as Chinese. Missionaries and refugees of various religions found a haven here. The Zoroastrian religion, which had arrived from Persia in the fifth century, was protected under the T'angs. When the Nestorians were expelled from the Christian church as heretics in the seventh century, many of them migrated from Syria to China; their arrival in Chang'an was even celebrated on a stele, which survived into modern times. The Chinese Emperor himself decreed that the Nestorian Christians should be free to practice and spread their religion, noting:

> The way has more than one name, and wise men have more than one method. Knowledge is such that it may suit all countries, so that all creatures may be saved. The virtuous...[Nestorians] came from afar, bringing books and pictures to our capital...it is right that this teaching should spread freely through the world.

Manichaeism, too, which would convulse the inquisitors of Europe for many centuries, found a home in T'ang China. Among these seekers of religious freedom were many merchants, who continued to trade along the Silk Road, their Western dialects mixing with those of Central and Eastern Asia.

The seventh century was a time of great change on the western end of the Silk Road as well. The Byzantine and Persian Empires had for centuries been in conflict, especially over Persia's monopoly on the silk trade; at times the Persians cut off the overland route altogether, supplying Byzantium only through the Spice Route. Over time, however, the continual struggle weakened them both and made them prey to a new power from Arabia: Islam. In just a few decades, the Moslems swept through Persian territory, making most of it their own, but leaving parts semi-independent, under the influence of Byzantium. Prime among these were Tabiristan, which ran around the southern rim of the Caspian Sea, and Armenia, between the Caspian and Black seas. The route from the East, around or across the Caspian to Tabriz or Artaxata (formerly a main silk mart between the Byzantines and the Persians) was temporarily in Byzantine hands. But not for long. By the middle of the eighth century the Arabs had completed ingesting the former Persian territories and had

even laid unsuccessful siege against Constantinople itself. Moving eastward, the Moslems and their new allies, the Tibetans, met the advance guard of the Chinese at the Talas River in 751. The Chinese were defeated, but the Arabs did not pursue them, the Talas River marking the dividing line between them for some time. One of the unanticipated results of the battle was that a number of skilled Chinese silk-weavers and papermakers were captured and taken to Syria, where they began to produce high-quality silk cloth and introduced Eastern papermaking to the West.

The various contenders on the western end of the Silk Road turned to China for help against each other. Persia had kept up diplomatic relations with China even while trade was suspended; when its king lost his throne to the Moslems, he found refuge in Chang'an (as did the last ruler of independent Tabiristan). Byzantium, bemoaning the severing of the Silk Road, tried to open a new northern route to China; but the Eurasian Steppe was too unsettled to be a reliable trade route. The Chinese received embassies from Fu-lin (Byzantium, or the Eastern Roman Empire) for centuries, but the proposed alliance came to naught. The great days of the silk trade were over, if only because Byzantium was able to supply sufficient silk to Europe, now poor and in disarray.

Silk Road traders are met by a Turkish chief on the shores of the Caspian Sea. (19th century, authors' archives)

Filing across the Iranian plateau, this caravan is headed for the caravanserai on the right. (By Engelbert Kaempfer, c. 1680, MS. Sloane 5232, British Library)

In any case, the Moslems themselves soon established relations with China. Within four decades of the Battle of the Talas River, the two were allied against the unruly Tibetans, who still harassed the Silk Road. While silk was no longer the prime product it once was, the Moslems found other things of value in the East. The Prophet Mohammed himself had said: "Seek for Learning, though it be as far away as China." Although most trade between Arabs and Chinese was carried on through the Spice Route, the overland Silk Road saw merchants, scholars, and travelers passing back and forth for centuries. These were sad days for the Buddhist religion, however. Where the Moslems came, they destroyed the—to them—idolatrous temples, leaving parts of ancient and beautiful cities like Balkh in ruins. In China, too, the old tolerance waned. In 845 A.D., the Confucians, powerful in the Chinese bureaucracy, outlawed all other religions; temples were smashed, and monks and nuns shorn of their religious mantles. Buddhism, Nestorian Christianity, and most other religions that had found a haven in China survived but never recovered their former strength.

This was a last ditch effort by the T'ang dynasty, however. Faced with internal revolts throughout its empire, China increasingly called on northern peoples to help

it restore order. In 755, Uighur Turks, from the Turfan region, helped put down a revolt in Chang'an, the capital itself. When, in the following century, the T'ang dynasty expired and China broke apart, a Turkish regime took the eastern end of the Silk Rod, shifting the capital to Kaifeng, east of Luoyang, near where the Huang River has split and shifted its course over the centuries. The Sung dynasty later established unity in central and southern China, but northern China was divided under the domination of various northern peoples for some centuries. In the first half of the 10th century, one Chinese general, attempting to remove the Turks from the Huang region, called for aid from a Mongol people called the Khitans, from Manchuria, north of the Gulf of Bo Hai. They came—and they stayed. Though the Khitans ruled only part of the Silk Road, sharing the eastern end of that route with other non-Chinese peoples, they were the first Mongols to rule in China, situating their capital north of the fortified wall and west of Bo Hai. Their name—in its Turkish form, Khitai—came to be applied to northern China and would be transformed by the Europeans into the romantic name of Cathay. The Sung, failing to win back its northern territories from these invaders, sued for peace, paying large amounts of tribute—mostly gold and silk—for centuries, to keep China's borders free from raids.

This was not, however, a time of barbarism along the eastern half of the Silk Road. The rougher peoples who settled along the route became increasingly sinicized, adopting not only Chinese technology but also the Buddhist religion, which was still very much alive in this period. Like their Christian contemporaries in Europe, Buddhist monks in Central Asia copied and recopied sacred texts, preserving them for posterity. It was during this time that the vast storehouse of manuscripts was collected in Dunhuang, some of them translations of Buddhist texts by Hsüan-Tsang himself, the room being sealed up—probably in some time of momentary danger—around 1015 A.D. In the 12th century, the Sung dynasty repeated the mistake it had made with the Khitans; it invited the Jurchens, an unbridled nomadic people from Siberia, far to the north, to help them drive out the Khitans. The Jurchens did so, and more, pushing the Sung south toward the Yangtze. This left the Silk Road completely in "foreign" hands. The Jurchens—quickly adopting Chinese coloration—founded the Chin dynasty, which stretched from Manchuria to the Huang and Wei Valleys. To their west were the Tibetans, with their Hsi-Hsia dynasty, reaching as far as the Jade Gate. Some Khitans emigrated to west, settling from the Corridor to the Oxus River,

while others remained in their homeland north of the Chin territory.

The Europeans knew little of all this, for they had long since lost contact with the East. Some trade goods, though much less than in previous times, had continued to filter through Moslem lands even in the early centuries of expansion, but—like the Persians before them—the Moslems blocked direct European access to the East. Instead, Syrians, Jews, and Greeks played their old roles as carriers, go-betweens for the Moslem and Christian worlds. This trade was temporarily disrupted in the 11th century when the Seljuk Turks irrupted from the Iranian Plateau onto the Mesopotamian plain. The Turks quickly adopted the higher culture of the people they had conquered, but in their case it took a fanatical twist. In Tabiristan, where the Silk Road passes south of the Caspian Sea, they founded a secret sect called the Assassins, whose use of murder as a weapon of political control has passed their name into our modern language. Further to their west, religious zeal caused these recent Moslem converts to bar Christian pilgrims from the holy places of the Near East. In response, the Europeans launched the Crusades, which resulted in a number of Christian states along the Syrian and Palestinian coasts. When trade later resumed, goods traveled along the western part of the Silk

Invaders from the steppe enter partly ruined Samarkand. (Authors' archives)

393

With the great days of the Silk Road long past, the bazaar in early 20th century Yarkand was more shabby than exotic. (Royal Geographic Society)

Road to Antioch (center of one Crusader's state), or via the northern route to Trebizond; they were then ferried to Europe in ships of the rising city-states of Italy, notably Genoa, Venice, and Pisa. When, in the 13th century, the Christian foothold in Syria was in danger, Europeans—like so many before them—attempted to find an ally on the far side of the Iranian Plateau. The Silk Road being closed, they sent their emissaries by the Eurasian Steppe Route—but their aim was not China. It was the rising new power in Central Asia: the Mongols.

In the first decade of the 13th century, a young leader named Temujin succeeded in uniting the disparate Mongol tribes of the Eurasian Steppe. Taking the name of Genghis Khan, he orchestrated one of the most astonishing series of military conquests in history. Within two decades the Mongols had swept westward, along the most northern course of the Silk Road, to Balkh and then on to Rayy (formerly Rhagae, near modern Tehran) and through Armenia to Tabriz and Tiflis in the Caucasus Mountains. (In a later wave, the Mongols exterminated the Assassins in this region, but, unfortunately, not their contribution to world politics.) In the same period, Genghis Khan pushed down through the Hindu Kush into India and began his drive toward China, in this first bite taking the Chin territory north of the Huang He. His successors quickly drove across the Eurasian Steppe as far

as Hungary. China, though closer to the Mongolian homeland, was conquered more slowly but more completely; by 1260, the Mongols had reunited China under a new dynasty: the Yuans. For the first—and last—time in history, virtually the whole Silk Road was in the hands of one power; although others held the Syrian coast, travelers could simply enter the Mongol-controlled Silk Road from the north, through Trebizond. More to the point, the Mongol Empire was open to the world, welcoming traders, envoys, and missionaries from abroad. For one brief century—the Pax Mongolica or Pax Tatarica between 1260 and 1368—travelers could cross the great land mass by not one but two routes: the Silk Road and the more northerly Eurasian Steppe Route. Indeed, since the Mongol headquarters was in Karakorum, and they made their Chinese capital in the northern city of Beijing (Peking), the Eurasian Steppe Route was, in some ways, far more important in this period. But the Silk Road had the weight of history and romance about it—and it had the benefit of a unique chronicler, Marco Polo, who gave us an invaluable picture of the route.

In the memoirs related to his secretary, Rustichello, Marco Polo shows the changes that had been wrought over the centuries. Entering the Silk Road in Armenia, he found that many cities in the region produced silk in abundance and weaving as fine as he had seen anywhere—a far cry from the Byzantine Empire of a millennium earlier, starved for silk. Passing through Tabriz he found:

The city is so favorably situated that it is a market for merchandise from India and Baghdad, from Mosul and Hormuz, and from many other places; and many Latin [Italian] merchants come here to buy merchandise imported from foreign lands.

On the Iranian Plateau, he found the local people had built a reputation for breeding horses, which they exported to India, and asses, which they supplied to traders on the Silk Road. These Polo found to be the "finest asses in the world"; the reasons were clear:

This is because they eat little, carry heavy loads, and travel long distances in a single day, enduring toil beyond the power of horses or mules. For the merchants of these parts, when they travel from one country to another, traverse vast deserts, that is to say dry, barren, sandy regions, producing no grass or fodder suitable for horses, and the wells and sources of fresh water lie so far apart that they must travel by long stages if their beasts are to have anything to drink. Since horses cannot endure this, the merchants use only these asses, because they are swift coursers and steady amblers, besides being less costly to keep...They also use camels, which likewise carry heavy loads and are cheap to maintain.

The Mongol—or, as he says, Tartar—rule had imposed some order along the route, he found:

Among the people of these kingdoms [of Persia] there are many who are brutal and bloodthirsty. They are forever slaughtering one another; and, were it not for fear of the government...they would do great mischief to traveling merchants. The government imposes severe penalties upon them and has ordered that along all dangerous routes the inhabitants at the request of the merchants shall supply good and efficient escorts from district to district for their safe conduct on payment of two or three groats for each loaded beast according to the length of the journey. Yet, for all that the government can do, these brigands are not to be deterred from frequent depradations. Unless the merchants are well-armed and equipped with bows, they slay and harry them unsparingly.

Passing across the Iranian Plateau, into the Pamirs and out into Sinkiang, Polo was struck time and again with the contrasts between the valley oases "where there is rich herbage, fine pasturage, fruit in plenty, and no lack of anything" and the long stretches of desert in which no water or even habitation was to be found. We also see, from Polo and from the writings of the indefatigable Moslem traveler Ibn Battuta 50 years later, pictures of once-great cities gone to ruin. Of Balkh, Polo found:

It used to be much greater and more splendid; but the Tartars and other invaders have sacked and ravaged it. For I can tell you that there used to be many fine palaces and mansions of marble, which are still to be seen, but shattered now and in ruins.

Not only were the old Buddhist temples gone, but the Moslem mosques—themselves now centuries old—were pulled down as well. Further north, Ibn Battuta found the same to be true:

...[Bukhara] was laid in ruins by the accursed Tankiz [Genghis], the Tatar...So at the present time its mosques, colleges and bazaars are in ruins, all but a few...

Elsewhere Ibn Battuta reported that this devastation was in punishment against the Moslems who had revolted against Mongol rule. Genghis had, he said, pardoned Bukhara and Samarkand, and much of the ruination had simply occurred over time. In Samarkand, "one of the greatest and finest cities, and most perfect of them in beauty," he found:

There were formerly great palaces on its bank, and constructions which bear witness to the lofty aspirations of the townsfolk, but most of this is obliterated, and most of the city itself has also fallen into ruins. It has no city wall, and no gates, and there are gardens inside it...

While Ibn Battuta left the Silk Road to enter India, Marco Polo continued on, giving us a picture of the Southern Way along the Takla Makan, 1,500 years after China had opened the way west. First he had to pass through the Pamirs, a region of "many narrow passes and natural fortresses, so that the inhabitants are not afraid of any invader breaking in to molest them. Their cities and towns are built on mountain tops or sites of great natural strength." Unlike many earlier chroniclers, especially the Chinese, Polo had mostly good words to say about the Pamirs, raving about the "lush growth," the "copious springs of the purest waters," the choice trout and other fish, and especially the pure, salubrious mountain air; his attitude perhaps stems from the fact that, fallen sick with a fever, he recuperated here and came to love—and adjust to—the people and the mountains.

The Mongols at this time had no one religion but honored the holy days of all to win favor from all the gods, so Polo reported. Such an attitude must have found favor in Sinkiang, where Polo found Moslems mixed with Nestorian Christians and "idolators," mostly Buddhists. He also encountered this variety of religions in Hotan, which he found "amply stocked with the means of life," with "vineyards, estates, and orchards in plenty." The same was true in Qarqan, which "used to be a splendid and fruitful country, but...much devastated by the Tartars." Like Silk Road travelers for centuries before him, he was dismayed at the prospect of crossing the salt flats of the Lop Nor desert:

> After leaving Charchan [Qarqan], the road runs for fully five days through sandy wastes, where the water is bad and bitter, except in a few places...At the end of the five days' journey...is a city which stands on the verge of the Great Desert. It is here that men take in provisions for crossing the desert...

There travelers rested for a week "to refresh themselves and their beasts." Such preparations were necessary because they had to travel "for a day and a night" between water holes; even then the water is often "bitter and brackish" and sufficient only for small parties of 50 to 100 men and their animals.

Polo also had to face the old fears—real and imaginary—always inspired by the towering, shifting dunes of the desert:

> When a man is riding by night through this desert and something happens to make him loiter and lose touch with his companions, by dropping asleep or for some other reason, and afterwards he wants to rejoin them, then he hears spirits talking in such a way that they seem to be his companions. Sometimes, indeed, they even hail him by name. Often these voices make him stray from the path, so that he never finds it again. And in this way many travelers have been lost and have perished. And sometimes in the night they are conscious of a noise like the clatter of a great cavalcade of riders away from the road; and, believing that these are some of their own company, they go where they hear the noise and, when day breaks, find they are victims of an illusion and in an awkward plight. And there are some who, in crossing this desert, have seen a host of men coming towards them and, suspecting that they were robbers, have taken flight; so, having left the beaten track and not knowing how to return to it, they have gone helplessly astray. Yes, and even by daylight men hear these spirit voices, and often you fancy you are listening to the strains of many instruments, especially drums, and the clash of arms. For this reason bands of travelers make a point of keeping very close together. Before they go to sleep they set up a sign pointing in the direction in which they have to travel. And round the necks of all their beasts they fasten little bells, so that by listening to the sound they may prevent them from straying off the path.

So far, Polo had followed the old main route of the Silk Road. But now he diverged to the north. The once-great cities of Dunhuang, Chang'an, Luoyang, and Kaifeng rated not even a mention. The change had come with the Mongols, who shifted the political center of China to the north, closer to their homeland. Their summer capital,

the famous Shang-tu (Xanadu), was out on the Mongolian plateau. Their winter capital and main administrative center lay between the Gulf of Bo Hai and the top of the Huang's great loop. The Mongols call it Khanbaligh (City of the Khan); the Chinese called it Ta-tu (Great Capital); in modern times it would be known as Beijing (Peking, or Northern Capital) or Beibing (Peiping, or Northern Peace). The eastern end of the old Silk Road now sank into relative insignificance as travelers focused on this new northern center.

Even so, for the Silk Road, the Mongol period was a last bright flash before darkness descended. With the accession of the Ming dynasty in 1368, the Silk Road was finished. Under the Mings, China was closed behind its borders tighter than ever before. Foreigners were driven from the land and kept out by new-built stone fortifications that would become world-famous as the Great Wall. Beyond the wall, Islam spread inexorably, by the 15th century being adopted by the Mongols and their successors, the Turks, and expunging most traces of the once-great Buddhist civilization that had flourished there. Under the Ch'ing dynasty of the Manchus, which replaced the Ming in the 17th century, China would once gain expand westward into Central Asia. But the old land route never revived. Northern Europe, not the Mediterranean, was now the major market. Had the Eurasian continent been at peace, the more natural overland route would have been the Eurasian Steppe Route. As it was, European ships sailing around the Cape of Good Hope largely replaced the old caravan routes.

By the 19th century, Central Asia was in the hands of mostly Mongolian or Turkic peoples in variety of small states, including Kokand, Bukhara, and Khiva, near the mouth of the Oxus River. China having relaxed her weak hold on these territories, the Europeans regarded them as potentially easy conquests during what was known as "The Great Game." Russians moving down from the Eurasian Steppe into the region now called Turkestan, and Britons crossing the Karakorum Mountains (the main route through Balkh being blocked by Afghans), braved fiercely antagonistic nomads and brigands to explore the desert heartland of Asia—to their own potential advantage. What they found was a world of much crudeness and little grace. The great days of the past had long since been forgotten, along with the remains of many once-prosperous settlements. What had not been destroyed by the iconoclastic Moslems was often covered by the drifting sands of the Takla Makan. The unlettered nomads carried with them only superstitious tales of hundreds of cities buried in the sand for religious perfidy—and of the horrible retribution awaiting anyone who attempted to dig for the treasure lying under the dunes.

It was tales such as these that attracted "foreign devils" to the route of the old Silk Road (which, indeed, was so dubbed only in this period). The Swedish explorer

Sven Hedin crossed the Karakorum to retrace the route of the old silk caravans, uncovering the buried caravan post of Loulan, near the Lop Nor desert; Aurel Stein made his discoveries at Dunhuang and elsewhere; and Europeans and East Asians began to race each other to find and cart off Central Asia's forgotten treasures.

But while the writings of these explorers brought the Silk Road back into the world's attention, there was no bringing it back to life. When the various principalities of Central Asia were once again brought under the rein of a few great powers, these had little love for each other. By the mid-20th century, China had once again expanded into Sinkiang, past Kashgar to the borders of Ferghana, home of the famous horses; in addition to Manchuria and Inner Mongolia, it had annexed Tibet, destroying many of the Buddhist temples that had survived over the centuries. West of that, the great Silk Road cities of Tashkent, Samarkand, Bukhara, and Merv, plus the Caucasus region on the far side of the Caspian, all were under the dominion of the Soviet Union. Afghanistan and Iran barred the rest of the once-traditional routes to the Mediterranean and India. Political borders led to strange choices, however. In modern times, with other routes foreclosed, the Karakorum Highway snakes across the mountains of Kashmir from Kashgar to Pakistan, China's only ally in a hostile land.

Even today, however, travelers still need their wits about them to travel on the old routes. On the heights of the Karakorum Highway, avalanches are routine and can wipe away a motor convoy as easily as they once did a camel caravan. And whether aboard a camel or a Land Rover, a traveler is wise to beware the dangerous mirages of the Takla Makan.

Selective Bibliography

Ibn Battuta. *Travels, A.D. 1325–1354,* in three vols. Translated by H. A. R. Gibb (Cambridge: University Press, 1958–71). Hakluyt Society Publications, Second Series. A fine edition, with helpful maps.

Blunt, Wilfrid. *The Golden Road to Samarkand* (New York: Viking, 1973). A well-illustrated work focusing on famous personages on the Silk Road, from Alexander to Aurel Stein.

Boulnois, L. *The Silk Road.* Translated from the French by Dennis Chamberlin (London: George Allen & Unwin, 1966). A helpful, somewhat idiosyncratically organized review of the route in classical and early medieval times.

Cable, Mildred, and Francesca French. *Through Jade Gate and Central Asia: An Account of Journeys in Kansu, Turkestan, and the Gobi Desert* (Boston: Houghton Mifflin, 1927). Travels by missionaries in China.

de Gaury, Gerald and H. V. F. Winstone, eds. *The Road to Kabul: An Anthology* (London: Quartet Books, 1981). Excerpts of works by modern travelers in Central Asia.

Edwardes, Michael. *East-West Passage: The Travel of Ideas, Arts, and Inventions between Asia and the Western World* (New York: Taplinger, 1971). An interesting review of cross-connections, weighted somewhat toward the modern period.

Grousset, René. *The Empire of the Steppes: A History of Central Asia.* Translated from the French by Naomi Walford (New Brunswick, New Jersey: Rutgers University Press, 1970). A detailed, comprehensive, classic political history.

———. *In the Footsteps of the Buddha.* Translated from the French by J. A. Underwood (New York: Grossman, 1971). Outlines the spread of Buddhism and the role of the great pilgrims of the East.

Hambly, Gavin, et al. *Central Asia* (London: Weidenfeld & Nicolson, 1969). Volume 16 of the publisher's Universal History. A political history by many hands, stressing modern times.

Hedin, Sven. *The Silk Road* (New York: Dutton, 1938). An account of his retracing of the route.

Herrmann, Albert. *An Historical Atlas of China,* New Edition (Edinburgh: Edinburgh University Press, 1966). An extremely useful, detailed work.

Hirth, F. *China and the Roman Orient: Researches into the Ancient and Medieval Relations as Represented in Old Chinese Records* (New York: Paragon, 1966; reprint of the 1885 Shanghai edition). Reprints and translates some basic texts, stressing identification of references to Western places and artifacts.

Hopkirk, Peter. *Foreign Devils on the Silk Road: The Search for the Lost Cities and Treasures of Chinese Central Asia* (London: John Murray, 1980). Focuses on the modern rediscoverers.

Hudson, G. F. *Europe and China: A Survey of Their Relations from the Earliest Times to 1800* (Boston: Beacon Press, 1961; reprint of the 1931 edition, London: Edward Arnold). An invaluable overview.

Journey Into China (Washington, D. C.: *National Geographic Society,* 1982). An unusually well-illustrated popular work, with sections on the Silk Road and the Great Wall.

Lattimore, Owen and Eleanor Lattimore, eds. *Silks, Spices and Empire: Asia Seen Through the Eyes of Its Discoverers* (New York: Delacorte Press, 1968). Part of the Great Explorers series. Selections of first-hand accounts from classical to modern times, with useful editorial overview and comments.

Legg, Stuart. *The Heartland* (New York: Capricorn, 1971). A useful history primarily of the modern period.

Miller, J. Innes. *The Spice Trade of the Roman Empire, 29 B.C.-A.D. 641* (Oxford: Clarendon Press, 1969). Has a scope far wider than the title might indicate, including sections on the trade routes and the carriers.

Mirsky, Jeannette, ed. *The Great Chinese Travelers* (New York: Pantheon, 1964). Well-edited firsthand accounts, longer but fewer in number than in the Lattimore work.

Needham, Joseph. *Science and Civilization in China* (Cambridge: The University Press, 1965–   ). Volume 1 of this incomparable work contains a useful historical overview of China's contacts with the West.

Polo, Marco. *The Travels.* Translated by Ronald Latham. (Harmondsworth, Middlesex: Penguin, 1958). A very readable translation of the classic work, with helpful introduction, notes, and index.

Rostovtzeff, M. *Caravan Cities* (Oxford: Clarendon, 1932). Includes an historical survey of the caravan trade, focusing on Mesopotamia.

Schreiber, Hermann. *The History of Roads: From Amber Route to Motorway.* Translated from the German by Stewart Thomson (London: Barrie and Rockliff, 1961). Includes two chapters on the Central Asian caravan routes.

Severin, Timothy. *The Oriental Adventure: Explorers of the East* (Boston: Little, Brown, 1976). Focuses on European travelers in the East, from Marco Polo on.

Stein, Sir Aurel. *On Ancient Central-Asian Tracks: Brief Narrative of Three Expeditions in Innermost Asia and Northwestern China.* Edited by Jeannette Mirsky (New York: Pantheon, 1965). A popular account of his journeys and discoveries.

Teggart, Frederick J. *Rome and China: A Study of Correlations in Historical Events* (Berkeley, California: University of California Press, 1939). A unique work, comparing the effects on each of events in Central Asia, focusing on 58 B.C. to A.D. 107

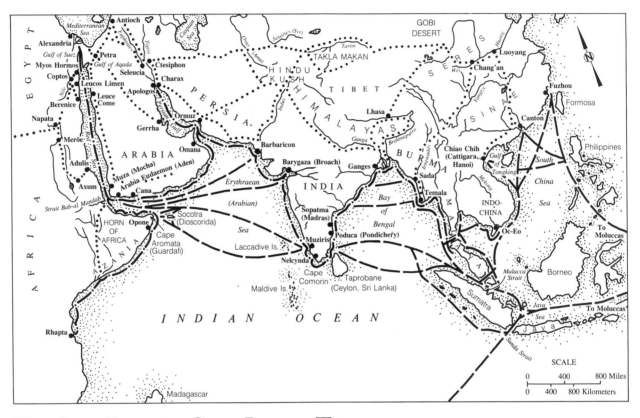

The Spice Route in Greco-Roman Times

—·—·— Early Sea Routes   · · · · · · Main Connecting Land Routes

— — — Sea Routes in Roman Times   ⟊ Main Portages

The Spice Route

*A*lmost 1,000 years before the birth of Christ, King Solomon of Israel and the Phoenician king Hiram of Tyre embarked on a famous joint venture, as related in 1 Kings 9 and 10:

> And King Solomon made a navy of ships in Ezion-geber [Aqaba]...on the shore of the Red Sea...And Hiram sent in the navy his servants, shipmen that had knowledge of the sea, with the servants of Solomon. And they came to Ophir, and fetched from hence gold...[and] algum trees and precious stones... Once in three years came the navy...bringing gold, and silver, ivory, and apes, and peacocks.

King Solomon, rich in his own right, needed the help of the Phoenicians because his land—indeed most of the land around the Red Sea and Persian Gulf—had no trees fit for ships, and, therefore, no skilled shipbuilders or sailors. King Hiram, drawing on long experience and on the famous cedars of Lebanon for wood, had both.

The destination of this expedition is unknown. Some believe that Ophir was on the East African coast, on or past the Horn of Africa, which juts out into the sea toward the Arabian Peninsula. Certainly that area was long an international trading center—for how long no one knows for sure—where goods from India and further east reached Western markets. The tip of the horn itself—now called Cape Guardafi—was known as Cape Aromata or the Cape of Spices. Others believe that Ophir was on the

west Indian coast, citing the particular mix of goods brought back by the expeditions and the length of time between trips. Some have even suggested that Ophir—or another of their destinations, Tarshish—was on the metal-rich Burmese-Malayan peninsula. Wherever Ophir was located, however, it was clearly goods from India and further east that were the magnet. The Western desire for Eastern goods laid the basis for the fabled Spice Route, a route so important in history that in Renaissance times, when the Moslem-controlled Near East made duties on these goods prohibitive, Europeans were forced to look for other routes to the East—the result being the discovery of the sea route around Africa and of the Americas.

The Spice Route linked the great civilizations of the Mediterranean, India, and Southeast Asia for thousands of years. What made this long-distance sea route possible was the Indian Ocean's pattern of monsoons that change direction twice a year, providing a steady northeast wind during winter and a reliable, though sometimes too-strong southwest wind during summer and early autumn. With these trade winds, even early sailors in primitive vessels could travel far over the seas.

The Spice Route itself was not a single sea lane, but more resembled a spider's web caught in the middle, or an old-fashioned child's "cat's cradle," with routes feeding in from east and west to India at the center. From the west, the route ran from the Red Sea and Persian Gulf, on either side of the Arabian Peninsula, and from the east coast of

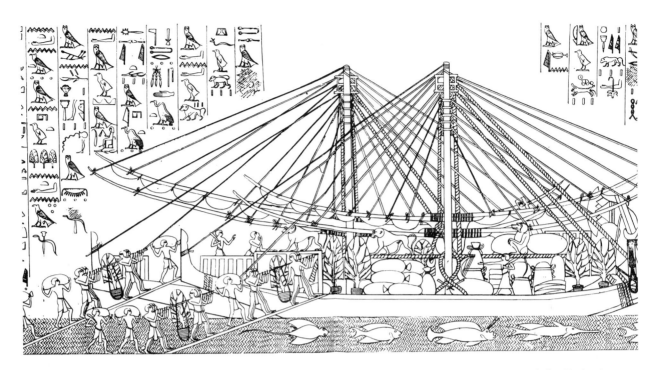

Queen Hatshepsut's expedition to the land of Punt was commemorated on a relief near Thebes in the 2nd century B.C., the basis for this drawing. (Authors' archives)

Africa as far south as Madagascar, these strands all crossing the Arabian Sea and twining together at the tip of the Indian Peninsula, between the mainland and the island of Ceylon. From the east, the route ran from China, Indochina, and the many islands of the Malay Archipelago (East Indies), either through the Malacca Strait between the Malayan Peninsula and Sumatra or through the Sunda Strait between the islands of Sumatra and Java; both routes crossed the Bay of Bengal to converge also at southern India. An errant strand of the route in some periods ran directly between East Africa and the Malay Archipelago. One group among these islands, the Moluccas, was later called the Spice Islands, giving the Spice Route its name. But, in truth, spices and other luxuries came from many parts of Southeast Asia for hungry Western buyers, who often had little but gold and silver to trade in return, except for ivory, ebony, and slaves they brought from Africa for the purpose.

The peoples at the western end of the Spice Route seem to have begun their seafaring activities before the always more self-sufficient Chinese. From southern Mesopotamia, the Sumerian people of Ur were trading with various ports along the Persian Gulf 5,000 years ago. Among Ur's main trading partners seem to have been the city of Dilmun, most likely the island of Bahrain, partway down the west side of the Gulf; the port of Magan, possibly near Muscat on the Omani coast; and a place called Melukkha, which was probably in the Indus Valley. Indian teak—an exceptionally hard wood, abundant on the

Malabar coast of southwest India—was used in buildings of Ur as early as 3000 B.C.

The Egyptians were also very early long-distance traders with the fabled land of Punt. The trade at first was overland, from the Upper Nile Valley, and was old by 2800 B.C., when the Egyptians decided to bypass the land route, sending expeditions down the Red Sea to Punt, whose location is unknown. Punt was mostly likely in East Africa or southwest Arabia, but may be a general term for the whole region, like "Asia." Egyptian hieroglyphics record that "a command was heard from the great throne, an oracle of the god himself, that the ways of Punt should be searched out, that the highways to the *'ntyw* [probably myrrh or frankincense] terraces should be penetrated." In addition to *'ntyw*, Egyptians also brought home ebony, ivory, gold, cinnamon wood (though perhaps not "true" cinnamon as we now know it), and two varieties of incense. At some point in the next millennium, they began receiving goods that were native only to India or places further east, including true cinnamon; in about 1500 B.C., for example, Queen Hatshepsut's expedition to Punt brought back a load of cinnamon, which was heavily used in embalming. The Egyptian and Israeli names for several special items of trade—including peacocks, cinnamon, apes, rice, and sandalwood—came from the Tamil dialects of southern India (not the northern dialects one would expect if the goods had arrived overland). So it seems likely that, at a very early period, traders—many of them probably Indian—operated in Arabian waters. Southern Arabians seem to have already been operating as middlemen, transshipping eastern goods along with their own spices along the Incense Road up the west coast of Arabia.

Lacking wood with which to build ships and metals appropriate to form nails, the early peoples of Arabia, Egypt, and Mesopotamia used reed boats or raftlike craft built of inflated animal skins stretched on pieces of precious wood. Later, when they imported wood from elsewhere, they generally used twine to bind their boats together; even into modern times Arabian boats were generally sewn, rather than nailed together. Indian sailors were better off, having ready supplies of hardwoods suited for use in tropical waters, which quickly caused most

woods to rot. Even so, the earliest vessels were not strong enough to stand up well against rough seas and generally hugged the coastlines on their trading runs.

The Red Sea and Persian Gulf posed many problems for early sailors. Drinking water was scarce, with much of the coastline desert. Piracy was common from early times, for the many islands in the area acted as ideal shelter for brigands. In addition, the Red Sea has hazardous coral reefs and a year-round northerly wind for its 1,200-mile length, making any Egypt-bound voyage difficult; certainly stories of shipwrecked sailors on Red Sea expeditions go back to the third millennium B.C. Partly because of these problems, the Egyptians very early

This Spice Route sailor is being rescued not only from drowning but also from the jaws of a fearsome shark. (From Borobudur, Java, 8th century A.D.)

403

opened up a caravan route along a *wadi* (a usually-dry streambed) between the Red Sea and the Nile, where the river bends to within 100 miles of the seashore; they provided wells and stations along the way for a caravan's five-to-six-day trek, generally between the seaport of Leucos Limen (White Harbor) and the city of Coptos, where it joined other goods from inland Africa being taken down the Nile to Memphis.

The Egyptians also—rather astonishingly—built a canal at the Gulf of Suez, one half of the forked head of the Red Sea (the other being the Gulf of Aqaba). Almost 4,000 years ago, they dug a canal along the line of an old *wadi* and some small lakes to connect the Red Sea with one arm of the Nile (not directly to the Mediterranean, like the modern canal). The Nile at its delta breaks up into many arms, none of which is a prime waterway to the Mediterranean, but this canal allowed ships to proceed directly from the Red Sea into the Nile and often back upstream, without the costly unloading and reloading required by the caravan route. This 30-mile canal was in use for centuries—Queen Hatshepsut sent her expedition down to Punt by way of it. However, it tended to silt up, and, although it was occasionally reopened, the caravan track was more often the preferred route.

Because neither the Egyptians nor the Mesopotamians were adept sailors, both sought wood and expertise from the experts: the Phoenicians. Well before the

second millennium B.C., the Egyptians were importing pine wood and resin (and probably artisans) from the Phoenician city of Gebāl and building ships to sail down the Red Sea to Punt. (This reliance on Phoenicians lasted a long time. Over 1,000 years later, in the seventh century A.D., the Assyrians had Phoenicians build ships and transport them from the Mediterranean to the head of the Persian Gulf, using inland rivers where possible and portaging overland where necessary.) During some periods, the Phoenicians themselves traded on the Red Sea, alone or in concert with others, such as King Solomon. It is not clear whether any of these early Red Sea sailors followed the Arabian coast around to India, though they are alleged to have sailed around Africa from the Red Sea. Indeed, the Phoenicians may originally have come from the western end of the Spice Route; according to the fifth century B.C. Greek historian Herodotus, "Persian learned men" said they came from the Persian Gulf. The Greek geographer Strabo, writing 500 years later, was more specific than that:

On sailing...south from Gerrha, there are other islands, Tyrus and Aradus, which have temples resembling those of the Phoenicians. The inhabitants of these islands (if we are to believe them) say that the islands and cities bearing the same name as those of the Phoenicians are their own colonies.

The outlines of this Indian-Malayan ship and its busy crew are sharply delineated on this 8th century A.D. bas-relief from Borobudur, Java.

These suggestions are tantalizing, especially since the islands are near modern Bahrain—ancient Dilmun.

The main sailors on the Spice Route in this early period were the Indians. But much of what we know of the early Indian sailors is fragmentary and conjectural, coming from poems and religious works that cannot easily be dated. The early Indus Valley civilizations, which had traded with the Sumerians from their centers at Mohenjodaro and Harappa, were destroyed after the invasion of Aryans (Indo-Europeans) from the north around 1500 B.C. Indian sea trade either continued or resumed, however, for the earliest Sanskrit records of the succeeding Vedic civilization contain many references to ships. River boats are clearly distinguished from vessels designed to go on the ocean, "where there is nothing to give support, nothing to rest upon or cling to." The *Rigveda* and other early writings describe in some detail construction of these sewn ships, the positioning of the cabins, and their decoration, including colorful paints, animal sculptures, and precious metals and gems. Clearly some of these boats were used for royal pleasure trips, but most were used for trade and transport of goods, with some being mobilized for use in naval warfare among the many rival Indian kingdoms. Many writings refer to Indian ships that held 500–800 passengers. While these figures seem phenomenally large, at least one experienced modern observer, Alan Villiers, avers that he views such numbers "with an informed eye" after his experience on a 20th century Arab *dhow:*

> Here we embarked 200 passengers, a feat that I would have believed impossible if I had not seen it done. The passengers came at the ship in sewn boats from all directions, and, when close by, each endeavored to heave something over the rail— preferably a piece of his belongings, if he had any…then…claimed that piece of the deck as his for the passage.

While such numbers must be taken with a large grain of salt, the carrying capacity of a ship should clearly not be judged by modern Western standards.

Indians seem to have been the first Spice Route sailors to hazard the open waters, looking east as well as west. Buddhist writings called *Jatakas,* referring to the period between 1000 and 500 B.C., describe merchants crossing the Bay of Bengal to trade with the land they called Suvarnabhumi (the Golden Land, now Burma and the Malayan Peninsula). The *Sankha-Jataka* describes one Brahman from Benares, on the Ganga River, who gave away so much of his money in alms that he was sailing to the "Gold Country" to replenish his wealth; when his ship sprang a leak in mid-ocean, he was saved by a magic ship with "three masts made of sapphire, cordage of gold, silver sails, and of gold also…the oars and the rudders." Burmese merchant-sailors also crossed the Bay of Bengal

to Indian ports, and sailors from the west coast of India, from such major ports as Barygaza (Bharukachchha, now Broach), joined in the eastern trade at an early period. When crossing open waters, these early captains apparently did not navigate by the stars but used birds to guide them, as the first century A.D. Roman writer Pliny described:

> …they carry birds on board with them and at fairly frequent intervals set them free, and follow the course they take as they make for the land.

While there is no way to assess the size of the ships used, they were large and strong enough (built completely without nails, although metal was available) to withstand the winds of the open seas.

At some point in the shadowy millennium before Christ, Indians began to move eastward as colonists. The east coast kingdom of Kalinga—by tradition founded "at least eight centuries before Christ"—took the key island of Ceylon and then, spurred by commerce and missionary zeal, began to settle in Suvarnabhumi, all the way to the island of Singapore at the tip of the Malayan Peninsula. Considered "lower class" and persecuted for their Buddhism, these Klings and other Indian migrants settled eastward in increasing numbers over the years.

On the far eastern end of the Spice Route, little took place in this early period. The Chinese showed scant interest in ocean travel and apparently did not venture onto the open seas until the fourth century B.C. By the third century B.C., they had moved across the sea to Japan and in the following century took Chiao Chih, better known in modern times as Hanoi, and its harbor, Haiphong. This, with Canton, would be China's major port for foreign trade for centuries. But Chinese merchant-adventurers seem not to have moved actively beyond Chiao Chih; instead they waited for foreign traders—mostly Indian-Malayans—to bring goods to them.

Activities on the western end of the Spice Route at the same time are rather unclear. Southwest Arabia had long been a prime producer of aromatic spices, particularly frankincense, balsam, and myrrh, trading these products and foreign goods to Egypt and the Levant over the Incense Road. Several centuries before the birth of Christ—some speculate as early as the eighth century B.C.—Arabs began to spread across the hazardous Strait of Bab al-Mandab (Gate of Tears) to the Horn of Africa and down the East African coast, mixing to some extent with the native population. There they established trading settlements and coastal colonies as far south as Rhapta (a name possibly referring to their characteristic sewn boats), near modern Dar es-Salaam. From both East Africa and South Arabia, they traded Eastern goods with Egypt and the Mediterranean lands. But whether the Arabs were actually sailing on the Spice Route is unclear; they may have been primarily acting as middlemen, receiving goods supplied by Indian traders.

This Indian pilot, surrounded by his navigational instruments, was working in a craft thousands of years old in India. (By Thomas Postans, c. 1835, Indian Office Library)

Indians may also have been active on the East African coast in the millennium before Christ. Tradition has it that the important trading island off the Cape of Spices was discovered independently by Indian sailors; its name—Socotra—is derived from the Sanskrit *Dvipa Sukhatara* (the Happy Isles). The question of cinnamon, queen of spices, most expensive and most sought-after of all spices in early times, may shed some light on the matter. Native to only a few places in southeast Asia, cinnamon and its alternative form, cassia, were heavily used in Egypt for millennia, and Mediterranean records consistently say that East Africa was "cinnamonland," the source of the fabulous spice, noting that it arrived at the Nile Valley overland. Since cinnamon cannot grow in that region, more than one historian has speculated that Indian traders brought the spice to Arab middlemen, who carefully kept secret the source of the luxury they monopolized. Some have even conjectured that the cinnamon was brought directly across the ocean from Malaya or Indonesia; Pliny said that men of great bravery brought it "over vast seas on rafts," which may refer to Indonesians on catamaran-style outrigger canoes. Also intriguing are the reports of striking similarity between the

languages of Indian-Malayans and some modern inhabitants of the island of Madagascar, far down the East African coast; some 15th century A.D. reporters even said that the two languages were mutually intelligible. But such conjectures tell us little about what actually was happening in the region before Greco-Roman times, when more written records are available.

The first recorded direct voyage between India and the Red Sea was sponsored by the Persians—hardly a sailing people—who arose on the east shore of the gulf that came to bear their name in the middle of the first millennium B.C. Darius the Great sent a fleet under a Greek sailor named Scylax down the Indus River and around Arabia to Egypt. The two-and-one-half-year voyage had little effect, however. The Arabs apparently offered to pay an annual tribute of incense to the Persians to forestall conquest. In any case, the Persians did not develop the gulf as a trade route in this period, either because of piracy or concern that their land empire would be made vulnerable to attack. Instead, Darius developed the Red Sea trade, with the actual sailing carried on primarily by Phoenicians and Arabs. He also reopened the old canal, trumpeting:

I am a Persian: with the power of Persia I conquered Egypt. I ordered this canal to be dug from the [Nile] river which flows in Egypt, to the sea...

So stood the Spice Route before the arrival of Alexander the Great who, in his 13-year reign between 336 and 323 B.C., built a unique empire, joining three continents. His plan was to unite this empire with trade routes, both on land and on sea. To this end he had a fleet of hundreds of vessels gathered and constructed on the Indus River and sent to explore the Persian Gulf, of which the expedition's leader, Nearchus, left the oldest surviving maritime account. Alexander's chronicler, Arrian, recorded the surprise of these Greeks, who found waters very different from their familiar Mediterranean:

In this foreign sea there live great whales and other large fish, much bigger than in our Mediterranean. Nearchus tells us of his encounter with them as follows: As we set sail we observed that in the sea to the east of us water was blown aloft, as happens with a strong whirlwind. We were terrified and asked our pilots what it was and whence it came. They replied that it was caused by whales, which inhabit this sea. Our sailors were so horrified that the oars fell from their hands. I went and spoke to them encouragingly. Then I walked round the fleet and ordered every steersman I met to steer straight at the whales, exactly as if they were going into a naval battle. All the men were to row hard and with as much noise as possible, including yells. The sailors regained their courage, and at a signal we all set off together. When we had approached the beasts, everyone shouted as loudly as they could. On top of that, trumpets were blown and the noise of the oars echoed across the sea. The whales, which could be seen just in front of the ships, dived terrified into the depths. Not long after, they surfaced again behind the fleet, blowing water into air as before. The sailors clapped their hands, rejoiced in their escape, and praised Nearchus for his courage and astuteness.

But these Greek explorations led to nought, for Alexander died prematurely and his empire was divided by his lieutenants. One of Alexander's heirs founded the Seleucid dynasty centered on what had been Persia. The Seleucids tried to institute regular trade down the Persian Gulf with India, but piracy from the Gerrhaeans of the east Arabian coast aborted their plans. Then in 165 B.C. the Parthians took over Persia, monopolizing land routes between West and East and charging heavy duties for passage of goods. The seagoing Spice Route, as a result, looked even more attractive; with the Persian Gulf trade hazardous, the bulk of the traffic began to flow to and from the Red Sea.

The lands at the head of the Red Sea, especially Egypt, had been taken over by another of Alexander's lieutenants, Ptolemy. He and his successors made the Greek city of Alexandria, at one mouth of the Nile, a major trading and manufacturing center of the Mediterranean where all the goods of the East could be found. With the native Egyptians generally confining themselves to the Nile, the Greek overlords began to develop the Red Sea's potential. The Ptolemies once again reopened the old canal at the Gulf of Suez; built new caravan routes to Coptos, one from Berenice, south of the old port of Leucos Limen, and another further north at Myos Hormos (Mussel Harbor); improved navigation in the difficult Gulf of Aqaba; and explored both coasts of the Red Sea, founding Adulis (destined later to become a major port) on the African side. Among the many items that the Ptolemies shipped from the East African coast to Berenice and the caravan route were African elephants—those tanks of the ancient world—to rival the Indian elephants of the Seleucids in Persia.

Indian sailors clearly continued to sail the Arabian Sea, although we have few direct records of their activities. In the late second century B.C., an Indian sailor stranded in the Red Sea offered to show the Greeks the route to India; one Eudoxus accepted the offer and made a successful trip to the west coast of India, inaugurating direct coastwise trade by the Greeks.

In the first century B.C., we begin to have fuller accounts of the Spice Route. Perhaps the most interesting work, *Periplus of the Erythraean (Red) Sea,* is a practical handbook, written by an anonymous Greek merchant-sailor, describing the main ports and routes of the Red

Sea. From Egypt, spice traders would set out from Myos Hormos, Berenice, or Arsinöe (at the head of the Gulf of Suez). It was by no means an easy trip, for—as the *Periplus* author tells us—the Red Sea was "without harbors, with bad anchorages, foul, inaccessible because of breakers and rocks, and terrible in every way." Ships headed down the African coast would follow the west side of the Red Sea, calling at the emerging port of Adulis or at several smaller ports before rounding the Cape of Spices; from there they moved down the arid, harborless coast to a group of islands, among them one now called Zanzibar, and "two days' sail beyond" to the Arabs' southernmost port of Rhapta. Beyond this, said the *Periplus,* "the unexplored ocean curves around toward the west, and running along by the regions to the south...it mingles with the western sea."

Ships heading from Egypt toward India generally followed the east coast of the Red Sea, stopping at small ports or watering places, and then at Muza (Mocha), where, the *Periplus* said:

...the whole place is crowded with Arab shipowners and seafaring men, and is busy with the affairs of commerce; for they carry on a trade with the far-side coast [Africa] and with Barygaza [in India], sending their own ships there.

From there ships passed through the Strait of Bab al-Mandab; for many years they would have stopped at the major port of Eudaemon Arabia (Blessed Arabia, or Arabia Felix, now called Aden), which had long been a meeting place for Egyptian and Indian merchants. But by the time the *Periplus* was written, it was no longer a port of call, being just "a village by the shore," possibly subdued by Greco-Roman trading rivals. From there ships would follow the southern coast of Arabia (the Hadramaut) as it curved up toward the Persian Gulf, to the Strait of Ormuz, where Arabia comes within 29 miles of Persia. Some might at that point head into the Persian Gulf, stopping at the port of Oman and proceeding up to Apologos (now al-Ubulla) on the Euphrates River. But most ships would cross the Gulf of Oman and follow the Indian coast southeast to the main ports, especially Barbaricon near the Indus River and Barygaza further south. In these ports, in major stops all along the Spice Route, local pilots guided foreign ships into port; at Barygaza, for example, the *Periplus* author noted that navigation up the long estuary was dangerous, so "local seamen in the king's service, in fully manned frigates, go out to meet incoming vessels—and pilot them from the mouth of the bay to berths already fixed." This route, hugging the coast all the way, was the standard early route for Western sailors, especially Arabs in their frail sewn boats, who did not dare venture onto the open seas.

Eventually, however, Greek sailors learned how to

exploit the Indian Ocean's monsoons and, leaving the coast, let the winds blow them in season straight across to India and back again. The northwest wind toward India was named Hippalus, after the Greek sailor credited with first using it in 45 A.D. (although Indian sailors had probably been using it for centuries before that). As Western sailors reached further down the Indian peninsula, other ports on the Malabar Coast came into heavy use, especially Muziris (later Cranganore) and Nelcynda. A Tamil poet talked of:

> The thriving town of Muziris, where the beautiful large ships of the Yavanas [Greeks], bringing gold, come splashing the white foam on the waters...and return laden with pepper.

Another Tamil poet added to the description:

> ...sacks of pepper are brought from the houses to the market; the gold received from ships, in exchange for articles sold, is brought to shore in barges at Muziris, where the music of the surging sea never ceases, and where Kudduvan [the king] presents to visitors the rare products of the seas and mountains.

By the time *Periplus* was actually written, sailing across the Arabian Sea had become commonplace. Ships bound directly for southern India would follow the Arabian coast past Aden to the port of Cana (near modern Mukalla), pass Socotra (which was inhabited by Arab, Greek, and Indian traders), and then cross the open waters to the Malabar ports. The more adventurous moved on around Cape Comorin, at the tip of the Indian peninsula, stopping at various east coast ports as far as the mouth of the Ganga, which was the eastern limit of the *Periplus* account.

The *Periplus* author also gave a unique report of activities on the East African coast. After describing a native Negro population "of very great stature" along the coast, he noted that "under some ancient right" they were ruled by a chief of Arab descent, explaining that:

> ...the people of Muza [Mocha] now hold it under his authority, and send thither many large ships, using Arab captains and agents who are familiar with the natives and intermarry with them and who know the whole coasts and understand the language.

Among the goods taken out of Africa were ivory, rhinoceros horn, and palm oil (from the coconut palm, which was introduced in East Africa by Indians, possibly as early as the sixth century B.C.). The *Periplus* author also provided the first record of slave trading on the Spice Route, noting that "slaves of the better sort...are brought to Egypt in increasing numbers." He also mentioned that Indian ships brought "to those far-side market-towns the products of their own places." Clearly trade had existed for some time in East Africa, but for the next 500 years we hear almost nothing more about it.

Of the Spice Route beyond the Ganga River, Western writers had less direct experience. According to the Roman geographer Ptolemy, writing half a century after the *Periplus*, the route from the Ganga followed the Burma coast past the mouth of the Irrawaddy River, to the Gulf of Thailand. So far so good. From that point on, however, Ptolemy's knowledge became hazy; he described two ports on the Indochina coast, but did not mention the long Malay Peninsula in between. Indeed, he thought that the Chinese coast curved around and met the African coast at Rhapta, both being the limits of Europe's geographical knowledge of the Indian Ocean. Ptolemy's errors and confusions were perpetuated for centuries, until Western sailors finally followed the eastern route and filled in the gaps.

There was good reason for this, for the eastern trade was primarily carried on by the Indians. Merchants and missionaries had carried to many parts of southeast Asia the Indian culture and religion—generally the Buddhist "reform" version of Hinduism—a process often followed by the importation of Indian rulers, although military conquest was generally not involved. In the first century A.D., largely autonomous Indianized states—together known as "Greater India"—emerged on the Malayan Peninsula, in the Mekong River delta area of southern Cambodia, and in the Malay Archipelago. The Chinese, also, had made modest contact with the eastern islands, and some Japanese traded directly with the Spice Islands.

The eastern end of the Spice Route in this period ran from India across the Bay of Bengal through the Malacca Strait, down and around the Malay Peninsula, across the Gulf of Thailand, to the port of Oc-Eo (probably in southern Cambodia), and then on to the Chinese ports of Chiao Chih and Canton. The Malay Peninsula forced a 1,000-mile detour, however, and the storms and pirates off its tip posed great hazards to ships. As a result, several portage routes—each at first controlled by a different kingdom—developed across the relatively narrow peninsula. One main route crossed midway down the peninsula, at the Isthmus of Kra, while another crossed further south at Pěnarikan (the Place Where Boats Were Hauled).

Sea trade in the East was relatively modest, however, until the rise of the Roman Empire in the West and the Chinese Empire in the East created two very large, stable, hungry markets on either end of the Spice Route. With the land route between them—the Silk Road—controlled by Parthian middlemen, who exacted heavy tolls and would let no foreigners pass through the territory, a large part of the great and growing trade followed the Spice Route.

The Indians made the most of their central posi-

This small Malayan proa is fighting the powerful currents of the Strait of Malacca. (Victoria and Albert Museum)

tion on the route. Greco-Roman and Arab traders came to the Malabar coast to buy goods the Indians had collected from the East. Under the Mauryan Dynasty, a superintendent of ships was in charge of the whole operation, building vessels under a government monopoly; training mariners in navigational skills; overseeing the collection of port dues; and ensuring obedience to harbor regulations. Each port's superintendent was charged to lend "the protecting hand of a father" to any battered, storm-weary ship arriving in his harbor; and the brick-and-mortar lighthouses marking the prime Indian ports were well-known throughout the classical world. A contemporary account, the *Paddinappalai,* describes the mix of wares at a typical crossroads market at Kaviripaddinam:

> Horses were brought from distant lands beyond the seas; pepper was brought in ships; gold and precious stones came from the northern mountains; sandal and aghil came from the mountains towards the West; pearls from the Southern seas, and coral from the Eastern seas.

In this period, Western traders — all now called *Yavanas* — became familiar figures in Indian ports, being lodged in separate quarters and closely watched or escorted elsewhere. The Roman gold coin, the *aureus,* and the silver coin, the *denarius,* became the standard currency along the Spice Route. The Indians were, according to Pliny, much impressed by the fact that "the denarii were all equal in weight, although the various figures on them showed

that they had been coined by several emperors." In the time of Christ, Strabo reported, 120 ships were leaving annually from Myos Hormos for India, up from only a few a year under the Ptolemies. In the first century A.D., Pliny sharply criticized the waste of Rome's precious metals on useless luxuries, like perfumes and silks, lamenting that there was "no year in which India did not drain the Roman Empire of fifty million sesterces," noting later "so dearly do we pay for our luxury and our women."

On the western end of the Spice Route, most of the trade came to be carried on by mariners of the Roman Empire. Arab trading declined sharply in the face of competition; Arabs shifted their center of trading activity to Socotra, and then gradually dropped out of shipping altogether. Some Western traders based themselves in India, among them Jews, Armenians, Syrians, and Nestorian Christians, who were obliged to leave the Middle East after religious and political differences with ruling Romans. (Some of these groups settled colonies that lasted into the 20th century, like the Jewish settlement in Cochin, India, which was an active community until after World War II.)

As the Western Roman Empire declined, others joined in the trade. In the East African region of Ethiopia, a mixed Arab and African population formed the kingdom of Axum; through their port of Adulis, they came to supply the Mediterranean with all the goods of the Spice Route, although Alexandria continued to be the main processing and distribution center for Europe. In the third century A.D., the Persian Empire revived under the

Sassanid dynasty, occupying lands from northern Mesopotamia almost to the Indus. They, too, entered the seagoing trade, and gradually the Persian Gulf replaced the Red Sea as the main western terminus of the Spice Route. For all of these traders, the main destination was the Tamil kingdoms of southern India. These kingdoms gradually came under the sway of Chola, on the southeast coast of India, which capped its control by making the island of Taprobane (Ceylon, now Sri Lanka) an international entrepôt, a place where Axum, Jewish, Syrian, Greek, and Persian traders met Indian and Malayan merchants.

The eastern end of the Spice Route also saw considerable growth in the heyday of the Roman and Chinese empires. Taking advantage of their position as middlemen, Indians moved throughout Southeast Asia, establishing protected way stations all the way to North Vietnam and China, especially to the ports of Chiao Chih (known to the West as Cattigara) and Canton. They were followed by colonists, rulers, and missionaries, who further "Indianized" the region. Tradition has it, for example, that Java was colonized by Klings in the 75th year after the birth of Christ. In the same period Indian-influenced colonies were established in Indochina, among them Champa in central Vietnam and Funan in southern Cambodia, with its main port at Oc Eo, which controlled the important portage routes across Malaya. Traders along these routes were mostly Indian; the rare Europeans who traversed the Spice Route all the way to the land of the Sinae (as the southern Chinese were then known) were notable. Chinese annals record the arrival of an ambassador from the Roman Emperor Aurelius Antonius in 166 A.D.; but this "envoy" was most likely an adventurous entrepreneur hoping to make his fortune in the East.

While the Chinese themselves generally continued to wait for others to come to them, they made some forays along the Spice Route, possibly as far as India. The fifth century *Sung-shu* is not quite clear on this point:

> As regards Ta-ts'in [Syria] and Shen-Tu [India], far out on the western ocean, we have to say that, although the envoys of the two Han dynasties have experienced the special difficulties of this route, yet traffic in merchandise has been effected, and goods have been sent out to the foreign tribes, the force of the winds driving them far away across the waves of the sea...All the precious things of land and water come from there, as well as the gems made of rhinoceros horns...also the doctrine of the abstraction of mind in devotion to the the lord of the world [Buddha]—all this having caused navigation and trade to be extended to those parts.

More often traders met at intermediate ports, such as those at the Malayan portages; one such entrepôt is described (with exaggeration) in a fifth century A.D. Chinese account:

Its market was a meeting ground between the east and west, frequented every day by more than 10,000 men, including merchants from India, Parthia and more distant kingdoms who came in large numbers to carry on trade.

With junks like this one, the Chinese would win the Spice Route—and then let it go. (By Manning de V. Lee, in Rupert Sargent Holland, Historic Ships, *1926)*

By the sixth century, Rome had fallen and the Chinese Empire, centered in the north, had come under attack from Central Asian nomads. The Middle East and the lands south and east of the Himalayan barrier were relatively untouched by the Eurasian turbulence in this period, however, so the Spice Route continued to thrive, running between Persia, still-prosperous India, and southern China, temporarily the main base of Chinese civilization. It was in this period that a new power arose in the eastern half of the Spice Route: Srivijaya.

Based on the island of Sumatra, with its capital at Palembang, Srivijaya was in the fifth century just one of many small kingdoms in southeast Asia, which generally dealt with China though Indochinese middlemen, portaging across the Malayan peninsula. But by the sixth century, formerly powerful Funan had declined, and various kingdoms, among them Srivijaya, began to send direct embassies to southern China. Srivijaya assumed control in the region, making the other countries its vassals. Srivijaya's greatest asset was its position, for the island of Sumatra helped form the two vital Spice Route straits: Malacca and Sunda. Srivijaya exploited its advantages by building a substantial navy, which cleared the area of the ubiquitous pirates and made the sea routes for the first time safer and more attractive than the cumbersome and costly portage routes. The new power also improved harbors for merchant sailors, initially its own, but later also Indian and Arab sailors; as the navy grew stronger, it began to force all foreign ships to visit a Srivijayan port, to pay appropriate tolls. This exaction they enforced for centuries,

Pirates like these roamed East Asian waters, attacking ships bound for Canton or other ports. (Authors' archives)

for as late as the 12th century, the Chinese writer Chao Ju-kua noted: "If some foreign ship passing this place should not enter here, an armed party would certainly come out and kill [them] to the last man."

But traders and political ambassadors were not the only ones to travel these waters. From the first century A.D., Buddhism had spread eastward from India along both the Silk Road and the Spice Route. Devout Buddhists from as far away as China and Japan made pilgrimages to India, sometimes by land in peaceful times but increasingly by the Spice Route. Many such pilgrims took years on their journeys, spending long periods in Buddhist monasteries and universities along the way, among them in Srivijaya. The seventh century Chinese Buddhist I-Ching is typical; he studied Sanskrit in a Srivijayan city for six months before going to India, where he spent 14 years. He recommended the same to other pilgrims, suggesting: "If a Chinese priest wishes to go to the west in order to hear and read he had better stay here [in Srivijaya] one or two years and practice the proper rules and proceed to Central India." For seven centuries, Srivijaya maintained its dominant position – although not without opposition – along the eastern portion of the Spice Route.

Meanwhile, great changes were taking place in the West. In the seventh century, the prophet Mohammed founded a new religion on the old Incense Road. Spreading with astonishing speed, the militant religion of Islam within a century conquered all of the lands at the far western terminus of the Spice Route – including Arabia, Mesopotamia, Syria, and Egypt – and beyond. A desert people themselves, who indeed forbade maritime activity for a few decades, these Moslems ultimately drew on the marine tradition and experience of the region to become a naval power on the Spice Route.

Surprisingly, the Moslem land wars did not seriously affect sea trade. Although various Moslem countries were intermittently at war with India for over 800 years from the eighth to the sixteenth centuries, as Islam moved to control the subcontinent, merchant-adventurers continued to trade freely in the international entrepôts of the Indian Ocean, unhindered by any state policy. Indeed, many of the merchants who sailed in "Arab" ships were actually Greeks, Syrians, Jews, Indians, and other non-Moslems. Moslem pressure did push many Indians from Gujarat, on the west coast, to emigrate, some to "Greater India," others to the islands of the Arabian Sea, where they took up piracy. Otherwise trading on the Spice Route continued much as before; whatever their ethnic or reli-

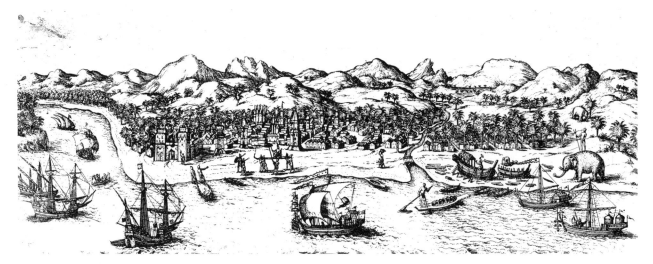

As portrayed by a 16th century European artist, Calicut was a prosperous, hospitable city. (From Civitates Orbis Terrarum, *1576)*

gious backgrounds, traders en route were housed in special foreign quarters of distant ports, where were found also warehousing and processing facilities, then called factories.

With Islamic power in the west and Srivijayan power in the east, the Spice Route was safer and more secure than at any time in its history, although pirates always existed at vulnerable points. The Red Sea and Persian Gulf both being under Islamic control after Persia's conversion to Islam, the Persian Gulf, with its more favorable sailing conditions, came to take the bulk of the trade. The main port of entry was at the head of the gulf, at first al-Ubulla (formerly Apologos), later Basra; from there goods were shipped up inland canals to the Islamic capital of Baghdad, and then on to Antioch in Syria, which replaced Alexandria as the main entrepôt for the Mediterranean.

But the Arab traders did not simply consolidate their hold on the Spice Route; they expanded. Persian ships were already trading directly with China, primarily Canton, by the sixth century; the Chinese pilgrim I-Ching took a Persian ship from Canton to Srivijaya in 671 A.D. The Moslem trade was highly regulated by the Chinese, as the anonymous Arabic author of *Akhbar al-Sin w-al-Hind* reported:

> When the seamen come in from the sea, the Chinese seize their goods and put them in the sheds; there they guard them securely for [up to] six months, until the last seaman has come in. After that, three-tenths of every consignment is taken as a duty, and the remainder is delivered to the merchants. Whatever the Government requires, it takes at the highest price and pays for promptly and fairly.

The aim, supposedly, was to provide a fair market—and incidentally to keep prices down; but merchants were often

left little time to sell their goods before they had to sail with the monsoon, and goods were often destroyed by the fire. Relations were often strained, sometimes erupting violently. Chinese records report that in 758: "The Arabs and Persians together sacked and burned the city of Canton and went back by sea." After this Canton was closed for half a century, replaced by Cattigara (Hanoi-Haiphong).

Moslems, whose ships were trading routinely from one end of the Spice Route to the other, exulted in their station; as al-Mansur expressed it: "This is the Tigris; there is no obstacle between us and China; everything on the sea can come to us." The Persian *dirhem*, which had replaced the Roman *aureus* and *dinarius* as the standard coin on the Spice Route, was itself ousted by the Arabian *dinar*. Some merchants apparently traveled all the way from Europe to China and back on the Spice Route. The ninth century Arab geographer Ibn Khurdadhbih described the itinerary of some contemporary Jewish merchants:

> These merchants speak Persian, Roman [Greek and Latin], Arabic, and the Frankish, Spanish, and Slav languages. They travel from West to East and from East to West, sometimes by land, sometimes by sea. From the West they bring back eunuchs, female slaves, boys, silk, furs, and spices. They sail from the country of the Franks, on the Western Sea [Mediterranean], and head towards Farama [near modern Port Said on the Suez Canal]; there they load their goods on the backs of beasts of burden and take the land route to Qulzum [Suez], a five days' journey...They set sail on the East [Red] Sea and make their way from Qulzum to Al Jar and Jidda; thence they go to Sind [the Indus region], India, and China. On their return they load up with musk, aloes, camphor, cinnamon, and other products of the Eastern countries, and come back to Qulzum,

and then to Farama, where they again set sail on the Western Sea. Some head to Constantinople to sell their goods; others make their way to the country of the Franks.

In this period, Arab ships generally left for the East in November; since navigation near Basra was difficult for large ships, they often left from the port of Siraf on the Persian shore, occasionally from Muscat on the Arabian shore. The northeast monsoon took them to Quilon, near the tip of southern India, so they could cross the Bay of Bengal in December, after the cyclone season was past. Ships then headed for the port of Kalah Bar (probably modern Kedah, near the portage at Kra), where they reprovisioned and sometimes exchanged goods with ships returning from China. With the northeast monsoon still blowing, ships moved down the Strait of Malacca and then with friendly winds across the South China Sea and up the coast of Indochina to Haiphong and Canton. Other ships, wishing to pick up spices on their way to China, headed from the Malacca Strait into the Java Sea and east to the Molucca Islands, that treasurehouse of spices, before heading north with their goods. Some ships went further north, to Fuzhou (Foochow), Hangzhou (Hangchow) at the mouth of the Yangtze, or even to Korea, before returning to summer at Canton. Then the winds would blow them back by the same route, with trading stops in the Malacca Strait, to the Persian Gulf 18 months after they had left it.

Moslems were also active along the East African portion of the Spice Route. The mixed Arabian, Indian, and African population that had long occupied the thin coastal strip was joined by Moslems beginning in the seventh century. Some, like the Omani migrants from East Arabia, had failed in a bid for independence; others belonged to the Shiite branch of Islam, including some Persians, seeking refuge over the centuries from their rivals, the Sunnis. Arriving piecemeal, and bringing their rivalries with them, the settlements along the coast— Mogadishu, Malindi, Mombasa, Pemba, Zanzibar (Negro Coast, a corruption of Zinj Bar), Kilwa, Mozambique, the southernmost gold-rich Sofala, and the many lesser towns—were independent cities, each behind fortified ramparts. Although occasionally one city would grow dominant over some others, no Arab empire existed, although all were converted to Islam by the ninth or tenth centuries. While Arabs ruled on land, long-resident Indians continued to run the businesses and ships in the "Arab" coastal trade.

Sailors headed for East Africa often followed a coastal route, probably stopping at the once-again major port of Aden (formerly Arabia Eudaemon) for trade—and to avoid the pirates around Socotra. Although the monsoons were favorable, the winds were sometimes strong for the sewn boats to handle; the 10th century traveler Al-Mas'udi reported that seamen said of the ocean:

...its waves are huge as the lofty mountains, and...they are "blind waves"; meaning by that that they rise up like mountains and sink down like valleys; the waves never break and there never appears on them any foam as at the breaking of the waves of the other seas. They also say that the waves are "mad."

Europeans and Asians alike would struggle for the port of Ormuz, which controlled the strait at the mouth of the Persian Gulf. (Authors' archives)

Moslem trade goods in East Africa consisted, more than anything else, of slaves, who were sent to Asia, especially to Turkey, Arabia, Persia, and India—so many of them that they sometimes formed a threat to the native Asian population. In the mid-ninth century, 400 Zinj (Negro) slaves taken into the army revolted and eventually took and sacked Basra, dominating the region for 14 years. Six centuries later, the king of Bengal had 8,000 African slaves; some promoted into the court murdered the king, and an African eunuch took the throne. For seven years, various Africans ruled Bengal, as regents for the Asian heir or as deposers; finally all Africans were expelled from the kingdom and forced to find refuge in Gujarat and the Deccan Peninsula. While this slave trade constituted a substantial portion of the activity on the western end of the Spice Route in these centuries, it apparently did not extend to China, for the occasional African slave mentioned in Chinese records is treated as a sensation.

Trade along the Spice Route was not untroubled in these times. After Canton was reopened in 792, Arabs and others resumed trade until 878, when Chinese rebels massacred merchants in the foreign quarter there—120,000 of them, according to one report supposedly based on a Chinese census. Whatever the true number, the incident had a chilling effect on Moslem trade in China. For some centuries thereafter, Moslems treated Kalah Bar, on the Malayan Peninsula, as their terminal port, there meeting merchants from further east. Some Jewish merchants did continue to trade all the way to China for another century or more, generally from the Red Sea. With the rise of the Fatimid dynasty in Egypt, the balance once again shifted away from the Persian Gulf, which was eclipsed by the Red Sea, especially the ports of Aden and Jiddah.

The China Sea also saw some changes. The main route of trade and influence historically had been from north China down the Korean Peninsula, then across the Korea Strait into Japan. But worsening relations between Korea and Japan in the eighth century led Japan to undertake direct contact across the 500-mile-wide sea to China. In the following century, Koreans—many of them forced out of their country by political unrest—came to dominate a triangular trade among the three countries, establishing merchant settlements in China, especially on the Shantung Peninsula, and Japan. While Japan exported much metal, including superior swords and other weapons, their main desires were for spices, medicines, and Buddhist materials, the religion having reached them by way of China. Toward the end of the ninth century, with Buddhism weakening in China (as it had earlier in India), and with political upheavals in the region, contacts in the region diminished. Japan, now resisting Chinese influence, had less impetus for trade, and when trading revived in the 12th century, it was in the hands of the Sung dynasty of southern China. So dominant were the Chinese in the Far East that Chinese coins were made legal Japanese tender in the 13th century, with the Japanese mint actually closing down.

While the Chinese were rising, the Indian traders along the middle of the Spice Route were declining. The Chola Empire of southern India resented the inroads Arabs had made in their trade; but fearing to directly attack them, they concentrated on the possessions of the Arabs' Indian allies, taking Quilon, Ceylon, and the Maldive Islands, where Arab ships were built of Indian teak and Maldive coconut fiber. Turning eastward, the Cholas then confronted Srivijaya, in the 10th century still a major power along the Spice Route, her ships seen from Canton to India. Making a forward base on the Andaman and Nicobar Islands in the Bay of Bengal in 1025, the Cholas soon captured Srivijaya's capital of Palembang and other major ports. Desiring primarily to break Srivijaya's monopoly, Chola withdrew for home, but the encounter weakened both empires. Other lesser powers arose in the region, notably on Java and at Malacca, where a polyglot traders' colony formed across the strait from Palembang.

The results were profound, for the region and for the Spice Route itself. With Srivijaya's monopoly broken, the Javanese began to develop products—especially cloves, mace, and nutmeg from the Molucca Islands—that had not before been standard goods on the Spice Route. Near Eastern and European markets responded enthusiastically, and Moslem and Indian merchants moved into the islands as they never had before. With hopes of independence from Srivijaya and of gain from the rich Arab trade, many of the lesser kingdoms in the region converted to Islam, a non-militant religious conversion once again sweeping Southeast Asia, as Buddhism had a millennium before. Buddhism, long since dormant in its homeland, continued its decline elsewhere; a Brahmanic ruling forbidding Hindus to participate in maritime activity assured Moslem dominance of the trade and increasingly of the religion of the region.

Moslem ships were not alone on the Spice Route, however. The Sungs, who had laid a strong basis for Chinese shipping, reaching as far as India, fell to the Mongols in the 13th century. After destroying the last Sung fleet, Kublai Khan had a new fleet built, in which he unsuccessfully attacked Japan and various parts of Southeast Asia as far south as Java. Toward the end of the 13th century, the Mongols took the more successful tack of trading. So began China's great era as a maritime power, during that unique century when Mongol power on land and open travel on the sea allowed travelers—including Europeans, for whom this region had been *terra incognita*—to wander the East as never before or since.

Large Chinese ships called junks plied between China and India, and Chinese merchants became a common sight on the Malabar Coast. On his return from China to Venice in the 13th century Marco Polo took one of these ships back to India and described how they were made:

> They have one deck; and above this deck, in most ships, are at least sixty cabins, each of which can comfortably accommodate one merchant. They have one steering-oar and four masts; often they add another two masts, which are hoisted and lowered at pleasure. The entire hull is of double thickness...caulked outside and in, and the fastening is done with iron nails.
> Some of the ships, that is the bigger ones, have also...partitions made of stout planks dovetailed into one another. This is useful in case the ship's hull should chance to be damaged in some place by striking on a reef or being rammed by a whale in search of food—a not infrequent occurrence, for if a whale happens to pass near the ship while she is sailing at night and churning the water to foam, he may infer from the white gleam in the water that there is food for him there and so charge full tilt against the ship and ram her, often breaching the hull at some point...Cargo is shifted from the damaged compartment into the neighboring ones; for the bulkheads are so stoutly built that the compartments are watertight.

Both Chinese and Moslem mariners still had to contend with pirates in the late 13th century; indeed, some of them were extremely well-organized, leaving their island bases in season and fanning out along the vulnerable parts

The clove trade of Amboina (Ambon) Island would later be the object of fierce competition between the Dutch and British. (Nederlandsch Historisch Scheepvaart Museum, Amsterdam)

of the Spice Route. Marco Polo described one such group in the Arabian Sea:

You must know that from Malabar and from a neighboring province called Gujarat, more than 100 ships cruise out every year as corsairs, seizing other ships and robbing the merchants. For they are pirates on a big scale. I assure you that they bring their wives and little children with them. They spend the whole summer on a cruise and work havoc among the merchants. Most of these villainous corsairs scatter here and there, scouring the sea in quest of merchant ships. But sometimes their evil-doing is more concerted. For they cruise in line, that is to say at distances of about five miles apart. In this way twenty ships cover 100 miles of sea. And as soon as they catch sight of a merchant ship, one signals to another by means of beacons, so that not a ship can pass through this sea undetected. But the merchants, who are quite familiar with the habits of these villainous corsairs and know that they are sure to encounter them, go so well-armed and equipped that they are not afraid to face them after they have been detected. They defend themselves stoutly and inflict great damage on their attackers. But of course it is inevitable that one should be captured now and then. When the corsairs do capture a merchant ship, they help themselves to the ship and the cargo; but they do not hurt the men. They say to them: "Go and fetch another cargo. Then, with luck, you may give us some more."

For the Chinese, pirates from the Japanese coasts – a mixed band of outcasts – were the worst predators. They were kept down somewhat during the early Mongol period but arose again as Mongol rule began to disintegrate in the late 14th century. It was up to the succeeding Ming dynasty to join with the Japanese government in suppressing them.

Under the Ming dynasty, China reached its greatest height as a maritime power. Reviving the old system of exacting tribute from other countries (which the Khans had tried to do and failed), the Mings sent missions throughout Southeast Asia, including India, exacting tribute – after which trading continued. Most impressive of these tribute expeditions were seven great voyages under Cheng Ho, nicknamed the "three-jeweled eunuch." Going beyond familiar territory, Cheng Ho's expeditions went to Ormuz on the Persian Gulf; to Aden, which contributed a giraffe for the Ming court; and all the way south along the East African coast to past Mogadishu. These voyages – with fleets of several dozen ships and tens of thousands of men – surely made China the leading power along the Spice Route, even over the longer-tenured Moslems. Cheng Ho himself saw his achievement this way:

The countries beyond the horizon and at the ends of the earth have all become subjects; and to the most western of the western or the most northern of the northern countries, however far they may be, the distances of the routes may be calculated...The barbarian countries we have visited are...more than thirty countries large and small. We have traversed more than one hundred thousand *li* of immense water spaces and have beheld in the ocean huge waves like mountains rising sky-high, and we have set eyes on barbarian regions far away hidden in a blue transparency of light vapors, while our sails, loftily unfurled like clouds, day and night continued their course, rapid like that of a star, traversing the savage waves as if we were treading a public thoroughfare.

But these voyages, between 1405 and 1433, led to nothing. Feeling within the Ming court turned against maritime adventures; indeed the eunchs' power aroused so much envy that Cheng Ho's records were mostly destroyed, so no one could follow up his great beginnings. China, which had had the Spice Route in the palm of the hand, let it fall.

The Moslems were, by default, the dominant power on the Spice Route, continuing trade and travel as they had for centuries. Moslem sailors—many of them still Indians, with much of the crew made up of African slaves—had long been navigating by the stars; even the *Koran* noted: "He it is who hath appointed for you the stars that ye guide yourselves thereby in the darkness of land and sea." But from Chinese sailors, they had obtained the mariner's compass; because it was still a crude device, the compass was primarily used when other navigational means were foreclosed, as an anonymous Chinese sailor explained:

> The shipmaster to ascertain his geographic position by night looks at the stars; by day he looks at the sun; in dark weather he looks at the south-pointing needle.

Even so, mariners on the Arab *dhows* in the turbulent waters of the Indian Ocean still had good reason to feel like "worms on a splinter."

Trade along the Spice Route in these centuries was rather a short-hop, pick-up affair. Some rich merchants had their own ships or could rent them, as did Sindbad in the *Arabian Nights:*

> I was again seized with the longing to travel and to see foreign countries and islands. Accordingly I bought costly merchandise suited to my purpose and, making it up into bales, repaired to Bassorah [Basra], where I walked about the river-quay till I found a tall fine ship, newly builded with gear unused and fitted ready for sea. She pleased me; so I bought her and, embarking my goods in her, hired a master and crew, over whom I set certain of my slaves and servants as inspectors. A number of merchants also brought their outfits and paid me freight and passage-money; then...we set sail over Allah's pool in all joy and cheer, promising ourselves a prosperous voyage and much profit.

Most merchants were simply peddlers, who paid passage on ships like Sindbad's and attempted to make a profit by trading one batch of goods for another in each successive port the ship visited. To these travelers were added another group: pilgrims. While few Buddhist pilgrims still voyaged to India, all Moslems were obliged—if they were able—to visit the holy city of Mecca at least once in their lives. The many Moslem countries of Southeast Asia sent large numbers of pilgrims west along the Spice Route, many of them to the port of Muscat, from where they crossed the desert to Mecca, others to Mecca's Red Sea port of Jiddah. For many, of course, religion was the excuse, and travel itself was the aim, for in those

prosperous times on the Spice Route many people had a hankering to see the world.

Then suddenly, life along the Spice Route was disrupted. From out of the untraveled waters south of Madagascar came ships of the Portuguese, barbarians who had only recently helped to push Moslem brothers back across the Strait of Gibraltar into North Africa. The Portuguese were not totally unprepared for what they found, for they had sent spies to the Near East to learn something of the faraway place they were aiming to visit. Still it must have been a great shock, after decades of working around the wild, mostly untenanted African coastline, to come upon the fine Moslem cities of the East African coast. One Portuguese sailor, Duarte Barbosa, described Kilwa, one of the main cities of the region:

> ...[it is] a Moorish town with many fair houses of stone and mortar, with many windows after our fashion, very well laid out in streets, with many flat roofs. The doors are of wood, well-carved, with excellent joinery. Around it are streams and orchards and fruit-gardens with many channels of sweet water...It is a place of great traffic and has a good harbor in which are always moored small craft of many kinds and also great ships, both of those which are bound to and from Sofala and others which come from Cambay and Malindi and others of which sail to the islands of Zanzibar.

The Portuguese were fortunate that the Moslem city-states had continued their rivalries, for although the first few ports were hostile, the port of Malindi welcomed them and gave them a first-class Indian navigator to guide them to Calicut, on the Malabar coast.

The Portuguese arrival in Asia in 1498 was less than earthshaking for the Indians. People who had been trading fine goods for gold and silver for thousands of years found the rough cloth and crude hardware of the Europeans laughable, if not insulting. The Portuguese, recognizing that they could not compete on the Spice Route on equal terms, realized that they would have to force their way in; after Vasco da Gama had returned home with his sample cargo of peppers and other spices, the Portuguese sent successive fleets around the Cape of Good Hope to do just that. Their goods might have been crude, but their guns were superior; by 1503, da Gama had exacted tribute from Kilwa, bombarded Calicut for its previous frosty reception, and defeated a larger Moslem fleet off Malabar. In the next decade, the Portuguese took the main East African ports—Sofala, Kilwa, Mombasa, and later Mozambique—as well as the island ports of Socotra and Ormuz; decisively defeated a multinational Moslem navy off Diu, on the Gujarat coast; took the shipbuilding island of Goa off Malabar; crossed the Bay of Bengal to take Malacca; and reached Canton and the Spice Islands. In a brilliantly orchestrated series of moves, the Portuguese

After the arrival of Europeans, Canton, shown here in the early 18th century, once again became the main Chinese port. (British Museum)

had taken the key points along the Spice Route; from there they were able to enforce control of trade, harassing any ships that had not been licensed by a Portuguese port—in effect, had not paid for their protection.

In short order, Portugal effectively destroyed the Spice Route as it had existed for thousands of years. Ships had formerly plied from China to Egypt and Mesopotamia, delivering goods for the Near East and Europe, most recently through the shipping services of Venice and Genoa. But now the Portuguese substituted a different route: goods gathered from local ports along the Spice Route went not to the Near East, but on the Cape of Good Hope Route around Africa to the European markets. While some old-style trade continued, as well as pilgrimages to Mecca, the western end of the Spice Route become—for the first time in its existence—a backwater. Ships out from Portugal, after resting up in the rich East African ports, often crossed the sea to India, bypassing both the Red Sea and Persian Gulf. From the Gujarat and Malabar coasts, they would pass onto the Malacca Strait, largely ignoring the Bengal ports, out to the Spice Islands and up to Canton.

In China itself, trade was in disorder. With Chinese fleets ill-kept and poorly deployed, piracy in the South China Sea had once again become extremely serious; the problem was further complicated because Japanese and Chinese merchants were forbidden to trade with one another, so pirates acted as middlemen between them. It was the Portuguese who finally put them down. The Portuguese had originally been allowed to trade at Canton, along with other foreigners, but were thrown out when one of their captains behaved very badly. But, for this help, they were allowed to establish themselves on the peninsula of Macao, downriver from Canton, in 1557. In the meantime, Portuguese merchants had begun trading with Japan, the first of them arriving on a Chinese junk blown off-course by a typhoon in 1542. Gradually the Portuguese took over as brokers between Japanese and Chinese merchants, and Portuguese became the commercial *lingua franca* all along the Spice Route.

The Portuguese were not the only Europeans in the region, however. The Spanish had arrived in 1522 from across the Pacific, Magellan's crew claiming the Philippine Islands for their sovereign. While they failed to establish themselves in the Spice Islands, the Spanish founded a major port at Manila in 1570, shuttling galleons annually between it and Acapulco in Mexico, providing the Mexican silver that oiled trade all along the Spice Route. The Spanish attempted to find a friendly port in Japan, which was on its route back toward California; there was hope of that for a time, and indeed Japan even sent ships across the Pacific to Acapulco in 1613 and 1616. But Japan did not take kindly to Spanish missionaries, and the relationship terminated a few years later. Toward the

417

This modern Chinese merchant ship, anchored along the coast, dwarfs the rowboats that bring traders to her side. (New York Public Library)

end of the 16th century—and the end of its tenure—the Ming dynasty revived its naval forces, and Chinese ships carried not only traders but large numbers of emigrants (many indentured to pay for their passage) throughout Southeast Asia, especially to Indonesia, Malaya, and the Philippines. There they settled, establishing full-fledged communities and trading with their home country, with the Portuguese, with the Spanish, and with the remaining Asian ships.

Then, near the end of the 16th century, other Europeans—with sailing experience gained on the North Atlantic and knowledge that had filtered out of Portuguese ports—made their appearance, notably the English and the Dutch. The Dutch, with superior ships and information, had the early edge and made the most of it. They were considerably aided by Jewish merchants, expelled from Portugal, who had settled in Amsterdam and had both practical experience in Asian trading and capital to finance overseas ventures. Penetrating the Spice Route first in 1596, at Bantam, on Java, the Dutch East India Company quickly established itself in the Molucca Islands as

well. The Portuguese, who had been strong enough to take the Spice Route away from the Moslems, were stretched too thin and were unable to keep out the intruders, especially when the Dutch and British combined forces against them. The British ambassador in India, Sir Thomas Roe, saw Portugal's weaknesses quite clearly:

> Look at the Portuguese. In spite of all their fine settlements they are beggared by the maintenance of military forces; and even their garrisons are only mediocre.

Indeed, Portugal had been forced increasingly to rely on native shippers to carry on the vital coastal trade that collected the products to be sent home around the Cape of Good Hope. Portugal was weakest in the East Indies, and there the Dutch concentrated.

Although Portugal withstood a four-year Dutch siege of Malacca and defeated a Dutch fleet off Macao in 1622, the first half of the 17th century saw its long slow decline. In 1612 the Portuguese lost a crucial battle to a smaller

418

British fleet off Surat, in 1622 also losing Ormuz; between 1638 and 1640 all Portuguese traders were expelled from Japan; in 1641, they finally gave up Malacca to the Dutch; and in the next 20 years they lost almost all of their Spice Route ports, except Goa, Macao, Mombasa, and the Mozambique region. No other power emerged as dominant, however. The Dutch were the strongest, especially in the East Indies; the British were considerably weaker, as were the French newcomers, both attempting to establish themselves primarily in India; and the Moslems retained control of the Arabian region and gradually regained power in East Africa.

With Portuguese power gone, and no other country able to replace it, the relative order they had imposed on the Spice Route collapsed. The following century was essentially a free-for-all time, in which European rivals preyed on each other according to a shifting set of alliances and rivalries, and all were fair game for the pirates that once again sprang up all along the route. Japanese pirates operated in the China Sea; and the East Indies were under continual attack from infamous Malay pirates, who attacked both the Spice Route traders and the Spanish-American galleons that traded in Manila.

In the Bay of Bengal, two groups of pirates operated in the islands, especially off Chittagong; the Muggs were primarily of native extraction, and the Feringhis were adventurers of Portuguese or other European ancestry;

a specially consitituted Mughal navy had to be assembled in India to bring these and the occasional British pirates in Bengal Bay under some control in the late 17th century. In the islands off India's Malabar Coast, Maratha pirates—Hindus disenfranchised by the ruling Moslem Mughals—established a pirating empire. Not until the second quarter of the 18th century did the British East India Company's Bombay Marine develop sufficient strength to make the waters safe for European shipping.

Further west was the province of the Omanis, Moslems occupying the horn of the Arabian Peninsula—a region called the Coast of Pirates—that forms the mouth of the Persian Gulf. With a navy modeled on that of the Portuguese, the Omanis took the main islands of the Persian Gulf, except Ormuz, and threatened Goa and Diu. As they turned from pirates to imperialists, the Omanis directed their attention toward the Portuguese possessions in East Africa, taking first Muscat, them Mombasa—which they took, lost, and took again between 1660 and 1698; they also moved down the coast to Pemba and Zanzibar, failing only to dislodge the Portuguese from Mozambique. A fledgling Persian fleet, allied with the Portuguese, slowed the Omanis somewhat in the early 18th century, allowing Portugal to retake Mombasa in 1728, but the Omani sailors were strong enough to continue operations into the 19th century, when the Bombay Marine finally cleared them from the waters and reopened unharassed

Before the opening of the Suez Canal, travelers tried to shorten the route to the East by crossing the shifting sands of the Suez Isthmus. (Illustrated London News, *April 25, 1857*)

navigation in the Persian Gulf. The Omanis continued to hold much of East Africa, however, and Moslems for the most part kept Europeans from maintaining any strong foothold in the Red Sea.

During this period the main trade along the Spice Route was what the English called the "country trade," a pattern of trading originated by the Dutch. They established a central port, Batavia (Jakarta) on Java, to which came their long-distance ships from Europe on annual voyages; the distribution of Dutch goods and the gathering of products to take back to Europe were all done by smaller ships built for the purpose, who plied among the many ports of the Spice Route. These "country traders" were operating well-maintained ships—not vessels that had just made the trying voyage around the Cape of Good Hope—and had no worries about how to unload a boatful of European goods in a small coastal town. Initially the English, and later the French and Danish, used their long-distance ships for coastal trading, but once established, they also adopted the country trading style. The eastern-built coastal ships had the advantage of being made of almost indestructible teak, far better wood than European oak for tropical waters; they were often manned by native traders, especially the Indian sailors who had worked the Spice Route for so long.

This country trade also held the prospect of riches for many a captain and sailor. Sailors were given a space on the boat for their own trade goods (often in lieu of wages), with the captain's share larger than the rest; some were employed privately by moneyed "gentlemen traders," who remained in the main ports, like the Bantam traders in this early Dutch account:

> The merchants who are wealthy in general stay at home, then when some ships are ready to leave they give those going with them a sum of money to be repaid doubly, [the amount] more or less according to the length of the voyages, of which they make an obligation, and if the voyage is prosperously completed then the giver is paid according to the contract, and if the drawer cannot pay the money because of some misfortune then he must give his wife and children in pledge for the whole time until the debt is paid, unless the ship be wrecked— then the former loses the money he lent...

Though the risks were great, the prospects were tantalizing to traders all along the route; as Jan Coen, governor of the Dutch East India Company, wrote to his directors in 1623 of their efforts to force the Chinese out of trade on the Spice Route:

> ...the Chinese say that [the risk of] losing the goods will not make them abandon the trade on Manila, but that if we want to keep them from there we will have to imprison or kill all the people we get hold

of in order to make the fear of losing life and property greater for the poor than the hope of making profit, for as long as the poor are not in bodily danger the rich will always venture the goods...

Trade was made difficult by national trade restrictions. Some of the strongest restrictions were laid down by the Chinese and the Japanese, both of whom deeply resented attempts by Catholic missionaries to convert them. When in 1640 Catholics were expelled from Japan and many Japanese converts massacred, the Dutch alone were allowed to stay, for they did not proselytize; but even they were sequestered, being restricted to an artificial island called Deshima in the port of Hirado for over two centuries, while Japan withdrew from the rest of the world. (The Dutch were allowed to stay partly because a British pilot named William Adams, shipwrecked with a Dutch vessel in the early 1600's and made adviser to the shogun, had influenced Japanese opinion in favor of the Northern European Protestants.)

But the Dutch themselves set up strong restrictions. They had to give up attempts to control the pepper market (since some of the best pepper came from the Malabar Coast, where other Europeans operated), but they rigorously enforced their monopoly on cloves and nutmeg. Having set aside particular areas as spice farms, the Dutch destroyed stands of clove and nutmeg trees elsewhere in Indonesia, wrecking the local economy; so seriously did they regard a breach of their monopoly that in 1722 a Dutch governor beheaded 26 employees in one day, all for smuggling the precious spices. An anonymous contemporary wrote: "No lover ever guarded his beloved more jealously than did the Dutch the island of Amboina where the clove trees grow." By the early 18th century, however, French colonists obtained the precious plants and spread them to the western parts of the Indian Ocean, most notably Zanzibar and Pemba, which became a second major source of spices.

In China, European traders were limited to two Chinese ports—Macao and its upriver neighbor Canton—and could deal only with Chinese merchant associations called *hongs* in their foreign quarters. Originally the Chinese wanted little other than Spanish dollars, brought to the region by Manila galleons and the standard currency of the region from the 16th through the 18th centuries. Enterprising traders eventually found other articles of interest, however. American traders—from around either the Cape of Good Hope or Cape Horn—brought highly prized ginseng and exotic goods from the Pacific; British traders, following the lead of Captain Cook, joined in the trade of furs, birds' nests, and such items from the Pacific. But these did not benefit the East India Company, which found something that did: opium, grown in India and extremely attractive—but illegal—in China. Under unofficial East India Company auspices, country traders began to

Spices gradually replaced slaves as the main "products" handled in Zanzibar's markets. (Graphic, *1873*)

supply China with opium in exchange for silks and tea, which became England's national drink (along with coffee, imported from Mocha, in Arabia). Dealing through many rivers and harbors along China's unpatrolled coastline, these country traders gradually opened up contacts outside Canton.

The late 18th and early 19th centuries saw the Age of Pirates give way to the Age of Rivalry along the Spice Route. The Dutch continued to operate along the eastern end of the Spice Route, though without their former strength; they also maintained their trading monopoly (except for occasional Chinese merchants) with the Japanese. But the main battle was between the English and the French for dominance in the Indian Ocean, a rivalry paralleling that in Europe and North America at the same time. In a series of wars between 1740 and 1815, the French—with bases in the Mascarenes and on the Indian coast, especially at Pondichéry—sometimes allied with the Dutch, gradually lost ground to the English. Indeed the French might have been pushed out of the Indian Ocean altogether in the late 18th century, had not Napoleon Bonaparte launched an expedition to Egypt, threatening English interests from the Red Sea and relieving pressure on the French and Dutch forces elsewhere. With a typically grand design, Napoleon assigned an engineer to explore the possibilities of a canal at Suez, between the Red Sea and the Mediterranean; although incomplete, this lay the groundwork for the revival of the Spice Route as a long-distance route, far preferable to the Cape of Good Hope Route. By the end of the Napoleonic Wars, the British had gained clear ascendancy along the Spice Route, with virtually total control of India and Ceylon. Although, by treaty, the British returned Java and Malacca to the Dutch, they established their own key port in 1819 at the island of Singapore, at the tip of Malaya, which became a main

entrepôt on the Spice Route.

In the process, the British re-established order along the old Spice Route—an order it had not had since the decline of Portuguese dominance. The old Portuguese ways, which had persisted for three centuries, long after the decline of Portugal as an international power, finally were replaced by British ways. The Portuguese language—or a creole version of it—had been the standard trading language along the Spice Route until the 19th century; each ship carried Portuguese interpreters, and ports were well-stocked with Portuguese dictionaries for country traders' use. Now the *lingua franca* increasingly came to be English (a process speeded because it was spoken also by American traders). The money standard also changed; for centuries it had been based on Spanish silver dollars, generally brought from Mexico in the Acapulco galleons, or at least made from Mexican silver. With the rise of the British and the end of the galleon runs, the standard coin along the Spice Route became the Indian *rupee*.

Through all the years the English had been active along the Spice Route, the East India Company had had a monopoly on trade. But in the late 18th and early 19th centuries, the East India Company laid the basis for its own downfall. In its eagerness to supply illegal opium to China, it employed non-Company captains, who traded with equally unofficial Chinese counterparts; opium ships—often fast clippers, of a type developed in Baltimore in the 1830's—even had a race to be the first to bring each crop of the Bengal-grown opium from Calcutta to the Pearl River near Canton. While legitimate European merchants traded with the official *hongs* in Whampoa, the port of Canton, private merchants headquartered on Lintin Island, in Canton Bay, from where they and a wide variety of smugglers traded along the ill-patrolled Chinese river and sea coast. At the turn of the 19th century, approximately 4,500 chests of opium are estimated to have been brought to Canton yearly; by the late 1830's, the amount was almost 10 times that. The Chinese, who had ineffectually forbidden the opium trade, tried to cut it off in 1838, seizing British goods, forcing the British to withdraw to Macao and then to Hong Kong, and cutting off their food and water. Continuing their trading temporarily through the medium of the Americans, the British mounted an expedition to open China's ports, blockading the Yangtze River and taking positions along the coast up to Shanghai. The Chinese, who felt their Celestial Empire invulnerable, had found the British challenge ridiculous; but British ambassador Lord Macartney had seen better than they, noting with appropriate maritime metaphor:

> The Empire of China is an old, crazy, first-rate man of war, which a fortunate succession of able and vigilant officers have continued to keep afloat for 150 years past, and to overawe their neighbours merely by her bulk and appearance, but whenever an insufficient man happens to have the command upon deck, adieu to the discipline and safety of the ship...she can never be rebuilt on the old bottom.

The British readily forced China's hand, and in August 1842 the first Opium War ended with Britain gaining Hong Kong island and rights of free trade in Canton (Guangzhou), Amoy (Xiamen), Fuzhou, Ningbo (Ningpo), and Shanghai. The Americans and French quickly won similar rights. The British Navy immediately began the task of clearing the China Sea of pirates, who had proliferated through China's inattention. The East India Company lost its monopoly on Eastern trade in the same period, and private merchants took on more and more of the trade, increasingly in European ships. Chinese junks, which had continued to operate over the centuries of European presence, were forced out of the long-distance trade on the Spice Route, although many Chinese merchants continued active as liaisons for European traders in such cities as the growing entrepôt of Hong Kong, or Shanghai, a fine deep-water port at the mouth of the Yangtze River, which soon outpaced Canton. By the 1850's the Europeans were seeking further trade concessions, which the beleaguered Chinese emperor was not disposed to grant. As a result the British and French launched a further expedition (partly delayed by a recall of some British troops to deal with the 1857 mutiny in India) against the weakened giant. After occupying Canton in 1858, they arranged for the opening of 11 more ports, including Tianjin (Tientsin), Nanking, and Taipei, on the island of Taiwan (Formosa); disagreement on fulfillment of other terms led the expeditionary forces inland, where they took and looted Peking, destroying the famous Summer Palace. At the end of this second Opium War, trading in the drug was legalized, and the British were granted further concessions and indemnities, among them the peninsula of Kowloon, which was added to their colony of Hong Kong.

Other major changes were taking place on the eastern end of the Spice Route. Japan continued its isolation from Europeans other than the Dutch, but—seeing the handwriting on the wall—had begun to modernize behind its rice-paper curtain. Dutch learning in such areas as astronomy, geography, and medicine was highly regarded; recognizing that the powers who had opened China would eventually turn toward them, the Japanese began to develop their army, metal industries, and shipyards. When the American Commodore Matthew Perry arrived with his warships in 1853, therefore, they were not totally surprised, but not yet prepared to effectively resist. The result was that the Japanese agreed to open Shimoda and Hakodate to America, not for trading, but for repair and reprovisioning of ships for the long return trip across the Pacific (a boon Spain had long wished for, before her Manila galleons had ceased to cross the ocean). Within five years, however, the Japanese were forced to open these and the additional ports of Kanagawa and Nagasaki to European traders: within a decade, several other ports, including Kobe (Hyogo) were opened for trading, and the Western merchants had begun to develop the fishing village of Yokohama (near the older port of Kanagawa) into a major international port. Joining the other European countries in the Far East was a newcomer: Russia. Having pushed to the Pacific by land and sea, the Russians had established a main port at Vladivostok, just north of Korea. Failing in the early 19th century to open trade with Japan, they contented themselves with attacking Japanese settlements on the disputed island of Sakhalin, until they joined in the opening of both the China and Japan trade.

Since the arrival of the Portuguese in the late 15th century, the Spice Route had been a somewhat fragmented, localized route, along which traders gathered goods piecemeal to be stored in the major national entrepôts until they were shipped in the long-distance ships on the Cape of Good Hope Route to Europe. But in the mid-19th century, with peace in Europe and in the Mediterranean, and with Europe, especially Britain, controlling almost all of the Spice Route, attention once again began to turn to the western end of the Spice Route. While not yet under European dominance, Moslem control in the area was weak, and European eyes sparkled at the prospect of a shorter route to Europe.

The most attractive idea was a canal at Suez. Some suggested reopening the old canal to Alexandria; others recommended a straight cut from the Red Sea through the Pelusic arm of the Nile to the Mediterranean, a choice muddied for some years by the mistaken impression that there was a 30-foot difference in the levels of the two seas. While the talk went on, some individuals made other

At the opening of the Suez Canal, a great international procession of ships passed through the cut that was to change the history of the region. (Authors' archives)

arrangements. In 1829–30 a British lieutenant, Thomas Waghorn, pioneered a route from London through the Mediterranean, across the Suez Isthmus, down the Red Sea, and on to Bombay, arriving in a little over 40 days—an astonishing record at the time. In 1837 he opened regular service along that route for mail and passengers, with East India Company ships plying between Bombay and Suez; carriages, donkeys, camels, and horses overland to Cairo: steamer up the Nile and inland canal to Alexandria; then steamship from Alexandria through the Mediterranean via Malta to England. Once in working order, with hotel accommodations provided for passengers at Suez, Cairo, and Alexandria, the route took 60 days off the previous time to India around the Cape of Good Hope; as a result, messages and travelers requiring speed adopted this as the preferred route, though slow and bulky traffic continued the long slog around the Cape. By 1854 another enterprising soul had put in a railroad between Cairo and Alexandria. Even so, these routes required costly unloading and reloading, so the idea of a canal continued to grow.

By luck, a Frenchman named Ferdinand de Lesseps had a friendship with the Egyptian viceroy of the time, supposedly subject to Turkey, but in truth very much influenced by France and England. The viceroy warmly welcomed the idea of a canal, granting a concession for the purpose; more difficult was the politicking involved in getting approval of the European powers, especially as the British feared the opening of a new route would render their monopoly of the Cape of Good Hope Route almost valueless. The British had good reason for such a fear; agreeing with Napoleon Bonaparte that "in order to

destroy England it is necessary for us to possess Egypt," the French minister Talleyrand in 1798 wrote:

The revival of the Suez route will have an effect upon her [England]...as fatal as the discovery of the Cape of Good Hope was to the Genoese and Venetians in the sixteenth century.

In the event, de Lesseps succeeded in gaining both approval and financing for a joint stock company, which began digging the canal in the spring of 1859, the first cut being a freshwater canal for transport and water supply in the wasteland they were carving. Originally undertaken by a body of 60,000 forced laborers, protests later led to increased reliance on heavy machinery to do the excavating. When completed 10 years later, the Suez Canal ran 100 miles, from the port of Suez, through the Little and Great Bitter Lakes and some other smaller lakes, to the new city of Ismailia (soon a crossing point for a rail line between Palestine and Egypt), and out to the new settlement of Port Said on the Mediterranean. A relatively straight cut, with no locks and few curves, the canal at its narrowest was 150 feet wide, but at eight stations was wide enough to allow vessels to pass each other.

The opening was attended by a generous number of the crowned heads of Europe, along with thousands of visitors drawn by the momentous occasion. The French Empress Eugenie cried with pride; as de Lesseps put it: "...sobs which do her honor, for it was French patriotism overflowing from her heart." Two flotillas—one Egyptian from the Red Sea, the other an international grouping

Pilgrims for Mecca who arrived by sea were brought into Jiddah harbor by these small sailing dhows. (From Richard H. Sanger, The Arabian Peninsula, *Cornell University Press)*

from the Mediterranean—started from either end of the canal to meet near the middle at Ismailia. This sight was not all that astonished onlookers, for in the process of building the canal, de Lesseps had transformed a wasteland. Sir Frederick Arrow observed of the passage from the north:

> ...after going about 20 miles, we came on the true features of the desert: unbroken sand, as far as the eye could reach, hot, dry, and arid-looking, everywhere except where the stations were. There (supplied by tapping the pipes which take the water from the freshwater canal at Ismailia to Port Said) irrigation and Nile water had made a veritable oasis; huts covered with verdant creepers in full bloom, cane and the date palms growing freely; in truth, the prophesy is fulfilled. "The desert *hath* blossomed like the rose."

With the Suez Canal open, the Spice Route once again became the dominant long-distance trading route in the region; the Cape of Good Hope Route was eclipsed, except for travel to and from Australia and the Cape Colony in South Africa. The success of the Suez Canal also spelled death for the sailing ships on the Spice Route, for ill winds and hidden reefs made the Red Sea inhospitable for the great clippers and East Indiamen, which also re-

quired a prohibitively expensive tow through the canal itself. While sail remained dominant on the Cape of Good Hope route (for sailing ships did not require massive infusions of coal, as steamships did), steamships gradually took over on the Spice Route, ferrying goods and, increasingly, people from China, Indochina, the East Indies, Malaya, India, and East Africa on through the Suez Canal and into European waters. The western end of the Spice Route, which had languished for centuries, was re-established as the key juncture between Asia and Europe. Only the Persian Gulf remained a relatively local route, except for the continual stream of Moslem pilgrims from the East, who sailed up the Persian Gulf to Muscat and across the desert to Mecca.

The 19th century also brought massive social changes to the Spice Route. With Europe brought close by the Suez Canal, a different presence came to be felt. The early Europeans in the Indian Ocean had been few in number, arriving only after an arduous journey of many months. Mostly male, these early adventurers had, with their governments' encouragement, intermingled with the local population. This was especially true of the early Portuguese. The Dutch had originally attempted to recreate in the East Indies the family life they had known at home, but too many wives and daughters had fallen prey to shipwreck or piracy, so the government changed its stance, recommending intermarriage between the Dutch and the local population. The English and French had taken a different tack, establishing a pattern called nabobism. The weakness of native principalities, especially in India, allowed Europeans to set themselves up as nabobs (a corruption of the Indian word *nawab*), or Mughal princes. The process was widespread, as witnessed by the late 19th century popular song, "I've Got Rings on My Fingers":

> Jim O'Shea was cast away
> Upon an Indian isle.
> The natives there, they liked his hair,
> They liked his Irish smile.
> They named him chief panjandrum,
> The nabob of them all.
> They called him Jitty-Bob Jay,
> And rigged him out so gay...

While earlier Europeans had largely operated from trading colonies, under rights and concessions granted by the Eastern rulers, these 19th century nabobs were moving into both political and commercial control of countries in a way not seen before along the Spice Route. In the security of the peaceful mid-19th century, they also came in increasing numbers, bringing their families. The result was a clash of cultures that shocked many of the staid Victorians who arrived in the East; when Jim O'Shea's fiancée arrived from Ireland, for example, she was most unhappy to be shown Jitty-Bob Jay's "harem/ Where he had wives galore," and was not cheered by the reassurance that he was "keeping these wives here/ Just for ornyment, my dear."

The opening of the Suez Canal reinforced this new, wider-scale imperialism. East Africa felt the effects most sharply. Europeans had paid little attention to East Africa, largely leaving that to the Moslems, who—following the traditional pattern—had confined themselves to a coastal strip, with only occasional trading forays into the hinterland. The coast and its slave trade had been controlled by the Sultan of Muscat since he defeated the Portuguese in 1698; then in 1841, the sultan had established a Zinj (Negro) Empire, centered on the island of Zanzibar. The British made some ineffectual attempts to stop the East African slave trade, after outlawing slavery in their own dominions in the early 19th century. But after the opening of the Suez Canal, the British and others focused on East Africa; explorers, missionaries, traders, and settlers increasingly began to probe the inner lands of East Africa beyond the thin strip under Zinj control. Joining the British were others, colonial latecomers who wanted their own piece of the imperial pie. The French moved to take Djibouti (French Somaliland) just south of the Strait of Bab al-Mandab; the Italians made an entrée further down the Somali coast, and the Germans moved inland from Zanzibar to Tanganyika and Kenya.

For all of these countries, the Suez Canal made East Africa more attainable and attractive. Events made it especially so for the British. While the Suez Canal had changed the international scene, it was not a financial success; high cost and improvidence by the Egyptian ruler brought almost half of the shares of the Suez Canal on the market. Bought by British Prime Minister Benjamin Disraeli in a startling coup, they brought the Suez Canal for the first time under effective control of a government, not simply international stockholders. Anti-foreign feeling ran high in Egypt, however; by the 1880's, when rioting began to take European lives, British forces stepped in. The French and Turks, who did not join the British, lost control of Egypt, which became a British protectorate. From there, Britain moved successively to the Sudan, to Somaliland, and to Kenya (eventually, by agreement, retaining it, but leaving Tanganyika to the Germans). Italy in the meantime had atempted to establish itself as an imperial power in Ethiopia (Abyssinia), but was soundly repulsed.

Other social changes were transforming the Spice Route. In Europe the Industrial Revolution was giving the Northern Europeans technical capabilities they had never had before. Skilled metalwork and fine cloths, which had been a large proportion of the goods shipped from the East to Europe, were now available in abundance at home. Skilled artisans of India, China, and elsewhere in the East were thrown out of work, replaced by the weavers and metalworkers of Northern Europe, especially England. In response, the imperialists expanded colonial cultivation of agricultural products and raw materials. As the Dutch had done so long before, Europeans now moved into the Spice Route region as planters and miners, but on a large scale, developing coffee, tea, and rubber plantations in Ceylon, the Philippines, Malaya, East Africa, and all along the route. Slavery gradually died out in the region, but cheap labor was still needed, so "coolies"— mostly from India and China—moved throughout the Indian Ocean in enormous numbers to fill the demand. As large numbers of immigrants moved into foreign lands, the local economy was distorted and ethnic hatreds ran high, breaking into dreadful violence. As the Chinese and Japanese mobs had often, in history, massacred foreigners, so they faced xenophobia themselves elsewhere. In the mid-18th century, the Dutch governor tried to deport all Chinese settlers from Batavia; they resisted and, in the resulting riot, thousands of Chinese were slaughtered by Dutch and Indonesian mobs and troops. The pattern was laid and continues to this day, when any day news comes of strife between the majority group and ethnic minorities, some of whom have been resident for centuries. These immigrants not only supplied plantation labor but also operated as crews on the many trading ships, all with European officers. With their help, Europeans continued the division of the East, with the Netherlands taking Indonesia; Britain extending beyond India and Ceylon to

Burma, Malaya, and even into Borneo; France establishing itself in Indochina; and the United States replacing Spain in the Philippines. The Japanese, too, burst on the scene. While their modern navy was only decades old, they were strong enough to break China's hold on the island of Taiwan and the peninsula of Liaodong. By 1905 they had taken Korea and defeated the Russian Empire, driving the Russians from Manchuria (and from their only warm-water port on the Pacific, Port Arthur, established only in 1897) and from southern Sakhalin.

World War I had few direct effects on the Spice Route. Japan was well able to stave off any Russian threat, and the British had no great difficulty handling the Germans in East Africa. The main effect of the war was probably the change of domination in the Middle East, where Britain took control after 1918. The Suez Canal, although not open to all belligerents as had been its intended international status, continued to operate through the war, closed only briefly by Turkish air attacks. Surveying the whole region, the British soon discovered and started to develop the resource for which the region is now best known: oil. Much oil had traveled through the Suez Canal from Russia to the Far East before the war, but the 1917 Revolution cut off oil from the Black Sea. The finds in Indonesia and the Middle East made the Spice Route now an important oil route.

The post-war years were also the time of the great passenger liners, grande dames of the ocean, now designed for passenger comfort. As always, some were merchants, traveling on business, but more often these days, the passengers were civil servants or army officers on administrative service, or just plain tourists. The Grand Tour of Europe, after all, paled next to a voyage that included Aden, Coromandel, Ceylon, Bengal, Singapore, Shanghai, and Peking as its stops. But fast they were not. Passengers lolled the long weeks in the sumptuous quarters of the great liners, learning a slower pace to suit their speed, as Rudyard Kipling described:

Twelve knots an hour, be they more or less—
Oh slothful mother of much idleness,
Whom neither rivals spur nor contracts speed!
Nay, bear us gently! Wherefore need we press?
How runs the old indictment? "Dear and slow,"
So much and twice so much. We gird but go.
For all the soul of our sad East is there,
Beneath the house-flag of the P. and O.

But all was not peaceful on the Spice Route. Proud Eastern nations, imbibing Western ideas of freedom and spurred by Europe's post-war nationalist movements, increasingly agitated to regain independence. Imperialism was far from dead, however, and indeed others were still embarking on that course. In 1935, Italians moved against Ethiopia; they would be expelled by the British a few years later, but they heralded a new time of troubles on the

western end of the Spice Route. On the eastern end, a more successful power was still growing: Japan. Moving against a disorganized China in the 1930's, she stunned the world in 1941 by smashing the American navy at Pearl Harbor and moving rapidly against much of Southeast Asia: Indochina, Malaya, Burma, Indonesia, and the Philippines. Worse than that, the English-crafted Japanese Navy even raided India and Ceylon, threatened northern Australia, and forced the remains of the British Navy to retreat to Mombasa, after the defeat of combined British and Dutch forces in the Java Sea in 1942 and after the fall of Singapore. Had they pressed further into the Indian Ocean, the Japanese might have come to control the whole route; seasoned Indian Ocean sailor Alan Villiers noted that "it was a good thing for the allies...that the Japanese, for some reason, did not venture into that ocean in strength again. They lost thereby their chance of gaining its overwhelming mastery—a chance which was within their grasp, but did not come their way again." By mid-1942, the revived Allies defeated the Japanese in the Coral Sea, and the tide of war on the eastern Spice Route had turned. German submarines and raiders operated in the region, and the Desert Fox, Rommel, threatened the Suez Canal from North Africa. But they did not come close to controlling the western part of the Spice Route.

With the war over, life on the Spice Route changed again. The short life of the passenger liners was speeding to a close, with the rise of airplane travel. Meanwhile, the oil fields of the region came under heavier exploitation than before the war, to fuel the airplanes and cars that now spread across the face of the Earth. Oil tankers came to form an increasing proportion of the traffic on the Spice Route. Long-repressed nationalist desires also changed the face of the region. While Japan was being rehabilitated as an industrial nation, and China was once again closing itself off from the world, this time under a Communist regime, the rest of the countries gradually began throwing off the imperial mantle, most importantly with the independence of India. Though a few old-style colonies would remain—notably Macao and eastern Timor—in the next few decades direct European political control fell away, though certainly not European cultural or commercial influence. Nor was the process always peaceful, sometimes leading to complicated tragedies such as that in Vietnam.

On the western end of the Spice Route, all was not quiet, either. In the years following World War II, Egypt's agitation for control of the Suez Canal increased; and the international status of this key waterway was negated when Egypt refused to allow passage of ships from the newly created country of Israel. Then, in 1956, Egypt nationalized the Suez Canal. British, French, and Israeli forces attacked Egypt to regain control of the canal, but pressure from the United Nations, especially from the United States and Soviet Union, forced them to withdraw. Egypt was

426

left in control, but despite all agreements, refused to allow Israeli ships through the canal. Then in 1967 the Israelis took matters into their own hands, moving across the Sinai Desert to take the east bank of the Canal. For the first time, the canal was well and truly closed, by ships sunk in the channel; it remained so for eight long years, during which time all ships had to use the long Cape of Good Hope Route again. Not until 1979 did the first Israeli ship pass through the canal. But during those years of closure, supertankers were developed that could no longer fit through the canal; these now pass from the oil-rich countries around the Cape of Good Hope Route once again.

The colonial policies of the last few centuries sadly distorted the ancient trade of the Spice Route. The economies of many Eastern countries had been shaped primarily with European markets in mind, and the "country trade" that once bound together the peoples along the Asian and East African coasts almost disappeared. It remains to be seen whether, in the post-imperial age, traders from around the Indian Ocean and China Seas will once again resume control of the great Spice Route that played so large a part in their history. Some things never change, however: Yachters braving the waters of the Spice Route would still be wise to beware pirates off Singapore, home of freebooters for thousands of years.

Selective Bibliography

Coupland, R. *East Africa and Its Invaders: From the Earliest Times to the Death of Seyyid Said in 1856* (Oxford: Clarendon Press, 1938). A detailed history.

Furber, Holden. *Rival Empires of Trade in the Orient, 1600–1800* (Minneapolis: University of Minnesota Press, 1976). Volume 2 of the Europe and the World in the Age of Expansion series. Primarily an economic history.

Hoskins, Halford Lancaster. *British Routes to India* (New York: Octagon, 1966; reprint of 1928 edition). Focuses on the Near Eastern overland routes, especially at Suez.

Hourani, George Fadlo. *Arab Seafaring: In the Indian Ocean in Ancient and Early Medieval Times* (New York: Octagon, 1975; reprint of 1951 edition). Volume 13 of Princeton Oriental Studies; a lively, well-focused study.

Howe, Sonia E. *In Quest of Spices* (London: Herbert Jenkins, Ltd., 1939). Covers early European activities in the spice trade.

Huzayyin, S. A. *Arabia and the Far East: Their Commercial and Cultural Relations in Graeco-Roman and Irano-Arabian Times* (Cairo: Publications de la Société Royale de Géographie D'Egypte, 1942). A very useful overview of both land and sea routes.

Miller, J. Innes. *The Spice Trade of the Roman Empire, 29 B.C. to A.D. 641* (Oxford: Clarendon Press, 1969). A fascinating and extremely useful review of the land and sea trade, and the spices themselves.

Mirsky, Jeannette. *The Great Chinese Travelers* (New York: Pantheon, 1964). An anthology of historical travel writings.

Mookerji, R. K. *Indian Shipping: A History of the Sea-Borne Trade and Maritime Activity of the Indians from the Earliest Times* (Bombay: Longman, 1957). A detailed work, focusing on written records.

Panikkar, K. M. *India and the Indian Ocean: An Essay on the Influence of Sea Power on Indian History* (London: George Allen & Unwin, 1945). A brief but useful overview.

Schonfield, Hugh J. *The Suez Canal: In Peace and War 1869–1969,* Revised Edition (Coral Gables, Florida: University of Miami Press, 1969). An historical review with a political emphasis.

Schurmann, Franz, and Orville Schell. *Imperial China: The Last Dynasty and the Origins of Modern China, the 18th and 19th Centuries* (New York: Random House, 1967). Volume 1 of the China Reader series. "A documentary history based on contemporary accounts and historical examinations..."

Simkin, C. G. F. *The Traditional Trade of Asia* (London: Oxford University Press, 1968). An invaluable survey of land and sea contacts.

Toussaint, Auguste. *History of the Indian Ocean* (Chicago: University of Chicago Press, 1966). Translated from the French. Wider-ranging than the title indicates, covering the whole Spice Route.

Van Leur, J. C. *Indonesian Trade and Society: Essays in Asian Social and Economic History* (The Hague: W. van Hoeve Ltd., 1955). Volume 1 of Selected Studies on Indonesia. A compilation of evidence and interpretations, in English.

Villiers, Alan. *Monsoon Seas: The Story of the Indian Ocean* (New York: McGraw-Hill, 1952). Part of the Oceans of the World series. A popular history by an experienced sailor.

Wilson, Arnold T. *The Persian Gulf: An Historical Sketch From the Earliest Times to the Beginning of the Twentieth Century* (London: George Allen & Unwin, 1928). Stresses modern colonial times; includes many interesting quotations.

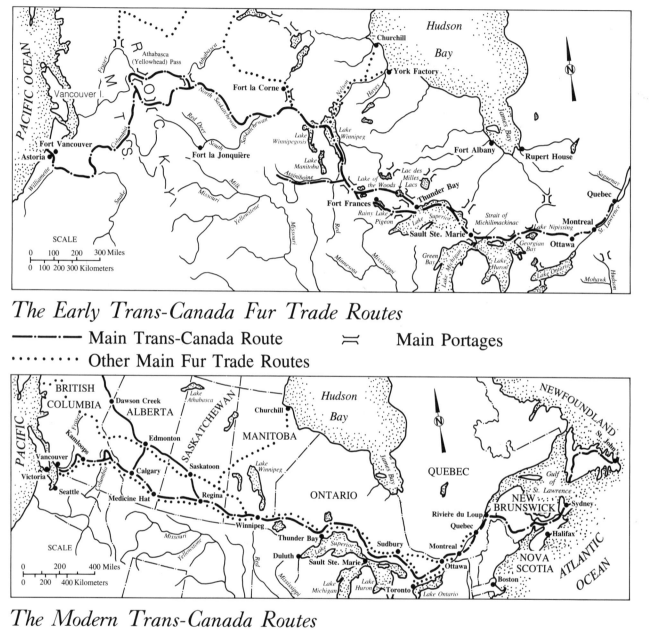

The Early Trans-Canada Fur Trade Routes

—·—·— Main Trans-Canada Route   ⇌ Main Portages

·········· Other Main Fur Trade Routes

The Modern Trans-Canada Routes

—·—·— Trans-Canada Highway   ——·—— U.S. - Canada Boundaries

—— Alaska Highway   ——·—— State or Province Boundaries

·········· Main Railroad Routes

The Trans-Canada Route

Alexander Mackenzie, from Canada by land, the twenty-second of July, one thousand seven hundred and ninety-three.

That was the inscription written "in large characters" of vermilion and grease by Alexander Mackenzie on a rock in Dean Channel, north of what we now call Vancouver Island. Two hundred and fifty-nine years after Jacques Cartier had entered the mouth of the St. Lawrence River, Alexander Mackenzie had finished the European journey across North America. George Vancouver saw the inscription a few days later, exploring up the coast by sea; but he missed Mackenzie, who had by then started his return trip to Lake Athabasca, on the east side of the Rockies. The inscription might just as easily have read:

Alexander Mackenzie, Leif Ericson, Jacques Cartier, John Cabot, Henry Hudson, Samuel de Champlain, Robert La Salle, Jean Nicolet, Jacques Marquette, Pierre Radisson, Anthony Henday, Simon Fraser, David Thompson, and others, by land and waterway across Canada from sea to sea.

They and scores of others contributed; their story is the story of the way west across Canada, the quest for the Northwest Passage, the exploration of Canada, and the growth and consolidation of the Canadian nation.

In reality, there were two ways west across Canada.

The principal Trans-Canada Route followed the St. Lawrence River to the Ottawa River, then continued westward via Lake Nipissing to Lakes Huron and Superior, the most northerly of the Great Lakes. In this eastern portion, the story of the way west is very much that of the St. Lawrence-Great Lakes Route. Beyond the Great Lakes, the route crossed difficult, marshy land dotted by many smaller lakes; with no natural pathway to follow, early travelers generally angled northwest toward Lake Winnipeg. Once out of the lake country, the route headed across the Canadian plains, whose flat, rather well-drained surfaces provided much better ground for traveling. Making their way over the Rocky Mountains by a variety of routes, travelers on the far side linked up with the Columbia River system, which they followed down to Vancouver and the Pacific Ocean. Though the routes might vary in detail, Canada and its roads and railroads have developed generally along this axis laid down by early voyageurs and explorers. A secondary Trans-Canada Route also existed, always more a trade than travel route. From the western side of Hudson Bay, reached by sea from the North Atlantic, this route cut southwest to Lake Winnipeg, where it joined the main Trans-Canada Route. This was the pathway taken by the trappers and traders of the Hudson's Bay Company, rulers of much of western Canada for centuries.

As they began pushing westward from the St. Lawrence, the French were not, however, entering a virgin

At many portages in western Canada, like this one at Kakabeka Falls, travelers placed rows of logs in the ground to ease hauling. (By William Armstrong, Canadian Illustrated News, *1871)*

land. The canoe trails that made up the way west were all Native American routes. The journeys west were only voyages of discovery for the Europeans who made them; for the Native Americans, North America was a well-known, well-settled continent. A thousand years before Champlain arrived on the scene, the great Hopewell culture, centered in the Ohio Valley, had developed an almost continent-wide trade network, over which traveled such goods as shells from the Gulf of Mexico, obsidian from the west, and copper and lead from the Lake Superior region. Even in the 16th century, when the French were beginning to push westward, copper was being traded on the great continental trade routes.

Europeans made contact with the Native American trading network almost as soon as they arrived in North America. One trail led out of the interior of the continent to Tadoussac, at the mouth of the Saguenay River, near where the St. Lawrence begins to widen from a river to a gulf. There a lively trade in furs and European tools and other trade goods developed in the early 16th century. Furs were brought from remote tribes deep in the

interior through various tribes acting as middlemen: in return, tools and other European trade goods flowed inland from Tadoussacc. Indeed, they had done so even before Cartier's arrival on the St. Lawrence in 1534. Since John Cabot's North Atlantic voyage in 1497, European fishermen had been very actively trading with Native Americans along the North Atlantic Coast. It is not surprising that in 1534, when Jacques Cartier entered Chaleur Bay on the coast of New Brunswick, he was met by:

...two fleets of Indian canoes that were crossing from one side to the other, which numbered in all some forty or fifty canoes. Upon one of the fleets reaching this point, there sprang out and landed a large number of Indians, who set up a great clamour and made frequent signs to us to come on shore, holding up to us some furs on sticks...

And the next day, after both parties had indicated peaceful intentions, Cartier

430

...sent two men on shore to offer them some knives and other iron goods, and a red cap to give to their chief. Seeing this, they sent on shore part of their people with some of their furs, and the two parties traded together. The savages showed a marvellously great pleasure in possessing these iron wares and other commodities, dancing and going through many ceremonies, and throwing salt water over their heads with their hands. They bartered all they had to such an extent that all went back naked without anything on them; and they made signs to us that they would return on the morrow with more furs.

Soon after Cartier's arrival, the French began working their way west in Canada, while the British were still largely confined to the east coast of North America by the mountain ranges that bar access to the inland regions. In their earliest explorations of North America, the French opened the way along the St. Lawrence as far as the Lachine Rapids past Montreal. The geographical position of the St. Lawrence was vital, for it was (aside from the Mohawk River to the south) the only passage that cut through the mountains to the heart of the continent. Whoever held the St. Lawrence could open up North America; the French did precisely that.

The Trans-Canada Route left the St. Lawrence at Montreal, however. The Iroquois played a part in this decision. The five Native American nations that formed the Iroquois confederacy have aptly been called the "Romans" of eastern North America. This was the greatest Native American power east of the Mississippi, perhaps on the continent. It was an imperial power, as well; the Iroquois had been moving east from the Mississippi Valley since the 13th century and had, early in the 17th century, consolidated their hold on much of the country south of the Great Lakes and east to the Hudson River and Lake Champlain, the land traversed by what was later known as the Mohawk Trail. They effectively barred the French from the southern Great Lakes and from the routes south of the lakes until well into the 17th century, forcing the main travel and trade route to go north of the lakes.

Geography did the rest. It was far easier—and shorter—to follow the path of exploration and trade west out of Montreal along the Ottawa than to negotiate the almost 200 miles of very difficult waterway between Montreal and Lake Ontario. So it was that the main route out of Montreal started at the junction of the Ottawa and the St. Lawrence rivers and went due west along the Ottawa. This was the route that Champlain took, starting the westward trek in Canada.

Champlain's first trip west along the Ottawa was in pursuit of the two great goals that dominated French thinking in North America: the Northwest Passage to Asia and the fur trade. As had been true since Cartier's time, three-quarters of a century earlier, the main fur was beaver, highly prized in Europe for men's hats and other clothing. Champlain was following the route of the fur brigades of

British fur trade traffic, here at Fort Edmonton on the Saskatchewan, was dominated by the all-powerful Hudson's Bay Company. (Confederation Life Association)

the Ottawas, who had been trading for many years with the French in Montreal. Searching for new supplies of beaver, as the old ones became exhausted, he was traveling to meet the Hurons, who acted as middlemen in the fur trade between the French in Montreal and the tribes further west; with French encouragement, they would eagerly push expansion of the trade westward. Beaver would continue to be prized for two and a half centuries after Champlain, until the North American beaver had been all but destroyed by late in the 19th century. The westward pursuit of the vanishing beaver fueled much of the exploration of Canada, as well as that of the United States Northwest.

As to the Northwest Passage, Champlain was in pursuit of a will-of-the-wisp. One of his young followers, Robert Vignau, who had spent the winter of 1611–12 with an Algonquin tribe out beyond the present site of Ottawa near Allumette Lake on the Ottawa, claimed that he "had seen the northern sea," and that:

In seventeen days one could go from the St. Louis [Lachine] rapids to this sea and back again. He also said that he had seen pieces of the wreck of an English ship which had been lost on that coast.

Not entirely convinced, Champlain set off with Vignau to "discover" this northern sea and with it the passage to Cathay. Instead, he discovered that Vignau was a great liar. But this liar had started Champlain on the way west, for after his trip up the Ottawa to Allumette Island in 1613, he was convinced that there was indeed a great sea to the west—an inland sea.

In 1615, Champlain went west again, this time much further out along the Ottawa, past Allumette Lake and the mouth of the Mattawa River. His birchbark canoes—light, ingenious craft, adopted from the Native Americans by the French voyageurs—continued to serve him well on smaller streams as he went the short distance to Lake Nipissing. From there he took the French River west to Georgian Bay, at the eastern end of Lake Huron. He had reached the inland sea. Although Champlain went no further west than this, he had blazed the way for others.

The first of these was Etienne Brûlé, who had traveled west with Champlain. He is thought to have stayed in the Lake Huron country and to have traveled on the north shore of Lake Huron as far as the eastern end of Lake Superior in the period 1615–1620. If so, he was the first of the French to travel the next leg of the main Trans-Canada Route.

After Brûlé came Jean Nicolet, who had also traveled west with Champlain in 1615. Nineteen years later, in 1634, he traveled to the western end of Lake Huron and the Strait of Michilimackinac. Leaving what would be the main Trans-Canada Route, he passed through the strait to the north shore of Lake Michigan and to Green Bay, opening that route further for those who would later explore the Mississippi.

Other French explorers continued westward, opening up the mid-continent portions of what would ultimately be the main route from the Atlantic to the Pacific. In 1641, Father Isaac Jogues and Charles Raymbault, traveling northwest along the northern shores of Georgian Bay and Lake Huron, reached Sault St. Marie, which lay between Lakes Huron and Superior. In the 1650's, Pierre Radisson and his brother-in-law Médard Chouart explored the southern shore of Lake Superior and a considerable portion of the western and northern shores; they also traveled by land as far north as James Bay, at the southern end of Hudson Bay. By the 1660's several missions, including that of Father Jacques Marquette, had been established along the south shore of Lake Superior. And by 1679, Daniel Duluth had gone further west, beyond Lake Superior and into the country of the Sioux in what is now northern Minnesota.

In this period, the main westward routes of travel, trade, and early settlement were along the south shore of Lake Superior. The south shore was—and is—far more hospitable country, and the main Native American cultures and trading opportunities west of the lakes were to the south rather than in the northern portion of the Great Plains.

Had politics played no part in the matter, the shape of the land would have led the French and then the British into the Mississippi-Missouri system. The main Canadian route would have fed from the south shore of Lake Superior and the north shore of Lake Michigan to the Mississippi, then south on that mighty river to the Gulf of Mexico and west to the Pacific along its tributary, the Missouri—on the Lewis and Clark route. Those were, indeed, the routes that Jolliet, Marquette, La Salle, Radisson,

and Duluth began to explore. But continental political arrangements would make further Canadian explorations along these routes impossible, and the Trans-Canada Route itself would later be forced northward.

At this juncture, the British entered the picture on the Trans-Canada Route. Pierre Radisson and Médard Chouart, who had fallen out with the French in Quebec, went to England, there exciting interest in the profits that were to be gained by the Canadian fur trade; meeting Charles II; and initiating the formation of the Hudson's Bay Company, which was to have such a powerful influence on the development of western Canada.

What Radisson did was to convince the English that there were enormous profits to be made in the fur trade, especially from a base on Hudson Bay, in Cree country, from which trading could proceed without middlemen. He described the country and its people in this fashion:

> We went from Isle to Isle all that summer. We pluckt aboundance of Ducks, as of all other sort of fowles; we wanted nor fish nor fresh meate. We weare well beloved, and weare overjoyed that we promised them to come with such shipps as we invented...
> They [the Cree] is a wandering nation, and containeth a vast countrey, in winter they live ye land for the hunting sake, and in summer by the water for fishing. They are of a good nature, and not great whore masters, having but one wife, and are [more] satisfied then any others that I knewed. They cloath themselves all over with castors' [beavers'] skins in winter, in summer of staggs' skins. They are the best huntsmen of all America, and scorns to catch a castor in a trappe.

Meanwhile, the French continued to develop a route across Canada, going north and west beyond Lake Superior. Daniel Duluth had built a trading post at the mouth of the Kaministikwia River, at what is now Thunder Bay on Lake Superior. From there, French trappers and traders began to explore the country leading out to Lake Winnipeg and the Great Plains. But their progress was slow. Beyond the Great Lakes, the country was very difficult, without a single main water route west. It was almost two decades after Duluth, in 1688, that Jacques de Noyon made the long, difficult journey up the Kaministikwia to Lac des Mille Lacs, then to the Rainy River and further west to Lake of the Woods. And it was almost three decades more before Zacharie de la Noüe built Fort Frances on Rainy Lake in 1717.

During those decades, the British Hudson's Bay Company had established bases on Hudson Bay and was actively trading and beginning an exploration that would ultimately take Canadians west to the Pacific and north to the Arctic Ocean.

Radisson had clearly seen that whoever traded for western furs directly out of Hudson Bay would be able to profit greatly by elimination of Native American middlemen and also by the ability to ship furs and trade goods directly by sea to Europe. The Hudson's Bay Company did precisely that, trading south and west out of York Factory and Churchill, on the west side of Hudson Bay, from the 1670's on. While the French were opening up the Canadian plains from the Great Lakes, the British were carrying on some modest explorations of their own. August Kelsey went west on the plains out of York Factory in 1690. He apparently went as far as the Saskatchewan River, perhaps even to the Assiniboine, his mission "to discover and bring to commerce" a western tribe, perhaps the Mandans.

The last of the great French traders and explorers was Pierre Gaultier de Varennes, Sieur de la Vérendrye. During the 1730's, he and his sons journeyed to Lake Winnipeg, to Portage la Prairie, and northwest to link up with the main Native American-English trading routes west from Hudson Bay.

He built trading posts at the mouth of the Assiniboine River, at what is now Winnipeg, on the Saskatchewan, Winnipeg, and Red rivers, and at Rainy Lake, Lake of the Woods, and Lake Manitoba. La Vérendrye also went considerably south, to the Mandan country on the Missouri, anticipating and seeking the water route west along the Missouri that would later be followed to the Pacific by Lewis and Clark. He even sent his sons all the way out into the Yellowstone country, but was unable to pursue the path westward beyond the plains.

La Vérendrye also found and used a more southerly westward route past Lake of the Woods to Rainy Lake and out into the Great Plains. Advised by a local Native American guide, he went south from the Kaministikwia to the Pigeon River and then west on the Pigeon through the Grand Portage to Rainy Lake. This Grand Portage route west, roughly following what is now the Canada-United States border, became the main choice of westbound travelers for a time.

After La Vérendrye came the British. Anthony Henday explored westward out of York Factory in 1753–54. Traveling much further than his countryman, Kelsey, he went far over the plains, across the South Saskatchewan, North Saskatchewan, and Red Deer rivers into the country of the powerful Blackfeet, people with whom he wintered. He found that the Blackfeet had horses, hunted buffalo, and were skeptical as to the possible benefits of trade, as indicated by this entry from his journal, dated October 15, 1754:

Froze a little last night. Our women employed dressing beaver skins for cloathing. About 10 o'clock A.M. I was invited to the...Leader's tent: when by an interpreter I told him what I was sent for, and desired of him to allow some of his young men to go down to the Fort with me, where they would be kindly received, and get Guns. But he answered, it was far off, and they could not leave their horses

&c: and many other obstacles, though all might be got over if they were acquainted with a Canoe, and could eat Fish, which they never do. The Chief further said they never wanted food, as they followed the Buffalo and killed them with the Bows and Arrows; and he was informed the Natives that frequented the Settlements, were oftentimes starved on their journey. Such remarks I thought exceedingly true...

In the half century after Henday and La Vérendrye, that part of the Great Plains that is now in Manitoba, Saskatchewan, and Alberta was thoroughly explored and mapped, while the exploration of the Rockies and the Arctic was beginning. The plains offered no great obstacles to the British, and the potential rewards from the fur trade provided strong incentives for exploration, mapping, surveying, and building trading posts and forts.

While these French and British explorers were still pushing westward in search of the valuable furs, their two countries were struggling for control of North America, with the decision finally going to Britain. This quite altered the role and direction of the Trans-Canada Route. Before the Treaty of 1763, the British had held the east coast of the continent from north of Florida to Newfoundland, while the British Hudson's Bay Company had held the north, in a large arc extending outward from Hudson Bay. After 1763, when the British took French Canada, British explorers and traders rapidly began replacing the French, moving out along the main southern Trans-Canada Route from Montreal, Ottawa, and the Great Lakes, as well as from Hudson Bay. The French voyageurs and traders were still there, but leadership, finance, and ownership were British. The Northwest Company, operating out of Montreal, was organized in 1795; taking over the old French routes, it soon controlled three-quarters of that trade. The tremendous competition between the new Northwest Company and the older Hudson's Bay Company considerably accelerated the opening of the Canadian West to exploration and trade. In the following 25 years, both companies established a far-flung network of trading posts and forts throughout the Canadian West.

The last barrier to the Canadian journey from sea to sea was the Rockies. Alexander Mackenzie reached the Pacific first, in 1793. But his journey provided no usable route for others to follow, as he had started down the terribly difficult Fraser River and abandoned that route to cut across country and down to the sea much north of Vancouver.

In 1808, Simon Fraser set out from Fort George, on the east slope of the Rockies, to explore the river that would be named for him. He thought it was the "River of Oregon," the Columbia, leading across the mountains to the Willamette Valley and Fort Vancouver, later the destination of thousands of Americans on the Oregon

Corduroy roads of logs, sometimes built out into balconies like this one, were the forerunners of the elaborate wooden trestles that would bear the railroad westward. (From W. C. Bryant, Picturesque America, *1872)*

Trail. Instead, it was the route that Mackenzie had been forced to abandon 16 years earlier. Like Mackenzie, he found the Fraser River's rapids daunting:

> This immense body of water passing through this narrow space in a turbulent manner, forming numerous gulfs and cascades and making a tremendous noise, had an awful and forbidding appearance.

Fraser and his party could find no portage route around the turbulent waters, so they ran the rapids, as they did many more further down the river, eventually reaching the sea at what is now Vancouver. Because of the difficulty of the passage, however, Fraser had not found a workable pathway across the mountains to the Pacific, any more than Mackenzie had before him. Only later road building would enable the lower Fraser to become part of the main Trans-Canada Route, eventually to be traversed by both main railroads and motor roads.

It remained for the great Canadian explorer, surveyor, and geographer David Thompson to provide a workable route across the mountains to the Pacific, the final leg of the Canadian way west. Between 1808 and 1812, Thompson explored, surveyed, and mapped the entire Columbia River, from its source to the sea, in the process crossing Howse Pass, the main early Canadian way west across the Rockies, and thereby reaching the Columbia River system.

With Thompson, the main Canadian way west was complete. But for some decades yet, the route would be heavily used only from the St. Lawrence to the eastern end of Lake Huron, along a corridor that is still the most populous in Canada. As late as 1900, the population of Sault St. Marie was only about 7,000, and that of Sudbury, on the north shore of Lake Huron, abut 2,000.

But in the late 18th and in the 19th centuries, a number of changes occurred that would transform the Trans-Canada Route. After the American Revolution against the British, the territory west of the Great Lakes became disputed, including the Pigeon River portion of La Vérendrye's westward route, which became part of the United States when the dispute was finally resolved in 1842. As a result, Canadians were forced north of the international boundary and were obliged once again to use the older, more circuitous route north of Lake Superior, via the Kaministikwia River. The settlement of the Oregon-British Columbia boundary, also in the 1840's, had a similar effect: it cut Canadians off from the rich Columbia River basin, forcing them to cut a passage through the lower Fraser to the Pacific. Also, after the Louisiana Purchase, in 1803, the southern portion of the Great Plains—previously but tenuously held by the Canadians—became American territory, and Canadian trading access was severely limited.

The Trans-Canada Route was dealt a further blow by the 1821 merger of the two main fur companies into a single Hudson's Bay Company. The main traffic of the fur trade began to head toward York Factory and Churchill, and the fur trade route from Montreal west lost much of its importance.

Then, in 1869, two years after Canadian Confederation and the creation of the Dominion of Canada, the Hudson's Bay Company gave up the territorial rights it had held in northern and western Canada. Only then did the settlement of the Canadian West really begin, with emigrants replacing fur traders as the main travelers westward.

All these changes laid the basis for the transformation of the Trans-Canada Route from a canoe route to an overland road.

In western Canada, all the early waterway routes, including both the main east-west route and the route from Hudson Bay, had crossed at Lake Winnipeg. From there, the Hayes and Nelson rivers reached northeast out to Hudson Bay; from there, explorers could move to the Athabasca River and its lake, to the Great Slave Lake, and out the Mackenzie to the Arctic Ocean; and from there, the route crossed the plains to the Rockies via the Saskatchewan or the Athabasca River, and then through the Rockies to the Pacific by way of the Columbia or Fraser River. But settlers traveled by wagon, not canoe, creating rough wagon roads across the plains where they could. Later, when the Canadian National Railway came, the way west across the plains no longer needed waterways and cut a new route even more directly west across the plains, and then south of Howse Pass, through Kicking Horse, Rogers, and Eagle passes.

In 1871, only two years after the Dominion of Canada was created, planning for the first Trans-Canadian railroad began. It was to go through financial scandals and changes of route. More seriously, the railroad—and Canada itself—had to contend with wars and rebellions in the West, with Native Americans, and with the French-speaking mixed population called the Métis, led by Louis Riel, who wanted an independent, Catholic, French-oriented counry of their own in the West. But the railroad and the idea of the nation prevailed. The last spike of the railroad was driven on November 7, 1885, and from then on the railroad was to be the main way west. It followed the old route generally out beyond the Great Lakes and then headed west across the Great Plains through Winnipeg, Regina, Medicine Hat, Calgary, and over the mountains through Kicking Horse, Rogers, and Eagle passes to Kamloops. Finally, it swung south beside the Fraser River to Vancouver. The railroad opened the Canadian West and provided a very needed material basis for transforming Canada into a united nation.

In 1962, the transcontinental railroad was joined by a highway, the 4,860-mile Trans-Canada Highway, stretching all the way from St. John's, Newfoundland, to Victoria, British Columbia. From just inside the Gulf of St. Lawrence, at Rivière du Loup, all the way to Vancouver-Victoria, the highway roughly parallels the old main Canadain route west, the route of Cartier and all the others.

Many of the world's historic travel and trade routes are used no more, or else in such altered forms as to be almost unrecognizable. In Canada, the way west is still the way west.

This view of the modern railroad route shows the beauty and difficulty early travelers met in British Columbia. (Canadian Pacific Railroad)

Selective Bibliography

Berton, Pierre. *The Impossible Railway* (New York: Knopf, 1972). A comprehensive account of the building of the Canadian Pacific, the first Canadian transcontinental railway.

Brebner, John Bartlett. *The Discovery of North America, 1492–1806* (New York: Doubleday, 1955). A comprehensive history of the early exploration of North America.

Burpee, Lawrence J. *An Historical Atlas of Canada* (Toronto: Nelson, 1927). An excellent historical atlas, with notes relating to maps, historical population statistics, useful chronologies, place-name changes, and bibliography.

———. *The Search for the Western Sea*, 2 vols. (New York: Macmillan, 1936). An excellent, comprehensive work on the exploration of the Canadian Northwest.

———. *The Discovery of Canada* (Toronto: Macmillan, 1944). A brief, simply written, useful history of Canadian exploration, written primarily for young people but worthwhile for adult nonspecialist readers as well.

Creighton, Donald. *A History of Canada* (Boston: Houghton Mifflin, 1954). A good, standard general history of Canada.

Cumming, W. P., et al. *The Exploration of North America* (New York: Putnam's, 1974). A large, heavily illustrated work, containing a good deal of material quoted from early explorers, accompanied by editorial commentary.

De Voto, Bernard. *The Course of Empire* (Boston: Houghton Mifflin, 1952). A substantial, anecdotal history of the exploration and conquest of North America. Focuses on the United States but also contains useful Canadian trade and travel route material.

Glazebrook, G. P. de T. *A History of Transportaion In Canada* (New York: Greenwood, 1969; reprint of the 1938 edition). A detailed, comprehensive, useful work covering the entire history of land and water transport in Canada, from French Canadian beginnings through the mid-1930's.

Guillet, Edwin C. *The Story of Canadian Roads* (Toronto: University of Toronto Press, 1966). A comprehensive, well-illustrated history of major Canadian roads.

Josephy, Alvin M. *The Indian Heritage of America* (New York: Knopf, 1969). Excellent, comprehensive general work on the history and culture of the Native Americans of the Americas.

Lavender, David. *Winner Take All* (New York: McGraw-Hill, 1977). A substantial work on the Trans-Canada canoe trail, with emphasis on rivalries in the Canadian fur trade.

Munro, William Bennett. *Crusaders of New France*, vol 4. in the Chronicles of America series (New Haven: Yale University Press, 1918). A good, now standard work on early French exploration in North America.

Parkman, Francis. *France and England in North America.* Edited by Samuel Eliot Morison (London: Faber & Faber, 1954). A substantial selection from the works of Francis Parkman, covering the history of early French exploration of the St. Lawrence and Canada through the end of the British-French contest for North America.

———. *La Salle and the Discovery of the Great West* (Boston: Little, Brown, 1897). Parkman's classic work on La Salle, his explorations, and those with whom he was associated.

Wrong, George M. *The Conquest of New France*, vol. 10 in the Chronicles of America series (New Haven: Yale University Press, 1918). A good, now standard work on the British-French struggle for North America.

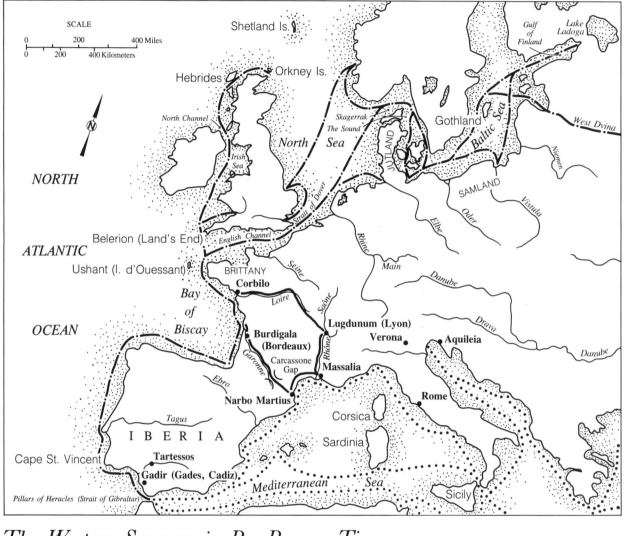

The Western Seaways in Pre-Roman Times

—·—·— Western Seaways · · · · · · · Main Connecting Sea Routes

———— Tin Routes

The Western Seaways and the Tin Routes

At some point in the late fourth or early third century B.C., a Greek explorer named Pytheas slipped through the Phoenician blockade at the Pillars of Heracles (Strait of Gibraltar) and sailed into the Western Ocean, known to us as the Atlantic. Heading up the Iberian coast, Pytheas's ship passed the Phoenician stronghold of Gadir (later Gades, now Cadiz) on a headland 70 miles from Gibraltar; five days beyond that he rounded the Sacred Headland (Cape St. Vincent) where the line of coastal cliffs begins to face straight west, fronting the open ocean. From here up to the northwesternmost promontory of Spain, Pytheas faced the danger of heavy tides, strong westerly (onshore) winds, dense fogs, and unpredictable gales. Sailing on around the deep curve of the Bay of Biscay, along the coast of Spain and southwest France, he reached Brittany, the peninsula projecting out from northwestern France into the Atlantic. But, rather than continuing to follow the coastline, as would be expected of a Mediterranean sailor, he apparently headed straight across the English Channel from Land's End in Brittany to Land's End in Cornwall. That he did so, presumably on good information from local guides, indicates that sea routes in the region were well-established. In truth, people had been abroad on the Western Seaways for some thousands of years before Pytheas arrived.

The Western Seaways run around Europe's coast from the Strait of Gibraltar past the British Isles and Scandinavia to Finland and Russia. The first leg of the Western Seaways faces the Atlantic, making a wide S-curve around the Iberian Peninsula and the Bay of Biscay to Brittany and the English Channel. From here, one main branch of the Seaways extends along Pytheas's route, from the tip of Brittany to the tip of Cornwall and on into the Irish Sea, past the Isle of Man and through the narrow North Channel between Ireland and Scotland; swinging northwest past the Western Isles of Scotland—including the Inner and Outer Hebrides—this branch continues on to the Orkneys, the Shetlands, and to the Faeroes, there meeting and merging with the North Atlantic Route to the Americas.

The other main branch of the Western Seaways runs from the tip of Brittany into the English Channel and through the narrower Strait of Dover, with its famous white chalk cliffs; on the way it links with some of the great northern European rivers: the Seine, the Thames, and the Rhine. Heading into the stormy North Sea, this branch curves northeastward around Jutland (Denmark) through the difficult passageway known as the Skaggerak and the wide channel called The Sound. Rounding the southern tip of Sweden, the route heads into the Baltic Sea, past the Oder, Vistula, Niemen, and West Dvina rivers and on into the Gulf of Finland, where it links with the Russian River Routes. Other, smaller branches of the Western Seaways feed between Norway and northeastern Britain and Scotland, and between Sweden and Poland, especially to the region of Königsberg (Kaliningrad) and Gdansk (Danzig).

As Europeans were opening up world ocean routes, and discovering a wide variety of new beings in the process, the oceans seemed full of strange monsters. (From Sebastian Munster, Cosmographia, *1550, Staatliche Museen zu Berlin)*

While the many sheltered harbors of the Western Seaways were attractive to sailors, the numerous capes proved difficult, with treacherous winds, tides, and currents. As a result, traders and travelers for many thousands of years took shortcuts across peninsulas, often using a combination of river routes and overland portages. Several such routes developed across peninsulas in Cornwall, Ireland, Scotland, and Wales; some crossed Britain itself, between the Severn River in the west and the Thames River in the east, and between the Firth of Forth and the Firth of Clyde. By the same token, the passage around Denmark through the Skaggerak was so arduous that a special route developed across the waist of Jutland, entered by a small river on either side; boats were pulled across to the head of navigation on the far river, sometimes on a roller-way.

Considerations of difficulty, distance, and politics also led to the development of overland routes across the "isthmus" of France, which sometimes replaced sea routes around the Iberian Peninsula. From the Bay of Biscay,

one of these routes entered the Gironde estuary and followed the Garonne River from the port of Bordeaux to the region of Toulouse; it then passed through the Carcassone Gap, emerging on the Mediterranean at Narbonne. The other route followed the Loire River to its headwaters and then portaged overland to the major Gallic crossroads city of Lyon, following the Rhône down to the Mediterranean and the great port of Marseilles. (Indeed, a few scholars believe that Pytheas was unable to break through the Phoenician blockade of Gibraltar and traveled overland, beginning his explorations on the Bay of Biscay.) These are known collectively as the Tin Routes, that metal being a most prized commodity in early times.

Travel on the Western Seaways goes back thousands of years, but we have very little hard evidence to tell us about the sea routes in early times. Much of what we know comes from inference, from obvious associations of peoples across tens or even hundreds of miles of open water, of the presence in grave sites and ancient garbage heaps of materials from across the seas. We know that the Western

Seaways could not have been used before around 5500 B.C., for they did not exist at that time. The British Isles, connected to Europe during the last Ice Age, gradually subsided over the millennia, and the waters of the Atlantic flowed in, forming the Strait of Dover and the North Sea where land bridges had once existed. The peoples of northwest Europe, still deep in the Stone Age, apparently began crossing the seas soon after they opened.

By 3500 B.C., when the seas reached approximately their modern configuration (although parts of the British Isles are still sinking), there is clear evidence of contact along the Western Seaways. From southern France, Cornwall, northeast Ireland, and the Isle of Man in the Irish Sea to the Western Isles of Scotland, peoples used the same kinds of tools and implements, indicating maritime connections, if not necessarily regular travel. These peoples presumably used boats made from skins sewn on frames, possibly sealed with pitch, as they did later; they also used dugouts, some of which have been preserved from this period in Danish peat bogs, though these were better suited to river use than for the open seas. Peoples along the eastern branch of the Western Seaways also shared some aspects of their culture, with influences from central Europe spreading from the southern Baltic coast across the waters to the Scandinavian littoral and southeastern Britain. Stone axes manufactured in factory sites, some of them on islands, were transported across the water along these main lines of the Western Seaways.

By one or both of these routes, the practices of farming and of domesticating animals reached across the seas into the British Isles by the third millennium B.C. Some time after that, the practice of building Megalithic (great stone) communal graves appeared along the Western Seaways, especially on the Atlantic side. While archaeologists once thought this practice was adopted from the western Mediterranean, others now disagree. In any case, the seas certainly tied together the Megalithic peoples; their great stone circles, like Stonehenge, which appear from Brittany to Scotland, attest to that. Indeed, for many archaeologists, this ranks as the golden age of the Western Seaways; as V. Gordon Childe put it: "...the grey waters of the Irish Sea were as bright with Neolithic [New Stone Age] argonauts as the Western Pacific is today."

In about the beginning of the second millennium B.C., techniques of metalworking reached Atlantic Europe. From the Danube region of Eastern Europe, the Bell-Beaker Folk—so-named for their distinctive pottery—spread through much of Western Europe; some of these people, probably an Indo-European group who came to be known as the Celts, apparently brought knowledge of copperworking across the sea to the British Isles in about 1800 B.C. Knowledge of bronzeworking followed soon after, and it was this that would play such an important part in the development of the Western Seaways. Copper hardened with tin becomes a material far superior to either soft copper alone or to stones; but, while copper is relatively plentiful, tin is more rare. The attempts to find, develop, and hold sources of precious tin—located in Cornwall, Brittany, and Spain—were a main motivation for trade and travel in this period.

While Western Europe was nominally in the Bronze Age, its needs were at first small, probably served by itinerant bronzesmiths skilled at making daggers and axes or by traders distributing such products from a few central sites. Interestingly, although Ireland had little or no tin, many specialized bronzeworking sites are found in the northeastern region around modern Belfast; since this was also the site of many stoneworking factories in earlier times, the inhabitants clearly had a long tradition as skilled artisans, supplying their neighbors in Ireland and Britain with many of their metal implements. In this period, roughly the middle of the second millennium B.C., the main route connecting the British Isles with Europe seems to have been that across the English Channel and the North Sea. Nor was the contact all one way. Fine Irish and British metalwork was exported into Europe and was sometimes even copied by continental smiths. While trade was being carried on rather peacefully on the overland Amber Routes, traffic apparently declined on the Atlantic branch of the Western Seaways.

Trading all along the Western Seaways seems to have revived later in the second millennium B.C., possibly because a new series of invasions by various Indo-European peoples temporarily disrupted the overland Amber Routes. Archaeological finds from this late Bronze Age period attest to the spread of trading contacts. A merchant ship which sank off northwest Spain (near the site of Columbus's later port of embarkation) in this period contained jewelry not only from the British Isles but also from Sicily. Similarly, Mediterranean glass, amber from the Baltic, and continental bronzework are found on the island of Lewis, in the Outer Hebrides, the Orkneys and Shetlands also sharing in this trade; and Irish and British goods were still reaching the coasts of the North and Baltic Seas. But still all is conjecture and inference; we know almost nothing directly about the people who traveled the Western Seaways.

Nor does the picture change with the appearance of Mediterranean traders. Seeking to supplement their own meager metal resources, peoples from the eastern Mediterranean were moving westward toward Spain in this same period. The first to do so, possibly even before the second millennium B.C., were probably sailors from Crete, who may even have penetrated the Strait of Gibraltar to trade on the metal-rich Guadalquivir River. Whether they traded with other peoples further along the Atlantic coast, we do not know. Like most early Mediterranean venturers, they were traders, not colonists, and they established only minimal trading posts on their routes. In any case, invasions and earthquakes in their homeland disrupted

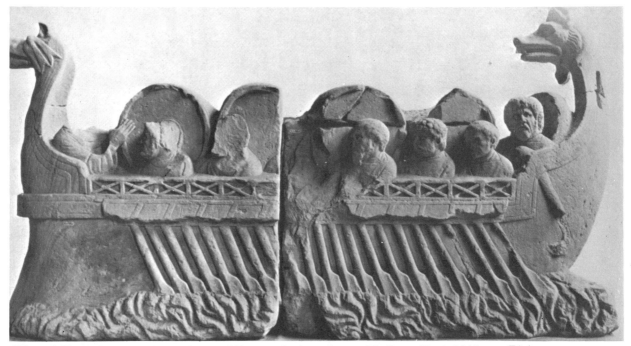

Using craft like this Roman wine boat, traders crossed France on the river-and-portage Tin Routes. (Provincial Museum, Trier)

the Mediterranean routes, putting an end to Cretan trading.

In this period, new waves of Celts were moving across Europe, settling in the regions of modern France and Germany, and spreading also to the coasts of Iberia. By the time Mediterranean traders reappeared on the Western Seaways, about the beginning of the first millennium B.C., these Celts controlled much of the Atlantic seaboard of France, Spain, and Portugal.

Tradition has it that the Phoenicians, far from their homeland in the Middle East, founded the island stronghold of Gadir (Gades to the Romans, now Cadiz) past Gibraltar in about 1200 B.C. But archaeologists suggest that they actually arrived some centuries later and may have been preceded by Greek traders. The fifth century B.C. Greek historian Herodotus certainly was unequivocal on that point:

> The Phocaeans [founders of Massalia, or Marseilles] were the first of the Greeks to undertake long sea voyages. It was they who made...known...Iberia and Tartessos.

According to Herodotus, Tartessos, most likely the metal-rich region above Seville on the Guadalquivir River, was an "untouched virgin market" before the arrival of the Greeks in around the mid-seventh century B.C. Since the region had large resources of copper, gold, silver, and the precious tin, the Greeks eagerly—and profitably—traded their manufactures for raw metal ingots.

If the Greeks were first, the Phoenicians were not far behind, founding and fortifying Gadir and the site of Algeciras just a few miles beyond the nine-mile-wide Strait of Gibraltar. By about 530 B.C., they were strong enough to close the strait to all but Phoenician (Punic) ships and to raze the rival trading city of Tartessos. (Some people think the destruction of Tartessos may have sparked, in some convoluted way, the legend of the lost civilization of Atlantis, mentioned by Plato.) About 70 years later, they apparently sent north an explorer named Himilco; as far as we know, he reached only the northwestern cape of Spain. Greek writers suggest that the Phoenicians sailed all the way up the coast to Brittany for Cornish and Breton tin, but archaeological finds do not confirm this. It seems more likely that Celtic traders brought tin south to trade with the Phoenicians, supplementing the dwindling supply of tin from traditional Spanish sources.

The Phoenicians are peculiarly unhelpful on this point. Although the Phoenicians gave the world the alphabetic system of writing, they were themselves remarkably secretive. Not only did they keep no surviving records, which might have fallen into the hands of competitors, but they actively obscured the picture by spreading stories filled with deliberate errors and fanciful horrors. In fairness, some of these might have had their basis in fact; the monsters that they averred haunted the Western Ocean might well have been the whales that, in those early times, abounded in the Bay of Biscay. In later times, we are told, when a Roman ship tried to follow a Phoenician vessel to learn about its route, the Phoenician captain deliberately ran his ship aground, causing the Roman ship to be wrecked and destroyed. So important was secrecy to the Phoenicians that the Phoenician captain was reportedly reimbursed for his loss by his countrymen in gratitude for his guarding the knowledge of the Western Seaways. In any case, they were successful in their attempt; their knowledge died with them.

Whether or not the Phoenicians did sail all the way north on the Western Seaways—as their general sailing prowess and the finding of some Carthaginian coins 900 miles out in the Atlantic on the Azores Islands indicate they may have—the Celts certainly traveled along the Atlantic seaboard. Indeed, the route from the Atlantic coast of Spain and France across the tips of Brittany and Cornwall and into the Irish Sea and beyond might well be called the Celtic Seaway, for this great maritime pathway united the Celtic peoples for many centuries, until the rise of the great ocean-going routes of the Renaissance made the old coastal routes less important.

Meanwhile Greeks—cut off from the Western Seaways for at least three centuries by the Phoenician blockade—were forced to develop alternative routes from the western Mediterranean to northern sources of tin. Celtic traders on the sea portion of the route operated primarily from islands, which were protected and therefore somewhat neutral ground. Drawing on earlier sources, the first century B.C. writer Diodorus gives us a picture of trade on the Tin Routes. He noted that the people of Belerion (Land's End in Cornwall) are "very fond of strangers, and, from their intercourse with foreign merchants, are civilized in their manner of life." Mining and preparing the tin into fist-shaped ingots, they carry it to a "certain island lying off Britain called Ictis." This is clearly identified as St. Michael's Mount, off Belerion, which is an island or peninsula, depending on the tide, as Diodorus describes:

> During the ebb of the tide the intervening space is left dry, and they carry over into this island the tin in abundance in their wagons...Here then the merchants buy the tin from the natives and carry it over to Gaul...

Celtic ships apparently made a similar stop off Land's End in Brittany, where the Île d'Ouessant (Ushant, known to the Greeks and Romans as Uxisame) functioned likewise as an entrepôt for Breton tin. (Later Roman writers would note that Tartessians also visited the islands off Brittany.) The trading vessels would then put in at the Celtic settlement of Corbilo, near modern Nantes, on the Loire River. From there, some goods and merchants would make their way inland along the Loire River as it curves east and then south through Gaul, around the Central Massif. A short portage would then take them across to the Rhône-Saône system which cuts north-south through eastern Gaul, down to the Greek city of Massalia (Marseilles). But most traffic in these centuries seems to

have continued by sea from Corbilo, the land routes most likely being more dangerous and time-consuming. Trading vessels from Corbilo would move down the Biscay coast to the Celtic town of Burdigala (Bordeaux) on the Gironde estuary. Following the Garonne River upstream to near modern Toulouse, merchants would then cut overland through the Carcassone Gap, emerging at the Greek settlement of Narbo (Narbonne); from there goods were probably transshipped on the coast road, the Heraclean Way, to Massalia, the Greeks' home base in the region. Diodorus himself gives little information on this point, noting only that:

> ...the merchants buy the tin from the natives and carry it over to Gaul, and after traveling over land for about thirty days, they finally bring their loads on horses to the mouth of the Rhône.

These Tin Routes apparently operated for some centuries; even when tin was no longer so vital, as Europeans were replacing bronze with iron, merchants brought fine goldwork from Ireland and amber from Jutland over this route, sending north wine and oil.

The Greeks were, however, consummate sailors. And, in about the third century B.C., they seized the opportunity to slip through the Carthaginian (Phoenician) blockade at Gibraltar; they may have been able to do so because Carthage was preoccupied by its wars with Rome. Pytheas's exploratory expedition, sponsored by the citizens of Massalia, was apparently aimed at opening profitable routes to the Cassiterides (Tin Islands, possibly the Scilly Isles off Cornwall) along the Western Seaways.

Pytheas did not stop at Cornwall, however, but went on to circumnavigate Britain via the North and Irish Seas, and possibly to land in Kantion (Kent), in southeastern Britain, and explore overland to Cornwall, prime source of the sought-after tin. He moved beyond even these explorations into the unknown waters of the North Atlantic past the Orkney Islands (which he knew as the Orcas), to a place called Thule. Pytheas's own writings are lost, and we know of his travels only second- and third-hand through references in the work of others. From such descriptions, Thule has been variously identified as the Shetlands, the coast of Norway, the Faeroes, even Iceland. He also reached far enough north, possibly above the Arctic Circle, to encounter heavy chunks of ice in the seas, the first Mediterranean sailor to do so, as far as we know. Pytheas's reputation suffered for many years because the eminent classical Greek geographer Strabo rightly supposed, on the basis of his knowledge of northern Europe, that so far north the seas would have been frozen; he therefore assumed that Pytheas was a liar, a judgment accepted for many centuries. But Strabo could not have known of the Gulf Stream, which so warms these northern waters that flowers bloom on the Scilly Isles in January and palm trees flourish in western Scotland. Pytheas's explorations even extended into the Baltic Seas, possibly as far as the Polish coast near modern Gdansk (Danzig) and Königsberg (Kaliningrad) at the mouth of the Vistula River; here, in the region he called Samland, he sought and may have found the source of Baltic amber which had crossed Europe overland for many centuries, being distributed around the Mediterranean primarily by Greek merchants.

Pytheas was undoubtedly one of the greatest explorers of classical times, though it is clear that he was traversing sea lanes that had long been used by native sailors. His explorations had little effect on Greek trade, however. The Carthaginian blockade of the Strait of Gibraltar was reimposed after Pytheas's time, remaining more or less in place until the beginning of the third century B.C., when Carthage fell before Rome. But even then, Massalian Greeks, allied with Rome, did not attempt to

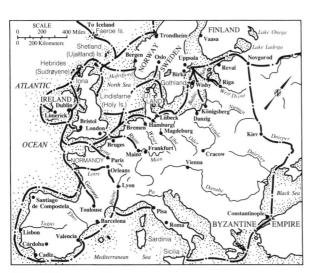

The Western Seaways in the 10th and 11th Centuries

———·——·—— Main Viking Routes

open trading on the Western Seaways. The reason was simple; Pytheas himself saw that "the portion of Spain that faces north is more readily accessible by way of the Celtic land than by sailing the Ocean." Indeed, the overland distance between Narbo and Burdigala on the Gironde was less than 300 miles, while the sea route around the Iberian Peninsula between those two points was more like 1,700 miles. So the overland Tin Routes remained dominant from the fourth to the first centuries B.C., while the southern part of the Western Seaways languished.

The Tin Routes declined only when the Romans absorbed into their empire both the Iberian Peninsula and the Greek trading colonies on the Gallic coast. In the first century B.C., the Romans found new sources of tin in Spain, diminishing their dependence on the more northerly sources. But more to the point, the Romans moved to take all of Gaul. Long before setting foot in Britain, Julius Caesar dealt a severe blow to the British Isles for, in 56 B.C., he conquered the Celtic peoples of Brittany and destroyed the fleet of wooden ships with leather sails in which they had carried tin across the English Channel and Bay of Biscay. The great days of the Tin Routes were over.

The Western Seaways were eclipsed altogether for some centuries in the wake of the Romans. Always landlubbers, the Romans relied on their magnificent roads for trade and travel, using the sea only for necessary crossings. For many centuries after the Romans arrived on the Atlantic coast, the Western Seaways operated less as trade and travel routes than as migration and missionary routes.

It was the migrations that came first. Flying before Caesar and Claudius, who in 43 A.D. conquered Britain, many Celts emigrated from southwestern Gaul and Brittany along the Western Seaways, especially to Cornwall. Peoples from Southern Britain, fleeing the double invasion by both Gallic Celts and Romans, emigrated further north; blocked by the powerful Brigantes, who held the Midlands, these refugees followed the long-established sea routes northward. Settling first in the Western Isles of Scotland, especially on Skye and Tiree, where they developed their distinctive *brochs* (large stone towers) and Iron Age culture, they soon moved to the Outer Hebrides, the Orkneys, the Shetlands, and the Scottish Highlands, merging with the other peoples who had settled these regions over the previous centuries. Though little trade was carried on among these rather self-sufficient peoples, they continued to live a life focused on the seaways, using their sewn-skin-on-wicker curraghs and smaller coracles for fishing, whaling, and inter-island communication.

The Western Seaways became important once again after the departure of the Romans from Britain around 400 A.D. Along the sea routes, emigrants invaded Britain from the North Sea; these were Angles and Saxons from the lands between the Rhine and Elbe Rivers and Jutes from Jutland. Pressing into Britain from the east, they settled most of southern, central, and northeastern England, pushing many Britons into the western lands bordering the Irish Sea, especially into Wales and Cornwall.

The stage was set for the Western Seaways to become missionary routes. Christianity had arrived in Britain under the Romans. But in the fifth century, when Europe was being invaded by waves of "barbarians" from the Eurasian Steppe, many Celts migrated along the old Tin Routes—from cities like Lyon and Bordeaux—and the

Western Seaways to the British Isles, especially to Cornwall and Wales. They brought with them a form of Christianity that emphasized the ascetic, with monks, hermits, and *peregrini* (pilgrims) playing an important role in their religion. Meanwhile, many Britons—pressed by the Angles and Saxons—had brought their Roman Christianity with them to the western lands. Roman and Gallic Christianity fused along the Western Seaways, most notably along the Severn estuary and in the Cotswolds, into a distinctive Celtic Christianity, which would flourish along the Atlantic sea routes for centuries; Ireland produced a heretical form of Christianity called Pelagianism, but this was effectively exterminated after the pope in Rome sent some representatives along the Western Seaways for the purpose. In the fifth and sixth centuries, the Roman church began to send other emissaries to introduce Christianity to Anglo-Saxon England and to act as bishops for the Celtic Christians.

But the movement was not all one way. Celtic Christianity, especially Irish Christianity, was impelled outward by religious zeal. In what came to be known as the Age of the Saints, culminating in the seventh century, roving monks and pilgrims fanned out along the Western Seaways to spread their faith. The routes of these roving missionaries can be traced by the remains of churches dedicated to particular saints on coastlines and peninsulas all along the Western Seaways.

Some of these saints reversed the trend of migration and headed south. St. Samson, for example, crossed from Wales, Ireland, and Cornwall across to Brittany, founding there a famous monastery. Such missionaries often preferred trans-peninsular crossings, their aim, after all, being to convert or revive adherents. St. Samson's seventh century biographer, for example, reported that when he landed at Cornwall, he sent his ship on ahead and "arranged for a cart to convey his holy vessels and books and harnessed two horses to his chariot which he had brought with him from Ireland." Celtic Christian missionaries even reached along the old sea routes as far south as northwestern Spain, where they established the missionary of Santa Maria de Bretoña in the late fifth or early sixth century.

Missionaries also operated in the northern parts of the Western Seaways. Religious ambassadors like St. Patrick and St. Columba established churches and monasteries in northern Ireland, the Isle of Man, western Scotland, Iona, and across the isthmus between the Forth and Clyde estuaries in southern Scotland and Northumbria, especially on the Holy Island of Lindisfarne.

In the seventh and eight centuries, when the Arab Moslems moved into Spain and even took Bordeaux and the surrounding region of Aquitaine for a time, these Celtic Christian connections were broken along the Western Seaways. But missionaries continued to press northward. Celtic—especially Irish—missionaries, who

had in previous centuries moved across the northern seas in their curraghs and coracles to the Orkneys, the Shetlands, and the Faeroes, moved even further northwest to Iceland, hundreds of miles out in the North Atlantic. There they were found by the "pagan" Vikings, who arrived somewhat later.

During the many centuries when the rest of the Western Seaways had been maritime highways, the Baltic Sea had been a backwater, while the North Sea had lain in the shadow of the Irish Sea. Cultural achievements spread slowly across these seas, first to the Scandinavian coast and only much later inland; much of Scandinavia had languished in the Stone Age while the Germans and Britons were using bronze, and the use of iron likewise came late to Scandinavia. A few centuries before Christ, Pytheas may have visited the Gutones (Goths), who handled the Baltic end of the amber trade, but the Romans largely ignored the lands east of the Rhine. What trade there was in these early centuries generally followed the south coast of the North and Baltic Seas, avoiding the hazardous passage through the Skaggerak by portaging across lower Jutland; this overland traffic made the fortune of the city of Schleswig, in the region of Holstein, in medieval times.

In the early sixth century, merchant-adventurers from the Frisian Islands off the German coast between the Rhine and the Elbe rivers began to operate trading routes between northwestern Europe and the less-developed peoples of the Baltic, using the traditional overland route to avoid the Skaggerak. They developed numerous trading connections around the Baltic, often on easy-to-defend islands or peninsulas, like their forebears on the Western Seaways. Among the cities they traded with were Birka, in east-central Sweden; old Lübeck, just beyond the eastern side of the neck of Jutland; and island posts at the mouth of the Oder and the Vistula, the latter near modern Gdansk. The Frisians were so dominant that, until the ninth century, the North Sea was often called the Frisian Sea. They had a significant problem with piracy from all shores of the Baltic, however, and from among these raiding peoples sprang one group that would transform the character of the Western Seaways, making the North and Baltic sea routes for the first time equal partners with the Atlantic routes. This group, known popularly as the Vikings (pirates), actually included three main peoples: the Norse, or Northmen, from Norway; the Danes from Jutland (Denmark); and the Swedes (Varangians, also called Rus).

Bursting out in all directions from Scandinavia in the ninth century, the Vikings made the northern seas the center of their world. The Varangians concentrated on Eastern Europe. Penetrating Slavic territory at the head of the Gulf of Finland, they moved inland to build the great trading city of Novgorod on Lake Ilmen. Pressing southward from here, they opened the Russian River

Crossing the Channel to take England, the Normans still had boats much like their not-long removed Viking forebears. (From the Bayeux Tapestry, authors' archives)

Routes to the Black and Caspian seas, where they traded with Byzantium, Moslem Persia, and the peoples of Central Asia. The overland routes of Europe being in disarray at this time, the Russian River Routes became the main trans-European route, as attested by the large number of Arab coins found along the Baltic coastline from the eighth and ninth centuries. After an initial period of raiding, these Varangian traders made the Baltic a central waterway, with centers at Birka and at the large island of Gothland off Sweden.

The Norse and the Danes took a different course, toward Western Europe, with the Norse concentrating on the northern islands and the circle of the Irish Sea, while the Danes focused on eastern England and northwestern France. From the region of Bergen, Norse adventurers first moved to the Shetlands and Orkneys, using them as bases for their invasion of northern England, Scotland, and Ireland. With their narrow, single-sailed, oared ships, they appeared out of the blue at Lindisfarne in 793 and Iona in 795, using these as closer stepping-stones for attacks elsewhere in the region. These being settled and literate lands, the depredations produced many written records of horror; by 820, the *Annals of Ulster* lamented that: "...the sea spewed forth floods of foreigners over Erin, so that no haven, no landing place, no stronghold, no fort, no castle might be found but it was submerged by waves of Vikings and pirates." Celtic monks built high cylindrical towers as refuges for themselves and their religious treasures, but to little avail.

By the mid-ninth century, Norse raiders were supplanted by Norse settlers, who took Armagh in the north-east and built fortified bases at several key sites around Ireland, including Dublin and Waterford and perhaps Cork and Limerick (though they may have been settled somewhat later). It was in this period that Norse groups, including some Irish members, began to settle in Iceland. Other waves of Norse raiders arrived in the late ninth and early tenth centuries, making seasonal raids during the warm months and returning to winter in the northern islands; later they sometimes adopted bases closer to Ireland, especially the Isle of Man, which became the base for the 11th–13th century kingdom of Man and the Sudreys (the Western Isles of Scotland, "southern isles" in Norse). By the early 11th century, the Norse raids had virtually ended, and the Norse settlers in Celtic lands began to form a new fusion, centered on the Christian religion, which the newcomers adopted.

The Danish Vikings had yet another focus. From Jutland and its eastern islands, they swung through the Skaggerak and aimed at England, notably at Yorkshire; the Fen Country around the Wash; East Anglia, which bulges into the North Sea; and the lands around the Thames estuary, especially Kent, to the south. After long battles with the Angles, Saxons, and Jutes, their predecessors, they too settled down into uneasy stasis in England. But the Danes (along with some Norse raiders via Ireland) also cut deep into the continent along Europe's many navigable rivers. Down the Rhine, Seine, Loire, and Gironde-Garonne they pushed. A ninth-century observer, Ermentarius of Noirmoutier, an island off the mouth of the Loire, gives a graphic picture of the effect of the Viking invasions:

Medieval Bordeaux built its prosperity on transporting wine to the British Isles and pilgrims to the continent. (From Antoine du Pinet, Planz, *1564)*

The number of ships grows: the endless stream of Vikings never ceases to increase. Everywhere the Christians are victims of massacres, burnings, plunderings: the Vikings conquer all in their path, and no one resists them: they seize Bordeaux, Périgueux, Limoges, Angoulême and Toulouse. Angers, Tours and Orleans are annihilated and an innumerable fleet sails up the Seine and the evil grows in the whole region. Rouen is laid waste, plundered and burnt: Paris, Beauvais and Meaux taken, Melun's strong fortress leveled to the ground, Chartres occupied, Evreux and Bayeux plundered, and every town besieged. Scarcely a town, scarcely a monastery is spared: all the people fly, and few are those who dare to say, "Stay and fight, for our land, children, homes!" In their trance, preoccupied with rivalry, they ransom for tribute what they ought to defend with the sword, and allow the kingdom of the Christians to perish.

The Viking visit to Noirmoutier itself is particularly memorable, for here, in 842, they elected to stay the winter rather than returning home at the end of the raiding season. Other groups gradually did the same along the coast of France, eventually forming the basis of the Norman people, who would in 1066 conquer England from

the south in a new wave of invasion. Vikings headed further south, as well, penetrating across the Tin Route, threatening Lisbon, and entering the Guadalquivir to attack Seville, where they met the Moors who had recently arrived in Spain. Proceeding along the Western Seaways, the Vikings even attacked North Africa and entered the Mediterranean, some settling in southern France, near the termini of the old Tin Routes. Most Vikings, or Normans, remained in northern Europe, however. And as they gradually adopted Christianity, more peaceful trade and travel returned to the Western Seaways.

Celtic-Norman Christianity still had a strong bias toward saints and pilgrimages. As calm returned, Christians once more set out on the Western Seaways to visit shrines. Their routes often followed those of the saints they honored, especially along and across the peninsulas of Wales and Cornwall. The seventeenth century Welsh historian George Owen noted that the famous chapel of St. David's in Pembrokeshire and its subsidiary chapels to other saints were all:

...near to the sea side and adjoining the places where those that come by sea commonly landed. They

447

were placed here to draw the devotion of the seamen and passengers when they first came ashore: other pilgrims us'd likewise to come to them.

Also prominent among pilgrimage sites on the Western Seaways were St. Michael's Mount, where once traders had brought their tin to trade, and Mont St. Michel, across the English Channel at the head of the Gulf of St.-Malo scooped out of Brittany. But perhaps most prominent of the pilgrimage sites on the Western Seaways came to be Santiago de Compostela, the supposed tomb of the Apostle St. James (Santiago). Though the overland routes through France to this shrine are most famous, many pilgrims came by sea to this region in northwest Spain long linked by the Western Seaways with Celtic Christianity. Some followed the old Tin Route to Bordeaux on the Gironde estuary, cutting south to join the main

Staples like the food carried in this Latvian boat were the mainstay of the Hanseatic League's trade. (New York Public Library)

overland pilgrimage route; but many others took ships directly from the north to the port of La Coruña, near Compostela itself. Trade and pilgrimage went hand in hand during medieval times, and many pilgrims sailed on the ships that bore wine and oil from France to the British Isles.

During early medieval times, the main port on the North Sea coast was Bruges, in Flanders (now Belgium). Taking advantage of its easily defended island position in the marshy lowlands and its contact with both the growing international trade fairs of Western Europe and the wool producers of Britain, Bruges built a thriving textile industry. Medieval ships of low draft could readily come up by river to Bruges and its artificially deepened port of Damme, but as the river began to silt up, new canals and a lock at nearby Sluys had to be built to attempt to keep shipping lanes open to Bruges. These water control activities served as prototypes for the land reclamation projects that would allow much of the Netherlands and Flanders to arise from the sea in the coming centuries.

But in the years following the Viking invasions, the center of activity on the Western Seaways shifted into the Baltic Sea, terminus for trade routes to Russia and the Orient. Drawn by this attractive trade, German traders began moving around the Baltic in the 12th century, establishing bases all along the seacoast from Lübeck to Riga, with a major trading colony at Wisby, on the island of Gothland. With the Skaggerak still difficult, the overland crossing of Jutland remained important. It is no accident that when the cities of the Baltic and North Seas formed a cooperative network known as the Hanseatic League, Lübeck and Hamburg, on either side of Jutland's land bridge, were among its most powerful members. Both had become "free" cities, able to carry on trade without interference from the lords of the region, in the early 13th century. Led by Lübeck, Cologne, and Hamburg, the Hanseatic League, formed in the second half of the 13th century, spread throughout the Baltic and North seas to include almost 100 cities, not only seacoast cities, but also many river ports deep in the continent, like Cracow on the Vistula and Frankfurt on the Main. Hanseatic traders also pushed overland deeper into Europe, meeting Italian traders pressing northward from the Mediterranean, in the process reviving overland trade.

But it was the sea trade that formed the heart of the Hanseatic League's activities. Throughout its circle of influence, Hansa ports supplied warehouses and docks for the collection and shipment of goods from the interior, in exchange for manufactured goods from elsewhere. It also established depots for its merchants in foreign cities like London, Bruges, Novgorod, and Bergen, on the west coast of Norway, and even at lesser ports like Britain's Boston, Hull, Yarmouth, and Lynn. The trade goods varied with the port. For London, trade revolved around wool, lead, and still-important tin; at Bruges, textiles were prime, along with wine and metalwork; at Bergen, salt fish, whale oils, and timber topped the list; while at Novgorod furs, honey, wax, and flax from the hinterland were joined by more exotic luxuries such as silks, spices, and pearls from the great trading marts to the south.

Strong as they were, however, the Hansards never enjoyed a real monopoly of the Baltic trade. In the 14th century, English and Dutch merchants began to make their presence known. Britain, which had long exported wool to Bruges, now sent it to Calais across the English Channel. More to the point, British and Dutch traders moved into the Baltic itself, sailing around Jutland to trade at various ports, especially Danzig (Gdansk). British and Norwegian fishers and traders were dominant on the North Atlantic routes toward Iceland, as well, while Britain and France both drew strength from trade on the Tin Routes—now becoming wine and pilgrimage routes—to France.

Realizing that there was money to be made from their control of the sea routes around Jutland, the Danes,

This lively, crowded merchant ship is just setting off onto the Western Seaways. (By Hans Holbein the Younger, 1533, Städelsches Kunstinstitut, Frankfurt-on-Main)

in about 1430, began to charge heavy tolls on ships sailing into the Baltic; the Hanseatic League, with its control of the overland crossing, at first benefited from this pressure on their competition. The Hansards also established a temporary dominance over the North Sea and North Atlantic trade, wresting control from the British and the Norwegians. In addition, Lübeck, still leader of the league, controlled the prosperous herring fishing rights in the Sound, the main channel eastward from the Skagerrak to the Baltic proper. With the Mongols in control of the Eurasian Steppe Route between the mid-13th and mid-14th centuries, traders from Hansa cities such as Cracow and Frankfurt followed Marco Polo's lead and traveled thousands of miles to trade for exotic Eastern luxuries.

But just as the Hanseatic League seemed to be at its height, several events conspired to weaken it. One was the reopening of the Western Seaways from the Mediterranean. During the long years of Moslem control, the Strait of Gibraltar was effectively closed to European traf-

fic, and the ancient Atlantic ports of the Iberian peninsula had languished. But with the decline of Moslem power and the rise of the Italian city-states, Mediterranean sailors once more moved out onto the Western Seaways into what they called the "Great Sea of Darkness." At the turn of the 14th century, both Genoa and Venice began to send galleys directly to Bruges, London, and Southampton. Also, in the early 15th century, the North Sea herring for unknown reasons ceased their seasonal migration into the Sound for the summer; Lübeck's and the Hansards' loss was the Netherlands' gain, for Dutch fishermen now reaped the herring harvest in the North Sea, laying the basis for their rise as a maritime power. In 1361, the rising Danes destroyed the central Hanseatic base of Wisby, on Gothland, which never recovered. In addition, the continental routes, which had sparked the rise of the Hansa towns, fell into disarray. The 14th century saw the infamous Black Plague, from which perhaps one-quarter of Europe's population died; peasant risings and, after the rise of Protestantism in the 15th century, religious wars completed the breakdown. But the worst blow to the Hanseatic League came with the European Age of Discovery, when the Baltic Sea once again became a backwater on the Western Seaways.

These European explorations were sparked largely by the Venetian and Genoese sailors who had reopened the Iberian portion of the Western Seaways. While Spain and Portugal were throwing off the last of Moslem control, cities like Cadiz, Seville, and Lisbon were becoming ports of call for Venetian ships. All along the Atlantic waters, sailors and merchants gained knowledge from their contact with experienced Italian sea-traders. But the Italian city-states were themselves in decline. Their sources of Eastern goods were increasingly being pinched off by the Turks, newly arrived in the Middle East; extra duties sent prices soaring, while lack of product left many Genoese and Venetian sailors out of work. These migrated to the Western Seaways, supplying many of the skilled sailors for the great European explorations. It is well known that Columbus was Genoese, as were many of the early explorers of the Cape of Good Hope Route around Africa and of the routes to and around South America. What is less well known is that many of these Italian sailors penetrated northern waters as well: the great British explorer John Cabot was, in truth, Venetian-born Giovanni Caboto, who explored out of Bristol under a patent granted by Henry VII.

Gradually the center of gravity on the Western Seaways shifted north to the English Channel, especially to the Netherlands and Britain; by the 16th century, Venice, short of timber, was even having her ships built by the Dutch. It was during this period that the great modern ports of northern Europe first came into prominence, as many of the older, smaller ports, such as Bruges and Narbonne, silted up. Antewerp replaced Bruges in the early 16th century, but was ruined during a war and was itself replaced as the international capital for trade and finance in the 17th century by Amsterdam, which benefited from the active Dutch land reclamation projects. Amsterdam's rise was fueled, in part, by the arrival of many Jews expelled from Spain and Portugal, who made good use of their experience in overseas trade. London's rise as a dominant seaport came in the next century, as Britain's eastern empire grew. The 17th century also saw the development of newer ports such as Le Havre, on the estuary of the Seine River.

Trained in the difficult Atlantic waters with the help of Italian experts, mariners from the Western Seaways explored, opened, developed, and ran routes around the world, beginning in the late 15th century. At first, the Portuguese and Spanish were dominant, while later the Dutch, English, and French came to control these global waterways. But in these modern times, the Western Seaways were gradually eclipsed, as the old coastal routes were replaced by the great circle routes of ships braving the open seas. For Europe's ocean-going ships, first tiny *caravels*, later larger *nãos* and galleons, still later clipper ships and packets, and finally liners and supertankers, the Western Seaways were simply an entryway to the world.

Yet the coastal waters have not been abandoned. Fishermen continue to ply their trade all along the ragged coasts of Western Europe. As for the missionaries and pilgrims who once followed the "Celtic Seaway," they have their closest counterpart in the recreational mariners who sail their yachts toward the Mediterranean—and who might be forgiven for avoiding the icy and turbulent waters of the Baltic and North Seas.

Selective Bibliography

Bautier, Robert-Henri. *The Economic Development of Medieval Europe* (London: Thames and Hudson, 1971). A well-illustrated, readable work, with separate chapters on the trade of the Western Seaways.

Bowen, E. G. *Britain and the Western Seaways* (London: Thames and Hudson, 1972). Part of the Ancient Peoples and Places series. A very useful view of the Atlantic routes as seen from the north, emphasizing archaeological evidence.

Braudel, Fernand. *The Wheels of Commerce.* Translated from the French by Siân Reynolds (New York: Harper & Row, 1979). Volume 2 of *Civilization and Capitalism, 15th–18th Century.* A general work with much fascinating detail.

Carpenter, Rhys. *Beyond the Pillars of Heracles: The Classical World Seen Through the Eyes of its Discoverers* (New York: Delacorte, 1966). Part of the Great Explorers series. Includes several chapters of text and quotations on Mediterranean sailors exploring the Atlantic.

Clark, J. G. D. *Prehistoric Europe: The Economic Basis* (London: Methuen, 1974; reprint of 1952 edition). A fine overview, with separate chapters on trade and on travel and transport.

East, W. Gordon. *An Historical Geography of Europe,* Third Edition Revised (London: Methuen, 1948). A very useful overview, with chapters on the sea routes in late medieval and early Renaissance times.

Great Rivers of Europe. (London: Weidenfeld and Nicolson, 1966). Illustrated articles by various authors.

Herrmann, Paul. *Conquest by Man.* Translated from the German by Michael Bullock (New York: Harper, 1954). A popularly written work with several early chapters touching on the Atlantic routes.

Karmon, Yehuda. *Ports Around the World* (New York: Crown, 1980). An illustrated work, stressing modern times.

Lewis, Archibald R. *The Northern Seas: Shipping and Commerce in Northern Europe A.D. 300–1100* (Princeton, New Jersey: Princeton University Press, 1958). A detailed political and economic history.

Piggott, Stuart. *Ancient Europe: From the Beginnings of Agriculture to Classical Antiquity* (Chicago: Aldine, 1965). A fine survey of the archaeological background, with many useful distribution maps.

Pounds, Norman J. G. *An Historical Geography of Europe, 450 B.C.–A.D. 1330* (Cambridge: At the University Press, 1973).

———. *An Historical Geography of Europe: 1500–1840* (Cambridge: At the University Press, 1979). A comprehensive and useful two-volume work.

Stefansson, Vihjalmur. *Great Adventures and Explorations: From the Earliest Times to the Present as Told by the Explorers Themselves,* Revised Edition (New York: Dial, 1952). Starts with the Mediterranean entry into the Atlantic waters, with useful explanatory text.

Tavernier, Bruno. *Great Maritime Routes: An Illustrated History.* Translated from the French by Nicholas Fry (London: Macdonald, 1972). A popularly written pictorial work, with chapters on the Viking and the Hanseatic Routes.

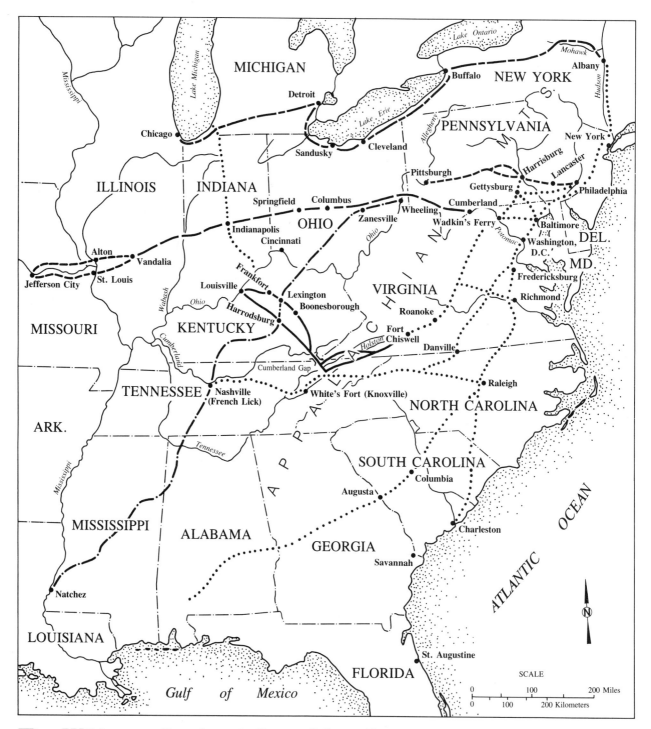

The Wilderness Road and Other Main Roads to the West in the Early 19th Century

———————— Wilderness Road

— — — — National Road

- - - - - Uncompleted

- - - - - - Pennsylvania Road

—--—--—-- Mohawk Trail and Chicago Turnpike

—·—·—·— Natchez Trace (Chickasaw Trail) and Zane's Trace

· · · · · · · · Main Connecting Roads

The Wilderness Road and Other Trans-Appalachian Routes

In the early spring of 1775, land speculator Colonel Thomas Henderson, with Daniel Boone as his aide, met with many of the leaders of the Cherokee nation, at Sycamore Shoals, on the Watauga River, near where Tennessee, North Carolina, and Virginia meet today. There, for some thousands of pounds worth of goods and 2,000 pounds in cash, these Cherokees "sold" to Henderson and his associates in the Transylvania Land Company all the land south of the Ohio River between the Cumberland and Kentucky rivers, a huge area containing an estimated 20 million acres, including a right of way through Cumberland Gap.

The son of one of the Cherokee chiefs, a young man named Dragging-Canoe, made an impassioned speech opposing the sale, and later told Boone:

> You have bought a fair land, but there is a cloud hanging over it. You will find its settlement dark and bloody.

These are much-quoted words, and good prophecy, for the evidence seems to indicate that the Cherokees had just sold Henderson and Boone Shawnee land, rather than their own. At the very least, it was hotly disputed land, a no-man's land. It is even possible to infer that the statesmenlike Cherokees had, by virtue of this "sale," found a way to pour the American settlers westward through the difficult mountain passes, diverting them from the old,

easy, and quite natural path around the mountains, going south on the Great Indian Warpath into Cherokee country, and then back north on the Warrior's Path.

The Wilderness Road and the other trans-Appalachian routes were a long time a-borning, for they faced both geographical and political obstacles. The geography is, at heart, very simple. The Appalachian Mountains, running from mid-Georgia in the south all the way to Canada, form a natural barrier between the plains of the East Coast and the plateaus and rivers facing the great Mississippi basin. Though far from impassable, the mountains are troublesome to traverse, and satisfactory passes through them are limited. As a result, travelers headed for the trans-Appalachian lands—especially Kentucky, Tennessee, Ohio, Indiana, and the whole Mississippi basin beyond—developed just a few main routes through the mountains. The Wilderness Board is perhaps the best known. Travelers from the Potomac River region would head southward toward Roanoke, being joined on the way by a spur from Richmond, Virginia. In western Virginia the Wilderness Road proper began, cutting southwest to the upper reaches of the Holston River, then angling sharply northwest through the Cumberland Gap into Kentucky; crossing the Kentucky plains, the road struck the Ohio River at Louisville, while a spur cut southwest to Nashville on the Cumberland River.

The other two main trans-Appalachian routes lay further north. The Pennsylvania Road ran from Philadelphia through Lancaster and Harrisburg over the Appalachians to meet the Ohio at Pittsburgh. The National Road arced from Cumberland, Maryland, through Wheeling, West Virginia, on the Ohio, and straight across Ohio, Indiana, and Illinois to St. Louis on the Mississippi. The river connections on these routes, especially with the Ohio, were extremely important for, in the days when overland travel was long and hard, the Ohio and the other westward-flowing tributaries of the Mississippi offered easy routes west, once emigrants had crossed beyond the Appalachians.

These were not the most natural routes into North America, however. The interior of the continent opens most easily to Europe from the Gulf of St. Lawrence down the Great Lakes and via the Mississippi to the Gulf of Mexico. With the Appalachians as a natural barrier, interior westward routes developed rather late in the history of the continent. Perhaps more to the point, the main thrust of European exploration and settlement had little to do with the logic of continental geography and very much to do with the politics of conquest, as Great Britain, France, Spain, and later the United States struggled for dominance in North America. Their early choices much influenced the development of the trans-Appalachian routes.

For the Spanish, coming from the south, North America was a distant and not terribly desirable outpost of empire. For the French, North America was a very attractive set of trading opportunities, but settlement was small, even two centuries after Cartier's arrival in the 1530's, and even then mostly concentrated in the St. Lawrence Valley. For the British, early settlement was relatively heavy, but only in the narrow coastal strip running from Maine to southern Georgia. Until 1763, the French territories in the interior were wrapped around the British colonies; in addition to their settlements to the north, they explored and claimed the Mississippi Valley a century before the British began to move west across the Appalachians.

But the French were not the only obstacles to westward movement by British colonists. The Native Americans in the region also played a part. The Iroquois Confederacy, the most powerful Native American force in eastern North America, had allied itself with the British and played a key role in the ultimate British victory over France in North America. In return, British colonial policy barred substantial migration west into Iroquois territory, blocking use of the open, easy-to-traverse Mohawk Valley, which cuts through the Appalachians in modern New York State on what would later be the heavily used

This post-Civil War view of Cumberland Gap shows both Daniel Boone's road and a later, straighter military road. (From Picturesque America, *1872)*

454

Mohawk Trail. South of the Appalachians, occupying similarly easy-to-traverse territory, was a group of powerful Indian confederations, including the Iroquois-speaking Cherokees and the Creeks. They were also either allied with the British or neutral in the British-French struggle, so the southern pathway around the mountains through the flat country of mid-Georgia was closed as well.

So it was that the British colonists were essentially penned into the coastal plain of eastern North America for 150 years, breaking out and through the Appalachians in great numbers only after the American Revolution, when the British-Native American treaties were no longer in force. They would then complete the journey of conquest west to the Pacific in less than half the time it had taken them to cross the Appalachians and begin to settle the Mississippi River basin.

The modest amount of movement west in pre-Revolutionary times was largely directed across the Appalachians and into Kentucky, which was open ground contested by Europeans and Native Americans alike. Its main Native American occupants—weaker than either the Iroquois or the southern confederations—were loosely allied with the French further west on the Mississippi rather than with the British. Early venturers were not trail-blazers, but generally followed trails laid down long before them. The Appalachians had been traversed by woods buffalo and Native Americans for some thousands of years before the Europeans came. The only real natural difficulties encountered by the colonists were caused by the heavy forest cover they had to penetrate. These mountain trails through thickly forested country were suitable for people on foot or on mounts, but not for wagons or even light-wheeled carts.

Although a few British explorers entered the southern Appalachians as early as the 1670's, it was not until the middle of the 17th century that the British began to filter through the mountain passes west. By then, the tide of settlement had spread south in Virginia and North Carolina through the Shenandoah Valley and into the Great Valley of the Appalachians, which runs between the Blue Ridge Mountains and the Alleghenies. The road later known as the Great Pennsylvania Wagon Road had begun to develop, running west out of Philadelphia to Gettysburg and Wadkins Ferry, and then south to Roanoke, generally following the route of the Great Indian Warpath, which ran from the lands of the eastern Iroquois nations to the Cherokee country, in what is now western North Carolina and eastern Tennessee. Even in the mid-17th century, though, the presence of the French to the west served to discourage deep exploration.

The Hunter-Salley party, exploring west from southern Virginia during the spring and summer of 1642, for example, had little difficulty in crossing the mountains to the Woods River, a tributary of the Ohio. Once on the Ohio, they passed the Falls of the Ohio, at what would

later be Louisville, Kentucky, noting that: "...without much danger or difficulty, and in a time of a fresh in the river, men may pass either up or down, they being active or careful..." In truth, there was no major natural impediment to travel all the way from the Falls of the Ohio to the mouth of the Mississippi, a distance of well over a thousand miles.

But political impediments still hampered travel, as the Hunter-Salley party found only 300 miles upriver from New Orleans:

> ...we were suddenly surprised by a company of men...to the number of ninety, consisting of Frenchmen, Negroes, and Indians, who took us prisoners and carried us to the Town of New Orleans, which was about one hundred leagues from us when we were taken, and after being examined upon oath before the Governor first separately one by one, and then all together, we were committed to close Prison.

They were imprisoned for two years before being allowed to return home to Virginia; the political questions needed solution before hundreds of thousands of Americans could follow these early venturers across the mountains and into the Mississippi basin. Until then, there would only be a trickle of American emigrants west.

In 1750, Dr. Thomas Walker crossed the mountains from the vicinity of what is now Kingsport, Tennessee, to examine land west of the mountains on behalf of a London land company. It was he who first described Cave Gap, which would be the main emigrant pass through the Cumberland Mountains and onto the plains of eastern Kentucky; he later called it Cumberland Gap, the name with which it passed into American history. His diary entry records the scene:

> April 13th. We went four miles to a large creek, which we called Cedar Creek, being a branch of Bear-Grass, and from thence six miles to Cave Gap, the land being level. On the north side of the Gap is a large spring, which falls very fast, and just above the spring is a small entrance to a large cave, which the spring runs through, and there is a constant stream of cool air issuing out. The spring is sufficient to turn a mill. Just at the foot of the hill is a laurel thicket, and the spring water runs through it. On the south side is a plain Indian road. The mountain on the north side of the gap is very steep and rocky, but on the south side it is not so. We called it Steep Ridge. At the foot of the hill on the north west side we came to a branch, that made a great deal of flat land. We kept down it two miles, several other branches coming in to make it a large creek, and we called it Flat Creek. We camped where we found very good coal. I did not see any lime stone beyond this ridge. We rode 13 miles this day.

At the Falls of the Ohio (later Louisville, Kentucky), early settlers cleared a space and built a fort in 1778. (Author's archives)

The "plain Indian road" Walker had discovered was part of the great Native American trail called the Warrior's Path, which ran from the Shawnee villages along the Scioto River, a tributary of the Ohio, south through the Cumberland Gap into the country of the Catawbas and Cherokees. Substantial portions of the Great Indian Warpath and the Warrior's Path would become part of the Wilderness Road.

A few years later, a year before the start of the American Revolution, Colonel Henderson made his famous purchase of Kentucky and other trans-Appalachian lands. The governor of Virginia, Lord Dunmore, called the Henderson purchase illegal, and it was seriously questioned by many in the southern colonies, including George Washington. But the main fact that emerged from the Cherokees' "sale" of disputed and Shawnee land was the opening of what would become the Wilderness Road. Henderson employed Daniel Boone and his party of 30 axmen to clear a road through the Cumberland Gap and into Kentucky. They started west from Long Island, where the Great Wagon Road out of Philadelphia met the Holston River, on March 10, 1775. Mainly following Native American paths and buffalo traces, and doing a minimum of path-straightening and brush-clearing on the way, they pushed through Cumberland Gap, joining and following the Warrior's Path for about 20 miles beyond. Leaving the old trail, they cut a path through the woods out of the mountains and onto low, rolling Kentucky country, headed for the Kentucky River. Near what is now Richmond, Indiana, their inadequately picketed camp was successfully—and quite predictably—attacked by Shawnees. The Shawnees did not press their attack, however, so Boone was able to reach the Kentucky River and set up camp there, to be joined later that year by Henderson and a much larger body of settlers; together they founded Boonesborough.

Here is Boone's version of what happened, as told to a biographer:

I undertook to mark out a road in the best passage from the settlement through the wilderness to Kentucke. I soon began this work, having collected a number of enterprising men, well armed. We pro-ceeded with all possible expedition until we came within fifteen miles of where Boonsborough now stands, and where we were fired upon by a party of Indians that killed two, and wounded two of our number; yet, although surprised and taken at a disadvantage, we stood our ground. This was on the 20th of March, 1775. Three days after that we were fired upon again, and had two men killed, and three wounded. Afterwards we proceeded on to Kentucky river without opposition; and on the first day of April began to erect the fort of Boonsborough at a salt lick, about sixty yards from the river, on the south side.

Benjamin Logan, traveling with the Henderson party, split off south of Boonesborough at Hazel Patch, traveling west on the route that would complete the main line of the Wilderness Road, through what would be Harrodsburg. Later travelers extended the Wilderness Road a little further to its terminus at the Falls of the Ohio, at Louisville.

Geographer Ellen Churchill Semple supplies an excellent description of the web of trans-Appalachian trails collectively known as the Wilderness Road:

The Cumberland Gap route was the natural avenue to the West for emigrants from Virginia and the Carolinas, but it was preferred also by colonists from Philadelphia when they carried little baggage,

From this small settlement in 1796, Pittsburgh grew into a major city, as travelers funneled westward to the Ohio River. (From Victor Collot, Atlas in Voyage dans l'Amèrique Septentrionale, *1826, New York Public Library)*

457

though the distance from that city to the interior of Kentucky was eight hundred miles. From Philadelphia an established line of travel led across the Potomac by Wadkin's Ferry, and up the Valley of Virginia along the old war-trail of the Iroquois and Cherokee, over the low watershed to the New River. The pioneers crossed that stream and continued up its western affluent, Reed Creek, which on an almost level divide interlocks with the head streams of the Holston. Here the western trail was joined by another path from Richmond, Virginia, and here at the "forks of the road" was Fort Chissel, the blockhouse built in 1758 to hold the Cherokees in check. At this point began the Wilderness Road. The distance to Cumberland Gap was two hundred miles.

From the upper Holston, the Wilderness Road turned west, and by a maze of gaps and their approaching streams which furrowed the mountain sides, it crossed the parallel ranges of Clinch, Powell, and Walden mountains to the Powell River, and turned down this valley to Cumberland Gap, an old "wind-gap" which opened an easy gateway (1600 feet elevation) through Cumberland Mountain to the West. Just beyond the pass the frontiersman struck the "Warrior's Path," an Indian trail which ran between the Shawnee villages at the mouth of the Scioto in Ohio and the Cherokee lands in eastern Tennessee. The Wilderness Road, as tracked in 1775, by Daniel Boone for Colonel Henderson, followed this Indian trail across the ford of the Cumberland, where this river breaks through Pine Mountain, and down the stream for a few miles to Flat Lick; but here it turned northwest, and followed a buffalo trace along the ridges over to Rockcastle River. In Kentucky the pioneer, following the example of the buffalo, avoided the immediate watercourses, for in contrast to the broad basins of the Allegheny rivers, these streams had carved out the surface of the Cumberland Plateau into deep V-shaped valleys, which afforded only precarious foothold for the traveler and necessitated continous crossing of their rushing currents.

By buffalo trace the road continued north from the Rockcastle River through Boone's Gap in the rugged barrier of the Big Hill range (present route of the Louisville and Nashville Railroad) to Otter Creek and the Kentucky River at Fort Boonesborough, thence to Lexington and the smiling lands of the Bluegrass. From Rockcastle River another branch of the Wilderness Road, blazed by Logan in 1775, turned northwest and, by a natural gateway near Crab Orchard, reached level land near the present town of Stanford, where Logan built Station St. Asaphs. This track became more important than Boone's trail to the north because it led more directly to the attractive level lands of Kentucky, and, passing through Danville, Bardstown, and Bullitt's Lick, terminated at the Falls of the Ohio, whence was the readiest connection with the old French tradingposts on the Mississippi and the Wabash.

The route to the Tennessee country followed the Wilderness Road beyond Cumberland Gap, and then turned southwest, guided largely by buffalo traces seeking pools and salt-licks, to the "bend of the Cumberland," where Nashville grew up; but the women, children, and baggage for the new settlement made a long and dangerous journey in flatboats, dugouts, and canoes down the winding course of the Tennessee River to the Ohio, and up the Cumberland to the little stockade on the bluffs. But later (1783) a new road from the confluence of the Holston and the Clinch rivers passed by easy ascent over Cumberland Mountain to the valley of the Cumberland and Nashville. This route was joined by a trail also from North Carolina, and at the mouth of the French Broad River by still another from South Carolina. Thus several roads from the east converged upon the upper Tennessee, just as Cumberland Gap was a plexus of the other routes aiming at Kentucky and the West.

The Wilderness Road soon proved to be an enormously attractive way west for emigrants from Virginia and the Carolinas and from as far north as Philadelphia. Even during the American Revolution, with war raging on the frontier, several thousand settlers a year came through Cumberland Gap into Kentucky. After the Revolution, the trickle became a flood. By 1792, when Kentucky became a state in the new United States, an estimated 70,000 people had poured west through Cumberland Gap. As the danger of Shawnee attack along the Ohio receded, they were joined by tens of thousands more, coming out of Philadelphia directly west through Pennsylvania or pushing across New York and then turning south to the Ohio. By 1800, the population of Kentucky was 221,000; a decade later it had reached 407,000; by the early 1780's, emigrants were also crossing south of the Gap on the Tennessee Path, out to Nashville and beyond to the Mississippi. By 1820 Kentucky and Tennessee accounted for one-tenth of the country's total population of nearly 10 million. The westward movement across the Appalachians had indeed been a massive one for the new nation.

After the Revolution, emigrants from the mid-Atlantic States began to head more directly west. The main immediate destination of emigrants headed west from Philadelphia was Pittsburgh, at the Forks of the Ohio, where the Allegheny and Monongahela rivers join to form the Ohio itself. From late in the 18th century until late in the 19th century, millions of emigrants poured through Pittsburgh on the way west. There was also considerable east-west commercial traffic between the substantial cities that developed along the Pennsylvania Road. This route generally follows the course of modern Route 30, running from Philadelphia through Lancaster, once the state capital; through Harrisburg, the present state capital; and then over the Appalachians into western Pennsylvania and on to Pittsburgh.

Its eastern section, the Philadelphia and Lancaster Turnpike, was completed in 1796; it was one of the earliest gravel—as opposed to plain dirt or log—roads in the country. Its westernmost portion was early called Forbes Road, after the British general who used this route to supply his forces during the successful campaign to take Fort Du-quesne (at the present site of Pittsburgh) from the French in 1758. After the American Revolution the entire route was called the Pennsylvania Road. From the mid-18th century, and especially during the first third of the 19th century, this road carried a great volume of vehicles, from the pack trains and light carts of the early period to the massive Conestoga freight wagons and swift express stagecoaches that characterized the later period. Later, with the coming of the railroad and the completion of the Pennsylvania Canal—really a combined canal and railway system—the western section of the Pennsylvania Road fell into disuse, and the eastern sections came to carry mainly local traffic.

Another main route west flourished for a short time during the first half of the 19th century. This was the National Road, also called the National Pike or the Cumberland Road, which generally followed the course of what is now U.S. Route 40 from Cumberland, Maryland, through Wheeling, West Virginia, and then west through southern Ohio, Indiana, and Illinois to meet the Mississippi at St. Louis. The original road did not get as far as St. Louis, but only to Vandalia, Illinois, although the state of Illinois later built a connecting link between Vandalia and St. Louis. The National Road is notable for both the volume of traffic it carried during the American expansion west and because it was the first major American federal interstate highway.

By the turn of the 19th century, trans-Appalachian settlers had developed great pressure on the new American federal government for construction of a major road from the east, linking the coast and the Mississippi. In response, the federal government in 1802 authorized dedication of a portion of the revenue from the sale of Ohio public lands for road construction, and in 1806 it approved the building of the National Road. The first construction contracts were awarded in 1811, and the earliest section of the road—a well-constructed, 30-foot-wide road on an 80-foot-wide right of way from Cumberland to Wheeling—was completed in 1818. Thomas B. Searight, early chronicler of the National Road, noted that:

> Its numerous and stately stone bridges, with handsome, turned arches, its iron mile-posts, and its old iron gates, attest to the skill of the workmen engaged on its construction...

This section of the road alone was of great importance for the American westward expansion, as Wheeling is on the Ohio River; large numbers of emigrants and traders took this road to the Ohio and exchanged wagons for flatboats as they continued westward.

Here is Searight's view of the amount and kind of traffic carried by this part of the National Road in its heyday:

> As many as twenty four-horse coaches have been counted in line at one time on the road, and large, broad-wheeled wagons, covered with white canvas stretched over bows laden with merchandise and drawn by six Conestoga horses were visible all the day long at every point, and many times until late in the evening, besides innumerable caravans of horses, mules, cattle, hogs and sheep. It looked more like a leading avenue of a great city than a road through rural districts...
>
> Excitement followed in the wake of the coaches all along the road. Their arrival in the towns was the leading event of each day, and they were so regular in transit that farmers along the road knew the exact hour of their coming without the aid of watch or clock. They ran night and day alike. Relays of fresh horses were placed at intervals of twelve miles as nearly as practicable...Teams were changed almost in the twinkling of an eye. The coach was driven rapidly to the station, where a fresh team stood ready harnessed waiting on the roadside. The moment the team came to a halt the driver threw down the reins and almost instantly the incoming team was detached, a fresh one attached, the reins thrown back to the driver, who did not leave his seat, and away again went the coach at full speed.

The first section of the National Road, running 131 miles from Cumberland to Wheeling, continued in heavy use as emigrants poured into the Mississippi basin down the Ohio. But political troubles were to delay the building of the much longer portion of the originally projected road, which was to run 530 miles more to St. Louis. The road was completed to Columbus, Ohio, only in 1833, 15 crucial years after it had reached Wheeling, and did not reach Vandalia, then the Illinois state capital, until 1852. As a result, later sections of the National Road served more local than national traffic. Though it did largely define the future development of several midwestern cities, including Columbus, Ohio, and Indianapolis, Indiana, time had somewhat passed it by.

The fate of the National Road was mirrored by that of the Wilderness Road and the Pennsylvania Road. By the mid-19th century, the Mississippi Valley had long been settled and American pioneers had already started the great movement west from the Mississippi and the Missouri along the Oregon and California Trails. The great wave of trans-Appalachian emigration had passed. More to the point, the Americans had eliminated other contenders for the eastern half of the country and were free to bring into play the emerging technology of the 19th century—railroads and canals—which generally replaced roads for both trade and long-distance traffic.

But if the Wilderness Road, the Pennsylvania Road, and the National Road declined to relative insignificance after their brief glory days, these routes still carry with them a very special sense of history for the descendants of those early trans-Appalachian emigrants who settled the heart of North America.

In the post-Revolutionary days, this road pushed west from Baltimore, past the rough tavern shown in the left foreground. (From Columbian Magazine, *Library of Congess)*

Selective Bibliography

Billington, Ray Allen. *The Westward Movement in the United States* (New York: Van Nostrand Reinhold, 1959). A concise, useful general history of American westward movement from sea to sea.

Cumming, W. P., et. al. *The Exploration of North America* (New York: Putnam's, 1974). A large, heavily illustrated work, containing a good deal of material quoted from early explorers, accompanied by editorial commentary.

De Voto, Bernard. *The Course of Empire* (Boston: Houghton Mifflin, 1952). A substantial, anecdotal history of the exploration and conquest of North America.

Dunbar, Seymour. *History of Travel in America* (New York: Bobbs-Merrill, 1915). A comprehensive early history of travel in the United States, from colonial times through the completion of the first transcontinental railway.

Hulbert, Archer B. *The Paths of Inland Commerce* (New Haven: Yale, 1921). A classic short work on American trails, roads, and waterways.

Josephy, Alvin M. *The Indian Heritage of America* (New York: Knopf, 1969). An excellent, comprehensive general work on the history and culture of the Native Americans.

Kincaid, Robert L. *The Wilderness Road* (New York: Bobbs-Merrill, 1947). A comprehensive, anecdotal history of the Wilderness Road and related routes.

Merk, Frederick. *History of the Westward Movement* (New York: Knopf, 1978). A comprehensive, detailed history of the entire American westward movement from sea to sea.

Rose, Albert C. *Historic American Roads: From Frontier Trails to Superhighways* (New York: Crown, 1967). A brief popular work, with color paintings and maps.

Rouse, Park, Jr. *The Great Wagon Road* (New York: McGraw-Hill, 1973). A detailed history of this road, with a section on the Wilderness Road.

Semple, Ellen Churchill. *American History and Its Geographic Conditions* (Boston and New York: Houghton, Mifflin, 1903). A classic, comprehensive work on the influence of geography upon patterns of development and settlement in the United States, with excellent maps.

Stewart, George R. *U.S. 40* (Boston: Houghton, Mifflin, 1953). A detailed, section-by-section treatment of U.S. 40 from coast to coast; includes historical material on the National Road, as precursor of some eastern portions.

Index

Abd-er-Razzak—84
'Abjib al-Kafuta—264
About, Edmund—318
Abraham—113, 169ff
Abulfeda—226
Abyssinia—87ff, 173ff
Acapulco—50, 65, 87, 328ff, 417
Actium, Battle of—39
Adams, William—420
Aden—87, 169ff, 407ff
Adige River—18ff
Adriatic Sea—18ff, 33ff, 208ff
Adulis—260ff, 407ff
Aegean Sea—35ff, 208ff
Aeneas—35, 211
Aeneid—211
Aeschylus—214
Afghanistan, Afghans—6, 188ff
Africanus, Leo—337, 344
Agamemnon—210
Agatharchides—170ff
aghil—409ff
Agra—199ff
Agricola—130
Ahaggar Mountains—338ff
Aix-en-Provence—150ff
Akbar—196, 199
Akhbar al-Sin w-al-Hind—412
Alans—101
al-Bakri—154
Albany—243ff
Albuquerque—363ff
Aleppo—111, 169ff
Alexander the Great—35, 116ff, 147,
    171, 187ff, 218, 377ff, 406ff
Alexander, Boyd—268
Alexandretta—120ff, 220
Alexandria—218ff, 260ff, 407
Alfonso V—81
Algiers—228, 349
Algonquins—244
al-Ifrani—346ff
Alleghenies—455
Allegheny River—458
Allumette Island—356, 431

Almalik—105
al-Mansur—346ff, 412
Al-Mas'udi—413
Almeida, Francisco de—86ff
aloes—412ff
Alps—18ff, 147, 317ff
Alta California—51ff
Altai Mountains—96ff
Alwa—261ff
Amazon River—159ff
Ambassador's Road—1ff
amber—17ff, 441ff
Amber Routes—17ff, 312ff, 441
Amboina—415ff
Ambrosius—39
Americans: See United States
Amman—169ff
Amritsar—200
Amsterdam—450
Amundsen, Roald—289
Amur River—107
Anasazi—364
Andes Mountains—160ff
angareion—115
Anglo-Saxons—25ff, 131ff, 444ff
Angola—87ff
Anhsi—381ff
Anian, Strait of—50, 287
Ankara—111ff
Annals of Ulster—446
Annam, Annamese—1ff
Antarctica—67
Antibes—149ff
Antioch—117ff, 173, 220, 379ff, 412
Antique Land, The—202
Antisuyu Road—166
Antonine Wall—130
Antony, Mark—38ff, 220ff
Antwerp—27, 88, 450
Anxi—105, 378ff
Anza, Juan Bautista de—54
Anza Trail—54
apachetas—163
Apaches—364
apes—191ff, 401ff

Apollonia—34ff, 215ff
Appalachian Mountains—453ff
Appian Way—33ff, 149, 317ff
Applegate, Jesse—297
Appleton, Nathaniel—68
Apuleius—20
Apurimac Bridge—163ff
Apurimac River—160ff
Aqaba—172
Aqaba, Gulf of—404ff
Aquileia—22, 311ff
Arabia, Arabians—12, 116ff, 169ff,
    219ff, 385, 401ff
Arabia Eudaemon—169ff, 407ff
Arabian Nights—416
Arabs—9, 80, 111ff, 154, 222ff, 261ff,
    341ff 391ff, 445
Aral Sea—96, 379ff
Archangel—284ff
Arguim Island—81
Aricia—34
Aristeas—98
Aristotle—213
Arkansas River—235ff, 363ff
Arlberg Orient Express—319
Arlberg Pass—20ff
Arles—20ff, 147ff
Armenia—113ff, 194ff, 391ff, 409ff
armor—382ff
Arnold, Benedict—243
Arrian—406
Arrow, Frederick—424
Arsu—117
Aryans: See Indo-Europeans—187
Askia the Great—346
Aśoka—191ff
as-Sahali—343
assassins—319
Assassins—393
asses—22, 113ff, 395ff
Assiniboine River—433
Assyrians—112ff, 171, 260, 404
Astarte—217
Astor, John Jacob—302
Astrakhan—95ff

Aswan—257ff
Atahuallpa—164
Atbara—255ff
Athabasca, Lake—429ff
Athens—210ff, 319
Athtar-Dhu-Gabdim—171
Atlantis—442
Atlas Mountains—338ff
Attila—100
Attock—189ff
Augsburg—20ff, 312ff
Augusta Taurinorum—20ff
Augusta Vindelicum—20ff
Augustus Caesar—20, 151, 172, 220, 384
Australia—78ff
Austria, Austrians—17ff, 316ff
automobiles—58ff, 126, 184, 349
avant-couriers—369
Avars—22, 42, 100ff, 313ff
Awdoghast—341ff
Axum—173, 260ff, 409ff
Aydhab—176ff, 263ff, 342
Azizu—117
Azores Islands—443
Azov, Sea of—95, 208ff
Aztecs—364
Azurara, Gomes Eannes de—80

Bab al-Mandab Strait—405ff
Babur—199
Babylon—113ff, 379ff
Bactra—6, 191ff, 378ff
Bactria—117
Baghdad—119ff, 176ff, 379ff, 412
Bahrain—402ff
Baikal, Lake—96ff, 100ff
Baja California—51ff
Baker, Mr. and Mrs. Samuel—266
Balboa, Vasco Núñuz de—63, 326
Balearic Islands—208ff
Balkans—34ff, 100, 309ff
Balkh—200, 378ff
Balkhash, Lake—100ff
The Ballad of the King's Jest—187
balsam—170ff
Baltic Sea—96ff, 439ff
Balts—97
bamboo—5, 381
Bantam—77ff, 418ff
Barani, Ziau'ddin—198
Barbaricon—192, 407ff
Barbarossa—226
Barbary—226, 337ff
Barbosa, Duarte—416
Barcelona—155
Barents, William—285
barges—10
Bari—34
Barlow Road—299
Barth, Henry—348
Bartleson Party—303
Bartram, John—246
Barygaza—192, 405ff
Basel, Basle—19, 319
basheer—119, 175
bashi—119ff, 174ff

Basra—112ff, 176ff, 412ff
Basutos—142
Batavia—89ff, 420ff
bateaux—250
bayrakdar—119
Beagle Channel—70
Bear River—299
beaver—246, 355ff, 431ff
Beawes, William—119, 122ff
bêche-de-mer—67
Bechuanaland, Bechuanas—144
Beijing—10ff, 96ff, 103ff, 377ff
Beirut—120
Beit Allah—175ff
Belgrade—100, 309ff
Bell-Beaker Folk—441
Belle Isle Strait—233, 275ff, 355
Bello, Muhammed—267
Belon, Pierre—45
Beneventum—34ff
Bengal—2ff, 195ff
Bengal, Bay of—77ff, 86, 191, 402
Benin—80
ben Jonah, Benjamin—224
Bent, Charles—371, 373
Bent, William—371
Benton, Fort—238, 239
Benton, Thomas Hart—303, 368
Berbers—154, 339ff
Berenice—407ff
Bergen—273, 446ff
berid—119ff, 177ff
Bering, Vitus—287
Bering Strait—160, 283ff
Berlin—317ff
Berlin-to-Baghdad Railway—126
Bertinoro, Obadiah de—225
Beshbalik—105
Big Horn River—302
Bilma—339ff
Bingham, Hiram—166
Binghamton—244
birds' nests—63ff, 420
biremes—212ff
Biscay, Bay of—439ff
Black Africans—80ff, 256ff, 274ff, 339ff, 408ff
Blackfeet—301, 433
Black Gravel Mountains—189ff
Black Sea—35ff, 95ff, 111ff, 207ff, 311ff, 379ff
Black Sea Routes—207ff
Black Death—225, 449
Black Stone—169ff
Blanchard, R.—173
Blesberg River—143
Blood River—143
Blue Mountains—299
Blue Ridge Mountains—455
boat bridges—116ff, 216ff
Boers—92ff
Boer Trek—141ff
Bojador, Cape—80
Boliadou, Soados—118
Bolsón de Mapimi—363
Bombay Marine—419
Bonavista Cape—355

Bonn—28
Boone, Daniel—453ff
Boonesborough—457
Bordeaux—23, 440ff
Boreas—215
Bornu—261ff, 349
Bosporus—34ff, 118, 153, 309ff
Boston—70
Botany Bay—91
Bourges—23
Bovill, E.L.—348
Bradford, Ernie—225, 229
Bratislava—19, 311ff
Brazil—83ff
Brendan, St.—273
Brenner Pass—17ff, 314
Brenner Pass Route—17ff
Breslau—25
Bridge of San Luis Rey—166
Bridger, Jim—298
Brindisi—34ff, 317
Bristol—272ff, 450
Britain, British—13, 20, 46, 49ff, 65, 82ff, 88, 121ff, 129ff, 140ff, 200ff, 228, 237ff, 243ff, 264ff, 275, 283ff, 328ff, 354ff, 418, 431ff, 439ff, 454
British East India Company—88, 200ff, 419ff
Brittany—150, 275ff, 353, 439ff
bronze—18ff, 259, 441ff
Bronze Age—18ff, 98, 209, 441ff
Brotherhood of the Long House—244
Brougham, Lord—155
Bruce, James—265
Bruges—25ff, 448ff
Brûlé, Etienne—356, 432
Brundisium—34
Brussels—27
Brutus—39
Bryce, James—140
Bucharest—319
Budapest—25, 311ff
Buddha—189ff, 386ff
Buenos Aires—66, 164ff
Buffalo—248ff, 356
buffalo—192ff
Bug River—101ff
Bukhara—103, 379ff
Bulgars—42ff, 100ff, 315
Bulla, Felix—39
bullocks—190ff
Bunau-Varilla, Phillippe—332
Burckhardt, John L.—264
Burgos—23
Burma, Burmese—1ff, 187ff, 401ff
Burma—405ff
Burma Road—1ff
Burn, A.R.—210
Burroughs, Steven—284
Burton, Richard—176, 267
Busbecq, Count—316
Bushmen—140ff
Butterfield Southern Overland Mail Route—58, 373
Byblos—209ff
Byzantine Empire—261, 309ff

Byzantium—33ff, 100, 119ff, 176, 215ff, 387ff

Cabot, Sebastian—284
Cabral, Pedro—79ff
Cabot, John—275, 353, 450
Cabrillo, Juan—50ff
cacao—160
Cadiz—79, 147ff, 209ff, 324, 439ff
Caesar, Julius—19ff, 38ff, 129, 150ff, 219ff, 444
Cahors—23
Cahuenga Pass—55ff
Caillié, René—342-343, 348
Cairo—120, 176ff, 262ff, 423
Cajamarca—164
Calcutta—200ff, 421ff
Calgacus—130
Calicut—84ff, 416ff
California—49ff, 67ff, 295ff
California Mission Trail—49ff
California Trail—295ff
Caligula—152
Callao—65, 164, 327ff
cambric—108
camels—95ff, 113ff, 170ff, 187ff, 260ff, 316ff, 337ff, 379ff
Camin Aurelian, lu—155
camphor—412ff
Canaan—113, 169
Canada, Canadians—243ff, 353ff, 429ff
Canojoharie—244
canals—36, 229, 250ff, 258ff, 290ff, 327ff, 359-360, 404, 422ff
Canandaigua—249
Canary Current—273ff
Canary Islands—77ff, 324ff
canoes—236, 244, 355, 406ff, 430ff
Canosa—34ff
Canton—1ff, 86ff, 405ff
Capac Nãn—159
Cape Colony—92, 139ff
Cape Horn—87ff
Cape Horn Route—55, 63ff, 330, 420
Cape of Good Hope—77ff, 396
Cape of Good Hope Route—63, 67, 77ff, 121ff, 200, 226, 264, 416ff, 450
Cape of Spices—401ff
Cape Town—90ff, 139ff
Cape Verde Islands—67ff, 77ff, 325
Capua—34ff
caravels—80ff, 450
caravansarais—124ff, 177ff, 198ff
carbuncle—339ff
Carcassone Gap—23, 440ff
Carchemish—113
Caribbean Sea—90, 324ff
Carmel—51ff
carnelian—113ff
Carnuntum—17, 312
Carpathian Mountains—96
Carpini, John de Plano—104
carriages—39ff, 133
Carson, Kit—302, 371
Carson River—300
Carson Route—300

Carsstensz, Jan—89
Cartagena—328
Carthage, Carthaginians—37, 79, 148, 209ff, 339ff, 443ff
Carthago Nova—149ff, 219ff
Cartier, Jacques—233, 353ff, 430
carts—8, 19, 39, 55, 115ff, 130, 164, 249, 370, 459
Casa de Contratación—326ff
Casalis, Edouard—142
Cascades Mountains—296ff
Caspian Gates—379
Caspian Sea—95ff, 113ff, 379ff
Cassell's Magazine—73
Cassiterides—443ff
Cassius—39
Cathay—11, 95ff, 275, 284ff, 392ff
Catherine the Great—287
Catskill Trail—244
Cattigara—6ff
cattle—260
Caucasus Mountains—100
Cave Gap—455
Cavendish, Thomas—66
Cave of the Thousand Buddhas—377ff
Cayugas—244ff
cedars of Lebanon—209ff, 401
Celtic Seaway—443ff
Celts—35, 97, 130, 148, 273, 311ff, 354, 441ff
Ceuta—79, 147ff, 207ff
Ceylon—90ff, 402ff
Chad, Lake—261, 339ff
Chagres River—325ff
Champlain, Lake—243ff
Champlain, Samuel de—353ff, 430ff
Chancellor, Richard—284
Chan Chan—160ff
Chandra, Moti—188
Chang'an—2ff, 377ff
Chang Ch'ien—6ff, 380ff
Chang Chiu-ling—9
Chang River—1ff
Chao Ju-kua—411
chariots—6, 8, 20ff, 39ff, 97ff, 112, 130, 152ff, 189ff, 259ff, 311ff, 338ff, 379ff
chasquis—163
Chelyuskin, Cape—287
Chengdu—2ff
Cheng Ho—415
Cherokees—453ff
Cherokee Trail—305
Chenoweth, F.A.—303
Chiao Chih—2ff, 405ff
Chihuahua—366ff
Chihuahua Trail—363ff
Childe, V. Gordon—441
Chile—159ff
Chimney Rock—297
Chimor, Chimus—160ff
China, Chinese—1ff, 67ff, 95ff, 187ff, 377ff, 402ff
China ships—329ff
Ch'in Dynasty—5ff, 380
Chin Dynasty—393ff
Ch'ing Dynasty—1ff, 396
Chisdai Abu-Yusuf—223

chocolate—329
Chongging—6ff
Chouart, Médard—432
Chou Dynasty—5ff
Chukot peninsula—286ff
Churchill—433
Churchill, Winston—189
Chuviscar River—365
Cicero—37, 151, 219
Cilician Gates—112ff
Cimarron Cutoff—363ff
Cimmerians—97ff, 115
cinnabar—5
cinnamon—85, 170ff, 402ff
Clarke, E.D.—108
Claudius—20, 129, 220, 444
Claudius Appius—33
Clemens, Samuel—233ff
Cleopatra—39, 220
Clinton, DeWitt—250
clipper ships—70ff, 91ff, 421ff, 450
Clodius—33
cloth—84ff, 108, 192, 244, 261, 448ff
cloves—85, 414ff
coal—92
Coast of Pirates—419
coca—160
cod—276
Coen, Jan—420
coffee—421ff
Cohoes Falls—244
Colles, Christopher—250
Cologne—19ff, 309ff, 448ff
Colorado River—51
Columba, St.—445
Columbia River—299, 429ff
Columbus, Christopher—83, 323ff, 450
Comanches—364
Commerce of the Prairies—363, 365, 368-370
Comnena, Anna—309ff
Comnenus, Alexius—45, 314
Compagnie Internationale des Wagons-Litts—316ff
Company for Distant Lands—77ff
Compostela—23ff
Comstock Lode—305
Conestoga wagons—370, 459
Congo—82ff
Connecticut Path—248
Connecticut River—248
Conques—23
Conrad, Joseph—208
Constantine—22, 39, 119, 153, 313
Constantinople—23, 33ff, 102ff, 119ff, 153, 215ff, 309ff, 387ff
Constanza—215, 312ff
Cook, Captain James—67, 91, 420
Cook's Tour—28
copper—18ff, 72, 113ff, 148ff, 209ff, 234, 259, 430, 441ff
Coptos—258ff, 404
coolies—425
coracles—444ff
coral—84ff, 341, 409ff
coral moss—67

Corfu—35, 215
Corinth—35ff, 210ff
Corniche—155
Cornwall—129, 150, 439ff
Corsica—208ff
Cortés, Hernando
corvus—219
cosmetics—386ff
Cossacks—108, 286
Côte d'Azur—155
Cottius—151
cotton—160, 192ff, 277, 379ff
Council Grove—368
country trading—90ff, 420ff
corduroy roads—18ff, 247, 251, 434
couriers—111ff, 132ff, 163ff, 175ff, 199ff, 228ff, 244, 264, 369
Cracow—25, 96, 448
Creeks—455
Crees—432
Crespî, Juan—52
Crete, Cretans—19ff, 208ff, 441ff
Crimea—215ff
Cristóbal—333
Croats—42ff
Croesus—111
Croton—215ff
Crusaders—23, 45, 120, 224ff, 309ff, 393
Ctesiphon—117, 379ff
Cuba—325
Culebra Cut—332ff
Cumae—215
Cumberland Gap—453ff
Cumberland, Maryland—454
Cumberland River—235ff, 453ff
curraghs—444ff
Cuzco—159ff
Cycladic Islands—210
Cyprus—210
Cypsala—35ff
Cyrene—216, 340
Cyrus the Great—115
Czechoslovakia—17ff

Dablon, Claude—236
dacoits—198ff
d'Albuquerque, Alfonso—86
Dana, Richard Henry Jr.—69ff
daleel—119, 175
Dalhousie, Governor-General—200
Damascus—113ff, 169ff
Dante—23
Danube River—18, 35, 96ff, 111ff, 207ff, 309ff
Darb el-Hajj—176ff
Darbe el-Sitt Zubayda—176ff
Darb es-Sa'i—126
Dardanelles—35, 208ff, 311ff
Darfur—256ff
Darius—35, 99, 115ff, 171, 191, 217, 406
Darwin, Charles—70
Davis, John—88
De Administrando Imperio
Dean Channel—429ff
De Barros, João—81

Dee, John—284
Defoe, Daniel—133
Dei, Benedeto—345
de la Noüe, Zacharie—432
de la Penne, Barras—226
Delhi—197ff
Denmark, Danes—90ff, 130, 200ff, 420, 439ff
Denmark Strait—271ff, 353
Derib el Arba'in—256ff
Deshima—420
De Smet, Pierre-Jean—296
De Soto, Hernando—233
Dewald, Johann Eberhard—27
dhows—84ff, 405ff
Diamond Sutra—377
Dias, Bartholomeu—82ff
Dickens, Charles—135, 279
Dickson, Port—287
Dido—211ff
Dijon—25ff
Dingane—142ff
Dio Cassius—313
Diodorus—147
Diogo Cao—82
Disraeli, Benjamin—425
Diu—416ff
Dnieper River—96ff
Dniester River—101ff
Dobrudja—96ff, 311ff
Dongola Reach—255ff
Dongting Lake—2ff
donkeys—113ff, 192ff, 258, 339ff
Donner Pass—300
Don River—98ff, 379ff
Doughty, Charles M.—180ff
Dover, Strait of—439ff
Dragging-Canoe—453
Drake, Francis—50, 65, 83, 329
Drakensberg Mountains—139ff
Drake's Bay—50
Drava River—19ff, 311ff
dugouts—209, 237, 441
du Jarric, Pierre—188
Duluth, Daniel—358, 432
dumb barter: See silent trade
Dunhuang—377ff
Dura-Europos—117, 384ff
Durance River—147ff
Durazzo—34ff
Durham boats—250
Dutch: See Netherlands
Dutch East India Company—140, 418ff
dye—210, 384ff
Dyrrhachium—34ff
Dzungarian Gap—96ff, 388ff

Earth Girdle—96
East Africa—401ff
East Indiamen—90ff, 424
East, W. Gordon—314
ebony—259, 402ff
Ebro River—148ff, 207
Ecbatana—116, 379ff
Edinburgh—129ff

Egnatian Way—33ff, 215, 311ff
Egypt, Egyptians—6, 116, 169ff, 209ff, 257ff, 402ff
Elbe River—18ff
El Camino del Diablo—51ff
El Camino Real—53ff, 365
Eleanor of Aquitaine—314
Elephantine Island—257ff
elephants—37, 149, 191ff, 267, 407ff
El Fasher—256ff
El Kharga Oasis—256ff
Elmina—82ff
El Obeid—264
El Paso—363ff
Emigrant Road—295
Emporiae—149ff, 216
English Channel—25ff, 129, 439ff
Ephesus—115
Ericson, Leif—274
Eric the Red—274, 354
Erie Canal—250ff, 359
Erie, Lake—243, 356
Erhhai Lake—6
Ermentarius—446
Ermine Street—129ff
Ethiopia, Ethiopians—255ff
Etruria, Etruscans—18ff, 148, 213ff
Eudoxus—79, 407
Euphrates River—111ff, 379ff, 407ff
Eurasian Steppe—22, 35, 42, 95ff, 311ff
Eurasian Steppe Route—95ff, 313ff, 379ff, 449ff

Fabri, Felix—25, 224
Faeroe Islands—271ff, 439ff
Fages, Captain Pedros—49
Fa-Hsien—194ff, 388
Falkland Islands—66
Falls of the Ohio—238, 455ff
Fan Yeh—385
Farragut, David G.—239
fatakas—405
feathers—5
Ferghana—380ff
Fernando Po Island—81
ferries—36, 57, 116ff, 190ff, 298
Fertile Crescent—111ff, 169ff
Fez—263, 341ff
Fezzan—338ff
Finger Lakes—243
fish—160, 275, 448
Five Foot Way—6
flatboats—237,459
flax-448ff
Florence—154
Florence, Nebraska—296
Florida Strait—273
flotas—328ff
fly-whisks—259
Font, Pedro—53
Formia—34ff
Fosse Way—130
Fox River—235
France, Franks, French—17ff, 46, 53, 90ff, 100ff, 122, 147ff, 154, 200ff,

233ff, 244ff, 275, 309ff, 354ff, 366, 420, 431, 439ff, 454
Frankfurt-on-Main—18ff, 96, 311ff, 448
frankincense—170ff
Fraser, David—203
Fraser River—433
Fraser, Simon—433
Frémont, John—57, 303
French and Indian War—243
French Foreign Legion—349
frigates—407
Frisian Islands—445
fur—63ff, 99ff, 192ff, 233ff, 244ff, 276, 286, 339ff, 355, 386ff, 412, 420, 430ff, 448ff

Gades—79, 147ff, 439ff
Galapagos Islands—68
Galaup, Jean François—54
Galinée, René—355
galleons—328ff, 417ff, 450
galleys—226ff, 449
Galilee—173
Gallipoli Peninsula—35, 208ff, 311ff
Gálvez, Jose de—51
Gama, Vasco da—83, 200, 416
Ganga River—2ff, 187ff, 379, 408ff
Gansu Corridor—96, 378ff
Gao—343ff
Garamantes road—339ff
Garonne River—440ff
Gaviota Pass—57ff
Gaza—171
Gdansk—19ff, 439ff
Gebāl—211ff, 404
Genesee River—244
Genesee Valley Trails—244
Genghis Khan—103ff, 394ff
Geneva, Lake—20ff
Genoa, Genoese—25, 79ff, 120ff, 147ff, 223ff, 315ff, 394, 449ff
Geoffrey of Villehardouin—45
Georgian Bay—356, 432
Germany, Germans—17ff, 96, 100ff, 309ff, 442ff
Gerrha—170ff, 404
Gestes de Louis VII—314
Ghadames—340ff
Ghana—81ff, 340ff
Ghori, Mohammed—197
Gibraltar, Strait of—79ff, 147ff, 207ff, 439ff
Gila River—365
ginger—85
ginseng—63ff
giraffes—259, 415
Gironde estuary—440ff
glass—211ff, 348, 386ff, 441ff
Goa—86, 416ff
Gobi Desert—96, 378ff
Goes, Benedict—200
Goethals, George W.—333
gold—69ff, 80, 85, 92ff, 98ff, 113ff, 169ff, 192, 194ff, 212ff, 238, 259ff, 337ff, 379ff, 401ff, 442ff
Gold Coast—81ff, 261

Golden Fleece—214ff
Golden Horn—222ff
Golden Milestone—33ff, 149
Gomes, Fernão—81
Gordian Knot—116
Gordon, Charles George—255, 267-268
Gorki—109
Goths, Gothland—22, 42, 100, 153, 313ff, 445
grain—10, 22, 72, 92, 151ff, 211ff, 260, 287, 316
Grain Coast—81ff
Grand Canal (China)—9ff
Grande Corniche—155
Grand Trunk Road—186ff
Grant, Christina—176
Grant, Ulysses S.—239, 331
grapes—150ff
Great Bulgar—100ff
Great Carrying Place—244
Great Desert Route—92ff, 111ff, 169ff, 171ff, 228ff
Greater Headache Mountains—384
Greater India—408
Great Fish River—83, 139ff
Great Genesee Road—249
Great Indian Warpath—453ff
Great Khan—10ff
Great Lakes—244ff, 429ff
Great Medicine Road—295
Great North Road—129ff
Great North Trail—364
Great Pennsylvania Wagon Road—455
Great St. Bernard Pass—19ff
Great Slave Lake—435
Great Trek Route—139ff
Great Valley of the Appalachians—455
Great Wall (China)—2, 96ff, 377ff
Great Wall (Peru)—161
Great Western Turnpike—251
Greece, Greeks—19ff, 34ff, 97ff, 111ff, 147ff, 187ff, 207ff, 260, 311ff, 354, 380ff, 406ff, 439ff
Greek fire—216ff
Green Bay—235, 356, 432
Greenland—271ff, 353
Green River—298
Gregg, Josiah—363, 365, 368-370
grizzly bear teeth—234
Grousset, René—96
Guadalquivir River—63, 148ff, 212ff, 441ff
guano—72
Guide du Pelerin—23
Gulf Stream—272ff, 325, 443
gum trees—401ff
Gupta Dynasty—194ff
Gypsies—316ff

Hadramaut—169ff
Hadrian—150
Hadrianapolis—35ff, 312
Hadrian's Wall—130ff
Haiphong—2ff, 405ff
hajj—176ff, 262ff, 342
Hall, Fort—299

Hamburg—18ff, 448ff
Hami—388ff
Hamilton, Ian—203
Han Dynasty—6ff, 380ff
Hangzhou—10ff, 413ff
Han Jen—9
Hannibal—36ff, 149ff, 219
Hanoi—2ff, 405ff
Hanseatic League—25, 448ff
Harappa—190, 405
Harare—140ff
hardware—85
Harkhuf—258
Harpies—215
Harsha—196
Harun el-Rashid—176
Hatshepsut—259, 402ff
Haughton, H.L.—203
Haun, Catherine—295
Hausa—263, 348
Hawaiian Islands—67, 330
heavenly horses—381ff
Hebrides—439ff
Hebros River—35ff
Hedin, Sven—397
Hegira—174
Hejaz—174ff
Helen—210
Hellespont—35, 208ff
Henday, Anthony—433
Henderson, Thomas—453
Hennepin, Louis—357
Henry the Navigator—79, 323
Heraclea—35ff
Heraclean Way—147ff, 443ff
Herculaneum—34
Herodotus—78ff, 98, 111, 115, 147ff, 212ff, 339, 404, 442
herring—449ff
Hesiod—208
hides—55, 67, 192ff, 339ff
High Veld—139ff
highwaymen—39, 129ff
Himilco—442
Hindu Kush—188ff, 380
Hippalus—408
Hiram—401
Hispaniola—325ff
Hittites—97, 114ff, 210
Holland: See Netherlands
Holland Land Company—248
Hollywood—55
Holston River—453
Holy Land—23ff, 224ff, 314
Homer—207, 210
Homs—116, 171
honey—448
Hong Kong—422ff
hongs—1, 420ff
Honolulu—69
Hopewell culture—234, 430
Horace—208
Horn of Africa—77ff, 401ff
horses—22, 95ff, 115ff, 133, 149ff, 164, 169, 192ff, 247ff, 259ff, 316ff, 339ff, 379ff, 409ff
Hotan—378ff

Hottentots—140ff
Hou Han Shu—7, 385
Hsia-Hsia Dynasty—393ff
Hsiung—nu—5, 98ff, 380ff
Hsi Wang Mu—380ff
Hsüan-tsang—193ff, 388
Huai River—5ff
Huancabamba—164
Huang He (River)—1ff, 377ff
Huang Ti—5
Huascar—164
Huayna Capac—163
Hudson Bay—355ff, 429ff
Hudson, G.F.—98
Hudson, Henry—244, 285
Hudson River—243ff
Hudson's Bay Company—299, 429ff
Humayan—199
Humber River—129ff
Humboldt, Alexander von—166
Humboldt Current—160
Humboldt River—300
Hungary—17ff, 309ff
Huns—5, 22, 95ff, 187ff, 313ff, 380ff
Huron, Lake—235, 356, 429ff
Hurons—356, 431
Hyperboreans—98
Hyde, W.E.—215

Iberia—79ff, 147ff, 201ff, 439ff
Ibn Battuta—11, 105ff, 176ff, 263, 344, 395
Ibn Haukal—341
Ibn Khurdadhbih—412
ibn Majid, Ahmed—84
Ibn Rusta—102
Ica-Nazca culture—160
ice—63ff
icebreakers—290
Iceland—271ff, 353, 443ff
I-Ching—411
ihram—179
Iliad—210
Ilium—35, 210ff, 311ff
Ilmen, Lake—102, 445
Inca Royal Road—159ff
Incas—160ff
incense—402ff
Incense Road—116ff, 169ff, 342, 403ff, 411
Inchtuthil—130
Independence—296, 368
Independence Rock—298
India, Indians—6ff, 77ff, 117, 120ff, 170ff, 187ff, 219ff, 401ff
Indian Grand Road—111, 187ff, 379
Indian Ocean—12, 77ff, 401ff
Indians (American): See Native Americans or specific tribes
Indochina, Indochinese—10, 402ff
Indo-Europeans—35ff, 95ff, 114ff, 187ff, 210ff, 311ff, 379ff, 405, 441ff
Indus River—188ff, 379, 402ff
inns—37, 152, 249
Innsbruck—18, 319
Iona—445ff
Ionian Sea—208ff

Ipuwer Papyrus—258
Iranians: See Persians
Ireland, Irish—273, 439ff
Irish Sea—271, 439ff
Irkutsk—109
iron—210ff
Iron Age—98
Iron Gate—379ff
Iron Gates—311ff
iron ships—92
Iroquois—243ff, 354ff, 431, 454
Iroquois Trail—243
Irrawaddy River—2ff, 408
Israel—169ff, 212
Istanbul—33ff, 112, 215ff, 309ff, 387ff
Italy, Italians—33ff, 79ff, 147ff, 207ff, 315
Itil—103
Ivan the Terrible—284
I've Got Rings On My Fingers—425
ivory—5, 17, 175ff, 259ff, 339ff, 401ff
Ivory Coast—81ff

Jackson Hole—302
jade—378ff
Jade Gate—96, 378ff
Jakarta—89ff, 420ff
James Bay—432
Janissaries—316
Japan, Japanese—86, 387ff, 408
Jason and the Argonauts—147, 214ff
Jathrib—171
Java—77ff, 402ff
Jaxartes River—97ff, 379ff
Jebel-al-Tariq—223
Jefferson, Thomas—301
Jerome, St.—100
Jerusalem—23, 118, 153, 169, 224ff, 309ff
Jesuits—13, 51
Jesus—173
jewels, jewelry—85, 92ff, 108, 113ff, 169ff, 192ff, 210ff, 259ff, 339ff, 379ff, 401ff, 441ff
Jews—26, 45, 79ff, 117ff, 194ff, 221ff, 309ff, 324, 340ff, 386ff, 409ff, 450
Jiddah—176ff, 263ff, 342, 414ff
Jogues, Isaac—358, 432
Johannesburg—139ff
Johnson, Samuel—129
Johnson, William—247
John II
Jolliet, Louis—235ff
Jonah, Benjamin ben—224
Jordan—169ff
Jordan River—113ff
Jornada del Muerto—365ff
Juan Fernando Island—69
Juarez, Ciudad—373
Juba—259
junks—414ff
Jusserand, J.J.—130
Jutland—17ff, 439ff

Ka'bah—169ff

Kabul—379ff
kafilas—121ff, 187ff
Kafilat al-Tayyarah—182ff
Kaffir Wars—140
Kahn, Peter—246
kahweji—119
Kaifeng—10ff, 392ff
Kalah Bar—413
Kaliningrad—19ff, 439ff
Kamchatka Peninsula—108, 283ff
Kaministikwia River—432
Kanauj—191ff
Kandahar—380
Kanishka—194ff
Kano—263, 346ff
Kansas City—296
Kansas River—235ff, 296ff, 363ff
Kan Ying—385
Kapisa—191ff
Karakorum—96ff, 394
Karakorum Highway—204, 397
Karakorum Mountains—189ff
Karakorum Pass—379
Kara Sea—284ff
Kashgar—378ff
Kashmir—189ff, 397
Katsina—263, 348
Kaye, John—201
Keats, John—323
keelboats—237
Kelsey, August—433
Kemp, Harry—73
Kentucky River—453ff
Kertch Strait—208ff
Khanbaligh—10, 103ff, 396
khangahs—199
khans—124ff, 177ff
Khartoum—255ff
Khushal Khan Khatak—199
Khazars—101ff, 223ff
Khiva—103
Khusrau, Amir—198
Khyber Pass—187ff
Kiachta—107
Kidd, Captain—90
Kiev—101ff
Kilwa—86ff, 413ff
Kim—201
Kimberly—139
King's Highway—247
Kingston—356
Kino, Eusebio Francisco—51ff
Kipling, Rudyard—187, 201, 426
Kirghiz Steppe—96, 388ff
Kiswa—178
Kitchener, N.H.—268
Knight, E.F.—203
Knights of St. John Hospitallers—225
Kokand—382ff
Koko Nor—379
Kolima River—286ff
Konya—118ff
Koran—416
Korea—380ff, 413ff
Kra Isthmus—408
Kublai Khan—11, 104ff, 414
Kumbi Saleh—341ff

Kunming Lakes—6ff
Kush—258ff
Kushans—194, 385ff

Lac Des Mille Lacs—432ff
lace—329
Lachine Canal—359
Lachine Rapids—355
Ladoga, Lake—101ff
Land's End—439ff
Laing, Alexander
    Gordon—348
Lake of the Woods—432ff
Lalemant, Jerome—358
lapis lazuli—113ff, 379ff
Laramie, Fort—297ff
La Salle, Robert—234, 238, 356
Las Cruces—327
lateen sails—223
Lawrence of Arabia—184
lead—212, 238, 430
leather—192
Lebanon—113ff, 216ff
Lebanon Springs—248
Lecomte, Louis—13
Legazpi, Miguel Lopez de—328
Leh—194ff, 379
Le Havre—275ff, 450
Leipzig—25
Le Maire, Jacob—66
Le Maire, Strait of—70ff
Lemberg—96
Le Moyne, Pierre—237
Lena River—286ff
León—23
León, Pedro de Cieza de—159
Leptis Magna—211, 339ff
Le Puy—23
Lescarbot, Marc—276
Lesseps, Ferdinand de—332, 423
Leuce Come—171
Leucos Limen—404ff
Levant Company—121
Lewis and Clark expedition—235, 301
Lhasa—379
Libertalia—90
Li-chien—381ff
Life On the Mississippi—233ff
lighthouses—219ff, 260, 409
Lima—160ff, 164ff
Limoges—23
Limón Bay—325
Limpopo River—139ff
Lincoln—129ff
Lindisfarne—445ff
linen—192ff
liners—92ff, 278ff, 426, 450
Linked Cloud Road—6, 8
Lion River—188ff
Lisbon—81ff, 155, 447
Listening For the Drums—203
litters—9, 39ff, 152, 192ff
Little Falls—250
Little Ice Age—275
Little St. Bernard Pass—20
Liverpool—92, 272ff

Livingstone, David—144
llamas—160, 162ff
Logan, Benjamin—457
Loire River—440ff
London—25, 92, 129ff, 448ff
longships—278ff
Lop Nor—378ff
Loreto—51ff
Los Angeles—49ff
Louis VII—314
Louisbourg—271
Louisiana—237ff
Louisville—238, 453ff
Loulan—378ff
Lourdes—23
Lübeck—445
Luchow—13
Lucian—220
Lugdunum—20ff
Luoyang—2ff, 377ff
Lychnidos—35ff
Lyle, Evelyn—126
Lyon—20ff, 129, 440ff

Macao—13, 87ff, 417
Macartney, Lord—1, 422
Mackenzie, Alexander—429ff
Mackenzie River—435
Macchu Picchu—164ff
Madagascar—77ff, 402ff
Madeira—79
Mafeking—139
Magdeburg—18
Magellan, Ferdinand—63, 327, 417
Magellan, Strait of—64
Maghreb—338ff
Magic Canal—9
Magna Graecia—35, 215
Magoffin, James Wiley—372
Magoffin, Susan Shelby—372
Magyars—22, 101ff, 313ff
Mahabharata—192
Mahdi—255ff
mahmil—178ff
Mahmud—197
Mai Ali b. 'Umar—264
Main River—18ff
Mainz—18ff, 309ff
Malacca—86
Malacca Strait—402ff
Malaya, Malayans—6ff, 88, 401ff
Mali—343
Malindi—84, 413ff
Malta—207ff
Mamelukes—178, 262ff
Manchu Dynasty, Manchus—107, 396
Mandalay—13
Mandans—236, 433
Manibadra—190
Manila—65, 87, 417ff
Manila galleons—51ff, 329
Man, Isle of—439
Mansa Musa—343
Marathon—217
Marches of Hindustan, The—203
Mare Nostrum—208ff

Ma'rib—171
Marmara, Sea of—35ff, 208ff, 311ff
Marquette, Jacques—235ff, 358, 432
Marrakech—263, 342
Marryat, Frank—58
Marseilles—19ff, 149ff, 209ff, 443ff
Martyr, Peter—87
Massalia, Massilia—19ff, 149ff, 216ff,
    443ff
Massawa—87, 260ff
Mathura—190ff
Mauritius—77ff
Maury, Matthew Fontaine—70, 279
Maurya, Chandragupta—191
Mauryan Dynasty—191ff
Maximilian I—27
mace—414ff
McAdam, John—135
meat—92ff
Mecca—169ff, 262ff, 337ff, 342, 416ff
Median Wall—115
medicines—67, 329, 414ff
Medina—171ff
Mediolanum—25
Mediterranean Routes—207ff
Mediterranean Sea—17ff, 78ff, 103,
    111ff, 147ff, 169ff, 207ff, 377ff, 439ff
Megapolensis, Johannes—244
Megasthenes—191
Mei-ling Pass—13
Mekong River—2ff, 408
Melville, Herman—68
Memphis—258ff, 404
Menaham, Meshullah ben R.—225
Menelaus—210
Menes—257
Merchant of Venice—226
Merv—379ff
Meshed Ali—125ff
Messina, Strait of—207ff
metalwork—329
Métis—435
Mexico—51ff, 65ff, 363ff
Mexico City—328, 364ff
Mfecane—142
Michigan, Lake—235, 356, 432
Michilimackinac—235
Michilimackinac Strait—356, 432
Midas—111
Midlands—129ff
Milan—25ff, 319
Miletus—210ff
miliarium aureum—33ff
Milo—33
Ming Dynasty—12, 107, 396, 415
Minnesota—355
Missionary Road—139ff
Mississippian culture—236
Mississippi River—233ff, 296ff, 354ff,
    432, 454
Mississippi Route—233ff
Missouri River—234ff, 295ff, 363ff
Mithridates—38
Moby Dick—68
Mocha—407ff
Mochica culture—160ff
Mocquet, Jean—87ff

Moffat, Robert—144
Mogadishu—413ff
Mohammed—174, 197, 261, 392, 411
Mohawk River—243ff
Mohawks—244ff
Mohawk Trail—243ff
Mohawk Turnpike—249
Mohenjodaro—190, 405
molasses—237
Moldau River—18ff
Moluccas—77ff, 402ff
Mombasa—84ff, 413ff
Monaco—149ff, 216
Monastir Gap—35ff
Mongolia, Mongols—2ff, 95ff, 177ff,
    187ff, 377ff, 414
Monongahela River—458
Mons Graupius—130
monsoons—401ff
Montalvo, Garcia Ordonez de—50
Mont Cenis Pass—23, 317
Monterey—49ff
Montevideo—64ff
Mont Genèvre Pass—147ff
Montreal—243, 250, 354ff, 431ff
Mont St. Michel—448
Moorcroft, William—203
Moors—80ff, 226, 337ff, 447
Morand, Paul—319
Morava River—19ff, 312
Morgan, Henry—329
Mormon Battalion—300
Mormon Trail—296ff
Mormons—296ff
Mormon's Ferry—298
Morocco, Moroccans—80, 212
Moscow—106ff
Moslems—9
Mosul—113ff
mother-of-pearl—67
Mozambique—413ff
Mozambique Channel—77ff
Mozambique Current—86
muezzin—119
Mughal Dynasty—199
Muhammed Ali—265ff
mulberry trees—388
mules—51, 133, 152, 327, 364, 371,
    386ff
Munich—311ff
Murmansk—289ff
Muscat—402ff
Muscovy Company—284
musk—412ff
Mussolini, Benito—46, 229
Mu-Wang—380
Mycenae—210
Myos Hormos—407ff
myrrh—170ff
Mzilikazi—142ff

nadeer—119, 175ff
Nagelmackers, Georges—317ff
Nahum—260
Nancy—28
Nan-hai—2ff

Nanking—12, 422
Nan Shan—378ff
nãos—83, 450
Napier, George—144
Naples—34ff, 215ff
Napoleon—90ff, 155, 264ff, 421
Narbonne—23, 147ff, 440
Narrows, The—207ff
Nashville—453
Natal—84, 139ff
National Road—454ff
Native Americans—49ff, 159ff, 233ff,
    244ff, 295ff, 323ff, 354ff, 364ff,
    430ff, 454ff
Naucratis—216
Nauvoo—298
Navajos—364
Neapolis—34ff, 215ff
Nearchus—406
Negroes: See Black Africans
Nelson, Horatio—264
Nero—17, 260
Nestor—210
Netherlands, Holland, Dutch—13, 66,
    77ff, 200ff, 228ff, 244ff, 275, 283,
    418, 448ff
Nevsky, Alexander—106
New Amsterdam—244
Newfoundland—271, 355
New Mexico—363ff
New Orleans—238ff, 250
New South Wales—91
New Spain—49ff
New York Central Railroad—251
New York City—243ff, 271ff
New Zealand—89
Niagara Falls—243, 357
Niagara River—244, 356
Nice—149ff, 216
Nicetas—314
Nicolet, Jean—235, 356, 432
Niger River—81, 338ff
Nile River—87, 191, 209ff, 255ff, 402ff
Niña—324
Nineveh—113ff
Nipissing, Lake—429ff
nitrates—72
Nizhni Novgorod—106ff
Nombre de Dios—325ff
Nordenskiöld, Nils—287
Normans—45, 223ff, 446ff
Norse—273ff
North Atlantic Route—271ff, 439ff
North Cape—283ff
Northeast Passage—283ff
Northern Sea Route—289ff
Northern Trestle Road—8
Northern Way—378ff
North Sea—439ff
North Star—211
Northwest Company—433
Northwest Passage—233, 289, 300,
    353, 431
Norval's Pont—143
Norway, Norwegians—271ff, 439ff
Nova Scotia—271

Novaya Zemlya—284ff
Novgorod—101ff, 445
Noyes, Alfred—129
Noyon, Jacques de—432
Nubia—257ff
Nuremburg—25
nutmeg—414ff

Ob River—284ff
obsidian—430
Oc-Eo—408ff
Ochrid—35ff
Octavian: See Augustus
Oder River—25
Odysseus—207ff
Odyssey—207ff
Ohio River—234ff, 244, 453ff
Ohio Steamship Navigation
    Company—238
oil—211ff, 230, 443ff
oils—259
oil tankers—93, 426, 450
Old Bay Path—248
Old Transport Road—139ff
olives—150ff
Oman, Hazrat—187
Omdurman—264ff
Oñate, Don Juan de—365
Oneida Lake—243ff
Oneidas—244ff
On First Looking Into Chapman's
    Homer—323
Onion Mountains—378ff
Onondagas—244ff, 356
Ontario, Lake—243ff, 356
Ophir—87, 401ff
opium—420ff
Opium Wars—13, 422ff
Orange, Fort—244
Orange River—139ff
ordinaries—249
Oregon—50ff, 295ff
Oregon Trail—295ff
Orient Express—311ff
Orient Route—23, 35, 96, 309ff
Oriskany—243, 248
Orkhon River—100
Orkney Islands—271ff, 439ff
Orléans—23
Ormuz—87ff
Ormuz Strait—407
Orpheus—214
Ostia—220ff
ostrich products—259, 339ff, 383
Oswego River—243ff
Otranto—34
Otrar—105
Ottawa River—356, 429ff
Ottawas—234
Ovalle, Alonso de—326
Overland Trail—295ff
Owen, George—447
Ox-Bow Route—57
oxen—95ff, 139, 189ff, 339ff
Oxus River—97ff, 379

Pachacuti—162ff
Pacific Mail Steamship Company—332
packets—251, 278ff, 450
Paddinappalai—409
padrões—82
Pakistan—187ff
palanquins—192ff
Palermo—217
Palestine—169ff
Palmers—23
palm oil—408ff
Palmyra—117ff, 220, 384ff
Palos—324
Pamirs—188ff, 378ff
Pamplona—23
Panama—70, 327ff
Panama Canal—63, 92, 323ff
Panama Railroad—332
Panama Route—164, 323ff
Pan-American Highway—166
Pan Ch'ao—385
Paramonga—162
Paris—23, 317ff
Parker, E. H.—13
Parkman, Frances—295
Parry, J. H.—328
Parthians—117ff, 194ff, 381ff, 407ff
Patagonia, Patagonians—64ff
Pataliputra—191ff
pathikrits—190
Patrick, St.—445
Paul, St.—41, 118, 173, 207ff, 221
Pavia—25, 154
Pawnee Rock—369
Pax Brittanica—228
Pax Hellenica—218
Pax Mongolica—394
Pax Romana—221
Pax Tatarica—394
Peacock River—188ff
peacocks—191ff, 401ff
pearls—5, 192ff, 226, 329, 409ff, 448ff
Pechenegs—102ff, 315
Pegolotti, Francesco di Balduccio—95
Pei Shih—386
Peking—1ff, 377ff
Penarikan—408ff
Pennsylvania Canal—459
Pennsylvania Road—453ff, 458
Pepi II—258
pepper—81ff, 408ff
peregrini—152, 445ff
perfumes—175ff, 259, 386ff, 409ff
Pergamum—118
Perinthus—37ff
Periplus of the Erythraean Sea—170, 407
Perry, Matthew—422
Persepolis—111ff
Persia, Persians—10, 99ff, 102, 111ff, 187ff, 216ff, 379ff, 406ff
Persian Gulf—78ff, 111ff, 401ff
Persian Royal Road—111ff
Perthus, Le—147
Peru, Peruvians—164ff
Peshawar—187ff

Peter the Great—287
Petra—171ff
Petronius—220
Petropavlovsk—108
Philippi—35ff
Phillippines—51ff, 65, 87, 328ff, 417
Philip of Macedon—218
Philip II—35
Phillips, Wendell—171
Phoenicia, Phoenicians—19ff, 78ff, 116ff, 148ff, 273, 339ff, 354, 384ff, 401, 439ff, 442ff
Picaud, Aimery—23
Pickwick Papers—135
Picts—130
Pigafetta, Antonio—64
pigeon post—119ff, 177ff
Pighius, Stefan—45
Pike, Zebulon—367
Pilgrimage Road—169ff, 263ff
pilgrims, pilgrimages—21ff, 120, 131ff, 174ff, 192ff, 224ff, 262ff, 309, 314, 342ff, 411, 445ff
Pillars of Heracles (Hercules)—79ff, 147ff, 212ff, 439ff
pilots—79, 174ff, 191
pilots, caravan—386
Pinta—324
pirates—51ff, 66, 88ff, 170ff, 213ff, 328ff, 403ff, 414ff
pirogues—237
Pisa—25, 120ff, 150ff, 223ff, 394
Pitts, Joseph—179ff
Pittsburgh—235ff, 454ff
Pizarro, Francisco—164ff
Pizarro, Hernando—159
Plains of Abraham—359
Plaisted, Bartholomew—111, 123ff
plank roads—251
Plato—442
Platte River—235ff, 296ff
Pliny—17, 117, 151, 152, 171, 194, 340, 386, 405
Plutarch—152
Poitiers—23
Poland, Poles—17ff, 96, 101, 439ff
Polo, Maffeo—104
Polo, Marco—10ff, 50, 89, 104ff, 284, 377ff, 414
Polo, Nicolo—104
Pompeii—34
Pompey—38, 150
Pontine Marshes—34ff
Pontius Euxinus—214ff
pontoon bridges—20, 312ff
Pony Express—305
Pope Pius II—45
porcelain—1ff, 67ff, 108, 329, 388ff
Po River—20
porters—343
Portolá, Gaspar de—51
Portugal, Portuguese—13, 63, 79ff, 120ff, 139ff, 155, 179, 200, 226, 323ff, 416, 442ff, 450
post roads—5, 11, 37, 105ff, 129ff, 177ff
Pouqueville, François—45

Powder River—299
Pozzuoli—34ff
Practice of Commerce, The—95
Prague—309ff
Prayaga—191ff
Prester John—82ff, 262
Pretoria—139ff
Pretorius, Andries—143ff
Procopius—36
Propontis—35ff, 208ff
Provence—151
Pseudo-Aristotle—149
Ptolemy—171, 194, 260, 340, 407, 408
Pueblos—364
Puerto Bello—325ff
Punjab—189
Punt—402ff
Puteoli—34ff, 220
Pylus—210
pyramids—257ff
Pyrrhus—36
Pytheas—19, 216, 273, 439ff

Qusair—176ff, 263ff, 342
Quebec—355ff
Quebec City—354ff
Qin Ling Shan—2ff
quipus—163
Quito—159ff

Radisson, Pierre—358, 432
rafeek—124
Raft River—299
rafts—113ff, 209, 238, 406ff
railroads—126, 135, 184, 239, 251, 305, 317ff, 373, 459
Rainy Lake—432ff
Rainy River—432ff
Raton Pass—363ff
Rattray, Lieutenant—200
Ravenna—42, 153, 221
Raymbault, Charles—358, 432
Red River—235ff
Red Sea—78ff, 170ff, 255ff, 401ff
reed boats—403
Regensburg—18, 309ff
Remus—35
Rensselaer and Columbia Turnpike—249
Retief, Piet—141
Réunion—77ff
Rhapta—405ff
Rhine River—18ff, 309ff, 311ff, 439ff
rhinoceros horns—7, 408ff
Rhodes—210ff
Rhodes, Cecil—144
Rhône River—19ff, 147ff, 207ff, 440ff
Rhône-Saône Route—19ff
Ricci, Matteo—13
rice—402ff
Richmond—453ff
Rideau Canal—359
Riel, Louis—435
Riga—448
Rio de Janiero—63ff, 68
Rio de la Plata—63ff

Rio Grande—363
riverboats—256ff
River of Golden Sand—1ff
Riviera—147ff, 208ff
Road Through the Willows—388
Roanoke—453
Roaring Forties—64, 84, 88ff
robbers—39, 122, 129ff, 190ff, 260, 316ff, 390ff
Rochester, New York—250
Roe, Thomas—418
roller tramway—218, 440
Rome, Romans—7ff, 17ff, 27, 33ff, 99, 111ff, 129ff, 147ff, 171ff, 219ff, 260ff, 340, 381ff, 407
Rome, New York—243ff
Romers—23ff
Romulus—35
Roof of the World—378
Roosevelt, Theodore—73, 333
Ross, Fort—54
Rostovtzeff, Michael—117
Round Mound—369
Route du Littoral—155
rowboats—209
Roxana—191, 381
Rubrick, William de—104
rugs—329
rum—237
Rumania—316ff
Runciman, Steven—120
Rus—223, 283
Russell, John—144
Russia, Russians—53ff, 96ff, 200ff, 283ff, 422, 439ff
Russian River—54
Russian River Routes—95ff, 314ff, 439ff

Saale River—18ff
Sacramento—58, 300
Sagres—79
Saguenay River—355
Sahara Camel Corps—349
Sahara Desert—80, 255ff, 337ff
Sahara Routes—337ff
Sahel Corridor—255ff, 338ff
sailing ships—92ff, 209ff
St. Catherine, Cape—82
St. Denis—23
St. Gotthard Pass—20ff
St. Helena Island—81ff
St. Jean Pied-de-Port—23ff
St. John's—271ff
St. Lawrence-Great Lakes Route—250, 271, 353ff
St. Lawrence, Gulf of—353
St. Lawrence River—244, 353ff, 429ff
St. Lawrence Seaway—252, 359ff
St. Louis—367, 454ff
St.-Malo—353
St. Petersburg—286
St. Vincent, Cape—79, 439
St. Vrain, Céran—371
Sakhalin—422
Saladin—225
Salamis—217

salt—10, 17, 35, 160, 260, 337ff
Salt Lake City—296ff
Salvatierra, Juan Maria—51
Salween River—2ff
Samarkand—103, 191, 379ff
Samland—444
Samson, St.—445
San Antonio de Padua Mission—53ff
San Carlos Borromeo Mission—50ff
sandalwood—67, 192ff, 402ff
San Diego—49ff
San Francisco—51ff, 66, 288
San Francisco de Asis Mission—53ff
San Gabriel Arcangel—53ff
Sangre de Cristo Mountains—363
San Juan Capistrano Mission—53ff
Sankha Fataka—405
San Lucas, Cape—51
San Luis Obispo—52ff
San Luis Obispo de Tolosa Mission—53ff
San Pedro—69
San Simeon—52ff
Santa Ana—52
Santa Barbara—50ff
Santa Clara Mission—53ff
Santa Cruz—163
Santa Fe—363ff
Santa Fe Trail—296, 363ff
Santa Lucia, Sierra de—52ff
Santa Maria—51ff
Santa Maria—324
Santa María Island—68
Santiago, Chile—166
Santiago de Compostela—23ff, 448
Santiago de Compostela Routes—23ff
Saône River—19ff, 443ff
São Roque, Cape—70, 83
São Thomé—82
Saracen Route—102ff
Sarai—95ff
sarais—198ff
Sardes—111ff, 217
Sargasso Sea—324
Sargon II—115
Sarmatians—100
sārtha vāha—190ff
Saskatchewan River—433
The Satyricon—220
Saudis—180ff
Sault St. Marie—359ff, 432
Sault St. Marie Canals—359
Sava River—19ff, 311ff
Saxons—130, 444ff
scarlet—84ff
Schaden, Adolph von—26
Schenectady—244
Schouten, William—66
Schreiber, Hermann—155
Schuyler, Hon Yost—243
Scilly Isles—443ff
Scotland, Scotch—129ff, 439ff
Scott's Bluff—297
scurvy—51, 84ff, 228
Scylax—406
Scythia, Scythians—95ff, 115, 194, 311ff, 380ff

seals—67
sea otters—67ff
Searight, Thomas B.—459
seaweed—160
Seine River—23, 439ff
Seleucia—117, 379ff
Seleucus, Seleucids—171, 191, 380
Selfridge, Thomas S.—332
Semple, Ellen Churchill—374, 457
Seneca Falls—250
Senecas—39, 152, 244ff
Senegal River—81, 339ff
Sennar—261ff
Sera Metropolis—385
Serbs—42ff
Seres—383ff
Serra, Junipero—51ff
Seville—154ff, 212ff, 442ff
sewan—244
sewn boats—403ff
Shaanxi—2ff
Shabwah—171
Shaka—142
Shakespeare, William—226
Shang—4
Shanghai—422ff
Shang-tu—96ff, 396
Shawnees—453ff
Sheba—169
shells—4, 17, 160, 234, 430
Shendi—259ff
Sherman, William Tecumseh—55
Sher Shah—199
Shetland Islands—271ff, 439ff
Shipton, Diana—202
Shu—2ff
Siberia—96ff
Sichuan—2ff, 381
Sicily, Sicilians—207ff
Siddhartha—189
Sidon—171, 211ff
Sierra Leone—81
Sierra Madre Occidental—363
Sierra Madre Oriental—363
Sierra Nevada Mountains—300
Sijilmasa—263, 341ff
silent trade—79, 107, 192, 212, 341ff, 386
silk—1ff, 100ff, 192, 226, 329, 348, 382ff, 409ff, 448ff
Silk Road—95ff, 113ff, 171ff, 187ff, 223ff, 377ff
silver—51, 85, 100ff, 113ff, 148ff, 150, 175ff, 212ff, 238, 329, 382ff, 401ff, 417ff, 442ff
simooms—266
Simplon Orient Express—319
Simplon Pass—20ff
Sinae—385ff
Sinae Metropolis—385
Sinai Desert—169ff
Sindbad—416
Singapore—405
Sinkiang—390ff
Sioux—432
Skaggerak—439ff
slaves—25, 39ff, 80ff, 102ff, 141, 215ff,

226ff, 259ff, 277, 329, 339ff, 386ff, 402ff, 408ff
Slavs—22, 97ff, 283, 313ff
sledges—113
sleighs—248
Smith, Jedediah—57
Smolensk—101ff
Smollett, Tobias—154
Smyrna—115
Snake River—299
Snefru—209, 257
Snowy Mountains—197, 390
Socotra—87, 406ff
Soda Springs—299
Sofala—86ff, 413ff
Sofia—312
Sogdiana—381ff
Solis, Juan Diaz de—63
Solomon—87, 169, 401ff
Sound, The—439ff
South Africa, South Africans—83ff, 139ff
South China Sea—413
Southern Way—378ff
South Pass—298
Spain, Spanish—13, 23ff, 49ff, 63ff, 79ff, 82ff, 147ff, 159ff, 226ff, 237, 323ff, 417, 439ff, 454
Spanish Main—325
Sparta—210ff, 214ff
Spartacus—39
Speke, John—267
Spice Islands—77ff, 402ff
Spice Route—2, 3, 77ff, 111ff, 117ff, 170ff, 194ff, 222ff, 260, 384ff, 401
spices—87, 169ff, 329, 448ff
Sport and Folklore in the Himalaya—203
Srinigar—379
Srivijaya—410ff
Ssuma-Ch'ien—6, 8, 380ff
stagecoaches—53, 57, 58, 129ff, 249, 305, 318ff, 373, 459
Stamford—130ff
Stanwix, Fort—243ff
Stark, Eliphalet—248, 250
Stawianski, Fort—54
steamboats—238ff, 317ff
steamships—70, 92ff, 126, 230, 237ff, 279, 432ff
steel ships—92
steerage—277ff
Stephen, St.—314
Stein, Marc Aurel—377, 397
Stonehenge—441
Stone Tower—384ff
Strabo—20ff, 148, 170ff, 404, 409, 443
Strasbourg—311ff
Strata Diocletiana—118, 172ff
Strauss, Levi—71
Sublette, William—302
Sublette's Cutoff—298ff
Suchow—13
Sudan, Sudanese—81, 255ff, 337ff
Suez—228ff
Suez Canal—46, 92ff, 126, 183, 267, 421ff

Suez, Gulf of—258, 404ff
sugar—73, 237
Sukraniti—202
Suleimans—188
Sumatra—77ff, 402ff
Sumer, Sumerians—113ff, 402ff
Summer Palace—422
Sunda Strait—77ff, 402ff
Sung Dynasty—10ff, 392ff, 414
Sung-shu—410
Superior, Lake—356, 429ff
Surat—88, 419
Susa—111ff
Susquehanna River—244
Sutter's Fort—300
Suvarnabhumi—405ff
Svyatoslav—103
Sweden, Swedes—283, 314, 439ff
Sweetwater River—298
Switzerland, Swiss—17ff, 317ff
swords—414ff
Sycamore Shoals—453
Sydney—91
Syracuse—215ff
Syracuse, New York—248ff
Syria, Syrians—7ff, 26, 111ff, 169ff, 194ff, 210ff, 379ff, 409ff

Tabari—174
Table Bay—140
Ta-Ch'in—7, 383ff
Tacitus—130
Tadoussac—430
Taghaza—337ff
Tahoe, Lake—300
Ta-Hsia—6, 381ff
Tahuantinsuyu—162ff
Taimir Peninsula—287
Taiwan—422
Taj Mahal—200
Takla Makan—378ff
takshif—344ff
Talas River—379ff
Talleyrand—423
tallow—55, 67, 287
Tamerlane—107
tampus—164ff
Tamralipti—191
Tanais—95, 215
Tanawunda—243
T'ang Dynasty—1ff, 390ff
Tangier—79, 211
T'ang Jen—9
Taodeni—346ff
Taos—366
Taos Trail—369
Taranto—34, 215ff
Tarim River—378ff
Tarracina—34ff
Tarshish—212ff
Tarsus—112ff, 210ff, 212ff
Tartessos, Tartessus—212ff, 442ff
Tashkent—379ff
Tashkurgan—384ff
Tasman, Alfred—89
Tasmania, Tasmanians—89ff
tatars—121ff, 177ff

Taureg—344ff
Taxila—189ff
Taxis—26
tea—1, 67, 107ff, 329, 421ff
Telford, Thomas—135
Temujin—103, 394
Tennessee Path—458
Tennessee River—235ff
Tennyson, Alfred—271
Thackery, William Makepeace—228
Thames River—439ff
Thebes—258ff
The Dalles—299
Thermopylae—217
Thessalonica—35ff, 312, 319
Thomas, Benjamin E.—349
Thompson, David—435
Thorn—19ff
Thucydides—213
Thung Chien Kang Mu—384
Tiber River—35
Tibesti Massif—261, 338ff
Tibet—190, 379ff
T'iao-chih—381ff
T'ien An Men—13
Tien Shan—96ff, 378ff
Tierra del Fuego—65
Tigris River—111ff, 379ff, 412
Timbuktu—80, 337
tin—18ff, 113ff, 148ff, 209ff, 273, 379ff, 441ff
Tin Routes—150, 439ff
Titicaca, Lake—160ff
Titanic—271, 280
tobacco—160
Topeka—296
Torres Strait—89
tortoise shells—5
Toulouse—23, 440ff
Tours—23
Tower of Babel—113
trackers—113ff
Track of the Forty Days—256ff
Trajan—42, 150, 152, 310ff
Trans-Appalachian Routes—453ff
Trans-Canada Highway—435
Trans-Canada Route 354, 429ff
Transvaal—139ff
Trapezus—118, 172, 215ff, 379ff
Trebizond—118, 172, 215ff, 379ff
Trekboers—140ff
Trekker's Road—143
trestle roads—6, 434
Trevisan, Angelo—79
triangle trade—277ff
Trieste—19, 28, 311ff
Tripoli—228, 263, 339ff
trireme—217ff
Tristram, W. Outram—133ff
Troy, Trojans—35, 119, 210ff, 311ff
Troyes—25ff
Tumbes—164ff
Tunis—226
Tupa Inca—163
Turfan Depression—379
Turin—20ff, 147ff
Turkey, Turks—35ff, 97ff, 111ff,

177ff, 187ff, 208ff, 215ff, 223ff, 226, 263ff, 309ff, 388ff, 423ff, 450
turnpikes—134ff, 249ff
turquoise—379ff
Tuthmosis I—259
Tuscaroras—244ff
Twain, Mark: See Clemens, Samuel
Tweed River—129ff
Two Years Before the Mast—69ff
Tyne River—129ff
Tyre—171, 211ff
Tyrrhenian Sea—208ff

Ugarit—210
Ukraine—95ff
Ultima Thule—273
Ulysses: See Odysseus
Umatilla River—299
United States, Americans—49ff, 63ff, 90, 236ff, 243ff, 277ff, 330ff, 363ff, 420ff
Ural Mountains—96ff
Ur—113
Urgenj—95ff
Utica—211ff
Utica, New York—248ff

Vaal River—139ff
Valley of the Kings—258
Valparaiso—69ff
Vancouver Island—429ff
Vancouver, George—429ff
Vandalia—459
Vandals—22, 153, 222
van dan Bogaert, Herman Meyndertz—244
Varanasi—194ff
Varangians—101ff, 283, 445ff
Varangian Route—102ff
Varennes, Pierre Gaultier de—433
Vasquez, Louis—298
Vega—288
vegetables—92ff
Vegkop—139ff
Venice—18ff, 23ff, 79ff, 120ff, 224ff, 311ff, 314, 394, 449ff
Vera Cruz—328ff, 364ff
veredus—119
Verona—18ff
Vertomannus, Ludovicus—177ff
Vespucci, Amerigo—325
Vesuvius, Mt.—34, 39
Vézelay—23
Via Aemilia Scauri—150

Via Appia—33ff
Via Appia Traiana—34ff
Via Argenta—150ff
Via Augusta—150ff
Via Aurelia—149ff
Via Claudia Augusta—20
Via Domitia—150ff
Via Egnatia—33ff
Via Gaditana—152
Via Herculea—147ff
Via Julia Augusta—150ff
Via Maxima—150ff
Vicksburg—239
Vienna—96, 311ff
Vikings—101, 216ff, 273ff, 283, 314, 353, 445ff
Vilcabamba—164ff
Vilkitski, Boris—289
Villiers, Alan—405, 426
Villiers, Alexander von—28
Virgil—211
Visigoths—42, 153, 155
Vistula River—101, 439ff
Vistula Route—19ff
Vita Nuova, La—23
Vizcaino, Sebastián—51, 60
Vladivostok—109, 288, 422
Volga River—96ff, 379ff
Volturno River—36ff
von Hagen, Victor—166
Voyage Around the World—64

Wadi Halfa—258ff
Waghorn, Thomas—423
wagons—36, 55, 95ff, 133, 139, 143, 149ff, 249, 300, 311ff, 366, 435
Wahhabis—180ff
Walata—342ff
Walker, Thomas—455
Wallachs—42ff
Walla Walla River—299
wampum—244
Wangara—341ff
Warring States period—5
Warrior's Path—453ff
Warsaw—25
Watling Street—130
wax—448ff
Wei He (River)—1ff, 377ff
Welland Canal—359
Wells Fargo—58
Western Isles—439ff
Western Seaways—26, 103, 439ff
West India Company—244

whales, whaling—67, 68, 448ff
Wheeling—454ff
Where Three Empires Meet—203
White Sea Canal—290
Whitney, Eli—277
Wilderness Road—238, 453ff
Wilder, Thornton—166
Willamette River—299
Wilson, Peter—252
Winburg—143
wine—35ff, 73, 211ff, 443ff
Winnepeg, Lake—429ff
Wisconsin River—235
wood—113ff, 339ff, 402ff, 448ff
wool—92ff, 160, 284, 448ff
Wuhan—14
Wu-Ti—380
Wyeth, Nathaniel—299, 301
Wyse, Lucien Napoleon Bonaparte—332

Xanadu—96ff, 396
Xerxes—35, 217
Xi'an—2ff, 377ff
Xi River—2ff

yaks—386ff
Yamuna River—190ff
Yangtze River—1ff
Yarkand—378ff
Yavanas—408ff
Yellow River—1ff
Yellowstone River—302ff
Yemen—169ff, 340
Yenesei River—286ff
Yokohama—422
York—129ff
York Factory—433
Young, Brigham—298
Yuan Dynasty—10ff, 394
Yüeh-Chih—98ff, 380ff
Yumen—378ff
Yunnan—2ff
Yupanqui—162ff

Zagreb—319
Zagros Mountains—111, 379ff
Zanzibar—267, 407ff
Zemarchus—100
Zenobia—118
Zeugma—117ff
Zimbabwe—139ff
Zubayda—176
Zuk, Mary—280
Zulus—139ff